THE LOEB CLASSICAL LIBRARY

FOUNDED BY JAMES LOEB, LL.D.

EDITED BY

† T. E. PAGE, C.H., LITT.D.

† E. CAPPS, PH.D., LL.D.   † W. H. D. ROUSE, LITT.D.

L. A. POST, L.H.D.   E. H. WARMINGTON, M.A., F.R.HIST.SOC.

DEMOSTHENES

II

DE CORONA AND DE FALSA LEGATIONE
XVIII, XIX

DEMOSTHENES.
VATICAN MUSEUM.

DEMOSTHENES

II

DE CORONA
AND
DE FALSA LEGATIONE
XVIII, XIX

WITH AN ENGLISH TRANSLATION BY

C. A. VINCE, M.A.
FORMERLY FELLOW OF CHRIST'S COLLEGE, CAMBRIDGE

AND

J. H. VINCE, M.A.
FORMERLY SCHOLAR OF CHRIST'S COLLEGE, CAMBRIDGE

CAMBRIDGE, MASSACHUSETTS
HARVARD UNIVERSITY PRESS
LONDON
WILLIAM HEINEMANN LTD
MCMLXIII

First printed 1926
Reprinted 1939, 1953, 1963

Printed in Great Britain

68A37925

CONTENTS

	PAGE
ORDER OF THE ORATIONS ACCORDING TO BLASS'S TEXT	vii
XVIII. DE CORONA—	
Introduction	3
Text	18
XIX. DE FALSA LEGATIONE—	
Introduction	232
Text	246
INDEX OF NAMES	475

CONTENTS

THE ORATIONS OF
DEMOSTHENES

*The numbers of the Orations are those used in Blass's
text and generally followed by editors.*

ORATION	TITLE	L.C.L. VOLUME
I.	Olynthiac I	I
II.	Olynthiac II	I
III.	Olynthiac III	I
IV.	Philippic I	I
V.	On the Peace	I
VI.	Philippic II	I
VII.	On Halonnesus	I
VIII.	On the Chersonese	I
IX.	Philippic III	I
X.	Philippic IV	I
XI.	Answer to Philip's Letter	I
XII.	Philip's Letter	I
XIII.	On Organization	I
XIV.	On the Navy-boards	I
XV.	For the Liberty of the Rhodians	I
XVI.	For the People of Megalopolis	I

THE ORATIONS OF DEMOSTHENES

ORATION	TITLE	L.C.L. VOLUME
XVII.	On the Treaty with Alexander	I
XVIII.	De Corona	II
XIX.	De Falsa Legatione	II
XX.	Against Leptines	I
XXI.	Against Meidias	III
XXII.	Against Androtion	III
XXIII.	Against Aristocrates	III
XXIV.	Against Timocrates	III
XXV.	Against Aristogeiton I	III
XXVI.	Against Aristogeiton II	III
XXVII.	Against Aphobus I	IV
XXVIII.	Against Aphobus II	IV
XXIX.	Against Aphobus III	IV
XXX.	Against Onetor I	IV
XXXI.	Against Onetor II	IV
XXXII.	Against Zenothemis	IV
XXXIII.	Against Apaturius	IV
XXXIV.	Against Phormio	IV
XXXV.	Against Lacritus	IV
XXXVI.	For Phormio	IV
XXXVII.	Against Pantaenetus	IV
XXXVIII.	Against Nausimachus	IV
XXXIX.	Against Boeotus I	IV
XL.	Against Boeotus II	IV
XLI.	Against Spudias	V
XLII.	Against Phaenippus	V

THE ORATIONS OF DEMOSTHENES

ORATION	TITLE	L.C.L. VOLUME
XLIII.	Against Macartatus	V
XLIV.	Against Leochares	V
XLV.	Against Stephanus I	V
XLVI.	Against Stephanus II	V
XLVII.	Against Evergus	V
XLVIII.	Against Olympiodorus	V
XLIX.	Against Timotheüs	V
L.	Against Polycles	VI
LI.	On the Trierarchic Crown	VI
LII.	Against Callippus	VI
LIII.	Against Nicostratus	VI
LIV.	Against Conon	VI
LV.	Against Callicles	VI
LVI.	Against Dionysodorus	VI
LVII.	Against Eubulides	VI
LVIII.	Against Theocrines	VI
LIX.	Against Neaera	VI
LX.	Funeral Speech	VII
LXI.	Erotic Essay	VII
	Exordia	VII
	Letters	VII

DE CORONA

INTRODUCTION TO THE DE CORONA

THE speech *On the Crown* (or, *In Defence of Ctesiphon*) was delivered in August, 330 B.C., before a jury of more than five hundred Athenian citizens. Six years earlier Ctesiphon had proposed and carried in the Council or Senate (βουλή) a Provisional Decree (προβούλευμα), needing ratification by the Assembly, by which a golden crown was awarded, not for the first time [83],[a] to Demosthenes in recognition of his public services. Ctesiphon was immediately indicted for unconstitutional action (παράνομα) by Aeschines, the leading orator of the party opposed to Demosthenes. In Athenian politics this indictment was very frequently used as a means of opposition or obstruction, insomuch that the name of a statesman who had never been so arraigned was remembered as a singular exception to the common experience [251]. Until the suit had been tried and determined, the decree could not be put to the vote of the Assembly. The postponement of the trial for so many years is unexplained; perhaps the assassination of Philip a few weeks after the date of the indictment, and uncertainty as to the temper and policy of his successor, Alexander the Great, made both sides shrink from a forensic contest in which

[a] References in square brackets are to the sections of the Speech.

the relations of Athens to the Macedonian monarchy could not but be treated with the utmost freedom. In the interval Demosthenes narrowly escaped being put to silence by another process, for Alexander, who shortly after his accession had punished the recalcitrance of the Thebans to his authority by razing their city to the ground, followed up his revenge by demanding from Athens the surrender of Demosthenes and seven (or nine) other politicians [41]. In the year 330, however, Alexander was far away from Greece, and busy with his vast schemes of oriental conquest—for he had won his victory over the Persians at Arbela in the autumn of 331 ; and the case of Ctesiphon was at last brought to trial.

The result was a complete victory for Demosthenes and Ctesiphon. Aeschines became subject to the penalties incurred by a prosecutor who failed to obtain the votes of one-fifth of the jury (τὸ μέρος τῶν ψηφῶν) ; and in the following year Demosthenes duly received his crown by vote of the Assembly.

According to the prosecution, Ctesiphon's motion had been illegal for three reasons : (1) because he had proposed to crown a man who still held responsible office, and had not yet submitted his accounts and official acts to scrutiny at the public audit (εὔθυνα) ; (2) because he had proposed to proclaim the award in the Theatre at the Great Dionysia; and (3) because his decree, which, if ratified, would become a public record, contained false statements as to the public merits of the recipient of the crown. The third count enabled the prosecutor to attack, and compelled the defendant to justify, the whole of the political career of Demosthenes.

4

INTRODUCTION TO THE DE CORONA

Aeschines, in his speech, deals with these several counts in their proper order. Demosthenes, on the other hand, exercising a right which he claims with much solemnity at the outset, arranges his topics of defence in the order which he deems most effective for his purpose ; and does not discuss the technicalities of the first two counts [110–121] until he has already fixed the attention of the jury upon the larger issue, appealed to their patriotism, and elicited symptoms of their goodwill [52]. Further, he is not content merely to vindicate his own acts and words ; he assails both the public and the private life of his antagonist, perhaps mendaciously, certainly with extreme virulence. Such personalities were permitted by the rules of the game, and contributed to the enjoyment of an Athenian jury.

In reading the speech, it should be borne in mind that the policy of resistance to Macedonian aggression, for which Demosthenes accepts responsibility, was a policy that had failed. It may even be condemned, by historians judging it in the light of the event, as hopeless and ill-advised throughout. Eight years before the trial (338 B.C., autumn) the coalition of Athens and Thebes, the formation of which was, in the orator's own opinion, the greatest service he had rendered to his country, had been disastrously defeated at " that dishonest victory at Chaeronea, fatal to liberty,"—fatal also to all the hopes and purposes of Demosthenes. No modern parallel can be cited ; but one, sufficiently exact, may be imagined. Suppose that Napoleon's career of conquest had been as successful as Philip's ; that Mr. Pitt had lived to see Europe, as Demosthenes saw Hellas, subjugated and helpless, and his policy of resistance

5

discredited by final failure; and that, after the crowning disaster, one of his friends had moved the House of Commons to honour him with a public statue. Suppose also that the mover could be, and had been, prosecuted before a very large jury, fairly representing the whole body of the citizens, and entitled to deliver the judgement of the nation; that he had entrusted his defence to Mr. Pitt himself; that, apart from technical pleas, treated lightly both by the defence and by the court, the prosecutors had supported their case by holding up Mr. Pitt to obloquy as the author of his country's misfortunes; and that he, unable to deny that his purposes had been baffled, his enemy victorious, and his country impoverished, had been forced to maintain the position that a people which had successfully resisted the aggressions of Philip of Spain and Louis of France was committed by its character and its traditions to the high-spirited policy that he had pursued, and that it was vastly better to have resisted and failed than to have yielded timidly to the ambition of an adventurer. If, on such an issue, Mr. Pitt had won the verdict, history, to say the least, could not have refused to do justice both to the genius and sincerity of the orator and to the magnanimity of the nation. Such was the case, and such the triumph, of Demosthenes.

The judgement of posterity, less decisive and less generous than the verdict of the Athenians, has fluctuated from time to time in sympathy with the ebb and flow of liberal opinion. In the days of Tory ascendancy Demosthenes was grievously defamed by the partisan historian Mitford. After the democratic triumph of 1832 he found vindicators in the

[handwritten margin note:] Suppose Napoleon had had designs only on a few countries.

6 *[handwritten:]* Suppose the leaders had only invented and provoked a threat to increase their power and hide their domestic failures.

Whig Bishop, Thirlwall, and the philosophical Radical, Grote. Later in the century the hero-worship of Carlyle and Froude, and the Caesarism of Bismarck and Mommsen, induced a reaction in favour of the successful military autocrat, and against the man of words, deaf to the signs of the times, and protesting vainly against the inevitable march of events. Perhaps the Great War may be followed by another swing of the pendulum; aggressive militarism may lose its attraction for the picturesque historian; and Athens and her statesman, fighting a losing battle for the small democracies, may again be held worthy of the sympathy of communities which have themselves passed, not unscathed, through the fires of a similar trial.

At the time when Demosthenes first entered public life, Athens had so far recovered from the disastrous effects of the Peloponnesian War, and of the successive hegemonies of Sparta and Thebes, that her lost empire had been in great part restored. The expedition by which the Thebans were expelled from the island of Euboea [99] took place in the year 357, when Demosthenes was twenty-seven. The power of the City again prevailed, not only over the islands of the Aegean, but over the coast of Thrace, the Thracian Chersonese—a peninsula of great importance in the wars and intrigues of that time, and now once more famous in the history of European warfare under the name of Gallipoli—and along the coast of the narrow waters that part Europe from Asia, as far as Byzantium. In the year 355, however, came a reverse of fortune; for the islands of Cos, Chios, and Rhodes, and the city of Byzantium, made good their revolt against Athens. At the same time

a new and unexpected menace to Athenian empire
and to Hellenic independence was already imminent ;
for in the year 359 Philip, a young king excelling
in capacity and determination all the bygone enemies
of Athens, succeeded to the throne of Macedonia.
The Athenian empire was essentially maritime, to
be secured by command of the sea, and by the
efficiency of that navy to the organization of which
Demosthenes devoted so much attention [102]. Communication with the Thracian peninsulas, as well as
with the islands, was by water,—though Athenian
statesmen were never unconscious of the strategical
importance of the famous pass of Thermopylae [32],
as the position of defence of central Greece against
invasion by land from the north. Until Philip had
given practical proof of his ambition, and of his
military genius, Athens was little concerned with
the neighbourhood of the Macedonian clans to her
northern possessions, or with the apprehension that,
given secrecy of preparation, a Macedonian army
might reach the Hellespont in advance of a naval
expedition from Peiraeus.

The Macedonian people were Hellenic in race and
in language. But their civilization and their political
institutions, as compared with those of central Greece,
were primitive, and their dialect mean and unfit for
literary uses. Their Hellenic character was not fully
recognized ; they were commonly ignored in Panhellenic politics ; they sent no representatives to the
Amphictyonic Council. In the eyes of Athenians, the
exemplars and the champions of the democratic
principle, their submission to hereditary monarchy
marked them as a people in a low stage of development ; and Demosthenes' fear of Macedonia was

tinged, and perhaps misguided, by the disdain of the Greek for the barbarian. He was to learn by experience [235] with what advantage a tyrant, commanding his own armies, obeyed with superstitious respect, keeping his own counsel, and able to conceal his ulterior purposes, could contend with a state in which nothing could be done without open debate in a popular assembly, and where prompt action was thwarted by party spirit and personal jealousy.

The earliest aggressions of Philip were made in the country lying north-east of his own proper dominions, that is, in the direction of the Hellespont. The consequent menace to Byzantium and the Straits concerned, in the view of Demosthenes, not only Athens, but all Greece ; for control of the narrow waters would give him also control of the transport of corn ($\sigma\iota\tauο\piο\mu\pi\acute{\iota}\alpha$) from the Black Sea [87. 241]. The occasion, however, of the first, or Amphipolitan, war between Philip and Athens was the seizure by him, in the year 357, of Amphipolis, Pydna, and Potidaea [69], places belonging to the Athenian alliance or protectorate. The war was languidly conducted, except at times when the apprehensions of Athens were stimulated by the foresight or eloquence of Demosthenes ; for there was always a party, and sometimes a majority, disposed to conciliation, and, if Demosthenes is right, no lack, in Athens as in other Greek cities [295], of " philippizing " politicians, whose patriotism had been undermined by the flattery or the bribes of Philip. The Amphipolitan War was brought to an end at last by the Peace of Philocrates in the year 346, Philip remaining in possession of all his acquisitions. Both Demosthenes and Aeschines were members both of

But United They Stand in Our Way towards independence from foolish alliances.

the first [25] and of the second [30] embassy sent to
Macedonia in that and the following year—the first
before, the second after, the acceptance of the peace
by the Assembly. The question of responsibility for
the deplorable terms of the peace-treaty became the
subject of persistent recrimination between the two
orators ; and the accounts of the conduct of the two
embassies which they offer, each to the detriment of
the other, are hopelessly inconsistent, and, it may
be, equally misleading. Of the recapitulation of
these conflicting narratives in the two speeches *On
the Crown* it must, however, be said that some of the
statements of Aeschines are demonstrably mendacious, while those of Demosthenés [18–49] are at least
consistent with his own speech *On the Embassy*, made
fourteen years earlier.

Meanwhile events had given a new direction to
Macedonian ambitions. The Amphictyonic Council
was a venerable assembly, representing a primitive
coalition of twelve Hellenic tribes, and charged with
the protection of the Temple and Oracle of Apollo
at Delphi. It might also, apparently, claim jurisdic-
tion over other great Apolline temples ; for in the
year 340 the citizens of Delos besought the Amphictyons to abrogate the right of control exercised by
Athens over the temple of Apollo's nativity in that
island [134]. The twenty-four Amphictyonic votes,
two for each tribe, were cast by Remembrancers
(ἱερομνήμονες) [148], nominated severally by the
qualified cities, at the Pylaean Synod [147], so called
because the place of meeting was near Pylae or
Thermopylae. Phocis held two votes ; Athens one
only of the two Ionian votes. Each hieromnemon
was supported by one or more **Pylaean Orators**

(πυλάγοροι) [149], who might speak but not vote. In the year 357 the Thebans prosecuted their neighbours, the Phocians, who were firm allies of Athens, before the Amphictyons for occupying lands dedicated to Apollo. The Phocians not only refused to pay the fine inflicted, but seized the Temple at Delphi, and so became involved in a Sacred War with Thebes, in which, with the help of the Delphian treasures, they won important successes. The division of sympathy among the Greek states afforded to Philip his opportunity of intervening in Hellenic affairs [18, 19]; and in 352 he was provoked by the Phocians, who had sent aid to his enemy, Lycophron of Pherae in Thessaly. He defeated them and hunted them out of Thessaly; and would have followed them into central Greece, had not an Athenian expedition prevented his occupation of the pass of Thermopylae [32]. The war dragged on until the year 346, when Philip at last gained possession of the pass. In the following year the Amphictyons expelled the Phocians from the Council, transferred their two votes to Philip, and, through his agency, punished them with an unprecedented severity, scandalous to Hellenic feeling. The Athenians were especially indignant, and with good cause; for although Philip, in making peace with the Athenians and their allies, had expressly excluded the Phocians from the benefit of the treaty, on the plea of avoiding offence to Thebes, the Assembly had accepted, on the assurance of the traitor Philocrates who gave his name to the peace, an unwritten promise, said to have been made by Philip, that he would deal with the Phocians as the Athenians wished. The guilt of this deceit, according to Demo-

sthenes, was shared by Aeschines [35]. Aeschines
was also accused of joining in the carousals with
which Philip and the Thebans celebrated the destruction of the Phocians [287].

Popular sympathy with the injured Phocians gave
new strength to the war-party at Athens; and
Demosthenes was encouraged to pursue with vigour
his anti-Macedonian policy. In the year 344 he
was engaged in a roving mission to the cities of the
Peloponnesus, by way of counteracting the intrigues
of Philip, who was trying to turn to his own account
the quarrels of city with city and party with party
[79]: but he is unable to boast of any considerable
success. In the following year the peace was finally
discredited by the impeachment and flight of its
author Philocrates. About a year later the people
of Peparethus attacked and captured the Macedonian
garrison in Halonnesus, an island which Philip had
refused to restore to Athens except on terms rejected
by the Athenians as dishonourable. Reprisals followed, and Peparethus itself was ravaged by the
Macedonian fleet [70]. War being now inevitable,
Philip asked the Byzantines to promise him their
aid against Athens; but Demosthenes had already
persuaded them to renew their old alliance with
Athens [87]. They rejected Philip's overtures, and
the Macedonians laid siege to their city [71]. Athens
prepared for war by adopting the naval reforms
devised by Demosthenes.[a] In 340 Philip sent to

[a] War-galleys (τριήρεις) were built and equipped at the
cost of 1200 citizens of sufficient wealth, who were divided
into twenty Naval Boards (συμμορίαι). Each Board or
Symmory, on being called upon to provide a certain number
of triremes, divided itself into contributing associations
(συντέλειαι), each responsible for one vessel. If naval

12

Athens a letter of remonstrance ending with a declaration of war [76] ; but, in the view of Demosthenes, he had already begun the war by the seizure of Athenian merchantmen in the Hellespont [73].

At a Pylaean Synod held in the spring of 339, Aeschines, attending as deputy for the Athenian hieromnemon, and acting, as Demosthenes suspected [149], in collusion with Philip, accused the Locrians of Amphissa of the sin of tilling the Plain of Cirrha, a territory that had been condemned to perpetual sterility by an Amphictyonic decree made two-and-a-half centuries before. The protest of Demosthenes at Athens was disregarded [143] ; the absurd accusation was pressed home ; and the Council declared war against the Amphissians. In the speech Demosthenes fortifies his long account of these proceedings, and his asseveration that Aeschines provoked the Amphissian War to serve the purposes of Philip, by a solemn imprecation [141]. The Amphictyons, finding themselves unable to prosecute the war because of the failure of their levies [151], revived a proposition made by the Thebans eight years earlier, and invited Philip to

requirements were moderate, the association might number as many as sixteen contributors [104]. The expense being equally distributed, rich men escaped lightly, while the poorer contributors were reluctant or unable to meet their obligation ; and the ships were therefore badly found. Demosthenes' Trierarchic Law [102–109] provided for a redistribution of the liability ($\lambda\eta\tau o\nu\rho\gamma\iota\alpha$) in proportion to the assessed wealth of the several contributors ; but further details are wanting. In his disparagement of this just and useful law, Aeschines was fishing for the votes of wealthy jurors, who were aggrieved by the change. Demosthenes accuses him of accepting money subscribed by this class as a reward for his obstruction of the measure [312].

13

act as their commander-in-chief [152]. He accepted the commission ; but, instead of marching to the Cirrhaean Plain and clearing it of the sacrilegious Locrians, he seized and fortified Elateia, a derelict fortress of the Phocians, well adapted by its position to serve as a base of operations either against Attica or Thebes. From this point in the story it is unnecessary either to anticipate or to explain the brilliant narrative of Demosthenes [153 ff.].

Arrangement of Topics.—For the purposes of his attack, Aeschines had divided the public life of Demosthenes into four periods, the terminal points being the Peace of Philocrates (346), the renewal of war (340), and the battle of Chaeroneia (338). With the first period Demosthenes deals in sections 18–52, dwelling chiefly upon the events of 346, and on the responsibility of Aeschines for the faults of the treaty of peace, and for the mischievous delay in obtaining Philip's ratification. To charges relating to the second period he replies in sections 60–109 ; here he claims the special gratitude of the jury (that is, of his countrymen) for the Trierarchical Law by which he had increased the resources and the efficiency of the navy. With the third period, that of the second war with Philip, he deals in sections 160–187, and 211–251, vehemently demanding the gratitude due to him for his suggestion, and negotiation, of the alliance between Athens and Thebes. Of events later than Chaeroneia—Aeschines' fourth period—he says little, except that he refers with indignation to efforts made by the Macedonians and their Athenian friends to worry and ruin him [320–323].

A summary analysis of the whole speech may be completed as follows : exordium, 1–8 ; protest

14

against irrelevant charges, 9 ; reply to charges against private life, 10, 11 ; introduction to discussion of public policy, 12–17. (First Period, 18–52.) Introduction to charges relevant to the indictment, 53–59. (Second Period, 60–109.) Reply to the two minor counts, 110–125 ; attack on the private character of Aeschines, 126–131 ; and on his public misdeeds, 132–138 ; and, in particular, on his provocation of the Amphissian War, 139–159. (Third Period, 160–187.) General defence of the Athenian policy of resistance, 188–210. (Third Period resumed, 211–251.) Renewed attack on the life and character of Aeschines, 252–275 ; reply to the imputation of rhetorical artfulness, 276–284 ; claim that the orator's public acts had already received the approval of the people, 285–296 ; epilogue and recapitulation, 297–323 ; short peroration, 324.

By this irregular, and, at first sight, haphazard, arrangement of his topics, involving as it does many digressions and sudden transitions, Demosthenes gains some important advantages. The unremitting attention of the jury is secured by the alternation of passages of narrative with rhetorical argument, and of defence with retort ; passages of lofty eloquence are distributed through the oration, instead of being reserved to the end ; and the orator's reply to the technical pleas, on which—as it is commonly suspected, though, in the absence of the full text of the statutes cited, it cannot be certain—his defence is weak and fallacious,[a] is kept in the background of the argument. Moreover, the general effect of the

---

[a] Many inscriptions, however, prove that the proclamation of the crown in the theatre, whether legal or not, was regular and customary. See Goodwin's note on 120.

speech is undoubtedly climactic in a degree attainable only by consummate art.

Aeschines, secure of the votes of any friends of Macedonia who might be on the jury, had striven to win the support of patriots by concealing his own philippizing sentiments, and by attacking Demosthenes, not as the opponent, but as the unsteady and ineffective opponent, of Philip. With equal rhetorical skill, and more candour, Demosthenes poses as the defender, not merely of his own acts and words, but of the deliberate policy of Athens, approved by that democratic assembly which the jury represented: in condemning him, they would be condemning themselves. He addresses the jury as though they were not merely representative of the people, but the people itself. For this reason a literal translation of the plural pronoun " you "—or of " these (jurymen) " in sentences addressed to the prosecutor—would fail to convey the orator's meaning ; and periphrasis is necessary. It may be added that when, as frequently, he ceases to address the jury and accosts Aeschines, the change of address is easily marked in the Greek by the change from the plural to the singular of the second person—a method forbidden by our English idiom. These transitions are indicated in the English text by inserting a dash ; occasionally the vocative " Aeschines " has been interpolated where, in the Greek, it is only implied by the change from ὑμεῖς to σύ.

The Documents.—In the course of the speech thirty-eight documents (at least), put in by the orator, were read to the jury by the Clerk of the Court. The places of these interruptions are indicated in the text ; but the documents themselves, whether included or omitted by Demosthenes when he published his oration, have all disappeared. Those which do appear in all manuscripts were forged, with very little skill, by some exceptionally ignorant editor. They are bracketed as spurious in all modern editions ; and the reader is advised to take no notice of them. The Chaeroneia epitaph [289] stands on a different footing. It is absent from the best manuscripts, and therefore got into the tradition at another point. It is a poor composition, very clumsily versified ; but this does not prove it to be spurious—the Muse has so often refused her inspiration to an official poet. It is, of course, open to suspicion ; but it is not bracketed in this edition, because, on the whole, it seems more probable that a laureate should have failed than that an Alexandrian editor should have been unable to obtain a true copy of the inscription engraved on so important a monument.

The Greek Text.—The text here printed is based on the third edition of W. Dindorf (Leipzig, 1871). In revising this text, we have followed, without notice, the example of more recent editors in avoiding hiatus by elision, and sometimes by crasis; and also by correcting the spelling of a few words in accordance with the testimony of Attic inscriptions. Further, in many places we have substituted the reading of the Paris MS., the superiority of which is now universally admitted, for the reading of Dindorf ; and wherever our text differs from that of Dindorf, and no note is added, it is to be understood that we have deferred to the authority of that manuscript. A few other variations are indicated by footnotes. The numbers in square brackets are those of Reiske's pages.

ΔΗΜΟΣΘΕΝΟΥΣ

XVIII

ΠΕΡΙ ΤΟΥ ΣΤΕΦΑΝΟΥ

Πρῶτον μέν, ὦ ἄνδρες Ἀθηναῖοι, τοῖς θεοῖς εὔχομαι πᾶσι καὶ πάσαις, ὅσην εὔνοιαν ἔχων ἐγὼ δια-
[226] τελῶ τῇ τε πόλει καὶ πᾶσιν ὑμῖν, τοσαύτην ὑπάρξαι
μοι παρ᾽ ὑμῶν εἰς τουτονὶ τὸν ἀγῶνα, ἔπειθ᾽ ὅπερ
ἐστὶ μάλισθ᾽ ὑπὲρ ὑμῶν καὶ τῆς ὑμετέρας εὐ-
σεβείας τε καὶ δόξης, τοῦτο παραστῆσαι τοὺς θεοὺς
ὑμῖν, μὴ τὸν ἀντίδικον σύμβουλον ποιήσασθαι
2 περὶ τοῦ πῶς ἀκούειν ὑμᾶς ἐμοῦ δεῖ (σχέτλιον
γὰρ ἂν εἴη τοῦτό γε), ἀλλὰ τοὺς νόμους καὶ τὸν
ὅρκον, ἐν ᾧ πρὸς ἅπασι τοῖς ἄλλοις δικαίοις καὶ
τοῦτο γέγραπται, τὸ ὁμοίως ἀμφοῖν ἀκροάσασθαι.
τοῦτο δ᾽ ἐστὶν οὐ μόνον τὸ μὴ προκατεγνωκέναι
μηδέν, οὐδὲ τὸ τὴν εὔνοιαν ἴσην ἀποδοῦναι,
ἀλλὰ τὸ καὶ τῇ τάξει καὶ τῇ ἀπολογίᾳ, ὡς βεβού-
ληται καὶ προῄρηται τῶν ἀγωνιζομένων ἕκαστος,
οὕτως ἐᾶσαι χρήσασθαι.
3 Πολλὰ μὲν οὖν ἔγωγ᾽ ἐλαττοῦμαι κατὰ τουτονὶ
τὸν ἀγῶν᾽ Αἰσχίνου, δύο δ᾽, ὦ ἄνδρες Ἀθηναῖοι,
καὶ μεγάλα, ἓν μέν, ὅτι οὐ περὶ τῶν ἴσων ἀγωνί-
ζομαι· οὐ γάρ ἐστιν ἴσον νῦν ἐμοὶ τῆς παρ᾽ ὑμῶν
εὐνοίας διαμαρτεῖν, καὶ τούτῳ μὴ ἑλεῖν τὴν γραφήν,
18

DEMOSTHENES

XVIII

ON THE CROWN

LET me begin, men of Athens, by beseeching all the Powers of Heaven that on this trial I may find in Athenian hearts such benevolence towards me as I have ever cherished for the city and the people of Athens. My next prayer is for you, and for your conscience and honour. May the gods so inspire you that the temper with which you listen to my words shall be guided, not by my adversary—that would be monstrous indeed !—but by the laws and by the judicial oath, by whose terms among other obligations you are sworn to give to both sides an impartial hearing. The purpose of that oath is, not only that you shall discard all prejudice, not only that you shall show equal favour, but also that you shall permit every litigant to dispose and arrange his topics of defence according to his own discretion and judgement.

Among many advantages which Aeschines holds over me in this contention, there are two, men of Athens, of great moment. In the first place, I have a larger stake on the issue ; for the loss of your favour is far more serious to me than the loss of your

ἀλλ' ἐμοὶ μὲν—οὐ βούλομαι δυσχερὲς εἰπεῖν οὐδὲν
ἀρχόμενος τοῦ λόγου, οὗτος δ' ἐκ περιουσίας μου
κατηγορεῖ. ἕτερον δ', ὃ φύσει πᾶσιν ἀνθρώποις
ὑπάρχει, τῶν μὲν λοιδοριῶν καὶ τῶν κατηγοριῶν
ἀκούειν ἡδέως, τοῖς ἐπαινοῦσι δ' αὑτοὺς ἄχθεσθαι·
4 τούτων τοίνυν ὃ μέν ἐστι πρὸς ἡδονήν, τούτῳ δέδοται,
ὃ δὲ πᾶσιν ὡς ἔπος εἰπεῖν ἐνοχλεῖ, λοιπὸν ἐμοί.
κἂν μὲν εὐλαβούμενος τοῦτο μὴ λέγω τὰ πεπραγμέν'
ἐμαυτῷ, οὐκ ἔχειν ἀπολύσασθαι τὰ κατηγορημένα
δόξω, οὐδ' ἐφ' οἷς ἀξιῶ τιμᾶσθαι δεικνύναι· ἐὰν
δ' ἐφ' ἃ καὶ πεποίηκα καὶ πεπολίτευμαι βαδίζω,
πολλάκις λέγειν ἀναγκασθήσομαι περὶ ἐμαυτοῦ.
[227] πειράσομαι μὲν οὖν ὡς μετριώτατα τοῦτο ποιεῖν·
ὅ τι δ' ἂν τὸ πρᾶγμα αὔτ' ἀναγκάζῃ, τούτου τὴν
αἰτίαν οὗτός ἐστι δίκαιος ἔχειν ὁ τοιοῦτον ἀγῶν'
ἐνστησάμενος.
5 Οἶμαι δ' ὑμᾶς, ὦ ἄνδρες Ἀθηναῖοι, πάντας ἂν
ὁμολογῆσαι κοινὸν εἶναι τουτονὶ τὸν ἀγῶν' ἐμοὶ
καὶ Κτησιφῶντι, καὶ οὐδὲν ἐλάττονος ἄξιον
σπουδῆς ἐμοί· πάντων μὲν γὰρ ἀποστερεῖσθαι
λυπηρόν ἐστι καὶ χαλεπόν, ἄλλως τε κἂν ὑπ'
ἐχθροῦ τῳ τοῦτο συμβαίνῃ, μάλιστα δὲ τῆς παρ'
ὑμῶν εὐνοίας καὶ φιλανθρωπίας, ὅσῳπερ καὶ τὸ
6 τυχεῖν τούτων μέγιστόν ἐστιν. περὶ τούτων δ'
ὄντος τουτουὶ τοῦ ἀγῶνος, ἀξιῶ καὶ δέομαι πάντων
ὁμοίως ὑμῶν ἀκοῦσαί μου περὶ τῶν κατηγορημένων ἀπολογουμένου δικαίως, ὥσπερ οἱ νόμοι
κελεύουσιν, οὓς ὁ τιθεὶς ἐξ ἀρχῆς Σόλων, εὔνους
ὢν ὑμῖν καὶ δημοτικός, οὐ μόνον τῷ γράψαι
κυρίους ᾤετο δεῖν εἶναι, ἀλλὰ καὶ τῷ τοὺς δικά-
7 ζοντας ὀμωμοκέναι, οὐκ ἀπιστῶν ὑμῖν, ὥς γ'
ἐμοὶ φαίνεται, ἀλλ' ὁρῶν ὅτι τὰς αἰτίας καὶ τὰς

verdict to him. For me, indeed—but let me say nothing inauspicious at the outset of my speech: I will only say that he accuses me at an advantage. Secondly, there is the natural disposition of mankind to listen readily to obloquy and invective, and to resent self-laudation. To him the agreeable duty has been assigned ; the part that is almost always offensive remains for me. If, as a safeguard against such offence, I avoid the relation of my own achievements, I shall seem to be unable to refute the charges alleged against me, or to establish my claim to any public distinction. Yet, if I address myself to what I have done, and to the part I have taken in politics, I shall often be obliged to speak about myself. Well, I will endeavour to do so with all possible modesty ; and let the man who has initiated this controversy bear the blame of the egoism which the conditions force upon me.

You must all be agreed, men of Athens, that in these proceedings I am concerned equally with Ctesiphon, and that they require from me no less serious consideration Any loss, especially if inflicted by private animosity, is hard to bear ; but to lose your goodwill and kindness is the most painful of all losses, as to gain them is the best of all acquisitions. Such being the issues at stake, I implore you all alike to listen to my defence against the accusations laid, in a spirit of justice. So the laws enjoin—the laws which Solon, who first framed them, a good democrat and friend of the people, thought it right to validate not only by their enactment but by the oath of the jury ; not distrusting you, if I understand him aright, but

διαβολάς, αἷς ἐκ τοῦ πρότερος λέγειν ὁ διώκων
ἰσχύει, οὐκ ἔνι τῷ φεύγοντι παρελθεῖν, εἰ μὴ τῶν
δικαζόντων ἕκαστος ὑμῶν, τὴν πρὸς τοὺς θεοὺς
εὐσέβειαν φυλάττων, καὶ τὰ τοῦ λέγοντος ὑστέρου
δίκαια εὐνοϊκῶς προσδέξεται, καὶ παρασχὼν
ἑαυτὸν ἴσον καὶ κοινὸν ἀμφοτέροις ἀκροατήν,
οὕτω τὴν διάγνωσιν ποιήσεται περὶ ἁπάντων.

8 Μέλλων δὲ τοῦ τ' ἰδίου βίου παντός, ὡς ἔοικε,
λόγον διδόναι τήμερον καὶ τῶν κοινῇ πεπολιτευμένων, βούλομαι πάλιν τοὺς θεοὺς παρακαλέσαι
καὶ ἐναντίον ὑμῶν εὔχομαι, πρῶτον μέν, ὅσην
εὔνοιαν ἔχων διατελῶ τῇ πόλει, τοσαύτην ὑπάρξαι
[228] μοι εἰς τουτονὶ τὸν ἀγῶνα, ἔπειθ' ὅ τι μέλλει
συνοίσειν καὶ πρὸς εὐδοξίαν κοινῇ καὶ πρὸς εὐσέβειαν ἑκάστῳ, τοῦτο παραστῆσαι πᾶσιν ὑμῖν
περὶ ταυτησὶ τῆς γραφῆς γνῶναι.

9 Εἰ μὲν οὖν περὶ ὧν ἐδίωκε μόνον κατηγόρησεν
Αἰσχίνης, κἀγὼ περὶ αὐτοῦ τοῦ προβουλεύματος
εὐθὺς ἂν ἀπελογούμην· ἐπειδὴ δ' οὐκ ἐλάττω
λόγον τἄλλα διεξιὼν ἀνήλωκε καὶ τὰ πλεῖστα
κατεψεύσατό μου, ἀναγκαῖον εἶναι νομίζω καὶ
δίκαιον ἅμα βραχέ', ὦ ἄνδρες Ἀθηναῖοι, περὶ
τούτων εἰπεῖν πρῶτον, ἵνα μηδεὶς ὑμῶν τοῖς
ἔξωθεν λόγοις ἠγμένος ἀλλοτριώτερον τῶν ὑπὲρ
τῆς γραφῆς δικαίων ἀκούῃ μου.

10 Περὶ μὲν δὴ τῶν ἰδίων ὅσα λοιδορούμενος
βεβλασφήμηκε περὶ ἐμοῦ, θεάσασθ' ὡς ἁπλᾶ
καὶ δίκαια λέγω. εἰ μὲν ἴστε με τοιοῦτον οἷον
οὗτος ᾐτιᾶτο (οὐ γὰρ ἄλλοθί που βεβίωκα ἢ παρ'
ὑμῖν) μηδὲ φωνὴν ἀνάσχησθε, μηδ' εἰ πάντα τὰ
κοίν' ὑπέρευ πεπολίτευμαι, ἀλλ' ἀναστάντες κατα-

22

perceiving that no defendant can defeat the charges and calumnies which the prosecutor prefers with the advantage of prior speech, unless every juryman receives with goodwill the pleas of the second speaker, as an obligation of piety to the gods by whom he has sworn, and forms no final conclusion upon the whole case until he has given a fair and impartial hearing to both sides.

It appears that I have to-day to render account of the whole of my private life as well as of my public transactions. I must therefore renew my appeal to the gods ; and in your presence I now beseech them, first that I may find in your hearts such benevolence towards me as I have ever cherished for Athens, and secondly that they will guide you to such a judgement upon this indictment as shall redound to the good repute of the jury, and to the good conscience of every several juryman.

If then Aeschines had confined his charges to the matters alleged in the prosecution, I should have immediately addressed my defence to the resolution of the Council ; but as he has wastefully devoted the greater part of his speech to irrelevant topics, mostly false accusations, I conceive it to be both fair and necessary, men of Athens, to say a few words first on those matters, lest any of you, misled by extraneous arguments, should listen with estrangement to my justification in respect of the indictment.

To his abusive aspersion of my private life, I have, you will observe, an honest and straightforward reply. I have never lived anywhere but in your midst. If then you know my character to be such as he alleges, do not tolerate my voice, even if all my public conduct has been beyond praise, but rise and

23

ψηφίσασθ' ἤδη· εἰ δὲ πολλῷ βελτίω τούτου καὶ
ἐκ βελτιόνων, καὶ μηδενὸς τῶν μετρίων, ἵνα
μηδὲν ἐπαχθὲς λέγω, χείρονα κἀμὲ καὶ τοὺς
ἐμοὺς ὑπειλήφατε καὶ γιγνώσκετε, τούτῳ μὲν
μηδ' ὑπὲρ τῶν ἄλλων πιστεύετε (δῆλον γὰρ ὡς
ὁμοίως ἅπαντ' ἐπλάττετο), ἐμοὶ δ', ἢν παρὰ
πάντα τὸν χρόνον εὔνοιαν ἐνδέδειχθ' ἐπὶ πολλῶν
ἀγώνων τῶν πρότερον, καὶ νυνὶ παράσχεσθε.

11 κακοήθης δ' ὤν, Αἰσχίνη, τοῦτο παντελῶς εὔηθες
ᾠήθης, τοὺς περὶ τῶν πεπραγμένων καὶ πεπολιτευμένων λόγους ἀφέντα με, πρὸς τὰς λοιδορίας
τὰς παρὰ σοῦ τρέψεσθαι. οὐ δὴ ποιήσω τοῦτο·
[229] οὐχ οὕτω τετύφωμαι· ἀλλ' ὑπὲρ μὲν τῶν πεπολιτευμένων ἃ κατεψεύδου καὶ διέβαλλες ἐξετάσω,
τῆς δὲ πομπείας ταύτης τῆς ἀνέδην γεγενημένης
ὕστερον, ἂν βουλομένοις ἀκούειν ᾖ τουτοισί,
μνησθήσομαι.

12 Τὰ μὲν οὖν κατηγορημένα πολλά, καὶ περὶ ὧν
ἐνίων μεγάλας καὶ τὰς ἐσχάτας οἱ νόμοι διδόασι
τιμωρίας· τοῦ δὲ παρόντος ἀγῶνος ἡ προαίρεσις
αὕτη[1] ἐχθροῦ μὲν ἐπήρειαν ἔχει καὶ ὕβριν καὶ
λοιδορίαν καὶ προπηλακισμὸν ὁμοῦ καὶ πάντα τὰ
τοιαῦτα· τῶν μέντοι κατηγοριῶν καὶ τῶν αἰτιῶν
τῶν εἰρημένων, εἴπερ ἦσαν ἀληθεῖς, οὐκ ἔνι τῇ
13 πόλει δίκην ἀξίαν λαβεῖν, οὐδ' ἐγγύς. οὐ γὰρ
ἀφαιρεῖσθαι δεῖ τὸ προσελθεῖν τῷ δήμῳ καὶ λόγου
τυχεῖν, οὐδ' ἐν ἐπηρείας τάξει καὶ φθόνου τοῦτο
ποιεῖν· οὔτε μὰ τοὺς θεοὺς ὀρθῶς ἔχον οὔτε πολι-
τικὸν οὔτε δίκαιόν ἐστιν, ὦ ἄνδρες Ἀθηναῖοι· ἀλλ'
ἐφ' οἷς ἀδικοῦντά μ', ἑώρα τὴν πόλιν, οὖσί γε τηλι-
κούτοις ἡλίκα νῦν ἐτραγῴδει καὶ διεξῄει, ταῖς ἐκ
τῶν νόμων τιμωρίαις παρ' αὐτὰ τἀδικήματα χρῆ-

condemn me incontinently. But if, in your judgement and to your knowledge, I am a better man and
better born than Aeschines, if you know me and my
family to be, not to put it offensively, as good as the
average of respectable people, then refuse credence
to all his assertions, for clearly they are all fictitious,
and treat me to-day with the same goodwill which
throughout my life you have shown to me in many
earlier contentions. Malicious as you are, Aeschines,
you were strangely innocent when you imagined
that I should turn aside from the discussion of
public transactions to reply to your calumnies. I
shall do nothing of the sort : I am not so infatuated.
Your false and invidious charges against my political
life I will examine ; but later, if the jury wish to hear
me, I will return to your outrageous ribaldry.

The crimes he has laid to my charge are many,
and to some of them the law has assigned severe
and even capital punishment. But the purpose of
this prosecution goes further : it includes private
malice and violence, railing and vituperation, and
the like ; and yet for none of these accusations, if
made good, is there any power at all in the state
to inflict an adequate penalty, or anything like it.
It is not right to debar a man from access to the
Assembly and a fair hearing, still less to do so by
way of spite and jealousy. No, by heavens, men
of Athens, it is neither just, nor constitutional, nor
honest ! If he ever saw me committing crimes
against the commonwealth, especially such frightful
crimes as he described just now so dramatically,
his duty was to avail himself of the legal penalties

---

¹ αὕτη Q : αὐτή Dind. with most mss. (S doubtful).

DEMOSTHENES

σθαι, εἰ μὲν εἰσαγγελίας ἄξια πράττονθ᾽ ἑώρα,
εἰσαγγέλλοντα καὶ τοῦτον τὸν τρόπον εἰς κρίσιν
καθιστάντα παρ᾽ ὑμῖν, εἰ δὲ γράφοντα παράνομα,
παρανόμων γραφόμενον· οὐ γὰρ δήπου Κτησιφῶντα
μὲν δύναται διώκειν δι᾽ ἐμέ, ἐμὲ δ᾽, εἴπερ ἐξελέγξειν
14 ἐνόμιζεν, αὐτὸν οὐκ ἂν ἐγράψατο. καὶ μὴν εἴ τι
τῶν ἄλλων, ὧν νυνὶ διέβαλλε καὶ διεξῄει, ἢ καὶ ἄλλ᾽
ὁτιοῦν ἀδικοῦντά μ᾽ ὑμᾶς ἑώρα, εἰσὶ νόμοι περὶ
πάντων καὶ τιμωρίαι καὶ ἀγῶνες καὶ κρίσεις πικρὰ
καὶ μεγάλ᾽ ἔχουσαι τἀπιτίμια, καὶ τούτοις ἐξῆν
ἅπασι χρῆσθαι· καὶ ὁπηνίκ᾽ ἐφαίνετο ταῦτα πεποιη-
[230] κώς, καὶ τοῦτον τὸν τρόπον κεχρημένος τοῖς πρὸς
ἐμέ, ὡμολογεῖτ᾽ ἂν ἡ κατηγορία τοῖς ἔργοις αὐτοῦ.
15 νῦν δ᾽ ἐκστὰς τῆς ὀρθῆς καὶ δικαίας ὁδοῦ, καὶ
φυγὼν τοὺς παρ᾽ αὐτὰ τὰ πράγματ᾽ ἐλέγχους,
τοσούτοις ὕστερον χρόνοις αἰτίας καὶ σκώμματα
καὶ λοιδορίας συμφορήσας ὑποκρίνεται· εἶτα κατηγορεῖ μὲν ἐμοῦ, κρίνει δὲ τουτονί, καὶ τοῦ μὲν
ἀγῶνος ὅλου τὴν πρὸς ἔμ᾽ ἔχθραν προΐσταται,
οὐδαμοῦ δ᾽ ἐπὶ ταύτην ἀπηντηκὼς ἐμοί, τὴν ἑτέρου
16 ζητῶν ἐπιτιμίαν ἀφελέσθαι φαίνεται. καίτοι πρὸς
ἅπασιν, ὦ ἄνδρες Ἀθηναῖοι, τοῖς ἄλλοις οἷς ἂν
εἰπεῖν τις ὑπὲρ Κτησιφῶντος ἔχοι, καὶ τοῦτ᾽ ἔμοιγε
δοκεῖ καὶ μάλ᾽ εἰκότως ἂν λέγειν, ὅτι τῆς ἡμετέρας
ἔχθρας ἡμᾶς ἐφ᾽ ἡμῶν αὐτῶν δίκαιον ἦν τὸν
ἐξετασμὸν ποιεῖσθαι, οὐ τὸ μὲν πρὸς ἀλλήλους
ἀγωνίζεσθαι παραλείπειν, ἑτέρῳ δ᾽ ὅτῳ κακόν τι
δώσομεν ζητεῖν· ὑπερβολὴ γὰρ ἀδικίας τοῦτό γε.
17 Πάντα μὲν τοίνυν τὰ κατηγορημέν᾽ ὁμοίως ἐκ
τούτων ἄν τις ἴδοι, οὔτε δικαίως οὔτ᾽ ἐπ᾽ ἀληθείας

26

as soon as they were committed, impeaching me, and so putting me on my trial before the people, if my sins deserved impeachment, or indicting me for breach of the constitution, if I had proposed illegal measures. For, of course, if he prosecutes Ctesiphon now on my account, it is impossible that he would not have indicted me, with a certain hope of conviction! Yet if he detected me in any of the acts which he has recounted to my prejudice, or in any other iniquity, there are statutes dealing with those offences, punishments, legal processes, trials involving severe penalties and heavy fines; and any of these proceedings he might have taken. Had he so acted, had he in that way employed the methods applicable to my case, his denunciations would have been consistent with his conduct; but in fact he has deserted the path of right and justice, he has flinched from the proof of recent guilt, and then, after a long interval, he makes a hotchpotch of imputation and banter and scurrility, and stands on a false pretence, denouncing me, but indicting Ctesiphon. He sets in the forefront of the controversy his private quarrel with me, in which he has never confronted me fairly; yet he is avowedly seeking to disfranchise somebody else. There are many other arguments, men of Athens, to be pleaded on Ctesiphon's behalf, but this surely is eminently reasonable, that the honest course was to fight out our own quarrels by ourselves, not to turn aside from our antagonism and try to find some one else to injure. That is carrying iniquity too far!

It is a fair inference that all his accusations are equally dishonest and untruthful. I wish, however,

οὐδεμιᾶς εἰρημένα· βούλομαι δὲ καὶ καθ' ἓν ἕκαστον
αὐτῶν ἐξετάσαι, καὶ μάλισθ' ὅσ' ὑπὲρ τῆς εἰρήνης
καὶ τῆς πρεσβείας κατεψεύσατό μου, τὰ πεπραγμέν'
ἑαυτῷ μετὰ Φιλοκράτους ἀνατιθεὶς ἐμοί. ἔστι δ'
ἀναγκαῖον, ὦ ἄνδρες Ἀθηναῖοι, καὶ προσῆκον ἴσως,
ὡς κατ' ἐκείνους τοὺς χρόνους εἶχε τὰ πράγματ'
ἀναμνῆσαι, ἵνα πρὸς τὸν ὑπάρχοντα καιρὸν ἕκαστα
θεωρῆτε.

18 Τοῦ γὰρ Φωκικοῦ συστάντος πολέμου, οὐ δι' ἐμέ
(οὐ γὰρ ἔγωγ' ἐπολιτευόμην πω τότε), πρῶτον μὲν
ὑμεῖς οὕτω διέκεισθε ὥστε Φωκέας μὲν βούλεσθαι
[231] σωθῆναι, καίπερ οὐ δίκαια ποιοῦντας ὁρῶντες,
Θηβαίοις δ' ὁτιοῦν ἂν ἐφησθῆναι παθοῦσιν, οὐκ
ἀλόγως οὐδ' ἀδίκως αὐτοῖς ὀργιζόμενοι· οἷς γὰρ
ηὐτυχήκεσαν ἐν Λεύκτροις, οὐ μετρίως ἐκέχρηντο·
ἔπειθ' ἡ Πελοπόννησος ἅπασα διειστήκει, καὶ οὔθ'
οἱ μισοῦντες Λακεδαιμονίους οὕτως ἴσχυον ὥστ'
ἀνελεῖν αὐτούς, οὔθ' οἱ πρότερον δι' ἐκείνων ἄρχον-
τες κύριοι τῶν πόλεων ἦσαν, ἀλλά τις ἦν ἄκριτος
καὶ παρὰ τούτοις καὶ παρὰ τοῖς ἄλλοις ἅπασιν ἔρις
19 καὶ ταραχή. ταῦτα δ' ὁρῶν ὁ Φίλιππος (οὐ γὰρ
ἦν ἀφανῆ), τοῖς παρ' ἑκάστοις προδόταις χρήματ'
ἀναλίσκων, πάντας συνέκρουε καὶ πρὸς αὐτοὺς
ἐτάραττεν· εἶτ' ἐν οἷς ἡμάρτανον ἄλλοι καὶ κακῶς
ἐφρόνουν, αὐτὸς παρεσκευάζετο καὶ κατὰ πάντων
ἐφύετο. ὡς δὲ ταλαιπωρούμενοι τῷ μήκει τοῦ
πολέμου οἱ τότε μὲν βαρεῖς, νῦν δ' ἀτυχεῖς Θηβαῖοι,
φανεροὶ πᾶσιν ἦσαν ἀναγκασθησόμενοι καταφεύγειν
ἐφ' ὑμᾶς, ὁ Φίλιππος, ἵνα μὴ τοῦτο γένοιτο μηδὲ
συνέλθοιεν αἱ πόλεις, ὑμῖν μὲν εἰρήνην, ἐκείνοις δὲ
20 βοήθειαν ἐπηγγείλατο. τί οὖν συνηγωνίσατ' αὐτῷ

to examine them one by one, and especially the falsehoods he told to my discredit about the peace and the embassy, attributing to me what was really done by himself with the aid of Philocrates. It is necessary, men of Athens, and not improper, to remind you of the position of affairs in those days, so that you may consider each transaction with due regard to its occasion.

When the Phocian war began—not by my fault, for I was still outside politics—you were at first disposed to hope that the Phocians would escape ruin, although you knew that they were in the wrong, and to exult over any misfortune that might befall the Thebans, with whom you were justly and reasonably indignant because of the immoderate use they had made of the advantage they gained at Leuctra. The Peloponnesus was divided. The enemies of the Lacedaemonians were not strong enough to destroy them ; and the aristocrats whom the Lacedaemonians had put into power had lost control of the several states. In those states and everywhere else there was indiscriminate strife and confusion. Philip, observing these conditions, which were apparent enough, spent money freely in bribing traitorous persons in all the cities, and tried to promote embroilment and disorder. He based his designs on the errors and follies of others, and the growth of his power was perilous to us all. When it was evident that the Thebans, now fallen from arrogance to disaster, and much distressed by the prolongation of the war, would be compelled to seek the protection of Athens, Philip, to forestall such an appeal and coalition, offered peace to you and succour to them. Now what contributed to his

πρὸς τὸ λαβεῖν ὀλίγου δεῖν ὑμᾶς ἑκόντας ἐξαπατω-
μένους; ἢ τῶν ἄλλων Ἑλλήνων, εἴτε χρὴ κακίαν εἴτ᾽
ἄγνοιαν εἴτε καὶ ἀμφότερα ταῦτ᾽ εἰπεῖν, οἳ πόλεμον
συνεχῆ καὶ μακρὸν πολεμούντων ὑμῶν, καὶ τοῦτον
ὑπὲρ τῶν πᾶσι συμφερόντων, ὡς ἔργῳ φανερὸν
γέγονεν, οὔτε χρήμασιν οὔτε σώμασιν οὔτ᾽ ἄλλῳ
οὐδενὶ τῶν ἁπάντων συνελάμβανον ὑμῖν· οἷς καὶ
δικαίως καὶ προσηκόντως ὀργιζόμενοι, ἑτοίμως
ὑπηκούσατε τῷ Φιλίππῳ. ἡ μὲν οὖν τότε συγ-
[232] χωρηθεῖσ᾽ εἰρήνη διὰ ταῦτ᾽, οὐ δι᾽ ἐμέ, ὡς οὗτος
διέβαλλεν, ἐπράχθη· τὰ δὲ τούτων ἀδικήματα καὶ
δωροδοκήματ᾽ ἐν αὐτῇ τῶν νυνὶ παρόντων πραγ-
21 μάτων, ἄν τις ἐξετάζῃ δικαίως, αἴτι᾽ εὑρήσει. καὶ
ταυτὶ πάνθ᾽ ὑπὲρ τῆς ἀληθείας ἀκριβολογοῦμαι καὶ
διεξέρχομαι. εἰ γὰρ εἶναί τι δοκοίη τὰ μάλιστ᾽ ἐν
τούτοις ἀδίκημα, οὐδέν ἐστι δήπου πρὸς ἐμέ, ἀλλ᾽
ὁ μὲν πρῶτος εἰπὼν καὶ μνησθεὶς ὑπὲρ τῆς εἰρήνης
Ἀριστόδημος ἦν ὁ ὑποκριτής, ὁ δ᾽ ἐκδεξάμενος καὶ
γράψας καὶ ἑαυτὸν μετὰ τούτου μισθώσας ἐπὶ ταῦτα,
Φιλοκράτης ὁ Ἁγνούσιος, ὁ σός, Αἰσχίνη, κοινωνὸς
οὐχ ὁ ἐμός, οὐδ᾽ ἂν σὺ διαρραγῇς ψευδόμενος, οἱ δὲ
συνειπόντες ὅτου δήποθ᾽ ἕνεκα (ἐῶ γὰρ τοῦτό γ᾽ ἐν τῷ
παρόντι), Εὔβουλος καὶ Κηφισοφῶν· ἐγὼ δ᾽ οὐδὲν
22 οὐδαμοῦ. ἀλλ᾽ ὅμως τούτων τοιούτων ὄντων καὶ
ἐπ᾽ αὐτῆς τῆς ἀληθείας οὕτω δεικνυμένων, εἰς τοῦθ᾽
ἧκεν ἀναιδείας ὥστ᾽ ἐτόλμα λέγειν ὡς ἄρ᾽ ἐγὼ πρὸς
τῷ τῆς εἰρήνης αἴτιος γεγενῆσθαι, καὶ κεκωλυκὼς
εἴην τὴν πόλιν μετὰ κοινοῦ συνεδρίου τῶν Ἑλλήνων
ταύτην ποιήσασθαι. εἶτ᾽ ὦ—τί ἂν εἰπών σέ τις
30

success, when he found you ready to fall into his
trap almost eagerly, was the baseness, or, if you
prefer the term, the stupidity, or both, of the other
Greek states. You were fighting a long and incessant war for purposes in which, as the event has
proved, they were all concerned, and yet they
helped you neither with money, nor with men, nor
with anything else ; and so, in your just and natural
indignation, you readily accepted Philip's suggestion.
The peace conceded to him at that time was due
to the causes I have named, and not, as Aeschines
maliciously insists, to me ; and the misdeeds and
the corruption of Aeschines and his party during
that peace will be found, on any honest inquiry,
to be the true cause of our present troubles. These
distinctions and explanations I offer merely for the
sake of accuracy ; for if you should suppose that
there was any guilt, or ever so much guilt, in that
peace-making business, the suspicion does not
concern me. The first man to raise the question
of peace in a speech was Aristodemus, the actor,
and the man who took up the cue, moved the
resolution, and, with Aeschines, became Philip's
hired agent, was Philocrates of Hagnus — your
confederate, Aeschines, not mine, though you lie
till you are black in the face. Their supporters in
the debate were Eubulus and Cephisophon — on
whose motives I have at present nothing to say.
I never spoke in favour of the peace. And yet, though
the facts are such and demonstrated to be such,
he has the amazing impudence to tell you that I
am to blame for the terms of peace, and that I
stopped the city from arranging the terms in con-
junction with a congress of the Greek states. Why,

ὀρθῶς προσείποι; ἔστιν ὅπου σὺ παρών, τηλικαύτην
πρᾶξιν καὶ συμμαχίαν, ἡλίκην νυνὶ διεξῄεις, ὁρῶν
ἀφαιρούμενόν με τῆς πόλεως, ἠγανάκτησας, ἢ
παρελθὼν ταῦθ' ἃ νῦν κατηγόρεις ἐδίδαξας καὶ δι-
23 εξῆλθες; καὶ μὴν εἰ τὸ κωλῦσαι τὴν τῶν Ἑλλήνων
κοινωνίαν ἐπεπράκειν ἐγὼ Φιλίππῳ, σοὶ τὸ μὴ
σιγῆσαι λοιπὸν ἦν, ἀλλὰ βοᾶν καὶ διαμαρτύρεσθαι
καὶ δηλοῦν τουτοισί. οὐ τοίνυν ἐποίησας οὐδαμοῦ
[233] τοῦτο, οὐδ' ἤκουσέ σου ταύτην τὴν φωνὴν οὐδείς·
οὔτε γὰρ ἦν πρεσβεία πρὸς οὐδέν' ἀπεσταλμένη τότε
τῶν Ἑλλήνων, ἀλλὰ πάλαι πάντες ἦσαν ἐξεληλεγ-
μένοι, οὔθ' οὗτος ὑγιὲς περὶ τούτων εἴρηκεν οὐδέν.
24 χωρὶς δὲ τούτων καὶ διαβάλλει τὴν πόλιν τὰ μέγιστ'
ἐν οἷς ψεύδεται· εἰ γὰρ ὑμεῖς ἅμα τοὺς μὲν Ἕλληνας εἰς πόλεμον παρεκαλεῖτε, αὐτοὶ δὲ πρὸς
Φίλιππον περὶ εἰρήνης πρέσβεις ἐπέμπετε, Εὐρυ-
βάτου πρᾶγμα, οὐ πόλεως ἔργον οὐδὲ χρηστῶν
ἀνθρώπων διεπράττεσθε. ἀλλ' οὐκ ἔστι ταῦτ',
οὐκ ἔστι· τί γὰρ καὶ βουλόμενοι μετεπέμπεσθ' ἂν
αὐτοὺς ἐν τούτῳ τῷ καιρῷ; ἐπὶ τὴν εἰρήνην; ἀλλ'
ὑπῆρχεν ἅπασιν. ἀλλ' ἐπὶ τὸν πόλεμον; ἀλλ'
αὐτοὶ περὶ εἰρήνης ἐβουλεύεσθε. οὔκουν οὔτε τῆς
ἐξ ἀρχῆς εἰρήνης ἡγεμὼν οὐδ' αἴτιος ὢν ἐγὼ φαίνομαι, οὔτε τῶν ἄλλων ὧν κατεψεύσατό μου οὐδὲν
ἀληθὲς ὂν δείκνυται.
25 Ἐπειδὴ τοίνυν ἐποιήσατο τὴν εἰρήνην ἡ πόλις,
ἐνταῦθα πάλιν σκέψασθε τί ἡμῶν ἑκάτερος προείλετο
πράττειν· καὶ γὰρ ἐκ τούτων εἴσεσθε τίς ἦν ὁ
Φιλίππῳ πάντα συναγωνιζόμενος, καὶ τίς ὁ πράττων
ὑπὲρ ὑμῶν καὶ τὸ τῇ πόλει συμφέρον ζητῶν. ἐγὼ

you, you—but I can find no epithet bad enough for
you—was there any single occasion when you, having
observed me in your presence trying to rob the state
of a negotiation and of an alliance which you have
just described as of the greatest importance, either
made any protest, or rose to give the people any
information whatsoever about the proceeding which
you now denounce ? Yet if I had really intrigued
with Philip to stop a Panhellenic coalition, it was your
business not to hold your peace, but to cry aloud, to
protest, to inform the people. You did nothing of
the sort. No one ever heard that fine voice of yours.
Of course not ; for at that time there was no
embassy visiting any of the Greek states, but all
the states had long ago been sounded, and there
is not an honest word in his whole story. Moreover,
his falsehoods are the worst of slanders upon Athens.
If at one and the same time you were inviting the
Greeks to make war and sending envoys to Philip to
negotiate peace, you were playing a part worthy of
Eurybatus [a] the impostor, not of a great city or of
honest men. But it is false ; it is false ! For what
purpose could you have summoned them at that
crisis ? For peace ? They were all enjoying peace.
For war ? You were already discussing terms of
peace. Therefore it is clear that I did not promote,
and was in no way responsible for, the original peace,
and that all his other calumnies are equally false.

Now observe what policy we severally adopted
after the conclusion of peace. You will thereby
ascertain who acted throughout as Philip's agent,
and who served your interests and sought the good

[a] Eurybatus, of Ephesus, a proverbial knave, gave to
Cyrus military money entrusted to him by Croesus.

DEMOSTHENES

μὲν τοίνυν ἔγραψα βουλεύων ἀποπλεῖν τὴν ταχίστην
τοὺς πρέσβεις ἐπὶ τοὺς τόπους ἐν οἷς ἂν ὄντα Φίλιππον πυνθάνωνται, καὶ τοὺς ὅρκους ἀπολαμβάνειν·
οὗτοι δ' οὐδὲ γράψαντος ἐμοῦ ταῦτα ποιεῖν ἠθέλησαν.
26 τί δὲ τοῦτ' ἐδύνατ', ὦ ἄνδρες Ἀθηναῖοι; ἐγὼ
διδάξω. Φιλίππῳ μὲν ἦν συμφέρον ὡς πλεῖστον
τὸν μεταξὺ χρόνον γενέσθαι τῶν ὅρκων, ὑμῖν δ' ὡς
ἐλάχιστον. διὰ τί; ὅτι ὑμεῖς μὲν οὐκ ἀφ' ἧς
ὠμόσαθ' ἡμέρας μόνον, ἀλλ' ἀφ' ἧς ἠλπίσατε τὴν
[234] εἰρήνην ἔσεσθαι, πάσας ἐξελύσατε τὰς παρασκευὰς
τὰς τοῦ πολέμου, ὁ δὲ τοῦτ' ἐκ παντὸς τοῦ χρόνου
μάλιστ' ἐπραγματεύετο, νομίζων, ὅπερ ἦν ἀληθές,
ὅσα τῆς πόλεως προλάβοι πρὸ τοῦ τοὺς ὅρκους
ἀποδοῦναι, πάντα ταῦτα βεβαίως ἕξειν· οὐδένα γὰρ
27 τὴν εἰρήνην λύσειν τούτων εἵνεκα. ἀγὼ προορώμενος, ἄνδρες Ἀθηναῖοι, καὶ λογιζόμενος τὸ
ψήφισμα τοῦτο γράφω, πλεῖν ἐπὶ τοὺς τόπους ἐν
οἷς ἂν ᾖ Φίλιππος, καὶ τοὺς ὅρκους τὴν ταχίστην
ἀπολαμβάνειν, ἵν' ἐχόντων τῶν Θρᾳκῶν, τῶν
ὑμετέρων συμμάχων, ταῦτα τὰ χωρί' ἃ νῦν οὗτος
διέσυρε, τὸ Σέρριον καὶ τὸ Μυρτηνὸν καὶ τὴν
Ἐργίσκην, οὕτω γίγνοιθ' οἱ ὅρκοι, καὶ μὴ προλαβὼν ἐκεῖνος τοὺς ἐπικαίρους τῶν τόπων κύριος
τῆς Θρᾴκης κατασταίη, μηδὲ πολλῶν μὲν χρημάτων πολλῶν δὲ στρατιωτῶν εὐπορήσας, ἐκ τούτων
28 ῥᾳδίως τοῖς λοιποῖς ἐπιχειροίη πράγμασιν. εἶτα
τοῦτο μὲν οὐχὶ λέγει τὸ ψήφισμ' οὐδ' ἀναγιγνώσκει·
εἰ δὲ βουλεύων ἐγὼ προσάγειν τοὺς πρέσβεις ᾤμην
δεῖν, τοῦτό μου διαβάλλει. ἀλλὰ τί ἐχρῆν με
ποιεῖν; μὴ προσάγειν γράψαι τοὺς ἐπὶ τοῦθ' ἥκον-
τας, ἵν' ὑμῖν διαλεχθῶσιν; ἢ θέαν μὴ κατανεῖμαι
τὸν ἀρχιτέκτον' αὐτοῖς κελεῦσαι; ἀλλ' ἐν τοῖν δυοῖν

34

of the city. I proposed in the Council that the
ambassadors should sail without delay to any place
where they might learn that Philip was to be found,
and there receive from him the oath of ratification;
but in spite of my resolution they refused to go.
What was the reason of that refusal? I will tell
you. It suited Philip's purposes that the interval
should be as long, and ours that it should be as
short as possible; for you had suspended all your
preparations for war, not merely from the day of
ratification, but from that on which you first began
to expect peace. That was just what Philip was
contriving all the time, expecting with good reason
that he would hold safely any Athenian possessions
which he might seize before the ratification, as no
one would break the peace to recover them. Fore-
seeing that result, and appreciating its importance,
I moved that the embassy should repair to the place
where they would find Philip and swear him in without delay, in order that the oath might be taken
while your allies the Thracians were still holding the
places about which Aeschines was so sarcastic—
Serrium, Myrtenum, and Ergisce—and that Philip
might not get control of Thrace by seizing the
positions of advantage and so providing himself
amply with men and money for the furtherance of
his ulterior designs. That decree Aeschines neither
cites nor reads; though he mentions to my discredit that I suggested in Council that the Macedonian ambassadors should be introduced. What
ought I to have done? Objected to the introduction
of men who had come expressly to confer with
you? Ordered the lessee not to give them reserved
seats in the theatre? But they could have sat in

ὀβολοῦν ἐθεώρουν ἄν, εἰ μὴ τοῦτ' ἐγράφη. ἢ τὰ
μικρὰ συμφέροντα τῆς πόλεως ἔδει με φυλάττειν,
τὰ δ' ὅλα, ὥσπερ οὗτοι, πεπρακέναι; οὐ δήπου.
λέγε τοίνυν μοι τὸ ψήφισμα τουτὶ λαβών, ὃ σαφῶς
οὗτος εἰδὼς παρέβη.

29   ΨΗΦΙΣΜΑ ΔΗΜΟΣΘΕΝΟΤΣ

[235] ['Επὶ ἄρχοντος Μνησιφίλου, ἑκατομβαιῶνος ἔνῃ καὶ
νέᾳ, φυλῆς πρυτανευούσης Πανδιονίδος, Δημοσθένης Δημοσθένους Παιανιεὺς εἶπεν· ἐπειδὴ Φίλιππος ἀποστείλας
πρέσβεις περὶ τῆς εἰρήνης ὁμολογουμένας πεποίηται συνθήκας, δεδόχθαι τῇ βουλῇ καὶ τῷ δήμῳ τῷ Ἀθηναίων,
ὅπως ἂν ἡ εἰρήνη ἐπιτελεσθῇ ἡ ἐπιχειροτονηθεῖσα ἐν τῇ
πρώτῃ ἐκκλησίᾳ, πρέσβεις ἑλέσθαι ἐκ πάντων Ἀθηναίων
ἤδη πέντε, τοὺς δὲ χειροτονηθέντας ἀποδημεῖν μηδεμίαν
ὑπερβολὴν ποιουμένους, ὅπου ἂν ὄντα πυνθάνωνται τὸν
Φίλιππον, καὶ τοὺς ὅρκους λαβεῖν τε παρ' αὐτοῦ καὶ
δοῦναι τὴν ταχίστην ἐπὶ ταῖς ὡμολογημέναις συνθήκαις
αὐτῷ πρὸς τὸν Ἀθηναίων δῆμον, συμπεριλαμβάνοντας καὶ
τοὺς ἑκατέρων συμμάχους. πρέσβεις ᾑρέθησαν Εὔβουλος
Ἀναφλύστιος, Αἰσχίνης Κοθωκίδης, Κηφισοφῶν Ῥαμνού-
σιος, Δημοκράτης Φλυεύς, Κλέων Κοθωκίδης.]

30   Ταῦτα γράψαντος ἐμοῦ τότε καὶ τὸ τῇ πόλει συμφέρον, οὐ τὸ Φιλίππῳ ζητοῦντος, βραχὺ φρον-
τίσαντες οἱ χρηστοὶ πρέσβεις οὗτοι καθῆντ' ἐν
Μακεδονίᾳ τρεῖς ὅλους μῆνας, ἕως ἦλθε Φίλιππος
ἐκ Θρᾴκης πάντα καταστρεψάμενος, ἐξὸν ἡμερῶν
δέκα, ἴσως[1] δὲ τριῶν ἢ τεττάρων, εἰς τὸν Ἑλλήσποντον ἀφῖχθαι καὶ τὰ χωρία σῶσαι, λαβόντας τοὺς
ὅρκους πρὶν ἐκεῖνον ἐξελεῖν αὐτά· οὐ γὰρ ἂν ἥψατ'
αὐτῶν παρόντων ἡμῶν, ἢ οὐκ ἂν ὡρκίζομεν αὐτόν,

_____
[1] ἴσως Blass: μᾶλλον Dind.: ὁμοίως S.

36

the threepenny seats, if I had not moved my resolution. Or was it my business to take care of the public pence, and put up the state for sale, like Aeschines and his friends ? Surely not. Please take and read this decree, which the prosecutor omitted, though he knows it well.

(The Decree of Demosthenes is read)

[In the archonship of Mnesiphilus, on the thirtieth day of Hecatombaeon, the tribe Pandionis then holding the presidency, Demosthenes, son of Demosthenes, of Paeania, proposed that, whereas Philip has sent ambassadors and has agreed to articles of peace, it be resolved by the Council and People of Athens, with a view to the ratification of the peace as accepted by vote of the first Assembly, to choose at once five ambassadors from all the citizens ; and that those so elected repair without delay wheresoever they ascertain Philip to be, and take and administer to him the oaths with all dispatch according to the articles agreed on between him and the People of Athens, including the Allies on either side. The ambassadors chosen were Eubulus of Anaphlystus, Aeschines of Cothocidae, Cephisophon of Rhamnus, Democrates of Phlya, Cleon of Cothocidae.]

My object in moving this decree was to serve Athens, not Philip. Nevertheless these excellent envoys took so little heed of it that they loitered in Macedonia for three whole months, until Philip returned from Thrace, having subdued the whole country ; though they might have reached the Hellespont in ten or perhaps in three or four days, and rescued the outposts by receiving the oaths of ratification before Philip captured them. He dared not have touched them in our presence, or we should not have accepted his oath, and so he

37

ὥστε τῆς εἰρήνης ἂν διημαρτήκει καὶ οὐκ ἂν
[236] ἀμφότερ' εἶχε, καὶ τὴν εἰρήνην καὶ τὰ χωρία.
31 Τὸ μὲν τοίνυν ἐν τῇ πρεσβείᾳ πρῶτον κλέμμα
μὲν Φιλίππου, δωροδόκημα δὲ τῶν ἀδίκων τούτων
ἀνθρώπων τοιοῦτον ἐγένετο· ὑπὲρ οὗ καὶ τότε καὶ
νῦν καὶ ἀεὶ ὁμολογῶ καὶ πολεμεῖν καὶ διαφέρεσθαι
τούτοις. ἕτερον δ' εὐθὺς ἐφεξῆς ἔτι τούτου μεῖζον
32 κακούργημα θεάσασθε. ἐπειδὴ γὰρ ὤμοσε[1] τὴν
εἰρήνην ὁ Φίλιππος προλαβὼν τὴν Θρᾴκην διὰ τούτους, οὐχὶ πεισθέντας τῷ ἐμῷ ψηφίσματι, πάλιν
ὠνεῖται παρ' αὐτῶν ὅπως μὴ ἄπιμεν[2] ἐκ Μακεδονίας,
ἕως τὰ τῆς στρατείας τῆς ἐπὶ τοὺς Φωκέας εὐτρεπῆ
ποιήσαιτο, ἵνα μή, δεῦρ' ἀπαγγειλάντων ἡμῶν ὅτι
μέλλει καὶ παρασκευάζεται πορεύεσθαι, ἐξέλθοιθ'
ὑμεῖς καὶ περιπλεύσαντες ταῖς τριήρεσιν εἰς Πύλας
ὥσπερ πρότερον κλείσαιτε τὸν τόπον, ἀλλ' ἅμ'
ἀκούοιτε ταῦτ' ἀπαγγελλόντων ἡμῶν, κἀκεῖνος
ἐντὸς εἴη Πυλῶν καὶ μηδὲν ἔχοιθ' ὑμεῖς ποιῆσαι.
33 οὕτω δ' ἦν ὁ Φίλιππος ἐν φόβῳ καὶ πολλῇ ἀγωνίᾳ,
μὴ καὶ ταῦτα προειληφότος αὐτοῦ, εἰ πρὸ τοῦ τοὺς
Φωκέας ἀπολέσθαι ψηφίσαισθε βοηθεῖν, ἐκφύγοι τὰ
πράγματ' αὐτόν, ὥστε μισθοῦται τὸν κατάπτυστον
τουτονί, οὐκέτι κοινῇ μετὰ τῶν ἄλλων πρέσβεων,
ἀλλ' ἰδίᾳ καθ' αὑτόν, τοιαῦτα πρὸς ὑμᾶς εἰπεῖν καὶ
34 ἀπαγγεῖλαι δι' ὧν ἅπαντ' ἀπώλετο. ἀξιῶ δ', ὦ
ἄνδρες Ἀθηναῖοι, καὶ δέομαι τοῦτο μεμνῆσθαι παρ'
ὅλον τὸν ἀγῶνα, ὅτι μὴ κατηγορήσαντος Αἰσχίνου
[237] μηδὲν ἔξω τῆς γραφῆς οὐδ' ἂν ἐγὼ λόγον οὐδέν'
ἐποιούμην ἕτερον, πάσαις δ' αἰτίαις καὶ βλασφημίαις
ἅμα τούτου κεχρημένου, ἀνάγκη κἀμοὶ πρὸς ἕκαστα

---

[1] ὤμοσε A: ὡμολόγησε Dind., S.
[2] ἄπιμεν Cobet: ἀπίωμεν Dind., S.

would have missed his peace, instead of gaining both his objects — peace and the strongholds as well.

Such then is the history of the first act of knavery on Philip's part, and venality on the part of these dishonest men at the time of the embassy. For that act I avow that I was then, am still, and ever shall be their enemy and their adversary. I will next exhibit an act of still greater turpitude which comes next in order of time. When Philip had sworn to the peace, having first secured Thrace because of their disobedience to my decree, he bribed them to postpone our departure from Macedonia until he had made ready for his expedition against the Phocians. He was afraid that, if we reported that he intended and was already preparing to march, you would turn out and sail round with your fleet to Thermopylae, and block the passage, as you did before; and his object was that you should not receive our report until he had reached this side of Thermopylae and you were powerless. He was so nervous, and so much worried by the fear that, in spite of his Thracian success, his enterprise would slip from his fingers if you should intervene before the Phocians perished, that he made a new bargain with this vile creature — all by himself this time, not in common with his colleagues — to make that speech and to render that report to you, by which all was lost. I earnestly beg you, men of Athens, to bear in mind throughout this trial that, if Aeschines had not gone outside the articles of indictment in his denunciation of me, I too would not have digressed; but as he has resorted to every sort of imputation and slander, I am compelled to

DEMOSTHENES

35 τῶν κατηγορημένων μίκρ' ἀποκρίνασθαι. τίνες
οὖν ἦσαν οἱ παρὰ τούτου λόγοι τότε ῥηθέντες, καὶ
δι' οὓς ἅπαντ' ἀπώλετο; ὡς οὐ δεῖ θορυβεῖσθαι τῷ
παρεληλυθέναι Φίλιππον εἴσω Πυλῶν· ἔσται γὰρ
ἅπανθ' ὅσα βούλεσθ' ὑμεῖς, ἂν ἔχηθ' ἡσυχίαν, καὶ
ἀκούσεσθε δυοῖν ἢ τριῶν ἡμερῶν, οἷς μὲν ἐχθρὸς
ἥκει, φίλον αὐτὸν γεγενημένον, οἷς δὲ φίλος, τοὐναντίον ἐχθρόν. οὐ γὰρ τὰ ῥήματα τὰς οἰκειότητας
ἔφη βεβαιοῦν, μάλα σεμνῶς ὀνομάζων, ἀλλὰ τὸ
ταὐτὰ συμφέρειν· συμφέρειν δὲ Φιλίππῳ καὶ Φωκεῦσι καὶ ὑμῖν ὁμοίως ἅπασι τῆς ἀναλγησίας καὶ
τῆς βαρύτητος ἀπαλλαγῆναι τῆς τῶν Θηβαίων.
36 ταῦτα δ' ἀσμένως τινὲς ἤκουον αὐτοῦ διὰ τὴν τόθ'
ὑποῦσαν ἀπέχθειαν πρὸς τοὺς Θηβαίους. τί οὖν
συνέβη μετὰ ταῦτ' εὐθύς, οὐκ εἰς μακράν; τοὺς
μὲν Φωκέας ἀπολέσθαι καὶ κατασκαφῆναι τὰς πόλεις
αὐτῶν, ὑμᾶς δ' ἡσυχίαν ἀγαγόντας καὶ τούτῳ πεισθέντας μικρὸν ὕστερον σκευαγωγεῖν ἐκ τῶν ἀγρῶν,
τοῦτον δὲ χρυσίον λαβεῖν, κἄτι πρὸς τούτοις τὴν μὲν
ἀπέχθειαν τὴν πρὸς Θηβαίους καὶ Θετταλοὺς τῇ
πόλει γενέσθαι, τὴν δὲ χάριν τὴν ὑπὲρ τῶν πεπραγ-
37 μένων Φιλίππῳ. ὅτι δ' οὕτω ταῦτ' ἔχει, λέγε μοι
τό τε τοῦ Καλλισθένους ψήφισμα καὶ τὴν ἐπιστολὴν
τοῦ Φιλίππου, ἐξ ὧν ἀμφοτέρων ταῦθ' ἅπανθ' ὑμῖν
ἔσται φανερά. λέγε.

ΨΗΦΙΣΜΑ

['Επὶ Μνησιφίλου ἄρχοντος, σύγκλητος ἐκκλησία ὑπὸ
στρατηγῶν καὶ πρυτάνεων, [καὶ] βουλῆς γνώμῃ, μαι-
μακτηριῶνος δεκάτῃ ἀπιόντος, Καλλισθένης Ἐτεονίκου
Φαληρεὺς εἶπε μηδένα Ἀθηναίων μηδεμιᾷ παρευρέσει ἐν
40

reply briefly to all his charges in turn. What then were the speeches he made at that crisis—the speeches that brought everything to ruin ? He told you that you need not be excited because Philip had passed Thermopylae ; that, if only you kept quiet, you would get all you wanted, and would within two or three days learn that Philip was now the friend of those to whom he came as enemy, and the enemy of those to whom he came as friend. The bonds of amity, he declared, with his most impressive eloquence, are fortified not by words but by community of interest; and it was an interest common to Philip, to the Phocians, and to all of you alike, to be quit of the unfeeling and offensive behaviour of the Thebans. Some of you were delighted to hear these remarks, for at that time we all disliked the Thebans. What was the result—not the distant, but the immediate result ? That the Phocians perished and their cities were demolished ; that you took his advice and kept quiet—and before long were carrying in your chattels from the country ; and that Aeschines pocketed his fee. A further result was that Athens got all the ill will of the Thebans and Thessalians, and Philip all their gratitude for these transactions. To prove the truth of these statements, please read the decree of Callisthenes and Philip's letter, which will make every point clear.

(The Decree of Callisthenes is read)

[In the archonship of Mnesiphilus, at an extraordinary assembly convened by the Generals and the Presidents, with the approval of the Council, on the twenty-first day of Maemacterion, Callisthenes, son of Eteonicus, of Phalerum, proposed that no Athenian be allowed upon any pretext

τῇ χώρᾳ κοιταῖον γίγνεσθαι, ἀλλ' ἐν ἄστει καὶ Πειραιεῖ,
ὅσοι μὴ ἐν τοῖς φρουρίοις εἰσὶν ἀποτεταγμένοι· τούτων δ
ἑκάστους ἣν παρέλαβον τάξιν διατηρεῖν μήτε ἀφημερεύον-
38 τας μήτε ἀποκοιτοῦντας. ὃς δ' ἂν ἀπειθήσῃ τῷδε τῷ
ψηφίσματι, ἔνοχος ἔστω τοῖς τῆς προδοσίας ἐπιτιμίοις,
ἐὰν μή τι ἀδύνατον ἐπιδεικνύῃ περὶ ἑαυτόν· περὶ δὲ τοῦ
ἀδυνάτου ἐπικρινέτω ὁ ἐπὶ τῶν ὅπλων στρατηγὸς καὶ ὁ
ἐπὶ τῆς διοικήσεως καὶ ὁ γραμματεὺς τῆς βουλῆς. κατακομίζειν δὲ καὶ τὰ ἐκ τῶν ἀγρῶν πάντα τὴν ταχίστην, τὰ
μὲν ἐντὸς σταδίων ἑκατὸν εἴκοσιν εἰς ἄστυ καὶ Πειραιᾶ, τὰ
δὲ ἐκτὸς σταδίων ἑκατὸν εἴκοσιν εἰς Ἐλευσῖνα καὶ
Φυλὴν καὶ Ἄφιδναν καὶ Ῥαμνοῦντα καὶ Σούνιον. εἶπε
Καλλισθένης Φαληρεύς.]

Ἆρ' ἐπὶ ταύταις ταῖς ἐλπίσι τὴν εἰρήνην ἐποιεῖσθε,
ἢ ταῦτ' ἐπηγγέλλεθ' ὑμῖν οὗτος ὁ μισθωτός;
39 Λέγε δὴ τὴν ἐπιστολὴν ἣν ἔπεμψε Φίλιππος μετὰ
ταῦτα.

ΕΠΙΣΤΟΛΗ

[Βασιλεὺς Μακεδόνων Φίλιππος Ἀθηναίων τῇ βουλῇ
καὶ τῷ δήμῳ χαίρειν. ἴστε ἡμᾶς παρεληλυθότας εἴσω
Πυλῶν καὶ τὰ κατὰ τὴν Φωκίδα ὑφ' ἑαυτοὺς πεποιημέ-
νους, καὶ ὅσα μὲν ἑκουσίως προσετίθετο τῶν πολισμάτων,
[239] φρουρὰς εἰσαγηοχότας, τὰ δὲ μὴ ὑπακούοντα κατὰ κράτος
λαβόντες καὶ ἐξανδραποδισάμενοι κατεσκάψαμεν. ἀκούων
δὲ καὶ ὑμᾶς παρασκευάζεσθαι βοηθεῖν αὐτοῖς γέγραφα
ὑμῖν, ἵνα μὴ πλεῖον ἐνοχλῆσθε περὶ τούτων. τοῖς μὲν
γὰρ ὅλοις οὐδὲ μέτριόν μοι δοκεῖτε ποιεῖν, τὴν εἰρήνην
συνθέμενοι καὶ ὁμοίως ἀντιπαρεξάγοντες, καὶ ταῦτα οὐδὲ
συμπεριειλημμένων τῶν Φωκέων ἐν ταῖς κοιναῖς ἡμῶν
συνθήκαις. ὥστε ἐὰν μὴ ἐμμένητε τοῖς ὡμολογημένοις,
οὐδὲν προτερήσετε ἔξω τοῦ ἐφθακέναι ἀδικοῦντες.]

40 Ἀκούεθ' ὡς σαφῶς δηλοῖ καὶ διορίζεται ἐν τῇ
πρὸς ὑμᾶς ἐπιστολῇ πρὸς τοὺς αὐτοῦ συμμάχους, ὅτι

whatsoever to pass the night in the country, but only in the City and Peiraeus, except those stationed in the garrison; that the latter keep each the post assigned to him, leaving it neither by day nor by night. Any person disobeying this decree shall be liable to the statutory penalty for treason, unless he can prove inability to obey in his own case, such plea of inability to be judged by the General of the Infantry, the Paymaster-General, and the Secretary of the Council. All property in the country shall be immediately removed, if within a radius of 120 furlongs, to the City and Peiraeus; if outside this radius, to Eleusis, Phyle, Aphidna, Rhamnus, or Sunium. Proposed by Callisthenes of Phalerum.]

Was it with such expectations that you made the peace? Were these the promises of this hireling?

Now read the letter sent to Athens afterwards by Philip.

(*Philip's Letter is read*)

[Philip, King of Macedonia, to the Council and People of Athens, greeting. Know that we have passed within the Gates, and have subdued the district of Phocis. We have put garrisons in all the fortified places that surrendered voluntarily; those that did not obey we have stormed and razed to the ground, selling the inhabitants into slavery. Hearing that you are actually preparing an expedition to help them, I have written to you to save you further trouble in this matter. Your general policy strikes me as unreasonable, to agree to peace, and yet take the field against me, and that although the Phocians were not included in the terms upon which we agreed. Therefore if you decline to abide by your agreements, you will gain no advantage save that of being the aggressors.]

Though the letter is addressed to you, it contains, as you hear, a distinct intimation intended for his

43

" ἐγὼ ταῦτα πεποίηκ᾽ ἀκόντων Ἀθηναίων καὶ λυπου-
μένων, ὥστ᾽ εἴπερ εὖ φρονεῖτ᾽, ὦ Θηβαῖοι καὶ Θετταλοί, τούτους μὲν ἐχθροὺς ὑπολήψεσθε, ἐμοὶ δὲ
πιστεύσετε,᾽᾽ οὐ τούτοις τοῖς ῥήμασιν γράψας, ταῦτα
δὲ βουλόμενος δεικνύναι. τοιγαροῦν ἐκ τούτων
ᾤχετ᾽ ἐκείνους λαβὼν εἰς τὸ μηδ᾽ ὁτιοῦν προορᾶν
τῶν μετὰ ταῦτα μηδ᾽ αἰσθάνεσθαι, ἀλλ᾽ ἐᾶσαι πάντα
τὰ πράγματ᾽ ἐκεῖνον ὑφ᾽ αὑτῷ ποιήσασθαι· ἐξ ὧν
ταῖς παρούσαις συμφοραῖς οἱ ταλαίπωροι κέχρηνται.

41 ὁ δὲ ταύτης τῆς πίστεως αὐτῷ συνεργὸς καὶ συναγω-
νιστής, καὶ ὁ δεῦρ᾽ ἀπαγγείλας τὰ ψευδῆ καὶ φενακίσας ὑμᾶς, οὗτός ἐσθ᾽ ὁ τὰ Θηβαίων ὀδυρόμενος νῦν
πάθη καὶ διεξιὼν ὡς οἰκτρά, καὶ τούτων καὶ τῶν ἐν
Φωκεῦσι κακῶν καὶ ὅσ᾽ ἄλλα πεπόνθασιν οἱ Ἕλληνες ἁπάντων αὐτὸς ὢν αἴτιος. δῆλον γὰρ ὅτι σὺ
μὲν ἀλγεῖς ἐπὶ τοῖς συμβεβηκόσιν, Αἰσχίνη, καὶ
τοὺς Θηβαίους ἐλεεῖς, κτήματ᾽ ἔχων ἐν τῇ Βοιωτίᾳ
καὶ γεωργῶν τὰ ἐκείνων, ἐγὼ δὲ χαίρω, ὃς εὐθὺς
[240] ἐξῃτούμην ὑπὸ τοῦ ταῦτα πράξαντος.

42 Ἀλλὰ γὰρ ἐμπέπτωκ᾽ εἰς λόγους, οὓς αὐτίκα μᾶλλον ἴσως ἁρμόσει λέγειν. ἐπάνειμι δὴ πάλιν εἰς
τὰς ἀποδείξεις, ὡς τὰ τούτων ἀδικήματα τῶν νυνὶ
παρόντων πραγμάτων γέγονεν αἴτια.

Ἐπειδὴ γὰρ ἐξηπατήσθε μὲν ὑμεῖς ὑπὸ τοῦ Φιλίππου διὰ τούτων τῶν ἐν ταῖς πρεσβείαις μισθω-
σάντων ἑαυτοὺς ἐκείνῳ[1] καὶ οὐδὲν ἀληθὲς ὑμῖν ἀπαγγειλάντων, ἐξηπάτηντο δ᾽ οἱ ταλαίπωροι Φωκεῖς
43 καὶ ἀνῄρηνθ᾽ αἱ πόλεις αὐτῶν, τί ἐγένετο; οἱ μὲν

---

[1] ἐκείνῳ papyrus : τῷ Φιλίππῳ S : Dind. om.

a the perpetrator: Alexander, who, in the year 335,
destroyed Thebes, and then demanded from Athens the
surrender of Demosthenes. See Introd. p. 4.

own allies : " I have done this against the wishes and the interests of the Athenians. Therefore, if you Thebans and Thessalians are wise, you will treat them as your enemies, and put your confidence in me." That is the meaning conveyed, though not in those words. By such delusions he carried them off their feet so completely that they had no foresight nor any inkling whatever of the sequel, but allowed him to take control of the whole business ; and that is the real cause of their present distresses. And the man who was hand-in-glove with Philip, and helped him to win that blind confidence, who brought lying reports to Athens and deluded his fellow-citizens, was this same Aeschines who to-day bewails the sorrows of the Thebans and recites their pitiful story, being himself guilty of those sorrows, guilty of the distresses of the Phocians, guilty of all the sufferings of every nation in Greece. Yes, Aeschines, beyond a doubt, you are sincerely grieved by that tale of woe, you are wrung with pity for the poor Thebans, you, who hold estates in Boeotia, you, who till the farms that once were theirs ; it is I who exult—I, who was at once claimed as a victim by the perpetrator [a] of those wrongs !

However, I have digressed to topics that will perhaps be more appropriately discussed later on. I return to my proof that the misdeeds of these men are the real cause of the present situation.

When you had been deluded by Philip through the agency of the men who took his pay when on embassy and brought back fictitious reports, and when the unhappy Phocians were likewise deluded, and all their cities destroyed, what happened ?

45

κατάπτυστοι Θετταλοὶ καὶ ἀναίσθητοι Θηβαῖοι
φίλον, εὐεργέτην, σωτῆρα τὸν Φίλιππον ἡγοῦντο.
πάντ' ἐκεῖνος ἦν αὐτοῖς· οὐδὲ φωνὴν ἤκουον, εἴ τις
ἄλλο τι βούλοιτο λέγειν. ὑμεῖς δ' ὑφορώμενοι τὰ
πεπραγμένα καὶ δυσχεραίνοντες, ἤγετε τὴν εἰρήνην
ὅμως· οὐ γὰρ ἦν ὅ τι ἂν ἐποιεῖτε. καὶ οἱ ἄλλοι δ'
Ἕλληνες, ὁμοίως ὑμῖν πεφενακισμένοι καὶ διημαρ-
τηκότες ὧν ἤλπισαν, ἦγον τὴν εἰρήνην αὐτοὶ τρόπον
44 τιν' ἐκ πολλοῦ πολεμούμενοι. ὅτε γὰρ περιιὼν
Φίλιππος Ἰλλυριοὺς καὶ Τριβαλλούς, τινὰς δὲ καὶ
τῶν Ἑλλήνων κατεστρέφετο, καὶ δυνάμεις πολλὰς
καὶ μεγάλας ἐποιεῖθ' ὑφ' ἑαυτῷ, καί τινες τῶν ἐκ
τῶν πόλεων ἐπὶ τῇ τῆς εἰρήνης ἐξουσίᾳ βαδίζοντες
ἐκεῖσε διεφθείροντο, ὧν εἷς οὗτος ἦν, τότε πάντες,
ἐφ' οὓς ταῦτα παρεσκευάζετ' ἐκεῖνος, ἐπολεμοῦντο.
εἰ δὲ μὴ ᾐσθάνοντο, ἕτερος λόγος οὗτος, οὐ πρὸς ἐμέ.
45 ἐγὼ μὲν γὰρ προύλεγον καὶ διεμαρτυρόμην καὶ παρ'
ὑμῖν ἀεὶ καὶ ὅποι πεμφθείην· αἱ δὲ πόλεις ἐνόσουν,
τῶν μὲν ἐν τῷ πολιτεύεσθαι καὶ πράττειν δωρο-
[241] δοκούντων καὶ διαφθειρομένων ἐπὶ χρήμασι, τῶν δ'
ἰδιωτῶν καὶ πολλῶν τὰ μὲν οὐ προορωμένων, τὰ
δὲ τῇ καθ' ἡμέραν ῥᾳστώνῃ καὶ σχολῇ δελεαζο-
μένων, καὶ τοιουτονί τι πάθος πεπονθότων ἁπάντων,
πλὴν οὐκ ἐφ' ἑαυτοὺς ἑκάστων οἰομένων τὸ δεινὸν
ἥξειν, καὶ διὰ τῶν ἑτέρων κινδύνων τὰ ἑαυτῶν
46 ἀσφαλῶς σχήσειν ὅταν βούλωνται. εἶτ', οἶμαι,
συμβέβηκε, τοῖς μὲν πλήθεσιν ἀντὶ τῆς πολλῆς καὶ
ἀκαίρου ῥᾳθυμίας τὴν ἐλευθερίαν ἀπολωλεκέναι,

46

Those vile Thessalians and those ill-conditioned Thebans regarded Philip as their friend, their benefactor, and their deliverer. He was all in all to them ; they would not listen to the voice of anyone who spoke ill of him. You Athenians, though suspicious and dissatisfied, observed the terms of peace, for you could do nothing. The rest of the Greeks, though similarly overreached and disappointed, observed the peace ; and yet in a sense the war against them had already begun ; for when Philip was moving hither and thither, subduing Illyrians and Triballians, and some Greeks as well, when he was gradually getting control of large military resources, and when certain Greek citizens, including Aeschines, were availing themselves of the liberty of the peace to visit Macedonia and take bribes, all these movements were really acts of war upon the states against which Philip was making his preparations. That they failed to perceive it is another story, and does not concern me. My forebodings and expostulations were unceasing ; I uttered them in the Assembly and in every city to which I was sent. But all the cities were demoralized. The active politicians were venal and corrupted by the hope of money : the unofficial classes and the people in general were either blind to the future or ensnared by the listlessness and indolence of their daily life ; in all the malady had gone so far that they expected the danger to descend anywhere but upon themselves, and even hoped to derive their security at will from the perils of others. In the result, of course, the excessive and inopportune apathy of the common people has been punished by the loss of their independence, while

DEMOSTHENES

τοῖς δὲ προεστηκόσι καὶ τἆλλα πλὴν ἑαυτοὺς
οἰομένοις πωλεῖν πρώτους ἑαυτοὺς πεπρακόσιν
αἰσθέσθαι· ἀντὶ γὰρ φίλων καὶ ξένων ἃ τότ' ὠνο-
μάζοντο ἡνίκ' ἐδωροδόκουν, νῦν κόλακες καὶ θεοῖς
ἐχθροὶ καὶ τἆλλ' ἃ προσήκει πάντ' ἀκούουσιν.
47 εἰκότως· οὐδεὶς γάρ, ἄνδρες Ἀθηναῖοι, τὸ τοῦ
προδιδόντος συμφέρον ζητῶν χρήματ' ἀναλίσκει,
οὐδ' ἐπειδὰν ὧν ἂν πρίηται κύριος γένηται, τῷ
προδότῃ συμβούλῳ περὶ τῶν λοιπῶν ἔτι χρῆται·
οὐδὲν γὰρ ἂν ἦν εὐδαιμονέστερον προδότου. ἀλλ'
οὐκ ἔστι ταῦτα· πόθεν; πολλοῦ γε καὶ δεῖ. ἀλλ'
ἐπειδὰν τῶν πραγμάτων ἐγκρατὴς ὁ ζητῶν ἄρχειν
καταστῇ, καὶ τῶν ταῦτ' ἀποδομένων δεσπότης
ἐστί, τὴν δὲ πονηρίαν εἰδὼς τότε δή, τότε καὶ
48 μισεῖ καὶ ἀπιστεῖ καὶ προπηλακίζει. σκοπεῖτε δέ·
καὶ γὰρ εἰ παρελήλυθ' ὁ τῶν πραγμάτων καιρός, ὁ
τοῦ γ' εἰδέναι τὰ τοιαῦτα καιρὸς ἀεὶ πάρεστι τοῖς
εὖ φρονοῦσι. μέχρι τούτου Λασθένης φίλος ὠνο-
μάζετο, ἕως προὔδωκεν Ὄλυνθον· μέχρι τούτου
Τιμόλαος, ἕως ἀπώλεσε Θήβας· μέχρι τούτου Εὔ-
δικος καὶ Σῖμος ὁ Λαρισαῖος, ἕως Θετταλίαν ὑπὸ
Φιλίππῳ ἐποίησεν. εἶτ' ἐλαυνομένων καὶ ὑβρι-
[242] ζομένων καὶ τί κακὸν οὐχὶ πασχόντων πᾶσ' ἡ
οἰκουμένη μεστὴ γέγονεν. τί δ' Ἀρίστρατος ἐν
Σικυῶνι, καὶ τί Περίλαος ἐν Μεγάροις; οὐκ
49 ἀπερριμμένοι; ἐξ ὧν καὶ σαφέστατ' ἄν τις ἴδοι
ὅτι ὁ μάλιστα φυλάττων τὴν ἑαυτοῦ πατρίδα, καὶ
πλεῖστ' ἀντιλέγων τούτοις, οὗτος ὑμῖν, Αἰσχίνη,
τοῖς προδιδοῦσι καὶ μισθαρνοῦσι τὸ ἔχειν ἐφ' ὅτῳ
48

their leaders, who fancied they were selling everything except themselves, discover too late that
their own liberty was the first thing they sold.
Instead of the name of trusty friend, in which they
rejoiced when they were taking their bribes, they
are dubbed toad-eaters and scoundrels, and other
suitable epithets. What did they expect? Men
of Athens, it is not because he wants to do a traitor
a good turn that a man spends his money; nor,
when he has once got what he paid for, has he any
further use for the traitor's counsels. Otherwise
treason would be the most profitable of all trades.
But it is not so. How could it be? Far from it! As
soon as the man who grasps at power has achieved
his purpose, he is the master of those who sold him
his mastery; and then — yes, then! — knowing
their baseness, he loathes them, mistrusts them,
and reviles them. Look at these instances, because, though the right time for action is past,
for wise men it is always the right time to understand history. Lasthenes was hailed as friend—
until he betrayed Olynthus; Timolaus, until he
brought Thebes to ruin; Eudicus and Simus of
Larissa, until they put Thessaly under Philip's heel.
Since then the whole world has become crowded with
men exiled, insulted, punished in every conceivable
way. What of Aristratus at Sicyon? or Perilaus[a]
at Megara? Are they not outcasts? From these
examples it may be clearly discerned that the man
who is most vigilant in defence of his country and
most vigorous in his opposition to treason—he is
the man, Aeschines, who provides you traitors and

---

[a] *Perilaus*: so mss. here, and, with variations, in 295;
according to Greek lexicographers the name was Perillus.

δωροδοκήσετε περιποιεῖ, καὶ διὰ τοὺς πολλοὺς
τουτωνὶ καὶ τοὺς ἀνθισταμένους τοῖς ὑμετέροις
βουλήμασιν ὑμεῖς ἐστὲ σῷοι καὶ ἔμμισθοι, ἐπεὶ διά
γ᾽ ὑμᾶς αὐτοὺς πάλαι ἂν ἀπωλώλειτε.

50 Καὶ περὶ μὲν τῶν τότε πραχθέντων ἔχων ἔτι
πολλὰ λέγειν, καὶ ταῦθ᾽ ἡγοῦμαι πλείω τῶν ἱκανῶν
εἰρῆσθαι. αἴτιος δ᾽ οὗτος, ὥσπερ ἑωλοκρασίαν
τινά μου τῆς πονηρίας τῆς ἑαυτοῦ καὶ τῶν ἀδικημάτων κατασκεδάσας, ἣν ἀναγκαῖον ἦν πρὸς τοὺς
νεωτέρους τῶν πεπραγμένων ἀπολύσασθαι. παρ-
ηνώχλησθε δ᾽ ἴσως οἳ καὶ πρὶν ἔμ᾽ εἰπεῖν ὁτιοῦν
51 εἰδότες τὴν τούτου τότε μισθαρνίαν. καίτοι
φιλίαν γε καὶ ξενίαν αὐτὴν ὀνομάζει, καὶ νῦν εἶπέ
που λέγων "ὁ τὴν Ἀλεξάνδρου ξενίαν ὀνειδίζων
ἐμοί." ἐγώ σοι ξενίαν Ἀλεξάνδρου; πόθεν
λαβόντι, ἢ πῶς ἀξιωθέντι; οὔτε Φιλίππου ξένον
οὔτ᾽ Ἀλεξάνδρου φίλον εἴποιμ᾽ ἂν ἐγώ σε, οὐχ
οὕτω μαίνομαι, εἰ μὴ καὶ τοὺς θεριστὰς καὶ τοὺς
ἄλλο τι μισθοῦ πράττοντας φίλους καὶ ξένους δεῖ
52 καλεῖν τῶν μισθωσαμένων. ἀλλ᾽ οὐκ ἔστι ταῦτα·
πόθεν; πολλοῦ γε καὶ δεῖ. ἀλλὰ μισθωτὸν ἐγώ σε
Φιλίππου πρότερον καὶ νῦν Ἀλεξάνδρου καλῶ, καὶ
οὗτοι πάντες· εἰ δ᾽ ἀπιστεῖς, ἐρώτησον αὐτούς,
μᾶλλον δ᾽ ἐγὼ τοῦθ᾽ ὑπὲρ σοῦ ποιήσω. πότερον
ὑμῖν, ὦ ἄνδρες Ἀθηναῖοι, δοκεῖ μισθωτὸς Αἰσχίνης
[243] ἢ ξένος εἶναι Ἀλεξάνδρου; ἀκούεις ἃ λέγουσιν.

53 Βούλομαι τοίνυν ἤδη καὶ περὶ τῆς γραφῆς αὐτῆς
ἀπολογήσασθαι καὶ διεξελθεῖν τὰ πεπραγμέν᾽ ἐμαυτῷ, ἵνα καίπερ εἰδὼς Αἰσχίνης ὅμως ἀκούσῃ δι᾽

50

mercenaries with something that you can betray for a bribe ; and, if you are still secure and still drawing your pay, you owe this to the great majority of these citizens, and to those who thwarted your purposes—for your own efforts would long ago have brought you to destruction.

I could say much more about the history of that time, but I suppose that what has been said is more than enough. My antagonist is to blame, for he has so bespattered me with the sour dregs of his own knavery and his own crimes, that I was obliged to clear myself in the eyes of men too young to remember those transactions. But it has perhaps been wearisome to you, who, before I said a word, knew all about his venality. However, he calls it friendship and amity ; and only just now he spoke of " the man who taunts me with the friend-ship of Alexander." I taunt you with the friend-ship of Alexander ! Where did you get it ? How did you earn it ? I am not out of my mind, and I would never call you the friend either of Philip or Alexander, unless we are to call a harvester or other hired labourer the friend of the man who pays him for his job. But it is not so. How could it be ? Far from it ! I call you Philip's hireling of yesterday, and Alexander's hireling of to-day, and so does every man in this Assembly. If you doubt my word, ask them ; or rather I will ask them myself. Come, men of Athens, what do you think ? Is Aeschines Alexander's hireling, or Alexander's friend ?—You hear what they say.

I propose then at last to come to my defence against the actual indictment, and to a recital of my public acts, that Aeschines may hear from me what

51

ἅ φημι καὶ τούτων τῶν προβεβουλευμένων καὶ
πολλῷ μειζόνων ἔτι τούτων δωρεῶν δίκαιος εἶναι
τυγχάνειν. καί μοι λέγε τὴν γραφὴν αὐτὴν λαβών.

ΓΡΑΦΗ

54 [Ἐπὶ Χαιρώνδου ἄρχοντος, ἐλαφηβολιῶνος ἕκτῃ ἰστα-
μένου, Αἰσχίνης Ἀτρομήτου Κοθωκίδης ἀπήνεγκε πρὸς
τὸν ἄρχοντα παρανόμων κατὰ Κτησιφῶντος τοῦ Λεω-
σθένους Ἀναφλυστίου, ὅτι ἔγραψε παράνομον ψήφισμα, ὡς
ἄρα δεῖ στεφανῶσαι Δημοσθένην Δημοσθένους Παιανιέα
χρυσῷ στεφάνῳ, καὶ ἀναγορεῦσαι ἐν τῷ θεάτρῳ Διονυσίοις
τοῖς μεγάλοις, τραγῳδοῖς καινοῖς, ὅτι στεφανοῖ ὁ δῆμος
Δημοσθένην Δημοσθένους Παιανιέα χρυσῷ στεφάνῳ ἀρετῆς ἕνεκα καὶ εὐνοίας ἧς ἔχων διατελεῖ εἴς τε τοὺς Ἕλληνας ἅπαντας καὶ τὸν δῆμον τὸν Ἀθηναίων, καὶ ἀνδρ-
αγαθίας, καὶ διότι διατελεῖ πράττων καὶ λέγων τὰ
βέλτιστα τῷ δήμῳ καὶ πρόθυμός ἐστι ποιεῖν ὅ τι ἂν
55 δύνηται ἀγαθόν, πάντα ταῦτα ψευδῆ γράψας καὶ παράνομα,
τῶν νόμων οὐκ ἐώντων πρῶτον μὲν ψευδεῖς γραφὰς εἰς τὰ
δημόσια γράμματα καταβάλλεσθαι, εἶτα τὸν ὑπεύθυνον
στεφανοῦν (ἔστι δὲ Δημοσθένης τειχοποιὸς καὶ ἐπὶ τῷ
θεωρικῷ τεταγμένος), ἔτι δὲ μὴ ἀναγορεύειν τὸν στέφανον
[244] ἐν τῷ θεάτρῳ Διονυσίοις τραγῳδῶν τῇ καινῇ, ἀλλ' ἐὰν
μὲν ἡ βουλὴ στεφανοῖ, ἐν τῷ βουλευτηρίῳ ἀνειπεῖν, ἐὰν
δὲ ἡ πόλις, ἐν πυκνὶ τῇ ἐκκλησίᾳ. τίμημα τάλαντα
πεντήκοντα. κλήτορες Κηφισοφῶν Κηφισοφῶντος Ῥαμ-
νούσιος, Κλέων Κλέωνος Κοθωκίδης.]

56 Ἃ μὲν διώκει τοῦ ψηφίσματος, ὦ ἄνδρες Ἀθηναῖοι, ταῦτ' ἐστίν. ἐγὼ δ' ἀπ' αὐτῶν τούτων πρῶτον οἶμαι δῆλον ὑμῖν ποιήσειν ὅτι πάντα δικαίως
ἀπολογήσομαι· τὴν γὰρ αὐτὴν τούτῳ ποιησάμενος
τῶν γεγραμμένων τάξιν περὶ πάντων ἐρῶ καθ'
57 ἕκαστον ἐφεξῆς καὶ οὐδὲν ἑκὼν παραλείψω. τοῦ
52

he knows perfectly well, the grounds on which I claim that I deserve even larger rewards than those proposed by the Council. Please take and read the indictment.

(The Indictment is read)

[In the archonship of Chaerondas, on the sixth day of Elaphebolion, Aeschines, son of Atrometus, of Cothocidae, indicted Ctesiphon, son of Leosthenes, of Anaphlystus, before the Archon for a breach of the constitution, in that he proposed an unconstitutional decree, to wit, that Demosthenes, son of Demosthenes, of Paeania should be crowned with a golden crown, and that proclamation should be made in the Theatre at the Great Dionysia, when the new tragedies are produced, that "the People crown Demosthenes, son of Demosthenes, of Paeania, with a golden crown for his merit and for the goodwill which he has constantly displayed both towards all the Greeks and towards the people of Athens, and also for his steadfastness, and because he has constantly by word and deed promoted the best interests of the people, and is forward to do whatever good he can," all these proposals being false and unconstitutional, inasmuch as the laws forbid, first, the entry of false statements in the public records ; secondly, the crowning of one liable to audit (now Demosthenes is Commissioner of Fortifications and a trustee of the Theatrical Fund) ; thirdly, the proclamation of the crown in the Theatre at the Dionysia on the day of the new tragedies ; but if the crowning is by the Council, it shall be proclaimed in the Council-house, if by the State, in the Assembly on the Pnyx. Fine demanded : fifty talents. Witnesses to summons : Cephisophon, son of Cephisophon, of Rhamnus, Cleon, son of Cleon, of Cothocidae.]

These are the clauses of the decree against which this prosecution is directed ; but from these very clauses I hope to prove to your satisfaction that I have an honest defence to offer. For I will take the charges one by one in the same order as the prosecutor, without any intentional omission. Now take

μὲν οὖν γράψαι πράττοντα καὶ λέγοντα τὰ βέλτιστά
με τῷ δήμῳ διατελεῖν, καὶ πρόθυμον εἶναι ποιεῖν ὅ
τι ἂν δύνωμαι ἀγαθόν, καὶ ἐπαινεῖν ἐπὶ τούτοις, ἐν
τοῖς πεπολιτευμένοις τὴν κρίσιν εἶναι νομίζω· ἀπὸ
γὰρ τούτων ἐξεταζομένων εὑρεθήσεται, εἴτ' ἀληθῆ
περὶ ἐμοῦ γέγραφε Κτησιφῶν ταῦτα καὶ προσήκοντα
58 εἴτε καὶ ψευδῆ· τὸ δὲ μὴ προσγράψαντ' '' ἐπειδὰν
τὰς εὐθύνας δῷ '' στεφανοῦν, καὶ ἀνειπεῖν ἐν τῷ
θεάτρῳ τὸν στέφανον κελεῦσαι, κοινωνεῖν μὲν
ἡγοῦμαι καὶ τοῦτο τοῖς πεπολιτευμένοις, εἴτ' ἄξιός
εἰμι τοῦ στεφάνου καὶ τῆς ἀναρρήσεως τῆς ἐν τούτοις εἴτε καὶ μή, ἔτι μέντοι καὶ τοὺς νόμους δεικτέον
εἶναί μοι δοκεῖ, καθ' οὓς ταῦτα γράφειν ἐξῆν τούτῳ.
οὑτωσὶ μέν, ὦ ἄνδρες Ἀθηναῖοι, δικαίως καὶ ἁπλῶς
τὴν ἀπολογίαν ἔγνωκα ποιεῖσθαι, βαδιοῦμαι δ' ἐπ'
59 αὔθ' ἃ πέπρακταί μοι. καί με μηδεὶς ὑπολάβῃ
ἀπαρτᾶν τὸν λόγον τῆς γραφῆς, ἐὰν εἰς Ἑλληνικὰς
πράξεις καὶ λόγους ἐμπέσω· ὁ γὰρ διώκων τοῦ
[245] ψηφίσματος τὸ λέγειν καὶ πράττειν τἄριστά με καὶ
γεγραμμένος ταῦθ' ὡς οὐκ ἀληθῆ, οὗτός ἐστιν ὁ
τοὺς περὶ ἁπάντων τῶν ἐμοὶ πεπολιτευμένων λόγους
οἰκείους καὶ ἀναγκαίους τῇ γραφῇ πεποιηκώς. εἶτα
καὶ πολλῶν προαιρέσεων οὐσῶν τῆς πολιτείας, τὴν
περὶ τὰς Ἑλληνικὰς πράξεις εἱλόμην ἐγώ, ὥστε καὶ
τὰς ἀποδείξεις ἐκ τούτων δίκαιός εἰμι ποιεῖσθαι.
60 Ἃ μὲν οὖν πρὸ τοῦ πολιτεύεσθαι καὶ δημηγορεῖν ἐμὲ προὔλαβε καὶ κατέσχε Φίλιππος,
ἐάσω· οὐδὲν γὰρ ἡγοῦμαι τούτων εἶναι πρὸς
ἐμέ· ἃ δ' ἀφ' ἧς ἡμέρας ἐπὶ ταῦτ' ἐπέστην ἐγὼ

first the clause which recites that in word and deed I have constantly done my best for the common weal, and that I am ever zealous to do all the good in my power, and which commends me on those grounds. Your judgement on that clause must, I take it, depend simply on my public acts, by examining which you will discover whether Ctesiphon has given a true and proper, or a false, description of my conduct. As for his proposing that a crown should be given to me, and the decoration proclaimed in the Theatre, without adding the words, " provided he shall first have rendered his accounts," I conceive that that also is related to my public acts, whether I am, or am not, worthy of the crown and of the proclamation before the people ; but I have, however, also to cite the statutes that authorize such a proposal. In this way, men of Athens, I am resolved to offer an honest and straightforward defence. I will proceed at once to the history of my own actions ; and let no one imagine that I am straying from the indictment if I touch upon Hellenic policy and Hellenic questions ; for by attacking as mendacious that clause of the decree which alleges that in word and deed I have acted for the common good, it is Aeschines who has made a discussion of the whole of my public life necessary and pertinent to the indictment. Further, out of many spheres of public activity I chose Hellenic affairs as my province, and therefore I am justified in taking Hellenic policy as the basis of my demonstration.

Well, I pass by those successes which Philip achieved and maintained before I became a politician and a public speaker, as I do not think that they concern me. I will, however, remind you of enterprises of

διεκωλύθη, ταῦτ' ἀναμνήσω καὶ τούτων ὑφέξω
λόγον, τοσοῦτον ὑπειπών. πλεονέκτημ', ἄνδρες
61 Ἀθηναῖοι, μέγ' ὑπῆρξεν Φιλίππῳ. παρὰ γὰρ
τοῖς Ἕλλησιν, οὐ τισίν, ἀλλ' ἅπασιν ὁμοίως,
φορὰν προδοτῶν καὶ δωροδόκων καὶ θεοῖς ἐχθρῶν
ἀνθρώπων συνέβη γενέσθαι τοσαύτην ὅσην οὐδείς
πω πρότερον μέμνηται γεγονυῖαν· οὓς συναγωνι-
στὰς καὶ συνεργοὺς λαβών, καὶ πρότερον κακῶς
τοὺς Ἕλληνας ἔχοντας πρὸς ἑαυτοὺς καὶ στα-
σιαστικῶς ἔτι χεῖρον διέθηκε, τοὺς μὲν ἐξαπατῶν,
τοῖς δὲ διδούς, τοὺς δὲ πάντα τρόπον διαφθείρων,
καὶ διέστησεν εἰς μέρη πολλά, ἑνὸς τοῦ συμφέροντος ἅπασιν ὄντος, κωλύειν ἐκεῖνον μέγαν
62 γίγνεσθαι. ἐν τοιαύτῃ δὲ καταστάσει καὶ ἔτ'
ἀγνοίᾳ τοῦ συνισταμένου καὶ φυομένου κακοῦ
τῶν ἁπάντων Ἑλλήνων ὄντων, δεῖ σκοπεῖν ὑμᾶς,
ἄνδρες Ἀθηναῖοι, τί προσῆκον ἦν ἑλέσθαι πράττειν
καὶ ποιεῖν τὴν πόλιν, καὶ τούτων λόγον παρ'
ἐμοῦ λαβεῖν· ὁ γὰρ ἐνταῦθ' ἑαυτὸν τάξας τῆς
63 πολιτείας εἴμ' ἐγώ. πότερον αὐτὴν ἐχρῆν, Αἰ-
[246] σχίνη, τὸ φρόνημ' ἀφεῖσαν καὶ τὴν ἀξίαν τὴν
αὑτῆς, ἐν τῇ Θετταλῶν καὶ Δολόπων τάξει συγ-
κατακτᾶσθαι Φιλίππῳ τὴν τῶν Ἑλλήνων ἀρχήν,
καὶ τὰ τῶν προγόνων καλὰ καὶ δίκαι' ἀναιρεῖν;
ἢ τοῦτο μὲν μὴ ποιεῖν, δεινὸν γὰρ ὡς ἀληθῶς,
ἃ δ' ἑώρα συμβησόμεν', εἰ μηδεὶς κωλύσει, καὶ
προῃσθάνεθ', ὡς ἔοικεν, ἐκ πολλοῦ, ταῦτα περι-
64 ιδεῖν γιγνόμενα; ἀλλὰ νῦν ἔγωγε τὸν μάλιστ' ἐπι-
τιμῶντα τοῖς πεπραγμένοις ἡδέως ἂν ἐροίμην,
τῆς ποίας μερίδος γενέσθαι τὴν πόλιν ἐβούλετ'

56

his which were thwarted after the day on which I entered public life. Of these I will render an account, premising only that Philip started with this enormous advantage. In all the Greek states— not in some but in every one of them—it chanced that there had sprung up the most abundant crop of traitorous, venal, and profligate politicians ever known within the memory of mankind. These persons Philip adopted as his satellites and accomplices. The disposition of Greeks towards one another was already vicious and quarrelsome ; and he made it worse. Some he cajoled ; some he bribed ; some he corrupted in every possible way. He split them into many factions, although all had one common interest—to thwart his aggrandizement. Now seeing that all Greece was in such a plight, and still unconscious of a gathering and ever-growing evil, what was the right policy for Athens to adopt, and the right action for her to take ? That is the question, men of Athens, which you ought to consider, and that is the issue on which I ought to be called to account ; for I was the man who took up a firm position in that department of your public affairs. Was it the duty of our city, Aeschines, to abase her pride, to lower her dignity, to rank herself with Thessalians and Dolopians, to help Philip to establish his supremacy over Greece, to annihilate the glories and the prerogatives of our forefathers ? Or, if she rejected that truly shameful policy, was she to stand by and permit aggressions which she must have long foreseen, and knew would succeed if none should intervene ? I would now like to ask the man who censures our past conduct most severely, what party he would have wished our city to join.

ἄν, πότερον τῆς συναιτίας τῶν συμβεβηκότων
τοῖς Ἕλλησι κακῶν καὶ αἰσχρῶν, ἧς ἂν Θετταλοὺς
καὶ τοὺς μετὰ τούτων εἴποι τις, ἢ τῆς περιεορα-
κυίας ταῦτα γιγνόμενα ἐπὶ τῇ τῆς ἰδίας πλεονεξίας
ἐλπίδι, ἧς ἂν Ἀρκάδας καὶ Μεσσηνίους καὶ
65 Ἀργείους θείημεν. ἀλλὰ καὶ τούτων πολλοί,
μᾶλλον δὲ πάντες, χεῖρον ἡμῶν ἀπηλλάχασιν.
καὶ γὰρ εἰ μὲν ὡς ἐκράτησε Φίλιππος ᾤχετ᾽
εὐθέως ἀπιὼν καὶ μετὰ ταῦτ᾽ ἦγεν ἡσυχίαν, μήτε
τῶν αὑτοῦ συμμάχων μήτε τῶν ἄλλων Ἑλλήνων μηδένα μηδὲν λυπήσας, ἦν ἄν τις κατὰ τῶν
ἐναντιωθέντων οἷς ἔπραττεν ἐκεῖνος μέμψις καὶ
κατηγορία· εἰ δ᾽ ὁμοίως ἁπάντων τὸ ἀξίωμα,
τὴν ἡγεμονίαν, τὴν ἐλευθερίαν περιείλετο, μᾶλλον
δὲ καὶ τὰς πολιτείας, ὅσων ἐδύνατο, πῶς οὐχ
ἁπάντων ἐνδοξόταθ᾽ ὑμεῖς ἐβουλεύσασθ᾽ ἐμοὶ πεισθέντες;
66   Ἀλλ᾽ ἐκεῖσ᾽ ἐπανέρχομαι. τί τὴν πόλιν, Αἰσχίνη, προσῆκε ποιεῖν ἀρχὴν καὶ τυραννίδα τῶν
Ἑλλήνων ὁρῶσαν ἑαυτῷ κατασκευαζόμενον Φίλ-
[247] ιππον; ἢ τί τὸν σύμβουλον ἔδει λέγειν ἢ γράφειν
τὸν Ἀθήνησιν (καὶ γὰρ τοῦτο πλεῖστον διαφέρει),
ὃς συνῄδειν μὲν ἐκ παντὸς τοῦ χρόνου μέχρι τῆς
ἡμέρας ἀφ᾽ ἧς αὐτὸς ἐπὶ τὸ βῆμ᾽ ἀνέβην, ἀεὶ
περὶ πρωτείων καὶ τιμῆς καὶ δόξης ἀγωνιζο-
μένην τὴν πατρίδα, καὶ πλείω καὶ χρήματα καὶ
σώματ᾽ ἀνηλωκυῖαν ὑπὲρ φιλοτιμίας καὶ τῶν
πᾶσι συμφερόντων ἢ τῶν ἄλλων Ἑλλήνων ὑπὲρ
67 αὑτῶν ἀνηλώκασιν ἕκαστοι, ἑώρων δ᾽ αὐτὸν τὸν
Φίλιππον, πρὸς ὃν ἦν ἡμῖν ἀγών, ὑπὲρ ἀρχῆς
καὶ δυναστείας τὸν ὀφθαλμὸν ἐκκεκομμένον, τὴν

The party that shares the guilt of all the disasters and dishonours that have befallen Greece,—the party, as one may say, of the Thessalians and their associates ? Or that which permitted those disasters in the hope of selfish gain, the party in which we may include the Arcadians, the Messenians, and the Argives ? Why, the fate of many, indeed of all, of those nations is worse than ours. For if, after his victory, Philip had at once taken himself off, and relapsed into inactivity, harassing neither his own allies nor any other Greeks, there might have been some reason for finding fault with the opponents of his enterprises ; but seeing that, wherever he could, he destroyed the prestige, the authority, the independence, and even the constitution of every city alike, who can deny that you chose the most honourable of all policies when you followed my advice ?

To resume my argument : I ask you, Aeschines, what was the duty of Athens when she perceived that Philip's purpose was to establish a despotic empire over all Greece ? What language, what counsels, were incumbent upon an adviser of the people at Athens, of all places in the world, when I was conscious that, from the dawn of her history to the day when I first ascended the tribune, our country had ever striven for primacy, and honour, and renown, and that to serve an honourable ambition and the common welfare of Greece she had expended her treasure and the lives of her sons far more generously than any other Hellenic state fighting only for itself ; and knowing as I did that our antagonist Philip himself, contending for empire and supremacy, had endured the loss of his eye, the

κλεῖν κατεαγότα, τὴν χεῖρα, τὸ σκέλος πεπηρω-
μένον, πᾶν ὅ τι βουληθείη μέρος ἡ τύχη τοῦ
σώματος παρελέσθαι, τοῦτο προϊέμενον, ὥστε
68 τῷ λοιπῷ μετὰ τιμῆς καὶ δόξης ζῆν; καὶ μὴν
οὐδὲ τοῦτό γ' οὐδεὶς ἂν εἰπεῖν τολμήσαι, ὡς τῷ
μὲν ἐν Πέλλῃ τραφέντι, χωρίῳ ἀδόξῳ τότε γ'
ὄντι καὶ μικρῷ, τοσαύτην μεγαλοψυχίαν προσῆκεν ἐγγενέσθαι ὥστε τῆς τῶν Ἑλλήνων ἀρχῆς
ἐπιθυμῆσαι καὶ τοῦτ' εἰς τὸν νοῦν ἐμβαλέσθαι,
ὑμῖν δ' οὖσιν Ἀθηναίοις, καὶ κατὰ τὴν ἡμέραν
ἑκάστην ἐν πᾶσι καὶ λόγοις καὶ θεωρήμασι τῆς
τῶν προγόνων ἀρετῆς ὑπομνήμαθ' ὁρῶσι, τοσαύτην
κακίαν ὑπάρξαι ὥστε τῆς ἐλευθερίας αὐτεπ-
69 αγγέλτους ἐθελοντὰς παραχωρῆσαι Φιλίππῳ. οὐδ'
ἂν εἷς ταῦτα φήσειεν. λοιπὸν τοίνυν ἦν καὶ
ἀναγκαῖον ἅμα πᾶσιν οἷς ἐκεῖνος ἔπραττεν ἀδικῶν
ὑμᾶς ἐναντιοῦσθαι δικαίως. τοῦτ' ἐποιεῖτε μὲν
ὑμεῖς ἐξ ἀρχῆς εἰκότως καὶ προσηκόντως, ἔγραφον
δὲ καὶ συνεβούλευον καὶ ἐγὼ καθ' οὓς ἐπολι-
[248] τευόμην χρόνους. ὁμολογῶ. ἀλλὰ τί ἐχρῆν με
ποιεῖν; ἤδη γάρ σ' ἐρωτῶ, πάντα τἄλλ' ἀφείς,
Ἀμφίπολιν, Πύδναν, Ποτείδαιαν, Ἀλόννησον· οὐ-
70 δενὸς τούτων μέμνημαι· Σέρριον δὲ καὶ Δορίσκον
καὶ τὴν Πεπαρήθου πόρθησιν καὶ ὅσ' ἄλλ' ἡ
πόλις ἠδικεῖτο, οὐδ' εἰ γέγονεν οἶδα. καίτοι
σύ γ' ἔφησθά με ταῦτα λέγοντ' εἰς ἔχθραν ἐμβαλεῖν
τουτουσί, Εὐβούλου καὶ Ἀριστοφῶντος καὶ Διο-
πείθους τῶν περὶ τούτων ψηφισμάτων ὄντων,
οὐκ ἐμῶν, ὦ λέγων εὐχερῶς ὅ τι ἂν βουληθῇς.
71 οὐδὲ νῦν περὶ τούτων ἐρῶ. ἀλλ' ὁ τὴν Εὔβοιαν
ἐκεῖνος σφετεριζόμενος καὶ κατασκευάζων ἐπι-
τείχισμ' ἐπὶ τὴν Ἀττικήν, καὶ Μεγάροις ἐπιχει-
60

fracture of his collar-bone, the mutilation of his hand and his leg, and was ready to sacrifice to the fortune of war any and every part of his body, if only the life of the shattered remnant should be a life of honour and renown? Surely no man will dare to call it becoming that in a man reared at Pella, then a mean and insignificant city, such lofty ambition should be innate as to covet the dominion of all Greece, and admit that aspiration to his soul, while you, natives of Athens, observing day by day, in every speech you hear and in every spectacle you behold, memorials of the high prowess of your forefathers, should sink to such cowardice as by a spontaneous, voluntary act to surrender your liberty to a Philip. No one will make that assertion. The only remaining, and the necessary, policy was to resist with justice all his unjust designs. That policy was adopted by you from the start in a spirit that well became you, and forwarded by me in all my proposals, according to the opportunities of my public life. I admit the charge. Tell me; what ought I to have done? I put the question to you, Aeschines, dismissing for the moment everything else—Amphipolis, Pydna, Potidaea, Halonnesus. I have no recollection of those places. Serrium, Doriscus, the sack of Peparethus, and all other injuries of our city—I ignore them utterly. Yet you told us that I entangled the citizens in a quarrel by my talk about those places, though every resolution that concerned them was moved by Eubulus, or Aristophon, or Diopeithes, not by me; only you allege so glibly whatever suits your purpose! Even now I will not discuss them. But here was a man annexing Euboea and making it a basis of operations against Attica,

ρῶν, καὶ καταλαμβάνων Ὠρεόν, καὶ κατασκάπτων
Πορθμόν, καὶ καθιστὰς ἐν μὲν Ὠρεῷ Φιλιστίδην
τύραννον, ἐν δ' Ἐρετρίᾳ Κλείταρχον, καὶ τὸν
Ἑλλήσποντον ὑφ' αὑτῷ ποιούμενος, καὶ Βυζάντιον πολιορκῶν, καὶ πόλεις Ἑλληνίδας τὰς
μὲν ἀναιρῶν, εἰς τὰς δὲ[1] τοὺς φυγάδας κατάγων,
πότερον ταῦτα ποιῶν ἠδίκει καὶ παρεσπόνδει
καὶ ἔλυε τὴν εἰρήνην, ἢ οὔ; καὶ πότερον φανῆναί
τινα τῶν Ἑλλήνων τὸν ταῦτα κωλύσοντα ποιεῖν
72 αὐτὸν ἐχρῆν, ἢ μή; εἰ μὲν γὰρ μὴ ἐχρῆν, ἀλλὰ
τὴν Μυσῶν λείαν καλουμένην τὴν Ἑλλάδ' οὖσαν
ὀφθῆναι ζώντων καὶ ὄντων Ἀθηναίων, περι-
είργασμαι μὲν ἐγὼ περὶ τούτων εἰπών, περι-
είργασται δ' ἡ πόλις ἡ πεισθεῖσ' ἐμοί, ἔστω δ'
ἀδικήματα πάνθ' ἃ πέπρακται καὶ ἁμαρτήματ'
ἐμά. εἰ δ' ἔδει τινὰ τούτων κωλυτὴν φανῆναι,
τίν' ἄλλον ἢ τὸν Ἀθηναίων δῆμον προσῆκε γενέ-
[249] σθαι; ταῦτα τοίνυν ἐπολιτευόμην ἐγώ, καὶ ὁρῶν
καταδουλούμενον πάντας ἀνθρώπους ἐκεῖνον ἠναντιούμην, καὶ προλέγων καὶ διδάσκων μὴ προΐεσθαι διετέλουν.
73 Καὶ μὴν τὴν εἰρήνην γ' ἐκεῖνος ἔλυσε τὰ πλοῖα
λαβών, οὐχ ἡ πόλις, Αἰσχίνη. φέρε δ' αὐτὰ τὰ
ψηφίσματα καὶ τὴν ἐπιστολὴν τὴν τοῦ Φιλίππου,
καὶ λέγ' ἐφεξῆς· ἀπὸ γὰρ τούτων τίς τίνος αἴτιός
ἐστι γενήσεται φανερόν.

ΨΗΦΙΣΜΑ

[Ἐπὶ ἄρχοντος Νεοκλέους, μηνὸς βοηδρομιῶνος, ἐκκλησία σύγκλητος ὑπὸ στρατηγῶν, Εὔβουλος Μνησιθέου

---

[1] τὰς μὲν . . . τὰς δὲ Butcher, with slight ms. authority:
ἃς μὲν . . . ἃς δὲ Dind., S.

attacking Megara, occupying Oreus, demolishing
Porthmus, establishing the tyranny of Philistides
at Oreus and of Cleitarchus at Eretria, subjugating
the Hellespont, besieging Byzantium, destroying
some of the Greek cities, reinstating exiled traitors
in others : by these acts was he, or was he not,
committing injustice, breaking treaty, and violating
the terms of peace ? Was it, or was it not, right
that some man of Grecian race should stand forward
to stop those aggressions ? If it was not right, if
Greece was to present the spectacle, as the phrase
goes, of the looting of Mysia,ᵃ while Athenians still
lived and breathed, then I am a busybody, because
I spoke of those matters, and Athens, too, is a
busybody because she listened to *me*; and let all
her misdeeds and blunders be charged to my
account ! But if it was right that some one should
intervene, on whom did the duty fall, if not on the
Athenian democracy ? That then was my policy. I
saw a man enslaving all mankind, and I stood in his
way. I never ceased warning you and admonishing
you to surrender nothing.

The peace was broken by Philip, when he seized
those merchantmen ; not by Athens, Aeschines.
Produce the decrees, and Philip's letter, and read
them in their proper order. They will show who
was responsible for each several proceeding.

(*A Decree is read*)

[In the archonship of Neocles, in the month Boëdromion,
at an extraordinary meeting of the Assembly convened by
the Generals, Eubulus, son of Mnesitheus, of Coprus,

ᵃ *looting of Mysia*, by pirates; the proverbial example
of cowardly non-resistance.

Κόπρειος εἶπεν· ἐπειδὴ προσήγγειλαν οἱ στρατηγοὶ ἐν τῇ
ἐκκλησίᾳ, ὡς ἄρα Λεωδάμαντα τὸν ναύαρχον καὶ τὰ μετ'
αὐτοῦ ἀποσταλέντα σκάφη εἴκοσιν ἐπὶ τὴν τοῦ σίτου παρα-
πομπὴν εἰς Ἑλλήσποντον ὁ παρὰ Φιλίππου στρατηγὸς
Ἀμύντας καταγήοχεν εἰς Μακεδονίαν καὶ ἐν φυλακῇ ἔχει,
ἐπιμεληθῆναι τοὺς πρυτάνεις καὶ τοὺς στρατηγοὺς ὅπως
ἡ βουλὴ συναχθῇ καὶ αἱρεθῶσι πρέσβεις πρὸς Φίλιππον,
74 οἵτινες παραγενόμενοι διαλέξονται πρὸς αὐτὸν περὶ τοῦ
ἀφεθῆναι τὸν ναύαρχον καὶ τὰ πλοῖα καὶ τοὺς στρατιώτας,
καὶ εἰ μὲν δι' ἄγνοιαν ταῦτα πεποίηκεν ὁ Ἀμύντας, ὅτι
οὐ μεμψιμοιρεῖ ὁ δῆμος οὐδέν· εἰ δέ τι πλημμελοῦντα
παρὰ τὰ ἐπεσταλμένα λαβών, ὅτι ἐπισκεψάμενοι Ἀθηναῖοι
ἐπιτιμήσουσι κατὰ τὴν τῆς ὀλιγωρίας ἀξίαν· εἰ δὲ
μηδέτερον τούτων ἐστίν, ἀλλ' ἰδίᾳ ἀγνωμονοῦσιν ἢ ὁ
[250] ἀποστείλας ἢ ὁ ἀπεσταλμένος, καὶ τοῦτο λέγειν, ἵνα
αἰσθανόμενος ὁ δῆμος βουλεύσηται τί δεῖ ποιεῖν.]

75 Τοῦτο μὲν τοίνυν τὸ ψήφισμ' Εὔβουλος ἔγραψεν,
οὐκ ἐγώ, τὸ δ' ἐφεξῆς Ἀριστοφῶν, εἶθ' Ἡγήσ-
ιππος, εἶτ' Ἀριστοφῶν πάλιν, εἶτα Φιλοκράτης, εἶτα
Κηφισοφῶν, εἶτα πάντες· ἐγὼ δ' οὐδὲν περὶ τούτων.
λέγε.

ΨΗΦΙΣΜΑ

[Ἐπὶ Νεοκλέους ἄρχοντος, βοηδρομιῶνος ἔνῃ καὶ νέᾳ,
βουλῆς γνώμῃ, πρυτάνεις καὶ στρατηγοὶ ἐχρημάτισαν τὰ
ἐκ τῆς ἐκκλησίας ἀνενεγκόντες, ὅτι ἔδοξε τῷ δήμῳ πρέσβεις ἑλέσθαι πρὸς Φίλιππον περὶ τῆς τῶν πλοίων
ἀνακομιδῆς καὶ ἐντολὰς δοῦναι κατὰ τὰ ἐκ τῆς ἐκκλησίας
ψηφίσματα. καὶ εἵλοντο τούσδε, Κηφισοφῶντα Κλέωνος
Ἀναφλύστιον, Δημόκριτον Δημοφῶντος Ἀναγυράσιον,
Πολύκριτον Ἀπημάντου Κοθωκίδην. πρυτανεία φυλῆς
Ἱπποθωντίδος, Ἀριστοφῶν Κολλυτεὺς πρόεδρος εἶπεν.]

76 Ὥσπερ τοίνυν ἐγὼ ταῦτα δεικνύω τὰ ψηφίσματα, οὕτω σὺ δεῖξον, Αἰσχίνη, ὁποῖον ἐγὼ

proposed that, whereas the generals have announced in
the assembly that the admiral Leodamas and the twenty
ships under his command, sent to the Hellespont to convoy
corn, have been removed to Macedonia by Philip's officer,
Amyntas, and are there kept in custody, it shall be the concern
of the presidents and of the generals that the Council be
convened and ambassadors chosen to go to Philip ; that
on their arrival they shall confer with him about the seizure
of the admiral and the ships and the soldiers, and, if Amyntas
acted in ignorance, they shall say that the people attach
no blame to him ; or, if the admiral was caught exceeding
his instructions, that the Athenians will investigate the
matter, and punish him as his carelessness shall deserve ;
if, on the other hand, neither of these suppositions is true,
but it was a deliberate affront on the part either of the
officer or of his superior, they shall state the same, in order
that the people, being apprised of it, may decide what
course to take.]

This decree was drawn up by Eubulus, not by me ;
the next in order by Aristophon ; then we have
Hegesippus, then Aristophon again, then Philocrates,
then Cephisophon, and so on. I proposed no decree
dealing with these matters. Go on reading.

(*Another Decree is read*)

[In the archonship of Neocles, on the thirtieth day of
Boëdromion, by sanction of the Council, the Presidents and
Generals introduced the report of the proceedings in the
Assembly, to wit, that the People had resolved that ambassadors be chosen to approach Philip concerning the re-
moval of the vessels, and that instructions be given them in
accordance with the decrees of the Assembly. The following
were chosen : Cephisophon, son of Cleon, of Anaphlystus,
Democritus, son of Demophon, of Anagyrus, Polycritus,
son of Apemantus, of Cothocidae. In the presidency of the
tribe Hippothontis, proposed by Aristophon, of Collytus, a
president.]

As I cite these decrees, Aeschines, you must cite

γράψας ψήφισμ' αἴτιός εἰμι τοῦ πολέμου. ἀλλ'
οὐκ ἂν ἔχοις· εἰ γὰρ εἶχες, οὐδὲν ἂν αὐτοῦ πρότερον νυνὶ παρέσχου. καὶ μὴν οὐδ' ὁ Φίλιππος
οὐδὲν αἰτιᾶται ἔμ' ὑπὲρ τοῦ πολέμου, ἑτέροις
ἐγκαλῶν. λέγε δ' αὐτὴν τὴν ἐπιστολὴν τὴν
τοῦ Φιλίππου.

ΕΠΙΣΤΟΛΗ

77 [Βασιλεὺς Μακεδόνων Φίλιππος Ἀθηναίων τῇ βουλῇ
[251] καὶ τῷ δήμῳ χαίρειν. παραγενόμενοι πρὸς ἐμὲ οἱ παρ'
ὑμῶν πρεσβευταί, Κηφισοφῶν καὶ Δημόκριτος καὶ
Πολύκριτος, διελέγοντο περὶ τῆς τῶν πλοίων ἀφέσεως
ὧν ἐναυάρχει Λεωδάμας. καθ' ὅλου μὲν οὖν ἔμοιγε
φαίνεσθε ἐν μεγάλῃ εὐηθείᾳ ἔσεσθαι, εἰ οἴεσθ' ἐμὲ
λανθάνειν, ὅτι ἐξαπεστάλη ταῦτα τὰ πλοῖα πρόφασιν
μὲν ὡς τὸν σῖτον παραπέμψοντα ἐκ τοῦ Ἑλλησπόντου
εἰς Λῆμνον, βοηθήσοντα δὲ Σηλυμβριανοῖς τοῖς ὑπ' ἐμοῦ
μὲν πολιορκουμένοις, οὐ συμπεριειλημμένοις δὲ ἐν ταῖς
78 τῆς φιλίας κοινῇ κειμέναις ἡμῖν συνθήκαις. καὶ ταῦτα
συνετάχθη τῷ ναυάρχῳ ἄνευ μὲν τοῦ δήμου τοῦ
Ἀθηναίων, ὑπὸ δέ τινων ἀρχόντων καὶ ἑτέρων ἰδιωτῶν
μὲν νῦν ὄντων, ἐκ παντὸς δὲ τρόπου βουλομένων τὸν
δῆμον ἀντὶ τῆς νῦν ὑπαρχούσης πρὸς ἐμὲ φιλίας τὸν
πόλεμον ἀναλαβεῖν, πολλῷ μᾶλλον φιλοτιμουμένων
τοῦτο συντετελέσθαι ἢ τοῖς Σηλυμβριανοῖς βοηθῆσαι·
καὶ ὑπολαμβάνουσιν αὐτοῖς τὸ τοιοῦτο πρόσοδον ἔσεσθαι.
οὐ μέντοι μοι δοκεῖ τοῦτο χρήσιμον ὑπάρχειν οὔθ' ὑμῖν
οὔτ' ἐμοί. διόπερ τά τε νῦν καταχθέντα πλοῖα πρὸς
ἡμᾶς ἀφίημι ὑμῖν, καὶ τοῦ λοιποῦ, ἐὰν βούλησθε μὴ
ἐπιτρέπειν τοῖς προεστηκόσιν ὑμῶν κακοήθως πολιτεύεσθαι, ἀλλ' ἐπιτιμᾶτε, πειράσομαι κἀγὼ διαφυλάττειν
τὴν εἰρήνην. εὐτυχεῖτε.]

79 Ἐνταῦθ' οὐδαμοῦ Δημοσθένην γέγραφεν, οὐδ'
αἰτίαν οὐδεμίαν κατ' ἐμοῦ. τί ποτ' οὖν τοῖς

some decree by proposing which I became responsible
for the war. But you cannot cite one ; if you could,
there is no document which you would have produced
more readily just now. Why, even Philip's letter
casts no blame upon me in respect of the war : he
imputes it to other men. Read Philip's actual letter.

(Philip's Letter is read)

[Philip, King of Macedonia, to the Council and People
of Athens, greeting.—Your ambassadors, Cephisophon and
Democritus and Polycritus, visited me and discussed the
release of the vessels commanded by Leodamas. Now,
speaking generally, it seems to me that you will be very
simple people if you imagine that I do not know that the
vessels were sent ostensibly to convey corn from the Hellespont to Lemnos, but really to help the Selymbrians, who are
being besieged by me and are not included in the articles
of friendship mutually agreed upon between us. These
instructions were given to the admiral, without the cognisance
of the Athenian People, by certain officials and by others
who are now out of office, but who were anxious by every
means in their power to change the present friendly attitude
of the people towards me to one of open hostility, being
indeed much more zealous for this consummation than
for the relief of the Selymbrians. They conceive that such
a policy will be a source of income to themselves ; it does
not, however, strike me as profitable either for you or for
me. Therefore the vessels now in my harbours I hereby
release to you ; and for the future, if, instead of permitting
your statesmen to pursue this malicious policy, you will
be good enough to censure them, I too will endeavour to
preserve the peace. Farewell.]

In this letter there is no mention of the name of
Demosthenes, nor any charge against me. Why does

ἄλλοις ἐγκαλῶν τῶν ἐμοὶ πεπραγμένων οὐχὶ
μέμνηται; ὅτι τῶν ἀδικημάτων ἂν ἐμέμνητο
[252] τῶν αὑτοῦ, εἴ τι περὶ ἐμοῦ γ' ἔγραφεν·[1] τούτων
γὰρ εἰχόμην ἐγὼ καὶ τούτοις ἠναντιούμην. καὶ
πρῶτον μὲν τὴν εἰς Πελοπόννησον πρεσβείαν
ἔγραψα, ὅτε πρῶτον ἐκεῖνος εἰς Πελοπόννησον
παρεδύετο, εἶτα τὴν εἰς Εὔβοιαν, ἡνίκ' Εὐβοίας
ἥπτετο, εἶτα τὴν ἐπ' Ὠρεὸν ἔξοδον, οὐκέτι πρεσβείαν, καὶ τὴν εἰς Ἐρέτριαν, ἐπειδὴ τυράννους
ἐκεῖνος ἐν ταύταις ταῖς πόλεσιν κατέστησεν.
80 μετὰ ταῦτα δὲ τοὺς ἀποστόλους ἅπαντας ἀπ-
έστειλα, καθ' οὓς Χερρόνησος ἐσώθη καὶ Βυζάντιον
καὶ πάντες οἱ σύμμαχοι. ἐξ ὧν ὑμῖν μὲν τὰ
κάλλιστα, ἔπαινοι, δόξαι, τιμαί, στέφανοι, χάριτες
παρὰ τῶν εὖ πεπονθότων ὑπῆρχον· τῶν δ' ἀδικου-
μένων τοῖς μὲν ὑμῖν τότε πεισθεῖσιν ἡ σωτηρία
περιεγένετο, τοῖς δ' ὀλιγωρήσασι τὸ πολλάκις
ὧν ὑμεῖς προείπατε μεμνῆσθαι, καὶ νομίζειν
ὑμᾶς μὴ μόνον εὔνους ἑαυτοῖς, ἀλλὰ καὶ φρονίμους
ἀνθρώπους καὶ μάντεις εἶναι· πάντα γὰρ ἐκβέβηκεν
81 ἃ προείπατε. καὶ μὴν ὅτι πολλὰ μὲν ἂν χρήματ'
ἔδωκε Φιλιστίδης ὥστ' ἔχειν Ὠρεόν, πολλὰ δὲ
Κλείταρχος ὥστ' ἔχειν Ἐρέτριαν, πολλὰ δ' αὐτὸς
ὁ Φίλιππος ὥστε ταῦθ' ὑπάρχειν ἐφ' ὑμᾶς αὐτῷ,
καὶ περὶ τῶν ἄλλων μηδὲν ἐλέγχεσθαι, μηδ' ἃ
ποιῶν ἠδίκει μηδέν' ἐξετάζειν πανταχοῦ, οὐδεὶς
82 ἀγνοεῖ, καὶ πάντων ἥκιστα σύ· οἱ γὰρ παρὰ τοῦ
Κλειτάρχου καὶ τοῦ Φιλιστίδου τότε πρέσβεις
δεῦρ' ἀφικνούμενοι παρὰ σοὶ κατέλυον, Αἰσχίνη,
καὶ σὺ προὐξένεις αὐτῶν· οὓς ἡ μὲν πόλις ὡς

---

[1] γ' ἔγραφεν Droysen: γέγραφεν S and other mss.:
ἐγεγράφει Dind.

he forget my acts, when he blames others ? Because
he could not mention me without recalling his own
transgressions, on which I fixed my attention, and
which I strove to resist. I began by proposing the
embassy to Peloponnesus, when first he tried to get
a footing there ; then the embassy to Euboea, when
he was tampering with Euboea ; then an expedition — not an embassy — to Oreus, and again to
Eretria, when he had set up tyrants in those cities.
Subsequently I dispatched all those squadrons by
which the Chersonese was rescued from him, and
Byzantium, and all our allies. By this policy you
gained much glory, receiving commendations, eulo-
gies, compliments, decorations, and votes of thanks
from the recipients of your favours. Of the nations
that suffered aggression, those who followed your
advice gained their salvation, while those who scorned
it have had many occasions since to remember your
warnings, and to acknowledge not only your goodwill but your sagacity and foresight, for everything
has turned out as you predicted. Now that Philistides would have paid a large sum for possession of
Oreus, and Cleitarchus for possession of Eretria, and
Philip himself to get those advantages of position
against you, or to escape conviction in other matters
or any inquiry into his wrongdoing in every quarter,
is well known to all—and to no one better than
to you, Aeschines. For the ambassadors who came
here from Cleitarchus and Philistides lodged at your
house and you entertained them. The govern-

ἐχθροὺς καὶ οὔτε δίκαι' οὔτε συμφέροντα λέγοντας ἀπήλασε, σοὶ δ' ἦσαν φίλοι. οὐ τοίνυν
ἐπράχθη τούτων οὐδέν, ὦ βλασφημῶν περὶ ἐμοῦ
καὶ λέγων ὡς σιωπῶ μὲν λαβών, βοῶ δ' ἀναλώ-
[253] σας. ἀλλ' οὐ σύ, ἀλλὰ βοᾷς μὲν ἔχων, παύσει
δ' οὐδέποτ', ἐὰν μή σ' οὗτοι παύσωσιν ἀτιμώ-
σαντες τήμερον.

83 Στεφανωσάντων τοίνυν ὑμῶν ἔμ' ἐπὶ τούτοις
τότε, καὶ γράψαντος Ἀριστονίκου τὰς αὐτὰς
συλλαβὰς ἅσπερ οὑτοσὶ Κτησιφῶν νῦν γέγραφε,
καὶ ἀναρρηθέντος ἐν τῷ θεάτρῳ τοῦ στεφάνου,
καὶ δευτέρου κηρύγματος ἤδη μοι τούτου γιγνο-
μένου, οὔτ' ἀντεῖπεν Αἰσχίνης παρὼν οὔτε τὸν
εἰπόντ' ἐγράψατο. καί μοι λέγε καὶ τοῦτο τὸ
ψήφισμα λαβών.

ΨΗΦΙΣΜΑ

84 [Ἐπὶ Χαιρώνδου Ἡγήμονος ἄρχοντος, γαμηλιῶνος ἕκτῃ
ἀπιόντος, φυλῆς πρυτανευούσης Λεοντίδος, Ἀριστόνικος
Φρεάρριος εἶπεν· ἐπειδὴ Δημοσθένης Δημοσθένους Παιανιεὺς πολλὰς καὶ μεγάλας χρείας παρέσχηται τῷ δήμῳ
τῷ Ἀθηναίων, καὶ πολλοῖς τῶν συμμάχων καὶ πρότερον
καὶ ἐν τῷ παρόντι καιρῷ βεβοήθηκε διὰ τῶν ψηφισμάτων,
καί τινας τῶν ἐν τῇ Εὐβοίᾳ πόλεων ἠλευθέρωκε, καὶ
διατελεῖ εὔνους ὢν τῷ δήμῳ τῷ Ἀθηναίων, καὶ λέγει καὶ
πράττει ὅ τι ἂν δύνηται ἀγαθὸν ὑπέρ τε αὐτῶν Ἀθηναίων
καὶ τῶν ἄλλων Ἑλλήνων, δεδόχθαι τῇ βουλῇ καὶ τῷ
δήμῳ τῷ Ἀθηναίων ἐπαινέσαι Δημοσθένην Δημοσθένους
Παιανιέα καὶ στεφανῶσαι χρυσῷ στεφάνῳ, καὶ ἀναγορεῦσαι τὸν στέφανον ἐν τῷ θεάτρῳ Διονυσίοις, τραγῳδοῖς
καινοῖς, τῆς δὲ ἀναγορεύσεως τοῦ στεφάνου ἐπιμεληθῆναι
τὴν πρυτανεύουσαν φυλὴν καὶ τὸν ἀγωνοθέτην. εἶπεν
[254] Ἀριστόνικος Φρεάρριος.]

ment expelled them as enemies, and as men whose proposals were dishonest and unacceptable ; but to you they were friends. Well, no part of their business was successful,—you backbiter, who tell me that I hold my tongue with a fee in my pocket, and cry aloud when I have spent it ! That is not your habit ; you cry aloud without ceasing, and nothing will ever stop your mouth,—except perhaps a sentence of disfranchisement this very day.

Although at that time you decorated me for my services, although Aristonicus drafted the decree in the very same terms that Ctesiphon has now used, although the decoration was proclaimed in the theatre, so that this is the second proclamation of my name there, Aeschines, who was present, never opposed the decree, nor did he indict the proposer. Take and read the decree in question.

(The Decree is read)

[In the archonship of Chaerondas, son of Hegemon, on the twenty-fifth day of Gamelion, the tribe Leontis holding the presidency, Aristonicus of Phrearrii proposed that, whereas Demosthenes, son of Demosthenes, of Paeania, has conferred many great obligations on the People of Athens, and has aided many of the Allies by his decrees both heretofore and upon the present occasion, and has liberated some of the cities of Euboea, and is a constant friend of the Athenian People, and by word and deed does his utmost in the interests of the Athenians themselves as well as of the other Greeks, it be resolved by the Council and People of Athens to commend Demosthenes, son of Demosthenes, of Paeania, and to crown him with a golden crown, and to proclaim the crown in the Theatre at the Dionysia at the performance of the new tragedies, the proclamation of the crown being entrusted to the tribe holding the presidency and to the steward of the festival. Proposed by Aristonicus of Phrearrii.]

85 Ἔστιν οὖν ὅστις ὑμῶν οἶδέ τιν' αἰσχύνην τῇ
πόλει συμβᾶσαν διὰ τοῦτο τὸ ψήφισμ' ἢ χλευα-
σμὸν ἢ γέλωτα, ἃ νῦν οὗτος ἔφη συμβήσεσθαι,
ἂν ἐγὼ στεφανῶμαι; καὶ μὴν ὅταν ᾖ νέα καὶ
γνώριμα πᾶσι τὰ πράγματα, ἐάν τε καλῶς ἔχῃ,
χάριτος τυγχάνει, ἐάν θ' ὡς ἑτέρως, τιμωρίας·
φαίνομαι τοίνυν ἐγὼ χάριτος τετυχηκὼς τότε,
καὶ οὐ μέμψεως οὐδὲ τιμωρίας.

86 Οὐκοῦν μέχρι μὲν τῶν χρόνων ἐκείνων, ἐν οἷς
ταῦτ' ἐπράχθη, πάντως[1] ἀνωμολόγημαι τἄριστα
πράττειν τῇ πόλει, τῷ νικᾶν, ὅτ' ἐβουλεύεσθε,
λέγων καὶ γράφων, τῷ καταπραχθῆναι τὰ γραφέντα, καὶ στεφάνους ἐξ αὐτῶν τῇ πόλει καὶ
ἐμοὶ καὶ πᾶσιν γενέσθαι, τῷ θυσίας τοῖς θεοῖς
καὶ προσόδους ὡς ἀγαθῶν τούτων ὄντων ὑμᾶς
πεποιῆσθαι.

87 Ἐπειδὴ τοίνυν ἐκ τῆς Εὐβοίας ὁ Φίλιππος ὑφ'
ὑμῶν ἐξηλάθη τοῖς μὲν ὅπλοις, τῇ δὲ πολιτείᾳ
καὶ τοῖς ψηφίσμασι, κἂν διαρραγῶσί τινες τούτων, ὑπ' ἐμοῦ, ἕτερον κατὰ τῆς πόλεως ἐπιτει-
χισμὸν ἐζήτει. ὁρῶν δ' ὅτι σίτῳ πάντων ἀνθρώπων πλείστῳ χρώμεθ' ἐπεισάκτῳ, βουλόμενος τῆς σιτοπομπίας κύριος γενέσθαι, παρελθὼν
ἐπὶ Θρᾴκης Βυζαντίους συμμάχους ὄντας αὑτῷ
τὸ μὲν πρῶτον ἠξίου συμπολεμεῖν τὸν πρὸς ὑμᾶς
πόλεμον, ὡς δ' οὐκ ἤθελον οὐδ' ἐπὶ τούτοις ἔφασαν
τὴν συμμαχίαν πεποιῆσθαι, λέγοντες ἀληθῆ, χά-
ρακα βαλόμενος πρὸς τῇ πόλει καὶ μηχανήματ'
ἐπιστήσας ἐπολιόρκει. τούτων δὲ γιγνομένων,

88 ὅ τι μὲν προσῆκε ποιεῖν ὑμᾶς, οὐκ ἐπερωτήσω·

[1] πάντως Dobree: πάντας S: πάντας ... τοὺς χρόνους
Dind.

72

Is any one of you aware of any dishonour, contempt, or ridicule that has befallen the city in consequence of that decree, such as he now tells you will follow, if I am crowned ? While acts are still recent and notorious, they are requited with gratitude, if good, and with punishment, if evil, and from this decree it appears that I received on that occasion gratitude, not censure nor punishment.

Therefore, up to the date of those transactions it is shown by common consent that my conduct was entirely beneficial to the commonwealth. The proofs are, that my speeches and motions were successful at your deliberations ; that my resolutions were carried into effect ; that thereby decorations came to the city and to all of you as well as to me ; and that for these successes you thanked the gods with sacrifices and processions.

When Philip was driven out of Euboea by your arms, and also,—though these men choke themselves with their denials,—by my policy and my decrees, he cast about for a second plan of attack against Athens ; and observing that we consume more imported corn than any other nation, he proposed to get control of the carrying trade in corn. He advanced towards Thrace, and the first thing he did was to claim the help of the Byzantines as his allies in the war against you. When they refused, declaring with entire truth that the terms of alliance included no such obligation, he set up a stockade against their city, planted artillery, and began a siege. I will not further ask what was your proper course in those circumstances,—the answer is too

DEMOSTHENES

[255] δῆλον γάρ ἐστιν ἅπασιν. ἀλλὰ τίς ἦν ὁ βοη-
θήσας τοῖς Βυζαντίοις καὶ σώσας αὐτούς; τίς ὁ
κωλύσας τὸν Ἑλλήσποντον ἀλλοτριωθῆναι κατ᾽
ἐκείνους τοὺς χρόνους; ὑμεῖς, ἄνδρες Ἀθηναῖοι.
τὸ δ᾽ ὑμεῖς ὅταν εἴπω, τὴν πόλιν λέγω. τίς
δ᾽ ὁ τῇ πόλει λέγων καὶ γράφων καὶ πράττων
καὶ ἁπλῶς ἑαυτὸν εἰς τὰ πράγματ᾽ ἀφειδῶς δούς;
89 ἐγώ. ἀλλὰ μὴν ἡλίκα ταῦτ᾽ ὠφέλησεν ἅπαντας,
οὐκέτ᾽ ἐκ τοῦ λόγου δεῖ μαθεῖν, ἀλλ᾽ ἔργῳ πε-
πείρασθε· ὁ γὰρ τότ᾽ ἐνστὰς πόλεμος, ἄνευ τοῦ
καλὴν δόξαν ἐνεγκεῖν, ἐν πᾶσι τοῖς κατὰ τὸν
βίον ἀφθονωτέροις καὶ εὐωνοτέροις διῆγεν ὑμᾶς
τῆς νῦν εἰρήνης, ἣν οὗτοι κατὰ τῆς πατρίδος
τηροῦσιν οἱ χρηστοί, ἐπὶ ταῖς μελλούσαις ἐλπίσιν,
ὧν διαμάρτοιεν, καὶ μετάσχοιεν ὧν ὑμεῖς οἱ τὰ
βέλτιστα βουλόμενοι τοὺς θεοὺς αἰτεῖτε, μὴ μετα-
δοῖεν ὑμῖν ὧν αὐτοὶ προῄρηνται. λέγε δ᾽ αὐτοῖς
καὶ τοὺς τῶν Βυζαντίων στεφάνους καὶ τοὺς
τῶν Περινθίων, οἷς ἐστεφάνουν ἐκ τούτων τὴν
πόλιν.

ΨΗΦΙΣΜΑ ΒΥΖΑΝΤΙΩΝ

90 [Ἐπὶ ἱερομνάμονος Βοσπορίχω Δαμάγητος ἐν τᾷ ἁλίᾳ
ἔλεξεν, ἐκ τᾶς βωλᾶς λαβὼν ῥήτραν, ἐπειδὴ ὁ δᾶμος ὁ
Ἀθαναίων ἔν τε τοῖς προγεναμένοις καιροῖς εὐνόεων διατελεῖ Βυζαντίοις καὶ τοῖς συμμάχοις καὶ συγγενέσι Περιν-
θίοις καὶ πολλὰς καὶ μεγάλας χρείας παρέσχηται, ἔν τε
τῷ παρεστακότι καιρῷ Φιλίππω τῶ Μακεδόνος ἐπιστρα-
τεύσαντος ἐπὶ τὰν χώραν καὶ τὰν πόλιν ἐπ᾽ ἀναστάσει
Βυζαντίων καὶ Περινθίων καὶ τὰν χώραν δαίοντος καὶ
[256] δενδροκοπέοντος, βοαθήσας πλοίοις ἑκατὸν καὶ εἴκοσι καὶ
σίτῳ καὶ βέλεσι καὶ ὁπλίταις ἐξείλετο ἁμὲ ἐκ τῶν μεγάλων
κινδύνων καὶ ἀποκατέστασε τὰν πάτριον πολιτείαν καὶ
74

obvious. But who sent reinforcements to the Byzantines and delivered them ? Who prevented the
estrangement of the Hellespont at that crisis ? You,
men of Athens ; and when I say you, I mean the
whole city. Who advised the city, moved the resolutions, took action, devoted himself whole-heartedly
and without stint to that business ? I did ; and I
need not argue how profitable my policy was, for
you know it by experience. The war in which we
then engaged, apart from the renown it brought to
you, made all the necessaries of life more abundant
and cheaper than the peace we now enjoy, the peace
which these worthies cherish to the disadvantage
of the city, in view of future expectations ! May
those expectations fail ! May they share only the
blessings for which you men of honest intent suppli-
cate the gods ! And may they never bestow upon
you any share in the principles they have chosen !
Now read of the crowns of the Byzantines and of the
Perinthians, conferred by them upon the city for
these services.

(*The Decree of the Byzantines is read*)

[In the recordership of Bosporichus, Damagetus proposed
in the Assembly, with the sanction of the Council, that,
whereas the Athenian People in former times have been
constant friends of the Byzantines and of their allies
and kinsmen the Perinthians, and have conferred many
great services upon them, and recently, when Philip of
Macedon attacked their land and city to exterminate the
Byzantines and Perinthians, burning and devastating the
land, they came to our aid with a hundred and twenty ships
and provisions and arms and infantry, and extricated us
from great dangers, and restored our original constitution

75

DEMOSTHENES

91 τὼς νόμως καὶ τὼς τάφως, δεδόχθαι τῷ δάμῳ τῷ Βυζαντίων καὶ Περινθίων Ἀθαναίοις δόμεν ἐπιγαμίαν, πολιτείαν, ἔγκτασιν γᾶς καὶ οἰκιᾶν, προεδρίαν ἐν τοῖς ἀγῶσι, πόθοδον ποτὶ τὰν βωλὰν καὶ τὸν δᾶμον πράτοις πεδὰ τὰ ἱερά, καὶ τοῖς κατοικεῖν ἐθέλουσι τὰν πόλιν ἀλειτουργήτοις ἦμεν πασᾶν τᾶν λειτουργιᾶν· στᾶσαι δὲ καὶ εἰκόνας τρεῖς ἑκκαιδεκαπάχεις ἐν τῷ Βοσπορείῳ, στεφανούμενον τὸν δᾶμον τὸν Ἀθαναίων ὑπὸ τῶ δάμω τῶ Βυζαντίων καὶ Περινθίων· ἀποστεῖλαι δὲ καὶ θεαρίας ἐς τὰς ἐν τᾷ Ἑλλάδι παναγύριας, Ἴσθμια καὶ Νέμεα καὶ Ὀλύμπια καὶ Πύθια, καὶ ἀνακαρῦξαι τὼς στεφάνως οἷς ἐστεφάνωται ὁ δᾶμος ὁ Ἀθαναίων ὑφ' ἀμέων, ὅπως ἐπιστέωνται οἱ Ἕλλανες τάν τε Ἀθαναίων ἀρετὰν καὶ τὰν Βυζαντίων καὶ Περινθίων εὐχαριστίαν.]

92 Λέγε καὶ τοὺς παρὰ τῶν ἐν Χερρονήσῳ στεφάνους.

ΨΗΦΙΣΜΑ ΧΕΡΡΟΝΗΣΙΤΩΝ

[Χερρονησιτῶν οἱ κατοικοῦντες Σηστόν, Ἐλαιοῦντα, Μάδυτον, Ἀλωπεκόννησον, στεφανοῦσιν Ἀθηναίων τὴν βουλὴν καὶ τὸν δῆμον χρυσῷ στεφάνῳ ἀπὸ ταλάντων ἑξήκοντα, καὶ Χάριτος βωμὸν ἱδρύονται καὶ Δήμου Ἀθηναίων, ὅτι πάντων τῶν μεγίστων ἀγαθῶν παραίτιος γέγονε Χερρονησίταις, ἐξελόμενος ἐκ τῆς Φιλίππου καὶ ἀποδοὺς [257] τὰς πατρίδας, τοὺς νόμους, τὴν ἐλευθερίαν, τὰ ἱερά. καὶ ἐν τῷ μετὰ ταῦτα αἰῶνι παντὶ οὐκ ἐλλείψει εὐχαριστῶν καὶ ποιῶν ὅ τι ἂν δύνηται ἀγαθόν. ταῦτα ἐψηφίσαντο ἐν κοινῷ βουλευτηρίῳ.]

93 Οὐκοῦν οὐ μόνον τὸ Χερρόνησον καὶ Βυζάντιον σῶσαι, οὐδὲ τὸ κωλῦσαι τὸν Ἑλλήσποντον ὑπὸ Φιλίππῳ γενέσθαι τότε, οὐδὲ τὸ τιμᾶσθαι τὴν πόλιν ἐκ τούτων ἡ προαίρεσις ἡ ἐμὴ καὶ ἡ πολιτεία διεπράξατο, ἀλλὰ καὶ πᾶσιν ἔδειξεν ἀνθρώποις

76

and our laws and our sepulchres, it be resolved by the People of Byzantium and Perinthus to grant to the Athenians rights of intermarriage, citizenship, tenure of land and houses, the seat of honour at the games, access to the Council and the people immediately after the sacrifices, and immunity from all public services for those who wish to settle in our city; also to erect three statues, sixteen cubits in height, in the Bosporeum, representing the People of Athens being crowned by the Peoples of Byzantium and Perinthus; also to send deputations to the Panhellenic gatherings, the Isthmian, Nemean, Olympian, and Pythian games, and there to proclaim the crown wherewith the Athenian People has been crowned by us, that the Greeks may know the merits of the Athenians and the gratitude of the Byzantines and the Perinthians.]

Read also of the crowns awarded by the inhabitants of the Chersonese.

(*The Decree of the Chersonesites is read*)

[The peoples of the Chersonesus inhabiting Sestus, Elaeus, Madytus, and Alopeconnesus, do crown the Council and People of Athens with a golden crown of sixty talents' value,[a] and erect an altar to Gratitude and to the People of Athens, because they have been a contributory cause of all the greatest blessings to the peoples of the Chersonesus, having rescued them from Philip and restored their fatherland, their laws, their freedom, and their temples; also in all time to come they will not fail to be grateful and to do them every service in their power. This decree was passed in Confederate Council.]

Thus my considered policy was not only successful in delivering the Chersonese and Byzantium, in preventing the subjugation of the Hellespont to Philip, and in bringing distinction to the city, but it exhibited

[a] These can hardly be standard talents. Perhaps they were the later conventional talents, mentioned by Philemon, which were equal to three gold staters or didrachmas (say 4s. 6d.); or perhaps the Chersonesus had an unknown standard of its own; or perhaps the forger of these documents was generous in disbursing other people's gold.

77

τήν τε τῆς πόλεως καλοκαγαθίαν καὶ τὴν Φιλίππου κακίαν. ὁ μὲν γὰρ σύμμαχος ὢν τοῖς
Βυζαντίοις πολιορκῶν αὐτοὺς ἑωρᾶθ᾽ ὑπὸ πάντων,
94 οὗ τί γένοιτ᾽ ἂν αἴσχιον ἢ μιαρώτερον; ὑμεῖς
δ᾽ οἳ καὶ μεμψάμενοι πολλὰ καὶ δίκαι᾽ ἂν ἐκείνοις
εἰκότως περὶ ὧν ἠγνωμονήκεσαν εἰς ὑμᾶς ἐν τοῖς
ἔμπροσθεν χρόνοις, οὐ μόνον οὐ μνησικακοῦντες
οὐδὲ προϊέμενοι τοὺς ἀδικουμένους, ἀλλὰ καὶ
σῴζοντες ἐφαίνεσθε, ἐξ ὧν δόξαν, εὔνοιαν παρὰ
πάντων ἐκτᾶσθε. καὶ μὴν ὅτι μὲν πολλοὺς
ἐστεφανώκατ᾽ ἤδη τῶν πολιτευομένων ἅπαντες
ἴσασι· δι᾽ ὅντινα δ᾽ ἄλλον ἡ πόλις ἐστεφάνωται,
σύμβουλον λέγω καὶ ῥήτορα, πλὴν δι᾽ ἔμ᾽, οὐδ᾽
ἂν εἷς εἰπεῖν ἔχοι.

95 Ἵνα τοίνυν καὶ τὰς βλασφημίας, ἃς κατὰ τῶν
Εὐβοέων καὶ τῶν Βυζαντίων ἐποιήσατο, εἴ τι
δυσχερὲς αὐτοῖς ἐπέπρακτο πρὸς ὑμᾶς ὑπο-
μιμνήσκων, συκοφαντίας οὔσας ἐπιδείξω μὴ μόνον
τῷ ψευδεῖς εἶναι (τοῦτο μὲν γὰρ ὑπάρχειν ὑμᾶς
εἰδότας ἡγοῦμαι), ἀλλὰ καὶ τῷ, εἰ τὰ μάλιστ᾽
ἦσαν ἀληθεῖς, οὕτως ὡς ἐγὼ κέχρημαι τοῖς πράγμασι συμφέρειν χρήσασθαι, ἓν ἢ δύο βούλομαι
[258] τῶν καθ᾽ ὑμᾶς πεπραγμένων καλῶν τῇ πόλει
διεξελθεῖν, καὶ ταῦτ᾽ ἐν βραχέσι· καὶ γὰρ ἄνδρ᾽
ἰδίᾳ καὶ πόλιν κοινῇ πρὸς τὰ κάλλιστα τῶν ὑπαρχόντων ἀεὶ δεῖ πειρᾶσθαι τὰ λοιπὰ πράττειν.
96 ὑμεῖς τοίνυν, ἄνδρες Ἀθηναῖοι, Λακεδαιμονίων
γῆς καὶ θαλάττης ἀρχόντων, καὶ τὰ κύκλῳ τῆς
Ἀττικῆς κατεχόντων ἁρμοσταῖς καὶ φρουραῖς,
Εὔβοιαν, Τάναγραν, τὴν Βοιωτίαν ἅπασαν, Μέ-
γαρ᾽, Αἴγιναν, Κέων, τὰς¹ ἄλλας νήσους, οὔτε

¹ Κέων, τὰς Dobree : Κλεωνὰς S : Κλεωνὰς, τὰς Dind.

to mankind the noble spirit of Athens and the depravity of Philip. For he, the ally of the Byzantines, was besieging them in the sight of all men : could anything be more discreditable and outrageous ? But you, who might with justice have found fault with them for earlier acts of trespass, so far from being vindictive and deserting them in their distress, appeared as their deliverers, and by that conduct won renown,—the goodwill of the whole world. Moreover all know that you have awarded crowns to many politicians ; but no one can name any man—I mean any statesman or orator—except me, by whose exertions the city itself has been crowned.

I wish to show you that the attack Aeschines made on the Euboeans and the Byzantines by raking up old stories of their disobliging conduct towards you, was mere spiteful calumny,—not only because, as I think you all must know, those stories are false, but because, even if they were entirely true, the merits of my policy are not affected,—by relating, with due brevity, two or three of the noble actions of your own commonwealth ; for the public conduct of a state, like the private conduct of a man, should always be guided by its most honourable traditions. When the Lacedaemonians, men of Athens, had the supremacy of land and sea, and were holding with governors and garrisons all the frontiers of Attica, Euboea, Tanagra, all Boeotia, Megara, Aegina, Ceos, and the other islands, for at that time Athens had

DEMOSTHENES

ναῦς οὔτε τείχη τῆς πόλεως τότε κεκτημένης,
ἐξῆλθετ᾽ εἰς Ἁλίαρτον καὶ πάλιν οὐ πολλαῖς
ἡμέραις ὕστερον εἰς Κόρινθον, τῶν τότ᾽ Ἀθηναίων
πόλλ᾽ ἂν ἐχόντων μνησικακῆσαι καὶ Κορινθίοις
καὶ Θηβαίοις τῶν περὶ τὸν Δεκελεικὸν πόλεμον
πραχθέντων· ἀλλ᾽ οὐκ ἐποίουν τοῦτ᾽, οὐδ᾽ ἐγγύς.
97 καίτοι τότε ταῦτ᾽ ἀμφότερ᾽, Αἰσχίνη, οὔθ᾽ ὑπὲρ
εὐεργετῶν ἐποίουν οὔτ᾽ ἀκίνδυν᾽ ἑώρων. ἀλλ᾽
οὐ διὰ ταῦτα προΐεντο τοὺς καταφεύγοντας ἐφ᾽
αὑτούς, ἀλλ᾽ ὑπὲρ εὐδοξίας καὶ τιμῆς ἤθελον τοῖς
δεινοῖς αὑτοὺς διδόναι, ὀρθῶς καὶ καλῶς βου-
λευόμενοι. πέρας μὲν γὰρ ἅπασιν ἀνθρώποις
ἐστὶ τοῦ βίου θάνατος, κἂν ἐν οἰκίσκῳ τις αὑτὸν
καθείρξας τηρῇ· δεῖ δὲ τοὺς ἀγαθοὺς ἄνδρας
ἐγχειρεῖν μὲν ἅπασιν ἀεὶ τοῖς καλοῖς, τὴν ἀγαθὴν
προβαλλομένους ἐλπίδα, φέρειν δ᾽ ὅ τι ἂν ὁ θεὸς
98 διδῷ γενναίως. ταῦτ᾽ ἐποίουν οἱ ὑμέτεροι πρόγονοι, ταῦθ᾽ ὑμεῖς οἱ πρεσβύτεροι, οἳ Λακεδαιμονίους οὐ φίλους ὄντας οὐδ᾽ εὐεργέτας, ἀλλὰ
πολλὰ τὴν πόλιν ἡμῶν ἠδικηκότας καὶ μεγάλα,
ἐπειδὴ Θηβαῖοι κρατήσαντες ἐν Λεύκτροις ἀνελεῖν ἐπεχείρουν, διεκωλύσατε, οὐ φοβηθέντες τὴν
τότε Θηβαίοις ῥώμην καὶ δόξαν ὑπάρχουσαν,
[259] οὐδ᾽ ὑπὲρ οἷα πεποιηκότων ἀνθρώπων κινδυνεύ-
99 σετε διαλογισάμενοι. καὶ γάρ τοι πᾶσι τοῖς
Ἕλλησιν ἐδείξατ᾽ ἐκ τούτων ὅτι, κἂν ὁτιοῦν τις
εἰς ὑμᾶς ἐξαμάρτῃ, τούτων τὴν ὀργὴν εἰς τἄλλ᾽
ἔχετε, ἐὰν δ᾽ ὑπὲρ σωτηρίας ἢ ἐλευθερίας κίνδυνός

80

no ships and no walls, you marched out to Haliartus,[a] and again a few days later to Corinth. The Athenians of those days had good reason to bear malice against the Corinthians and the Thebans for their conduct during the Decelean War; but they bore no malice whatever. Yet in making both these expeditions, Aeschines, they were not requiting benefits received, and they knew they were taking risks. They did not use those pleas as excuses for deserting men who had sought their protection. For the sake of honour and glory they willingly encountered those perils,—a righteous and a noble resolve! For every man death is the goal of life, though he keep himself cloistered in his chamber; but it behoves the brave to set their hands to every noble enterprise, bearing before them the buckler of hope, and to endure gallantly whatever fate God may allot. So your forefathers played their part; so also did the elder among yourselves. The Lacedaemonians were no friends or benefactors of ours; they had done many grievous wrongs to our commonwealth; but when the Thebans, after their victory at Leuctra, threatened to exterminate them, you balked that revenge, without fear of the prowess and high repute of the Thebans, without thought of the past misdeeds of the people for whom you imperilled yourselves. And so you taught to all Greece the lesson that, however gravely a nation may have offended against you, you keep your resentment for proper occasions, but if ever their life or their liberty is endangered, you

---

[a] Haliartus, 395 B.C.; Corinth, 394 B.C.; Decelean war, the last period, 413–404, of the Peloponnesian War, when the Spartans held the fortified position of Decelea in Attica.

τις αὐτοὺς καταλαμβάνῃ, οὔτε μνησικακήσετ'
οὔθ' ὑπολογιεῖσθε.

Καὶ οὐκ ἐπὶ τούτων μόνων οὕτως ἐσχήκατε,
ἀλλὰ πάλιν σφετεριζομένων Θηβαίων τὴν Εὔβοιαν,
οὐ περιείδετε, οὐδ' ὧν ὑπὸ Θεμίσωνος καὶ Θεο-
δώρου περὶ Ὠρωπὸν ἠδίκησθ' ἀνεμνήσθητε, ἀλλ'
ἐβοηθήσατε καὶ τούτοις, τῶν ἐθελοντῶν τότε
τριηράρχων πρῶτον γενομένων τῇ πόλει, ὧν
100 εἷς ἦν ἐγώ. ἀλλ' οὔπω περὶ τούτων. καὶ
καλὸν μὲν ἐποιήσατε καὶ τὸ σῶσαι τὴν νῆσον,
πολλῷ δ' ἔτι τούτου κάλλιον τὸ καταστάντες
κύριοι καὶ τῶν σωμάτων καὶ τῶν πόλεων ἀποδοῦναι ταῦτα δικαίως αὐτοῖς τοῖς ἐξημαρτηκόσιν
εἰς ὑμᾶς, μηδὲν ὧν ἠδίκησθε ἐν οἷς ἐπιστεύθηθ'
ὑπολογισάμενοι. μυρία τοίνυν ἕτερ' εἰπεῖν ἔχων
παραλείπω, ναυμαχίας, ἐξόδους πεζάς, στρατείας,
καὶ πάλαι γεγονυίας καὶ νῦν ἐφ' ὑμῶν αὐτῶν,
ἃς ἁπάσας ἡ πόλις τῆς τῶν ἄλλων Ἑλλήνων
101 ἐλευθερίας καὶ σωτηρίας πεποίηται. εἶτ' ἐγὼ
τεθεωρηκὼς ἐν τοσούτοις καὶ τοιούτοις τὴν πόλιν
ὑπὲρ τῶν τοῖς ἄλλοις συμφερόντων ἐθέλουσαν
ἀγωνίζεσθαι, ὑπὲρ αὐτῆς τρόπον τινὰ τῆς βουλῆς
οὔσης τί ἔμελλον κελεύσειν, ἢ τί συμβουλεύσειν
αὐτῇ ποιεῖν; μνησικακεῖν νὴ Δία πρὸς τοὺς
βουλομένους σῴζεσθαι, καὶ προφάσεις ζητεῖν δι'
[260] ἃς ἅπαντα προησόμεθα· καὶ τίς οὐκ ἂν ἀπέκτεινέ
με δικαίως, εἴ τι τῶν ὑπαρχόντων τῇ πόλει καλῶν
λόγῳ μόνον καταισχύνειν ἐπεχείρησα; ἐπεὶ τό
γ' ἔργον οὐκ ἂν ἐποιήσαθ' ὑμεῖς, ἀκριβῶς οἶδ'
ἐγώ· εἰ γὰρ ἐβούλεσθε, τί ἦν ἐμποδών; οὐκ
ἐξῆν; οὐχ ὑπῆρχον οἱ ταῦτ' ἐροῦντες οὗτοι;

102 Βούλομαι τοίνυν ἐπανελθεῖν ἐφ' ἃ τούτων

will not indulge your rancour or take your wrongs into account.

Not only towards the Lacedaemonians have you so demeaned yourselves; but when the Thebans were trying to annex Euboea, you were not indifferent; you did not call to mind the injuries you had suffered from Themiso and Theodorus in the matter of Oropus; you carried aid even to them. That was in the early days of the volunteer trierarchs, of whom I was one; but I say nothing of that now. Your deliverance of the island was a generous act, but still more generously, when you had their lives and their cities at your mercy, you restored them honestly to men who had sinned against you, forgetting your wrongs where you found yourselves trusted. I pass over ten thousand instances I could cite,—battles by sea, expeditions by land, campaigns of ancient date and of our own times, in all of which Athens engaged herself for the freedom and salvation of Greece. Having before my eyes the spectacle of a city in all those great enterprises ready to fight the battles of her neighbours, what advice was I to give and what policy to urge, when her deliberations in some measure concerned herself? To bear malice against men who were seeking deliverance? To search for excuses for deserting the common cause? Should I not have deserved death if even in word I had sought to tarnish our honourable traditions? In word, I say; for the deed you would never have done. Of that I am well assured, for if you so wished, what stood in your way? Was it not in your power? Were not Aeschines and his friends there to advise you?

I will now return to my next ensuing public actions;

83

ἑξῆς ἐπολιτευόμην· καὶ σκοπεῖτ' ἐν τούτοις πάλιν
αὖ, τί τὸ τῇ πόλει βέλτιστον ἦν. ὁρῶν γάρ,
ὦ ἄνδρες 'Αθηναῖοι, τὸ ναυτικὸν ὑμῶν κατα-
λυόμενον, καὶ τοὺς μὲν πλουσίους ἀτελεῖς ἀπὸ
μικρῶν ἀναλωμάτων γιγνομένους, τοὺς δὲ μέτρι'
ἢ μικρὰ κεκτημένους τῶν πολιτῶν τὰ ὄντα ἀπολ-
λύοντας, ἔτι δ' ὑστερίζουσαν ἐκ τούτων τὴν
πόλιν τῶν καιρῶν, ἔθηκα νόμον καθ' ὃν τοὺς μὲν
τὰ δίκαια ποιεῖν ἠνάγκασα, τοὺς πλουσίους,
τοὺς δὲ πένητας ἔπαυσ' ἀδικουμένους, τῇ πόλει
δ' ὅπερ ἦν χρησιμώτατον, ἐν καιρῷ γίγνεσθαι
103 τὰς παρασκευὰς ἐποίησα. καὶ γραφεὶς τὸν ἀγῶνα
τοῦτον εἰς ὑμᾶς εἰσῆλθον κἀπέφυγον, καὶ τὸ
μέρος τῶν ψήφων ὁ διώκων οὐκ ἔλαβεν. καίτοι
πόσα χρήματα τοὺς ἡγεμόνας τῶν συμμοριῶν
ἢ τοὺς δευτέρους καὶ τρίτους οἴεσθέ μοι διδόναι,
ὥστε μάλιστα μὲν μὴ θεῖναι τὸν νόμον τοῦτον,
εἰ δὲ μή, καταβάλλοντ' ἐᾶν ἐν ὑπωμοσίᾳ; τοσαῦτ',
ὦ ἄνδρες 'Αθηναῖοι, ὅσ' ὀκνήσαιμ' ἂν πρὸς ὑμᾶς
104 εἰπεῖν. καὶ ταῦτ' εἰκότως ἔπραττον ἐκεῖνοι.
ἦν γὰρ αὐτοῖς ἐκ μὲν τῶν προτέρων νόμων συνεκ-
καίδεκα λῃτουργεῖν, αὐτοῖς μὲν μικρὰ καὶ οὐδὲν
[261] ἀναλίσκουσι, τοὺς δ' ἀπόρους τῶν πολιτῶν ἐπι-
τρίβουσιν, ἐκ δὲ τοῦ ἐμοῦ νόμου τὸ γιγνόμενον
κατὰ τὴν οὐσίαν ἕκαστον τιθέναι, καὶ δυοῖν ἐφάνη
τριήραρχος ὁ τῆς μιᾶς ἕκτος καὶ δέκατος πρότερον
συντελής· οὐδὲ γὰρ τριηράρχους ἔτ' ὠνόμαζον
ἑαυτούς, ἀλλὰ συντελεῖς. ὥστε δὴ ταῦτα λυ-
θῆναι καὶ μὴ τὰ δίκαια ποιεῖν ἀναγκασθῆναι,
105 οὐκ ἔσθ' ὅ τι οὐκ ἐδίδοσαν. καί μοι λέγε πρῶτον

ᵃ ὑπωμοσία, in general an affidavit to arrest proceedings;
here the oath taken in the Assembly by the party engaging

84

consider them once again in relation to the best interests of the commonwealth. Observing that the navy was going to pieces, that the wealthy were let off with trifling contributions, while citizens of moderate or small means were losing all they had, and that as a result the government was missing its opportunities, I made a statute under which I compelled the wealthy to take their fair share of expense, stopped the oppression of the poor, and, by a measure of great public benefit, caused your naval preparations to be made in good time. Being indicted for this measure, I stood my trial before this court and was acquitted, the prosecutor not getting the fifth part of the votes. Now how much money do you think the first, second, and third classes of contributors on the Naval Boards offered me not to propose the measure, or, failing that, to put it on the list and then drop it on demurrer [a] ? It was so large a sum, men of Athens, that I hardly like to name it. It was natural that they should make this attempt. Under the former statutes they might discharge their public services in groups of sixteen, spending little or nothing themselves, but grinding down the needy citizens, whereas by my statute they had to return the full assessment according to their means, and a man who was formerly one of sixteen contributors to a single trireme—for they were dropping the term trierarch and calling themselves contributors—might have to furnish two complete vessels. They offered any amount to get the new rules abrogated and escape their just obligation. Read first the decree,

to prosecute the author of a law or a decree for violation of the constitution. Its effect was to keep the law in abeyance, at whatever stage it had arrived, until the suit was decided.

μὲν τὸ ψήφισμα, καθ' ὃ εἰσῆλθον τὴν γραφήν,
εἶτα τοὺς καταλόγους, τόν τ' ἐκ τοῦ προτέρου
νόμου καὶ τὸν κατὰ τὸν ἐμόν. λέγε.

ΨΗΦΙΣΜΑ

[Ἐπὶ ἄρχοντος Πολυκλέους, μηνὸς βοηδρομιῶνος ἕκτῃ
ἐπὶ δέκα, φυλῆς πρυτανευούσης Ἱπποθωντίδος, Δημοσθένης Δημοσθένους Παιανιεὺς εἰσήνεγκε νόμον τριηραρχικὸν ἀντὶ τοῦ πρότερον, καθ' ὃν αἱ συντέλειαι ἦσαν τῶν
τριηράρχων· καὶ ἐπεχειροτόνησεν ἡ βουλὴ καὶ ὁ δῆμος·
καὶ ἀπήνεγκε παρανόμων Δημοσθένει Πατροκλῆς Φλυεύς,
καὶ τὸ μέρος τῶν ψήφων οὐ λαβὼν ἀπέτεισε τὰς πεντα-
κοσίας δραχμάς.]

Φέρε δὴ καὶ τὸν καλὸν κατάλογον.

[262]   ### ΚΑΤΑΛΟΓΟΣ

[Τοὺς τριηράρχους καλεῖσθαι ἐπὶ τὴν τριήρη συνεκ-
καίδεκα ἐκ τῶν ἐν τοῖς λόχοις συντελειῶν, ἀπὸ εἴκοσι
καὶ πέντε ἐτῶν εἰς τετταράκοντα, ἐπὶ ἴσον τῇ χορηγίᾳ
χρωμένους.]

106   Φέρε δὴ παρὰ τοῦτον τὸν ἐκ τοῦ ἐμοῦ νόμου
κατάλογον.

ΚΑΤΑΛΟΓΟΣ

[Τοὺς τριηράρχους αἱρεῖσθαι ἐπὶ τὴν τριήρη ἀπὸ τῆς
οὐσίας κατὰ τίμησιν, ἀπὸ ταλάντων δέκα· ἐὰν δὲ πλειόνων ἡ οὐσία ἀποτετιμημένη ᾖ χρημάτων, κατὰ τὸν ἀνα-
λογισμὸν ἕως τριῶν πλοίων καὶ ὑπηρετικοῦ ἡ λειτουργία
ἔστω. κατὰ τὴν αὐτὴν δὲ ἀναλογίαν ἔστω καὶ οἷς ἐλάττων οὐσία ἐστὶ τῶν δέκα ταλάντων, εἰς συντέλειαν συν-
αγομένοις εἰς τὰ δέκα τάλαντα.]

for which I was indicted and tried, and then the schedules as compiled under the old statute and under my statute.

(The Decree is read)

[In the archonship of Polycles, on the sixteenth of the month Boëdromion, the tribe Hippothontis holding the presidency, Demosthenes, son of Demosthenes, of Paeania, introduced a bill to amend the former law constituting the syndicates for the equipment of triremes. The bill was passed by the Council and the People, and Patrocles of Phlya indicted Demosthenes for a breach of the constitution, and, not obtaining the required proportion of votes, paid the fine of five hundred drachmas.]

Now read that fine schedule.

(The Old Schedule is read)

[The trierarchs to be called up, sixteen for each trireme, from the associations of joint contributors, from the age of twenty-five to that of forty, paying equal contributions to the public service.]

Now read for comparison the schedule under my statute.

(The New Schedule is read)

[The trierarchs to be chosen according to the assessment of their property at ten talents to a trireme ; if the property be assessed above that sum, the public service shall be fixed proportionately up to three triremes and a tender. The same proportion shall be observed where those whose property is under ten talents form a syndicate to make up that sum.]

DEMOSTHENES

107 Ἆρα μικρὰ βοηθῆσαι τοῖς πένησιν ὑμῶν δοκῶ,
ἢ μίκρ᾿ ἀναλῶσαι ἂν τοῦ μὴ τὰ δίκαια ποιεῖν οἱ
πλούσιοι; οὐ τοίνυν μόνον τῷ μὴ καθυφεῖναι
ταῦτα σεμνύνομαι, οὐδὲ τῷ γραφεὶς ἀποφυγεῖν,
ἀλλὰ καὶ τῷ συμφέροντα θεῖναι τὸν νόμον καὶ
τῷ πεῖραν ἔργῳ δεδωκέναι. πάντα γὰρ τὸν
πόλεμον τῶν ἀποστόλων γιγνομένων κατὰ τὸν
νόμον τὸν ἐμόν, οὐχ ἱκετηρίαν ἔθηκε τριήραρχος
οὐδεὶς πώποθ᾿ ὡς ἀδικούμενος παρ᾿ ὑμῖν, οὐκ
ἐν Μουνιχίας[1] ἐκαθέζετο, οὐχ ὑπὸ τῶν ἀποστολέων
ἐδέθη, οὐ τριήρης οὔτ᾿ ἔξω καταλειφθεῖσ᾿ ἀπώλετο
τῇ πόλει, οὔτ᾿ αὐτοῦ ἀπελείφθη οὐ δυναμένη
108 ἀνάγεσθαι. καίτοι κατὰ τοὺς προτέρους νόμους
ἅπαντα ταῦτ᾿ ἐγίγνετο. τὸ δ᾿ αἴτιον, ἐν τοῖς
πένησιν ἦν τὸ λῃτουργεῖν· πολλὰ δὴ τἀδύνατα
συνέβαινεν. ἐγὼ δ᾿ ἐκ τῶν ἀπόρων εἰς τοὺς
εὐπόρους μετήνεγκα τὰς τριηραρχίας· πάντ᾿ οὖν
τὰ δέοντ᾿ ἐγίγνετο. καὶ μὴν καὶ κατ᾿ αὐτὸ
τοῦτ᾿ ἄξιός εἰμ᾿ ἐπαίνου τυχεῖν, ὅτι πάντα τὰ
τοιαῦτα προηρούμην πολιτεύματα, ἀφ᾿ ὧν ἅμα
δόξαι καὶ τιμαὶ καὶ δυνάμεις συνέβαινον τῇ πόλει·
[263] βάσκανον δὲ καὶ πικρὸν καὶ κακόηθες οὐδέν ἐστι
πολίτευμ᾿ ἐμόν, οὐδὲ ταπεινόν, οὐδὲ τῆς πόλεως
109 ἀνάξιον. ταὐτὸ τοίνυν ἦθος ἔχων ἔν τε τοῖς
κατὰ τὴν πόλιν πολιτεύμασι καὶ ἐν τοῖς Ἑλληνικοῖς φανήσομαι· οὔτε γὰρ ἐν τῇ πόλει τὰς
παρὰ τῶν πλουσίων χάριτας μᾶλλον ἢ τὰ τῶν
πολλῶν δίκαι᾿ εἱλόμην, οὔτ᾿ ἐν τοῖς Ἑλληνικοῖς
τὰ Φιλίππου δῶρα καὶ τὴν ξενίαν ἠγάπησ᾿ ἀντὶ
τῶν κοινῇ πᾶσι τοῖς Ἕλλησι συμφερόντων.
110 Ἡγοῦμαι τοίνυν λοιπὸν εἶναί μοι περὶ τοῦ

---
[1] Μουνιχίας Kirchhoff : Μουννιχίᾳ Dind., S.

88

Do you think it was a trifling relief I gave to the poor, or a trifling sum that the rich would have spent to escape their obligation ? I pride myself not only on my refusal of compromise and on my acquittal, but also on having enacted a beneficial law and proved it such by experience. During the whole war, while the squadrons were organized under my regulations, no trierarch made petition as aggrieved, or appeared as a suppliant in the dockyard temple,[a] or was imprisoned by the Admiralty, and no ship was either abandoned at sea and lost to the state, or left in harbour as unseaworthy. Such incidents were frequent under the old regulations, because the public services fell upon poor men, and impossible demands were often made. I transferred the naval obligations from needy to well-to-do people, and so the duty was always discharged. I also claim credit for the very fact that all the measures I adopted brought renown and distinction and strength to the city, and that no measure of mine was invidious, or vexatious, or spiteful, or shabby and unworthy of Athens. You will find that I maintained the same character both in domestic and in Hellenic policy. At home I never preferred the gratitude of the rich to the claims of the poor ; in foreign affairs I never coveted the gifts and the friendship of Philip rather than the common interests of all Greece.

My remaining task, I think, is to speak of the

[a] *dockyard temple*: lit. temple of (Artemis) Munichia : the " Bluejackets' Church " at Peiraeus.

κηρύγματος εἰπεῖν καὶ τῶν εὐθυνῶν· τὸ γὰρ
ὡς τἄριστά τ᾽ ἔπραττον καὶ διὰ παντὸς εὔνους
εἰμὶ καὶ πρόθυμος εὖ ποιεῖν ὑμᾶς, ἱκανῶς ἐκ
τῶν εἰρημένων δεδηλῶσθαί μοι νομίζω. καίτοι
τὰ μέγιστά γε τῶν πεπολιτευμένων καὶ πεπραγμένων ἐμαυτῷ παραλείπω, ὑπολαμβάνων πρῶτον
μὲν ἐφεξῆς τοὺς περὶ αὐτοῦ τοῦ παρανόμου λόγους
ἀποδοῦναί με δεῖν, εἶτα, κἂν μηδὲν εἴπω περὶ
τῶν λοιπῶν πολιτευμάτων, ὁμοίως παρ᾽ ὑμῶν
ἑκάστῳ τὸ συνειδὸς ὑπάρχειν μοι.

111   Τῶν μὲν οὖν λόγων, οὓς οὗτος ἄνω καὶ κάτω
διακυκῶν ἔλεγε περὶ τῶν παραγεγραμμένων νόμων, οὔτε μὰ τοὺς θεοὺς ὑμᾶς οἶμαι μανθάνειν,
οὔτ᾽ αὐτὸς ἐδυνάμην συνεῖναι τοὺς πολλούς· ἁπλῶς
δὲ τὴν ὀρθὴν περὶ τῶν δικαίων διαλέξομαι. τοσούτου γὰρ δέω λέγειν ὡς οὐκ εἴμ᾽ ὑπεύθυνος,
ὃ νῦν οὗτος διέβαλλε καὶ διωρίζετο, ὥσθ᾽ ἅπαντα
τὸν βίον ὑπεύθυνος εἶναι ὁμολογῶ ὧν ἢ διακε-
112 χείρικ᾽ ἢ πεπολίτευμαι παρ᾽ ὑμῖν. ὧν μέντοι
γ᾽ ἐκ τῆς ἰδίας οὐσίας ἐπαγγειλάμενος δέδωκα
τῷ δήμῳ, οὐδεμίαν ἡμέραν ὑπεύθυνος εἶναί φημι
[264] (ἀκούεις, Αἰσχίνη;) οὐδ᾽ ἄλλον οὐδένα, οὐδ᾽ ἂν
τῶν ἐννέ᾽ ἀρχόντων τις ὢν τύχῃ. τίς γάρ ἐστι
νόμος τοσαύτης ἀδικίας καὶ μισανθρωπίας μεστὸς
ὥστε τὸν δόντα τι τῶν ἰδίων καὶ ποιήσαντα
πρᾶγμα φιλάνθρωπον καὶ φιλόδωρον τῆς χάριτος
μὲν ἀποστερεῖν, εἰς τοὺς συκοφάντας δ᾽ ἄγειν,
καὶ τούτους ἐπὶ τὰς εὐθύνας ὧν ἔδωκεν ἐφιστάναι;
οὐδὲ εἷς. εἰ δέ φησιν οὗτος, δειξάτω, κἀγὼ
90

proclamation and of the audit ; for I hope that what I have already said has been sufficient to satisfy you that my policy was the best, and that I have been the people's friend, and zealous in your service. Yet I pass by the most important of my public actions, first, because I conceive that my next duty is to submit my explanations in respect of the actual charge of illegality, secondly, because, though I say nothing further about the rest of my policy, your own knowledge will serve my purpose equally well.

As for Aeschines' topsy-turvy miscellany of arguments about the statutes transcribed for comparison,[a] I vow to Heaven that I do not believe that you understand the greater part of them, and I am sure they were quite unintelligible to me. I can only offer a plain, straightforward plea on the rights of the matter. So far from claiming, as he invidiously suggested just now, that I am not to be called to account, I fully admit that all my life long I have been accountable for all my official acts and public counsels ; but for the donations that I promised and gave at my own expense I do say that I am not accountable at any time—you hear that, Aeschines —nor is any other man, though he be one of the nine archons. Is there any law so compact of iniquity and illiberality that, when a man out of sheer generosity has given away his own money, it defrauds him of the gratitude he has earned, drags him before a set of prying informers, and gives them authority to hold an audit of his free donations ? There is no such law. If he contradicts me, let him produce the

---

[a] The laws alleged to be violated were posted in court side by side with the law or decree which was the object of the prosecution.

DEMOSTHENES

113 στέρξω καὶ σιωπήσομαι. ἀλλ' οὐκ ἔστιν, ἄνδρες
'Αθηναῖοι, ἀλλ' οὗτος συκοφαντῶν, ὅτι ἐπὶ τῷ
θεωρικῷ τότ' ὢν ἐπέδωκα τὰ χρήματα, '' ἐπήνεσεν αὐτόν'' φησὶν '' ὑπεύθυνον ὄντα.'' οὐ
περὶ τούτων γ' οὐδενός, ὧν ὑπεύθυνος ἦν, ἀλλ'
ἐφ' οἷς ἐπέδωκ', ὦ συκοφάντα. '' ἀλλὰ καὶ
τειχοποιὸς ἦσθα.'' καὶ διά γε τοῦτ' ὀρθῶς
ἐπηνούμην, ὅτι τἀνηλωμέν' ἔδωκα καὶ οὐκ ἐλο-
γιζόμην. ὁ μὲν γὰρ λογισμὸς εὐθυνῶν καὶ τῶν
ἐξετασόντων προσδεῖται, ἡ δὲ δωρεὰ χάριτος
καὶ ἐπαίνου δικαία ἐστὶ τυγχάνειν· διόπερ ταῦτ'
114 ἔγραψεν ὁδὶ περὶ ἐμοῦ. ὅτι δ' οὕτω ταῦτ' οὐ
μόνον ἐν τοῖς νόμοις, ἀλλὰ καὶ ἐν τοῖς ὑμετέροις
ἤθεσιν ὥρισται, ἐγὼ ῥᾳδίως πολλαχόθεν δείξω.
πρῶτον μὲν γὰρ Ναυσικλῆς στρατηγῶν, ἐφ' οἷς
ἀπὸ τῶν ἰδίων προεῖτο, πολλάκις ἐστεφάνωται
ὑφ' ὑμῶν· εἶθ' ὅτε τὰς ἀσπίδας Διότιμος ἔδωκε
καὶ πάλιν Χαρίδημος, ἐστεφανοῦντο· εἶθ' οὑτοσὶ
Νεοπτόλεμος, πολλῶν ἔργων ἐπιστάτης ὤν, ἐφ'
οἷς ἐπέδωκε τετίμηται. σχέτλιον γὰρ ἂν εἴη
τοῦτό γε, εἰ τῷ τιν' ἀρχὴν ἄρχοντι ἢ διδόναι τῇ
πόλει τὰ ἑαυτοῦ διὰ τὴν ἀρχὴν μὴ ἐξέσται, ἢ
[265] τῶν δοθέντων ἀντὶ τοῦ κομίσασθαι χάριν εὐθύνας
115 ὑφέξει. ὅτι τοίνυν ταῦτ' ἀληθῆ λέγω, λέγε
τὰ ψηφίσματά μοι τὰ τούτοις γεγενημέν' αὐτὰ
λαβών. λέγε.

law, and I will be satisfied and hold my peace. But no, the law does not exist, men of Athens ; only this man, with his pettifogging spite, because, when I was in charge of the theatric fund, I added gifts of my own to that fund, says, " Ctesiphon gave him a vote of thanks before he had rendered his accounts." Yes, but the vote of thanks did not concern the accounts which I had to render ; it was for my own donations, you pettifogger ! " But you were also a Commissioner of Fortifications." Why, that is how I earned my vote of thanks : I made a present of the money I had spent, and did not charge it to the public account. The account requires an audit and checkers ; the benefaction deserves gratitude and formal thanks, and that is the very reason for Ctesiphon's proposition. That this distinction is re- cognized both in the statutes and in your moral feelings I can prove by many instances. Nausicles, for example, has been repeatedly decorated by you for the money he spent out of his own pocket when serving as military commander. When Diotimus, and on another occasion Charidemus, had made a present of shields, they were crowned. Then there is our friend Neoptolemus, who has received distinc- tions for donations given by him as Commissioner for sundry public works. It would be quite intoler- able that it should either be illegal for a man holding any office to make presents to the government, or that, when he has made them, instead of receiving thanks, he should be subjected to an audit. To prove the truth of my statement, please take and read the actual words of the decrees made in the cases I have cited. Read.

DEMOSTHENES

["Αρχων Δημόνικος Φλυεύς, βοηδρομιῶνος ἕκτῃ μετ᾽
εἰκάδα, γνώμῃ βουλῆς καὶ δήμου, Καλλίας Φρεάρριος
εἶπεν, ὅτι δοκεῖ τῇ βουλῇ καὶ τῷ δήμῳ στεφανῶσαι
Ναυσικλέα τὸν ἐπὶ τῶν ὅπλων, ὅτι Ἀθηναίων ὁπλιτῶν
δισχιλίων ὄντων ἐν Ἴμβρῳ καὶ βοηθούντων τοῖς κατοι-
κοῦσιν Ἀθηναίων τὴν νῆσον, οὐ δυναμένου Φίλωνος τοῦ
ἐπὶ τῆς διοικήσεως κεχειροτονημένου διὰ τοὺς χειμῶνας
πλεῦσαι καὶ μισθοδοτῆσαι τοὺς ὁπλίτας, ἐκ τῆς ἰδίας
οὐσίας ἔδωκε καὶ οὐκ εἰσέπραξε τὸν δῆμον, καὶ ἀναγορεῦσαι τὸν στέφανον Διονυσίοις τραγῳδοῖς καινοῖς.]

ΕΤΕΡΟΝ ΨΗΦΙΣΜΑ

116 [Εἶπε Καλλίας Φρεάρριος, πρυτάνεων λεγόντων, βουλῆς γνώμῃ· ἐπειδὴ Χαρίδημος ὁ ἐπὶ τῶν ὁπλιτῶν, ἀπο-
σταλεὶς εἰς Σαλαμῖνα, καὶ Διότιμος ὁ ἐπὶ τῶν ἱππέων,
ἐν τῇ ἐπὶ τοῦ ποταμοῦ μάχῃ τῶν στρατιωτῶν τινῶν ὑπὸ
τῶν πολεμίων σκυλευθέντων, ἐκ τῶν ἰδίων ἀναλωμάτων
καθώπλισαν τοὺς νεανίσκους ἀσπίσιν ὀκτακοσίαις, δεδόχθαι τῇ βουλῇ καὶ τῷ δήμῳ στεφανῶσαι Χαρίδημον καὶ
Διότιμον χρυσῷ στεφάνῳ, καὶ ἀναγορεῦσαι Παναθηναίοις
τοῖς μεγάλοις ἐν τῷ γυμνικῷ ἀγῶνι καὶ Διονυσίοις τραγῳδοῖς καινοῖς· τῆς δὲ ἀναγορεύσεως ἐπιμεληθῆναι θεσμο-
[266] θέτας, πρυτάνεις, ἀγωνοθέτας.

117 Τούτων ἕκαστος, Αἰσχίνη, τῆς μὲν ἀρχῆς ἧς
ἦρχεν ὑπεύθυνος ἦν, ἐφ᾽ οἷς δ᾽ ἐστεφανοῦτ᾽ οὐχ
ὑπεύθυνος. οὐκοῦν οὐδ᾽ ἐγώ· ταὐτὰ γὰρ δίκαι᾽
ἐστί μοι περὶ τῶν αὐτῶν τοῖς ἄλλοις δήπου.
ἐπέδωκα· ἐπαινοῦμαι διὰ ταῦτα, οὐκ ὢν ὧν
ἔδωκα ὑπεύθυνος. ἦρχον· καὶ δέδωκά γ᾽ εὐθύνας ἐκείνων, οὐχ ὧν ἐπέδωκα. νὴ Δί᾽, ἀλλ᾽
ἀδίκως ἦρξα; εἶτα παρών, ὅτε μ᾽ εἰσῆγον οἱ
λογισταί, οὐ κατηγόρεις;

94

(Sundry Decrees are read)

[Archonship of Demonicus of Phlya, on the twenty-sixth day of Boëdromion, with sanction of Council and People: Callias of Phrearrii proposed that the Council and People resolve to crown Nausicles, the commander of the infantry, because, when Philo, the official paymaster, was prevented by storms from sailing with pay for the two thousand Athenian infantry serving in Imbros to assist the Athenian residents in that island, he paid them from his private means, and did not send in a claim to the people ; and that the crown be proclaimed at the Dionysia at the performance of the new tragedies.]

[Proposed by Callias of Phrearrii, and put to the vote by the presidents, with sanction of Council : that, whereas Charidemus, dispatched to Salamis in command of the infantry, and Diotimus, commanding the cavalry, when in the battle at the river some of the soldiers had been disarmed by the enemy, did at their own expense arm the younger men with eight hundred shields, it be resolved by the Council and People to crown Charidemus and Diotimus with a golden crown, and to proclaim it at the great Panathenaea during the gymnastic contest, and at the Dionysia at the performance of the new tragedies ; and that the proclamation be entrusted to the judicial archons, the presidents, and the stewards of the festival.]

Every one of the persons mentioned, Aeschines, was liable to audit in respect of the office he held, but not of the services for which he was decorated. It follows that I am not liable ; for, surely, I have the same rights under the same conditions as anybody else ! I made donations. For those donations I am thanked, not being subject to audit for what I gave. I held office. Yes, and I have submitted to audit for my offices, though not for my gifts. Ah, but perhaps I was guilty of official misconduct ? Well, the auditors brought me into court—and no complaint from you !

118 Ἵνα τοίνυν ἴδηθ᾽ ὅτι αὐτὸς οὗτός μοι μαρτυρεῖ
ἐφ᾽ οἷς οὐχ ὑπεύθυνος ἦν ἐστεφανῶσθαι, λαβὼν
ἀνάγνωθι τὸ ψήφισμ᾽ ὅλον τὸ γραφέν μοι. οἷς
γὰρ οὐκ ἐγράψατο τοῦ προβουλεύματος, τούτοις
ἃ διώκει συκοφαντῶν φανήσεται. λέγε.

ΨΗΦΙΣΜΑ

[Ἐπὶ ἄρχοντος Εὐθυκλέους, πυανεψιῶνος ἐνάτῃ ἀπιόντος, φυλῆς πρυτανευούσης Οἰνῆδος, Κτησιφῶν Λεω-
σθένους Ἀναφλύστιος εἶπεν· ἐπειδὴ Δημοσθένης Δημοσθένους Παιανιεὺς γενόμενος ἐπιμελητὴς τῆς τῶν τειχῶν
ἐπισκευῆς, καὶ προσαναλώσας εἰς τὰ ἔργα ἀπὸ τῆς ἰδίας
οὐσίας τρία τάλαντα, ἐπέδωκε ταῦτα τῷ δήμῳ, καὶ ἐπὶ
τοῦ θεωρικοῦ κατασταθείς, ἐπέδωκε τοῖς ἐκ πασῶν τῶν
φυλῶν θεωροῖς ἑκατὸν μνᾶς εἰς θυσίας, δεδόχθαι τῇ βουλῇ
καὶ τῷ δήμῳ τῷ Ἀθηναίων ἐπαινέσαι Δημοσθένην Δημοσθένους Παιανιέα ἀρετῆς ἕνεκα καὶ καλοκαγαθίας ἧς ἔχων
διατελεῖ ἐν παντὶ καιρῷ εἰς τὸν δῆμον τὸν Ἀθηναίων,
[267] καὶ στεφανῶσαι χρυσῷ στεφάνῳ, καὶ ἀναγορεῦσαι τὸν
στέφανον ἐν τῷ θεάτρῳ Διονυσίοις τραγῳδοῖς καινοῖς·
τῆς δὲ ἀναγορεύσεως ἐπιμεληθῆναι τὸν ἀγωνοθέτην.]

119 Οὐκοῦν ἃ μὲν ἐπέδωκα, ταῦτ᾽ ἐστίν, ὧν οὐδὲν
σὺ γέγραψαι· ἃ δέ φησιν ἡ βουλὴ δεῖν ἀντὶ τούτων
γενέσθαι μοι, ταῦτ᾽ ἔσθ᾽ ἃ διώκεις. τὸ λαβεῖν
οὖν τὰ διδόμεν᾽ ὁμολογῶν ἔννομον εἶναι, τὸ χάριν
τούτων ἀποδοῦναι παρανόμων γράφει. ὁ δὲ
παμπόνηρος ἄνθρωπος καὶ θεοῖς ἐχθρὸς καὶ
βάσκανος ὄντως, ποῖός τις ἂν εἴη πρὸς θεῶν;
οὐχ ὁ τοιοῦτος;

120 Καὶ μὴν περὶ τοῦ γ᾽ ἐν τῷ θεάτρῳ κηρύττεσθαι,
τὸ μὲν μυριάκις μυρίους κεκηρῦχθαι παραλείπω

To prove that Aeschines himself testifies that I have been crowned for matters in which I was audit-free, take and read the whole of the decree that was drawn in my favour. The proof that his prosecution is vindictive will appear from those sentences in the provisional decree which he has not indicted. Read.

(The Decree is read)

[In the archonship of Euthycles, on the twenty-third day of Pyanepsion, the tribe Oeneis then holding the presidency, Ctesiphon, son of Leosthenes, of Anaphlystus, proposed that, whereas Demosthenes, son of Demosthenes, of Paeania, having been appointed superintendent of the repair of the fortifications, and having spent upon the works three talents from his private means, has made the same a benevolence to the people ; and whereas, having been appointed treasurer of the Theatrical Fund, he gave to the representatives of all the tribes one hundred minas for sacrifices, it be resolved by the Council and People of Athens to commend the said Demosthenes, son of Demosthenes, of Paeania, for his merits and for the generosity which he has constantly displayed on every occasion towards the People of Athens, and to crown him with a golden crown, and to proclaim the crown in the theatre at the Dionysia at the performance of the new tragedies ; and that the proclamation be entrusted to the steward of the festival.]

Here, then, are my donations, in the decree—but not in your indictment. Your prosecution is directed to the rewards which the Council says that I ought to receive for them. Acceptance of gifts you admit to be legal ; gratitude for gifts you indict for illegality. In Heaven's name, what do we mean by dishonesty and malignity, if you are not dishonest and malignant ?

As for the proclamation in the Theatre, I will not insist that thousands of names have been a thousand

καὶ τὸ πολλάκις αὐτὸς ἐστεφανῶσθαι πρότερον.
ἀλλὰ πρὸς θεῶν οὕτω σκαιὸς εἶ καὶ ἀναίσθητος,
Αἰσχίνη, ὥστ' οὐ δύνασαι λογίσασθαι ὅτι τῷ
μὲν στεφανουμένῳ τὸν αὐτὸν ἔχει ζῆλον ὁ στέ-
φανος ὅπου ἂν ἀναρρηθῇ, τοῦ δὲ τῶν στεφανούντων
εἴνεκα συμφέροντος ἐν τῷ θεάτρῳ γίγνεται τὸ
κήρυγμα; οἱ γὰρ ἀκούσαντες ἅπαντες εἰς τὸ
ποιεῖν εὖ τὴν πόλιν προτρέπονται, καὶ τοὺς ἀπο-
διδόντας τὴν χάριν μᾶλλον ἐπαινοῦσι τοῦ στε-
φανουμένου· διόπερ τὸν νόμον τοῦτον ἡ πόλις
γέγραφεν. λέγε δ' αὐτόν μοι τὸν νόμον λαβών.

ΝΟΜΟΣ

["Οσους στεφανοῦσί τινες τῶν δήμων, τὰς ἀναγορεύ-
σεις τῶν στεφάνων ποιεῖσθαι ἐν αὐτοῖς ἑκάστους τοῖς
ἰδίοις δήμοις, ἐὰν μή τινας ὁ δῆμος ὁ τῶν Ἀθηναίων
ἢ ἡ βουλὴ στεφανοῖ· τούτους δ' ἐξεῖναι ἐν τῷ θεάτρῳ
Διονυσίοις ἀναγορεύεσθαι.]

121 Ἀκούεις, Αἰσχίνη, τοῦ νόμου λέγοντος σαφῶς,
[268] "πλὴν ἐάν τινας ὁ δῆμος ἢ ἡ βουλὴ ψηφίσηται·
τούτους δ' ἀναγορευέτω." τί οὖν, ὦ ταλαίπωρε,
συκοφαντεῖς; τί λόγους πλάττεις; τί σαυτὸν
οὐκ ἐλλεβορίζεις ἐπὶ τούτοις; ἀλλ' οὐδ' αἰσχύνει
φθόνου δίκην εἰσάγων, οὐκ ἀδικήματος οὐδενός,
καὶ νόμους μεταποιῶν, τῶν δ' ἀφαιρῶν μέρη,
οὓς ὅλους δίκαιον ἦν ἀναγιγνώσκεσθαι τοῖς γ'
122 ὀμωμοκόσι κατὰ τοὺς νόμους ψηφιεῖσθαι; ἔπειτα
τοιαῦτα ποιῶν λέγεις πόσα[1] δεῖ προσεῖναι τῷ
δημοτικῷ, ὥσπερ ἀνδριάντ' ἐκδεδωκὼς κατὰ συγ-
γραφήν, εἶτ' οὐκ ἔχονθ' ἃ προσῆκεν ἐκ τῆς συγ-
γραφῆς κομιζόμενος, ἢ λόγῳ τοὺς δημοτικούς,

---

[1] πόσα Blass: πρὸς ἃ S: ἃ Dind.

times so proclaimed, nor that I myself have been crowned again and again before now. But, really now, are you so unintelligent and blind, Aeschines, that you are incapable of reflecting that a crown is equally gratifying to the person crowned wheresoever it is proclaimed, but that the proclamation is made in the Theatre merely for the sake of those by whom it is conferred? For the whole vast audience is stimulated to do service to the commonwealth, and applauds the exhibition of gratitude rather than the recipient; and that is the reason why the state has enacted this statute. Please take and read it.

(*The Statute is read*)

[In cases where crowns are bestowed by any of the townships, the proclamation of the crown shall be made within the respective townships, unless the crown is bestowed by the People of Athens or by the Council, in which case it shall be lawful to proclaim it in the Theatre at the Dionysia.]

You hear, Aeschines, how the statute expressly makes an exception : " persons named in any decree of the Council or the Assembly always excepted. They are to be proclaimed." Then why this miserable pettifogging? Why these insincere arguments? Why do you not try hellebore for your complaint? Are you not ashamed to prosecute for spite, not for crime ; misquoting this statute, curtailing that statute, when they ought to be read in their entirety to a jury sworn to vote according to their direction? And, while behaving like that, you treat us to your definition of all the qualities proper to a patriotic politician—as though you had bespoken a statue according to specification, and it had been delivered without the qualities specified! As though talk, not

99

DEMOSTHENES

ἀλλ' οὐ τοῖς πράγμασι καὶ τοῖς πολιτεύμασιν
γιγνωσκομένους. καὶ βοᾷς ῥητὰ καὶ ἄρρητ'
ὀνομάζων, ὥσπερ ἐξ ἁμάξης, ἃ σοὶ καὶ τῷ σῷ
γένει πρόσεστιν, οὐκ ἐμοί.

123 Καίτοι καὶ τοῦτ', ὦ ἄνδρες Ἀθηναῖοι· ἐγὼ
λοιδορίαν κατηγορίας τούτῳ διαφέρειν ἡγοῦμαι,
τῷ τὴν μὲν κατηγορίαν ἀδικήματ' ἔχειν, ὧν ἐν
τοῖς νόμοις εἰσὶν αἱ τιμωρίαι, τὴν δὲ λοιδορίαν
βλασφημίας, ἃς κατὰ τὴν αὐτῶν φύσιν τοῖς ἐχθροῖς
περὶ ἀλλήλων συμβαίνει λέγειν. οἰκοδομῆσαι δὲ
τοὺς προγόνους ταυτὶ τὰ δικαστήρι' ὑπείληφα,
οὐχ ἵνα συλλέξαντες ὑμᾶς εἰς ταῦτα ἀπὸ τῶν ἰδίων
κακῶς τἀπόρρητα λέγωμεν ἀλλήλους, ἀλλ' ἵν'
ἐξελέγχωμεν, ἐάν τις ἠδικηκώς τι τυγχάνῃ τὴν
124 πόλιν. ταῦτα τοίνυν εἰδὼς Αἰσχίνης οὐδὲν ἧττον
ἐμοῦ πομπεύειν ἀντὶ τοῦ κατηγορεῖν εἵλετο. οὐ
μὴν οὐδ' ἐνταῦθ' ἔλαττον ἔχων δίκαιός ἐστιν
ἀπελθεῖν. ἤδη δ' ἐπὶ ταῦτα πορεύσομαι, τοσοῦτον
αὐτὸν ἐρωτήσας. πότερόν σέ τις, Αἰσχίνη, τῆς
πόλεως ἐχθρὸν ἢ ἐμὸν εἶναι φῇ; ἐμὸν δῆλον ὅτι.
[269] εἶθ' οὗ μὲν ἦν παρ' ἐμοῦ δίκην κατὰ τοὺς νόμους
ὑπὲρ τούτων λαβεῖν, εἴπερ ἠδίκουν, ἐξέλειπες,
ἐν ταῖς εὐθύναις, ἐν ταῖς γραφαῖς, ἐν ταῖς ἄλλαις
125 κρίσεσιν· οὗ δ' ἐγὼ μὲν ἀθῷος ἅπασι, τοῖς νόμοις,
τῷ χρόνῳ, τῇ προθεσμίᾳ, τῷ κεκρίσθαι περὶ
πάντων πολλάκις πρότερον, τῷ μηδεπώποτ' ἐξ-
ελεγχθῆναι μηδὲν ὑμᾶς ἀδικῶν, τῇ πόλει δ' ἢ
πλέον ἢ ἔλαττον ἀνάγκη τῶν γε δημοσίᾳ πεπραγμένων μετεῖναι τῆς δόξης, ἐνταῦθ' ἀπήν-
100

deeds and policy, were the criterion of patriotism! And then you raise your voice, like a clown at a carnival,[a] and pelt me with epithets both decent and obscene, suitable for yourself and your kindred, but not for me.

Here is another point, men of Athens. The difference between railing and accusation I take to be this : accusation implies crimes punishable by law ; railing, such abuse as quarrelsome people vent upon one another according to their disposition. These law courts, if I am not mistaken, were built by our ancestors, not that we should convene you here to listen to us taunting one another with the secret scandal of private life, but that we should here bring home to the guilty offences against the public weal. Aeschines knows that as well as I do ; but he has a keener taste for scurrility than for accusation. However, even in that respect he deserves to get as good as he gives. I will come to that presently ; meantime I will ask him just one question. Are we to call you the enemy of Athens, Aeschines, or my enemy ? Mine, of course. Yet you let slip your proper opportunities of bringing me to justice on behalf of the citizens, if I had done wrong, by audit, by indictment, by any sort of legal procedure ; but here, where I am invulnerable on every ground, by law, by lapse of time, by limitation, by many earlier judgements covering every point, by default of any previous conviction for any public offence, here, where the country must take her share in the repute or disrepute of measures that were approved by the people, here you have met me face to face. You pose

---

[a] *like a clown at a carnival* : lit., as from a wagon, in the procession at a Dionysiac festival, when coarse raillery was customary. A similar expression is used in §§ 11 and 124.

τηκας; ὅρα μὴ τούτων μὲν ἐχθρὸς ᾖς, ἐμοὶ δὲ
προσποιῇ.

126 Ἐπειδὴ τοίνυν ἡ μὲν εὐσεβὴς καὶ δικαία ψῆφος
ἅπασι δέδεικται, δεῖ δέ μ᾽, ὡς ἔοικε, καίπερ οὐ
φιλολοίδορον ὄντα, διὰ τὰς ὑπὸ τούτου βλασφημίας εἰρημένας ἀντὶ πολλῶν καὶ ψευδῶν αὐτὰ
τἀναγκαιότατ᾽ εἰπεῖν περὶ αὐτοῦ, καὶ δεῖξαι τίς
ὢν καὶ τίνων ῥᾳδίως οὕτως ἄρχει τοῦ κακῶς λέγειν,
καὶ λόγους τινὰς διασύρει, αὐτὸς εἰρηκὼς ἃ τίς
οὐκ ἂν ὤκνησεν τῶν μετρίων ἀνθρώπων φθέγξα-
127 σθαι; εἰ γὰρ Αἰακὸς ἢ Ῥαδάμανθυς ἢ Μίνως
ἦν ὁ κατηγορῶν, ἀλλὰ μὴ σπερμολόγος, περίτριμμ᾽
ἀγορᾶς, ὄλεθρος γραμματεύς, οὐκ ἂν αὐτὸν οἶμαι
ταῦτ᾽ εἰπεῖν, οὐδ᾽ ἂν οὕτως ἐπαχθεῖς λόγους
πορίσασθαι, ὥσπερ ἐν τραγῳδίᾳ βοῶντα " ὦ γῆ
καὶ ἥλιε καὶ ἀρετή " καὶ τὰ τοιαῦτα, καὶ πάλιν
" σύνεσιν καὶ παιδείαν " ἐπικαλούμενον, " ᾗ τὰ
καλὰ καὶ τὰ αἰσχρὰ διαγιγνώσκεται." ταῦτα
128 γὰρ δήπουθεν ἠκούετ᾽ αὐτοῦ λέγοντος. σοὶ δ᾽
ἀρετῆς, ὦ κάθαρμα, ἢ τοῖς σοῖς τίς μετουσία;
ἢ καλῶν ἢ μὴ τοιούτων τίς διάγνωσις; πόθεν ἢ
πῶς ἀξιωθέντι; ποῦ δὲ παιδείας σοὶ θέμις μνησθῆναι; ἧς τῶν μὲν ὡς ἀληθῶς τετυχηκότων
[270] οὐδ᾽ ἂν εἷς εἴποι περὶ αὐτοῦ τοιοῦτον οὐδέν, ἀλλὰ
κἂν ἑτέρου λέγοντος ἐρυθριάσειε, τοῖς δ᾽ ἀπο-
λειφθεῖσι μέν, ὥσπερ σύ, προσποιουμένοις δ᾽
ὑπ᾽ ἀναισθησίας τὸ τοὺς ἀκούοντας ἀλγεῖν ποιεῖν,
ὅταν λέγωσιν, οὐ τὸ δοκεῖν τοιούτοις εἶναι περί-
εστιν.

129 Οὐκ ἀπορῶν δ᾽ ὅ τι χρὴ περὶ σοῦ καὶ τῶν σῶν

as my enemy ; are you sure you are not the enemy of the people ?

A righteous and conscientious verdict is now sufficiently indicated ; but I have still, as it seems—not because I have any taste for railing, but because of his calumnies — to state the bare necessary facts about Aeschines, in return for a great many lies. I must let you know who this man, who starts on vituperation so glibly—who ridicules certain words of mine though he has himself said things that every decent man would shrink from uttering—really is, and what is his parentage. Why, if my calumniator had been Aeacus, or Rhadamanthus, or Minos, instead of a mere scandal-monger, a market-place loafer, a poor devil of a clerk, he could hardly have used such language, or equipped himself with such offensive expressions. Hark to his melodramatic bombast : " Oh, Earth ! Oh, Sun ! Oh, Virtue," and all that vapouring ; his appeals to " intelligence and education, whereby we discriminate between things of good and evil report "—for that was the sort of rubbish you heard him spouting. Virtue ! you runagate ; what have you or your family to do with virtue ? How do you distinguish between good and evil report ? Where and how did you qualify as a moralist ? Where did you get your right to talk about education ? No really educated man would use such language about himself, but would rather blush to hear it from others ; but people like you, who make stupid pretensions to the culture of which they are utterly destitute, succeed in disgusting everybody whenever they open their lips, but never in making the impression they desire.

I am at no loss for information about you and your

εἰπεῖν, ἀπορῶ τοῦ πρώτου μνησθῶ· πότερ' ὡς ὁ
πατήρ σου Τρόμης ἐδούλευε παρ' Ἐλπίᾳ τῷ
πρὸς τῷ Θησείῳ διδάσκοντι γράμματα, χοίνικας
παχείας ἔχων καὶ ξύλον; ἢ ὡς ἡ μήτηρ τοῖς
μεθημερινοῖς γάμοις ἐν τῷ κλεισίῳ τῷ πρὸς τῷ
καλαμίτῃ Ἥρῳ χρωμένη τὸν καλὸν ἀνδριάντα
καὶ τριταγωνιστὴν ἄκρον ἐξέθρεψέ σε; ἀλλὰ
πάντες ἴσασι ταῦτα, κἂν ἐγὼ μὴ λέγω. ἀλλ'
ὡς ὁ τριηραύλης Φορμίων, ὁ Δίωνος τοῦ Φρεαρρίου
δοῦλος, ἀνέστησεν αὐτὴν ἀπὸ τῆς καλῆς ἐργασίας;
ἀλλὰ νὴ τὸν Δία καὶ θεούς, ὀκνῶ μὴ περὶ σοῦ τὰ
προσήκοντα λέγων αὐτὸς οὐ προσήκοντας ἐμαυτῷ
130 δόξω προῃρῆσθαι λόγους. ταῦτα μὲν οὖν ἐάσω,
ἀπ' αὐτῶν δ' ὧν αὐτὸς βεβίωκεν ἄρξομαι· οὐδὲ
γὰρ ὧν ἔτυχεν ἦν, ἀλλ' οἷς ὁ δῆμος καταρᾶται.
ὀψὲ γάρ ποτ'—ὀψὲ λέγω; χθὲς μὲν οὖν καὶ πρώην
ἅμ' Ἀθηναῖος καὶ ῥήτωρ γέγονε, καὶ δύο συλλαβὰς
προσθεὶς τὸν μὲν πατέρ' ἀντὶ Τρόμητος ἐποίησ'
Ἀτρόμητον, τὴν δὲ μητέρα σεμνῶς πάνυ Γλαυκο-
θέαν, ἣν Ἔμπουσαν ἅπαντες ἴσασι καλουμένην,
ἐκ τοῦ πάντα ποιεῖν καὶ πάσχειν δηλονότι ταύτης
131 τῆς ἐπωνυμίας τυχοῦσαν· πόθεν γὰρ ἄλλοθεν; ἀλλ'
ὅμως οὕτως ἀχάριστος εἶ καὶ πονηρὸς φύσει ὥστ'
[271] ἐλεύθερος ἐκ δούλου καὶ πλούσιος ἐκ πτωχοῦ διὰ
τουτουσὶ γεγονώς, οὐχ ὅπως χάριν αὐτοῖς ἔχεις,
ἀλλὰ μισθώσας σαυτὸν κατὰ τουτωνὶ πολιτεύει.

---

a *Heros the bone-setter* : this interpretation is doubtful ;
it assumes (1) identity with a person called, more respectfully,
Heros the physician, in a similar passage of the speech *On
the Embassy* ; (2) that καλαμίτης may mean one who uses
splints (κάλαμοι). Otherwise : near the shrine (or statue)
of the hero Calamites—unknown elsewhere, but perhaps

family ; but I am at a loss where to begin. Shall I relate how your father Tromes was a slave in the house of Elpias, who kept an elementary school near the Temple of Theseus, and how he wore shackles on his legs and a timber collar round his neck ? or how your mother practised daylight nuptials in an outhouse next door to Heros the bone-setter,[a] and so brought you up to act in tableaux vivants and to excel in minor parts on the stage ? However, everybody knows that without being told by me. Shall I tell you how Phormio the boatswain, a slave of Dio of Phrearrii, uplifted her from that chaste profession ? But I protest that, however well the story becomes you, I am afraid I may be thought to have chosen topics unbecoming to myself. I will pass by those early days, and begin with his conduct of his own life ; for indeed it has been no ordinary life, but such as is an abomination to a free people. Only recently —recently, do I say ? Why it was only the day before yesterday when he became simultaneously an Athenian and an orator, and, by the addition of two syllables, transformed his father from Tromes to Atrometus, and bestowed upon his mother the high-sounding name of Glaucothea, although she was universally known as the Banshee, a nickname she owed to the pleasing diversity of her acts and experiences—it can have no other origin. You were raised from servitude to freedom, and from beggary to opulence, by the favour of your fellow-citizens, and yet you are so thankless and ill-conditioned that, instead of showing them your gratitude, you take the pay of their enemies and conduct political intrigues

identical with the Lycian " Hero Physician." See Essay VI. in Goodwin's edition.

καὶ περὶ ὧν μὲν ἔστι τις ἀμφισβήτησις, ὡς ἄρ᾽
ὑπὲρ τῆς πόλεως εἴρηκεν, ἐάσω· ἃ δ᾽ ὑπὲρ τῶν
ἐχθρῶν φανερῶς ἀπεδείχθη πράττων, ταῦτ᾽ ἀναμνήσω.

132   Τίς γὰρ ὑμῶν οὐκ οἶδεν τὸν ἀποψηφισθέντ᾽
Ἀντιφῶντα, ὃς ἐπαγγειλάμενος Φιλίππῳ τὰ νεώρι᾽
ἐμπρήσειν εἰς τὴν πόλιν ἦλθεν; ὃν λαβόντος ἐμοῦ
κεκρυμμένον ἐν Πειραιεῖ καὶ καταστήσαντος εἰς
τὴν ἐκκλησίαν, βοῶν ὁ βάσκανος οὗτος καὶ
κεκραγώς, ὡς ἐν δημοκρατίᾳ δεινὰ ποιῶ τοὺς
ἠτυχηκότας τῶν πολιτῶν ὑβρίζων καὶ ἐπ᾽ οἰκίας
βαδίζων ἄνευ ψηφίσματος, ἀφεθῆναι ἐποίησεν.

133   καὶ εἰ μὴ ἡ βουλὴ ἡ ἐξ Ἀρείου πάγου τὸ πρᾶγμ᾽
αἰσθομένη, καὶ τὴν ὑμετέραν ἄγνοιαν ἐν οὐ δέοντι
συμβεβηκυῖαν ἰδοῦσα, ἐπεζήτησε τὸν ἄνθρωπον
καὶ συλλαβοῦσ᾽ ἐπανήγαγεν ὡς ὑμᾶς, ἐξήρπαστ᾽
ἂν ὁ τοιοῦτος καὶ τὸ δίκην δοῦναι διαδὺς ἐξ-
επέπεμπτ᾽ ἂν ὑπὸ τοῦ σεμνολόγου τουτουί· νῦν δ᾽
ὑμεῖς στρεβλώσαντες αὐτὸν ἀπεκτείνατε, ὡς ἔδει

134   γε καὶ τοῦτον.   τοιγαροῦν εἰδυῖα ταῦθ᾽ ἡ βουλὴ
ἡ ἐξ Ἀρείου πάγου τότε τούτῳ πεπραγμένα,
χειροτονησάντων αὐτὸν ὑμῶν σύνδικον ὑπὲρ τοῦ
ἱεροῦ τοῦ ἐν Δήλῳ ἀπὸ τῆς αὐτῆς ἀγνοίας ἧσπερ
πολλὰ προΐεσθε τῶν κοινῶν, ὡς προσείλεσθε
κἀκείνην καὶ τοῦ πράγματος κυρίαν ἐποιήσατε,
τοῦτον μὲν εὐθὺς ἀπήλασεν ὡς προδότην, Ὑπερείδῃ
δὲ λέγειν προσέταξε· καὶ ταῦτ᾽ ἀπὸ τοῦ βωμοῦ
[272] φέρουσα τὴν ψῆφον ἔπραξε, καὶ οὐδεμία ψῆφος
135   ἠνέχθη τῷ μιαρῷ τούτῳ.   καὶ ὅτι ταῦτ᾽ ἀληθῆ
λέγω, κάλει τούτων τοὺς μάρτυρας.

to their detriment. I will not deal with speeches which, on a disputable construction, may be called patriotic, but I will recall to memory acts by which he was proved beyond doubt to have served your enemies.

You all remember Antiphon, the man who was struck off the register, and came back to Athens after promising Philip that he would set fire to the dock-yard. When I had caught him in hiding at Peiraeus, and brought him before the Assembly, this malignant fellow raised a huge outcry about my scandalous and undemocratic conduct in assaulting citizens in distress and breaking into houses without a warrant, and so procured his acquittal. Had not the Council of the Areopagus, becoming aware of the facts, and seeing that you had made a most inopportune blunder, started further inquiries, arrested the man, and brought him into court a second time, the vile traitor would have slipped out of your hands and eluded justice, being smuggled out of the city by our bombastic phrase-monger. As it was, you put him on the rack and then executed him, and you ought to have done the same to Aeschines. In fact, the Council of the Areopagus knew well that Aeschines had been to blame throughout this affair, and there-fore when, after choosing him by vote to speak in support of your claims to the Temple at Delos, by a misapprehension such as has often been fatal to your public interests, you invited the co-operation of that Council and gave them full authority, they promptly rejected him as a traitor, and gave the brief to Hypereides. On this occasion the ballot was taken at the altar, and not a single vote was cast for this wretch. To prove the truth of my statement, please call the witnesses.

DEMOSTHENES

[Μαρτυροῦσι Δημοσθένει ὑπὲρ ἁπάντων οἵδε, Καλλίας Σουνιεύς, Ζήνων Φλυεύς, Κλέων Φαληρεύς, Δημόνικος Μαραθώνιος, ὅτι τοῦ δήμου ποτὲ χειροτονήσαντος Αἰσχίνην σύνδικον ὑπὲρ τοῦ ἱεροῦ τοῦ ἐν Δήλῳ εἰς τοὺς Ἀμφικτύονας, συνεδρεύσαντες ἡμεῖς ἐκρίναμεν Ὑπερείδην ἄξιον εἶναι μᾶλλον ὑπὲρ τῆς πόλεως λέγειν, καὶ ἀπεστάλη Ὑπερείδης.]

136 Οὐκοῦν ὅτε τοῦτον τοῦ λέγειν[1] ἀπήλασεν ἡ βουλὴ καὶ προσέταξεν ἑτέρῳ, τότε καὶ προδότην καὶ κακόνουν ὑμῖν ἀπέφηνεν.

Ἕν μὲν τοίνυν τοῦτο τοιοῦτο πολίτευμα τοῦ νεανίου τούτου, ὅμοιόν γ᾽, οὐ γάρ; οἷς ἐμοῦ κατηγορεῖ· ἕτερον δ᾽ ἀναμιμνήσκεσθε. ὅτε γὰρ Πύθωνα Φίλιππος ἔπεμψε τὸν Βυζάντιον καὶ παρὰ τῶν αὑτοῦ συμμάχων πάντων συνέπεμψε πρέσβεις, ὡς ἐν αἰσχύνῃ ποιήσων τὴν πόλιν καὶ δείξων ἀδικοῦσαν, τότ᾽ ἐγὼ μὲν τῷ Πύθωνι θρασυνομένῳ καὶ πολλῷ ῥέοντι καθ᾽ ὑμῶν οὐχ ὑπεχώρησα, ἀλλ᾽ ἀναστὰς ἀντεῖπον, καὶ τὰ τῆς πόλεως δίκαι᾽ οὐχὶ προὔδωκα, ἀλλ᾽ ἀδικοῦντα Φίλιππον ἐξήλεγξα φανερῶς οὕτως ὥστε τοὺς ἐκείνου συμμάχους αὐτοὺς ἀνισταμένους ὁμολογεῖν· οὗτος δὲ συνηγωνίζετο καὶ τἀναντί᾽ ἐμαρτύρει τῇ πατρίδι, καὶ ταῦτα ψευδῆ.

137 Καὶ οὐκ ἀπέχρη ταῦτ᾽, ἀλλὰ πάλιν μετὰ ταῦθ᾽ ὕστερον Ἀναξίνῳ τῷ κατασκόπῳ συνιὼν εἰς τὴν Θράσωνος οἰκίαν ἐλήφθη. καίτοι ὅστις τῷ ὑπὸ
[273] τῶν πολεμίων πεμφθέντι μόνος μόνῳ συνῄει καὶ ἐκοινολογεῖτο, οὗτος αὐτὸς ὑπῆρχε τῇ φύσει

---

[1] τοῦτον τοῦ λέγειν Pauly : τούτου λέγοντος Dind. (S doubtful).

(*The Depositions are read*)

[We, Callias of Sunium, Zeno of Phlya, Cleon of Phalerum, Demonicus of Marathon, on behalf of all the councillors, bear witness for Demosthenes that, when the people elected Aeschines state-advocate before the Amphictyons in the matter of the temple at Delos, we in Council judged Hypereides more worthy to speak on behalf of the state, and Hypereides was accordingly commissioned.]

Thus by rejecting this man from his spokesmanship, and giving the appointment to another, the Council branded him as a traitor and an enemy to the people.

So much for one of his spirited performances. Is it not just like the charges he brings against me ? Now let me remind you of another. Philip had sent to us Pytho of Byzantium in company with an embassy representing all his allies, hoping to bring dishonour upon Athens and convict her of injustice. Pytho was mightily confident, denouncing you with a full spate of eloquence, but I did not shrink from the encounter. I stood up and contradicted him, refusing to surrender the just claims of the commonwealth, and proving that Philip was in the wrong so conclusively that his own allies rose and admitted I was right ; but Aeschines took Philip's side throughout, and bore witness, even false witness, against his own country.

Nor did that satisfy him. At a later date he was caught again in the company of the spy Anaxinus at the house of Thraso. Yet a man who secretly met and conversed with a spy sent by the enemy must have been himself a spy by disposition and an enemy

109

κατάσκοπος καὶ πολέμιος τῇ πατρίδι. καὶ ὅτι
ταῦτ᾽ ἀληθῆ λέγω, κάλει μοι τούτων τοὺς μάρτυρας.

MΑΡΤΥΡΕΣ

[Τελέδημος Κλέωνος, Ὑπερείδης Καλλαίσχρου, Νικό-
μαχος Διοφάντου μαρτυροῦσι Δημοσθένει καὶ ἐπωμόσαντο
ἐπὶ τῶν στρατηγῶν εἰδέναι Αἰσχίνην Ἀτρομήτου Κοθωκίδην συνερχόμενον νυκτὸς εἰς τὴν Θράσωνος οἰκίαν καὶ
κοινολογούμενον Ἀναξίνῳ, ὃς ἐκρίθη εἶναι κατάσκοπος
παρὰ Φιλίππου. αὗται ἀπεδόθησαν αἱ μαρτυρίαι ἐπὶ Νικίου, ἑκατομβαιῶνος τρίτῃ ἱσταμένου.]

138 Μυρία τοίνυν ἕτερ᾽ εἰπεῖν ἔχων περὶ αὐτοῦ παραλείπω. καὶ γὰρ οὕτω πως ἔχει. πόλλ᾽ ἂν ἐγὼ
ἔτι τούτων ἔχοιμι δεῖξαι, ὧν οὗτος κατ᾽ ἐκείνους
τοὺς χρόνους τοῖς μὲν ἐχθροῖς ὑπηρετῶν, ἐμοὶ
δ᾽ ἐπηρεάζων εὑρέθη. ἀλλ᾽ οὐ τίθεται ταῦτα παρ᾽
ὑμῖν εἰς ἀκριβῆ μνήμην οὐδ᾽ ἣν προσῆκεν ὀργήν,
ἀλλὰ δεδώκατ᾽ ἔθει τινὶ φαύλῳ πολλὴν ἐξουσίαν
τῷ βουλομένῳ τὸν λέγοντά τι τῶν ὑμῖν συμφερόντων
ὑποσκελίζειν καὶ συκοφαντεῖν, τῆς ἐπὶ ταῖς λοιδο-
ρίαις ἡδονῆς καὶ χάριτος τὸ τῆς πόλεως συμφέρον
ἀνταλλαττόμενοι· διόπερ ῥᾷόν ἐστι καὶ ἀσφαλέστερον ἀεὶ τοῖς ἐχθροῖς ὑπηρετοῦντα μισθαρνεῖν ἢ τὴν
ὑπὲρ ὑμῶν ἑλόμενον τάξιν πολιτεύεσθαι.

139 Καὶ τὸ μὲν δὴ πρὸ τοῦ πολεμεῖν φανερῶς συν-
αγωνίζεσθαι Φιλίππῳ δεινὸν μέν, ὦ γῆ καὶ θεοί,
[274] πῶς γὰρ οὔ; κατὰ τῆς πατρίδος· δότε δ᾽, εἰ
βούλεσθε, δότ᾽ αὐτῷ τοῦτο. ἀλλ᾽ ἐπειδὴ φανερῶς
ἤδη τὰ πλοῖ᾽ ἐσεσύλητο, Χερρόνησος ἐπορθεῖτο,
ἐπὶ τὴν Ἀττικὴν ἐπορεύεθ᾽ ἄνθρωπος, οὐκέτ᾽ ἐν
ἀμφισβητησίμῳ τὰ πράγματ᾽ ἦν, ἀλλ᾽ ἐνειστήκει
πόλεμος, ὅ τι μὲν πώποτ᾽ ἔπραξεν ὑπὲρ ὑμῶν

110

of his country. To prove the truth of my statement, please call the witnesses.

(The Depositions are read)

[Teledemus, son of Cleon, Hypereides, son of Callaeschrus, Nicomachus, son of Diophantus, bear witness for Demosthenes, and have taken oath before the Generals that to their knowledge Aeschines, son of Atrometus, of Cothocidae, comes by night to the house of Thraso and holds communication with Anaxinus, who has been proved to be a spy from Philip. These depositions were lodged with Nicias on the third day of Hecatombaeon.]

I omit thousands of stories that I could tell you about him. The fact is, I could cite many clear instances of his conduct at that time, helping the enemy and maligning me ; only it is not your way to score up such offences for accurate remembrance and due resentment. You have a vicious habit of allowing too much indulgence to anyone who chooses by spiteful calumnies to trip up the heels of a man who gives you good advice. You give away a sound policy in exchange for the entertainment you derive from invective ; and so it is easier and safer for a public man to serve your enemies and pocket their pay than to choose and maintain a patriotic attitude.

Though it was a scandalous shame enough, God knows, openly to take Philip's side against his own country even before the war, make him a present, if you choose, make him a present of that. But when our merchantmen had been openly plundered, when the Chersonese was being ravaged, when the man was advancing upon Attica, when there could no longer be any doubt about the position, but war had already begun—even after that this malignant mumbler of

111

ὁ βάσκανος οὗτος ἰαμβειοφάγος, οὐκ ἂν ἔχοι
δεῖξαι, οὐδ' ἔστιν οὔτε μεῖζον οὔτ' ἔλαττον ψήφισμ'
οὐδὲν Αἰσχίνη περὶ τῶν συμφερόντων τῇ πόλει.
εἰ δέ φησι, νῦν δειξάτω ἐν τῷ ἐμῷ ὕδατι. ἀλλ'
οὐκ ἔστιν οὐδέν. καίτοι δυοῖν αὐτὸν ἀνάγκη
θάτερον, ἢ μηδὲν τοῖς πραττομένοις ὑπ' ἐμοῦ τότ'
ἔχοντ' ἐγκαλεῖν μὴ γράφειν παρὰ ταῦθ' ἕτερα, ἢ
τὸ τῶν ἐχθρῶν συμφέρον ζητοῦντα μὴ φέρειν εἰς
μέσον τὰ τούτων ἀμείνω.

140 Ἆρ' οὖν οὐδ' ἔλεγεν, ὥσπερ οὐδ' ἔγραφεν,
ἡνίκ' ἐργάσασθαί τι δέοι κακόν; οὐ μὲν οὖν ἦν
εἰπεῖν ἑτέρῳ· καὶ τὰ μὲν ἄλλα καὶ φέρειν ἐδύναθ',
ὡς ἔοικεν, ἡ πόλις καὶ ποιῶν οὗτος λανθάνειν·
ἐν δ' ἐπεξειργάσατ', ἄνδρες Ἀθηναῖοι, τοιοῦτον ὃ
πᾶσι τοῖς προτέροις ἐπέθηκεν τέλος· περὶ οὗ τοὺς
πολλοὺς ἀνήλωσε λόγους, τὰ τῶν Ἀμφισσέων
τῶν Λοκρῶν διεξιὼν δόγματα, ὡς διαστρέψων
τἀληθές. τὸ δ' οὐ τοιοῦτόν ἐστι· πόθεν; οὐδέποτ'
ἐκνίψει σὺ τἀκεῖ πεπραγμένα σαυτῷ· οὐχ οὕτω
πόλλ' ἐρεῖς.

141 Καλῶ δ' ἐναντίον ὑμῶν, ἄνδρες Ἀθηναῖοι, τοὺς
θεοὺς πάντας καὶ πάσας ὅσοι τὴν χώραν ἔχουσι
τὴν Ἀττικήν, καὶ τὸν Ἀπόλλω τὸν Πύθιον, ὃς
πατρῷός ἐστι τῇ πόλει, καὶ ἐπεύχομαι πᾶσι
τούτοις, εἰ μὲν ἀληθῆ πρὸς ὑμᾶς εἴποιμι καὶ
εἶπον καὶ τότ' εὐθὺς ἐν τῷ δήμῳ, ὅτε πρῶτον
[275] εἶδον τουτονὶ τὸν μιαρὸν τούτου τοῦ πράγματος
ἁπτόμενον (ἔγνων γάρ, εὐθέως ἔγνων), εὐτυχίαν
μοι δοῦναι καὶ σωτηρίαν, εἰ δὲ πρὸς ἔχθραν ἢ
φιλονικίας ἰδίας ἕνεκ' αἰτίαν ἐπάγω τούτῳ ψευδῆ,
πάντων τῶν ἀγαθῶν ἀνόνητόν με ποιῆσαι.

blank verse can point to no patriotic act. No profitable proposition, great or small, stands to the credit of Aeschines. If he claims any, let him cite it now, while my hour-glass [a] runs. But there is none. Now one of two things : either he made no alternative proposal because he could find no fault with my policy, or he did not disclose his amendments because his object was the advantage of the enemy.

Did he then refrain from speech as well as from moving resolutions, when there was any mischief to be done ? Why, no one else could get in a word ! Apparently the city could stand, and he could do without detection, almost anything ; but there was one performance of his that really gave the finishing touch to his earlier efforts. On that he has lavished all his wealth of words, citing in full the decrees against the Amphissians of Locri, in the hope of distorting the truth. But he can never disguise it. No, Aeschines, you will never wash out that stain ; you cannot talk long enough for that !

In your presence, men of Athens, I now invoke all the gods and goddesses whose domain is the land of Attica. I invoke also Pythian Apollo, the ancestral divinity of this city, and I solemnly beseech them all that, if I shall speak the truth now, and if I spoke truth to my countrymen when first I saw this miscreant putting his hand to that transaction—for I knew it, I knew it instantly—they may grant to me prosperity and salvation. But if with malice or in the spirit of personal rivalry I lay against him any false charge, I pray that they may dispossess me of everything that is good.

---

[a] *hour-glass*, the clepsydra or water-clock, used to measure the time allowed by the court to each speaker.

DEMOSTHENES

142 Τί οὖν ταῦτ' ἐπήραμαι καὶ διετεινάμην οὑτωσὶ
σφοδρῶς; ὅτι καὶ γράμματ' ἔχων ἐν τῷ δημοσίῳ
κείμενα, ἐξ ὧν ταῦτ' ἐπιδείξω σαφῶς, καὶ ὑμᾶς
εἰδὼς τὰ πεπραγμένα μνημονεύοντας, ἐκεῖνο φοβοῦμαι, μὴ τῶν εἰργασμένων αὐτῷ κακῶν ὑποληφθῇ
οὗτος ἐλάττων· ὅπερ πρότερον συνέβη, ὅτε τοὺς
ταλαιπώρους Φωκέας ἐποίησ' ἀπολέσθαι τὰ ψευδῆ
143 δεῦρ' ἀπαγγείλας. τὸν γὰρ ἐν Ἀμφίσσῃ πόλεμον,
δι' ὃν εἰς Ἐλάτειαν ἦλθε Φίλιππος καὶ δι' ὃν
ᾑρέθη τῶν Ἀμφικτυόνων ἡγεμών, ὃς ἅπαντ'
ἀνέτρεψε τὰ τῶν Ἑλλήνων, οὗτός ἐσθ' ὁ συγ-
κατασκευάσας καὶ πάντων εἷς ἀνὴρ μεγίστων
αἴτιος κακῶν. καὶ τότ' εὐθὺς ἐμοῦ διαμαρτυρο-
μένου καὶ βοῶντος ἐν τῇ ἐκκλησίᾳ "πόλεμον εἰς
τὴν Ἀττικὴν εἰσάγεις, Αἰσχίνη, πόλεμον Ἀμφικτυο-
νικόν," οἱ μὲν ἐκ παρακλήσεως συγκαθήμενοι
οὐκ εἴων με λέγειν, οἱ δ' ἐθαύμαζον καὶ κενὴν
αἰτίαν διὰ τὴν ἰδίαν ἔχθραν ἐπάγειν μ' ὑπελάμβανον
144 αὐτῷ. ἥτις δ' ἡ φύσις, ἄνδρες Ἀθηναῖοι, γέγονε
τούτων τῶν πραγμάτων, καὶ τίνος ἕνεκα ταῦτα
συνεσκευάσθη καὶ πῶς ἐπράχθη, νῦν ἀκούσατε,
ἐπειδὴ τότ' ἐκωλύθητε· καὶ γὰρ εὖ πρᾶγμα
συντεθὲν ὄψεσθε, καὶ μεγάλ' ὠφελήσεσθε πρὸς
ἱστορίαν τῶν κοινῶν, καὶ ὅση δεινότης ἦν ἐν τῷ
Φιλίππῳ θεάσεσθε.

145 Οὐκ ἦν τοῦ πρὸς ὑμᾶς πολέμου πέρας οὐδ'
[276] ἀπαλλαγὴ Φιλίππῳ, εἰ μὴ Θηβαίους καὶ Θετταλοὺς ἐχθροὺς ποιήσειε τῇ πόλει· ἀλλὰ καίπερ
ἀθλίως καὶ κακῶς τῶν στρατηγῶν τῶν ὑμετέρων
πολεμούντων αὐτῷ, ὅμως ὑπ' αὐτοῦ τοῦ πολέμου

114

This imprecation I address to Heaven, and this solemn averment I now make, because, though I have letters, deposited in the Record Office, enabling me to offer absolute proof, and though I am sure that you have not forgotten the transaction, I am afraid that his ability may be deemed inadequate for such enormous mischief. That mistake was made before, when by his false reports he contrived the destruction of the unhappy Phocians. The war at Amphissa, that is, the war that brought Philip to Elatea, and caused the election, as general of the Amphictyons, of a man who turned all Greece upside down, was due to the machinations of this man. In his own single person he was the author of all our worst evils. I protested instantly; I raised my voice in Assembly; I cried aloud, " You are bringing war into Attica, Aeschines, an Amphictyonic war; " but a compact body of men, sitting there under his direction, would not let me speak, and the rest were merely astonished and imagined that I was laying an idle charge in private spite. Men of Athens, you were not allowed to hear me then; but now you must and shall hear what was the real nature of that business, what was the purpose of the conspiracy, and how it was accomplished. You will see how skilfully it was contrived; you will get the benefit of new insight into your own politics; and you will form an idea of the supreme craftiness of Philip.

For Philip there could be no end or quittance of hostilities with Athens unless he should make the Thebans and Thessalians her enemies. Now, although your commanders were conducting the war against him without ability and without success, he

καὶ τῶν ληστῶν μυρί' ἔπασχεν κακά. οὔτε γὰρ
ἐξήγετο τῶν ἐκ τῆς χώρας γιγνομένων οὐδέν,
146 οὔτ' εἰσήγεθ' ὧν ἐδεῖτ' αὐτῷ· ἦν δ' οὔτ' ἐν τῇ
θαλάττῃ τότε κρείττων ὑμῶν, οὔτ' εἰς τὴν Ἀττικὴν
ἐλθεῖν δυνατός, μήτε Θετταλῶν ἀκολουθούντων,
μήτε Θηβαίων διιέντων· συνέβαινε δὲ αὐτῷ τῷ
πολέμῳ κρατοῦντι τοὺς ὁποιουσδήποθ' ὑμεῖς ἐξ-
επέμπετε στρατηγούς (ἐῶ γὰρ τοῦτό γε) αὐτῇ τῇ
φύσει τοῦ τόπου καὶ τῶν ὑπαρχόντων ἑκατέροις
147 κακοπαθεῖν. εἰ μὲν οὖν τῆς ἰδίας ἕνεκ' ἔχθρας
ἢ τοὺς Θετταλοὺς ἢ τοὺς Θηβαίους συμπείθοι
βαδίζειν ἐφ' ὑμᾶς, οὐδέν' ἡγεῖτο προσέξειν αὐτῷ
τὸν νοῦν· ἐὰν δὲ τὰς ἐκείνων κοινὰς προφάσεις
λαβὼν ἡγεμὼν αἱρεθῇ, ῥᾷον ἤλπιζε τὰ μὲν παρα-
κρούσεσθαι, τὰ δὲ πείσειν. τί οὖν; ἐπιχειρεῖ,
θεάσασθ' ὡς εὖ, πόλεμον ποιῆσαι τοῖς Ἀμφικτύοσι καὶ περὶ τὴν Πυλαίαν ταραχήν· εἰς γὰρ
ταῦτ' εὐθὺς αὐτοὺς ὑπελάμβανεν αὐτοῦ δεήσεσθαι.
148 εἰ μὲν τοίνυν τοῦτ' ἢ τῶν παρ' ἑαυτοῦ πεμπομένων
ἱερομνημόνων ἢ τῶν ἐκείνου συμμάχων εἰσηγοῖτό
τις, ὑπόψεσθαι τὸ πρᾶγμ' ἐνόμιζε καὶ τοὺς Θηβαίους καὶ τοὺς Θετταλοὺς καὶ πάντας φυλάξεσθαι,
ἂν δ' Ἀθηναῖος ᾖ καὶ παρ' ὑμῶν τῶν ὑπεναντίων
ὁ τοῦτο ποιῶν, εὐπόρως λήσειν· ὅπερ συνέβη.
149 Πῶς οὖν ταῦτ' ἐποίησεν; μισθοῦνται τουτονί.
οὐδενὸς δὲ προειδότος, οἶμαι, τὸ πρᾶγμ' οὐδὲ
[277] φυλάττοντος, ὥσπερ εἴωθε τὰ τοιαῦτα παρ' ὑμῖν
γίγνεσθαι, προβληθεὶς πυλάγορος οὗτος καὶ τριῶν
116

was vastly distressed both by the campaign and by
the privateers ; for he could neither export the pro-
ducts of his own country, nor import what he needed
for himself. At that time he had no supremacy at
sea, nor could he reach Attica by land unless the
Thessalians followed his banner and the Thebans
gave him free passage. In spite of his successes
against the commanders you sent out, such as they
were—I have nothing to say of their failure—he
found himself in trouble by reason of conditions of
locality and of the comparative resources of the two
combatants. Now, if he should invite the Thebans
or the Thessalians to take up his private quarrel and
march against you, he could expect no attention ; but
if he should espouse their joint grievances and be
chosen as their leader, he might hope to succeed by
a mixture of deception and persuasion. Very well ;
he sets to work — and observe how cleverly he
managed it—to throw the Pylaean Congress into
confusion and to implicate the Amphictyonic Council
in warfare, feeling certain that they would immediately beg him to deal with the situation. If, however, the question should be introduced by any of the
commissioners of religion sent by him or by any
allies of his, the Thebans and Thessalians, as he
expected, would be suspicious and all on their guard ;
but, if the operator should be an Athenian, representing his opponents, he conceived that he would
easily escape detection. And such was the actual
result.

How did he manage it ? By hiring Aeschines.
Nobody, of course, had any inkling ; nobody was
watching—according to your usual custom ! Aeschines
was nominated for the deputation to Thermopylae ;

DEMOSTHENES

ἢ τεττάρων χειροτονησάντων αὐτὸν ἀνερρήθη. ὡς
δὲ τὸ τῆς πόλεως ἀξίωμα λαβὼν ἀφίκετ' εἰς τοὺς
'Αμφικτύονας, πάντα τἄλλ' ἀφεὶς καὶ παριδὼν
ἐπέραινεν ἐφ' οἷς ἐμισθώθη, καὶ λόγους εὐπροσώ-
πους καὶ μύθους, ὅθεν ἡ Κιρραία χώρα καθιερώθη,
συνθεὶς καὶ διεξελθών, ἀνθρώπους ἀπείρους λόγων
καὶ τὸ μέλλον οὐ προορωμένους, τοὺς ἱερομνήμονας,
150 πείθει ψηφίσασθαι περιελθεῖν τὴν χώραν, ἣν οἱ
μὲν 'Αμφισσεῖς σφῶν αὐτῶν οὖσαν γεωργεῖν
ἔφασαν, οὗτος δὲ τῆς ἱερᾶς χώρας ᾐτιᾶτ' εἶναι,
οὐδεμίαν δίκην τῶν Λοκρῶν ἐπαγόντων ἡμῖν,
οὐδ' ἃ νῦν προφασίζεται, λέγων οὐκ ἀληθῆ.
γνώσεσθε δ' ἐκεῖθεν. οὐκ ἐνῆν ἄνευ τοῦ προσκαλέσασθαι δήπου τοῖς Λοκροῖς δίκην κατὰ τῆς
πόλεως τελέσασθαι. τίς οὖν ἐκλήτευσεν ἡμᾶς;
ἐπὶ ποίας ἀρχῆς; εἰπὲ τὸν εἰδότα, δεῖξον. ἀλλ'
οὐκ ἂν ἔχοις, ἀλλὰ κενῇ προφάσει ταύτῃ κατεχρῶ
καὶ ψευδεῖ.
151 Περιόντων τοίνυν τὴν χώραν τῶν 'Αμφικτυόνων
κατὰ τὴν ὑφήγησιν τὴν τούτου, προσπεσόντες οἱ
Λοκροὶ μικροῦ κατηκόντισαν ἅπαντας, τινὰς δὲ
καὶ συνήρπασαν τῶν ἱερομνημόνων. ὡς δ' ἅπαξ
ἐκ τούτων ἐγκλήματα καὶ πόλεμος πρὸς τοὺς
'Αμφισσεῖς ἐταράχθη, τὸ μὲν πρῶτον ὁ Κόττυφος
αὐτῶν τῶν 'Αμφικτυόνων ἤγαγε στρατιάν, ὡς δ'
οἱ μὲν οὐκ ἦλθον, οἱ δ' ἐλθόντες οὐδὲν ἐποίουν, εἰς
τὴν ἐπιοῦσαν πυλαίαν ἐπὶ τὸν Φίλιππον εὐθὺς
ἡγεμόν' ἦγον οἱ κατεσκευασμένοι καὶ πάλαι
118

three or four hands were held up, and he was declared elected. He repaired to the Council, invested with all the prestige of Athens, and at once, putting aside and disregarding everything else, addressed himself to the business for which he had taken pay. He concocted a plausible speech about the legendary origin of the consecration of the Cirrhaean territory, and by this narration induced the commissioners, men unversed in oratory and unsuspicious of consequences, to vote for a tour of survey of the land which the Amphissians said they were cultivating because it belonged to them, while Aeschines accused them of intruding on consecrated ground. It is not true that these Locrians were meditating any suit against Athens, or any other action such as he now falsely alleges in excuse. You will find a proof of his falsehood in this argument: — Of course it was not competent for the Locrians to take proceedings against Athens without serving a summons. Well, who served it? From what office was it issued? Name anyone who knows; point him out. You cannot; it was a false and idle pretext of yours.

With Aeschines as their trusty guide, the Amphictyons began their tour of the territory; but the Locrians fell upon them, were within an ace of spearing the whole crowd, and did actually seize and carry off the sacred persons of several commissioners. Complaints were promptly laid, and so war against the Amphissians was provoked. At the outset Cottyphus was commander of an army composed of Amphictyons; but some divisions never joined, and those who joined did nothing at all. The persons engaged in the plot, mostly scoundrels of old standing from Thessaly and other states, prepared

119

DEMOSTHENES

πονηροὶ τῶν Θετταλῶν καὶ τῶν ἐν ταῖς ἄλλαις
152 πόλεσι. καὶ προφάσεις εὐλόγους εἰλήφεσαν. ἢ
[278] γὰρ αὐτοὺς εἰσφέρειν καὶ ξένους τρέφειν ἔφασαν
δεῖν καὶ ζημιοῦν τοὺς μὴ ταῦτα ποιοῦντας
ἢ 'κεῖνον αἱρεῖσθαι. τί δεῖ τὰ πολλὰ λέγειν;
ᾑρέθη γὰρ ἐκ τούτων ἡγεμών. καὶ μετὰ ταῦτ'
εὐθέως δύναμιν συλλέξας καὶ παρελθὼν ὡς ἐπὶ
τὴν Κιρραίαν, ἐρρῶσθαι φράσας πολλὰ Κιρραίοις
153 καὶ Λοκροῖς, τὴν Ἐλάτειαν καταλαμβάνει. εἰ
μὲν οὖν μὴ μετέγνωσαν εὐθέως, ὡς τοῦτ' εἶδον,
οἱ Θηβαῖοι καὶ μεθ' ἡμῶν ἐγένοντο, ὥσπερ χειμάρ-
ρους ἂν ἅπαν τοῦτο τὸ πρᾶγμ' εἰς τὴν πόλιν
εἰσέπεσε· νῦν δὲ τό γ' ἐξαίφνης ἐπέσχον αὐτὸν
ἐκεῖνοι, μάλιστα μέν, ὦ ἄνδρες Ἀθηναῖοι, θεῶν
τινὸς εὐνοίᾳ πρὸς ὑμᾶς, εἶτα μέντοι καὶ ὅσον
καθ' ἕν' ἄνδρα, καὶ δι' ἐμέ. δὸς δέ μοι τὰ δόγματα
ταῦτα καὶ τοὺς χρόνους ἐν οἷς ἕκαστα πέπρακται,
ἵν' εἰδῆθ' ἡλίκα πράγμαθ' ἡ μιαρὰ κεφαλὴ ταράξασ'
154 αὕτη δίκην οὐκ ἔδωκε. λέγε μοι τὰ δόγματα.

ΔΟΓΜΑ ΑΜΦΙΚΤΥΟΝΩΝ

[Ἐπὶ ἱερέως Κλειναγόρου, ἐαρινῆς πυλαίας, ἔδοξε τοῖς
πυλαγόροις καὶ τοῖς συνέδροις τῶν Ἀμφικτυόνων καὶ τῷ
κοινῷ τῶν Ἀμφικτυόνων, ἐπειδὴ Ἀμφισσεῖς ἐπιβαίνουσιν
ἐπὶ τὴν ἱερὰν χώραν καὶ σπείρουσι καὶ βοσκήμασι κατα-
νέμουσιν, ἐπελθεῖν τοὺς πυλαγόρους καὶ τοὺς συνέδρους,
καὶ στήλαις διαλαβεῖν τοὺς ὅρους, καὶ ἀπειπεῖν τοῖς Ἀμ-
φισσεῦσι τοῦ λοιποῦ μὴ ἐπιβαίνειν.]

ΕΤΕΡΟΝ ΔΟΓΜΑ

155 [Ἐπὶ ἱερέως Κλειναγόρου, ἐαρινῆς πυλαίας, ἔδοξε τοῖς
120

to put the war into Philip's hands at the next congress. They found a plausible pretext : you must either, they said, pay contributions to a war-chest, maintain mercenary forces, and levy a fine on all recusants, or else elect Philip as commander-in-chief : and so, to cut a long story short, elected he was on this plea. He lost no time, collected his army, pretended to march to Cirrha, and then bade the Cirrhaeans and the Locrians alike good-bye and good luck, and seized Elatea. When the Thebans saw the trick, they promptly changed their minds and joined our side ; otherwise the whole business would have descended upon Athens like a torrent from the hills. In fact, the Thebans checked him for the moment ; and for that relief, men of Athens, you have first and chiefly to thank the kindness of some friendly god, but in a secondary degree, and so far as one man could help, you have to thank me. Hand me those decrees, with the dates of the several transactions. They will show you what a mass of trouble this consummate villain provoked ; and yet he was never punished. Please read the decrees.

(Sundry Resolutions of the Amphictyons are read)

[In the priesthood of Cleinagoras, at the spring session, it was resolved by the Wardens and Assessors of the Amphictyons, and by the General Synod of the Amphictyons, that, whereas Amphissians are encroaching upon the sacred territory and are sowing and grazing the same, the Wardens and Assessors shall attend and mark out the boundaries with pillars, and shall forbid the Amphissians hereafter to encroach.]

[In the priesthood of Cleinagoras, at the spring session,

DEMOSTHENES

[279] πυλαγόροις καὶ τοῖς συνέδροις τῶν Ἀμφικτυόνων καὶ τῷ κοινῷ τῶν Ἀμφικτυόνων, ἐπειδὴ οἱ ἐξ Ἀμφίσσης τὴν ἱερὰν χώραν κατανειμάμενοι γεωργοῦσι καὶ βοσκήματα νέμουσι, καὶ κωλυόμενοι τοῦτο ποιεῖν, ἐν τοῖς ὅπλοις παραγενόμενοι, τὸ κοινὸν τῶν Ἑλλήνων συνέδριον κεκωλύκασι μετὰ βίας, τινὰς δὲ καὶ τετραυματίκασι, τὸν στρατηγὸν τὸν ᾑρημένον τῶν Ἀμφικτυόνων Κόττυφον τὸν Ἀρκάδα πρεσβεῦσαι πρὸς Φίλιππον τὸν Μακεδόνα, καὶ ἀξιοῦν ἵνα βοηθήσῃ τῷ τε Ἀπόλλωνι καὶ τοῖς Ἀμφικτύοσιν, ὅπως μὴ περιίδῃ ὑπὸ τῶν ἀσεβῶν Ἀμφισσέων τὸν θεὸν πλημμελούμενον· καὶ διότι αὐτὸν στρατηγὸν αὐτοκράτορα αἱροῦνται οἱ Ἕλληνες οἱ μετέχοντες τοῦ συνεδρίου τῶν Ἀμφικτυόνων.]

Λέγε δὴ καὶ τοὺς χρόνους ἐν οἷς ταῦτ᾽ ἐγίγνετο· εἰσὶ γὰρ καθ᾽ οὓς ἐπυλαγόρησεν οὗτος. λέγε.

ΧΡΟΝΟΙ

[Ἄρχων Μνησιθείδης, μηνὸς ἀνθεστηριῶνος ἕκτῃ ἐπὶ δέκα.]

156 Δὸς δὴ τὴν ἐπιστολήν, ἥν, ὡς οὐχ ὑπήκουον οἱ Θηβαῖοι, πέμπει πρὸς τοὺς ἐν Πελοποννήσῳ συμμάχους ὁ Φίλιππος, ἵν᾽ εἰδῆτε καὶ ἐκ ταύτης σαφῶς ὅτι τὴν μὲν ἀληθῆ πρόφασιν τῶν πραγμάτων, τὸ ταῦτ᾽ ἐπὶ τὴν Ἑλλάδα καὶ τοὺς Θηβαίους καὶ ὑμᾶς πράττειν, ἀπεκρύπτετο, κοινὰ δὲ καὶ τοῖς Ἀμφικτύοσιν δόξαντα ποιεῖν προσεποιεῖτο· ὁ δὲ τὰς ἀφορμὰς ταύτας καὶ τὰς προφάσεις παρασχὼν οὗτος ἦν. λέγε.

ΕΠΙΣΤΟΛΗ

[280]

157 [Βασιλεὺς Μακεδόνων Φίλιππος Πελοποννησίων τῶν ἐν τῇ συμμαχίᾳ τοῖς δημιουργοῖς καὶ τοῖς συνέδροις καὶ

122

it was resolved by the Wardens, Assessors, and General Synod that, whereas the Amphissians who have occupied the sacred territory are tilling and grazing the same, and, when forbidden to do so, have appeared in arms and resisted the common assembly of the Greeks by force, and have actually wounded some of them, the general appointed by the Amphictyons, Cottyphus the Arcadian, shall go as an ambassador to Philip of Macedon and request him to come to the help of Apollo and the Amphictyons, that he may not suffer the god to be outraged by the impious Amphissians; he shall also announce that Philip is appointed General with full powers by the Greeks who are members of the Assembly of the Amphictyons.]

Now read the dates of these transactions. They are all dates at which he was our spokesman at the Congress of Thermopylae.

(*The Record of Dates is read*)

[Archonship of Mnesitheides, on the sixteenth of the month Anthesterion.]

Now hand me the letter which Philip dispatched to his Peloponnesian allies, when the Thebans disobeyed him. Even that letter will give you a clear proof that he was concealing the true reasons of his enterprise, namely his designs against Greece, and especially against Thebes and Athens, and was only pretending zeal for the national interests as defined by the Amphictyonic Council. But the man who provided him with that basis of action and those pretexts was Aeschines. Read.

(*Philip's Letter is read*)

[Philip, king of Macedonia, to the public officers and councillors of the allied Peloponnesians and to all his other

τοῖς ἄλλοις συμμάχοις πᾶσι χαίρειν. ἐπειδὴ Λοκροὶ οἱ
καλούμενοι Ὀζόλαι, κατοικοῦντες ἐν Ἀμφίσσῃ, πλημ-
μελοῦσιν εἰς τὸ ἱερὸν τοῦ Ἀπόλλωνος τοῦ ἐν Δελφοῖς
καὶ τὴν ἱερὰν χώραν ἐρχόμενοι μεθ' ὅπλων λεηλατοῦσι,
βούλομαι τῷ θεῷ μεθ' ὑμῶν βοηθεῖν καὶ ἀμύνασθαι
τοὺς παραβαίνοντάς τι τῶν ἐν ἀνθρώποις εὐσεβῶν· ὥστε
συναντᾶτε μετὰ τῶν ὅπλων εἰς τὴν Φωκίδα, ἔχοντες ἐπι-
σιτισμὸν ἡμερῶν τετταράκοντα, τοῦ ἐνεστῶτος μηνὸς λῴου,
ὡς ἡμεῖς ἄγομεν, ὡς δὲ Ἀθηναῖοι, βοηδρομιῶνος, ὡς δὲ
Κορίνθιοι, πανήμου. τοῖς δὲ μὴ συναντήσασι πανδημεὶ
χρησόμεθα τοῖς ἐν τοῖς συμβόλοις ἡμῖν κειμένοις ἐπι-
ζημίοις. εὐτυχεῖτε.]

158 Ὁρᾶθ' ὅτι φεύγει μὲν τὰς ἰδίας προφάσεις, εἰς
δὲ τὰς Ἀμφικτυονικὰς καταφεύγει. τίς οὖν ὁ
ταῦτα παρασκευάσας αὐτῷ; τίς ὁ τὰς προφάσεις
ταύτας ἐνδούς; τίς ὁ τῶν κακῶν τῶν γεγενημένων
μάλιστ' αἴτιος; οὐχ οὗτος; μὴ τοίνυν λέγετ', ὦ
ἄνδρες Ἀθηναῖοι, περιιόντες ὡς ὑφ' ἑνὸς τοιαῦτα
πέπονθεν ἡ Ἑλλὰς ἀνθρώπου. οὐχ ὑφ' ἑνός,
ἀλλ' ὑπὸ πολλῶν καὶ πονηρῶν τῶν παρ' ἑκάστοις,
159 ὦ γῆ καὶ θεοί· ὧν εἷς οὑτοσί, ὅν, εἰ μηδὲν εὐ-
λαβηθέντα τἀληθὲς εἰπεῖν δέοι, οὐκ ἂν ὀκνήσαιμ'
ἔγωγε κοινὸν ἀλειτήριον τῶν μετὰ ταῦτ' ἀπολωλότων ἁπάντων εἰπεῖν, ἀνθρώπων, τόπων, πόλεων·
ὁ γὰρ τὸ σπέρμα παρασχών, οὗτος τῶν φύντων
[281] αἴτιος. ὃν ὅπως ποτ' οὐκ εὐθὺς ἰδόντες ἀπ-
εστράφητε θαυμάζω. πλὴν πολύ τι σκότος, ὡς
ἔοικεν, ἐστὶ παρ' ὑμῖν πρὸ τῆς ἀληθείας.

160 Συμβέβηκε τοίνυν μοι τῶν κατὰ τῆς πατρίδος
τούτῳ πεπραγμένων ἁψαμένῳ εἰς ἃ τούτοις
ἐναντιούμενος αὐτὸς πεπολίτευμαι ἀφῖχθαι· ἃ
πολλῶν μὲν ἕνεκ' ἂν εἰκότως ἀκούσαιτέ μου,
124

Allies, greeting. Since the Ozolian Locrians, settled at Amphissa, are outraging the temple of Apollo at Delphi and come in arms to plunder the sacred territory, I consent to join you in helping the god and in punishing those who transgress in any way the principles of religion. Therefore meet under arms at Phocis with forty days' provisions in the next month, styled Loüs by us, Boëdromion by the Athenians, and Panemus by the Corinthians. Those who, being pledged to us, do not join us in full force, we shall treat as punishable. Farewell.]

You see how he avoids personal excuses, and takes shelter in Amphictyonic reasons. Who gave him his equipment of deceit? Who supplied him with these pretexts? Who above all others is to blame for all the ensuing mischief? Who but Aeschines? Then do not go about saying, men of Athens, that these disasters were brought upon Greece by Philip alone. I solemnly aver that it was not one man, but a gang of traitors in every state. One of them was Aeschines; and, if I am to tell the whole truth without concealment, I will not flinch from declaring him the evil genius of all the men, all the districts, and all the cities that have perished. Let the man who sowed the seed bear the guilt of the harvest. I marvel that you did not avert your faces the moment you set eyes on him; only, as it seems, there is a cloud of darkness between you and the truth.

In dealing with his unpatriotic conduct I have approached the question of the very different policy pursued by myself. For many reasons you may fairly be asked to listen to my account of that policy,

DEMOSTHENES

μάλιστα δ' ὅτι αἰσχρόν ἐστιν, ὦ ἄνδρες Ἀθηναῖοι,
εἰ ἐγὼ μὲν τὰ ἔργα τῶν ὑπὲρ ὑμῶν πόνων ὑπέμεινα,
161 ὑμεῖς δὲ μηδὲ τοὺς λόγους αὐτῶν ἀνέξεσθε. ὁρῶν
γὰρ ἐγὼ Θηβαίους, σχεδὸν δὲ καὶ ὑμᾶς, ὑπὸ τῶν
τὰ Φιλίππου φρονούντων καὶ διεφθαρμένων παρ'
ἑκατέροις, ὃ μὲν ἦν ἀμφοτέροις φοβερὸν καὶ
φυλακῆς πολλῆς δεόμενον, τὸ τὸν Φίλιππον ἐᾶν
αὐξάνεσθαι, παρορῶντας καὶ οὐδὲ καθ' ἓν φυλαττο-
μένους, εἰς ἔχθραν δὲ καὶ τὸ προσκρούειν ἀλλήλοις
ἑτοίμως ἔχοντας, ὅπως τοῦτο μὴ γένοιτο παρα-
τηρῶν διετέλουν, οὐκ ἀπὸ τῆς ἐμαυτοῦ γνώμης
162 μόνον ταῦτα συμφέρειν ὑπολαμβάνων, ἀλλ' εἰδὼς
Ἀριστοφῶντα καὶ πάλιν Εὔβουλον πάντα τὸν
χρόνον βουλομένους πρᾶξαι ταύτην τὴν φιλίαν,
καὶ περὶ τῶν ἄλλων πολλάκις ἀντιλέγοντας
ἑαυτοῖς τοῦθ' ὁμογνωμονοῦντας ἀεί. οὓς σὺ ζῶντας
μέν, ὦ κίναδος, κολακεύων παρηκολούθεις, τεθ-
νεώτων δ' οὐκ αἰσθάνει κατηγορῶν· ἃ γὰρ περὶ
Θηβαίων ἐπιτιμᾷς ἐμοί, ἐκείνων πολὺ μᾶλλον ἢ
ἐμοῦ κατηγορεῖς, τῶν προτέρων ἢ ἐγὼ ταύτην
163 τὴν συμμαχίαν δοκιμασάντων. ἀλλ' ἐκεῖσ' ἐπ-
άνειμ', ὅτι τὸν ἐν Ἀμφίσσῃ πόλεμον τούτου μὲν
ποιήσαντος, συμπερανάμενων δὲ τῶν ἄλλων τῶν
συνεργῶν αὐτῷ τὴν πρὸς Θηβαίους ἔχθραν, συνέβη
[282] τὸν Φίλιππον ἐλθεῖν ἐφ' ἡμᾶς, οὗπερ ἕνεκα τὰς
πόλεις οὗτοι συνέκρουον, καὶ εἰ μὴ προεξανέστημεν
μικρόν, οὐδ' ἀναλαβεῖν ἂν ἐδυνήθημεν· οὕτω
μέχρι πόρρω προήγαγον οὗτοι τὴν ἔχθραν. ἐν
126

but chiefly because it would be discreditable, men of Athens, that you should be impatient of the mere recital of those arduous labours on your behalf which I had patience to endure. When I saw that the Thebans, and perhaps even the Athenians, under the influence of the adherents of Philip and the corrupt faction in the two states, were disregarding a real danger that called for earnest vigilance, the danger of permitting Philip's aggrandizement, and were taking no single measure of precaution, but were ready to quarrel and attack each other, I persistently watched for opportunities of averting that danger, not merely because my own judgement warned me that such solicitude was necessary, but because I knew that Aristophon, and after him Eubulus, had always wished to promote a good understanding between Athens and Thebes. In that regard they were always of one mind, despite their constant disagreement on other points of policy. While those statesmen were alive, Aeschines, you pestered them with your flattery, like the sly fox you are ; now they are dead, you denounce them, unaware that, when you reproach me with a Theban policy, your censure does not affect me so much as the men who approved of a Theban alliance before I did. But that is a digression. I say that, when Aeschines had provoked the war in Amphissa, and when his associates had helped him to aggravate our enmity towards Thebes, the result was that Philip marched against us, in pursuance of the purpose for which they had embroiled the states, and that, if we had not roused ourselves a little just in time, we could never have retrieved our position ; so far had these men carried the quarrel. You will better un-

οἷς δ᾽ ἦτ᾽ ἤδη τὰ πρὸς ἀλλήλους, τουτωνὶ
τῶν ψηφισμάτων ἀκούσαντες καὶ τῶν ἀποκρίσεων
εἴσεσθε. καί μοι λέγε ταῦτα λαβών.

ΨΗΦΙΣΜΑ

164 [Ἐπ᾽ ἄρχοντος Ἡροπύθου, μηνὸς ἐλαφηβολιῶνος ἕκτῃ
φθίνοντος, φυλῆς πρυτανευούσης Ἐρεχθῆδος, βουλῆς καὶ
στρατηγῶν γνώμῃ· ἐπειδὴ Φίλιππος ἃς μὲν κατείληφε
πόλεις τῶν ἀστυγειτόνων, τινὰς δὲ πορθεῖ, κεφαλαίῳ δ᾽
ἐπὶ τὴν Ἀττικὴν παρασκευάζεται παραγίγνεσθαι, παρ᾽
οὐδὲν ἡγούμενος τὰς ἡμετέρας συνθήκας, καὶ τοὺς ὅρκους
λύειν ἐπιβάλλεται καὶ τὴν εἰρήνην, παραβαίνων τὰς
κοινὰς πίστεις, δεδόχθαι τῇ βουλῇ καὶ τῷ δήμῳ πέμπειν
πρὸς αὐτὸν πρέσβεις, οἵτινες αὐτῷ διαλέξονται καὶ
παρακαλέσουσιν αὐτὸν μάλιστα μὲν τὴν πρὸς ἡμᾶς
ὁμόνοιαν διατηρεῖν καὶ τὰς συνθήκας, εἰ δὲ μή, πρὸς τὸ
βουλεύσασθαι δοῦναι χρόνον τῇ πόλει καὶ τὰς ἀνοχὰς
ποιήσασθαι μέχρι τοῦ θαργηλιῶνος μηνός. ᾑρέθησαν
ἐκ βουλῆς Σῖμος Ἀναγυράσιος, Εὐθύδημος Φυλάσιος,
Βουλαγόρας Ἀλωπεκῆθεν.]

ΕΤΕΡΟΝ ΨΗΦΙΣΜΑ

165 [Ἐπ᾽ ἄρχοντος Ἡροπύθου, μηνὸς μουνυχιῶνος ἕνῃ
καὶ νέᾳ, πολεμάρχου γνώμῃ· ἐπειδὴ Φίλιππος εἰς ἀλλο-
τριότητα Θηβαίους πρὸς ἡμᾶς ἐπιβάλλεται καταστῆσαι,
παρεσκεύασται δὲ καὶ παντὶ τῷ στρατεύματι πρὸς τοὺς
[283] ἔγγιστα τῆς Ἀττικῆς παραγίγνεσθαι τόπους, παραβαίνων
τὰς πρὸς ἡμᾶς ὑπαρχούσας αὐτῷ συνθήκας, δεδόχθαι τῇ
βουλῇ καὶ τῷ δήμῳ πέμψαι πρὸς αὐτὸν κήρυκα καὶ πρέσβεις, οἵτινες ἀξιώσουσι καὶ παρακαλέσουσιν αὐτὸν
ποιήσασθαι τὰς ἀνοχάς, ὅπως ἐνδεχομένως ὁ δῆμος
βουλεύσηται· καὶ γὰρ νῦν οὐ κέκρικε βοηθεῖν ἐν οὐδενὶ
τῶν μετρίων. ᾑρέθησαν ἐκ βουλῆς Νέαρχος Σωσινόμου,
Πολυκράτης Ἐπίφρονος, καὶ κῆρυξ Εὔνομος Ἀναφλύστιος ἐκ τοῦ δήμου.]

128

derstand the state of feeling between the two cities, when you have heard the decrees and the answers sent thereto. Please take and read these papers.

(The Decrees are read)

[In the archonship of Heropythus, on the twenty-fifth day of the month Elaphebolion, the tribe Erechtheis then holding the presidency, on the advice of the Council and the Generals: whereas Philip has captured some of the cities of our neighbours and is besieging others, and finally is preparing to advance against Attica, ignoring our agreement with him, and is meditating a breach of his oaths and of the peace, violating all mutual pledges, be it resolved by the Council and People to send ambassadors to confer with him and to summon him to preserve in particular his agreement and compact with us, and, failing that, to give the City time for decision and to conclude an armistice until the month of Thargelion. The following members of Council were chosen: Simus of Anagyrus, Euthydemus of Phylae, Bulagoras of Alopece.]

[In the archonship of Heropythus, on the thirtieth of the month Munychion, on the advice of the Commander-in-chief: whereas Philip aims at setting the Thebans at variance with us, and has prepared to march with all his forces to the parts nearest to Attica, violating his existing arrangements with us, be it resolved by the Council and People to send a herald and ambassadors to request and exhort him to conclude an armistice, in order that the People may decide according to circumstances; for even now the People have not decided to send a force if they can obtain reasonable terms. The following were chosen from the Council: Nearchus, son of Sosinomus, Polycrates, son of Epiphron; and as herald from the People, Eunomus of Anaphlystus.]

129

166   Λέγε δὴ καὶ τὰς ἀποκρίσεις.

ΑΠΟΚΡΙΣΙΣ ΑΘΗΝΑΙΟΙΣ

[Βασιλεὺς Μακεδόνων Φίλιππος Ἀθηναίων τῇ βουλῇ
καὶ τῷ δήμῳ χαίρειν. ἣν μὲν ἀπ᾽ ἀρχῆς εἴχετε πρὸς
ἡμᾶς αἵρεσιν οὐκ ἀγνοῶ, καὶ τίνα σπουδὴν ἐποιεῖσθε
προσκαλέσασθαι βουλόμενοι Θετταλοὺς καὶ Θηβαίους,
ἔτι δὲ καὶ Βοιωτούς· βέλτιον δ᾽ αὐτῶν φρονούντων καὶ μὴ
βουλομένων ἐφ᾽ ὑμῖν ποιήσασθαι τὴν ἑαυτῶν αἵρεσιν, ἀλλὰ
κατὰ τὸ συμφέρον ἱσταμένων, νῦν ἐξ ὑποστροφῆς ἀπο-
στείλαντες ὑμεῖς πρός με πρέσβεις καὶ κήρυκα συνθηκῶν
μνημονεύετε καὶ τὰς ἀνοχὰς αἰτεῖσθε κατ᾽ οὐδὲν ὑφ᾽
ἡμῶν πεπλημμελημένοι. ἐγὼ μέντοι ἀκούσας τῶν πρε-
σβευτῶν συγκατατίθεμαι τοῖς παρακαλουμένοις καὶ ἕτοι-
μός εἰμι ποιεῖσθαι τὰς ἀνοχάς, ἄν περ τοὺς οὐκ ὀρθῶς
συμβουλεύοντας ὑμῖν παραπέμψαντες τῆς προσηκούσης
ἀτιμίας ἀξιώσητε. ἔρρωσθε.]

167   ΑΠΟΚΡΙΣΙΣ ΘΗΒΑΙΟΙΣ

[Βασιλεὺς Μακεδόνων Φίλιππος Θηβαίων τῇ βουλῇ καὶ
τῷ δήμῳ χαίρειν. ἐκομισάμην τὴν παρ᾽ ὑμῶν ἐπιστολήν,
[284] δι᾽ ἧς μοι τὴν ὁμόνοιαν καὶ τὴν εἰρήνην ἀνανεοῦσθε.
πυνθάνομαι μέντοι διότι πᾶσαν ὑμῖν Ἀθηναῖοι προσ-
φέρονται φιλοτιμίαν, βουλόμενοι ὑμᾶς συγκαταίνους
γενέσθαι τοῖς ὑπ᾽ αὐτῶν παρακαλουμένοις. πρότερον μὲν
οὖν ὑμῶν κατεγίγνωσκον ἐπὶ τῷ μέλλειν πείθεσθαι ταῖς
ἐκείνων ἐλπίσι καὶ ἐπακολουθεῖν αὐτῶν τῇ προαιρέσει.
νῦν δ᾽ ἐπιγνοὺς ὑμᾶς τὰ πρὸς ἡμᾶς ἐζητηκότας ἔχειν εἰρήνην
μᾶλλον ἢ ταῖς ἑτέρων ἐπακολουθεῖν γνώμαις, ἥσθην καὶ
μᾶλλον ὑμᾶς ἐπαινῶ κατὰ πολλά, μάλιστα δ᾽ ἐπὶ τῷ βουλεύσασθαι περὶ τούτων ἀσφαλέστερον καὶ τὰ πρὸς ἡμᾶς
ἔχειν ἐν εὐνοίᾳ· ὅπερ οὐ μικρὰν ὑμῖν οἴσειν ἐλπίζω ῥοπήν,
ἐάν περ ἐπὶ ταύτης μένητε τῆς προθέσεως. ἔρρωσθε.]

168   Οὕτω διαθεὶς ὁ Φίλιππος τὰς πόλεις πρὸς

Now read the replies.

(The Reply to the Athenians is read)

[Philip, King of Macedonia, to the Council and People of Athens, greeting.—I am not ignorant of the policy which you have adopted towards us from the first, nor of your efforts to win over the Thessalians and Thebans, and the Boeotians as well. They, however, are wiser, and will not submit their policy to your dictation, but take their stand upon self-interest. And now you change your tactics, and send ambassadors with a herald to me, reminding me of our compact and asking for an armistice, though we have done you no wrong. However, after hearing your ambassadors, I accede to your request, and am ready to conclude an armistice, if you will dismiss your evil counsellors, and punish them with suitable degradation. Farewell.]

(The Reply to the Thebans is read)

[Philip, King of Macedonia, to the Council and People of Thebes, greeting.—I have received your letter, in which you renew goodwill and peace with me. I understand, however, that the Athenians are displaying the utmost eagerness in their desire to win your acceptance of their overtures. Now formerly I used to blame you for a tendency to put faith in their hopes and to adopt their policy ; but now I am glad to learn that you have preferred to be at peace with me rather than to adopt the opinions of others. Especially do I commend you for forming a safer judgement on these matters and for retaining your goodwill toward us, which I expect will be of no small advantage to you, if you adhere to this purpose. Farewell.]

Having, through the agency of these men, pro-

DEMOSTHENES

ἀλλήλας διὰ τούτων, καὶ τούτοις ἐπαρθεὶς τοῖς
ψηφίσμασι καὶ ταῖς ἀποκρίσεσιν, ἧκεν ἔχων τὴν
δύναμιν καὶ τὴν Ἐλάτειαν κατέλαβεν, ὡς οὐδ᾽
ἂν εἴ τι γένοιτ᾽ ἔτι συμπνευσάντων ἂν ἡμῶν καὶ
τῶν Θηβαίων. ἀλλὰ μὴν τὸν τότε συμβάντ᾽ ἐν
τῇ πόλει θόρυβον ἴστε μὲν ἅπαντες μικρὰ δ᾽
ἀκούσαθ᾽ ὅμως αὐτὰ τἀναγκαιότατα.

169 Ἑσπέρα μὲν γὰρ ἦν, ἧκε δ᾽ ἀγγέλλων τις ὡς
τοὺς πρυτάνεις ὡς Ἐλάτεια κατείληπται. καὶ
μετὰ ταῦθ᾽ οἱ μὲν εὐθὺς ἐξαναστάντες μεταξὺ
δειπνοῦντες, τούς τ᾽ ἐκ τῶν σκηνῶν τῶν κατὰ
τὴν ἀγορὰν ἐξεῖργον καὶ τὰ γέρρ᾽ ἀνεπετάννυσαν,[1]
οἱ δὲ τοὺς στρατηγοὺς μετεπέμποντο καὶ τὸν
σαλπικτὴν ἐκάλουν· καὶ θορύβου πλήρης ἦν ἡ
πόλις. τῇ δ᾽ ὑστεραίᾳ, ἅμα τῇ ἡμέρᾳ, οἱ μὲν
πρυτάνεις τὴν βουλὴν ἐκάλουν εἰς τὸ βουλευτήριον,
[285] ὑμεῖς δ᾽ εἰς τὴν ἐκκλησίαν ἐπορεύεσθε, καὶ πρὶν
ἐκείνην χρηματίσαι καὶ προβουλεῦσαι, πᾶς ὁ
170 δῆμος ἄνω καθῆτο. καὶ μετὰ ταῦθ᾽ ὡς ἦλθεν
ἡ βουλὴ καὶ ἀπήγγειλαν οἱ πρυτάνεις τὰ προσηγ-
γελμέν᾽ ἑαυτοῖς καὶ τὸν ἥκοντα παρήγαγον κἀκεῖνος
εἶπεν, ἠρώτα μὲν ὁ κῆρυξ "τίς ἀγορεύειν βούλεται;"
παρῄει δ᾽ οὐδείς. πολλάκις δὲ τοῦ κήρυκος
ἐρωτῶντος, οὐδὲν μᾶλλον ἀνίστατ᾽ οὐδείς, ἁπάντων

---

[1] ἀνεπετάννυσαν Girard : ἐνεπίμπρασαν Dind.: so S and all
MSS.

a presiding councillors: the fifty representatives on the
Council of that one of the ten tribes within whose term of
administrative duty the meeting fell.

b unfolded the hurdles: they were tied together hinge-

132

moted such relations between the two cities, and
being encouraged by these decrees and these replies,
Philip came with his forces and occupied Elatea,
imagining that, whatever might happen, you and
the Thebans would never come to agreement. You
all remember the commotion that ensued at Athens ;
nevertheless let me recount some small but essential
details.

Evening had already fallen when a messenger
arrived bringing to the presiding councillors[a] the
news that Elatea had been taken. They were
sitting at supper, but they instantly rose from
table, cleared the booths in the market-place of their
occupants, and unfolded the hurdles,[b] while others
summoned the commanders and ordered the attend-
ance of the trumpeter. The commotion spread
through the whole city. At daybreak on the morrow
the presidents summoned the Council to the Council
House, and the citizens flocked to the place of
assembly. Before the Council could introduce the
business and prepare the agenda, the whole body of
citizens had taken their places on the hill. The
Council arrived, the presiding Councillors formally
reported the intelligence they had received, and the
courier was introduced. As soon as he had told his
tale, the marshal put the question, Who wishes to
speak ? No one came forward. The marshal repeated his question again and again, but still no

wise, and, when unfolded, formed barriers, either to keep
out strangers ([Dem.] *In Neaeram*, 90) or to block streets
leading from the market-place elsewhere than to the Pnyx,
where the Assembly met (Schol. on Aristoph. *Ach. 22*). *Unfolded* is a conjectural reading derived from the scholium
cited ; but no satisfactory explanation is forthcoming of the
reading of all mss., *set fire to the hurdles.*

DEMOSTHENES

μὲν τῶν στρατηγῶν παρόντων, ἀπάντων δὲ τῶν
ῥητόρων, καλούσης δὲ τῆς πατρίδος τῇ κοινῇ
φωνῇ[1] τὸν ἐροῦνθ' ὑπὲρ σωτηρίας· ἣν γὰρ ὁ κῆρυξ
κατὰ τοὺς νόμους φωνὴν ἀφίησι, ταύτην κοινὴν
171 τῆς πατρίδος δίκαιον ἡγεῖσθαι. καίτοι εἰ μὲν
τοὺς σωθῆναι τὴν πόλιν βουλομένους παρελθεῖν
ἔδει, πάντες ἂν ὑμεῖς καὶ οἱ ἄλλοι Ἀθηναῖοι
ἀναστάντες ἐπὶ τὸ βῆμ' ἐβαδίζετε· πάντες γὰρ
οἶδ' ὅτι σωθῆναι αὐτὴν ἐβούλεσθε· εἰ δὲ τοὺς
πλουσιωτάτους, οἱ τριακόσιοι· εἰ δὲ τοὺς ἀμφότερα
ταῦτα, καὶ εὔνους τῇ πόλει καὶ πλουσίους, οἱ
μετὰ ταῦτα τὰς μεγάλας ἐπιδόσεις ἐπιδόντες·
172 καὶ γὰρ εὐνοίᾳ καὶ πλούτῳ τοῦτ' ἐποίησαν. ἀλλ',
ὡς ἔοικεν, ἐκεῖνος ὁ καιρὸς καὶ ἡ ἡμέρα 'κείνη
οὐ μόνον εὔνουν καὶ πλούσιον ἄνδρ' ἐκάλει, ἀλλὰ
καὶ παρηκολουθηκότα τοῖς πράγμασιν ἐξ ἀρχῆς
καὶ συλλελογισμένον ὀρθῶς τίνος ἕνεκα ταῦτ'
ἔπραττεν ὁ Φίλιππος καὶ τί βουλόμενος· ὁ γὰρ
μὴ ταῦτ' εἰδὼς μηδ' ἐξητακὼς πόρρωθεν, οὔτ'
εἰ εὔνους ἦν οὔτ' εἰ πλούσιος, οὐδὲν μᾶλλον ἔμελλ'
ὅ τι χρὴ ποιεῖν εἴσεσθαι, οὐδ' ὑμῖν ἕξειν συμβου-
173 λεύειν. ἐφάνην τοίνυν οὗτος ἐν ἐκείνῃ τῇ ἡμέρᾳ
[286] ἐγὼ καὶ παρελθὼν εἶπον εἰς ὑμᾶς, ἅ μου δυοῖν
ἕνεκ' ἀκούσατε προσσχόντες τὸν νοῦν, ἑνὸς μέν,
ἵν' εἰδῆθ' ὅτι μόνος τῶν λεγόντων καὶ πολιτευομένων ἐγὼ τὴν τῆς εὐνοίας τάξιν ἐν τοῖς δεινοῖς
οὐκ ἔλιπον, ἀλλὰ καὶ λέγων καὶ γράφων ἐξηταζό-
μην τὰ δέονθ' ὑπὲρ ὑμῶν ἐν αὐτοῖς τοῖς φοβεροῖς,

---

[1] τῇ κοινῇ τῆς πατρίδος φωνῇ A : τῆς πατρίδος τῇ κοινῇ φωνῇ
Dind. : τῆς κοινῆς πατρίδος φωνῆς S.

one rose to speak, although all the commanders were there, and all the orators, and although the country with her civic voice was calling for the man who should speak for her salvation ; for we may justly regard the voice, which the crier raises as the laws direct, as the civic voice of our country. Now had it been the duty of every man who desired the salvation of Athens to come forward, all of you, aye, every Athenian citizen, would have risen in your places and made your way to the tribune, for that salvation, I am well assured, was the desire of every heart. If that duty had fallen upon the wealthy, the Three Hundred would have risen ; if upon those who were alike wealthy and patriotic, the men who thereafter gave those generous donations which signalized at once their wealth and their patriotism. But, it seems, the call of the crisis on that moment-ous day was not only for the wealthy patriot but for the man who from first to last had closely watched the sequence of events, and had rightly fathomed the purposes and the desires of Philip ; for anyone who had not grasped those purposes, or had not studied them long beforehand, however patriotic and however wealthy he might be, was not the man to appreciate the needs of the hour, or to find any counsel to offer to the people. On that day, then, the call was manifestly for me. I came forward and addressed you ; and I will now ask your careful attention to the speech I then made, for two reasons : first, that you may understand that I, alone among your orators and politicians, did not desert the post of patriotism in the hour of peril, but approved myself as one who in the midst of panic could, both in speech and in suggestion, do what duty bade on

ἑτέρου δ', ὅτι μικρὸν ἀναλώσαντες χρόνον, πολλῷ
πρὸς τὰ λοιπὰ τῆς πάσης πολιτείας ἔσεσθ' ἐμπει-
ρότεροι.

174 Εἶπον τοίνυν ὅτι " τοὺς μὲν ὡς ὑπαρχόντων
Θηβαίων Φιλίππῳ λίαν θορυβουμένους ἀγνοεῖν
τὰ παρόντα πράγμαθ' ἡγοῦμαι· εὖ γὰρ οἶδ' ὅτι,
εἰ τοῦθ' οὕτως ἐτύγχανεν ἔχον, οὐκ ἂν αὐτὸν
ἠκούομεν ἐν Ἐλατείᾳ ὄντα, ἀλλ' ἐπὶ τοῖς ἡμετέροις
ὁρίοις. ὅτι μέντοι ἵν' ἕτοιμα ποιήσηται τὰν
Θήβαις ἥκει, σαφῶς ἐπίσταμαι. ὡς δ' ἔχει "
175 ἔφην " ταῦτα, ἀκούσατέ μου. ἐκεῖνος ὅσους ἢ
πεῖσαι χρήμασιν Θηβαίων ἢ ἐξαπατῆσαι ἐνῆν
ἅπαντας ηὐτρέπισται· τοὺς δ' ἀπ' ἀρχῆς ἀνθ-
εστηκότας αὐτῷ καὶ νῦν ἐναντιουμένους οὐδαμῶς
πεῖσαι δύναται. τί οὖν βούλεται, καὶ τίνος
ἕνεκα τὴν Ἐλάτειαν κατείληφεν; πλησίον δύναμιν δείξας καὶ παραστήσας τὰ ὅπλα, τοὺς μὲν
ἑαυτοῦ φίλους ἐπᾶραι καὶ θρασεῖς ποιῆσαι, τοὺς
δ' ἐναντιουμένους καταπλῆξαι, ἵν' ἢ συγχωρήσωσι
φοβηθέντες ἃ νῦν οὐκ ἐθέλουσιν, ἢ βιασθῶσιν.
176 εἰ μὲν τοίνυν προαιρησόμεθ' ἡμεῖς " ἔφην " ἐν
τῷ παρόντι, εἴ τι δύσκολον πέπρακται Θηβαίοις
πρὸς ἡμᾶς, τούτου μεμνῆσθαι καὶ ἀπιστεῖν αὐτοῖς
ὡς ἐν τῇ τῶν ἐχθρῶν οὖσιν μερίδι, πρῶτον μὲν
ἂν εὔξαιτο Φίλιππος ποιήσομεν, εἶτα φοβοῦμαι
μὴ προσδεξαμένων τῶν νῦν ἀνθεστηκότων αὐτῷ
[287] καὶ μιᾷ γνώμῃ πάντων φιλιππισάντων, εἰς τὴν
Ἀττικὴν ἔλθωσιν ἀμφότεροι. ἂν μέντοι πεισθῆτ'
ἐμοί, καὶ πρὸς τῷ σκοπεῖν ἀλλὰ μὴ φιλονικεῖν
136

your behalf; and secondly, because at the cost of
a few minutes of study you may gain experience
which will stand you in good stead for your policy
in times to come.

What I said was this. " In my judgement the
present position of affairs is misunderstood by those
who are so much alarmed by the apprehension that
all Thebes is at the disposal of Philip. If that were
true, I am quite certain that we should have heard
of him not at Elatea but on our own frontiers.
But I know with certainty that he has come to complete his preparations at Thebes. Let me tell you
how he is situated. He has at his command all
those Thebans whom he was able to win by fraud
or corruption ; but he cannot by any means prevail
upon those who have resisted him from the first and
who are still his opponents. His present object, and
the purpose for which he has occupied Elatea, is
that, by an exhibition of his power in the neighbourhood of Thebes, and by bringing up armed forces,
he may encourage and embolden his friends, and
overawe his adversaries, hoping that the latter will
yield to intimidation or to compulsion and will so
concede what at present they refuse. If," I added,
" at this crisis we are determined to remember all
the provocative dealings of the Thebans with us in
past time, and to distrust them still on the score of
enmity, in the first place, we shall be acting exactly
as Philip would beg us to act; and secondly, I am
afraid that, if his present opponents give him a
favourable reception, and unanimously become
Philip's men, both parties will join in an invasion of
Attica. If, however, you will listen to my advice,
and apply your minds to consideration, but not to

περὶ ὧν ἂν λέγω γένησθε, οἶμαι καὶ τὰ δέοντα
λέγειν δόξειν καὶ τὸν ἐφεστηκότα κίνδυνον τῇ πόλει
177 διαλύσειν. τί οὖν φημὶ δεῖν; πρῶτον μὲν τὸν
παρόντ᾽ ἐπανεῖναι φόβον, εἶτα μεταθέσθαι καὶ
φοβεῖσθαι πάντας ὑπὲρ Θηβαίων· πολὺ γὰρ τῶν
δεινῶν εἰσιν ἡμῶν ἐγγυτέρω, καὶ προτέροις αὐτοῖς
ἐστιν ὁ κίνδυνος· ἔπειτ᾽ ἐξελθόντας Ἐλευσῖνάδε
τοὺς ἐν ἡλικίᾳ καὶ τοὺς ἱππέας δεῖξαι πᾶσιν ὑμᾶς
αὐτοὺς ἐν τοῖς ὅπλοις ὄντας, ἵνα τοῖς ἐν Θήβαις
φρονοῦσι τὰ ὑμέτερα ἐξ ἴσου γένηται τὸ παρρη-
σιάζεσθαι περὶ τῶν δικαίων, ἰδοῦσιν ὅτι, ὥσπερ
τοῖς πωλοῦσι Φιλίππῳ τὴν πατρίδα πάρεσθ᾽ ἡ
βοηθήσουσα δύναμις ἐν Ἐλατείᾳ, οὕτω τοῖς ὑπὲρ
τῆς ἐλευθερίας ἀγωνίζεσθαι βουλομένοις ὑπάρχεθ᾽
ὑμεῖς ἕτοιμοι καὶ βοηθήσετ᾽, ἐάν τις ἐπ᾽ αὐτοὺς ἴῃ.
178 μετὰ ταῦτα χειροτονῆσαι κελεύω δέκα πρέσβεις,
καὶ ποιῆσαι τούτους κυρίους μετὰ τῶν στρατηγῶν
καὶ τοῦ πότε δεῖ βαδίζειν ἐκεῖσε καὶ τῆς ἐξόδου.
ἐπειδὰν δ᾽ ἔλθωσιν οἱ πρέσβεις εἰς Θήβας, πῶς
χρῆσθαι τῷ πράγματι παραινῶ; τούτῳ πάνυ μοι
προσέχετε τὸν νοῦν. μὴ δεῖσθαι Θηβαίων μηδέν
(αἰσχρὸς γὰρ ὁ καιρός), ἀλλ᾽ ἐπαγγέλλεσθαι
βοηθήσειν, ἂν κελεύσωσιν, ὡς ἐκείνων μὲν ὄντων
ἐν τοῖς ἐσχάτοις, ἡμῶν δ᾽ ἄμεινον ἢ 'κεῖνοι προ-
ορωμένων· ἵν᾽ ἐὰν μὲν δέξωνται ταῦτα καὶ πει-
σθῶσιν ἡμῖν, καὶ ἃ βουλόμεθ᾽ ὦμεν διῳκημένοι
[288] καὶ μετὰ προσχήματος ἀξίου τῆς πόλεως ταῦτα
πράξωμεν, ἂν δ᾽ ἄρα μὴ συμβῇ κατατυχεῖν,
ἐκεῖνοι μὲν αὐτοῖς ἐγκαλῶσιν, ἄν τι νῦν ἐξαμαρ-
τάνωσιν, ἡμῖν δὲ μηδὲν αἰσχρὸν μηδὲ ταπεινὸν
ᾖ πεπραγμένον."

captious criticism, of what I lay before you, I believe
that you will find my proposals acceptable, and that
I shall disperse the perils that overhang our city.
Let me then tell you what to do. In the first place,
get rid of your present terror ; or rather direct it
elsewhere, and be as frightened as you will for the
Thebans. They lie nearer to peril ; the danger
threatens them first. Next, let all men of military
age, and all the cavalry, march out to Eleusis, and
show the world that you are under arms. Then
your partisans at Thebes will have equal freedom to
speak their minds for righteousness' sake, knowing
that, just as the men who have sold their country
to Philip are supported by a force at Elatea ready
to come to their aid, so also you are in readiness to
help men who are willing to fight for independence,
and will come to their aid, if they are attacked. In
the next place, I would have you appoint ten ambassadors, and give them authority, in consultation with
the military commanders, to determine the time of
the march to Thebes and the conduct of the campaign.
Now for my advice on the treatment of the difficulty
after the arrival of the ambassadors at Thebes. I
beg your careful attention to this. Do not ask any
favour of the Thebans : for that the occasion is not
creditable. Pledge yourselves to come to their aid at
their call, on the ground that they are in extremities,
and that we have a clearer foresight of the future than
they. And so, if they accept our overtures and take
our advice, we shall have accomplished our desires and
have acted on a principle worthy of our traditions ;
while, if success does not fall to our lot, they will have
themselves to blame for their immediate blunder, and
we shall have done nothing mean or discreditable.''

DEMOSTHENES

179 Ταῦτα καὶ παραπλήσια τούτοις εἰπὼν κατέβην. συνεπαινεσάντων δὲ πάντων καὶ οὐδενὸς εἰπόντος ἐναντίον οὐδέν, οὐκ εἶπον μὲν ταῦτ᾽, οὐκ ἔγραψα δέ, οὐδ᾽ ἔγραψα μέν, οὐκ ἐπρέσβευσα δέ, οὐδ᾽ ἐπρέσβευσα μέν, οὐκ ἔπεισα δὲ Θηβαίους, ἀλλ᾽ ἀπὸ τῆς ἀρχῆς ἄχρι τῆς τελευτῆς διεξῆλθον, καὶ ἔδωκ᾽ ἐμαυτὸν ὑμῖν ἁπλῶς εἰς τοὺς περιεστηκότας τῇ πόλει κινδύνους. καί μοι φέρε τὸ ψήφισμα τὸ τότε γενόμενον.

180 Καίτοι τίνα βούλει σ᾽, Αἰσχίνη, καὶ τίν᾽ ἐμαυτὸν ἐκείνην τὴν ἡμέραν εἶναι θῶ; βούλει ἐμαυτὸν μέν, ὃν ἂν σὺ λοιδορούμενος καὶ διασύρων καλέσαις, Βάτταλον, σὲ δὲ μηδ᾽ ἥρω τὸν τυχόντα, ἀλλὰ τούτων τινὰ τῶν ἀπὸ τῆς σκηνῆς, Κρεσφόντην ἢ Κρέοντα, ἢ ὃν ἐν Κολλυτῷ ποτ᾽ Οἰνόμαον κακῶς ἐπέτριψας; τότε τοίνυν κατ᾽ ἐκεῖνον τὸν καιρὸν ὁ Παιανιεὺς ἐγὼ Βάτταλος Οἰνομάου τοῦ Κοθωκίδου σοῦ πλείονος ἄξιος ὢν ἐφάνην τῇ πατρίδι. σὺ μέν γ᾽ οὐδὲν οὐδαμοῦ χρήσιμος ἦσθα· ἐγὼ δὲ πάνθ᾽ ὅσα προσῆκε τὸν ἀγαθὸν πολίτην ἔπραττον. λέγε τὸ ψήφισμά μοι.

ΨΗΦΙΣΜΑ ΔΗΜΟΣΘΕΝΟΥΣ

181 [Ἐπὶ ἄρχοντος Ναυσικλέους, φυλῆς πρυτανευούσης Αἰαντίδος, σκιροφοριῶνος ἕκτῃ ἐπὶ δέκα, Δημοσθένης Δη-
[239] μοσθένους Παιανιεὺς εἶπεν· ἐπειδὴ Φίλιππος ὁ Μακεδὼν ἔν τε τῷ παρεληλυθότι χρόνῳ παραβαίνων φαίνεται τὰς γεγενημένας αὐτῷ συνθήκας πρὸς τὸν Ἀθηναίων δῆμον περὶ τῆς εἰρήνης, ὑπεριδὼν τοὺς ὅρκους καὶ τὰ παρὰ πᾶσι τοῖς Ἕλλησι νομιζόμενα εἶναι δίκαια, καὶ πόλεις παραιρεῖται οὐδὲν αὐτῷ προσηκούσας, τινὰς δὲ καὶ Ἀθηναίων οὔσας δοριαλώτους πεποίηκεν οὐδὲν προαδικηθεὶς ὑπὸ τοῦ δήμου τοῦ Ἀθηναίων, ἔν τε τῷ παρόντι ἐπὶ πολὺ προάγει
140

In those words, or to that effect, I spoke, and left the tribune. My speech was universally applauded, and there was no opposition. I did not speak without moving, nor move without serving as ambassador, nor serve without convincing the Thebans. I went through the whole business from beginning to end, devoting myself ungrudgingly to your service in face of the perils that encompassed our city. Please produce the decree made at that time.

What part do you wish me to assign to you, Aeschines, and what to myself, in the drama of that great day? Am I to be cast for the part of Battalus,[a] as you dub me when you scold me so scornfully, and you for no vulgar rôle but to play some hero of legendary tragedy, Cresphontes, or Creon, or, shall we say, Oenomaus, whom you once murdered by your bad acting at Collytus? Anyhow, on that occasion Battalus of Paeania deserved better of his country than Oenomaus of Cothocidae. You were utterly useless; I did everything that became a good citizen. Please read the decree.

(*The Decree of Demosthenes is read*)

[In the archonship of Nausicles, the tribe Aeantis then holding the presidency, on the sixteenth day of Scirophorion, Demosthenes, son of Demosthenes, of Paeania, proposed that, whereas Philip of Macedon is proved in the past to have violated the terms of peace agreed to between him and the People of Athens, disregarding his oaths and the principles of equity as recognized among all the Greeks: and whereas he appropriates cities not belonging to him, and has captured in war some that actually belonged to the Athenians without provocation from the Athenian people, and is to-day

---

[a] *Battalus*, perhaps *stammerer*, a nickname of the nursery; capable also of an indecent interpretation, and therefore maliciously revived by Aeschines.

DEMOSTHENES

182 τῇ τε βίᾳ καὶ τῇ ὠμότητι· καὶ γὰρ Ἑλληνίδας πόλεις
ἃς μὲν ἐμφρούρους ποιεῖ καὶ τὰς πολιτείας καταλύει, τινὰς
δὲ καὶ ἐξανδραποδιζόμενος κατασκάπτει, εἰς ἐνίας δὲ καὶ
ἀντὶ Ἑλλήνων βαρβάρους κατοικίζει ἐπὶ τὰ ἱερὰ καὶ τοὺς
τάφους ἐπάγων, οὐδὲν ἀλλότριον ποιῶν οὔτε τῆς ἑαυτοῦ
πατρίδος οὔτε τοῦ τρόπου, καὶ τῇ νῦν αὐτῷ παρούσῃ
τύχῃ κατακόρως χρώμενος, ἐπιλελησμένος ἑαυτοῦ ὅτι ἐκ
183 μικροῦ καὶ τοῦ τυχόντος γέγονεν ἀνελπίστως μέγας· καὶ
ἕως μὲν πόλεις ἑώρα παραιρούμενον αὐτὸν βαρβάρους καὶ
ἰδίας, ὑπελάμβανεν ἔλαττον εἶναι ὁ δῆμος ὁ Ἀθηναίων τὸ
εἰς αὐτὸν πλημμελεῖσθαι· νῦν δὲ ὁρῶν Ἑλληνίδας πόλεις
τὰς μὲν ὑβριζομένας, τὰς δὲ ἀναστάτους γιγνομένας, δεινὸν ἡγεῖται εἶναι καὶ ἀνάξιον τῆς τῶν προγόνων δόξης
184 τὸ περιορᾶν τοὺς Ἕλληνας καταδουλουμένους· διὸ δεδόχθαι τῇ βουλῇ καὶ τῷ δήμῳ τῷ Ἀθηναίων, εὐξαμένους
καὶ θύσαντας τοῖς θεοῖς καὶ ἥρωσι τοῖς κατέχουσι τὴν
πόλιν καὶ τὴν χώραν τὴν Ἀθηναίων, καὶ ἐνθυμηθέντας
τῆς τῶν προγόνων ἀρετῆς, διότι περὶ πλείονος ἐποιοῦντο
[290] τὴν τῶν Ἑλλήνων ἐλευθερίαν διατηρεῖν ἢ τὴν ἰδίαν πατρίδα, διακοσίας ναῦς καθέλκειν εἰς τὴν θάλατταν καὶ τὸν
ναύαρχον ἀναπλεῖν ἐντὸς Πυλῶν, καὶ τὸν στρατηγὸν καὶ
τὸν ἵππαρχον τὰς πεζὰς καὶ τὰς ἱππικὰς δυνάμεις Ἐλευσῖνάδε ἐξάγειν, πέμψαι δὲ καὶ πρέσβεις πρὸς τοὺς ἄλλους
Ἕλληνας, πρῶτον δὲ πάντων πρὸς Θηβαίους διὰ τὸ ἐγ-
185 γυτάτω εἶναι τὸν Φίλιππον τῆς ἐκείνων χώρας, παρακαλεῖν
δὲ αὐτοὺς μηδὲν καταπλαγέντας τὸν Φίλιππον ἀντέχεσθαι
τῆς ἑαυτῶν καὶ τῆς τῶν ἄλλων Ἑλλήνων ἐλευθερίας, καὶ
ὅτι ὁ Ἀθηναίων δῆμος, οὐδὲν μνησικακῶν εἴ τι πρότερον
γέγονεν ἀλλότριον ταῖς πόλεσι πρὸς ἀλλήλας, βοηθήσει
καὶ δυνάμεσι καὶ χρήμασι καὶ βέλεσι καὶ ὅπλοις, εἰδὼς
ὅτι αὐτοῖς μὲν πρὸς ἀλλήλους διαμφισβητεῖν περὶ τῆς
ἡγεμονίας οὖσιν Ἕλλησι καλόν, ὑπὸ δὲ ἀλλοφύλου
ἀνθρώπου ἄρχεσθαι καὶ τῆς ἡγεμονίας ἀποστερεῖσθαι
ἀνάξιον εἶναι καὶ τῆς τῶν Ἑλλήνων δόξης καὶ τῆς τῶν

142

making great advances in violence and cruelty, for of some Greek cities he overthrows the constitution, putting a garrison in them, others he razes to the ground, selling the inhabitants into slavery, others he colonizes with barbarians instead of Greeks, handing over to them the temples and the sepulchres, acting as might be expected from his nationality and his character and making insolent use of his present fortune, forgetful of how he rose to greatness unexpectedly from a small and ordinary beginning ; and whereas, so long as the People of Athens saw him seizing barbarian states, belonging to themselves alone, they conceived that their own wrongs were of less account, but now, seeing Greek states outraged or wiped out, they consider it a scandal and unworthy of the reputation of their ancestors to suffer the Greeks to be enslaved ; therefore be it resolved by the Council and People of Athens, after offering prayers and sacrifices to the gods and heroes who guard the city and country of the Athenians, and after taking into consideration their ancestors' merits, in that they ranked the preservation of the liberties of Greece above the claims of their own state, that two hundred ships be launched, and that the Admiral sail into the Straits of Thermopylae, and that the General and commander of the cavalry march out with the infantry and cavalry to Eleusis ; also that ambassadors be sent to the other Greeks, but first of all to the Thebans, because Philip is nearest to their territory, and exhort them not to be dismayed at Philip, but to hold fast to their own liberty and the liberty of the other Greeks, assuring them that the people of Athens, harbouring no ill will for previous mutual differences between the states, will help them with troops, money, ammunition, and arms, knowing that, while it is an honourable ambition for Greeks to dispute with each other for the hegemony, yet to be ruled by a man of alien race and to be robbed by him of that hegemony is unworthy both of the reputation of the Greeks and of the merits of their

186 προγόνων ἀρετῆς. ἔτι δὲ οὐδὲ ἀλλότριον ἡγεῖται εἶναι ὁ
Ἀθηναίων δῆμος τὸν Θηβαίων δῆμον οὔτε τῇ συγγενείᾳ
οὔτε τῷ ὁμοφύλῳ· ἀναμιμνῄσκεται δὲ καὶ τὰς τῶν
προγόνων τῶν ἑαυτοῦ εἰς τοὺς Θηβαίων προγόνους εὐερ-
γεσίας· καὶ γὰρ τοὺς Ἡρακλέους παῖδας ἀποστερουμένους
ὑπὸ Πελοποννησίων τῆς πατρῴας ἀρχῆς κατήγαγον, τοῖς
ὅπλοις κρατήσαντες τοὺς ἀντιβαίνειν πειρωμένους τοῖς
Ἡρακλέους ἐγγόνοις, καὶ τὸν Οἰδίπουν καὶ τοὺς μετ'
ἐκείνου ἐκπεσόντας ὑπεδεξάμεθα, καὶ ἕτερα πολλὰ ἡμῖν
187 ὑπάρχει φιλάνθρωπα καὶ ἔνδοξα πρὸς Θηβαίους· διόπερ
[291] οὐδὲ νῦν ἀποστήσεται ὁ Ἀθηναίων δῆμος τῶν Θηβαίοις
τε καὶ τοῖς ἄλλοις Ἕλλησι συμφερόντων. συνθέσθαι δὲ
πρὸς αὐτοὺς καὶ συμμαχίαν καὶ ἐπιγαμίαν ποιήσασθαι
καὶ ὅρκους δοῦναι καὶ λαβεῖν. πρέσβεις Δημοσθένης
Δημοσθένους Παιανιεύς, Ὑπερείδης Κλεάνδρου Σφήττιος,
Μνησιθείδης Ἀντιφάνους Φρεάρριος, Δημοκράτης Σω-
φίλου Φλυεύς, Κάλλαισχρος Διοτίμου Κοθωκίδης.]

188 Αὕτη τῶν περὶ Θήβας ἐγίγνετο πραγμάτων ἀρχὴ
καὶ κατάστασις πρώτη, τὰ πρὸ τούτων εἰς ἔχθραν
καὶ μῖσος καὶ ἀπιστίαν τῶν πόλεων ὑπηγμένων
ὑπὸ τούτων. τοῦτο τὸ ψήφισμα τὸν τότε τῇ
πόλει περιστάντα κίνδυνον παρελθεῖν ἐποίησεν,
ὥσπερ νέφος. ἦν μὲν τοίνυν τοῦ δικαίου πολίτου
τότε δεῖξαι πᾶσιν εἴ τι τούτων εἶχεν ἄμεινον,
189 μὴ νῦν ἐπιτιμᾶν. ὁ γὰρ σύμβουλος καὶ ὁ συκοφάντης, οὐδὲ τῶν ἄλλων οὐδὲν ἐοικότες, ἐν τούτῳ
πλεῖστον ἀλλήλων διαφέρουσιν· ὁ μέν γε πρὸ
τῶν πραγμάτων γνώμην ἀποφαίνεται, καὶ δίδωσιν
ἑαυτὸν ὑπεύθυνον τοῖς πεισθεῖσι, τῇ τύχῃ, τοῖς
καιροῖς, τῷ βουλομένῳ· ὁ δὲ σιγήσας ἡνίκ' ἔδει
λέγειν, ἄν τι δύσκολον συμβῇ, τοῦτο βασκαίνει.
190 ἦν μὲν οὖν, ὅπερ εἶπον, ἐκεῖνος ὁ καιρὸς τοῦ γε φρον-

ancestors. Furthermore, the People of Athens regard the people of Thebes as in no way alien either in race or in nationality. They remember the services rendered by their own ancestors to the ancestors of the Thebans, for, when the sons of Heracles were dispossessed by the Peloponnesians of their paternal dominion, they restored them, overcoming in battle those who were trying to oppose the descendants of Heracles ; and we harboured Oedipus and his family when they were banished ; and many other notable acts of kindness have we done to the Thebans. Therefore now also the people of Athens will not desert the cause of Thebes and the other Greeks. An alliance shall be arranged with them, and rights of intermarriage established, and oaths exchanged. —Ambassadors appointed : Demosthenes, son of Demosthenes, of Paeania, Hypereides, son of Cleander, of Sphettus, Mnesitheides, son of Antiphanes, of Phrearrii, Democrates, son of Sophilus, of Phlya, Callaeschrus, son of Diotimus, of Cothocidae.]

Such was the first beginning and such the basis of our negotiations with Thebes ; the first, I say, for hitherto the two cities had been dragged by these men into mutual enmity, hatred, and distrust. The decree was made, and the danger that environed the city passed away like a summer cloud. Then was the time therefore for an honest man to point, if he could, to a better way ; now cavilling comes too late. That is the salient difference between the statesman and the charlatan, who are indeed in all respects unlike one another. The statesman declares his judgement before the event, and accepts responsibility to his followers, to fortune, to the chances of the hour, to every critic of his policy. The charlatan holds his peace when he ought to speak, and then croaks over any untoward result. That then, as I said, was the opportunity for

DEMOSTHENES

τίζοντος ἀνδρὸς τῆς πόλεως καὶ τῶν δικαίων
λόγων· ἐγὼ δὲ τοσαύτην ὑπερβολὴν ποιοῦμαι
ὥστ᾽, ἂν νῦν ἔχῃ τις δεῖξαί τι βέλτιον, ἢ ὅλως εἴ
τι ἄλλ᾽ ἐνῆν πλὴν ὧν ἐγὼ προειλόμην, ἀδικεῖν
ὁμολογῶ. εἰ γὰρ ἔσθ᾽ ὅ τι τις νῦν ἑόρακεν, ὃ
συνήνεγκεν ἂν τότε πραχθέν, τοῦτ᾽ ἐγώ φημι
δεῖν ἐμὲ μὴ λαθεῖν. εἰ δὲ μήτ᾽ ἔστι μήτ᾽ ἦν μήτ᾽
[292] ἂν εἰπεῖν ἔχοι μηδεὶς μηδέπω καὶ τήμερον, τί τὸν
σύμβουλον ἐχρῆν ποιεῖν; οὐ τῶν φαινομένων καὶ
191 ἐνόντων τὰ κράτισθ᾽ ἑλέσθαι; τοῦτο τοίνυν ἐποίησα, τοῦ κήρυκος ἐρωτῶντος, Αἰσχίνη, "τίς ἀγορεύειν βούλεται;" οὐ "τίς αἰτιᾶσθαι περὶ τῶν
παρεληλυθότων;" οὐδὲ "τίς ἐγγυᾶσθαι τὰ μέλλοντ᾽
ἔσεσθαι;" σοῦ δ᾽ ἀφώνου κατ᾽ ἐκείνους τοὺς
χρόνους ἐν ταῖς ἐκκλησίαις καθημένου, ἐγὼ παριὼν
ἔλεγον. ἐπειδὴ δ᾽ οὐ τότε, ἀλλὰ νῦν δεῖξον.
εἰπὲ τίς ἢ λόγος, ὅντιν᾽ ἐχρῆν εὑρεῖν, ἢ καιρὸς
συμφέρων ὑπ᾽ ἐμοῦ παρελείφθη τῇ πόλει; τίς δὲ
συμμαχία, τίς πρᾶξις, ἐφ᾽ ἣν μᾶλλον ἔδει μ᾽
ἀγαγεῖν τουτουσί;
192 Ἀλλὰ μὴν τὸ μὲν παρεληλυθὸς ἀεὶ παρὰ πᾶσιν
ἀφεῖται, καὶ οὐδεὶς περὶ τούτου προτίθησιν οὐδαμοῦ
βουλήν· τὸ δὲ μέλλον ἢ τὸ παρὸν τὴν τοῦ συμβούλου τάξιν ἀπαιτεῖ. τότε τοίνυν τὰ μὲν ἔμελλεν,
ὡς ἐδόκει, τῶν δεινῶν, τὰ δ᾽ ἤδη παρῆν, ἐν οἷς
τὴν προαίρεσίν μου σκόπει τῆς πολιτείας, μὴ τὰ
συμβάντα συκοφάντει. τὸ μὲν γὰρ πέρας, ὡς
ἂν ὁ δαίμων βουληθῇ, πάντων γίγνεται· ἡ δὲ
προαίρεσις αὐτὴ τὴν τοῦ συμβούλου διάνοιαν
193 δηλοῖ. μὴ δὴ τοῦθ᾽ ὡς ἀδίκημ᾽ ἐμὸν θῇς, εἰ
κρατῆσαι συνέβη Φιλίππῳ τῇ μάχῃ· ἐν γὰρ τῷ
θεῷ τὸ τούτου τέλος ἦν, οὐκ ἐμοί. ἀλλ᾽ ὡς οὐχ
146

any man who cared for Athens or for honest discussion. But I will make a large concession. If even now any man can point to a better way, nay, if any policy whatever, save mine, was even practicable, I plead guilty. If anyone has now discerned any course which might have been taken profitably then, I admit that I ought not to have missed it. But if there is none, if there never was any, if to this very day no one is able to name any, what was a statesman to do? Surely to choose the best policy among those that were visible and feasible. That is what I did, Aeschines, when the marshal put the question, " Who wishes to speak ? " He did not ask, " Who wishes to rake up old grievances ? " or, " Who wishes to be answerable for the future ? " In those days you sat speechless at every assembly ; I came forward and spoke. You had nothing to say then ; very well,—show us our duty now. Tell me what plan I ought to have discovered. Tell me what favourable opportunity was lost to the state by my default. Tell me of any alliance, or any negotiation, to which I ought by preference to have introduced the people.

Bygones are bygones, all the world over. No one proposes deliberation about the past ; it is the present and the future that call the statesman to his post. And at that time, as we all thought, there were future perils and there were present perils. Look at the policy I chose in the light of those perils ; do not carp at results. The issue depends on the will of a higher Power ; the mind of the statesman is manifested in his policy. You must not accuse me of crime, because Philip happened to win the battle ; for the event was in God's hands, not mine. Show me that I did not adopt,

147

ἅπανθ᾽ ὅσ᾽ ἐνῆν κατ᾽ ἀνθρώπινον λογισμὸν εἱλόμην,
καὶ δικαίως ταῦτα κἀπιμελῶς ἔπραξα καὶ φιλο-
πόνως ὑπὲρ δύναμιν, ἢ ὡς οὐ καλὰ καὶ τῆς πόλεως
ἄξια πράγματ᾽ ἐνεστησάμην καὶ ἀναγκαῖα, ταῦτά
194 μοι δεῖξον, καὶ τότ᾽ ἤδη κατηγόρει μου. εἰ δ᾽
ὁ συμβὰς σκηπτὸς μὴ μόνον ἡμῶν, ἀλλὰ καὶ
πάντων τῶν ἄλλων Ἑλλήνων μείζων γέγονε, τί
[293] χρὴ ποιεῖν; ὥσπερ ἂν εἴ τις ναύκληρον, πάντ᾽ ἐπὶ
σωτηρίᾳ πράξαντα, καὶ πᾶσι κατασκευάσαντα
τὸ πλοῖον ἀφ᾽ ὧν ὑπελάμβανεν σωθήσεσθαι, εἶτα
χειμῶνι χρησάμενον καὶ πονησάντων αὐτῷ τῶν
σκευῶν ἢ καὶ συντριβέντων ὅλως, τῆς ναυαγίας
αἰτιῷτο. ἀλλ᾽ οὔτ᾽ ἐκυβέρνων τὴν ναῦν, φήσειεν
ἄν, ὥσπερ οὐδ᾽ ἐστρατήγουν ἐγώ, οὔτε τῆς τύχης
κύριος ἦν, ἀλλ᾽ ἐκείνη τῶν πάντων.

195 Ἀλλ᾽ ἐκεῖνο λογίζου καὶ ὅρα· εἰ μετὰ Θηβαίων
ἡμῖν ἀγωνιζομένοις οὕτως εἵμαρτο πρᾶξαι, τί
χρῆν προσδοκᾶν, εἰ μηδὲ τούτους ἔσχομεν συμμάχους, ἀλλὰ Φιλίππῳ προσέθεντο, ὑπὲρ οὗ τότ᾽
ἐκεῖνος πάσας ἀφῆκε φωνάς; καὶ εἰ νῦν τριῶν
ἡμερῶν ἀπὸ τῆς Ἀττικῆς ὁδὸν τῆς μάχης γενο-
μένης, τοσοῦτος κίνδυνος καὶ φόβος περιέστη
τὴν πόλιν, τί ἄν, εἴ που τῆς χώρας ταὐτὸ τοῦτο
πάθος συνέβη, προσδοκῆσαι χρῆν; ἆρ᾽ οἶσθ᾽ ὅτι
νῦν μὲν στῆναι, συνελθεῖν, ἀναπνεῦσαι, πολλὰ μἵ᾽
ἡμέρα καὶ δύο καὶ τρεῖς ἔδοσαν τῶν εἰς σωτηρίαν
τῇ πόλει, τότε δ᾽—οὐκ ἄξιον εἰπεῖν, ἅ γε μηδὲ
πεῖραν ἔδωκε θεῶν τινὸς εὐνοίᾳ καὶ τῷ προβαλέσθαι τὴν πόλιν ταύτην τὴν συμμαχίαν, ἧς σὺ
κατηγορεῖς.

as far as human calculation could go, all the measures that were practicable, or that I did not carry them out with honesty and diligence, and with an industry that overtaxed my strength ; or else show me that the enterprises I initiated were not honourable, worthy of Athens, and inevitable. Prove that, and then denounce me ; but not till then. If the hurricane that burst upon us has been too strong, not for us alone, but for every Hellenic state,—what then? As if a shipowner, who had done everything in his power for a prosperous voyage, who had equipped his craft with every appliance he could think of to ensure her safety, should encounter a great storm, and then, because his tackle was overstrained or even shattered, should be accused of the crime of shipwreck ! " But," he might say, " I was not at the helm "—nor was I in command of the army—" and I could not control fortune, but fortune controls all."

Here is another point for your consideration. If we were destined to disaster when we fought with the Thebans at our side, what were we to expect if we had lacked even that alliance, and if they had joined Philip, a union for which he exerted all his powers of appeal ? And if, after a battle fought three days' march from the frontier, such danger and such alarm beset the city, what must we have expected after suffering the same defeat within our own borders ? Do you not see that, as it was, one, or two, or three days gave the city time for resistance, concentration, recovery, for much that made for deliverance ; as it might have been—but I will not mention an experience that we were spared by divine favour, and by the protection of that very alliance which you denounce.

196 Ἔστι δὲ ταυτὶ πάντα μοι, τὰ πολλά, πρὸς ὑμᾶς,
ἄνδρες δικασταί, καὶ τοὺς περιεστηκότας ἔξωθεν
κἀκροωμένους, ἐπεὶ πρός γε τοῦτον τὸν κατάπτυστον βραχὺς καὶ σαφὴς ἐξήρκει λόγος. εἰ μὲν
γὰρ ἦν σοὶ πρόδηλα τὰ μέλλοντα, Αἰσχίνη, μόνῳ
τῶν ἄλλων, ὅτ᾽ ἐβουλεύεθ᾽ ἡ πόλις περὶ τούτων,
τότ᾽ ἔδει προλέγειν· εἰ δὲ μὴ προῄδεις, τῆς αὐτῆς
[294] ἀγνοίας ὑπεύθυνος εἶ τοῖς ἄλλοις, ὥστε τί μᾶλλον
197 ἐμοῦ σὺ ταῦτα κατηγορεῖς ἢ ἐγὼ σοῦ; τοσοῦτον
γὰρ ἀμείνων ἐγὼ σοῦ πολίτης γέγον᾽ εἰς αὐτὰ
ταῦθ᾽ ἃ λέγω (καὶ οὔπω περὶ τῶν ἄλλων διαλέγομαι),
ὅσον ἐγὼ μὲν ἔδωκ᾽ ἐμαυτὸν εἰς τὰ πᾶσι δοκοῦντα συμφέρειν, οὐδένα κίνδυνον ὀκνήσας ἴδιον
οὐδ᾽ ὑπολογισάμενος, σὺ δ᾽ οὔθ᾽ ἕτερ᾽ εἶπες
βελτίω τούτων (οὐ γὰρ ἂν τούτοις ἐχρῶντο),
οὔτ᾽ εἰς ταῦτα χρήσιμον οὐδὲν σαυτὸν παρέσχες,
ὅπερ δ᾽ ἂν ὁ φαυλότατος καὶ δυσμενέστατος
ἄνθρωπος τῇ πόλει, τοῦτο πεποιηκὼς ἐπὶ τοῖς
συμβᾶσιν ἐξήτασαι, καὶ ἅμ᾽ Ἀρίστρατος ἐν
Νάξῳ καὶ Ἀριστόλεως ἐν Θάσῳ, οἱ καθάπαξ
ἐχθροὶ τῆς πόλεως, τοὺς Ἀθηναίων κρίνουσι
φίλους, καὶ Ἀθήνησιν Αἰσχίνης Δημοσθένους
198 κατηγορεῖ. καίτοι ὅτῳ τὰ τῶν Ἑλλήνων ἀτυ-
χήματ᾽ ἐνευδοκιμεῖν ἀπέκειτο, ἀπολωλέναι μᾶλλον
οὗτός ἐστι δίκαιος ἢ κατηγορεῖν ἑτέρου· καὶ
ὅτῳ συνενηνόχασιν οἱ αὐτοὶ καιροὶ καὶ τοῖς τῆς
πόλεως ἐχθροῖς, οὐκ ἔνι τοῦτον εὔνουν εἶναι τῇ
πατρίδι. δηλοῖς δὲ καὶ ἐξ ὧν ζῇς καὶ ποιεῖς
καὶ πολιτεύει καὶ πάλιν οὐ πολιτεύει. πράττεταί
τι τῶν ὑμῖν δοκούντων συμφέρειν· ἄφωνος Αἰσχίνης.

Gentlemen of the jury, all this long story is intended for you, and for that circle of hearers outside the barrier. For this contemptible fellow, I have a short, plain, and sufficient answer. Aeschines, if the future was revealed to you and to nobody else, you should have given us the benefit of your predictions when we were deliberating; if you had no foreknowledge, you are open to the charge of ignorance just like the rest of us. Then what better right have you to denounce me than I to denounce you? In respect of the business of which I am speaking—and at present I discuss nothing else—I am a better citizen than you, in so far as I devoted myself to a course of action that was unanimously approved, neither shirking nor even counting any personal danger. You made no more acceptable suggestion, otherwise mine would not have been adopted; and in carrying out mine you were not of the slightest use. You are proved after the event to have behaved throughout like a worthless and most unpatriotic citizen; and now, by a strange coincidence, those thorough-going enemies of Athens, Aristratus at Naxos and Aristolaus at Thasos, are bringing the friends of Athens to trial, while at Athens itself Aeschines is accusing Demosthenes. And yet he who built his reputation on the accumulated misfortunes of Greece deserves rather to perish himself than to prosecute his neighbour; and the man who has found his profit in the same emergencies as his country's foes can make no claim to patriotism. You stand revealed in your life and conduct, in your public performances and also in your public abstinences. A project approved by the people is going forward. Aeschines is speechless. A regret-

ἀντέκρουσέ τι καὶ γέγον᾽ οἷον οὐκ ἔδει· πάρεστιν
Αἰσχίνης· ὥσπερ τὰ ῥήγματα καὶ τὰ σπάσματα,
ὅταν τι κακὸν τὸ σῶμα λάβῃ, τότε κινεῖται.

199 Ἐπειδὴ δὲ πολὺς τοῖς συμβεβηκόσιν ἔγκειται,
βούλομαί τι καὶ παράδοξον εἰπεῖν. καί μου
πρὸς Διὸς καὶ θεῶν μηδεὶς τὴν ὑπερβολὴν θαυμάσῃ,
ἀλλὰ μετ᾽ εὐνοίας ὃ λέγω θεωρησάτω. εἰ γὰρ
ἦν ἅπασι πρόδηλα τὰ μέλλοντα γενήσεσθαι, καὶ
προῄδεσαν πάντες, καὶ σὺ προὔλεγες, Αἰσχίνη,
καὶ διεμαρτύρου βοῶν καὶ κεκραγώς, ὃς οὐδ᾽
[295] ἐφθέγξω, οὐδ᾽ οὕτως ἀποστατέον τῇ πόλει τούτων
ἦν, εἴπερ ἢ δόξης ἢ προγόνων ἢ τοῦ μέλλοντος
200 αἰῶνος εἶχε λόγον. νῦν μέν γ᾽ ἀποτυχεῖν δοκεῖ
τῶν πραγμάτων, ὃ πᾶσι κοινόν ἐστιν ἀνθρώποις,
ὅταν τῷ θεῷ ταῦτα δοκῇ· τότε δ᾽ ἀξιοῦσα προεστάναι τῶν ἄλλων, εἶτ᾽ ἀποστᾶσα τούτου, Φιλίππῳ
προδεδωκέναι πάντας ἂν ἔσχεν αἰτίαν. εἰ γὰρ
ταῦτα προεῖτ᾽ ἀκονιτεί, περὶ ὧν οὐδένα κίνδυνον
ὄντιν᾽ οὐχ ὑπέμειναν οἱ πρόγονοι, τίς οὐχὶ κατ-
έπτυσεν ἂν σοῦ; μὴ γὰρ τῆς πόλεώς γε, μηδ᾽
201 ἐμοῦ. τίσι δ᾽ ὀφθαλμοῖς, πρὸς Διός, ἑωρῶμεν ἂν
τοὺς εἰς τὴν πόλιν ἀνθρώπους ἀφικνουμένους, εἰ τὰ
μὲν πράγματ᾽ εἰς ὅπερ νυνὶ περιέστη, ἡγεμὼν δὲ
καὶ κύριος ᾑρέθη Φίλιππος ἁπάντων, τὸν δ᾽ ὑπὲρ
τοῦ μὴ γενέσθαι ταῦτ᾽ ἀγῶνα ἕτεροι χωρὶς ἡμῶν
ἦσαν πεποιημένοι, καὶ ταῦτα μηδεπώποτε τῆς
πόλεως ἐν τοῖς ἔμπροσθεν χρόνοις ἀσφάλειαν
ἄδοξον μᾶλλον ἢ τὸν ὑπὲρ τῶν καλῶν κίνδυνον
202 ᾑρημένης; τίς γὰρ οὐκ οἶδ᾽ Ἑλλήνων, τίς δὲ
βαρβάρων, ὅτι καὶ παρὰ Θηβαίων καὶ παρὰ τῶν

able incident is reported. Aeschines is in evidence. He reminds one of an old sprain or fracture : the moment you are out of health it begins to be active.

As he lays so much stress on results, let me venture on a paradox. If it seems extravagant, I beg that you will not be surprised, but that you will still give friendly consideration to what I am saying. Suppose that the future had been revealed to all of us, that every one had known what would happen, and that you, Aeschines, had predicted and protested, and shouted and stormed—though in fact you never opened your mouth—even then the city could not have departed from that policy, if she had any regard for honour, or for our ancestors, or for the days that are to come. All that can be said now is, that we have failed : and that is the common lot of humanity, if God so wills. But then, if Athens, after claiming the primacy of the nations, had run away from her claims, she would have been held guilty of betraying Greece to Philip. If, without striking a blow, she had abandoned the cause for which our forefathers flinched from no peril, is there a man who would not have spat in your face ? In your face, Aeschines : not at Athens, not at me ! How could we have returned the gaze of visitors to our city, if the result had been what it is—Philip the chosen lord paramount of all Greece—and if other nations had fought gallantly to avert that calamity without our aid, although never before in the whole course of history had our city preferred inglorious security to the perils of a noble cause ? There is no man living, whether Greek or barbarian, who does not know that the Thebans, or the Lacedaemonians,

153

ἔτι τούτων πρότερον ἰσχυρῶν γενομένων Λακεδαιμονίων καὶ παρὰ τοῦ Περσῶν βασιλέως μετὰ
πολλῆς χάριτος τοῦτ᾽ ἂν ἀσμένως ἐδόθη τῇ πόλει,
ὅ τι βούλεται λαβούσῃ καὶ τὰ ἑαυτῆς ἐχούσῃ τὸ κελευόμενον ποιεῖν καὶ ἐᾶν ἕτερον τῶν Ἑλλήνων
203 προεστάναι; ἀλλ᾽ οὐκ ἦν ταῦθ᾽, ὡς ἔοικε, τοῖς
Ἀθηναίοις πάτρι᾽ οὐδ᾽ ἀνέκτ᾽ οὐδ᾽ ἔμφυτα, οὐδ᾽
ἐδυνήθη πώποτε τὴν πόλιν οὐδεὶς ἐκ παντὸς τοῦ
χρόνου πεῖσαι τοῖς ἰσχύουσι μέν, μὴ δίκαια δὲ
πράττουσι προσθεμένην ἀσφαλῶς δουλεύειν, ἀλλ᾽
ἀγωνιζομένη περὶ πρωτείων καὶ τιμῆς καὶ δόξης,
204 κινδυνεύουσα πάντα τὸν αἰῶνα διατετέλεκε. καὶ
ταῦθ᾽ οὕτω σεμνὰ καὶ προσήκοντα τοῖς ὑμετέροις
[?96] ἤθεσιν ὑμεῖς ὑπολαμβάνετ᾽ εἶναι, ὥστε καὶ τῶν
προγόνων τοὺς ταῦτα πράξαντας μάλιστ᾽ ἐπαινεῖτε. εἰκότως· τίς γὰρ οὐκ ἂν ἀγάσαιτο τῶν
ἀνδρῶν ἐκείνων τῆς ἀρετῆς, οἳ καὶ τὴν χώραν καὶ
τὴν πόλιν ἐκλιπεῖν ὑπέμειναν εἰς τὰς τριήρεις
ἐμβάντες ὑπὲρ τοῦ μὴ τὸ κελευόμενον ποιῆσαι,
τὸν μὲν ταῦτα συμβουλεύσαντα Θεμιστοκλέα στρατηγὸν ἑλόμενοι, τὸν δ᾽ ὑπακούειν ἀποφηνάμενον
τοῖς ἐπιταττομένοις Κυρσίλον καταλιθώσαντες,
οὐ μόνον αὐτὸν ἀλλὰ καὶ αἱ γυναῖκες αἱ ὑμέτεραι
205 τὴν γυναῖκ᾽ αὐτοῦ. οὐ γὰρ ἐζήτουν οἱ τότ᾽
Ἀθηναῖοι οὔτε ῥήτορ᾽ οὔτε στρατηγὸν δι᾽ ὅτου
δουλεύσουσιν εὐτυχῶς, ἀλλ᾽ οὐδὲ ζῆν ἠξίουν, εἰ
μὴ μετ᾽ ἐλευθερίας ἐξέσται τοῦτο ποιεῖν. ἡγεῖτο
γὰρ αὐτῶν ἕκαστος οὐχὶ τῷ πατρὶ καὶ τῇ μητρὶ

---

[a] The Spartan hegemony lasted from 404 to 371, the
Theban from 371 to 362.

[b] *stoned Cyrsilus* : at Salamis, 479 B.C., when Athens was

154

who held supremacy before them,[a] or the king of
Persia himself, would cheerfully and gratefully have
given Athens liberty to keep what she had and to
take what she chose, if only she would do their behest
and surrender the primacy of Greece. But to the
Athenians of old, I suppose, such temporizing was
forbidden by their heredity, by their pride, by their
very nature. Since the world began, no man has
ever prevailed upon Athens to attach herself in the
security of servitude to the oppressors of mankind
however formidable : in every generation she has
striven without a pause in the perilous contention
for primacy, and honour, and renown. Such con-
stancy you deem so exemplary, and so congenial to
your character, that you still sing the praises of
those of your forefathers by whom it was most
signally displayed. And you are right. Who would
not exult in the valour of those famous men who,
rather than yield to a conqueror's behests, left city
and country and made the war-galleys their home ;
who chose Themistocles, the man who gave them
that counsel, as their commander, and stoned Cyrsilus[b]
to death for advising obedient submission ? Aye,
and his wife also was stoned by your wives. The
Athenians of that day did not search for a statesman
or a commander who should help them to a servile
security : they did not ask to live, unless they could
live as free men. Every man of them thought of
himself as one born, not to his father and his mother

held by the Persians ; see Herod. ix. 5, where, however, the
name is Lycides. Not 480 B.C., as Cicero, *Off.* iii. 11. 48,
implies ; though the rest of the sentence refers to the conditions of that year.

DEMOSTHENES

μόνον γεγενῆσθαι, ἀλλὰ καὶ τῇ πατρίδι. διαφέρει δὲ τί; ὅτι ὁ μὲν τοῖς γονεῦσι μόνον γεγενῆσθαι νομίζων τὸν τῆς εἱμαρμένης καὶ τὸν αὐτό-
ματον θάνατον περιμένει, ὁ δὲ καὶ τῇ πατρίδι
ὑπὲρ τοῦ μὴ ταύτην ἐπιδεῖν δουλεύουσαν ἀπο-
θνῄσκειν ἐθελήσει, καὶ φοβερωτέρας ἡγήσεται
τὰς ὕβρεις καὶ τὰς ἀτιμίας, ἃς ἐν δουλευούσῃ τῇ
πόλει φέρειν ἀνάγκη, τοῦ θανάτου.

206 Εἰ μὲν τοίνυν τοῦτ' ἐπεχείρουν λέγειν, ὡς ἐγὼ
προήγαγον ὑμᾶς ἄξια τῶν προγόνων φρονεῖν, οὐκ
ἔσθ' ὅστις οὐκ ἂν εἰκότως ἐπιτιμήσειέ μοι. νῦν
δ' ἐγὼ μὲν ὑμετέρας τὰς τοιαύτας προαιρέσεις
ἀποφαίνω, καὶ δείκνυμ' ὅτι καὶ πρὸ ἐμοῦ τοῦτ'
εἶχε τὸ φρόνημ' ἡ πόλις, τῆς μέντοι διακονίας
τῆς ἐφ' ἑκάστοις τῶν πεπραγμένων καὶ ἐμαυτῷ
207 μετεῖναί φημι, οὗτος δὲ τῶν ὅλων κατηγορῶν,
[207] καὶ κελεύων ὑμᾶς ἐμοὶ πικρῶς ἔχειν ὡς φόβων
καὶ κινδύνων αἰτίῳ τῇ πόλει, τῆς μὲν εἰς τὸ παρὸν
τιμῆς ἔμ' ἀποστερῆσαι γλίχεται, τὰ δ' εἰς ἅπαντα
τὸν χρόνον ἐγκώμι' ὑμῶν ἀφαιρεῖται. εἰ γὰρ
ὡς οὐ τὰ βέλτιστ' ἐμοῦ πολιτευσαμένου τουδὶ
καταψηφιεῖσθε, ἡμαρτηκέναι δόξετε, οὐ τῇ τῆς
208 τύχης ἀγνωμοσύνῃ τὰ συμβάντα παθεῖν. ἀλλ'
οὐκ ἔστιν, οὐκ ἔστιν ὅπως ἡμάρτετ', ἄνδρες
Ἀθηναῖοι, τὸν ὑπὲρ τῆς ἁπάντων ἐλευθερίας
καὶ σωτηρίας κίνδυνον ἀράμενοι, μὰ τοὺς Μαραθῶνι προκινδυνεύσαντας τῶν προγόνων, καὶ τοὺς
ἐν Πλαταιαῖς παραταξαμένους, καὶ τοὺς ἐν Σαλαμῖνι ναυμαχήσαντας καὶ τοὺς ἐπ' Ἀρτεμισίῳ,
καὶ πολλοὺς ἑτέρους τοὺς ἐν τοῖς δημοσίοις μνήμα-
σιν κειμένους ἀγαθοὺς ἄνδρας, οὓς ἅπαντας ὁμοίως
ἡ πόλις τῆς αὐτῆς ἀξιώσασα τιμῆς ἔθαψεν, Αἰσχίνη,
156

alone, but to his country. What is the difference ?
The man who deems himself born only to his parents
will wait for his natural and destined end ; the son
of his country is willing to die rather than see her
enslaved, and will look upon those outrages and
indignities, which a commonwealth in subjection is
compelled to endure, as more dreadful than death
itself.

If I had attempted to claim that you were first
inspired with the spirit of your forefathers by me,
every one would justly rebuke me. But I do not :
I am asserting these principles as your principles ;
I am showing you that such was the pride of Athens
long before my time,—though for myself I do claim
some credit for the administration of particular
measures. Aeschines, on the other hand, arraigns
the whole policy, stirs up your resentment against
me as the author of your terrors and your dangers,
and, in his eagerness to strip me of the distinction
of a moment, would rob you of the enduring praises
of posterity. For if you condemn Ctesiphon on the
ground of my political delinquency, you yourselves
will be adjudged as wrongdoers, not as men who
owed the calamities they have suffered to the un-
kindness of fortune. But no ; you cannot, men of
Athens, you cannot have done wrongly when you
accepted the risks of war for the redemption and the
liberties of mankind ; I swear it by our forefathers
who bore the brunt of warfare at Marathon, who
stood in array of battle at Plataea, who fought in
the sea-fights of Salamis and Artemisium, and by all
the brave men who repose in our public sepulchres,
buried there by a country that accounted them all
to be alike worthy of the same honour—all, I say,

οὐχὶ τοὺς κατορθώσαντας αὐτῶν οὐδὲ τοὺς κρα-
τήσαντας μόνους. δικαίως. ὃ μὲν γὰρ ἦν ἀνδρῶν ἀγαθῶν ἔργον ἅπασι πέπρακται· τῇ τύχῃ
δ᾽, ἣν ὁ δαίμων ἔνειμεν ἑκάστοις, ταύτῃ κέχρηνται.

209 Ἔπειτ᾽, ὦ κατάρατε καὶ γραμματοκύφων, σὺ
μὲν τῆς παρὰ τουτουὶ τιμῆς καὶ φιλανθρωπίας
ἔμ᾽ ἀποστερῆσαι βουλόμενος τρόπαια καὶ μάχας
καὶ παλαι᾽ ἔργ᾽ ἔλεγες, ὧν τίνος προσεδεῖθ᾽ ὁ
παρὼν ἀγὼν οὑτοσί; ἐμὲ δ᾽, ὦ τριταγωνιστά, τὸν
περὶ τῶν πρωτείων σύμβουλον τῇ πόλει παριόντα,
τὸ τίνος φρόνημα λαβόντ᾽ ἀναβαίνειν ἐπὶ τὸ βῆμ᾽
210 ἔδει; τὸ τοῦ τούτων ἀνάξι᾽ ἐροῦντος; δικαίως
[298] μέντἂν ἀπέθανον. ἐπεὶ οὐδ᾽ ὑμᾶς, ἄνδρες Ἀθηναῖοι, ἀπὸ τῆς αὐτῆς διανοίας δεῖ τάς τ᾽ ἰδίας
δίκας καὶ τὰς δημοσίας κρίνειν, ἀλλὰ τὰ μὲν τοῦ
καθ᾽ ἡμέραν βίου συμβόλαια ἐπὶ τῶν ἰδίων νόμων
καὶ ἔργων σκοποῦντας, τὰς δὲ κοινὰς προαιρέσεις
εἰς τὰ τῶν προγόνων ἀξιώματ᾽ ἀποβλέποντας·
καὶ παραλαμβάνειν γ᾽ ἅμα τῇ βακτηρίᾳ καὶ τῷ
συμβόλῳ τὸ φρόνημα τὸ τῆς πόλεως νομίζειν
ἕκαστον ὑμῶν δεῖ, ὅταν τὰ δημόσι᾽ εἰσίητε κρινοῦν-
τες, εἴπερ ἄξι᾽ ἐκείνων πράττειν οἴεσθε χρῆναι.

211 Ἀλλὰ γὰρ ἐμπεσὼν εἰς τὰ πεπραγμένα τοῖς
προγόνοις ὑμῶν, ἔστιν ἃ τῶν ψηφισμάτων παρέβην
καὶ τῶν πραχθέντων. ἐπανελθεῖν οὖν ὅποθεν
ἐνταῦθ᾽ ἐξέβην βούλομαι.

Ὡς γὰρ ἀφικόμεθ᾽ εἰς τὰς Θήβας, κατελαμ-
βάνομεν Φιλίππου καὶ Θετταλῶν καὶ τῶν ἄλλων
συμμάχων παρόντας πρέσβεις, καὶ τοὺς μὲν ἡμε-
τέρους φίλους ἐν φόβῳ, τοὺς δ᾽ ἐκείνου θρασεῖς.
ὅτι δ᾽ οὐ νῦν ταῦτα λέγω τοῦ συμφέροντος ἕνεκ᾽
ἐμαυτῷ, λέγε μοι τὴν ἐπιστολὴν ἣν τότ᾽ ἐπέμψα-

Aeschines, not the successful and the victorious alone.
So justice bids : for by all the duty of brave men
was accomplished : their fortune was such as Heaven
severally allotted to them.

And then a disreputable quill-driver like you, wanting to rob me of a distinction given me by the
kindness of my fellow citizens, talked about victories
and battles and ancient deeds of valour, all irrelevant
to the present trial. But I, who came forward to
advise my country how to retain her supremacy—
tell me, you third-rate tragedian, in what spirit did
it beseem me to ascend the tribune ? As one who
should give to the citizens counsel unworthy of their
traditions ? I should have deserved death ! Men
of Athens, you jurymen are not to judge public and
private causes in the same temper. You look at
contracts of everyday business in the light of relevant
statutes and facts, but at questions of public policy
with due regard to the proud traditions of our forefathers. If you feel bound to act in the spirit of
that dignity, whenever you come into court to give
judgement on public causes, you must bethink yourselves that with his staff and his badge every one of
you receives in trust the ancient pride of Athens.

However, in touching upon the achievements of
our ancestors, I have passed by some of my decrees
and other measures. I will now therefore return to
the point at which I digressed.

When we reached Thebes we found ambassadors
from Philip and from the Thebans and others of his
allies already there, our friends panic-stricken, and
his friends full of confidence. To prove that this is
not a statement made to-day to serve my own turn,
please read the dispatch which the ambassadors sent

212 μὲν εὐθὺς οἱ πρέσβεις. καίτοι τοσαύτῃ γ᾽ ὑπερ-
βολῇ συκοφαντίας οὗτος κέχρηται ὥστ᾽, εἰ μέν
τι τῶν δεόντων ἐπράχθη, τὸν καιρόν, οὐκ ἐμέ
φησιν αἴτιον γεγενῆσθαι, τῶν δ᾽ ὡς ἑτέρως συμβάντων ἁπάντων ἐμὲ καὶ τὴν ἐμὴν τύχην αἰτίαν
εἶναι. καὶ, ὡς ἔοικεν, ὁ σύμβουλος καὶ ῥήτωρ
ἐγὼ τῶν μὲν ἐκ λόγου καὶ τοῦ βουλεύσασθαι
πραχθέντων οὐδὲν αὐτῷ συναίτιος εἶναι δοκῶ,
τῶν δ᾽ ἐν τοῖς ὅπλοις καὶ κατὰ τὴν στρατηγίαν
ἀτυχηθέντων μόνος αἴτιος εἶναι. πῶς ἂν ὠμότε-
ρος συκοφάντης γένοιτ᾽ ἢ καταρατότερος; λέγε
τὴν ἐπιστολήν.

[299]

ΕΠΙΣΤΟΛΗ

213 Ἐπειδὴ τοίνυν ἐποιήσαντο τὴν ἐκκλησίαν, προσ-
ῆγον ἐκείνους προτέρους διὰ τὸ τὴν τῶν συμμάχων τάξιν ἐκείνους ἔχειν. καὶ παρελθόντες
ἐδημηγόρουν, πολλὰ μὲν Φίλιππον ἐγκωμιάζοντες,
πολλὰ δ᾽ ὑμῶν κατηγοροῦντες, πάνθ᾽ ὅσα πώποτ᾽
ἐναντί᾽ ἐπράξατε Θηβαίοις ἀναμιμνῄσκοντες. τὸ
δ᾽ οὖν κεφάλαιον, ἠξίουν ὧν μὲν εὖ ᾽πεπόνθεσαν
ὑπὸ Φιλίππου χάριν αὐτοὺς ἀποδοῦναι, ὧν δ᾽
ὑφ᾽ ὑμῶν ἠδίκηντο δίκην λαβεῖν, ὁποτέρως βούλονται, ἢ διέντας αὐτοὺς ἐφ᾽ ὑμᾶς ἢ συνεμβαλόντας
εἰς τὴν Ἀττικήν, καὶ ἐδείκνυσαν, ὡς ᾤοντο, ἐκ
μὲν ὧν αὐτοὶ συνεβούλευον τἀκ τῆς Ἀττικῆς
βοσκήματα καὶ ἀνδράποδα καὶ τἄλλ᾽ ἀγαθὰ εἰς τὴν
Βοιωτίαν ἥξοντα, ἐκ δ᾽ ὧν ἡμᾶς ἐρεῖν ἔφασαν τἀν
τῇ Βοιωτίᾳ διαρπασθησόμεν᾽ ὑπὸ τοῦ πολέμου.
καὶ ἄλλα πολλὰ πρὸς τούτοις, εἰς ταὐτὰ δὲ πάντα
214 συντείνοντ᾽ ἔλεγον. ἃ δ᾽ ἡμεῖς πρὸς ταῦτα, τὰ
μὲν καθ᾽ ἕκαστα ἐγὼ μὲν ἀντὶ παντὸς ἂν τιμησαίμην
160

at the time. The prosecutor is so extraordinarily malicious that he gives the credit of any duty successfully performed not to me but to opportunity, but holds me and my bad luck responsible for everything that miscarried. I am a speaker and a statesman, yet it would seem that, in his view, I am to have no credit for the results of discussion and deliberation, but am solely responsible for all the misadventures of our arms and our generalship. Can you imagine a cruder or more abominable calumny? Read the dispatch.

(The Ambassadors' Dispatch is read)

When the Thebans held their assembly, they introduced Philip's ambassadors first, on the ground that they were in the position of allies. They came forward and made their speech, full of eulogy of Philip, and of incrimination of Athens, and recalled everything you had ever done in antagonism to Thebes. The gist of the speech was that they were to show gratitude to Philip for every good turn he had done to them, and to punish you for the injuries they had suffered, in whichever of two ways they chose —either by giving him a free passage, or by joining in the invasion of Attica. They proved, as they thought, that, if their advice were taken, cattle, slaves, and other loot from Attica would come into Boeotia, whereas the result of the proposals they expected from us would be that Boeotia would be ravaged by the war. They added many other arguments, all tending to the same conclusion. I would give my life to recapitulate the reply that we made:

161

DEMOSTHENES

εἰπεῖν τοῦ βίου, ὑμᾶς δὲ δέδοικα, μὴ παρεληλυθότων
τῶν καιρῶν, ὥσπερ ἂν εἰ κατακλυσμὸν γεγενῆσθαι
τῶν πραγμάτων ἡγούμενοι, μάταιον ὄχλον τοὺς
περὶ τούτων λόγους νομίσητε· ὅ τι δ' οὖν ἐπεί-
σαμεν ἡμεῖς καὶ ἡμῖν ἀπεκρίναντο, ἀκούσατε·
λέγε ταυτὶ λαβών.

ΑΠΟΚΡΙΣΙΣ ΘΗΒΑΙΩΝ

215 Μετὰ ταῦτα τοίνυν ἐκάλουν ὑμᾶς καὶ μετεπέμποντο. ἐξῆτ', ἐβοηθεῖτε, ἵνα τἂν μέσῳ παραλείπω, οὕτως οἰκείως ὑμᾶς ἐδέχοντο ὥστ' ἔξω
[300] τῶν ὁπλιτῶν καὶ τῶν ἱππέων ὄντων εἰς τὰς οἰκίας
καὶ τὸ ἄστυ δέχεσθαι τὴν στρατιὰν ἐπὶ παῖδας
καὶ γυναῖκας καὶ τὰ τιμιώτατα. καίτοι τρί'
ἐν ἐκείνῃ τῇ ἡμέρᾳ πᾶσιν ἀνθρώποις ἔδειξαν
ἐγκώμια Θηβαῖοι καθ' ὑμῶν τὰ κάλλιστα, ἓν
μὲν ἀνδρείας, ἕτερον δὲ δικαιοσύνης, τρίτον δὲ
σωφροσύνης. καὶ γὰρ τὸν ἀγῶνα μεθ' ὑμῶν
μᾶλλον ἢ πρὸς ὑμᾶς ἑλόμενοι ποιήσασθαι, καὶ
ἀμείνους εἶναι καὶ δικαιότερ' ἀξιοῦν ὑμᾶς ἔκριναν
Φιλίππου· καὶ τὰ παρ' αὑτοῖς καὶ παρὰ πᾶσι δ'
ἐν πλείστῃ φυλακῇ, παῖδας καὶ γυναῖκας, ἐφ'
ὑμῖν ποιήσαντες σωφροσύνης πίστιν περὶ ὑμῶν
216 ἔχοντες ἔδειξαν. ἐν οἷς πᾶσιν, ἄνδρες Ἀθηναῖοι,
κατά γ' ὑμᾶς ὀρθῶς ἐφάνησαν ἐγνωκότες. οὔτε
γὰρ εἰς τὴν πόλιν εἰσελθόντος τοῦ στρατοπέδου,
οὐδεὶς οὐδὲν οὐδ' ἀδίκως ὑμῖν ἐνεκάλεσεν· οὕτω
σώφρονας παρέσχεθ' ὑμᾶς αὐτούς· δίς τε συμ-
παραταξάμενοι τὰς πρώτας μάχας, τήν τ' ἐπὶ τοῦ
ποταμοῦ καὶ τὴν χειμερινήν, οὐκ ἀμέμπτους
μόνον ὑμᾶς αὐτούς, ἀλλὰ καὶ θαυμαστοὺς ἐδείξατε
162

but I am afraid that, as that crisis is long past, and as you may think that all those transactions are now obliterated as by a flood, you would regard any discussion of them as useless and vexatious. I will only ask you to hear how far we prevailed upon them, and what answer they returned. Take and read this document.

(The Reply of the Thebans is read)

After that, the Thebans invited you to join them. You marched out : you reinforced them. I pass over the incidents of the march : but their reception of you was so friendly that, while their own infantry and cavalry lay outside the walls, they gave you access to their homes, to their citadel, to their wives and children and most precious possessions. On that day the Thebans publicly paid three fine compliments—to your valour, to your righteousness, and to your sobriety. When they decided to fight on your side rather than against you, they adjudged you to be braver men than Philip, and your claim to be more righteous than his ; and when they put into your power what they, like all other men, were most anxious to safeguard, namely their wives and their children, they exhibited their confidence in your sobriety. And thereby, men of Athens, they showed a just appreciation of your character. After the entry of your soldiers no man ever laid even a groundless complaint against them, so soberly did you conduct yourselves. Fighting shoulder to shoulder with them in the two earliest engagements, —the battle by the river, and the winter battle, —you approved yourselves irreproachable fighters,

163

τῷ κόσμῳ, ταῖς παρασκευαῖς, τῇ προθυμίᾳ. ἐφ᾽
οἷς παρὰ μὲν τῶν ἄλλων ὑμῖν ἐγίγνοντ᾽ ἔπαινοι,
217 παρὰ δ᾽ ὑμῶν θυσίαι καὶ πομπαὶ τοῖς θεοῖς. καὶ
ἔγωγ᾽ ἡδέως ἂν ἐροίμην Αἰσχίνην, ὅτε ταῦτ᾽ ἐπράττετο καὶ ζήλου καὶ χαρᾶς καὶ ἐπαίνων ἡ πόλις
ἦν μεστή, πότερον συνέθυε καὶ συνευφραίνετο τοῖς
πολλοῖς, ἢ λυπούμενος καὶ στένων καὶ δυσμεναίνων
τοῖς κοινοῖς ἀγαθοῖς οἴκοι καθῆτο. εἰ μὲν γὰρ
παρῆν καὶ μετὰ τῶν ἄλλων ἐξητάζετο, πῶς οὐ
δεινὰ ποιεῖ, μᾶλλον δ᾽ οὐδ᾽ ὅσια, εἰ ὧν ὡς ἀρίστων
αὐτὸς τοὺς θεοὺς ἐποιήσατο μάρτυρας, ταῦθ᾽ ὡς
οὐκ ἄριστα νῦν ὑμᾶς ἀξιοῖ ψηφίσασθαι τοὺς
[301] ὀμωμοκότας τοὺς θεούς; εἰ δὲ μὴ παρῆν, πῶς οὐκ
ἀπολωλέναι πολλάκις ἐστὶν δίκαιος, εἰ ἐφ᾽ οἷς
ἔχαιρον οἱ ἄλλοι, ταῦτ᾽ ἐλυπεῖθ᾽ ὁρῶν; λέγε δὴ καὶ
ταῦτα τὰ ψηφίσματά μοι.

ΨΗΦΙΣΜΑΤΑ ΘΥΣΙΩΝ

218 Οὐκοῦν ἡμεῖς μὲν ἐν θυσίαις ἦμεν τότε, Θηβαῖοι
δ᾽ ἐν τῷ δι᾽ ἡμᾶς σεσῶσθαι νομίζειν, καὶ περιειστήκει τοῖς βοηθείας δεήσεσθαι δοκοῦσιν ἀφ᾽ ὧν
ἔπραττον οὗτοι, αὐτοὺς βοηθεῖν ἑτέροις ἐξ ὧν
ἐπείσθητ᾽ ἐμοί. ἀλλὰ μὴν οἵας τότ᾽ ἠφίει φωνὰς
ὁ Φίλιππος καὶ ἐν οἵαις ἦν ταραχαῖς ἐπὶ τούτοις,
ἐκ τῶν ἐπιστολῶν τῶν ἐκείνου μαθήσεσθε, ὧν εἰς
Πελοπόννησον ἔπεμπεν. καί μοι λέγε ταύτας
λαβών, ἵν᾽ εἰδῆθ᾽ ἡ ἐμὴ συνέχεια καὶ πλάνοι καὶ
ταλαιπωρίαι καὶ τὰ πολλὰ ψηφίσματα, ἃ νῦν οὗτος
διέσυρεν, τί ἀπειργάσατο.

admirable alike in discipline, in equipment, and in
determination. Your conduct elicited the praises
of other nations, and was acknowledged by yourselves in services of thanksgiving to the gods. I
should like to ask Aeschines a question : when all
that was going on, when the whole city was a scene
of enthusiasm and rejoicing and thanksgiving, did
he take part in the worship and festivity of the
populace, or did he sit still at home, grieving and
groaning and sulking over public successes ? If he
was present as one of the throng, surely his behaviour
is scandalous and even sacrilegious, for after calling
the gods to witness that certain measures were very
good, he now asks a jury to vote that they were
very bad—a jury that has sworn by the gods ! If
he was not present, he deserves many deaths for
shrinking from a sight in which every one else
rejoiced. Please read these decrees.

(The Decrees appointing a Public Thanksgiving are read)

So we were engaged in thanksgiving, and the
Thebans in acknowledging the deliverance that they
owed to us. The situation was reversed, and a
nation that, thanks to the intrigues of Aeschines and
his party, seemed on the verge of suing for aid, was
now giving aid in pursuance of the advice which you
accepted from me. But indeed, what sort of language
Philip gave vent to at that time, and how seriously
he was discomposed, you shall learn from letters
sent by him to Peloponnesus. Please take and read
them, that the jury may learn the real effect of my
perseverance, of my journeys and hardships, and of
that profusion of decrees at which Aeschines was
just now scoffing.

165

219 Καίτοι πολλοὶ παρ᾽ ὑμῖν, ἄνδρες Ἀθηναῖοι,
γεγόνασι ῥήτορες ἔνδοξοι καὶ μεγάλοι πρὸ ἐμοῦ,
Καλλίστρατος ἐκεῖνος, Ἀριστοφῶν, Κέφαλος, Θρα-
σύβουλος, ἕτεροι μυρίοι· ἀλλ᾽ ὅμως οὐδεὶς πώποτε
τούτων διὰ παντὸς ἔδωκεν ἑαυτὸν εἰς οὐδὲν τῇ
πόλει, ἀλλ᾽ ὁ μὲν γράφων οὐκ ἂν ἐπρέσβευσεν, ὁ
δὲ πρεσβεύων οὐκ ἂν ἔγραψεν. ὑπέλειπε γὰρ
αὐτῶν ἕκαστος ἑαυτῷ ἅμα μὲν ῥαστώνην, ἅμα δ᾽,
220 εἴ τι γένοιτ᾽, ἀναφοράν. τί οὖν; εἴποι τις ἄν,
σὺ τοσοῦθ᾽ ὑπερῆρας ῥώμῃ καὶ τόλμῃ ὥστε πάντα
ποιεῖν αὐτός; οὐ ταῦτα λέγω, ἀλλ᾽ οὕτως ἐπεπείσμην μέγαν εἶναι τὸν κατειληφότα κίνδυνον τὴν
πόλιν ὥστ᾽ οὐκ ἐδόκει μοι χώραν οὐδὲ πρόνοιαν
οὐδεμίαν τῆς ἰδίας ἀσφαλείας διδόναι, ἀλλ᾽ ἀγα-
[302] πητὸν εἶναι, εἰ μηδὲν παραλείπων τις ἃ δεῖ πρά-
221 ξειεν. ἐπεπείσμην δ᾽ ὑπὲρ ἐμαυτοῦ, τυχὸν μὲν
ἀναισθητῶν, ὅμως δ᾽ ἐπεπείσμην, μήτε γράφοντ᾽
ἂν ἐμοῦ γράψαι βέλτιον μηδένα μήτε πράττοντα
πρᾶξαι, μήτε πρεσβεύοντα πρεσβεῦσαι προθυμό-
τερον μηδὲ δικαιότερον. διὰ ταῦτ᾽ ἐν πᾶσιν
ἐμαυτὸν ἔταττον. λέγε τὰς ἐπιστολὰς τὰς τοῦ
Φιλίππου.

ΕΠΙΣΤΟΛΑΙ

222 Εἰς ταῦτα κατέστησε Φίλιππον ἡ ἐμὴ πολιτεία,
Αἰσχίνη· ταύτην τὴν φωνὴν ἐκεῖνος ἀφῆκε, πολλοὺς
καὶ θρασεῖς τὰ πρὸ τούτων τῇ πόλει ἐπαιρόμε-
νος λόγους. ἀνθ᾽ ὧν δικαίως ἐστεφανούμην ὑπὸ
τουτουί, καὶ σὺ παρὼν οὐκ ἀντέλεγες, ὁ δὲ
γραψάμενος Διώνδας τὸ μέρος τῶν ψήφων οὐκ
166

Men of Athens, there have been many great and distinguished orators in your city before my time, — the famous Callistratus, Aristophon, Cephalus, Thrasybulus, and thousands more ; but no one of them ever devoted himself to any public business without intermission ; the man who moved a resolution would not go on embassy, and the man who went on embassy would not move a resolution. Each of them used to leave himself some leisure, and at the same time some loop-hole, in case anything happened. " What ! " some one may say, " were you so much stronger and bolder than others that you could do everything by yourself ? " That is not what I mean : but I was so firmly persuaded that the danger which overhung the city was very serious, that it did not seem to me to leave me any room for taking my personal safety into account ; but a man, I thought, must be content, without neglecting anything, to do his duty. As for myself, I was convinced, presumptuously, perhaps, but convinced I was, that there was no one more competent either to make sound proposals, or to carry them into effect, or to conduct an embassy diligently and honestly : and therefore I took my place in every field of action. Read Philip's letters.

(Philip's Letters are read)

To these straits had my policy, Aeschines, reduced Philip : and such was then the language uttered by a man who had hitherto lifted his voice vauntingly against Athens. And for that reason I was deservedly decorated by the citizens. You were present, but said nothing in opposition ; and Diondas, who arraigned the grant, did not get the fifth part of the

ἔλαβεν. καί μοι λέγε ταῦτα τὰ ψηφίσματα
τὰ τότε μὲν ἀποπεφευγότα, ὑπὸ τούτου δ᾽ οὐδὲ
γραφέντα.

ΨΗΦΙΣΜΑΤΑ

223 Ταυτὶ τὰ ψηφίσματ᾽, ἄνδρες ᾽Αθηναῖοι, τὰς
αὐτὰς συλλαβὰς καὶ ταὐτὰ ῥήματ᾽ ἔχει ἅπερ
πρότερον μὲν ᾽Αριστόνικος, νῦν δὲ Κτησιφῶν
γέγραφεν οὑτοσί. καὶ ταῦτ᾽ Αἰσχίνης οὔτ᾽ ἐδίωξεν αὐτός, οὔτε τῷ γραψαμένῳ συγκατηγόρησεν.
καίτοι τότε τὸν Δημομέλη τὸν ταῦτα γράφοντα
καὶ τὸν Ὑπερείδην, εἴπερ ἀληθῆ μου νῦν κατηγορεῖ,
224 μᾶλλον ἂν εἰκότως ἢ τόνδ᾽ ἐδίωκεν. διὰ τί;
ὅτι τῷδε μὲν γὰρ ἔστ᾽ ἀνενεγκεῖν ἐπ᾽ ἐκείνους καὶ
τὰς τῶν δικαστηρίων γνώσεις, καὶ τὸ τοῦτον
[303] αὐτὸν ἐκείνων μὴ κατηγορηκέναι ταῦτα γραψάντων
ἅπερ οὗτος νῦν, καὶ τὸ τοὺς νόμους μηκέτ᾽ ἐᾶν
περὶ τῶν οὕτω πραχθέντων κατηγορεῖν, καὶ
πόλλ᾽ ἕτερα· τότε δ᾽ αὐτὸ τὸ πρᾶγμ᾽ ἂν ἔκρινετ᾽
225 ἐφ᾽ αὑτοῦ, πρίν τι τούτων προλαβεῖν. ἀλλ᾽
οὐκ ἦν, οἶμαι, τόθ᾽ ὃ νυνὶ ποιεῖν, ἐκ παλαιῶν
χρόνων καὶ ψηφισμάτων πολλῶν ἐκλέξαντα, ἃ
μήτε προῄδει μηδεὶς μήτ᾽ ἂν ᾠήθη τήμερον
ῥηθῆναι, διαβάλλειν, καὶ μετενεγκόντα τοὺς χρόνους καὶ προφάσεις ἀντὶ τῶν ἀληθῶν ψευδεῖς
μεταθέντα τοῖς πεπραγμένοις δοκεῖν τι λέγειν.
226 οὐκ ἦν τότε ταῦτα, ἀλλ᾽ ἐπὶ τῆς ἀληθείας, ἐγγὺς
τῶν ἔργων, ἔτι μεμνημένων ὑμῶν καὶ μόνον οὐκ
ἐν ταῖς χερσὶν ἕκαστ᾽ ἐχόντων, πάντες ἐγίγνοντ᾽
ἂν οἱ λόγοι. διόπερ τοὺς παρ᾽ αὐτὰ τὰ πράγματ᾽

votes. Please read the decrees which were then by
that acquittal validated, and which Aeschines never
even arraigned.

(The Decrees are read)

These decrees, men of Athens, exhibit the same
wording and phrasing as those proposed formerly by
Aristonicus, and now by Ctesiphon. Aeschines did
not prosecute them himself, nor did he support the
accusation of the man who did arraign them. And
yet if there is any truth in his present denunciation,
he might then have prosecuted Demomeles, the
proposer, and Hypereides, with more reason than
Ctesiphon, who can refer to these precedents, to
the decision of the courts, to the observation that
Aeschines himself did not prosecute persons who
made the same proposals, to the statutory prohibition of repeated prosecution in such cases, and so
forth; whereas at that time the issue would have
been tried on its merits without such presumptions.
On the other hand, at that time, I imagine, there
was no chance of doing what he does now, when
out of a lot of old dates and decrees he selects for
slanderous purposes any that nobody knew beforehand or would expect to hear cited to-day, transposes
dates, substitutes fictitious reasons for the true
reasons of transactions, and so makes a show of
speaking to the point. That trick was not possible
then. All speeches must have been made on a
basis of truth, within a short time of the facts, when
the jury still remembered details and almost knew
them by heart. That is why, after shirking inquiry

ἐλέγχους φυγὼν νῦν ἥκει, ῥητόρων ἀγῶνα νομίζων,
ὥς γ᾽ ἐμοὶ δοκεῖ, καὶ οὐχὶ τῶν πεπολιτευμένων
ἐξέτασιν ποιήσειν ὑμᾶς, καὶ λόγου κρίσιν, οὐχὶ τοῦ
τῇ πόλει συμφέροντος ἔσεσθαι.

227 Εἶτα σοφίζεται καὶ φησὶν προσήκειν ἧς μὲν
οἴκοθεν ἥκετ᾽ ἔχοντες δόξης περὶ ἡμῶν ἀμελῆσαι,
ὥσπερ δ᾽, ὅταν οἰόμενοι περιεῖναι χρήματά τῳ
λογίζησθε, ἂν καθαραὶ ὦσιν αἱ ψῆφοι καὶ μηδὲν
περιῇ, συγχωρεῖτε, οὕτω καὶ νῦν τοῖς ἐκ τοῦ
λόγου φαινομένοις προσθέσθαι. θεάσασθε τοίνυν
ὡς σαθρόν, ὡς ἔοικεν, ἔστι φύσει πᾶν ὅ τι ἂν μὴ
228 δικαίως ᾖ πεπραγμένον. ἐκ γὰρ αὐτοῦ τοῦ
σοφοῦ τούτου παραδείγματος ὡμολόγηκε νῦν γ᾽
ἡμᾶς ὑπάρχειν ἐγνωσμένους ἐμὲ μὲν λέγειν ὑπὲρ
τῆς πατρίδος, αὐτὸν δ᾽ ὑπὲρ Φιλίππου· οὐ γὰρ
[304] ἂν μεταπείθειν ὑμᾶς ἐζήτει μὴ τοιαύτης ὑπαρ-
229 χούσης ὑπολήψεως[1] περὶ ἑκατέρου. καὶ μὴν ὅτι
γ᾽ οὐ δίκαια λέγει μεταθέσθαι ταύτην τὴν δόξαν
ἀξιῶν, ἐγὼ διδάξω ῥᾳδίως, οὐ τιθεὶς ψήφους (οὐ
γάρ ἐστιν ὁ τῶν πραγμάτων οὗτος λογισμός),
ἀλλ᾽ ἀναμιμνῄσκων ἕκαστ᾽ ἐν βραχέσι, λογισταῖς
ἅμα καὶ μάρτυσι τοῖς ἀκούουσιν ὑμῖν χρώμενος.
ἡ γὰρ ἐμὴ πολιτεία, ἧς οὗτος κατηγορεῖ, ἀντὶ
μὲν τοῦ Θηβαίους μετὰ Φιλίππου συνεμβαλεῖν
εἰς τὴν χώραν, ὃ πάντες ᾤοντο, μεθ᾽ ἡμῶν παρα-
230 ταξαμένους ἐκεῖνον κωλύειν ἐποίησεν· ἀντὶ δὲ τοῦ
ἐν τῇ Ἀττικῇ τὸν πόλεμον εἶναι, ἑπτακόσια
στάδι᾽ ἀπὸ τῆς πόλεως ἐπὶ τοῖς Βοιωτῶν ὁρίοις
γενέσθαι· ἀντὶ δὲ τοῦ τοὺς λῃστὰς ἡμᾶς φέρειν
καὶ ἄγειν ἐκ τῆς Εὐβοίας, ἐν εἰρήνῃ τὴν Ἀττικὴν
ἐκ θαλάττης εἶναι πάντα τὸν πόλεμον· ἀντὶ δὲ
τοῦ τὸν Ἑλλήσποντον ἔχειν Φίλιππον, λαβόντα

at the time when the events were recent, he has returned to the issue to-day, expecting, I suppose, that you will conduct a forensic competition rather than an inquiry into political conduct, and that the decision will turn upon diction rather than sound policy.

Then he resorts to sophistry, and tells you that you must ignore any opinion of himself and me which you brought with you from home ; and that, as, when you cast up a man's accounts, though you anticipate a surplus, you acquiesce in the result if the totals balance, so you must now accept the result of the calculation. Every dishonest contrivance, you will observe, is rotten to the core. By his ingenious apologue he has admitted that we are both here as acknowledged advocates—I of our country, he of Philip ; for if such had not been the view you take of us, he would not have been at pains to convert you. I shall prove without difficulty that he has no right to ask you to reverse that opinion—not by using counters, for political measures are not to be added up in that fashion, but by reminding you briefly of the several transactions, and appealing to you who hear me as both the witnesses and the auditors of my account. We owe it to that policy of mine which he denounces that, instead of the Thebans joining Philip in an invasion of our country, as everyone expected, they fought by our side and stopped him ; that, instead of the seat of war being in Attica, it was seven hundred furlongs away on the far side of Boeotia ; that, instead of privateers from Euboea harrying us, Attica was at peace on the sea-frontier throughout the war ; and that, instead of Philip taking Byzantium

---

[1] τοιαύτης ὑπαρχούσης ὑπολήψεως Oxyrh. pap.: τοιαύτης οὔσης τῆς ὑπαρχούσης ὑπολήψεως Dind., S.

Βυζάντιον, συμπολεμεῖν τοὺς Βυζαντίους μεθ'
231 ἡμῶν πρὸς ἐκεῖνον. ἆρά σοι ψήφοις ὅμοιος ὁ
τῶν ἔργων λογισμὸς φαίνεται; ἢ δεῖν ἀντανελεῖν
ταῦτα, ἀλλ' οὐχ ὅπως τὸν ἅπαντα χρόνον μνημο-
νευθήσεται σκέψασθαι; καὶ οὐκέτι προστίθημ'
ὅτι τῆς μὲν ὠμότητος, ἣν ἐν οἷς καθάπαξ τινῶν
κατέστη κύριος Φίλιππος ἔστιν ἰδεῖν, ἑτέροις
πειραθῆναι συνέβη, τῆς δὲ φιλανθρωπίας, ἣν τὰ
λοιπὰ τῶν πραγμάτων ἐκεῖνος περιβαλλόμενος
ἐπλάττετο, ὑμεῖς καλῶς ποιοῦντες τοὺς καρποὺς
κεκόμισθε. ἀλλ' ἐῶ ταῦτα.

232 Καὶ μὴν οὐδὲ τοῦτ' εἰπεῖν ὀκνήσω, ὅτι ὁ τὸν
ῥήτορα βουλόμενος δικαίως ἐξετάζειν καὶ μὴ
[305] συκοφαντεῖν οὐκ ἂν οἷα σὺ νῦν ἔλεγες, τοιαῦτα
κατηγόρει, παραδείγματα πλάττων καὶ ῥήματα
καὶ σχήματα μιμούμενος (πάνυ γὰρ παρὰ τοῦτ',
οὐχ ὁρᾷς; γέγονε τὰ τῶν Ἑλλήνων, εἰ τουτὶ τὸ
ῥῆμ' ἀλλὰ μὴ τουτὶ διελέχθην ἐγώ, ἢ δευρὶ τὴν
233 χεῖρ' ἀλλὰ μὴ δευρὶ παρήνεγκα), ἀλλ' ἐπ' αὐτῶν
τῶν ἔργων ἂν ἐσκόπει τίνας εἶχεν ἀφορμὰς ἡ
πόλις καὶ τίνας δυνάμεις, ὅτ' εἰς τὰ πράγματ'
εἰσῄειν, καὶ τίνας συνήγαγον αὐτῇ μετὰ ταῦτ'
ἐπιστὰς ἐγώ, καὶ πῶς εἶχε τὰ τῶν ἐναντίων. εἶτ'
εἰ μὲν ἐλάττους ἐποίησα τὰς δυνάμεις, παρ' ἐμοὶ
τἀδίκημ' ἂν ἐδείκνυεν ὄν, εἰ δὲ πολλῷ μείζους,
οὐκ ἂν ἐσυκοφάντει. ἐπειδὴ δὲ σὺ τοῦτο πέφευ-
γας, ἐγὼ ποιήσω· καὶ σκοπεῖτ' εἰ δικαίως χρήσομαι τῷ λόγῳ.

234 Δύναμιν μὲν τοίνυν εἶχεν ἡ πόλις τοὺς νησιώτας,
172

and holding the Hellespont, the Byzantines fought on our side against him. Do you see any resemblance between this computation of results and your casting up of counters? Are we to cancel the gains to balance the losses,[a] instead of providing that they shall never be forgotten? I need not add that other nations have had experience of that cruelty which is always observable whenever Philip has got people under his heel, whereas you have been lucky enough to enjoy the fruits of that factitious humanity in which he clothed himself with an eye to the future. But I pass that by.

I will not shrink from observing that any man who wished to bring an orator to the proof honestly, and not merely to slander him, would never have laid such charges as you have alleged, inventing analogies, and mimicking my diction and gestures. The fate of Greece, forsooth, depended on whether I used this word or that, or moved my hand this way or that way! No; he would have considered, in the light of actual facts, the means and resources possessed by the city when I entered on administration, and those accumulated by me when at the head of affairs; and also the condition of our adversaries. If I had impaired our resources, he would have proved that the fault lay at my door: if I had greatly increased them, he would have spared his slanders. As you avoided this test, I will apply it; and the jury will see whether I state the case fairly.

For resources, the city possessed the islanders—

[a] The metaphors here are taken from calculations on the abacus, where subtraction of counters from one side of the board would serve instead of addition to the other. Instead of showing the gains of Athens side by side with her losses, Aeschines would record only the adverse balance.

οὐχ ἅπαντας, ἀλλὰ τοὺς ἀσθενεστάτους· οὔτε
γὰρ Χίος οὔτε Ῥόδος οὔτε Κέρκυρα μεθ' ἡμῶν
ἦν· χρημάτων δὲ σύνταξιν εἰς πέντε καὶ τετταράκοντα τάλαντα, καὶ ταῦτ' ἦν προεξειλεγμένα· ὁπλίτην
δ' ἢ ἱππέα πλὴν τῶν οἰκείων οὐδένα. ὃ δὲ πάντων
καὶ φοβερώτατον καὶ μάλισθ' ὑπὲρ τῶν ἐχθρῶν,
οὗτοι παρεσκευάκεσαν τοὺς περιχώρους πάντας
ἔχθρας ἢ φιλίας ἐγγυτέρω, Μεγαρέας, Θηβαίους,
235 Εὐβοέας. τὰ μὲν τῆς πόλεως οὕτως ὑπῆρχεν
ἔχοντα, καὶ οὐδεὶς ἂν ἔχοι παρὰ ταῦτ' εἰπεῖν ἄλλ'
οὐδέν· τὰ δὲ τοῦ Φιλίππου, πρὸς ὃν ἦν ἡμῖν ὁ
ἀγών, σκέψασθε πῶς. πρῶτον μὲν ἦρχε τῶν
ἀκολουθούντων αὐτὸς αὐτοκράτωρ, ὃ τῶν εἰς τὸν
πόλεμον μέγιστόν ἐστιν ἁπάντων· εἶθ' οὗτοι τὰ
ὅπλ' εἶχον ἐν ταῖς χερσὶν ἀεί· ἔπειτα χρημάτων
[306] ηὐπόρει, καὶ ἔπραττεν ἃ δόξειεν αὐτῷ, οὐ προλέγων
ἐν τοῖς ψηφίσμασιν, οὐδ' ἐν τῷ φανερῷ βουλευό-
μενος, οὐδ' ὑπὸ τῶν συκοφαντούντων κρινόμενος,
οὐδὲ γραφὰς φεύγων παρανόμων, οὐδ' ὑπεύθυνος
ὢν οὐδενί, ἀλλ' ἁπλῶς αὐτὸς δεσπότης, ἡγεμών,
236 κύριος πάντων. ἐγὼ δ' ὁ πρὸς τοῦτον ἀντι-
τεταγμένος (καὶ γὰρ τοῦτ' ἐξετάσαι δίκαιον) τίνος
κύριος ἦν; οὐδενός. αὐτὸ γὰρ τὸ δημηγορεῖν
πρῶτον, οὗ μόνου μετεῖχον ἐγώ, ἐξ ἴσου προὔτίθεθ'
ὑμεῖς τοῖς παρ' ἐκείνου μισθαρνοῦσι καὶ ἐμοί,
καὶ ὅσ' οὗτοι περιγένοιντ' ἐμοῦ (πολλὰ δ' ἐγίγνετο
ταῦτα, δι' ἣν ἕκαστον τύχοι πρόφασιν), ταῦθ'
237 ὑπὲρ τῶν ἐχθρῶν ἀπῇτε βεβουλευμένοι. ἀλλ'
ὅμως ἐκ τοσούτων ἐλαττωμάτων, ἐγὼ συμμάχους
μὲν ὑμῖν ἐποίησ' Εὐβοέας, Ἀχαιούς, Κορινθίους,
Θηβαίους, Μεγαρέας, Λευκαδίους, Κερκυραίους,
ἀφ' ὧν μύριοι μὲν καὶ πεντακισχίλιοι ξένοι,
174

but not all, only the weakest, for neither Chios, nor Rhodes, nor Corcyra was on our side ; a subsidy of forty-five talents, all collected in advance ; and not a single private or trooper apart from our own army. But what was most alarming to us, and advantageous to the enemy, Aeschines and his party had made all our neighbours, Megarians, Thebans, and Euboeans, more disposed to enmity than to friendship. Such were the means of the city : and I defy anyone to name anything else. Now consider those of our antagonist Philip. In the first place, he was the despotic commander of his adherents : and in war that is the most important of all advantages. Secondly, they had their weapons constantly in their hands. Then he was well provided with money : he did whatever he chose, without giving notice by publishing decrees, or deliberating in public, without fear of prosecution by informers or indictment for illegal measures. He was responsible to nobody : he was the absolute autocrat, commander, and master of everybody and everything. And I, his chosen adversary — it is a fair inquiry — of what was I master ? Of nothing at all ! Public speaking was my only privilege : and that you permitted to Philip's hired servants on the same terms as to me. Whenever they had the advantage of me—and for one reason or another that often happened—you laid your plans for the enemy's benefit, and went your ways. In spite of all these drawbacks, I made alliance for you with Euboeans, Achaeans, Corinthians, Thebans, Megarians, Leucadians, and Corcyraeans : and from those states there was assembled a foreign division of fifteen thousand infantry and two thousand

175

δισχίλιοι δ' ἱππεῖς ἄνευ τῶν πολιτικῶν δυνάμεων
συνήχθησαν. χρημάτων δ' ὅσην¹ ἐδυνήθην ἐγὼ
238 πλείστην συντέλειαν ἐποίησα. εἰ δὲ λέγεις ἢ τὰ
πρὸς Θηβαίους δίκαι', Αἰσχίνη, ἢ τὰ πρὸς Βυζαντίους ἢ τὰ πρὸς Εὐβοέας, ἢ περὶ τῶν ἴσων νυνὶ
διαλέγει, πρῶτον μὲν ἀγνοεῖς ὅτι καὶ πρότερον
τῶν ὑπὲρ τῶν Ἑλλήνων ἐκείνων ἀγωνισαμένων
τριήρων, τριακοσίων οὐσῶν τῶν πασῶν, τὰς
διακοσίας ἡ πόλις παρέσχετο, καὶ οὐκ ἐλαττοῦσθαι
νομίζουσα, οὐδὲ κρίνουσα τοὺς ταῦτα συμβου-
λεύσαντας, οὐδ' ἀγανακτοῦσ' ἐπὶ τούτοις ἑωρᾶτο
(αἰσχρὸν γάρ), ἀλλὰ τοῖς θεοῖς ἔχουσα χάριν,
εἰ κοινοῦ κινδύνου τοῖς Ἕλλησι περιστάντος,
αὐτὴ διπλάσια τῶν ἄλλων εἰς τὴν ἁπάντων σωτη-
239 ρίαν παρέσχετο. εἶτα κενὰς χαρίζει χάριτας
[307] τουτοισὶ συκοφαντῶν ἐμέ. τί γὰρ νῦν λέγεις οἷ'
ἐχρῆν πράττειν, ἀλλ' οὐ τότ' ὢν ἐν τῇ πόλει καὶ
παρὼν ταῦτ' ἔγραφες, εἴπερ ἐνεδέχετο παρὰ τοὺς
παρόντας καιρούς, ἐν οἷς οὐχ ὅσ' ἐβουλόμεθα, ἀλλ'
ὅσα δοίη τὰ πράγματ' ἔδει δέχεσθαι· ὁ γὰρ
ἀντωνούμενος καὶ ταχὺ τοὺς παρ' ἡμῶν ἀπελαυ-
νομένους προσδεξόμενος καὶ χρήματα προσθήσων
ὑπῆρχεν ἕτοιμος.
240 Ἀλλ' εἰ νῦν ἐπὶ τοῖς πεπραγμένοις κατηγορίας
ἔχω, τί ἂν οἴεσθ', εἰ τότ' ἐμοῦ περὶ τούτων ἀκριβο-
λογουμένου, ἀπῆλθον αἱ πόλεις καὶ προσέθεντο
Φιλίππῳ, καὶ ἅμ' Εὐβοίας καὶ Θηβῶν καὶ Βυζαντίου κύριος κατέστη, τί ποιεῖν ἂν ἢ τί λέγειν τοὺς
241 ἀσεβεῖς ἀνθρώπους τουτουσί; οὐχ ὡς ἐξεδόθησαν;

_____

¹ ὅσην Dobree : ὅσων Dind., S.

_____

ᵃ that fought for Greece : at Salamis, 480 B.C.

176

cavalry, not counting their citizen-soldiery. I also obtained from them in money the largest subsidy I could. When you talk about fair terms with the Thebans, Aeschines, or with the Byzantines and the Euboeans, and raise at this time of day the question of equal contributions, in the first place, you must be unaware that of that famous fleet of three hundred galleys that fought for Greece *a* in former days, our city supplied two hundred ; and that she did not show any sign of complaining that she was unfairly treated, or impeaching the statesmen whose advice she took, or airing her dissatisfaction. That would have been discreditable indeed ! No, she gave thanks to the gods that, when all the Greeks alike were encompassed by a great peril, she had contributed twice as much as all the rest to the common deliverance. Secondly, when you grumble at me, you are doing an ill turn to your fellow-citizens. Why do you tell them to-day what they ought to have done then ? You were in Athens and at the Assembly : why did you not offer your suggestions at the time—if indeed they could possibly be offered during an imminent crisis, when we had to accept, not all that we wanted, but all that the conditions allowed ? There was a man lying in wait who was bidding against us, and was ready to welcome any allies we drove away, and pay them into the bargain.

If I am accused to-day for what was actually done, suppose that, while I was haggling over nice calculations, these cities had marched off and joined Philip —suppose he had become suzerain of Euboea, Thebes, and Byzantium—what do you think these unprincipled men would have done or said then ? Would they not have told you that we had made

οὐχ ὡς ἀπηλάθησαν βουλόμενοι μεθ' ἡμῶν εἶναι;
εἶτα τοῦ μὲν Ἑλλησπόντου διὰ Βυζαντίων ἐγκρατὴς
καθέστηκε, καὶ τῆς σιτοπομπίας τῆς τῶν Ἑλλήνων
κύριος, πόλεμος δ' ὅμορος καὶ βαρὺς εἰς τὴν
Ἀττικὴν διὰ Θηβαίων κεκόμισται, ἄπλους δ'
ἡ θάλαττα ὑπὸ τῶν ἐκ τῆς Εὐβοίας ὁρμωμένων
λῃστῶν γέγονεν; οὐκ ἂν ταῦτ' ἔλεγον, καὶ πολλά γε
242 πρὸς τούτοις ἕτερα; πονηρόν, ἄνδρες Ἀθηναῖοι,
πονηρὸν ὁ συκοφάντης ἀεὶ καὶ πανταχόθεν βάσκανον καὶ φιλαίτιον· τοῦτο δὲ καὶ φύσει κίναδος
τἀνθρώπιόν ἐστιν, οὐδὲν ἐξ ἀρχῆς ὑγιὲς πεποιηκὸς
οὐδ' ἐλεύθερον, αὐτοτραγικὸς πίθηκος, ἀρουραῖος
Οἰνόμαος, παράσημος ῥήτωρ. τί γὰρ ἡ σὴ
243 δεινότης εἰς ὄνησιν ἥκει τῇ πατρίδι; νῦν ἡμῖν
λέγεις περὶ τῶν παρεληλυθότων; ὥσπερ ἂν εἴ τις
ἰατρός, ἀσθενοῦσι μὲν τοῖς κάμνουσιν εἰσιὼν μὴ
[308] λέγοι μηδὲ δεικνύοι δι' ὧν ἀποφεύξονται τὴν
νόσον, ἐπειδὴ δὲ τελευτήσειέ τις αὐτῶν καὶ τὰ
νομιζόμεν' αὐτῷ φέροιτο, ἀκολουθῶν ἐπὶ τὸ
μνῆμα διεξίοι "εἰ τὸ καὶ τὸ ἐποίησεν ἄνθρωπος
οὑτοσί, οὐκ ἂν ἀπέθανεν." ἐμβρόντητ', εἶτα
νῦν λέγεις;
244   Οὐ τοίνυν οὐδὲ τὴν ἧτταν, εἰ ταύτῃ γαυριᾷς ἐφ'
ᾗ στένειν σ', ὦ κατάρατε, προσῆκεν, ἐν οὐδενὶ τῶν
παρ' ἐμοὶ γεγονυῖαν εὑρήσετε τῇ πόλει.   οὑτωσὶ δὲ
λογίζεσθε.   οὐδαμοῦ πώποτε, ὅποι πρεσβευτὴς
ἐπέμφθην ὑφ' ὑμῶν ἐγώ, ἡττηθεὶς ἀπῆλθον τῶν
παρὰ Φιλίππου πρέσβεων, οὐκ ἐκ Θετταλίας, οὐκ ἐξ
Ἀμβρακίας, οὐκ ἐξ Ἰλλυριῶν, οὐ παρὰ τῶν Θρᾳκῶν
βασιλέων, οὐκ ἐκ Βυζαντίου, οὐκ ἄλλοθεν οὐδαμόθεν,
178

Philip a present of our allies ? That they had been driven away when they wanted to join us ? That through the Byzantines he had gained the mastery of the Hellespont, and control of the corn-supply of all Greece ? That by means of the Thebans Attica had become the scene of a distressing war with her own neighbours ? That the sea had become useless for ships because of privateers with Euboea for their base ? Would they not have made all those complaints, and plenty more ? Oh, men of Athens, what a vile monster is the calumniator, gathering malice from everywhere, always backbiting ! But this fellow is by very nature a spiteful animal, absolutely incapable of honesty or generosity ; this monkey of melodrama, this bumpkin tragedy-king, this pinchbeck orator ! What use has all your cleverness ever been to your country ? What ! talk about bygones to-day ? It is as though a physician visiting his patients should never open his mouth, or tell them how to get rid of their complaint, so long as they are ill ; but, as soon as one of them dies, and the obsequies are celebrated, should follow the corpse to the grave, and deliver his prescription at last from the tombstone : " If our departed friend had done this or that, he would never have died ! " You lunatic ! what is the use of talking now ?

You will find that even our defeat, if this reprobate must needs exult over what he ought to have deplored, did not fall upon the city through any fault of mine. Make your reckoning in this way : wherever I was sent as your representative, I came away undefeated by Philip's ambassadors—from Thessaly, from Ambracia, from the Illyrians, from the kings of Thrace, from Byzantium, from every

οὐ τὰ τελευταῖ᾿ ἐκ Θηβῶν, ἀλλ᾿ ἐν οἷς κρατηθεῖεν οἱ
πρέσβεις αὐτοῦ τῷ λόγῳ, ταῦτα τοῖς ὅπλοις ἐπιὼν
245 κατεστρέφετο. ταῦτ᾿ οὖν ἀπαιτεῖς παρ᾿ ἐμοῦ, καὶ
οὐκ αἰσχύνει τὸν αὐτὸν εἴς τε μαλακίαν σκώπτων καὶ
τῆς Φιλίππου δυνάμεως ἀξιῶν ἕν᾿ ὄντα κρείττω
γενέσθαι; καὶ ταῦτα τοῖς λόγοις; τίνος γὰρ ἄλλου
κύριος ἦν ἐγώ; οὐ γὰρ τῆς γ᾿ ἑκάστου ψυχῆς, οὐδὲ
τῆς τύχης τῶν παραταξαμένων, οὐδὲ τῆς στρατηγίας
246 ἧς ἔμ᾿ ἀπαιτεῖς εὐθύνας· οὕτω σκαιὸς εἶ. ἀλλὰ
μὴν ὧν γ᾿ ἂν ὁ ῥήτωρ ὑπεύθυνος εἴη, πᾶσαν ἐξέτασιν λαμβάνετε· οὐ παραιτοῦμαι. τίν᾿ οὖν ἐστι
ταῦτα; ἰδεῖν τὰ πράγματ᾿ ἀρχόμενα, καὶ προαισθέσθαι, καὶ προειπεῖν τοῖς ἄλλοις. ταῦτα πέπρακταί
μοι. κἄτι τὰς ἑκασταχοῦ βραδυτῆτας, ὄκνους,
[309] ἀγνοίας, φιλονικίας, ἃ πολιτικὰ ταῖς πόλεσιν
πρόσεστιν ἁπάσαις καὶ ἀναγκαῖ᾿ ἁμαρτήματα, ταῦθ᾿
ὡς εἰς ἐλάχιστα συστεῖλαι, καὶ τοὐναντίον εἰς
ὁμόνοιαν καὶ φιλίαν καὶ τοῦ τὰ δέοντα ποιεῖν ὁρμὴν
προτρέψαι. καὶ ταῦτά μοι πάντα πεποίηται, καὶ
247 οὐδεὶς μήποθ᾿ εὕρῃ κατ᾿ ἔμ᾿ οὐδὲν ἐλλειφθέν. εἰ
τοίνυν τις ἔροιθ᾿ ὁντινοῦν τίσιν τὰ πλεῖστα Φίλιππος
ὧν κατέπραξε διῳκήσατο, πάντες ἂν εἴποιεν τῷ
στρατοπέδῳ καὶ τῷ διδόναι καὶ διαφθείρειν τοὺς ἐπὶ
τῶν πραγμάτων. οὐκοῦν τῶν μὲν δυνάμεων οὔτε
κύριος οὔθ᾿ ἡγεμὼν ἦν ἐγώ, ὥστ᾿ οὐδ᾿ ὁ λόγος τῶν
κατὰ ταῦτα πραχθέντων πρὸς ἐμέ. καὶ μὴν τῷ
διαφθαρῆναι χρήμασιν ἢ μὴ κεκράτηκα Φίλιππον·
ὥσπερ γὰρ ὁ ὠνούμενος νενίκηκε τὸν λαβόντ᾿, ἐὰν
πρίηται, οὕτως ὁ μὴ λαβὼν μηδὲ διαφθαρεὶς νενί-

other place, and finally from Thebes ; but wherever
Philip was beaten in diplomacy, he attacked the place
with an army and conquered it. And for those
defeats, Aeschines, you call me to account ! Are you
not ashamed to jeer at a man for cowardice, and then
to require that same man to overcome the whole
power of Philip single-handed, and to do it by mere
words ? For what else had I at my disposal ? Certainly not the personal courage of each man, not the
good fortune of the troops engaged, not that generalship for which you are unreasonable enough to hold
me responsible. Make as strict an inquiry as you
will into everything for which an orator is responsible ;
I ask no indulgence. But for what is he responsible ?
For discerning the trend of events at the outset, for
forecasting results, for warning others. That I have
always done. Further, he ought to reduce to a minimum those delays and hesitations, those fits of
ignorance and quarrelsomeness, which are the natural
and inevitable failings of all free states, and on the
other hand to promote unanimity and friendliness,
and whatever impels a man to do his duty. All
that also I have made my business : and herein no
man can find any delinquency on my part. Let
any man you like be asked by what means Philip
achieved most of his successes : the universal reply
will be, by his army and by bribing and corrupting
politicians. Well, I had no control or authority
over your forces, and therefore no question of their
performances can touch me. Moreover, in the
matter of corruption or purity I have beaten Philip.
In bribery, just as the purchaser has vanquished
the seller, whenever the bargain is struck, so
the man who refuses the price and remains in-

DEMOSTHENES

κηκε τὸν ὠνούμενον. ὥστ᾽ ἀήττητος ἡ πόλις τὸ κατ᾽ ἐμέ.

248 Ἃ μὲν τοίνυν ἐγὼ παρεσχόμην εἰς τὸ δικαίως τοιαῦτα γράφειν τουτονὶ περὶ ἐμοῦ, πρὸς πολλοῖς ἑτέροις ταῦτα καὶ παραπλήσια τούτοις ἐστίν· ἃ δ᾽ οἱ πάντες ὑμεῖς, ταῦτ᾽ ἤδη λέξω. μετὰ γὰρ τὴν μάχην εὐθὺς ὁ δῆμος, εἰδὼς καὶ ἑωρακὼς πάνθ᾽ ὅσ᾽ ἔπραττον ἐγώ, ἐν αὐτοῖς τοῖς δεινοῖς καὶ φοβεροῖς ἐμβεβηκώς, ἡνίκ᾽ οὐδ᾽ ἀγνωμονῆσαί τι θαυμαστὸν ἦν τοὺς πολλοὺς πρὸς ἐμέ, πρῶτον μὲν περὶ σωτηρίας τῆς πόλεως τὰς ἐμὰς γνώμας ἐχειροτόνει, καὶ πάνθ᾽ ὅσα τῆς φυλακῆς ἕνεκ᾽ ἐπράττετο, ἡ διάταξις

[310] τῶν φυλάκων, αἱ τάφροι, τὰ εἰς τὰ τείχη χρήματα, διὰ τῶν ἐμῶν ψηφισμάτων ἐγίγνετο· ἔπειθ᾽ αἱρούμενος σιτώνην ἐκ πάντων ἔμ᾽ ἐχειροτόνησεν ὁ δῆμος.

249 καὶ μετὰ ταῦτα συστάντων οἷς ἦν ἐπιμελὲς κακῶς ἐμὲ ποιεῖν, καὶ γραφάς, εὐθύνας, εἰσαγγελίας, πάντα ταῦτ᾽ ἐπαγόντων μοι, οὐ δι᾽ ἑαυτῶν τό γε πρῶτον, ἀλλὰ δι᾽ ὧν μάλισθ᾽ ὑπελάμβανον ἀγνοήσεσθαι (ἴστε γὰρ δήπου καὶ μέμνησθ᾽ ὅτι τοὺς πρώτους χρόνους κατὰ τὴν ἡμέραν ἑκάστην ἐκρινόμην ἐγώ, καὶ οὔτ᾽ ἀπόνοια Σωσικλέους, οὔτε συκοφαντία Φιλοκράτους, οὔτε Διώνδου καὶ Μελάντου μανία, οὔτ᾽ ἄλλ᾽ οὐδὲν ἀπείρατον ἦν τούτοις κατ᾽ ἐμοῦ), ἐν τοίνυν τούτοις πᾶσι μάλιστα μὲν διὰ τοὺς θεούς, δεύτερον δὲ δι᾽ ὑμᾶς καὶ τοὺς ἄλλους Ἀθηναίους ἐσῳζόμην. δικαίως· τοῦτο γὰρ καὶ ἀληθές ἐστι καὶ ὑπὲρ τῶν

250 ὀμωμοκότων καὶ γνόντων τὰ εὔορκα δικαστῶν. οὐκοῦν ἐν μὲν οἷς εἰσηγγελλόμην, ὅτ᾽ ἀπεψηφίζεσθέ μου καὶ τὸ μέρος τῶν ψήφων τοῖς διώκουσιν οὐ μετ-

182

corruptible has vanquished the purchaser. Therefore, in my person, Athens is undefeated.

These, and such as these, with many others are the grounds furnished by my conduct to justify the proposal of the defendant. I will now mention grounds furnished by all of you. Immediately after the battle, in the very midst of danger and alarm, at a time when it would not have been surprising if most of you had treated me unkindly, the people, with a full knowledge of all my doings, in the first place, adopted by vote my proposals for the safety of the city. All those measures of defence—the disposition of outposts, the entrenchments, the expenditure on the fortifications — were taken on resolutions moved by me. In the second place, they appointed me Food Controller, selecting me from the whole body of citizens. Then the men who made it their business to injure me formed a cabal, and set in motion all the machinery of indictments, audits, impeachments, and the like—not at first by their own agency, but employing persons by whom they imagined they would be screened. You will remember how, during that early period, I was put on my trial every day ; and how the recklessness of Sosicles, and the spite of Philocrates, and the frenzy of Diondas and Melantus, and everything else, were turned to account by them for my detriment. Nevertheless, by the favour, first of the gods, and secondly of you and the rest of the Athenians, I came through unscathed. And so I deserved. Yes ; that is true, and to the credit of juries that had taken the oath and gave judgement according to their oath. When, on my impeachment, you acquitted me, and did not give the prosecutors the fifth part of your votes,

ἐδίδοτε, τότ᾽ ἐψηφίζεσθε τἄριστά με πράττειν· ἐν
οἷς δὲ τὰς γραφὰς ἀπέφευγον, ἔννομα καὶ γράφειν
καὶ λέγειν ἀπεδεικνύμην· ἐν οἷς δὲ τὰς εὐθύνας ἐπ-
εσημαίνεσθε, δικαίως καὶ ἀδωροδοκήτως πάντα πε-
πρᾶχθαί μοι προσομολογεῖτε. τούτων οὖν οὕτως
ἐχόντων, τί προσῆκεν ἢ τί δίκαιον ἦν τοῖς ὑπ᾽ ἐμοῦ
πεπραγμένοις θέσθαι τὸν Κτησιφῶντ᾽ ὄνομα; οὐχ
ὃ τὸν δῆμον ἑώρα τιθέμενον, οὐχ ὃ τοὺς ὀμωμοκότας
δικαστάς, οὐχ ὃ τὴν ἀλήθειαν παρὰ πᾶσιν βεβαι-
οῦσαν;

251 Ναί, φησίν, ἀλλὰ τὸ τοῦ Κεφάλου καλόν, τὸ μηδεμίαν γραφὴν φυγεῖν. καὶ νὴ Δι᾽ εὔδαιμόν γε.
[311] ἀλλὰ τί μᾶλλον ὁ πολλάκις μὲν φυγών, μηδεπώποτε
δ᾽ ἐξελεγχθεὶς ἀδικῶν, ἐν ἐγκλήματι γίγνοιτ᾽ ἂν διὰ
τοῦτο δικαίως; καίτοι πρός γε τοῦτον, ἄνδρες
Ἀθηναῖοι, καὶ τὸ τοῦ Κεφάλου καλὸν εἰπεῖν ἔστι
μοι. οὐδεμίαν γὰρ πώποτ᾽ ἐγράψατό μ᾽ οὐδ᾽
ἐδίωξεν γραφήν, ὥσθ᾽ ὑπὸ σοῦ γ᾽ ὡμολόγημαι
μηδὲν εἶναι τοῦ Κεφάλου χείρων πολίτης.

252 Πανταχόθεν μὲν τοίνυν ἄν τις ἴδοι τὴν ἀγνωμο-
σύνην αὐτοῦ καὶ τὴν βασκανίαν, οὐχ ἥκιστα δ᾽ ἀφ᾽
ὧν περὶ τῆς τύχης διελέχθη. ἐγὼ δ᾽ ὅλως μέν,
ὅστις ἄνθρωπος ὢν ἀνθρώπῳ τύχην προφέρει,
ἀνόητον ἡγοῦμαι· ἣν γὰρ ὁ βέλτιστα πράττειν
νομίζων καὶ ἀρίστην ἔχειν οἰόμενος οὐκ οἶδεν εἰ
μενεῖ τοιαύτη μέχρι τῆς ἑσπέρας, πῶς χρὴ περὶ
ταύτης λέγειν ἢ πῶς ὀνειδίζειν ἑτέρῳ; ἐπειδὴ δ᾽
οὗτος πρὸς πολλοῖς ἄλλοις καὶ περὶ τούτων ὑπερ-
ηφάνως χρῆται τῷ λόγῳ, σκέψασθ᾽, ὦ ἄνδρες
Ἀθηναῖοι, καὶ θεωρήσατε ὅσῳ καὶ ἀληθέστερον
καὶ ἀνθρωπινώτερον ἐγὼ περὶ τῆς τύχης τούτου δια-
253 λεχθήσομαι. ἐγὼ τὴν τῆς πόλεως τύχην ἀγαθὴν

your verdict implied approval of my policy. When I was indicted, I satisfied you that my proposals and my speeches had been constitutional. When you put the seal on my accounts, you further admitted that I had done my business honestly and without corruption. That being so, what description could Ctesiphon properly and honestly have applied to my conduct, other than that which he had seen applied by the whole nation and by sworn juries, and confirmed by the truth in the eyes of all men?

Ah, says he, but look at that glorious boast of Cephalus—never once indicted! Yes, glorious, and also lucky. But why should a man who has been often indicted but never convicted be the more justly open to reproach? However, men of Athens, so far as Aeschines is concerned, I can repeat that glorious boast: for he never indicted me or prosecuted me on indictment; and so, by his own admission, I am no worse a citizen than Cephalus.

At every point his morose and spiteful temper is conspicuous, and especially in what he said about fortune. As a general remark, I must say that it is a stupid thing for any human being to reproach his brother man on the score of fortune. Seeing that a man who thinks he is doing very well and regards himself as highly fortunate, is never certain that his good fortune will last till the evening, how can it be right to boast about it, or use it to insult other people? But, since Aeschines has treated this topic, like many others, so vaingloriously, I beg you to observe, men of Athens, that my discourse on fortune will be more veracious, and more suitable to a mere man, than his. I attribute good fortune to

ἡγοῦμαι, καὶ ταῦθ' ὁρῶ καὶ τὸν Δία τὸν Δωδωναῖον
ὑμῖν μαντευόμενον, τὴν μέντοι τῶν πάντων ἀνθρώπων, ἢ νῦν ἐπέχει, χαλεπὴν καὶ δεινήν· τίς γὰρ
Ἑλλήνων ἢ τίς βαρβάρων οὐ πολλῶν κακῶν ἐν τῷ
254 παρόντι πεπείραται; τὸ μὲν τοίνυν προελέσθαι τὰ
κάλλιστα καὶ τὸ τῶν οἰηθέντων Ἑλλήνων, εἰ πρό-
οινθ' ἡμᾶς, ἐν εὐδαιμονίᾳ διάξειν, αὐτῶν ἄμεινον
πράττειν, τῆς ἀγαθῆς τύχης τῆς πόλεως εἶναι τίθημι·
[312] τὸ δὲ προσκροῦσαι καὶ μὴ πάνθ' ὡς ἐβουλόμεθ'
ἡμῖν συμβῆναι, τῆς τῶν ἄλλων ἀνθρώπων τύχης
τὸ ἐπιβάλλον ἐφ' ἡμᾶς μέρος μετειληφέναι νομίζω
255 τὴν πόλιν. τὴν δ' ἰδίαν τύχην τὴν ἐμὴν καὶ
τὴν ἑνὸς ἡμῶν ἑκάστου ἐν τοῖς ἰδίοις ἐξετάζειν
δίκαιον εἶναι νομίζω. ἐγὼ μὲν οὑτωσὶ περὶ τῆς
τύχης ἀξιῶ, ὀρθῶς καὶ δικαίως, ὡς ἐμαυτῷ δοκῶ,
νομίζω δὲ καὶ ὑμῖν· ὁ δὲ τὴν ἰδίαν τύχην τὴν ἐμὴν
τῆς κοινῆς τῆς πόλεως κυριωτέραν εἶναί φησι, τὴν
μικρὰν καὶ φαύλην τῆς ἀγαθῆς καὶ μεγάλης. καὶ
πῶς ἔνι τοῦτο γενέσθαι;

256 Καὶ μὴν εἴ γε τὴν ἐμὴν τύχην πάντως ἐξετάζειν,
Αἰσχίνη, προαιρεῖ, πρὸς τὴν σαυτοῦ σκόπει, κἂν
εὕρῃς τὴν ἐμὴν βελτίω τῆς σῆς, παῦσαι λοιδορούμενος αὐτῇ. σκόπει τοίνυν εὐθὺς ἐξ ἀρχῆς. καί
μου πρὸς Διὸς μηδεμίαν ψυχρότητα καταγνῷ μηδείς.
ἐγὼ γὰρ οὔτ' εἴ τις πενίαν προπηλακίζει νοῦν ἔχειν
ἡγοῦμαι, οὔτ' εἴ τις ἐν ἀφθόνοις τραφεὶς ἐπὶ τούτῳ
σεμνύνεται· ἀλλ' ὑπὸ τῆς τουτουὶ τοῦ χαλεποῦ
βλασφημίας καὶ συκοφαντίας εἰς τοιούτους λόγους
ἐμπίπτειν ἀναγκάζομαι, οἷς ἐκ τῶν ἐνόντων ὡς ἂν
δύνωμαι μετριώτατα χρήσομαι.

257 Ἐμοὶ μὲν τοίνυν ὑπῆρξεν, Αἰσχίνη, παιδὶ μὲν
ὄντι φοιτᾶν εἰς τὰ προσήκοντα διδασκαλεῖα, καὶ
186

our city, and so, I observe, does the oracle of Zeus at Dodona ; but the present fortune of all mankind I account grievous and distressing. Is there a man living, Greek or barbarian, who has not in these days undergone many evils ? I reckon it as part of the good fortune of Athens that she has chosen the noblest policy, and that she is better off than the Greeks who expected prosperity from their betrayal of us. If she has been unsuccessful, if everything has not fallen out as we desired, I regard that as our appointed share in the general ill-fortune of mankind. My personal fortune, or that of any man among you, must, I imagine, be estimated in the light of his private circumstances. That is my view of fortune : a just and correct view, as it seems to me, and, I think, also to you. But he declares that a poor, insignificant thing like my individual fortune has been more powerful than the great and good fortune of Athens. Now how is that possible ?

If, Aeschines, you are determined at all costs to investigate my fortune, compare it with your own ; and, should you find mine to be better than yours, stop your vilification. Begin your inquiry then at the beginning. And I beg earnestly that no one will blame me for want of generosity. No sensible man, in my judgement, ever turns poverty into a reproach, or prides himself on having been nurtured in affluence. But I am compelled by this troublesome man's scurrility and backbiting to deal with these topics ; and I will treat them with as much modesty as the state of the case permits.

In my boyhood, Aeschines, I had the advantage of attending respectable schools : and my means

DEMOSTHENES

ἔχειν ὅσα χρὴ τὸν μηδὲν αἰσχρὸν ποιήσοντα δι᾽
ἔνδειαν, ἐξελθόντι δ᾽ ἐκ παίδων ἀκόλουθα τούτοις
πράττειν, χορηγεῖν, τριηραρχεῖν, εἰσφέρειν, μηδεμιᾶς φιλοτιμίας μήτ᾽ ἰδίας μήτε δημοσίας ἀπολεί-
πεσθαι, ἀλλὰ καὶ τῇ πόλει καὶ τοῖς φίλοις χρήσιμον
εἶναι, ἐπειδὴ δὲ πρὸς τὰ κοινὰ προσελθεῖν ἔδοξέ μοι,
[313] τοιαῦτα πολιτεύμαθ᾽ ἑλέσθαι ὥστε καὶ ὑπὸ τῆς
πατρίδος καὶ ὑπ᾽ ἄλλων Ἑλλήνων πολλῶν πολλάκις
ἐστεφανῶσθαι, καὶ μηδὲ τοὺς ἐχθροὺς ὑμᾶς, ὡς οὐ
258 καλά γ᾽ ἦν ἃ προειλόμην, ἐπιχειρεῖν λέγειν. ἐγὼ
μὲν δὴ τοιαύτῃ συμβεβίωκα τύχῃ, καὶ πόλλ᾽ ἂν ἔχων
ἕτερ᾽ εἰπεῖν περὶ αὐτῆς παραλείπω, φυλαττόμενος
τὸ λυπῆσαί τιν᾽ ἐν οἷς σεμνύνομαι.

Σὺ δ᾽ ὁ σεμνὸς ἀνὴρ καὶ διαπτύων τοὺς ἄλλους,
σκόπει πρὸς ταύτην ποίᾳ τινὶ κέχρησαι τύχῃ, δι᾽ ἣν
παῖς μὲν ὢν μετὰ πολλῆς ἐνδείας ἐτράφης, ἅμα τῷ
πατρὶ πρὸς τῷ διδασκαλείῳ προσεδρεύων, τὸ μέλαν
τρίβων καὶ τὰ βάθρα σπογγίζων καὶ τὸ παιδα-
γωγεῖον κορῶν, οἰκέτου τάξιν, οὐκ ἐλευθέρου παιδὸς
259 ἔχων, ἀνὴρ δὲ γενόμενος τῇ μητρὶ τελούσῃ τὰς
βίβλους ἀνεγίγνωσκες καὶ τἄλλα συνεσκευωροῦ, τὴν
μὲν νύκτα νεβρίζων καὶ κρατηρίζων καὶ καθαίρων
τοὺς τελουμένους κἀπομάττων τῷ πηλῷ καὶ τοῖς
πιτύροις, καὶ ἀνιστὰς ἀπὸ τοῦ καθαρμοῦ κελεύων
λέγειν '' ἔφυγον κακόν, εὗρον ἄμεινον,'' ἐπὶ τῷ μη-

---

[a] *in her initiations*: she was an expert in Bacchic or
Sabazian rites imported from Phrygia.

were sufficient for one who was not to be driven by poverty into disreputable occupations. When I had come of age, my circumstances were in accordance with my upbringing. I was in a position to provide a chorus, to pay for a war-galley, and to be assessed to property-tax. I renounced no honourable ambition either in public or in private life : and rendered good service both to the commonwealth and to my own friends. When I decided to take part in public affairs, the political services I chose were such that I was repeatedly decorated both by my own country and by many other Grecian cities ; and even my enemies, such as you, never ventured to say that my choice was other than honourable. Such has been my fortune throughout my career. I could tell you more, but I forbear, fearing to weary you with details in which I take some pride.

But do you—you who are so proud and so contemptuous of others—compare your fortune with mine. In your childhood you were reared in abject poverty. You helped your father in the drudgery of a grammar-school, grinding the ink, sponging the benches, and sweeping the school-room, holding the position of a menial, not of a free-born boy. On arriving at manhood you assisted your mother in her initiations,[a] reading the service-book while she performed the ritual, and helping generally with the paraphernalia. At night it was your duty to mix the libations, to clothe the catechumens in fawn-skins, to wash their bodies, to scour them with the loam and the bran, and, when their lustration was duly performed, to set them on their legs, and give out the hymn :

> Here I leave my sins behind,
> Here the better way I find ;

DEMOSTHENES

δένα πώποτε τηλικοῦτ᾽ ὀλολύξαι σεμνυνόμενος (καὶ
ἔγωγε νομίζω· μὴ γὰρ οἴεσθ᾽ αὐτὸν φθέγγεσθαι
260 μὲν οὕτω μέγα, ὀλολύζειν δ᾽ οὐχ ὑπέρλαμπρον), ἐν
δὲ ταῖς ἡμέραις τοὺς καλοὺς θιάσους ἄγων διὰ τῶν
ὁδῶν, τοὺς ἐστεφανωμένους τῷ μαράθῳ καὶ τῇ
λεύκῃ, τοὺς ὄφεις τοὺς παρείας θλίβων καὶ ὑπὲρ τῆς
κεφαλῆς αἰωρῶν, καὶ βοῶν εὐοῖ σαβοῖ, καὶ ἐπορχού-
μενος ὑῆς ἄττης ἄττης ὑῆς, ἔξαρχος καὶ προηγεμὼν
καὶ κιττοφόρος καὶ λικνοφόρος καὶ τοιαῦθ᾽ ὑπὸ τῶν
[314] γρᾳδίων προσαγορευόμενος, μισθὸν λαμβάνων τούτων ἔνθρυπτα καὶ στρεπτοὺς καὶ νεήλατα, ἐφ᾽ οἷς
τίς οὐκ ἂν ὡς ἀληθῶς αὑτὸν εὐδαιμονίσειε καὶ τὴν
αὑτοῦ τύχην;
261   Ἐπειδὴ δ᾽ εἰς τοὺς δημότας ἐνεγράφης ὁπωσδή-
ποτε, ἐῶ γὰρ τοῦτ᾽, ἐπειδὴ δ᾽οὖν ἐνεγράφης, εὐθέως
τὸ κάλλιστον ἐξελέξω τῶν ἔργων, γραμματεύειν καὶ
ὑπηρετεῖν τοῖς ἀρχιδίοις. ὡς δ᾽ ἀπηλλάγης ποτὲ
καὶ τούτου, πάνθ᾽ ἃ τῶν ἄλλων κατηγορεῖς αὐτὸς
ποιήσας, οὐ κατῄσχυνας μὰ Δί᾽ οὐδὲν τῶν προϋπηρ-
262 μένων τῷ μετὰ ταῦτα βίῳ, ἀλλὰ μισθώσας σαυτὸν
τοῖς βαρυστόνοις ἐπικαλουμένοις ἐκείνοις ὑποκριταῖς
Σιμύλῳ καὶ Σωκράτει, ἐτριταγωνίστεις, σῦκα καὶ
βότρυς καὶ ἐλάας συλλέγων ὥσπερ ὀπωρώνης ἐκ τῶν
ἀλλοτρίων χωρίων, πλείω λαμβάνων ἀπὸ τούτων ἢ
τῶν ἀγώνων, οὓς ὑμεῖς περὶ τῆς ψυχῆς ἠγωνίζεσθε·
ἦν γὰρ ἄσπονδος καὶ ἀκήρυκτος ὑμῖν πρὸς τοὺς

190

and it was your pride that no one ever emitted that
holy ululation so powerfully as yourself. I can well
believe it ! When you hear the stentorian tones of
the orator, can you doubt that the ejaculations of
the acolyte were simply magnificent ? In day-time
you marshalled your gallant throng of bacchanals
through the public streets, their heads garlanded
with fennel and white poplar ; and, as you went,
you squeezed the fat-cheeked snakes, or brandished
them above your head, now shouting your *Euoi Saboi !*
now footing it to the measure of *Hyes Attes ! Attes
Hyes !*—saluted by all the old women with such
proud titles as Master of the Ceremonies, Fugleman,
Ivy-bearer, Fan-carrier ; and at last receiving
your recompense of tipsy-cakes, and cracknels, and
currant-buns. With such rewards who would not
rejoice greatly, and account himself the favourite of
fortune ?

After getting yourself enrolled on the register of
your parish—no one knows how you managed it ; but
let that pass—anyhow, when you were enrolled, you
promptly chose a most gentlemanly occupation, that
of clerk and errand-boy to minor officials. After committing all the offences with which you now reproach
other people, you were relieved of that employment ;
and I must say that your subsequent conduct did
no discredit to your earlier career. You entered the
service of those famous players Simylus and Socrates,
better known as the Growlers. You played small
parts to their lead, picking up figs and grapes and
olives, like an orchard-robbing costermonger, and
making a better living out of those missiles than by
all the battles that you fought for dear life. For
there was no truce or armistice in the warfare be-

DEMOSTHENES

θεατὰς πόλεμος, ὑφ' ὧν πολλὰ τραύματ' εἰληφὼς
εἰκότως τοὺς ἀπείρους τῶν τοιούτων κινδύνων ὡς
δειλοὺς σκώπτεις.

263 Ἀλλὰ γὰρ παρεὶς ὧν τὴν πενίαν αἰτιάσαιτ' ἄν τις,
πρὸς αὐτὰ τὰ τοῦ τρόπου σου βαδιοῦμαι κατηγορήματα. τοιαύτην γὰρ εἵλου πολιτείαν, ἐπειδή ποτε
καὶ τοῦτ' ἐπῆλθέ σοι ποιῆσαι, δι' ἣν εὐτυχούσης μὲν
τῆς πατρίδος λαγὼ βίον ἔζης δεδιὼς καὶ τρέμων καὶ
ἀεὶ πληγήσεσθαι προσδοκῶν ἐφ' οἷς σαυτῷ συνῄδεις
ἀδικοῦντι, ἐν οἷς δ' ἠτύχησαν οἱ ἄλλοι, θρασὺς ὢν
264 ὑφ' ἁπάντων ὦψαι. καίτοι ὅστις χιλίων πολιτῶν
ἀποθανόντων ἐθάρρησε, τί οὗτος παθεῖν ὑπὸ τῶν
ζώντων δίκαιός ἐστιν; πολλὰ τοίνυν ἕτερ' εἰπεῖν
[315] ἔχων περὶ αὐτοῦ παραλείψω· οὐ γὰρ ὅσ' ἂν δείξαιμι
προσόντ' αἰσχρὰ τούτῳ καὶ ὀνείδη, πάντ' οἶμαι δεῖν
εὐχερῶς λέγειν, ἀλλ' ὅσα μηδὲν αἰσχρόν ἐστιν εἰπεῖν
ἐμοί.

265 Ἐξέτασον τοίνυν παρ' ἄλληλα τὰ σοὶ κἀμοὶ βεβιω-
μένα, πράως, μὴ πικρῶς, Αἰσχίνη· εἶτ' ἐρώτησον
τουτουσὶ τὴν ποτέρου τύχην ἂν ἕλοιθ' ἕκαστος
αὐτῶν. ἐδίδασκες γράμματα, ἐγὼ δ' ἐφοίτων.
ἐτέλεις, ἐγὼ δ' ἐτελούμην. ἐγραμμάτευες, ἐγὼ δ'
ἠκκλησίαζον. ἐτριταγωνίστεις, ἐγὼ δ' ἐθεώρουν.
ἐξέπιπτες, ἐγὼ δ' ἐσύριττον. ὑπὲρ τῶν ἐχθρῶν
266 πεπολίτευσαι πάντα, ἐγὼ δ' ὑπὲρ τῆς πατρίδος. ἐῶ
τἄλλα, ἀλλὰ νυνὶ τήμερον, ἐγὼ μὲν ὑπὲρ τοῦ στεφα-

192

tween you and your audiences, and your casualties were so heavy, that no wonder you taunt with cowardice those of us who have no experience of such engagements.

However, passing by things for which your poverty may be blamed, I will address myself to actual charges against your way of living. When in course of time it occurred to you to enter public life, you chose such a line of political action that, so long as the city prospered, you lived the life of a hare, in fear and trembling and constant expectation of a sound thrashing for the crimes that burdened your conscience : although, when every one else is in distress, your confidence is manifest to all men.[a] What treatment does a man, who recovered his high spirits on the death of a thousand of his fellow-citizens, deserve at the hands of the survivors ? I shall omit a great many other facts that I might relate ; for I do not think that I ought to recount glibly all his discreditable and infamous qualities, but only such as I may mention without discredit to myself.

And now, Aeschines, I beg you to examine in contrast, quietly and without acrimony, the incidents of our respective careers : and then ask the jury, man by man, whether they would choose for themselves your fortune or mine. You were an usher, I a pupil ; you were an acolyte, I a candidate ; you were clerk-at-the-table, I addressed the House ; you were a player, I a spectator ; you were cat-called, I hissed ; you have ever served our enemies, I have served my country. Much I pass by ; but on this very day, I am on proof for the honour of a crown, and

---

[a] Since the battle of Chaeronea.

νωθῆναι δοκιμάζομαι, τὸ δὲ μηδ' ὁτιοῦν ἀδικεῖν
ἀνωμολόγημαι, σοὶ δὲ συκοφάντῃ μὲν εἶναι δοκεῖν
ὑπάρχει, κινδυνεύεις δ' εἴτε δεῖ σ' ἔτι τοῦτο ποιεῖν,
εἴτ' ἤδη πεπαῦσθαι μὴ μεταλαβόντα τὸ πέμπτον
μέρος τῶν ψήφων. ἀγαθῇ γ', οὐχ ὁρᾷς; τύχῃ
συμβεβιωκώς, τῆς ἐμῆς κατηγορεῖς.

267 Φέρε δὴ καὶ τὰς τῶν λῃτουργιῶν μαρτυρίας ὧν
λελῃτούργηκα ὑμῖν ἀναγνῶ. παρ' ἃς παρανάγνωθι
καὶ σὺ τὰς ῥήσεις ἃς ἐλυμαίνου,

ἥκω νεκρῶν κευθμῶνα καὶ σκότου πύλας

καὶ

κακαγγελεῖν μὲν ἴσθι μὴ θέλοντά με,

καὶ

κακὸν κακῶς σε

μάλιστα μὲν οἱ θεοί, ἔπειθ' οὗτοι πάντες ἀπολέσειαν,
πονηρὸν ὄντα καὶ πολίτην καὶ τριταγωνιστήν.
λέγε τὰς μαρτυρίας.

MAΡΤΥΡΙΑΙ

268 Ἐν μὲν τοίνυν τοῖς πρὸς τὴν πόλιν τοιοῦτος· ἐν
δὲ τοῖς ἰδίοις εἰ μὴ πάντες ἴσθ' ὅτι κοινὸς καὶ φιλ-
[316] άνθρωπος καὶ τοῖς δεομένοις ἐπαρκῶν, σιωπῶ καὶ
οὐδὲν ἂν εἴποιμ' οὐδὲ παρασχοίμην περὶ τούτων
οὐδεμίαν μαρτυρίαν, οὔτ' εἴ τινας ἐκ τῶν πολεμίων
ἐλυσάμην, οὔτ' εἴ τισιν θυγατέρας συνεξέδωκα, οὔτε
269 τῶν τοιούτων οὐδέν. καὶ γὰρ οὕτω πως ὑπείληφα.
ἐγὼ νομίζω τὸν μὲν εὖ παθόντα δεῖν μεμνῆσθαι
πάντα τὸν χρόνον, τὸν δὲ ποιήσαντ' εὐθὺς ἐπιλελῆ-
σθαι, εἰ δεῖ τὸν μὲν χρηστοῦ, τὸν δὲ μὴ μικροψύχου
ποιεῖν ἔργον ἀνθρώπου. τὸ δὲ τὰς ἰδίας εὐεργεσίας
ὑπομιμνήσκειν καὶ λέγειν μικροῦ δεῖν ὅμοιόν ἐστιν
194

acknowledged to be guiltless ; you have already the
reputation of an informer, and the question at hazard
for you is, whether you are still to continue in that
trade, or be stopped for ever by getting less than your
quota of votes. And that is the good fortune enjoyed
by you, who denounce the shabbiness of mine !

Let me now read to you the testimony of the public
services I have rendered, and you shall read for
comparison some of the blank-verse you used to
make such a hash of :

From gates of gloom and dwellings of the dead,[a]

or,

Tidings of woe with heavy heart I bear,

or,

Oh cruel, cruel fate !

Such a fate may the gods first, and the jury afterwards, allot to you—for your citizenship is as worthless as your mummery. Read the depositions.

(*The Depositions are read*)

Such has been my character in public life. In
private life, if any of you are not aware that I have
been generous and courteous, and helpful to the distressed, I do not mention it. I will never say a
word, or tender any evidence about such matters as
the captives I have ransomed, or the dowries I have
helped to provide, or any such acts of charity. It
is a matter of principle with me. My view is that
the recipient of a benefit ought to remember it all
his life, but that the benefactor ought to put it out
of his mind at once, if the one is to behave decently,
and the other with magnanimity. To remind a man
of the good turns you have done to him is very much

[a] Eurip. *Hec.* 1. The other quotations are unknown.

τῷ ὀνειδίζειν. οὐ δὴ ποιήσω τοιοῦτον οὐδέν, οὐδὲ προαχθήσομαι, ἀλλ᾽ ὅπως ποθ᾽ ὑπείλημμαι περὶ τούτων, ἀρκεῖ μοι.

270 Βούλομαι δέ, τῶν ἰδίων ἀπαλλαγείς, ἔτι μικρὰ πρὸς ὑμᾶς εἰπεῖν περὶ τῶν κοινῶν. εἰ μὲν γὰρ ἔχεις, Αἰσχίνη, τῶν ὑπὸ τοῦτον τὸν ἥλιον εἰπεῖν ἀνθρώπων, ὅστις ἀθῷος τῆς Φιλίππου πρότερον καὶ νῦν τῆς Ἀλεξάνδρου δυναστείας γέγονεν, ἢ τῶν Ἑλλήνων ἢ τῶν βαρβάρων, ἔστω, συγχωρῶ τὴν ἐμὴν εἴτε τύχην εἴτε δυστυχίαν ὀνομάζειν βούλει

271 πάντων αἰτίαν γεγενῆσθαι. εἰ δὲ καὶ τῶν μηδε-πώποτ᾽ ἰδόντων ἐμὲ μηδὲ φωνὴν ἀκηκοότων ἐμοῦ πολλοὶ πολλὰ καὶ δεινὰ πεπόνθασι, μὴ μόνον κατ᾽ ἄνδρ᾽, ἀλλὰ καὶ πόλεις ὅλαι καὶ ἔθνη, πόσῳ δικαιότερον καὶ ἀληθέστερον τὴν ἁπάντων, ὡς ἔοικεν, ἀνθρώπων τύχην κοινὴν καὶ φοράν τινα πραγμάτων χαλεπὴν καὶ οὐχ οἵαν ἔδει τούτων αἰτίαν

272 ἡγεῖσθαι. σὺ τοίνυν ταῦτ᾽ ἀφεὶς ἐμὲ τὸν παρὰ τουτοισὶ πεπολιτευμένον αἰτιᾷ, καὶ ταῦτ᾽ εἰδὼς ὅτι,

[317] καὶ εἰ μὴ τὸ ὅλον, μέρος γ᾽ ἐπιβάλλει τῆς βλασφη-μίας ἅπασι, καὶ μάλιστα σοί. εἰ μὲν γὰρ ἐγὼ κατ᾽ ἐμαυτὸν αὐτοκράτωρ περὶ τῶν πραγμάτων ἐβουλευόμην, ἦν ἂν τοῖς ἄλλοις ῥήτορσιν ὑμῖν ἔμ᾽

273 αἰτιᾶσθαι· εἰ δὲ παρῆτε μὲν ἐν ταῖς ἐκκλησίαις ἁπάσαις, ἀεὶ δ᾽ ἐν κοινῷ τὸ συμφέρον ἡ πόλις προὐτίθει σκοπεῖν, πᾶσι δὲ ταῦτ᾽ ἐδόκει τότ᾽ ἄριστ᾽ εἶναι, καὶ μάλιστα σοί (οὐ γὰρ ἐπ᾽ εὐνοίᾳ γ᾽ ἐμοὶ παρεχώρεις ἐλπίδων καὶ ζήλου καὶ τιμῶν, ἃ πάντα προσῆν τοῖς τότε πραττομένοις ὑπ᾽ ἐμοῦ, ἀλλὰ τῆς ἀληθείας ἡττώμενος δηλονότι καὶ τῷ μηδὲν ἔχειν

196

like a reproach. Nothing shall induce me to do anything of the sort; but whatever be my reputation in that respect, I am content.

I have finished with private matters, but I have still some trifling remarks to offer on public affairs. If you, Aeschines, can name any human being, Greek or barbarian, on whom yonder sun shines, who has escaped all injury from the domination, first of Philip, and to-day of Alexander, so be it: I grant you that my fortune—or my misfortune, if you prefer the word—has been the cause of the whole trouble. But if many people, who have never set eyes on me or heard the sound of my voice, have been grievously afflicted—I do not mean as individuals, but whole cities and nations—I say it is vastly more honest and candid to attribute these calamities to the common fortune of mankind, or to some distressing and untoward current of events. Yet you dismiss those causes, and put the blame upon me, who only took part in politics by the side of my fellow-citizens here, although you must be conscious that a part, if not the whole, of your invective is addressed to all of them, and particularly to yourself. If I had held sole and despotic authority when I offered my counsels, it would have been open to you other orators to incriminate me : but inasmuch as you were present at every assembly, as the state proposed a discussion of policy in which every one might join, and as my measures were approved at the time by every one, and especially by you,—for it was in no friendly spirit that you allowed me to enjoy all the hopes and enthusiasm and credit that were attached to my policy, but obviously because truth was too strong for you, and because you had nothing better to

εἰπεῖν βέλτιον), πῶς οὐκ ἀδικεῖς καὶ δεινὰ ποιεῖς τούτοις νῦν ἐγκαλῶν, ὧν τότ᾽ οὐκ εἶχες λέγειν βελτίω;

274 Παρὰ μὲν τοίνυν τοῖς ἄλλοις ἔγωγ᾽ ὁρῶ πᾶσιν ἀνθρώποις διωρισμένα καὶ τεταγμένα πως τὰ τοιαῦτα. ἀδικεῖ τις ἑκών· ὀργὴν καὶ τιμωρίαν κατὰ τούτου. ἐξήμαρτέ τις ἄκων· συγγνώμην ἀντὶ τῆς τιμωρίας τούτῳ. οὔτ᾽ ἀδικῶν τις οὔτ᾽ ἐξαμαρτάνων, εἰς τὰ πᾶσιν δοκοῦντα συμφέρειν ἑαυτὸν δοὺς οὐ κατώρθωσεν μεθ᾽ ἁπάντων· οὐκ ὀνειδίζειν οὐδὲ λοιδορεῖσθαι τῷ τοιούτῳ δίκαιον,
275 ἀλλὰ συνάχθεσθαι. φανήσεται ταῦτα πάνθ᾽ οὕτως οὐ μόνον τοῖς νόμοις, ἀλλὰ καὶ ἡ φύσις αὐτὴ τοῖς ἀγράφοις νομίμοις καὶ τοῖς ἀνθρωπίνοις ἤθεσιν[1] διώρικεν. Αἰσχίνης τοίνυν τοσοῦτον ὑπερβέβληκεν ἅπαντας ἀνθρώπους ὠμότητι καὶ συκοφαντίᾳ, ὥστε καὶ ὧν αὐτὸς ὡς ἀτυχημάτων ἐμέμνητο, καὶ ταῦτ᾽ ἐμοῦ κατηγορεῖ.

276 Καὶ πρὸς τοῖς ἄλλοις, ὥσπερ αὐτὸς ἁπλῶς καὶ μετ᾽ εὐνοίας πάντας εἰρηκὼς τοὺς λόγους, φυλάτ-
[318] τειν ἐμὲ καὶ τηρεῖν ἐκέλευεν, ὅπως μὴ παρακρούσομαι μηδ᾽ ἐξαπατήσω, δεινὸν καὶ γόητα καὶ σοφιστὴν καὶ τὰ τοιαῦτ᾽ ὀνομάζων, ὡς ἐὰν πρότερός τις εἴπῃ τὰ προσόνθ᾽ ἑαυτῷ περὶ ἄλλου, καὶ δὴ ταῦθ᾽ οὕτως ἔχοντα, καὶ οὐκέτι τοὺς ἀκούοντας σκεψομένους τίς ποτ᾽ αὐτός ἐστιν ὁ ταῦτα λέγων. ἐγὼ δ᾽ οἶδ᾽ ὅτι γιγνώσκετε τοῦτον ἅπαντες, καὶ πολὺ τούτῳ
277 μᾶλλον ἢ ἐμοὶ νομίζετε ταῦτα προσεῖναι. κἀκεῖν᾽ εὖ οἶδ᾽ ὅτι τὴν ἐμὴν δεινότητα — ἔστω γάρ. καίτοι ἔγωγ᾽ ὁρῶ τῆς τῶν λεγόντων δυνάμεως τοὺς ἀκούοντας τὸ πλεῖστον κυρίους· ὡς γὰρ ἂν ὑμεῖς ἀποδέξησθε καὶ πρὸς ἕκαστον ἔχητ᾽ εὐνοίας, οὕτως

---

[1] ἤθεσι mss. : ἔθεσι Dind. : S omits.

suggest—it is most iniquitous and outrageous to stigmatize to-day measures which at the time you were unable to amend.

Among other people I find this sort of distinction universally observed.—A man has sinned wilfully : he is visited with resentment and punishment. He has erred unintentionally : pardon takes the place of punishment Suppose that he has committed no sin or error at all, but, having devoted himself to a project approved by all, has, in common with all, failed of success. In that case he does not deserve reproach or obloquy, but condolence. This distinction will be found not only embodied in our statutes, but laid down by nature herself in her unwritten laws and in the moral sense of the human race. Now Aeschines so far surpasses all mankind in savagery and malignity that he turns even misadventures, which he has himself cited as such, into crimes for which I am to be denounced.

To crown all—as though all his own speeches had been made in a disinterested and patriotic spirit— he bids you be on your guard against me, for fear I should mislead and deceive you, calling me an artful speaker, a mountebank, an impostor, and so forth. He seems to think that if a man can only get in the first blow with epithets that are really applicable to himself, they must be true, and the audience will make no reflexions on the character of the speaker. But I am sure you all know him well, and will regard those epithets as more appropriate to him than to me. I am also sure that my artful-ness—well, be it so ; although I notice that in general an audience controls the ability of a speaker, and that his reputation for wisdom depends upon

ὁ λέγων ἔδοξε φρονεῖν. εἰ δ' οὖν ἐστι καὶ παρ'
ἐμοί τις ἐμπειρία τοιαύτη, ταύτην μὲν εὑρήσετε
πάντες ἐν τοῖς κοινοῖς ἐξεταζομένην ὑπὲρ ὑμῶν ἀεὶ
καὶ οὐδαμοῦ καθ' ὑμῶν οὐδ' ἰδίᾳ, τὴν δὲ τούτου
τοὐναντίον, οὐ μόνον τῷ λέγειν ὑπὲρ τῶν ἐχθρῶν,
ἀλλὰ καὶ εἴ τις ἐλύπησέ τι τοῦτον ἢ προσέκρουσέ
που, κατὰ τούτων. οὐ γὰρ αὐτῇ δικαίως, οὐδ' ἐφ'
278 ἃ συμφέρει τῇ πόλει, χρῆται. οὔτε γὰρ τὴν ὀργὴν
οὔτε τὴν ἔχθραν οὔτ' ἄλλ' οὐδὲν τῶν τοιούτων τὸν
καλὸν κἀγαθὸν πολίτην δεῖ τοὺς ὑπὲρ τῶν κοινῶν
εἰσεληλυθότας δικαστὰς ἀξιοῦν αὑτῷ βεβαιοῦν, οὐδ'
ὑπὲρ τούτων εἰς ὑμᾶς εἰσιέναι, ἀλλὰ μάλιστα μὲν μὴ
ἔχειν ταῦτ' ἐν τῇ φύσει, εἰ δ' ἄρ' ἀνάγκη, πράως καὶ
μετρίως διακείμεν' ἔχειν. ἐν τίσιν οὖν σφοδρὸν
εἶναι τὸν πολιτευόμενον καὶ τὸν ῥήτορα δεῖ; ἐν οἷς
τῶν ὅλων τι κινδυνεύεται τῇ πόλει, καὶ ἐν οἷς πρὸς
τοὺς ἐναντίους ἐστὶ τῷ δήμῳ, ἐν τούτοις· ταῦτα γὰρ
279 γενναίου κἀγαθοῦ πολίτου. μηδενὸς δ' ἀδικήματος
[319] πώποτε δημοσίου, προσθήσω δὲ μηδ' ἰδίου, δίκην
ἀξιώσαντα λαβεῖν παρ' ἐμοῦ μήθ' ὑπὲρ τῆς πόλεως
μήθ' ὑπὲρ αὑτοῦ, στεφάνου καὶ ἐπαίνου κατηγορίαν
ἥκειν συνεσκευασμένον καὶ τοσουτουσὶ λόγους ἀν-
ηλωκέναι ἰδίας ἔχθρας καὶ φθόνου καὶ μικροψυ-
χίας ἐστὶ σημεῖον, οὐδενὸς χρηστοῦ. τὸ δὲ δὴ καὶ
τοὺς πρὸς ἔμ' αὐτὸν ἀγῶνας ἐάσαντα νῦν ἐπὶ τόνδ'
280 ἥκειν καὶ πᾶσαν ἔχει κακίαν. καί μοι δοκεῖς ἐκ
τούτων, Αἰσχίνη, λόγων ἐπίδειξίν τινα καὶ φων-
ασκίας βουλόμενος ποιήσασθαι τοῦτον προελέσθαι
τὸν ἀγῶνα, οὐκ ἀδικήματος οὐδενὸς λαβεῖν τιμωρίαν.

your acceptance and your discriminating favour. Be that as it may, if I do possess any skill in speaking, you will all find that that skill has always been exercised on public concerns and for your advantage, never on private occasions and to your detriment. On the other hand the ability of Aeschines is applied not only to speaking on behalf of your enemies, but to the detriment of anyone who has annoyed or quarrelled with him. He never uses it honestly or in the interests of the commonweal. No upright and honourable citizen must ever expect a jury impanelled in the public service to bolster up his own resentment or enmity or other passions, nor will he go to law to gratify them. If possible he will exclude them from his heart : if he cannot escape them, he will at least cherish them calmly and soberly. In what circumstances, then, ought a politician or an orator to be vehement ? When all our national interests are imperilled ; when the issue lies between the people and their adversaries. Then such is the part of a chivalrous and patriotic citizen. But for a man who never once sought to bring me to justice for any public, nor, I will add, for any private offence, whether for the city's sake or for his own, to come into court armed with a denunciation of a crown and of a vote of thanks, and to lavish such a wealth of eloquence on that plea, is a symptom of a peevish, jealous, small-minded, good-for-nothing disposition. And the exhibition of his turpitude is complete when he relinquishes his controversy with me, and directs the whole of his attack upon the defendant. It really makes me think, Aeschines, that you deliberately went to law, not to get satisfaction for any transgression, but to make a display of your oratory

201

DEMOSTHENES

ἔστι δ' οὐχ ὁ λόγος τοῦ ῥήτορος, Αἰσχίνη, τίμιον,
οὐδ' ὁ τόνος τῆς φωνῆς, ἀλλὰ τὸ ταὐτὰ προαιρεῖσθαι
τοῖς πολλοῖς καὶ τὸ τοὺς αὐτοὺς μισεῖν καὶ φιλεῖν
281 οὕσπερ ἂν ἡ πατρίς. ὁ γὰρ οὕτως ἔχων τὴν ψυχήν,
οὗτος ἐπ' εὐνοίᾳ πάντ' ἐρεῖ· ὁ δ' ἀφ' ὧν ἡ πόλις
προορᾶται τινα κίνδυνον ἑαυτῇ, τούτους θεραπεύων
οὐκ ἐπὶ τῆς αὐτῆς ὁρμεῖ τοῖς πολλοῖς, οὔκουν οὐδὲ
τῆς ἀσφαλείας τὴν αὐτὴν ἔχει προσδοκίαν. ἀλλ',
ὁρᾷς; ἐγώ· ταὐτὰ γὰρ συμφέρονθ' εἱλόμην τουτοισί,
282 καὶ οὐδὲν ἐξαίρετον οὐδ' ἴδιον πεποίημαι. ἆρ'
οὖν οὐδὲ σύ; καὶ πῶς; ὃς εὐθέως μετὰ τὴν μάχην
πρεσβευτὴς ἐπορεύου πρὸς Φίλιππον, ὃς ἦν τῶν ἐν
ἐκείνοις τοῖς χρόνοις συμφορῶν αἴτιος τῇ πατρίδι,
καὶ ταῦτ' ἀρνούμενος πάντα τὸν ἔμπροσθε χρόνον
ταύτην τὴν χρείαν, ὡς πάντες ἴσασιν. καίτοι τίς ὁ
τὴν πόλιν ἐξαπατῶν; οὐχ ὁ μὴ λέγων ἃ φρονεῖ;
τῷ δ' ὁ κῆρυξ καταρᾶται δικαίως; οὐ τῷ τοιούτῳ;
τί δὲ μεῖζον ἔχοι τις ἂν εἰπεῖν ἀδίκημα κατ' ἀνδρὸς
[320] ῥήτορος, ἢ εἰ μὴ ταὐτὰ φρονεῖ καὶ λέγει; σὺ τοίνυν
283 οὗτος εὑρέθης. εἶτα σὺ φθέγγει καὶ βλέπειν εἰς τὰ
τούτων πρόσωπα τολμᾷς; πότερ' οὐχ ἡγεῖ γιγνώσκειν αὐτοὺς ὅστις εἶ; ἢ τοσοῦτον ὕπνον καὶ λήθην
ἅπαντας ἔχειν ὥστ' οὐ μεμνῆσθαι τοὺς λόγους οὓς
ἐδημηγόρεις ἐν τῷ πολέμῳ, καταρώμενος καὶ
διομνύμενος μηδὲν εἶναι σοὶ καὶ Φιλίππῳ πρᾶγμα,
ἀλλ' ἐμὲ τὴν αἰτίαν σοι ταύτην ἐπάγειν τῆς ἰδίας
284 ἕνεκ' ἔχθρας, οὐκ οὖσαν ἀληθῆ; ὡς δ' ἀπηγ-
γέλθη τάχισθ' ἡ μάχη, οὐδὲν τούτων φροντίσας
εὐθέως ὡμολόγεις, καὶ προσεποιοῦ φιλίαν καὶ
202

and your vocal powers. But it is not the diction of
an orator, Aeschines, or the vigour of his voice that
has any value : it is supporting the policy of the
people, and having the same friends and the same
enemies as your country. With such a disposition,
a man's speeches will always be patriotic : but the
man who pays court to those from whom the state
apprehends danger to herself, is not riding at the
same anchor as the people, and therefore does not
look to the same quarter for his security. I do ;
mark that ! My purposes are my countrymen's
purposes ; I have no peculiar or personal end to
serve. Can you say the same ? No, indeed ! Why,
immediately after the battle you went on embassy
to visit Philip, the author of all the recent calamities
of your country, although hitherto you had notori-
ously declined that employment. And who is
the deceiver of his country ? Surely the man who
does not say what he thinks. For whom does the
marshal read the commination ? For him. What
graver crime can be charged to an orator than that
his thoughts and his words do not tally ? In that
crime you were detected ; and yet you still raise
your voice, and dare to look your fellow-citizens in
the face ! Do you imagine that they do not know
who you are ? that they are sunk in such slumber
and oblivion that they do not remember the har-
angues you made while the war was still going on,
when you protested with oaths and curses that you
had no dealings with Philip—that I had laid that
charge against you out of private malice, and that
it was not true ? But no sooner had the news of
the battle reached us than you ignored all your pro-
tests, and confessed, or rather claimed, that you

203

ξενίαν εἶναί σοι πρὸς αὐτόν, τῇ μισθαρνίᾳ ταῦτα
μετατιθέμενος τὰ ὀνόματα· ἐκ ποίας γὰρ ἴσης ἢ
δικαίας προφάσεως Αἰσχίνη τῷ Γλαυκοθέας τῆς
τυμπανιστρίας ξένος ἢ φίλος ἢ γνώριμος ἦν Φίλιππος; ἐγὼ μὲν οὐχ ὁρῶ, ἀλλ' ἐμισθώθης ἐπὶ
τῷ τὰ τουτωνὶ συμφέροντα διαφθείρειν. ἀλλ' ὅμως,
οὕτω φανερῶς αὐτὸς εἰλημμένος προδότης, καὶ κατὰ
σαυτοῦ μηνυτὴς ἐπὶ τοῖς συμβᾶσι γεγονώς, ἐμοὶ
λοιδορεῖ καὶ ὀνειδίζεις ταῦτα, ὧν πάντας μᾶλλον
αἰτίους εὑρήσεις.

285   Πολλὰ καὶ καλὰ καὶ μεγάλ' ἡ πόλις, Αἰσχίνη, καὶ
προείλετο καὶ κατώρθωσεν δι' ἐμοῦ, ὧν οὐκ ἡμνημό-
νησεν. σημεῖον δέ· χειροτονῶν γὰρ ὁ δῆμος τὸν
ἐροῦντ' ἐπὶ τοῖς τετελευτηκόσιν παρ' αὐτὰ τὰ συμβάντα, οὐ σ' ἐχειροτόνησε προβληθέντα, καίπερ
εὔφωνον ὄντα, οὐδὲ Δημάδην, ἄρτι πεποιηκότα τὴν
εἰρήνην, οὐδ' Ἡγήμονα, οὐδ' ἄλλον ὑμῶν οὐδένα,
ἀλλ' ἐμέ. καὶ παρελθόντος σοῦ καὶ Πυθοκλέους
[321] ὠμῶς καὶ ἀναιδῶς, ὦ Ζεῦ καὶ θεοί, καὶ κατηγορούν-
των ἐμοῦ ταῦθ' ἃ καὶ σὺ νυνί, καὶ λοιδορουμένων,
286 ἔτ' ἄμεινον ἐχειροτόνησεν ἐμέ. τὸ δ' αἴτιον οὐκ
ἀγνοεῖς μέν, ὅμως δὲ φράσω σοι κἀγώ. ἀμφότερ'
ᾔδεσαν αὐτοί, τήν τ' ἐμὴν εὔνοιαν καὶ προθυμίαν μεθ'
ἧς τὰ πράγματ' ἔπραττον, καὶ τὴν ὑμετέραν ἀδικίαν·
ἃ γὰρ εὐθενούντων τῶν πραγμάτων ἠρνεῖσθε δι-
ομνύμενοι, ταῦτ' ἐν οἷς ἔπταισεν ἡ πόλις ὡμολογή-
σατε. τοὺς οὖν ἐπὶ τοῖς κοινοῖς ἀτυχήμασιν ὧν

were Philip's friend and Philip's guest—a euphemism for Philip's hired servant ; for with what show of equality or honesty could Philip possibly be the host or the friend or even the acquaintance of Aeschines, son of Glaucothea the tambourinist ? I cannot see : but the truth is, you took his pay to injure the interests of your countrymen. And yet you, a traitor publicly convicted on information laid by yourself after the fact, vilify and reproach me for misfortunes for which you will find I am less responsible than any other man.

Our city owes to me, Aeschines, both the inception and the success of many great and noble enterprises ; nor was she unmindful. It is a proof of her gratitude that, when the people wanted one who should speak over the bodies of the slain, shortly after the battle, you were nominated but they did not appoint you, in spite of your beautiful voice, nor Demades, although he had recently arranged the peace, nor Hegemon, nor any of your party : they appointed me. Then you came forward, and Pythocles with you—and, gracious Heavens ! how coarsely and impudently you spoke !—making the very same charges that you have repeated to-day ; but, for all your scurrility, they appointed me nevertheless. You know very well why ; but you shall hear the reason again from me. They were conscious both of the patriotism and energy with which I had conducted their business, and also of the dishonesty of you and your friends : for, when the city had made a false step, you had acknowledged relations which you had strenuously denied on oath in the days of prosperity. They conceived that men who found impunity for their ambitions in our national

ἐφρόνουν λαβόντας ἄδειαν ἐχθροὺς μὲν πάλαι,
287 φανεροὺς δὲ τόθ' ἡγήσανθ' αὑτοῖς γεγενῆσθαι. εἶτα
καὶ προσήκειν ὑπολαμβάνοντες τὸν ἐροῦντα ἐπὶ τοῖς
τετελευτηκόσι καὶ τὴν ἐκείνων ἀρετὴν κοσμήσοντα,
μήθ' ὁμωρόφιον μήθ' ὁμόσπονδον γεγενημένον εἶναι
τοῖς πρὸς ἐκείνους παραταξαμένοις, μηδ' ἐκεῖ μὲν
κωμάζειν καὶ παιωνίζειν ἐπὶ ταῖς τῶν Ἑλλήνων
συμφοραῖς μετὰ τῶν αὐτοχείρων τοῦ φόνου, δεῦρο δ'
ἐλθόντα τιμᾶσθαι, μηδὲ τῇ φωνῇ δακρύειν ὑποκρινό-
μενον τὴν ἐκείνων τύχην, ἀλλὰ τῇ ψυχῇ συναλγεῖν.
τοῦτο δ' ἑώρων παρ' ἑαυτοῖς καὶ παρ' ἐμοί, παρὰ δ'
ὑμῖν οὔ. διὰ ταῦτ' ἔμ' ἐχειροτόνησαν καὶ οὐχ ὑμᾶς.
288 καὶ οὐχ ὁ μὲν δῆμος οὕτως, οἱ δὲ τῶν τετελευτηκότων πατέρες καὶ ἀδελφοὶ οἱ ὑπὸ τοῦ δήμου τόθ'
αἱρεθέντες ἐπὶ τὰς ταφὰς ἄλλως πως, ἀλλὰ δέον
ποιεῖν αὐτοὺς τὸ περίδειπνον ὡς παρ' οἰκειοτάτῳ
τῶν τετελευτηκότων, ὥσπερ τἄλλ' εἴωθε γίγνεσθαι,
τοῦτ' ἐποίησαν παρ' ἐμοί. εἰκότως· γένει μὲν γὰρ
ἕκαστος ἑκάστῳ μᾶλλον οἰκεῖος ἦν ἐμοῦ, κοινῇ δὲ
πᾶσιν οὐδεὶς ἐγγυτέρω· ᾧ γὰρ ἐκείνους σωθῆναι
[322] καὶ κατορθῶσαι μάλιστα διέφερεν, οὗτος καὶ πα-
θόντων ἃ μήποτ' ὤφελον τῆς ὑπὲρ ἁπάντων λύπης
πλεῖστον μετεῖχεν.
289 Λέγε δ' αὐτῷ τουτὶ τὸ ἐπίγραμμα, ὃ δημοσίᾳ
προείλεθ' ἡ πόλις αὐτοῖς ἐπιγράψαι, ἵν' εἰδῇς,
Αἰσχίνη, καὶ ἐν αὐτῷ τούτῳ σαυτὸν ἀγνώμονα καὶ
συκοφάντην ὄντα καὶ μιαρόν. λέγε.

calamities had long been their secret, and were now their declared, enemies. They thought it becoming that the orator who should speak over the bodies of the slain, and magnify their prowess, should not be one who had visited the homes and shared the loving cup of their adversaries; that the man who in Macedonia had taken part with their murderers in revels and songs of exultation over the calamities of Greece, should not be chosen for high distinction at Athens; and that the chosen speaker should not lament their fate with the feigning voice of an actor, but express the mourning of his very soul. Such sympathy they discerned in themselves, and in me; but not in your party; and that is why they appointed me, and did not appoint you. The sentiments of the people were shared by those fathers and brothers of the dead who were chosen by the people to conduct the obsequies. In obedience to the custom that requires the funeral feast to be held in the home of the nearest relative of the dead, they ordered it to be held at my house; and with good reason. Each hero had some kinsman who by the ties of blood stood nearer to himself, but to the whole company of the fallen no man was nearer of kin than I. When they had met with their untimely fate, he who was most deeply concerned in their safety and their success, claimed the chief share in mourning for them all.

Read for his benefit the epitaph, which the state resolved by public vote to inscribe upon their monument. Even from these verses, Aeschines, you may learn something of your own callousness, and malignity, and brutality. Read.

DEMOSTHENES

ΕΠΙΓΡΑΜΜΑ

Οἵδε πάτρας ἕνεκα σφετέρας εἰς δῆριν ἔθεντο
ὅπλα, καὶ ἀντιπάλων ὕβριν ἀπεσκέδασαν·
μαρνάμενοι δ' ἀρετῆς καὶ δείματος οὐκ ἐσάωσαν
ψυχάς, ἀλλ' Ἀΐδην κοινὸν ἔθεντο βραβῆ,
οὕνεκεν Ἑλλήνων, ὡς μὴ ζυγὸν αὐχένι θέντες
δουλοσύνης στυγερὰν ἀμφὶς ἔχωσιν ὕβριν.
γαῖα δὲ πατρὶς ἔχει κόλποις τῶν πλεῖστα καμόντων
σώματ', ἐπεὶ θνητοῖς ἐκ Διὸς ἥδε κρίσις·
μηδὲν ἁμαρτεῖν ἐστι θεῶν καὶ πάντα κατορθοῦν,
ἐν βιοτῇ μοῖραν δ' οὔ τι φυγεῖν ἔπορεν.

290 ἀκούεις, Αἰσχίνη, καὶ ἐν αὐτῷ τούτῳ μηδὲν ἁμαρτεῖν ἐστι θεῶν καὶ πάντα κατορθοῦν; οὐ τῷ συμβούλῳ τὴν τοῦ κατορθοῦν τοὺς ἀγωνιζομένους ἀνέθηκε δύναμιν, ἀλλὰ τοῖς θεοῖς. τί οὖν, ὦ κατάρατ', ἐμοὶ περὶ τούτων λοιδορεῖ, καὶ λέγεις ἃ σοὶ καὶ τοῖς σοῖς οἱ θεοὶ τρέψειαν εἰς κεφαλήν;

291 Πολλὰ τοίνυν, ὦ ἄνδρες Ἀθηναῖοι, καὶ ἄλλα κατηγορηκότος αὐτοῦ καὶ κατεψευσμένου, μάλιστ' ἐθαύμασα πάντων, ὅτε τῶν συμβεβηκότων τότε τῇ πόλει μνησθείς, οὐχ ὡς ἂν εὔνους καὶ δίκαιος πολίτης

[323] ἔσχε τὴν γνώμην, οὐδ' ἐδάκρυσεν, οὐδ' ἔπαθε τοιοῦτον οὐδὲν τῇ ψυχῇ, ἀλλ' ἐπάρας τὴν φωνὴν καὶ γεγηθὼς καὶ λαρυγγίζων, ᾤετο μὲν ἐμοῦ κατηγορεῖν δηλονότι, δεῖγμα δ' ἐξέφερεν καθ' ἑαυτοῦ ὅτι τοῖς γεγενημένοις ἀνιαροῖς οὐδὲν ὁμοίως ἔσχε τοῖς

292 ἄλλοις. καίτοι τὸν τῶν νόμων καὶ τῆς πολιτείας φάσκοντα φροντίζειν, ὥσπερ οὗτος νυνί, καὶ εἰ μηδὲν ἄλλο, τοῦτό γ' ἔχειν δεῖ, ταὐτὰ λυπεῖσθαι καὶ ταὐτὰ χαίρειν τοῖς πολλοῖς, καὶ μὴ τῇ προαιρέσει τῶν κοινῶν ἐν τῷ τῶν ἐναντίων μέρει τετάχθαι· ὃ

Epitaph

> Here lie the brave, who for their country's right
> Drew sword, and put th' insulting foe to flight.
> Their lives they spared not, bidding Death decide
> Who flinched and lived, and who with courage died.
> They fought and fell that Greece might still be free,
> Nor crouch beneath the yoke of slavery.
> Zeus spoke the word of doom ; and now they rest
> Forspent with toil upon their country's breast.
> God errs not, fails not ; God alone is great ;
> But man lies helpless in the hands of fate.

Do you hear this admonition, that it is the gods alone who err not and fail not ? It attributes the power of giving success in battle not to the statesman, but to the gods. Accursed slanderer ! why do you revile me for their death ? Why do you utter words which I pray the gods to divert to the undoing of your children and yourself ?

Among all the slanders and lies which he launched against me, men of Athens, what amazed me most was that, when he recounted the disasters that befell our city at that time, his comments were never such as would have been made by an honest and loyal citizen. He shed no tears ; he had no emotion of regret in his heart ; he vociferated, he exulted, he strained his throat. He evidently supposed himself to be testifying against me, but he was really offering proof against himself that in all those distressing events he had had no feeling in common with other citizens. Yet a man who professes such solicitude, as he has professed to-day, for our laws and constitution, whatever else he lacks, ought at least to possess the quality of sympathizing both with the sorrows and the joys of the common people ; and, in choosing his political principles, he ought not to range himself

209

σὺ νυνὶ πεποιηκὼς εἶ φανερός, ἐμὲ πάντων αἴτιον
καὶ δι' ἔμ' εἰς πράγματα φάσκων ἐμπεσεῖν τὴν
πόλιν, οὐκ ἀπὸ τῆς ἐμῆς πολιτείας οὐδὲ προαιρέσεως
293 ἀρξαμένων ὑμῶν τοῖς "Ελλησι βοηθεῖν, ἐπεὶ ἔμοιγ'
εἰ τοῦτο δοθείη παρ' ὑμῶν, δι' ἔμ' ὑμᾶς ἠναντιῶσθαι
τῇ κατὰ τῶν Ἑλλήνων ἀρχῇ πραττομένῃ, μείζων ἂν
δοθείη δωρεὰ συμπασῶν ὧν τοῖς ἄλλοις δεδώκατε.
ἀλλ' οὔτ' ἂν ἐγὼ ταῦτα φήσαιμι (ἀδικοίην γὰρ ἂν
ὑμᾶς), οὔτ' ἂν ὑμεῖς εὖ οἶδ' ὅτι συγχωρήσαιτε·
οὗτός τ' εἰ δίκαι' ἐποίει, οὐκ ἂν ἕνεκα τῆς πρὸς ἔμ'
ἔχθρας τὰ μέγιστα τῶν ὑμετέρων καλῶν ἔβλαπτε
καὶ διέβαλλεν.

294 Ἀλλὰ τί ταῦτ' ἐπιτιμῶ, πολλῷ σχετλιώτερ' ἄλλα
κατηγορηκότος αὐτοῦ καὶ κατεψευσμένου; ὃς γὰρ
ἐμοῦ φιλιππισμόν, ὦ γῆ καὶ θεοί, κατηγορεῖ, τί
οὗτος οὐκ ἂν εἴποι; καίτοι, νὴ τὸν Ἡρακλέα καὶ
πάντας θεούς, εἴ γ' ἐπ' ἀληθείας δέοι σκοπεῖσθαι,
εἰ τὸ καταψεύδεσθαι καὶ δι' ἔχθραν τι λέγειν ἀνελόν-
τας ἐκ μέσου, τίνες ὡς ἀληθῶς εἰσὶν οἷς ἂν εἰκότως
καὶ δικαίως τὴν τῶν γεγενημένων αἰτίαν ἐπὶ τὴν
[324] κεφαλὴν ἀναθεῖεν ἅπαντες, τοὺς ὁμοίους τούτῳ παρ'
295 ἑκάστῃ τῶν πόλεων εὕροιτ' ἄν, οὐ τοὺς ἐμοί· οἵ, ὅτ'
ἦν ἀσθενῆ τὰ Φιλίππου πράγματα καὶ κομιδῇ μικρά,
πολλάκις προλεγόντων ἡμῶν καὶ παρακαλούντων
καὶ διδασκόντων τὰ βέλτιστα, τῆς ἰδίας ἕνεκ'
αἰσχροκερδίας τὰ κοινῇ συμφέροντα προΐεντο,
τοὺς ὑπάρχοντας ἕκαστοι πολίτας ἐξαπατῶντες καὶ
διαφθείροντες, ἕως δούλους ἐποίησαν, Θετταλοὺς
Δάοχος, Κινέας, Θρασύδαος· Ἀρκάδας Κερκιδᾶς,
210

with their enemies. But that is clearly what he has done, when he declares that I am responsible for everything, and that the city has fallen into trouble by my fault. Your policy of bearing succour to the Greeks did not originate in my statesmanship and my principles. If you were to acknowledge that my influence caused you to resist a despotism that threatened the ruin of Greece, you would bestow on me a favour greater than all the gifts you have ever conferred on anyone. I do not claim that favour ; I cannot claim it without injustice to you : and I am certain that you will not grant it. If Aeschines had acted an honest part, he would never have indulged his spite against me by impairing and defaming the noblest of your national glories.

But why reproach him for that imputation, when he has uttered calumnies of far greater audacity ? A man who accuses me of Philippism—Heaven and Earth, of what lie is he not capable ? I solemnly aver that, if we are to cast aside lying imputations and spiteful mendacity, and inquire in all sincerity who really are the men to whom the reproach of all that has befallen might by general consent be fairly and honestly brought home, you will find that they are men in the several cities who resemble Aeschines, and do not resemble me. At a time when Philip's resources were feeble and very small indeed, when we were constantly warning, exhorting, admonishing them for the best, these men flung away their national prosperity for private and selfish gain ; they cajoled and corrupted all the citizens within their grasp, until they had reduced them to slavery. So the Thessalians were treated by Daochus, Cineas, Thrasydaus, the Arcadians by Cercidas, Hieronymus,

211

Ἱερώνυμος, Εὐκαμπίδας· Ἀργείους Μύρτις, Τελέ-
δαμος, Μνασέας· Ἠλείους Εὐξίθεος, Κλεότιμος,
Ἀρίσταιχμος· Μεσσηνίους οἱ Φιλιάδου τοῦ θεοῖς
ἐχθροῦ παῖδες Νέων καὶ Θρασύλοχος· Σικυωνίους
Ἀρίστρατος, Ἐπιχάρης· Κορινθίους Δείναρχος,
Δημάρετος· Μεγαρέας Πτοιόδωρος, Ἕλιξος,
Περίλαος· Θηβαίους Τιμόλαος, Θεογείτων, Ἀνε-
μοίτας· Εὐβοέας Ἵππαρχος, Κλείταρχος, Σωσί-
296 στρατος. ἐπιλείψει με λέγονθ᾽ ἡ ἡμέρα τὰ τῶν
προδοτῶν ὀνόματα. οὗτοι πάντες εἰσίν, ἄνδρες
Ἀθηναῖοι, τῶν αὐτῶν βουλευμάτων ἐν ταῖς αὐτῶν
πατρίσιν ὧνπερ οὗτοι παρ᾽ ὑμῖν, ἄνθρωποι μιαροὶ
καὶ κόλακες καὶ ἀλάστορες, ἠκρωτηριασμένοι τὰς
ἑαυτῶν ἕκαστοι πατρίδας, τὴν ἐλευθερίαν προπε-
πωκότες πρότερον μὲν Φιλίππῳ, νῦν δ᾽ Ἀλεξάνδρῳ,
τῇ γαστρὶ μετροῦντες καὶ τοῖς αἰσχίστοις τὴν
εὐδαιμονίαν, τὴν δ᾽ ἐλευθερίαν καὶ τὸ μηδέν᾽ ἔχειν
δεσπότην αὐτῶν, ἃ τοῖς προτέροις Ἕλλησιν ὅροι τῶν
ἀγαθῶν ἦσαν καὶ κανόνες, ἀνατετροφότες.

297 Ταύτης τοίνυν τῆς οὕτως αἰσχρᾶς καὶ περιβοήτου
[325] συστάσεως καὶ κακίας, μᾶλλον δ᾽, ὦ ἄνδρες Ἀθηναῖοι, προδοσίας, εἰ δεῖ μὴ ληρεῖν, τῆς τῶν Ἑλλήνων
ἐλευθερίας ἥ τε πόλις παρὰ πᾶσιν ἀνθρώποις ἀν-
αίτιος γέγονεν ἐκ τῶν ἐμῶν πολιτευμάτων καὶ ἐγὼ
παρ᾽ ὑμῖν. εἶτά μ᾽ ἐρωτᾷς ἀντὶ ποίας ἀρετῆς ἀξιῶ
τιμᾶσθαι; ἐγὼ δέ σοι λέγω, ὅτι τῶν πολιτευομένων
παρὰ τοῖς Ἕλλησι διαφθαρέντων ἁπάντων, ἀρξαμένων ἀπὸ σοῦ, πρότερον μὲν ὑπὸ Φιλίππου, νῦν δ᾽
298 ὑπ᾽ Ἀλεξάνδρου, ἔμ᾽ οὔτε καιρὸς οὔτε φιλανθρωπία
λόγων οὔτ᾽ ἐπαγγελιῶν μέγεθος οὔτ᾽ ἐλπὶς οὔτε
φόβος, οὔτ᾽ ἄλλ᾽ οὐδὲν ἐπῆρεν οὐδὲ προηγάγετο, ὧν
ἔκρινα δικαίων καὶ συμφερόντων τῇ πατρίδι, οὐδὲν

Eucampidas, the Argives by Myrtis, Teledamus, Mnaseas, the Eleians by Euxitheus, Cleotimus, Aristaechmus, the Messenians by the sons of that god-forsaken Philiades, Neon and Thrasylochus, the Sicyonians by Aristratus and Epichares, the Corinthians by Deinarchus and Demaretus, the Megarians by Ptoeodorus, Helixus, Perilaus, the Thebans by Timolaus, Theogeiton, Anemoetas, the Euboeans by Hipparchus, Cleitarchus, and Sosistratus. I could continue this catalogue of traitors till the sun sets. Every one of them, men of Athens, is a man of the same way of thinking in the politics of his own country as Aeschines and his friends are in ours. They too are profligates, sycophants, fiends incarnate ; they have mutilated their own countries ; they have pledged away their liberty in their cups, first to Philip, and now to Alexander. They measure their happiness by their belly and their baser parts ; they have overthrown for ever that freedom and independence which to the Greeks of an earlier age were the very standard and canon of prosperity.

Of this disgraceful and notorious conspiracy, of this wickedness, or rather, men of Athens, if I am to speak without trifling, this betrayal of the liberties of Greece, you—thanks to my policy—are guiltless in the eyes of the world, as I am guiltless in your eyes. And then, Aeschines, you ask for what merit I claim distinction ! I tell you that, when all the politicians in Greece, starting with you, had been corrupted, first by Philip, and now by Alexander, neither opportunity, nor civil speeches, nor large promises, nor hope, nor fear, nor any other inducement, could provoke or suborn me to betray the just claims and the true interests of my country, as I conceived them ;

προδοῦναι, οὐδ᾽, ὅσα συμβεβούλευκα πώποτε τουτοισί, ὁμοίως ὑμῖν ὡσπερανεὶ τρυτάνη ῥέπων ἐπὶ
τὸ λῆμμα συμβεβούλευκα, ἀλλ᾽ ἀπ᾽ ὀρθῆς καὶ
δικαίας καὶ ἀδιαφθόρου τῆς ψυχῆς, καὶ μεγίστων δὴ
πραγμάτων τῶν κατ᾽ ἐμαυτὸν ἀνθρώπων προστὰς
299 πάντα ταῦθ᾽ ὑγιῶς καὶ δικαίως πεπολίτευμαι. διὰ
ταῦτ᾽ ἀξιῶ τιμᾶσθαι. τὸν δὲ τειχισμὸν τοῦτον ὃν
σύ μου διέσυρες, καὶ τὴν ταφρείαν ἄξια μὲν χάριτος
καὶ ἐπαίνου κρίνω, πῶς γὰρ οὔ; πόρρω μέντοι που
τῶν ἐμαυτῷ πεπολιτευμένων τίθεμαι. οὐ λίθοις
ἐτείχισα τὴν πόλιν οὐδὲ πλίνθοις ἐγώ, οὐδ᾽ ἐπὶ τούτοις μέγιστον τῶν ἐμαυτοῦ φρονῶ· ἀλλ᾽ ἐὰν τὸν
ἐμὸν τειχισμὸν βούλῃ δικαίως σκοπεῖν, εὑρήσεις
ὅπλα καὶ πόλεις καὶ τόπους, καὶ λιμένας καὶ ναῦς
καὶ ἵππους καὶ πολλοὺς τοὺς ὑπὲρ τούτων ἀμυνουμέ-
300 νους. ταῦτα προὐβαλόμην ἐγὼ πρὸ τῆς Ἀττικῆς,
ὅσον ἦν ἀνθρωπίνῳ λογισμῷ δυνατόν, καὶ τούτοις
ἐτείχισα τὴν χώραν, οὐχὶ τὸν κύκλον τοῦ Πειραιῶς
[326] οὐδὲ τοῦ ἄστεως. οὐδέ γ᾽ ἡττήθην ἐγὼ τοῖς
λογισμοῖς Φιλίππου, πολλοῦ γε καὶ δεῖ, οὐδὲ ταῖς
παρασκευαῖς, ἀλλ᾽ οἱ τῶν συμμάχων στρατηγοὶ καὶ
δυνάμεις τῇ τύχῃ. τίνες αἱ τούτων ἀποδείξεις; αἱ
ἐναργεῖς καὶ φανεραί. σκοπεῖτε δέ.

301 Τί χρῆν τὸν εὔνουν πολίτην ποιεῖν, τί τὸν μετὰ
πάσης προνοίας καὶ προθυμίας καὶ δικαιοσύνης ὑπὲρ
τῆς πατρίδος πολιτευόμενον; οὐκ ἐκ μὲν θαλάττης
τὴν Εὔβοιαν προβαλέσθαι πρὸ τῆς Ἀττικῆς, ἐκ δὲ
τῆς μεσογείας τὴν Βοιωτίαν, ἐκ δὲ τῶν πρὸς
Πελοπόννησον τόπων τοὺς ὁμόρους ταύτῃ; οὐ τὴν

and that, whatever counsels I have offered to my fellow-citizens here, I have not offered, like you, as if I were a false balance with a bias in favour of the vendor. With a soul upright, honest and incorruptible, appointed to the control of more momentous transactions than any statesman of my time, I have administered them throughout in all purity and righteousness. On those grounds I claim this distinction. As for my fortifications, which you treated so satirically, and my entrenchments, I do, and I must, judge these things worthy of gratitude and thanks ; but I give them a place far removed from my political achievements. I did not fortify Athens with masonry and brickwork : they are not the works on which I chiefly pride myself. Regard my fortifications as you ought, and you will find armies and cities and outposts, seaports and ships and horses, and a multitude ready to fight for their defence. These were the bastions I planted for the protection of Attica so far as it was possible to human forethought ; and therewith I fortified, not the ring-fence of our port and our citadel, but the whole country. Nor was I beaten by Philip in forethought or in armaments ; that is far from the truth. The generals and the forces of the allies were beaten by his good fortune. Have I any proofs of my claim ? Yes, proofs definite and manifest. I ask you all to consider them.

What course of action was proper for a patriotic citizen who was trying to serve his country with all possible prudence and energy and loyalty ? Surely it was to protect Attica on the sea-board by Euboea, on the inland frontier by Boeotia, and on the side towards Peloponnesus by our neighbours in that

σιτοπομπίαν, ὅπως παρὰ πᾶσαν φιλίαν ἄχρι τοῦ
302 Πειραιῶς κομισθήσεται, προϊδέσθαι; καὶ τὰ μὲν
σῶσαι τῶν ὑπαρχόντων ἐκπέμποντα βοηθείας καὶ
λέγοντα καὶ γράφοντα τοιαῦτα, τὴν Προκόννησον,
τὴν Χερρόνησον, τὴν Τένεδον, τὰ δ' ὅπως οἰκεῖα καὶ
σύμμαχ' ὑπάρξει πρᾶξαι, τὸ Βυζάντιον, τὴν Ἄβυδον,
τὴν Εὔβοιαν; καὶ τῶν μὲν τοῖς ἐχθροῖς ὑπαρχουσῶν
δυνάμεων τὰς μεγίστας ἀφελεῖν, ὧν δ' ἐνέλειπε τῇ
πόλει, ταῦτα προσθεῖναι; ταῦτα τοίνυν ἅπαντα
πέπρακται τοῖς ἐμοῖς ψηφίσμασι καὶ τοῖς ἐμοῖς
303 πολιτεύμασιν, ἃ καὶ βεβουλευμέν', ὦ ἄνδρες Ἀθηναῖοι, ἐὰν ἄνευ φθόνου τις βούληται σκοπεῖν, ὀρθῶς
εὑρήσει καὶ πεπραγμένα πάσῃ δικαιοσύνῃ, καὶ τὸν
ἑκάστου καιρὸν οὐ παρεθέντ' οὐδ' ἀγνοηθέντ' οὐδὲ
προεθένθ' ὑπ' ἐμοῦ, καὶ ὅσ' εἰς ἀνδρὸς ἑνὸς δύναμιν
καὶ λογισμὸν ἧκεν, οὐδὲν ἐλλειφθέν. εἰ δ' ἢ
δαίμονός τινος ἢ τύχης ἰσχύς, ἢ στρατηγῶν φαυ-
λότης, ἢ τῶν προδιδόντων τὰς πόλεις ὑμῶν κακία,
[327] ἢ πάντα ταῦτ' ἐλυμαίνετο τοῖς ὅλοις, ἕως ἀνέτρεψεν,
304 τί Δημοσθένης ἀδικεῖ; εἰ δ' οἷος ἐγὼ παρ' ὑμῖν
κατὰ τὴν ἐμαυτοῦ τάξιν, εἷς ἐν ἑκάστῃ τῶν Ἑλληνί-
δων πόλεων ἀνὴρ ἐγένετο, μᾶλλον δ' εἰ ἕν' ἄνδρα
μόνον Θετταλία καὶ ἕν' ἄνδρ' Ἀρκαδία ταὐτὰ
φρονοῦντ' ἔσχεν ἐμοί, οὐδένες[1] οὔτε τῶν ἔξω Πυλῶν
Ἑλλήνων οὔτε τῶν εἴσω τοῖς παροῦσι κακοῖς
305 ἐκέχρηντ' ἄν, ἀλλὰ πάντες ἂν ὄντες ἐλεύθεροι καὶ
αὐτόνομοι μετὰ πάσης ἀδείας ἀσφαλῶς ἐν εὐδαιμονίᾳ τὰς ἑαυτῶν ᾤκουν πατρίδας, τούτων τοσούτων
καὶ τοιούτων ἀγαθῶν ὑμῖν καὶ τοῖς ἄλλοις Ἀθηναίοις ἔχοντες χάριν δι' ἐμέ. ἵνα δ' εἰδῆθ' ὅτι

---

[1] οὐδένες . . . ἐκέχρηντ' ἄν Cobet: οὐδεὶς . . . ἐκέχρητ' ἄν
Dind.: οὐδεὶς . . . ἐκέχρηντ' ἄν S.

direction ; to make provision for the passage of our corn-supply along friendly coasts all the way to Peiraeus ; to preserve places already at our disposal, such as Proconnesus, Chersonesus, Tenedos, by sending succour to them and by suitable speeches and resolutions ; to secure the friendship and alliance of such places as Byzantium, Abydos, and Euboea ; to destroy the most important of the existing resources of the enemy, and to make good the deficiencies of our own city. All these purposes were accomplished by my decrees and my administrative acts. Whoever will study them, men of Athens, without jealousy, will find that they were rightly planned and honestly executed ; that the proper opportunity for each several measure was never neglected, or ignored, or thrown away by me : and that nothing within the compass of one man's ability or forethought was left undone. If the superior power of some deity or of fortune, or the incompetence of commanders, or the wickedness of traitors, or all these causes combined, vitiated and at last shattered the whole enterprise,—is Demosthenes guilty ? If in each of the cities of Greece there had been some one man such as I was in my appointed station in your midst, nay, if Thessaly had possessed one man and Arcadia one man holding the same sentiments that I held, no Hellenic people beyond or on this side of Thermopylae would have been exposed to their present distresses : they would still be dwelling prosperously in their own countries, in freedom and independence, securely and without fear, grateful to you and to all the Athenians for the great and manifold blessings they owed to me. To prove that,

πολλῷ τοῖς λόγοις ἐλάττοσι χρῶμαι τῶν ἔργων,
εὐλαβούμενος τὸν φθόνον, λέγε μοι ταυτὶ καὶ
ἀνάγνωθι λαβὼν τὸν ἀριθμὸν τῶν βοηθειῶν κατὰ
τἀμὰ ψηφίσματα.

ΑΡΙΘΜΟΣ ΒΟΗΘΕΙΩΝ

306 Ταῦτα καὶ τοιαῦτα πράττειν, Αἰσχίνη, τὸν καλὸν
κἀγαθὸν πολίτην δεῖ, ὧν κατορθουμένων μὲν μεγίστοις ἀναμφισβητήτως ὑπῆρχεν εἶναι καὶ τὸ δικαίως
προσῆν, ὡς ἑτέρως δὲ συμβάντων τὸ γοῦν εὐδοκι-
μεῖν περίεστι καὶ τὸ μηδένα μέμφεσθαι τὴν πόλιν
μηδὲ τὴν προαίρεσιν αὐτῆς, ἀλλὰ τὴν τύχην κακίζειν
307 τὴν οὕτω τὰ πράγματα κρίνασαν· οὐ μὰ Δι᾽ οὐκ
ἀποστάντα τῶν συμφερόντων τῇ πόλει, μισθώσαντα
δ᾽ αὑτὸν τοῖς ἐναντίοις, τοὺς ὑπὲρ τῶν ἐχθρῶν
καιροὺς ἀντὶ τῶν τῆς πατρίδος θεραπεύειν, οὐδὲ τὸν
μὲν πράγματ᾽ ἄξια τῆς πόλεως ὑποστάντα λέγειν καὶ
γράφειν καὶ μένειν ἐπὶ τούτων βασκαίνειν, ἂν δέ τις
ἰδίᾳ τι λυπήσῃ, τοῦτο μεμνῆσθαι καὶ τηρεῖν, οὐδέ γ᾽
ἡσυχίαν ἄγειν ἄδικον καὶ ὕπουλον, ὃ σὺ ποιεῖς
308 πολλάκις. ἔστι γάρ, ἔστιν ἡσυχία δικαία καὶ
[328] συμφέρουσα τῇ πόλει, ἣν οἱ πολλοὶ τῶν πολιτῶν
ὑμεῖς ἁπλῶς ἄγετε. ἀλλ᾽ οὐ ταύτην οὗτος ἄγει τὴν
ἡσυχίαν, πολλοῦ γε καὶ δεῖ, ἀλλ᾽ ἀποστὰς ὅταν
αὐτῷ δόξῃ τῆς πολιτείας (πολλάκις δὲ δοκεῖ)
φυλάττει πηνίκ᾽ ἔσεσθε μεστοὶ τοῦ συνεχῶς λέγοντος
ἢ παρὰ τῆς τύχης τι συμβέβηκεν ἐναντίωμα, ἢ ἄλλο
τι δύσκολον γέγονε (πολλὰ δὲ τἀνθρώπινα)· εἶτ᾽
218

as a precaution against envy, I am using words that
do less than justice to my deeds, please take these
papers, and read the list of expeditions sent in
pursuance of my decrees.

(*The List of Expeditions in Aid is read*)

It was the duty, Aeschines, of an upright and
honourable citizen to take these or similar measures.
If they had been successful, we should have been,
beyond controversy, the greatest of nations and a
nation that deserved its greatness : and, though
they have failed, there remains the result that our
reputation stands high, and that no man can find
fault with Athens or her policy, but lays the blame
on the fortune that so ordered the issue. Assuredly
it was not the duty of such a citizen to abandon the
cause of his country, to take the hire of her adversaries, to wait on the occasions, not of Athens, but
of her enemies. It was not his duty to look with an
evil eye upon a man who had made it his business
to support or propose measures worthy of our traditions, and was resolved to stand by such measures ;
nor to treasure vindictively the memory of private
annoyances. Nor was it his duty to hold his peace
dishonestly and deceptively, as you so often do.
There is, indeed, a silence that is honest and beneficial
to the city, such as is observed in all simplicity by
the majority of you citizens. Not such, but far, far
different, is the silence of Aeschines. Withdrawing
himself from public life whenever he thinks fit—and
that is very frequently—he lies in wait for the time
when you will be weary of the incessant speaker,
or when some unlucky reverse has befallen you, or
any of those vexations that are so frequent in the

ἐπὶ τούτῳ τῷ καιρῷ ῥήτωρ ἐξαίφνης ἐκ τῆς ἡσυ-
χίας ὥσπερ πνεῦμ᾽ ἐφάνη, καὶ πεφωνασκηκὼς καὶ
συνειλοχὼς ῥήματα καὶ λόγους συνείρει τούτους
σαφῶς καὶ ἀπνευστεί, ὄνησιν μὲν οὐδεμίαν φέρον-
τας οὐδ᾽ ἀγαθοῦ κτῆσιν οὐδενός, συμφορὰν δὲ τῷ
309 τυχόντι τῶν πολιτῶν καὶ κοινὴν αἰσχύνην. καίτοι
ταύτης τῆς μελέτης καὶ τῆς ἐπιμελείας, Αἰσχίνη,
εἴπερ ἐκ ψυχῆς δικαίας ἐγίγνετο καὶ τὰ τῆς πατρίδος
συμφέροντα προῃρημένης, τοὺς καρποὺς ἔδει γεν-
ναίους καὶ καλοὺς καὶ πᾶσιν ὠφελίμους εἶναι,
συμμαχίας πόλεων, πόρους χρημάτων, ἐμπορίου
κατασκευήν, νόμων συμφερόντων θέσεις, τοῖς
310 ἀποδειχθεῖσιν ἐχθροῖς ἐναντιώματα. τούτων γὰρ
ἁπάντων ἦν ἐν τοῖς ἄνω χρόνοις ἐξέτασις, καὶ ἔδωκεν
ὁ παρελθὼν χρόνος πολλὰς ἀποδείξεις ἀνδρὶ καλῷ τε
κἀγαθῷ, ἐν οἷς οὐδαμοῦ σὺ φανήσει γεγονώς, οὐ
πρῶτος, οὐ δεύτερος, οὐ τρίτος, οὐ τέταρτος, οὐ
πέμπτος, οὐχ ἕκτος, οὐχ ὁποστοσοῦν, οὔκουν ἐπί
311 γ᾽ οἷς ἡ πατρὶς ηὐξάνετο. τίς γὰρ συμμαχία σοῦ
πράξαντος γέγονε τῇ πόλει; τίς δὲ βοήθεια ἢ κτῆ-
σις εὐνοίας ἢ δόξης; τίς δὲ πρεσβεία, τίς διακονία
[329] δι᾽ ἣν ἡ πόλις ἐντιμοτέρα; τί τῶν οἰκείων ἢ
τῶν Ἑλληνικῶν καὶ ξενικῶν, οἷς ἐπέστης, ἐπηνώρ-
θωται; ποῖαι τριήρεις; ποῖα βέλη; ποῖοι νεώσ-
οικοι; τίς ἐπισκευὴ τειχῶν; ποῖον ἱππικόν; τί
τῶν ἁπάντων σὺ χρήσιμος εἶ; τίς ἢ τοῖς εὐπόροις ἢ
τοῖς ἀπόροις πολιτικὴ καὶ κοινὴ βοήθεια χρημάτων;
312 οὐδεμία. ἀλλ᾽, ὦ τᾶν, εἰ μηδὲν τούτων, εὔνοιά
γε καὶ προθυμία· ποῦ; πότε; ὅστις, ὦ πάντων

life of mortal men ; and then, seizing the occasion, he breaks silence and the orator reappears like a sudden squall, with his voice in fine training ; he strings together the words and the phrases that he has accumulated, emphatically and without a pause ; but, alas, they are all useless, they serve no good purpose, they are directed to the injury of this or that citizen, and to the discredit of the whole community. Yet if all that assiduous practice, Aeschines, had been conducted in a spirit of honesty and of solicitude for your country's well-being, it should have yielded a rich and noble harvest for the benefit of us all—alliances of states, new revenues, development of commerce, useful legislation, measures of opposition to our avowed enemies. In days of old all those services afforded the recognized test of statesmanship : and the time through which you have passed supplied to an upright politician many opportunities of showing his worth ; but among such men you won no position—you were neither first, second, third, fourth, fifth, sixth, nor anywhere in the race— at least when the power of your country was to be enlarged. What alliance does Athens owe to your exertions ?   What auxiliary expedition, what gain of amity or reputation ?   What embassy or service, by which the credit of the city has been raised ? What project in domestic, Hellenic, or foreign policy, of which you took charge, has ever been successful ? What war-galleys, or munitions, or docks, or fortifications, or cavalry, do we owe to you ?   Of what use in the wide world are you ?   What public-spirited assistance have you ever given to rich or to poor ? None whatever. But come, sir, without any of these things a man may show patriotism and zeal. Where ?

ἀδικώτατε, οὐδ᾽ ὅθ᾽ ἅπαντες, ὅσοι πώποτ᾽ ἐφθέγξαντ᾽
ἐπὶ τοῦ βήματος, εἰς σωτηρίαν ἐπεδίδοσαν, καὶ τὸ
τελευταῖον ᾿Αριστόνικος τὸ συνειλεγμένον εἰς τὴν
ἐπιτιμίαν, οὐδὲ τότ᾽ οὔτε παρῆλθες οὔτ᾽ ἐπέδωκας
οὐδέν, οὐκ ἀπορῶν, πῶς γάρ; ὅς γ᾽ ἐκεκληρονο-
μήκεις μὲν τῶν Φίλωνος τοῦ κηδεστοῦ χρημάτων
πλειόνων ἢ πεντεταλάντων, διτάλαντον δ᾽ εἶχες
ἔρανον δωρεὰν παρὰ τῶν ἡγεμόνων τῶν συμμοριῶν
313 ἐφ᾽ οἷς ἐλυμήνω τὸν τριηραρχικὸν νόμον. ἀλλ᾽
ἵνα μὴ λόγον ἐκ λόγου λέγων τοῦ παρόντος ἐμαυτὸν
ἐκκρούσω, παραλείψω ταῦτα. ἀλλ᾽ ὅτι γ᾽ οὐχὶ
δι᾽ ἔνδειαν οὐκ ἐπέδωκας, ἐκ τούτων δῆλον, ἀλλὰ
φυλάττων τὸ μηδὲν ἐναντίον γενέσθαι παρὰ σοῦ
τούτοις οἷς ἅπαντα πολιτεύει. ἐν τίσιν οὖν σὺ
νεανίας καὶ πηνίκα λαμπρός; ἡνίκ᾽ ἂν κατὰ τούτων
τι δέῃ, ἐν τούτοις λαμπροφωνότατος, μνημονικώ-
τατος, ὑποκριτὴς ἄριστος, τραγικὸς Θεοκρίνης.

314 Εἶτα τῶν πρότερον γεγενημένων ἀγαθῶν ἀνδρῶν
μέμνησαι. καὶ καλῶς ποιεῖς. οὐ μέντοι δίκαιόν
ἐστιν, ἄνδρες ᾿Αθηναῖοι, τὴν πρὸς τοὺς τετελευτη-
[330] κότας εὔνοιαν ὑπάρχουσαν προλαβόντα παρ᾽ ὑμῶν,
πρὸς ἐκείνους ἐξετάζειν καὶ παραβάλλειν ἐμὲ τὸν
315 νῦν ζῶντα μεθ᾽ ὑμῶν. τίς γὰρ οὐκ οἶδε τῶν
πάντων, ὅτι τοῖς μὲν ζῶσι πᾶσιν ὕπεστί τις ἢ
πλείων ἢ ἐλάττων φθόνος, τοὺς τεθνεῶτας δ᾽ οὐδὲ
τῶν ἐχθρῶν οὐδεὶς ἔτι μισεῖ; οὕτως οὖν ἐχόντων
τούτων τῇ φύσει, πρὸς τοὺς πρὸ ἐμαυτοῦ νῦν ἐγὼ
κρίνωμαι καὶ θεωρῶμαι; μηδαμῶς· οὔτε γὰρ
δίκαιον οὔτ᾽ ἴσον, Αἰσχίνη, ἀλλὰ πρὸς σὲ καὶ ἄλλον

ᵃ *Theocrines*, a notorious informer; prosecuted in a
speech attributed to Demosthenes.

222

When ? Why, you incorrigible knave, even at the
time when every man who ever spoke from the
tribune gave freely to the national defence, when at
last even Aristonicus gave the money he had collected
to redeem his citizenship, you never came forward
and put your name down for a farthing. And yet
you were certainly not without means, for you had
inherited more than five talents from the estate of
your father-in-law Philo, and you had a present of
two talents, subscribed by the chairmen of the Navy
Boards, as a reward for spoiling the Navy Reform
Bill. However, I will pass that by, for fear I should
stray from my immediate purpose by telling one
story after another. It is clear that you refused
to contribute, not because you were poor, but because
you were careful not to do anything in opposition
to the party you serve in politics. Then on what
occasions are you a man of spirit ? When are you
a shining light ? Whenever something is to be said
in prejudice of your fellow-citizens ; then your voice
is magnificent, then your memory is wonderful ;
then we hear the great tragedian, the Theocrines [a] of
the legitimate drama.

Then you remind us of the heroes of past genera-
tions. Quite right : but it is not fair, men of Athens,
to take advantage of the affection you cherish for
the departed, and analyse me, who am still living in
your midst, by comparing me with them. Everybody knows that against the living there is always
an undercurrent of more or less jealousy, while the
dead are no longer disliked even by their enemies.
Such is human nature ; am I then to be criticized
and canvassed by comparison with my predecessors ?
Heaven forbid ! No, Aeschines ; that is unfair and

εἴ τινα βούλει τῶν ταὐτά σοι προῃρημένων καὶ
316 ζώντων. κἀκεῖνο σκόπει. πότερον κάλλιον καὶ
ἄμεινον τῇ πόλει διὰ τὰς τῶν προτέρων εὐεργεσίας,
οὔσας ὑπερμεγέθεις, οὐ μὲν οὖν εἴποι τις ἂν ἡλίκας,
τὰς ἐπὶ τὸν παρόντα βίον γιγνομένας εἰς ἀχαριστίαν
καὶ προπηλακισμὸν ἄγειν, ἢ πᾶσιν, ὅσοι τι μετ᾽
εὐνοίας πράττουσι, τῆς τούτων τιμῆς καὶ φιλανθρω-
317 πίας μετεῖναι; καὶ μὴν εἰ καὶ τοῦτ᾽ ἄρα δεῖ μ᾽
εἰπεῖν, ἡ μὲν ἐμὴ πολιτεία καὶ προαίρεσις, ἄν τις
σκοπῇ, ταῖς τῶν τότ᾽ ἐπαινουμένων ἀνδρῶν ὁμοία
καὶ ταὐτὰ βουλομένη φανήσεται, ἡ δὲ σὴ ταῖς τῶν
τοὺς τοιούτους τότε συκοφαντούντων· δῆλον γὰρ
ὅτι καὶ κατ᾽ ἐκείνους ἦσάν τινες, οἳ διέσυρον μὲν
τοὺς ὄντας τότε, τοὺς δὲ πρότερον γεγενημένους
ἐπῄνουν, βάσκανον πρᾶγμα καὶ ταὐτὸ ποιοῦντες σοί.
318 εἶτα λέγεις ὡς οὐδὲν ὅμοιός εἰμ᾽ ἐκείνοις ἐγώ; σὺ δ᾽
ὅμοιος, Αἰσχίνη; ὁ δ᾽ ἀδελφὸς ὁ σός; ἄλλος δέ τις
τῶν νῦν ῥητόρων; ἐγὼ μὲν γὰρ οὐδένα φημί. ἀλλὰ
πρὸς τοὺς ζῶντας, ὦ χρηστέ, ἵνα μηδὲν ἄλλ᾽ εἴπω,
τὸν ζῶντ᾽ ἐξέταζε καὶ τοὺς καθ᾽ αὑτόν, ὥσπερ τἆλλα
[331] πάντα, τοὺς ποιητάς, τοὺς χορούς, τοὺς ἀγωνιστάς.
319 ὁ Φιλάμμων οὐχ ὅτι Γλαύκου τοῦ Καρυστίου καί
τινων ἑτέρων πρότερον γεγενημένων ἀθλητῶν
ἀσθενέστερος ἦν, ἀστεφάνωτος ἐκ τῆς Ὀλυμπίας
ἀπῄει, ἀλλ᾽ ὅτι τῶν εἰσελθόντων πρὸς αὐτὸν ἄριστ᾽
ἐμάχετο, ἐστεφανοῦτο καὶ νικῶν ἀνηγορεύετο. καὶ
σὺ πρὸς τοὺς νῦν ὅρα με ῥήτορας, πρὸς σαυτόν,
πρὸς ὅντινα βούλει τῶν ἁπάντων· οὐδέν᾽ ἐξίσταμαι.
320 ὧν, ὅτε μὲν τῇ πόλει τὰ βέλτισθ᾽ ἑλέσθαι παρῆν,
224

unjust : compare me with yourself, or with any
living man you choose, whose principles are identical
with yours. Consider this question : is it more
decent and patriotic that for the sake of the services
of men of old times, enormous as they were, nay,
great beyond expression, the services that are now
being rendered to the present age should be treated
with ingratitude and vituperation, or that every man
who achieves anything in a spirit of loyalty should
receive some share of the respect and consideration
of his fellow-citizens ? If I must deal with that
subject, I say that, if my policy and my principles
are considered, they will be found to resemble in
spirit and purpose those of the venerated names of
antiquity. Yours are like those of the men who
maligned them : for it is certain that, even in their
days, there were men who were always carping at
the living and commending the dead—a spiteful
vocation, and just like yours. You tell me I am not
at all like those great men. Are you like them,
Aeschines ? Or your brother ? Or any other orator
of this generation ? In my opinion, none. Then,
my honest friend—to call you nothing worse—assay
a living man by the standard of living men, men of
his own time. That is the test you apply to everything else—to dramatists, to choruses, to athletes.
Philammon did not leave Olympia without a crown,
because he was not so strong as Glaucus of Carystus,
or other bygone champions : he was crowned and
proclaimed victor, because he fought better than the
men who entered the ring against him. You must
compare me with the orators of to-day ; with yourself, for instance, or anyone you like : I exclude none.
When the commonwealth was at liberty to choose

DEMOSTHENES

ἐφαμίλλου τῆς εἰς τὴν πατρίδ' εὐνοίας ἐν κοινῷ πᾶσι
κειμένης, ἐγὼ κράτιστα λέγων ἐφαινόμην, καὶ τοῖς
ἐμοῖς καὶ ψηφίσμασι καὶ νόμοις καὶ πρεσβείαις
ἅπαντα διῳκεῖτο, ὑμῶν δ' οὐδεὶς ἦν οὐδαμοῦ, πλὴν εἰ
τούτοις ἐπηρεάσαι τι δέοι· ἐπειδὴ δ' ἃ μήποτ'
ὤφελεν συνέβη, καὶ οὐκέτι συμβούλων ἀλλὰ τῶν
τοῖς ἐπιταττομένοις ὑπηρετούντων, καὶ τῶν κατὰ
τῆς πατρίδος μισθαρνεῖν ἑτοίμων, καὶ τῶν κολα-
κεύειν ἕτερον βουλομένων ἐξέτασις ἦν, τηνικαῦτα σὺ
καὶ τούτων ἕκαστος ἐν τάξει καὶ μέγας καὶ λαμπρὸς
ἱπποτρόφος, ἐγὼ δ' ἀσθενής, ὁμολογῶ, ἀλλ' εὔνους
μᾶλλον ὑμῶν τουτοισί.

321 Δύο δ', ἄνδρες Ἀθηναῖοι, τὸν φύσει μέτριον
πολίτην ἔχειν δεῖ (οὕτω γάρ μοι περὶ ἐμαυτοῦ
λέγοντι ἀνεπιφθονώτατον εἰπεῖν), ἐν μὲν ταῖς
ἐξουσίαις τὴν τοῦ γενναίου καὶ τοῦ πρωτείου τῇ
πόλει προαίρεσιν διαφυλάττειν, ἐν παντὶ δὲ καιρῷ
καὶ πράξει τὴν εὔνοιαν· τούτου γὰρ ἡ φύσις κυρία,
τοῦ δύνασθαι δὲ καὶ ἰσχύειν ἕτερα. ταύτην τοί-
322 νυν παρ' ἐμοὶ μεμενηκυῖαν εὑρήσεθ' ἁπλῶς. ὁρᾶτε
δέ. οὐκ ἐξαιτούμενος, οὐκ εἰς Ἀμφικτύονας δίκας
[332] ἐπαγόντων, οὐκ ἀπειλούντων, οὐκ ἐπαγγελλομένων,
οὐχὶ τοὺς καταράτους τούτους ὥσπερ θηρία μοι
προσβαλλόντων, οὐδαμῶς ἐγὼ προδέδωκα τὴν εἰς
ὑμᾶς εὔνοιαν. τὸ γὰρ ἐξ ἀρχῆς εὐθὺς ὀρθὴν καὶ
δικαίαν τὴν ὁδὸν τῆς πολιτείας εἱλόμην, τὰς τιμάς,
τὰς δυναστείας, τὰς εὐδοξίας τὰς τῆς πατρίδος
323 θεραπεύειν, ταύτας αὔξειν, μετὰ τούτων εἶναι. οὐκ
ἐπὶ μὲν τοῖς ἑτέρων εὐτυχήμασι φαιδρὸς ἐγὼ καὶ

---

[a] To keep a stud of horses, whether for racing purposes
or for service in the cavalry, was at Athens the favourite
method of displaying wealth.

the best policy, when there was a competition of patriotism open to all comers, I made better speeches than any other man, and all business was conducted by my resolutions, my statutes, my diplomacy. Not one of you ever put in an appearance—except when you must needs fall foul of my measures. But when certain deplorable events had taken place, and there was a call, not for counsellors, but for men who would obey orders, who were ready to injure their country for pay, and willing to truckle to strangers, then you and your party were at your post, great men with gorgeous equipages.[a] I was powerless, I admit ; but I was still the better patriot.

There are two traits, men of Athens, that mark the disposition of the well-meaning citizen ;—that is a description I may apply to myself without offence. When in power, the constant aim of his policy should be the honour and the ascendancy of his country ; and on every occasion and in all business he should preserve his loyalty. That virtue depends on his natural disposition : ability and success depend upon other considerations. Such, you will find, has been my disposition, abidingly and without alloy. Look at the facts. They demanded that I should be given up ; they arraigned me before the Amphictyonic Council ; they tried me with threats, they tried me with promises : they set these miscreants to worry me like a pack of wolves ; but through it all I never renounced my loyalty to you. At the very outset of my career I had chosen once for all the path of political uprightness and integrity, and resolved to support, to magnify, and to associate myself with the honour, the power, and the glory of my native land. I do not perambulate the market-place, gaily

γεγηθὼς κατὰ τὴν ἀγορὰν περιέρχομαι, τὴν δεξιὰν
προτείνων καὶ εὐαγγελιζόμενος τούτοις οὓς ἂν ἐκεῖσ᾽
ἀπαγγέλλειν οἴωμαι, τῶν δὲ τῆς πόλεως ἀγαθῶν
πεφρικὼς ἀκούω καὶ στένων καὶ κύπτων εἰς τὴν
γῆν, ὥσπερ οἱ δυσσεβεῖς οὗτοι, οἳ τὴν μὲν πόλιν
διασύρουσιν, ὥσπερ οὐχ αὑτοὺς διασύροντες, ὅταν
τοῦτο ποιῶσιν, ἔξω δὲ βλέπουσι, καὶ ἐν οἷς ἀτυχησάν-
των τῶν Ἑλλήνων ηὐτύχησ᾽ ἕτερος, ταῦτ᾽ ἐπαινοῦσι
καὶ ὅπως τὸν ἅπαντα χρόνον μενεῖ φασὶ δεῖν τηρεῖν.

324   Μὴ δῆτ᾽, ὦ πάντες θεοί, μηδεὶς ταῦθ᾽ ὑμῶν ἐπι-
νεύσειεν, ἀλλὰ μάλιστα μὲν καὶ τούτοις βελτίω τινὰ
νοῦν καὶ φρένας ἐνθείητε, εἰ δ᾽ ἄρ᾽ ἔχουσιν ἀνιάτως,
τούτους μὲν αὐτοὺς καθ᾽ ἑαυτοὺς ἐξώλεις καὶ
προώλεις ἐν γῇ καὶ θαλάττῃ ποιήσατε, ἡμῖν δὲ τοῖς
λοιποῖς τὴν ταχίστην ἀπαλλαγὴν τῶν ἐπηρτημένων
φόβων δότε καὶ σωτηρίαν ἀσφαλῆ.

exulting in the good fortune of the alien, holding out my right hand, and telling the glad tidings to anyone I think likely to send word over yonder. When I hear of my country's successes, I do not shudder, and sigh, and hang down my head, like those blasphemers, who traduce Athens, forgetting that thereby they are traducing themselves; who turn their eyes abroad, and, when the alien has prospered by the distresses of Greece, applaud his good fortune, and declare that we must try to preserve it for ever.

Never, O ye Powers of Heaven, never vouchsafe to them the fulfilment of that desire. If it be possible, implant even in them a better purpose and a better spirit; but, if their malady is incurable, consign them, and them alone, to utter and untimely destruction by land and sea, and to us who remain grant speedy deliverance from the terrors that hang over our heads, and a salvation that shall never fail.

DE FALSA LEGATIONE

INTRODUCTION TO THE *DE FALSA LEGATIONE*

THE speech *On the Embassy* was delivered in the summer of the year 343 B.C., before a jury of 1501 citizens, sitting under the presidency of the Board of Auditors (Λογισταί), a body of ten Councillors, chosen by lot, whose duty was to examine the accounts and reports of all outgoing officials and to take cognizance of any charge of official misconduct. Demosthenes was prosecuting his political adversary, Aeschines, for malversation committed by him as a member of the embassy sent to Macedonia in the year 346. According to the prosecution, Aeschines had been (1) untruthful in his reports, (2) disobedient to his instructions, (3) dilatory, with treacherous intent, and (4) corrupt [4-8]; the last and most damaging charge being, however, inferential, and not made good by direct evidence.

The Greek name of the speech is derived from the verb παραπρεσβεύειν, to misconduct an embassy [191]; the Latin name, *De falsa legatione*, often used in references (*F.L.*), we owe to Cicero (*Orat.* 31. 111). Like the speech of Aeschines in defence, it has come down to us, not as delivered in court, but as subsequently revised and published by the orator. A curious interpolation in the text [149] seems to indicate that another edition of the speech once existed.

232

INTRODUCTION

The result of the trial was the acquittal of the defendant by the small plurality of thirty votes. That the jury was not altogether well disposed to Demosthenes had been shown by the clamour with which they interrupted him when he told the story of the Macedonian supper-party [196-8]; a story unsupported by evidence, and irrelevant to the accusation. A few weeks earlier the arch-deceiver, Philocrates, had been impeached by Hypereides [116], and driven from Athens. The guilt of Philocrates is unquestionable; but perhaps the majority of the jury was willing to believe that Aeschines had been the victim rather than the coadjutor of Philocrates' deceptions; or perhaps we have here an example of that unreasonable reaction from severity to indulgence, which was (and still is) characteristic of the Athenian populace, if not of democracy in general.

The speech deals with the negotiations and political intrigues that immediately preceded and followed the Peace of Philocrates. The sequence and the dating of events are, as Demosthenes insists, important to the argument; and it will be convenient to have them before us in a tabular form.[a]

	Olymp. 108.2	346 B.C.
Decree of Philocrates ordering the dispatch of ten envoys to Macedonia.	Gamelion.	February.

[a] The calculation of dates according to modern reckoning (taken from Goodwin's edition of *De corona*, pp. 300 ff.) assumes that the first day (Hecatombaeon 1) of the year in question fell on July 6th, 347 B.C. The year was a long year of 384 days, with an intercalated month.

Return of the First Embassy.	Anthesterion	March (end).
First Assembly : report of the Embassy.	Elaphebolion 18	April 15.
Second Assembly : Peace accepted.	Elaphebolion 19	April 16.
Second Embassy ordered.	Elaphebolion	April.
Assembly for ratification of the Peace by Allies ; Demosthenes in the Chair.	Elaphebolion 25	April 22.
The Council orders the Embassy to depart forthwith.	Munychion 3	April 29.
Return of the Second Embassy.	Scirophorion 13	July 7.
The Assembly requests the Phocians to surrender Delphi.	Scirophorion 16	July 10.
Departure of the Third Embassy to report to Philip.	Scirophorion 21	July 15.
Philip occupies Thermopylae.	Scirophorion 23	July 17.
The Embassy turns back on hearing that Philip is at Thermopylae.	Scirophorion 24	July 18.
The Assembly, meeting at Peiraeus, orders the Embassy to proceed to Philip.	Scirophorion 27	July 21.

In August, that is, in the first month of the Attic new year, the reports of the ambassadors came before the auditors for the statutory scrutiny (εὔθυνα); and notice of prosecution was then given by Demosthenes and Timarchus. Aeschines immediately retaliated by accusing Timarchus of unnatural crime, and obtained his disfranchisement (ἀτιμία) [241, 284 ff.], thus ridding himself of one of his prosecutors [2]. As the auditors had already dealt

234

with the reports of the First Embassy, the indictment laid by Demosthenes (of which we have no copy) must have been restricted to the defendant's misconduct of the Second Embassy. His speech, however, takes a wider range.

The first proposal to open negotiations for peace was made by Philocrates in the year 348. It was adopted ; but its author was prosecuted by Lycinus for proposing an illegal measure. Demosthenes spoke in his defence ; but it is unfair to draw any wider inference than that, at that time, he had no reason to regard Philocrates as the paid or secret agent of Philip. In the same year Olynthus, a city cursed with a pro-Macedonian party headed by Lasthenes and Euthycrates, who had taken Philip's bribes [265], fell into Philip's hands, after a battle in which the Olynthian cavalry was betrayed by its commander, Lasthenes [267]. The inhabitants were all sold into slavery ; and this fate was shared by many Athenians resident in the city, of whom some were afterwards ransomed at the expense of Demosthenes [169 f.]. The Athenians, who had given no adequate response to the appeals made on behalf of their allies by Demosthenes in his *Olynthiac Orations*, were filled with dismay and indignation. No action was taken in pursuance of the decree of Philocrates. Eubulus, an honest but short-sighted statesman, and the most powerful antagonist of Demosthenes—the same Eubulus who came forward to support Aeschines at the trial [290]—assumed the lead of the anti-Macedonian party, and proposed the dispatch of missionaries to stimulate the resentment of all the Greek cities, and to form a panhellenic coalition against the Macedonian intruder [304].

It was at this time that Aeschines, a strolling actor whose fine voice and robust presence were much envied by Demosthenes, first gained the ear of the Assembly by his vigorous denunciation of Philip's cruelty and ambition [303]. He had been strongly moved by a chance encounter with a gang of Olynthian slaves presented by Philip to his Arcadian friend Atrestidas [305]; he introduced a friendly Arcadian, Ischander, to the Council; and, in pursuance of the plan of Eubulus, he was sent as envoy to Arcadia, and there had the honour of addressing the Arcadian Assembly of ten thousand at Megalopolis [10]. At Athens futile resolutions denouncing the Olynthian traitors were adopted by the Assembly [267]; and Demosthenes enjoyed, for what it was worth, the satisfaction of seeing the men who had thwarted his policy converted to his sentiments, when it was too late for anything more practical than indignation meetings. On the other hand, the victory of Philip had put him in possession of property, wrested from allies of Athens, which he afterwards, according to the testimony of Olynthian witnesses, used to bribe or reward his Athenian friends [145-6], besides displaying his barbaric liberality in more creditable ways [192 ff.].

The propaganda of Eubulus failed; and its failure convinced both the old and the new enemies of Philip at Athens that the times required a policy of peace. Nor was Philip reluctant, for, in spite of all his victories by land, he found himself hampered and impoverished by the Athenian navy, which closed his ports and raided his seaboard [315]. Moreover, his ambition was turning in a new direction. The Amphictyonic Council had invited him

to take charge of their Sacred War against the
Phocians. The Phocians appealed to the Athenians
for succour, offering to them the command of the
Pass of Thermopylae. The Athenians, eager to
prevent a Macedonian invasion of central Greece,
resolved to send fifty war-galleys under the admiral
Proxenus ; but Phalaecus, the Phocian commander,
refused the proffered aid, and rudely dismissed
Proxenus [50 ff., 322], who returned to his station
at Oreus [155]. This unfortunate incident contributed to the readiness with which, a few months
later, the Assembly accepted the proposal of Philocrates that ten envoys should be sent to Macedonia
to confer with Philip, and report. The Ten included
Philocrates himself, Demosthenes, Aeschines, and
Aristodemus, another actor, who had made Philip's
acquaintance when paying a professional visit to
Macedonia. Others of the Ten, mentioned in the
speech, are Ctesiphon (not the Ctesiphon of the
speech *On the Crown*), Iatrocles, who had been
captured at Olynthus, but released without ransom,
Dercylus, and Phryno.

Of the many discrepancies between the accounts
of the First Embassy given by Demosthenes and
by Aeschines, it is sufficient here to observe that
the assertion that, before leaving Athens, Aeschines
suspected the good faith of Philocrates, and proposed
to Demosthenes that they two should keep an eye
on him [13], is contradicted by Aeschines, and is
not commended by probability. The ambassadors
had a long interview with the king at Pella ; and
brought back with them a courteous letter [38, 39],
in which Philip offered not only peace but alliance.
Demosthenes' suspicion, that this uncandid epistle

was actually composed by Aeschines, is commonly rejected by historians. The king, however, had dealt frankly with the embassy on one important point. They were unable to report any hope that he would admit the Athenian claim to Amphipolis, which had been the original issue of the war, or give up any of his acquisitions. Peace, in short, could be concluded only on a basis of *uti possidetis*. The Ten were ready to recommend the Assembly to accept peace on such terms ; but representatives of the several cities of the Athenian alliance, who were consulted after the return of the embassy to Athens, asked that the terms should be so amended as to offer the benefits of the peace to any Greek state that might choose to come in within three months. This proposal was made for the advantage of the Phocians and the Halians, with whom Philip was actively at war. It would, of course, have blocked those unavowed and unsuspected designs of Philip, for the sake of which he was willing to patch up peace with Athens.

At the first meeting of the Assembly Philocrates proposed an alliance between Philip and Athens and her allies, excluding by name the Phocians and the Halians ; but Aeschines joined with Demosthenes [14] in opposing this motion and in supporting the prayer of the allies. If Demosthenes is right, a resolution agreeable to that prayer would have been carried there and then, had not Aeschines intervened and procured an adjournment [144]. On the following day Aeschines threw the allies overboard [15, 16, 311], and supported the first proposal of Philocrates, from which the excluding clause had been artfully struck out. Aeschines, whose accounts

238

of the second meeting contradict each other, asserts that Demosthenes also changed sides; Demosthenes, that he continued to support the proposition of the allies [15]. Either of them may have learned in the interval, from Philip's envoys then present at Athens, that Philip would never make peace on the amended terms. The Macedonian terms were then accepted, on the strength of a verbal and unauthenticated assurance [321] that Philip, though unwilling to offend the Thebans and the Thessalians by making alliance with the Phocians, would give the latter such treatment as Athens desired. In this assurance lay the fatal deception of which Philocrates had been convicted, and of which Demosthenes — while acquitting the Macedonian envoys, Antipater and Parmenio [69] — accuses Aeschines. He also blames Eubulus for alarming the people by an exaggerated estimate of the sacrifices which a renewal of the war would entail [291]. In his eagerness to retaliate the charge of philippism, Aeschines was absurd enough to reproach Demosthenes with extending the customary diplomatic courtesies to the Macedonian ambassadors [235].

The peace was made and declared as between Philip and the Athenians "and their allies,"—an undefined term, of which the interpretation was sure to be disputed. Philip interpreted it to suit his own purposes, and excluded from the benefits of the peace not only the Phocians and the Halians, but also Cersobleptes [174, 334], a Thracian potentate who was bound to Athens by mutual obligations, and whose independence was an obstacle to Philip's designs upon the Hellespont. Six days after adopting the decree of Philocrates the Assembly met again to give representatives of the several allied cities an opportunity to swear to the peace in the presence of the Macedonian ambassadors. It is doubtful whether the oath was then tendered by the envoys of Cersobleptes; if tendered and accepted, it was afterwards disallowed by Philip. Of these proceedings Demosthenes says nothing ; Aeschines gives two accounts which contradict each other. In any case it is unfair to fix upon Demosthenes any responsibility for the exclusion of Cersobleptes, on the ground that he happened to be in the chair at this meeting ; for the consent of the Macedonians was clearly a necessary condition. Philip, who always acted while the Athenians were talking, pursued his Thracian campaign, and, when he at last met the second embassy, had already captured Serrium, Doriscus, and other towns, and had taken Cersobleptes prisoner at a place called the Sacred Mount.

The same ten ambassadors were reappointed, with a commission to return to Macedonia, accompanied by a representative of the allies, and there obtain Philip's oath to the peace, and swear in his allies. It was desirable that they should start as soon, and travel as rapidly, as possible, because, until Philip had taken the oath, he held himself at liberty to continue his operations against the northern allies ; but Demosthenes alone of the Ten recognized the importance of expedition.

Some preliminary knowledge of the sequence of events here summarized is necessary for the understanding of the speech, for the many allusions made to them by the orator are scattered and disorderly, and they are assumed to be within the recollection of the jury. It is, however, unnecessary to add here any account of the second embassy, because Demosthenes gives a continuous narrative of its proceedings, delays, and delinquencies, and of their unhappy results [150-81; compare also the speech *On the Crown*, 25-36]. Nor need we anticipate here the orator's account of the appointment of the third embassy [121 ff.]—a story irrelevant to the indictment, but adding some useful touches to the portraiture of Aeschines as a designing and philippizing knave. The narrative is distinct and orderly, as well as rhetorically effective; and Aeschines, while disputing the inferences, does not contradict it, except in minor details. It should, of course, be read with the sort of caution with which we commonly read history coloured by strong partisanship. Whether it convicts Aeschines of treason and corruption, or merely of levity and negligence, is a question upon which the jury, after hearing the evidence and the documents as well as the speeches, were nearly equally divided, and which the modern reader, if not himself both a historian and a partisan, may feel himself incompetent to decide.

Prosecution for *parapresbeia* had not been frequent; but there was one example of the offence and of its punishment of which Demosthenes repeatedly reminds the jury [31, 137, 191]. In the year 367 (that is, four years after the Battle of Leuctra) the Thebans had sent Pelopidas to Susa to persuade the king of Persia to recognize their hegemony; and Pelopidas had obtained from the king a rescript in which the Athenians were ordered to recall their fleet from active service, with a threat of Persian

DE FALSA LEGATIONE

intervention, if they refused. The Athenian ambassadors at Susa, Leon and Timagoras, having failed to procure any modification of the rescript, returned to Athens and reported. Leon immediately accused Timagoras of refusing to associate with him, of consorting and acting in collusion with Pelopidas, and of accepting presents from the king. Timagoras was found guilty, and condemned to death. (See Grote, ch. lxxix.) Demosthenes uses this leading case as a precedent both for his own unusual action in prosecuting a colleague, and for the severity with which he invited the jury to punish the crime imputed to Aeschines.

ANALYSIS OF THE SPEECH

I. *Prologue* 1-16
    (1) Protest against intimidation
[1, 2]; (2) general statement of
the charges [3-8]; (3) the charge
of corruption proved by the defendant's change of policy [9-16].

II. *First Narrative*: the story of the
making of the Peace of Philocrates,
proving the charge of deception . 17-66

III. *Amplification of the Charges* . . 67-149
    (1) Comments enhancing the
gravity of the charges, and reply
to pleas of extenuation or evasion
[67-120]; (2) treachery proved by
Aeschines' conduct on the appointment of the third embassy [121-
133]; (3) reply to the plea that a
conviction would be politically inexpedient [134-149].

INTRODUCTION

IV. *Second Narrative* : the story of the
second embassy and its results . 150-181
    Ending with a recapitulation of
    charges [177-181].

V. *Epilogue* : miscellaneous pleas and
    observations . . . 182-340
        (1) The plea that a man should
    not be punished for words [182-187];
    (2) reply to the reproach of accusing
    a colleague [188-191]; (3) anecdotes
    illustrating Aeschines' character
    [192-200]; (4) reply to the plea that
    Demosthenes was a party to the
    transactions in question [201-220];
    (5) proof that the prosecutor was
    disinterested [221-228]; (6) ethical
    results of acquittal [229-233]; (7)
    why Demosthenes entertained the
    Macedonian envoys [234-236]; (8)
    the defendant's compurgators [237-
    240]; (9) reminiscences of Aeschines'
    prosecution of Timarchus [241-255;
    285-287], interrupted by (10) a
    digression on political degeneracy
    and the good old times [256-284];
    (11) further results of the defendant's
    treachery, and proofs of his change
    of policy [288-314]; (12) recapitula-
    tion [315-331]; (13) Aeschines'
    attempt to blame the general,
    Chares [332-336]; (14) his eloquence
    [337-340].

VI. *Peroration* 341-343

DE FALSA LEGATIONE

The speech, though technically forensic, was composed for political purposes—to bring discredit upon a policy and a party, as well as to convict a culprit of a definite offence. For this reason it is discursive, and often irrelevant to the indictment; the epilogue, in particular, is exceptionally long and miscellaneous; and the arrangement of topics may seem disorderly. Yet the effect is cumulative; for each succeeding paragraph, though it may add nothing to the proof of the defendant's guilt, supplies new reason for a severe view of the heinousness of his offence, and of the gravity of its consequences. Demosthenes is striving, not merely for a conviction, but for a heavy punishment; and to that object, as well as to the political issue, everything he says is relevant.

THE GREEK TEXT

The Greek text here printed is based on that of Richard Shilleto (4th edition, Cambridge, 1874),—a skilful revision made by a great master of Greek idiom, and especially attractive to a translator, because Shilleto, who had undertaken at once to revise and to explain the text, always had an eye to the meaning of the orator as well as to the comparative merits of the manuscripts. We have not corrected his peculiar practice of writing αὐτὸν (rather than αὑτὸν), etc., "whenever the word refers either to the primary or secondary subject of the sentence." We have, however, (a) corrected

244

INTRODUCTION

not a few misprints, (*b*) mended the orthography
of a few words, and (*c*) marked many elisions, in
deference to the custom of more recent editors.
Further, we have often substituted the reading of
the Paris manuscript S, in places where Shilleto
stands alone among modern editors (Bekker and
his successors) in rejecting that reading ; but we
have not taken that liberty where Shilleto's annota-
tions show good reason against the S readings.
Footnotes are added where the reading given has
the authority neither of Shilleto nor of S.

The numbering of the sections is not Shilleto's,
but that of modern editors, except that from § 91
to § 109 we have ventured to re-number, in order to
avoid the clumsy expedient of jumping from 103 to
109. The numbers in square brackets are those of
Reiske's pages.

XIX

ΠΕΡΙ ΤΗΣ ΠΑΡΑΠΡΕΣΒΕΙΑΣ

[341] Ὅση μέν, ὦ ἄνδρες Ἀθηναῖοι, σπουδὴ περὶ τουτονὶ τὸν ἀγῶνα καὶ παραγγελία γέγονε, σχεδὸν οἶμαι πάντας ὑμᾶς ᾐσθῆσθαι, ἑορακότας ἄρτι τοὺς ὅτ᾽ ἐκληροῦσθ᾽ ἐνοχλοῦντας καὶ προσιόντας ὑμῖν. δεήσομαι δὲ πάντων ὑμῶν, ἃ καὶ τοῖς μὴ δεηθεῖσι δίκαιόν ἐστιν ὑπάρχειν, μηδεμίαν μήτε χάριν μήτ᾽ ἄνδρα ποιεῖσθαι περὶ πλείονος ἢ τὸ δίκαιον καὶ τὸν ὅρκον ὃν εἰσελήλυθεν ὑμῶν ἕκαστος ὀμωμοκώς, ἐνθυμουμένους ὅτι ταῦτα μέν ἐστιν ὑπὲρ ὑμῶν καὶ ὅλης τῆς πόλεως, αἱ δὲ τῶν παρακλήτων αὗται δεήσεις καὶ σπουδαὶ τῶν ἰδίων πλεονεξιῶν ἕνεκα γίγνονται, ἃς ἵνα κωλύηθ᾽ οἱ νόμοι συνήγαγον ὑμᾶς, οὐχ ἵνα κυρίας τοῖς ἀδικοῦσι ποιῆτε.

2 Τοὺς μὲν οὖν ἄλλους, ὅσοι πρὸς τὰ κοινὰ δικαίως προσέρχονται, κἂν δεδωκότες ὦσιν εὐθύνας, τὴν ἀειλογίαν ὁρῶ προτεινομένους, τουτονὶ δ᾽ Αἰσχίνην πολὺ τἀναντία τούτου· πρὶν γὰρ εἰσελθεῖν εἰς ὑμᾶς καὶ λόγον δοῦναι τῶν πεπραγμένων τὸν μὲν ἀνῄρηκε τῶν ἐπὶ τὰς εὐθύνας ἐλθόντων, τοῖς δ᾽ ἀπειλεῖ περιιών, δεινότατον πάντων ἔθος εἰς τὴν πολιτείαν εἰσάγων καὶ ἀσυμφορώτατον ὑμῖν· εἰ γὰρ ὁ πράξας τι τῶν κοινῶν καὶ διοικήσας τῷ

---

[a] For the selection of jurors.

XIX

ON THE EMBASSY

CITIZENS OF ATHENS, I do not doubt that you are all pretty well aware that this trial has been the centre of keen partisanship and active canvassing, for you saw the people who were accosting and annoying you just now at the casting of lots.[a] But I have to make a request which ought to be granted without asking, that you will all give less weight to private entreaty or personal influence than to the spirit of justice and to the oath which you severally swore when you entered that box. You will reflect that justice and the oath concern yourselves and the commonwealth, whereas the importunity and party spirit of advocates serve the end of those private ambitions which you are convened by the laws to thwart, not to encourage for the advantage of evil-doers.

Now I observe that men who enter public life with honest intentions, even after they have submitted to scrutiny, do still acknowledge a perpetual responsibility. But Aeschines, the defendant, reverses this practice. Before coming into court to justify his proceedings, he has put out of the way one of the men who called him to account, and the others he is constantly threatening. So he is trying to introduce into politics a most dangerous and deplorable practice ; for if a man who has undertaken and adminis-

καθ᾽ ἑαυτὸν φόβῳ καὶ μὴ τῷ δικαίῳ κατασκευάσει
[342] μηδέν᾽ εἶναι κατήγορον αὐτοῦ, παντάπασιν ἄκυροι
πάντων ὑμεῖς γενήσεσθε.

3 Τὸ μὲν οὖν ἐξελέγχειν πολλὰ καὶ δεινὰ πεποιηκότα τουτονὶ καὶ τῆς ἐσχάτης ὄντα τιμωρίας ἄξιον
θαρρῶ καὶ πάνυ πιστεύω· ὃ δὲ καίπερ ὑπειληφὼς
ταῦτα φοβοῦμαι, φράσω πρὸς ὑμᾶς καὶ οὐκ ἀπο-
κρύψομαι, ὅτι μοι δοκοῦσιν ἅπαντες οἱ παρ᾽ ὑμῖν
ἀγῶνες οὐχ ἧττον, ὦ ἄνδρες Ἀθηναῖοι, τῶν καιρῶν
ἢ τῶν πραγμάτων εἶναι, καὶ τὸ χρόνον γεγενῆσθαι
μετὰ τὴν πρεσβείαν πολὺν δέδοικα, μή τινα λήθην
ἢ συνήθειαν τῶν ἀδικημάτων ὑμῖν ἐμπεποίηκεν.
4 ὡς δή μοι δοκεῖτ᾽ ἂν ὅμως ἐκ τούτων καὶ γνῶναι
τὰ δίκαια καὶ δικάσαι νυνί, τοῦθ᾽ ὑμῖν λέξω. εἰ
σκέψαισθε παρ᾽ ὑμῖν αὐτοῖς, ὦ ἄνδρες δικασταί,
καὶ λογίσαισθε τίνων προσήκει τῇ πόλει λόγον
παρὰ πρεσβευτοῦ λαβεῖν. πρῶτον μὲν τοίνυν ὧν
ἀπήγγειλε, δεύτερον δ᾽ ὧν ἔπεισε, τρίτον δ᾽ ὧν
προσετάξατ᾽ αὐτῷ, μετὰ ταῦτα τῶν χρόνων, ἐφ᾽
ἅπασι δὲ τούτοις, εἰ ἀδωροδοκήτως ἢ μὴ πάντα
5 ταῦτα πέπρακται. τί δήποτε τούτων; ὅτι ἐκ μὲν
τῶν ἀπαγγελιῶν τὸ βουλεύσασθαι περὶ τῶν πραγμάτων ὑμῖν ἐστίν· ἂν μὲν οὖν ὦσιν ἀληθεῖς, τὰ
δέοντ᾽ ἔγνωτε, ἂν δὲ μὴ τοιαῦται, τἀναντία. τὰς
δὲ συμβουλίας πιστοτέρας ὑπολαμβάνετ᾽ εἶναι τὰς
τῶν πρέσβεων· ὡς γὰρ εἰδότων περὶ ὧν ἐπέμφθησαν
ἀκούετε· οὐδὲν οὖν ἐξελέγχεσθαι δίκαιός ἐστιν ὁ
πρεσβευτὴς φαῦλον οὐδ᾽ ἀσύμφορον ὑμῖν συμ-
6 βεβουλευκώς. καὶ μὴν περὶ ὧν γε προσετάξατ᾽
248

tered any public function can get rid of accusers not by his honesty but by the fear he inspires, the people will soon lose all control of public affairs.

While I have entire confidence that I shall prove that this man is guilty of serious delinquencies, and that he deserves the most severe punishment, yet, in spite of that assurance, I have a misgiving, which I will explain to you quite frankly. It appears to me, men of Athens, that the trials which come before you are affected quite as much by the conditions of the hour as by the facts ; and I am afraid that the long lapse of time since the embassy has inclined you to forget or to acquiesce in these iniquities. I will, then, suggest a method by which you may nevertheless reach a just conclusion and give a righteous verdict to-day. By consideration among yourselves, gentlemen, you should form a true conception of what should be included in the vindication which the state requires of any ambassador. He is responsible then, in the first place, for the reports he has made ; secondly, for the advice he has offered ; thirdly, for his observance of your instructions ; then there is the question of times and opportunities ; and, to crown all, whether he has done his business corruptly or with integrity. Why are these the topics of inquiry ? Your conclusions are derived from the ambassador's reports : you reach a right decision if they are true, a wrong decision if they are false. The advice of ambassadors you regard as the more trustworthy because it is given by men who presumably understand their own mission. No ambassador, then, ought ever to be convicted of defective or mischievous counsels. Thirdly, when he has been expressly instructed

εἰπεῖν ἢ πρᾶξαι καὶ διαρρήδην ἐψηφίσασθε ποιῆσαι, προσήκει διωκηκέναι. εἶεν· τῶν δὲ δὴ χρόνων
[343] διὰ τί; ὅτι πολλάκις, ὦ ἄνδρες Ἀθηναῖοι, συμβαίνει πολλῶν πραγμάτων καὶ μεγάλων καιρὸν ἐν
βραχεῖ χρόνῳ γίγνεσθαι, ὃν ἐάν τις ἑκὼν καθυφῇ
τοῖς ἐναντίοις καὶ προδῷ, οὐδ᾽ ἂν ὁτιοῦν ποιῇ πάλιν
7 οἷός τ᾽ ἔσται σῶσαι. ἀλλὰ μὴν ὑπέρ γε τοῦ προῖκ᾽
ἢ μή, τὸ μὲν ἐκ τούτων λαμβάνειν, ἐξ ὧν ἡ πόλις
βλάπτεται, πάντες οἶδ᾽ ὅτι φήσαιτ᾽ ἂν εἶναι δεινὸν
καὶ πολλῆς ὀργῆς ἄξιον. ὁ μέντοι τὸν νόμον τιθεὶς
οὐ διώρισε τοῦτο, ἀλλ᾽ ἁπλῶς εἶπε μηδαμῶς δῶρα
λαμβάνειν, ἡγούμενος, ὡς ἐμοὶ δοκεῖ, τὸν ἅπαξ
λαβόντα καὶ διαφθαρένθ᾽ ὑπὸ χρημάτων οὐδὲ
κριτὴν ἔτι τῶν συμφερόντων ἀσφαλῆ μένειν τῇ
8 πόλει. ἂν μὲν τοίνυν ἐξελέγξω καὶ δείξω σαφῶς
Αἰσχίνην τουτονὶ καὶ μηδὲν ἀληθὲς ἀπηγγελκότα
καὶ κεκωλυκότ᾽ ἐμοῦ τὸν δῆμον ἀκοῦσαι τἀληθῆ,
καὶ πάντα τἀναντία τῶν συμφερόντων συμβεβου-
λευκότα, καὶ μηδὲν ὧν προσετάξατ᾽ ἐν τῇ πρεσβείᾳ
πεποιηκότα, καὶ ἀνηλωκότα τοὺς χρόνους ἐν οἷς
πολλῶν καὶ μεγάλων πραγμάτων καιροὶ προεῖνται
τῇ πόλει, καὶ πάντων τούτων δῶρα καὶ μισθοὺς
εἰληφότα μετὰ Φιλοκράτους, καταψηφίσασθ᾽ αὐτοῦ
καὶ δίκην ἀξίαν τῶν ἀδικημάτων λάβετε· ἂν δὲ μὴ
δείξω ταῦτ᾽ ἢ μὴ πάντα, ἐμὲ μὲν φαῦλον ἡγεῖσθε,
τουτονὶ δ᾽ ἄφετε.
9 Πολλὰ δὲ καὶ δεινὰ κατηγορεῖν ἔχων ἔτι πρὸς
τούτοις ἕτερ᾽, ὦ ἄνδρες Ἀθηναῖοι, ἐξ ὧν οὐκ ἔσθ᾽
ὅστις ἂν οὐκ εἰκότως μισήσειεν αὐτόν, βούλομαι
πρὸ πάντων ὧν μέλλω λέγειν μνημονεύοντας
ὑμῶν οἶδ᾽ ὅτι τοὺς πολλοὺς ὑπομνῆσαι, τίνα τάξιν
ἑαυτὸν ἔταξεν Αἰσχίνης ἐν τῇ πολιτείᾳ τὸ πρῶτον,

what to say and what to do by resolution of the
Assembly, it is his duty to conduct his business
according to such instructions. Very well; but
how does the question of time arise? Because, men
of Athens, in important transactions opportunities
are often short-lived: once wilfully surrendered and
betrayed to the enemy, they cannot be recovered,
do what you will. Next, as for the question of
bribery or no bribery, of course you are agreed that
it is a scandalous and abominable offence to accept
money for acts injurious to the commonwealth. The
author of the statute, however, made no such distinction; he forbade the acceptance of rewards
absolutely, holding, as I suppose, that the man who
takes them and is thereby corrupted can no longer be
trusted by the state as a judge of sound policy. If,
then, I can establish by clear proofs that the reports
of the defendant, Aeschines, were entirely untruthful,
and that he prevented the Assembly from hearing
the truth from me; that his counsels were totally
opposed to your true interests; that he disobeyed
all your instructions when on embassy; that by his
waste of time many important opportunities were
lost to the city; and finally that for all these delinquencies he, as well as Philocrates, accepted presents
and rewards; pronounce him guilty and exact a
penalty adequate to his crimes. But if I fail to prove
all these five charges, or any one of them, then call
me an impostor, and acquit him.

I have many further charges to add, such as must
excite universal abhorrence; but, by way of preface,
I will first remind you of what doubtless most of you
remember,—of the party with which Aeschines at
first ranged himself in politics, and of the speeches

καὶ τίνας λόγους κατὰ τοῦ Φιλίππου δημηγορεῖν
[344] ᾤετο δεῖν, ἵν' εἰδῆθ' ὅτι τοῖς ὑφ' ἑαυτοῦ πεπραγμένοις καὶ δεδημηγορημένοις ἐν ἀρχῇ μάλιστ' ἐξελεγ-
10 χθήσεται δῶρ' ἔχων. ἔστι τοίνυν οὗτος ὁ πρῶτος
'Αθηναίων αἰσθόμενος Φίλιππον, ὡς τότε δημηγορῶν ἔφη, ἐπιβουλεύοντα τοῖς "Ελλησι καὶ δια-
φθείροντά τινας τῶν ἐν 'Αρκαδίᾳ προεστηκότων,
καὶ ἔχων "Ισχανδρον τὸν Νεοπτολέμου δευτερ-
αγωνιστὴν προσιὼν μὲν τῇ βουλῇ προσιὼν δὲ τῷ
δήμῳ περὶ τούτων, καὶ πείσας ὑμᾶς πανταχοῖ
πρέσβεις πέμψαι τοὺς συνάξοντας δεῦρο τοὺς
βουλευσομένους περὶ τοῦ πρὸς Φίλιππον πολέμου,
11 καὶ ἀπαγγέλλων μετὰ ταῦθ' ἥκων ἐξ 'Αρκαδίας
τοὺς καλοὺς ἐκείνους καὶ μακροὺς λόγους, οὓς ἐν
τοῖς μυρίοις ἐν Μεγάλῃ πόλει πρὸς 'Ιερώνυμον τὸν
ὑπὲρ Φιλίππου λέγονθ' ὑπὲρ ὑμῶν ἔφη δεδημηγο-
ρηκέναι, καὶ διεξιὼν ἡλίκα τὴν 'Ελλάδα πᾶσαν,
οὐχὶ τὰς ἰδίας ἀδικοῦσι μόνον πατρίδας, οἱ δωροδοκοῦντες καὶ χρήματα λαμβάνοντες παρὰ Φιλ-
12 ίππου. ἐπειδὴ τοίνυν ταῦτα πολιτευομένου τούτου
τότε καὶ τοῦτο τὸ δεῖγμ' ἐξενηνοχότος περὶ αὑτοῦ,
τοὺς περὶ τῆς εἰρήνης πρέσβεις πέμπειν ὡς Φίλιππον ἐπείσθητε ὑπ' 'Αριστοδήμου καὶ Νεοπτολέμου
καὶ Κτησιφῶντος καὶ τῶν ἄλλων τῶν ἐκεῖθεν ἀπαγγελλόντων οὐδ' ὁτιοῦν ὑγιές, γίγνεται τῶν πρέσβεων τούτων εἷς καὶ οὗτος, οὐχ ὡς τῶν ἀπο-
δωσομένων τὰ ὑμέτερα, οὐδ' ὡς τῶν πεπιστευκότων
τῷ Φιλίππῳ, ἀλλ' ὡς τῶν φυλαξόντων τοὺς ἄλλους·
διὰ γὰρ τοὺς προειρημένους λόγους καὶ τὴν πρὸς
τὸν Φίλιππον ἀπέχθειαν ταύτην εἰκότως περὶ
13 αὑτοῦ πάντες εἴχετε τὴν δόξαν. προσελθὼν τοίνυν
[345] ἐμοὶ μετὰ ταῦτα συνετάττετο κοινῇ πρεσβεύειν,
252

which he thought fit to make in opposition to Philip.
In this way I hope to satisfy you that his early acts
and speeches supply abundant proof of his present
corruption. Aeschines, then, was the first man in
Athens, as he claimed at the time in a speech, to
perceive that Philip had designs against Greece, and
was corrupting some of the magnates of Arcadia. It
was he who, with Ischander, son of Neoptolemus, as
his understudy, addressed the Council, and addressed
the Assembly, on this subject, and persuaded them
to send ambassadors to all the Greek states to
convene a conference at Athens for the consideration
of war with Philip. It was he who afterwards, on
his return from Arcadia, gave a report of the fine
long orations which he said he had delivered as your
spokesman before the Ten Thousand at Megalopolis in reply to Philip's champion Hieronymus, and
he made a long story of the enormous harm which
corrupt statesmen in the pay of Philip were doing
not only to their own countries but to the whole of
Greece. So on the strength of his policy at that
time, and of the sample he had exhibited of his
conduct, he was actually appointed as one of the
ambassadors when you were induced by Aristodemus,
Neoptolemus, Ctesiphon and others, who had brought
entirely misleading reports from Macedonia, to send
an embassy to negotiate peace with Philip. He was
chosen, not as one who would make traffic of your
interests, not as one who had any confidence in
Philip, but as one of the party that was to keep an
eye on the rest, for in view of his early speeches, and
of his known hostility to Philip, it was natural that
you should all have such an opinion of the man.
Then he came to me and proposed that we should

καὶ ὅπως τὸν μιαρὸν καὶ ἀναιδῆ φυλάξομεν ἀμφότεροι, τὸν Φιλοκράτην, πολλὰ παρεκελεύσατο.
καὶ μέχρι τοῦ δεῦρ' ἐπανελθεῖν ἀπὸ τῆς πρώτης
πρεσβείας ἐμὲ γοῦν, ὦ ἄνδρες Ἀθηναῖοι, δι-
εφθαρμένος καὶ πεπρακὼς ἑαυτὸν ἐλάνθανεν. χωρὶς
γὰρ τῶν ἄλλων ὧν, ὅπερ εἶπον, εἰρήκει πρότερον
ἀναστὰς τῇ προτέρᾳ τῶν ἐκκλησιῶν, ἐν αἷς περὶ τῆς
εἰρήνης ἐβουλεύεσθε, ἤρξατ' ἀρχήν, ἣν ἐγὼ καὶ τοῖς
ῥήμασιν οἶμαι τοῖς αὐτοῖς οἷσπερ οὗτος εἶπεν ἐν
14 ὑμῖν ἀπομνημονεύσειν. ''εἰ πάνυ πολύν,'' ἔφη,
''χρόνον ἐσκόπει Φιλοκράτης, ὦ ἄνδρες Ἀθηναῖοι,
πῶς ἂν ἄριστ' ἐναντιωθείη τῇ εἰρήνῃ, οὐκ ἂν αὐτὸν
ἄμεινον εὑρεῖν οἶμαι ἢ τοιαῦτα γράφοντα. ἐγὼ
δὲ ταύτην μὲν τὴν εἰρήνην, ἕως ἂν εἷς Ἀθηναίων
λείπηται, οὐδέποτ' ἂν συμβουλεύσαιμι ποιήσασθαι
τῇ πόλει, εἰρήνην μέντοι φημὶ δεῖν ποιεῖσθαι.''
καὶ τοιούτους τινὰς εἶπε βραχεῖς καὶ μετρίους
15 λόγους. ὁ δὲ ταῦτ' εἰπὼν τῇ προτεραίᾳ πάντων
ἀκουόντων ὑμῶν, εἰς τὴν ὑστεραίαν, ἐν ᾗ τὴν
εἰρήνην ἔδει κυροῦσθαι, ἐμοῦ τῷ τῶν συμμάχων
συνηγοροῦντος δόγματι καὶ τὴν εἰρήνην ὅπως ἴση
καὶ δικαία γένηται πράττοντος, καὶ ὑμῶν βουλομένων ταῦτα καὶ οὐδὲ φωνὴν ἐθελόντων ἀκούειν
τοῦ καταπτύστου Φιλοκράτους, ἀναστὰς ἐδημη-
16 γόρει καὶ συνηγόρει ἐκείνῳ πολλῶν ἀξίους, ὦ
Ζεῦ καὶ πάντες θεοί, θανάτων λόγους, ὡς οὔτε
τῶν προγόνων ὑμᾶς μεμνῆσθαι δέοι οὔτε τῶν τὰ
τρόπαια καὶ τὰς ναυμαχίας λεγόντων ἀνέχεσθαι,
νόμον τε θήσειν καὶ γράψειν μηδενὶ τῶν Ἑλλή-

act together on the embassy, being especially urgent that we should jointly keep watch upon that infamous scoundrel Philocrates. And until after our return from the first embassy I at least, men of Athens, had no suspicion that he was corrupt and had already sold himself. For apart from the speeches which, as I said, he had made on former occasions, he rose at the first of the two assemblies at which you discussed terms of peace, and began with an exordium which I believe I can repeat to you in the very words he used : " If Philocrates, men of Athens, had given many days to studying how best he could thwart the peace, I do not think he could have found a better way than the present proposal. Such a peace as this I for one will never advise the city to make, so long as a single Athenian remains alive ; yet I do say that we ought to make peace." In such terms he spoke, concisely and with moderation. And then on the next day, when the peace was to be ratified, when I supported the resolutions of our allies, and did what I could to secure fair and equitable terms, and when the people sympathized with my purpose and refused to hear a word from the contemptible Philocrates, up jumped the very man who had made the speech I have quoted in the hearing of all of you only the day before, and addressed you in support of Philocrates, using language for which, as Heaven is my witness, he deserves to die many times over. He told you that you ought to forget the achievements of your forefathers ; that you should not tolerate all that talk about old trophies and sea-fights ; and that he would draft and enact a law forbidding aid to any Greeks who had not previously

νων ὑμᾶς βοηθεῖν, ὃς ἂν μὴ πρότερος βεβοηθη-
[346] κὼς ὑμῖν ᾖ. καὶ ταῦθ' ὁ σχέτλιος καὶ ἀναιδὴς
οὗτος ἐτόλμα λέγειν ἐφεστηκότων ἔτι τῶν πρέσβεων καὶ ἀκουόντων, οὓς ἀπὸ τῶν Ἑλλήνων
μετεπέμψασθε ὑπὸ τούτου πεισθέντες, ὅτ' οὔπω
πεπρακὼς αὐτὸν ἦν.

17 Ὃν μὲν οὖν τρόπον, ὦ ἄνδρες Ἀθηναῖοι, χειροτονησάντων ὑμῶν ἐπὶ τοὺς ὅρκους αὐτὸν πάλιν τούς
τε χρόνους κατέτριψε καὶ τὰ πράγματα πάντ' ἐλυ-
μήνατο τῆς πόλεως, καὶ ὅσαι περὶ τούτων ἐμοὶ πρὸς
τοῦτον ἀπέχθειαι συνέβησαν βουλομένῳ κωλύειν,
αὐτίκ' ἀκούσεσθε. ἀλλ' ἐπειδὴ πάλιν ἥκομεν ἐκ
τῆς πρεσβείας ταύτης τῆς ἐπὶ τοὺς ὅρκους, ἧσπερ
εἰσὶν αἱ νῦν εὔθυναι, οὔτε μικρὸν οὔτε μέγ' οὐδ'
ὁτιοῦν εὑρημένοι τῶν ὅτε τὴν εἰρήνην ἐποιεῖσθε
λεχθέντων καὶ προσδοκηθέντων, ἀλλὰ πάντ' ἐξ-
ηπατημένοι, καὶ τούτων ἕτερ' αὖθις αὖ πεπραχότων
καὶ παρ' αὐτὸ τὸ ψήφισμα πεπρεσβευκότων,
προσῇμεν τῇ βουλῇ. καὶ ταυτὶ πολλοὶ συνίσασιν,
ἃ μέλλω λέγειν· τὸ γὰρ βουλευτήριον μεστὸν ἦν
18 ἰδιωτῶν. παρελθὼν δ' ἐγὼ πάντα τἀληθῆ πρὸς
τὴν βουλὴν ἀπήγγειλα, καὶ κατηγόρησα τούτων,
καὶ ἀνηριθμησάμην ἀπὸ τῶν πρώτων ἐλπίδων
ἐκείνων ὧν ὁ Κτησιφῶν καὶ ὁ Ἀριστόδημος ἀπήγγειλαν πρὸς ὑμᾶς, καὶ μετὰ ταῦτα, ὅτε τὴν εἰρήνην
ἐποιεῖσθε, ἃ οὗτος ἐδημηγόρησε, καὶ εἰς ἃ προ-
ήχασι τὴν πόλιν, καὶ περὶ τῶν ὑπολοίπων (ταῦτα
δ' ἦν Φωκεῖς καὶ Πύλαι) μὴ προέσθαι συνεβούλευον,
μηδὲ ταὐτὰ παθεῖν, μηδ' ἀναρτωμένους ἐλπίσιν ἐξ
256

brought aid to you. This speech the shameless reprobate found courage to make while the ambassadors, whom you summoned from the Greek cities at his own suggestion, before he had sold himself, were standing at his elbow and listening to what he said.

Well, you appointed him a second time, men of Athens, as an envoy to receive the oath of ratification; and I shall shortly have to tell you how he again wasted time, mishandled all the affairs of the commonwealth, and repeatedly fell out with me in regard to them when I tried to stand in his way. However, by reason of the persistent misconduct of these men, and their disobedience to instructions, we came back from the embassy for the oaths— that is the embassy which is the subject of the present scrutiny—without having realized any single one, great or small, of the advantages which were promised or expected when you approved the peace,—with nothing but deception and disappointment. Then we repaired to the Council. There are many eye-witnesses of what I am about to relate, for the Council-house was thronged with spectators. I came forward and reported the whole truth to the Council. I denounced these men, and told the whole story, point by point, beginning with those earlier hopes created by the reports of Ctesiphon and Aristodemus, going on to the more recent orations of Aeschines at the approval of the peace, and showing to what straits they had reduced the city. There remained the question of the Phocians and Thermopylae, and we must not — such was my advice— we must not repeat our experience, and throw them overboard, and so, in reliance upon a succession of

ἐλπίδων καὶ ὑποσχέσεσιν εἰς τοὔσχατον ἐλθεῖν τὰ
πράγματ' ἐᾶσαι. καὶ ἔπεισα ταῦτα τὴν βουλήν.

19
[347] ἐπειδὴ δ' ἧκεν ἡ ἐκκλησία καὶ πρὸς ὑμᾶς ἔδει λέγειν,
παρελθὼν Αἰσχίνης οὑτοσὶ πρῶτος ἡμῶν ἁπάντων
(καὶ πρὸς Διὸς καὶ θεῶν πειρᾶσθε συνδιαμνημο-
νεύειν ἂν ἀληθῆ λέγω· τὰ γὰρ πάντα τὰ πράγματα
λυμηνάμεν' ὑμῶν καὶ διαφθείρανθ' ὅλως ταῦτ' ἐστὶν
ἤδη) τοῦ μὲν ἀπαγγέλλειν τι τῶν πεπρεσβευμένων
ἢ περὶ τῶν ἐν τῇ βουλῇ ῥηθέντων, εἰ ἄρ' ἠμφι-
σβήτει μὴ ἀληθῆ λέγειν ἐμέ, μνησθῆναι πάμπληθες
ἀπέσχεν, εἶπε δὲ τοιούτους λόγους καὶ τηλικαῦτα
καὶ τοσαῦτ' ἔχοντας τἀγαθά, ὥσθ' ἅπαντας ὑμᾶς
20 λαβὼν ᾤχετο. ἔφη γὰρ ἥκειν πεπεικὼς Φίλιππον
ἅπανθ' ὅσα συμφέρει τῇ πόλει, καὶ περὶ τῶν ἐν
Ἀμφικτύοσιν καὶ περὶ τῶν ἄλλων ἁπάντων, καὶ
διεξῆλθε λόγον μακρὸν ὑμῖν, ὃν κατὰ Θηβαίων
εἰπεῖν πρὸς Φίλιππον ἔφη, καὶ τὰ κεφάλαι' ἀπήγγειλε πρὸς ὑμᾶς, καὶ ἀπελογίζετ' ἐκ τῶν αὐτῷ
πεπρεσβευμένων δυοῖν ἢ τριῶν ἡμερῶν ὑμᾶς, μένον-
τας οἴκοι καὶ οὐ στρατευομένους οὐδ' ἐνοχλουμέ-
νους, Θήβας μὲν πολιορκουμένας αὐτὰς καθ' αὑτὰς
21 χωρὶς τῆς ἄλλης Βοιωτίας ἀκούσεσθαι, Θεσπιὰς δὲ
καὶ Πλαταιὰς οἰκιζομένας, τῷ θεῷ δὲ τὰ χρήματ'
εἰσπραττόμεν' οὐ παρὰ Φωκέων ἀλλὰ παρὰ Θηβαίων
τῶν βουλευσάντων τὴν κατάληψιν τοῦ ἱεροῦ· διδάσκειν γὰρ αὐτὸς ἔφη τὸν Φίλιππον ὅτι οὐδὲν ἧττον
ἠσεβήκασιν οἱ βεβουλευκότες τῶν ταῖς χερσὶ
πραξάντων, καὶ διὰ ταῦτα χρήμαθ' ἑαυτῷ τοὺς
22 Θηβαίους ἐπικεκηρυχέναι. ἀκούειν δὲ καὶ τῶν
Εὐβοέων ἐνίων ἔφη πεφοβημένων καὶ τεταραγμένων

idle hopes and assurances, allow ourselves to fall into the last extremity of disaster. I convinced the Council ; but when the Assembly met, and we had to address the whole body of citizens, Aeschines took the first turn of all of us. And here I most earnestly entreat you to verify my account by your own recollections ; for I am now relating transactions which ultimately brought your affairs to complete and final ruin. He utterly ignored the duty of giving a report of the doings of the embassy. He never mentioned the speeches made to the Council, or told you whether he disputed the truth of my statement. But he made such a fine speech, so full of big promises, that he carried you all away with him. For he declared that he had completely converted Philip to the interests of Athens in respect of the Amphictyonic question and of everything else. He went through a long diatribe against the Thebans, which he said he had addressed to Philip himself, recapitulating the main points. He offered you a calculation that, thanks to his diplomacy, without leaving your homes, without any campaigning or worry, within two or three days you would hear the news of the beleaguerment of Thebes, independently of the rest of Boeotia, of the repopulation of Thespiae and Plataea, and of the recovery of Apollo's treasure, not from the Phocians, but from the Thebans, who had planned the seizure of the temple. It was himself, he added, who had instructed Philip that those who contrived the project were quite as sacrilegious as the men by whose hands it was executed ; and therefore the Thebans had set a price on his head ! He had even heard some Euboeans, who were thoroughly frightened by the friendship that had been cemented

τὴν πρὸς τὴν πόλιν οἰκειότητα Φιλίππῳ γεγενημένην,
[348] ὅτι '' οὐ λελήθαθ᾽ ἡμᾶς, ὦ ἄνδρες πρέσβεις, ἐφ᾽
οἷς πεποίησθε τὴν εἰρήνην πρὸς Φίλιππον, οὐδ᾽
ἀγνοοῦμεν ὅτι ὑμεῖς μὲν Ἀμφίπολιν δεδώκατ᾽
ἐκείνῳ, Φίλιππος δ᾽ ὑμῖν Εὔβοιαν ὡμολόγηκε
παραδώσειν.'' εἶναι μέντοι τι καὶ ἄλλο διῳκη-
μένον αὐτῷ, οὐ μήν πω τοῦτο βούλεσθαι λέγειν·
καὶ γὰρ νῦν φθονεῖν τινὰς αὐτῷ τῶν συμπρέσβεων.
ὑπῃνίττετο δ᾽ οὕτω καὶ παρεδήλου τὸν Ὠρωπόν.
23 εὐδοκιμῶν δ᾽ ἐπὶ τούτοις εἰκότως, καὶ δοκῶν καὶ
ῥήτωρ ἄριστος εἶναι καὶ ἀνὴρ θαυμαστός, κατέβη
μάλα σεμνῶς. ἀναστὰς δ᾽ ἐγὼ ταῦτά τ᾽ οὐκ ἔφην
εἰδέναι, καὶ ἐπειρώμην τι λέγειν τούτων ὧν εἰς
τὴν βουλὴν ἀπήγγειλα. καὶ παραστὰς ὁ μὲν ἔνθεν,
ὁ δ᾽ ἔνθεν, οὑτοσὶ καὶ Φιλοκράτης, ἐβόων, ἐξ-
έκρουόν με, τελευτῶντες ἐχλεύαζον. ὑμεῖς δ᾽ ἐγελᾶτε,
καὶ οὔτ᾽ ἀκούειν ἠθέλετ᾽ οὔτε πιστεύειν ἐβούλεσθ᾽
24 ἄλλα πλὴν ἃ οὗτος ἀπήγγελκε. καὶ νὴ τοὺς θεοὺς
εἰκός τι παθεῖν ἔμοιγε δοκεῖτε· τίς γὰρ ἂν ἠνέσχετο,
τηλικαῦτα καὶ τοσαῦτ᾽ ἔσεσθαι προσδοκῶν ἀγαθά,
ἢ ταῦθ᾽ ὡς οὐκ ἔσται λέγοντός τινος, ἢ κατηγοροῦντος τῶν πεπραγμένων τούτοις; πάντα γὰρ τἄλλ᾽,
οἶμαι, τότε δεύτερ᾽ ἦν τῶν ὑποκειμένων προσδοκιῶν
καὶ τῶν ἐλπίδων, οἱ δ᾽ ἀντιλέγοντες ὄχλος ἄλλως
καὶ βασκανία κατεφαίνετο, ταῦτα δὲ θαυμάσι᾽
ἡλίκα καὶ συμφέροντ᾽ ἐδόκει πεπρᾶχθαι τῇ πόλει.
25 Τοῦ χάριν δὴ ταῦθ᾽ ὑπέμνησα πρῶτα νῦν ὑμᾶς
καὶ διεξῆλθον τούτους τοὺς λόγους; ἑνὸς μέν, ὦ
260

between Philip and Athens, utter these very words :
" Gentlemen of the Embassy, we know all about the
terms on which you have concluded peace with
Philip, and we are aware that you have given up
Amphipolis to him, and that he has agreed to hand
over Euboea to you." He had also, he said, settled
another matter, but he thought it better not to
mention it just yet—some of his colleagues were
already so jealous of him. This was a veiled allusion
to Oropus. And so, in all the glory of these dis-
closures, with everybody regarding him as a grand
speaker and a marvellous man, he descended from
the tribune in his most majestic manner. Then I
rose, and said that the whole story was news to me.
I attempted to repeat the statement I had made to
the Council ; but Aeschines and Philocrates posted
themselves one on either side of me—shouting,
interrupting, and finally jeering. You were all
laughing ; you would not listen to me, and you did
not want to believe anything except what Aeschines
had reported. And I must say that your feeling
was quite natural. For how could anyone, filled
with anticipation of those wonderful benefits, be
patient of a speaker who told you that you would
never get them, and even denounced the conduct
of the benefactors ? At the moment, I imagine,
everything else was thrown into the shade by the
hopes and expectations that were suggested to you ;
contradiction seemed to be mere annoyance and
malice ; and these great achievements were thought
amazingly fine and most beneficial to the commonwealth.

Why have I begun by reviving these memories
and quoting those old speeches ? My first and chief

ἄνδρες Ἀθηναῖοι, μάλιστα καὶ πρώτου, ἵνα μηδεὶς
[349] ὑμῶν, ἐπειδάν τι λέγοντος ἀκούῃ μου τῶν πεπραγμένων καὶ δοκῇ δεινὸν αὐτῷ καὶ ὑπερβάλλον εἶναι,
"εἶτα τότ' οὐκ ἔλεγες παραχρῆμα ταῦτ' οὐδ'
26 ἐδίδασκες ἡμᾶς;" θαυμάζῃ, ἀλλὰ μεμνημένοι τὰς
ὑποσχέσεις τὰς τούτων, ἃς ἐφ' ἑκάστων ποιούμενοι
τῶν καιρῶν ἐξέκλειον λόγου τυγχάνειν τοὺς ἄλλους,
καὶ τὴν ἐπαγγελίαν τὴν τούτου ταύτην τὴν καλήν,
εἰδῆθ' ὅτι πρὸς ἅπασι τοῖς ἄλλοις καὶ τοῦτ' ἠδίκησθ'
ὑπ' αὐτοῦ, ὅτι τἀληθῆ παραχρῆμα καὶ ἡνίκ' ἔδει
πυνθάνεσθαι διεκωλύθητ' ἐλπίσι καὶ φενακισμοῖς
27 καὶ ὑποσχέσεσιν ἐξαπατώμενοι. πρώτου μὲν τούτου καὶ μάλισθ', οὗπερ εἶπον, ἕνεκα ταῦτα διεξῆλθον, δευτέρου δὲ τίνος; καὶ οὐδὲν ἐλάττονος ἢ
τούτου, ἵνα τὴν ὅτ' ἀδωροδόκητος ὑπῆρχε προαίρεσιν αὐτοῦ τῆς πολιτείας ἀναμνησθέντες, ὡς
προβεβλημένῃ καὶ ἄπιστος ἦν πρὸς τὸν Φίλιππον,
τὴν μετὰ ταῦτ' ἐξαίφνης γεγονυῖαν πίστιν καὶ φι-
28 λίαν σκέψησθε, εἶτ' εἰ μὲν ἐκβέβηκεν ὅσ' ἀπήγγειλε
πρὸς ὑμᾶς οὗτος καὶ καλῶς ἔχει τὰ πεπραγμένα,
διὰ τὴν ἀλήθειαν καὶ τὸ συμφέρον τῇ πόλει γεγενῆσθαι νομίσητε, εἰ δὲ πάντα τἀναντί' ὧν οὗτος
εἶπεν πέπρακται, καὶ πολλὴν αἰσχύνην καὶ μεγάλους
κινδύνους ταῦτ' ἔχει τῇ πόλει, διὰ τὴν αἰσχρο-
κέρδειαν τὴν ἑαυτοῦ καὶ τὸ χρημάτων ἀποδόσθαι
τἀληθῆ μεταβεβλημένον αὐτὸν εἰδῆτε.
29 Βούλομαι δ', ἐπειδήπερ εἰς τούτους προήχθην
τοὺς λόγους, ὃν τρόπον τὰ περὶ τοὺς Φωκέας
πράγμαθ' ὑμῶν παρείλοντο πρῶτον εἰπεῖν ἁπάντων.
δεῖ δὲ μηδέν' ὑμῶν, ὦ ἄνδρες δικασταί, εἰς τὸ τῶν
[350] πραγμάτων μέγεθος βλέψαντα μείζους τὰς κατηγορίας καὶ τὰς αἰτίας τῆς τούτου δόξης νομίσαι,

262

object, men of Athens, is that, when you hear me relate some performance that seems to you atrocious and incredible, no one may ask in surprise : " Then why did you not speak out and give us this information instantly ? " but that, by recalling the assurances by which on every occasion these men stopped others from getting your attention, and that magnificent promise of Aeschines, you may realize that you have to thank him for this crowning injury,—that you were precluded from learning the truth promptly and at the proper time, being cheated by hopes and impostures and vain assurances. That, I say, is my first and main purpose in this narration. What is my second purpose ? It is one of no less importance. I want you to remind yourselves of that policy of precaution and distrust of Philip which this man deliberately chose when he was still unbribed, and to compare the confidence and friendship that afterwards sprang up so suddenly ; and then, if the fair reports he laid before you have really proved true, and if all the results have been fortunate, to admit the view that that friendship was formed for truth's sake and in the best interests of the city ; but, if the sequel has given the lie to all his predictions, if it has involved the city in much dishonour and in grievous perils, then be assured that his own sordid greed has prompted this change of front, because he has sold the truth for a bribe.

Having allowed myself to refer to those old speeches, I wish to relate first of all how these men took the business of the Phocians out of your hands. Gentlemen of the jury, I hope that none of you will regard my charges and accusations as too big for the calibre of the defendant, measuring him against

ἀλλ' ἐκεῖν' ὁρᾶν, ὅτι ὄντιν' ἂν ὑμεῖς εἰς ταύτην τὴν
τάξιν κατεστήσατε καὶ τῶν συμβάντων καιρῶν
ἐποιήσατε κύριον, οὗτος, εἴπερ ὥσπερ οὗτος ἐβουλήθη μισθώσας αὑτὸν ἐξαπατᾶν ὑμᾶς καὶ φενακίζειν,
τῶν ἴσων αἴτιος ἦν ἂν κακῶν ὅσωνπερ καὶ οὗτος.
30 οὐ γὰρ εἰ φαύλοις χρῆσθ' ὑμεῖς εἰς τὰ κοινὰ πολλάκις
ἀνθρώποις, καὶ τὰ πράγματ' ἐστὶ φαῦλ' ὧν ἡ πόλις
ἀξιοῦται παρὰ τοῖς ἄλλοις, οὐδὲ πολλοῦ δεῖ· εἶτα
καὶ Φωκέας ἀπολώλεκε μέν, οἶμαι, Φίλιππος,
συνηγωνίσαντο δ' οὗτοι· τοῦτο δὴ δεῖ σκοπεῖν καὶ
ὁρᾶν, εἰ ὅσα τῆς Φωκέων σωτηρίας ἐπὶ τὴν πρεσβείαν ἧκε, ταῦθ' ἅπαντ' ἀπώλεσαν οὗτοι καὶ
διέφθειραν ἑκόντες, οὐχ ὡς ὅδε Φωκέας ἀπώλεσε
καθ' ἑαυτόν. πόθεν;
31 Δὸς δέ μοι τὸ προβούλευμα, ὃ πρὸς τὴν ἐμὴν
ἀπαγγελίαν ἐψηφίσαθ' ἡ βουλή, καὶ τὴν μαρτυρίαν
τὴν τοῦ γράψαντος αὐτὸ τότε, ἵν' εἰδῆθ' ὅτι ἐγὼ
μὲν οὐ τότε σιγήσας νῦν ἀφίσταμαι τῶν πεπραγμένων, ἀλλ' εὐθὺς κατηγόρουν καὶ προεώρων τὰ
μέλλοντα, ἡ βουλὴ δ' ἡ μὴ κωλυθεῖσ' ἀκοῦσαι τά-
ληθῆ παρ' ἐμοῦ οὔτ' ἐπήνεσε τούτους οὔτ' εἰς τὸ
πρυτανεῖον ἠξίωσε καλέσαι. καίτοι τοῦτ', ἀφ'
οὗ γέγονεν ἡ πόλις, οὐδεὶς πώποτέ φησι παθεῖν
οὐδένας πρέσβεις, οὐδὲ Τιμαγόραν, οὗ θάνατον
κατεχειροτόνησεν ὁ δῆμος. ἀλλ' οὗτοι πεπόν-
32 θασιν. λέγε δ' αὐτοῖς πρῶτον μὲν τὴν μαρτυρίαν,
εἶτα τὸ προβούλευμα.

the magnitude of the transactions. Reflect rather
that, if any man soever, placed by you in the position
he filled, and trusted to deal with the occasions that
arose, had taken hire, and had sought to deceive and
mislead you as Aeschines did, he would have brought
about exactly the same disaster as Aeschines. For
though you often employ insignificant men for public
business, it does not follow that those affairs are
insignificant for which the rest of the world acknow-
ledges our competence. Assuredly not. Again, it
was Philip, of course, who really destroyed the
Phocians ; but these men co-operated. The question
on which you are to fix your minds is whether they
purposely wasted and threw away any chances that
came to the embassy of saving the Phocians. I do
not suggest that Aeschines destroyed the Phocians
all by himself. How could he ?

Give me the resolution which the Council adopted
on my report, and the evidence of the member who
moved it on that occasion. These documents will
satisfy you that I did not hold my peace then, to run
away from my actions now,—for I was laying my
complaint, and trying to forecast results, at the first
opportunity ; and also that the Council, not being
debarred from hearing the truth from me, did not
give these men either a vote of thanks, or an invitation to the public dinner in the Town Hall. We are
told that these compliments had never before been
withheld from any ambassadors since the foundation
of Athens — not even from Timagoras,[a] whom the
Assembly condemned to death. These men, however,
had to go without them. Read first the deposition,
and then the resolution, to the jury.

[a] See Introduction, pp. 241-2.

ΜΑΡΤΥΡΙΑ. ΠΡΟΒΟΥΛΕΥΜΑ

Ἐνταῦθ' οὔτ' ἔπαινος οὔτε κλῆσις εἰς τὸ πρυτα-
νεῖόν ἐστι τῶν πρέσβεων ὑπὸ τῆς βουλῆς. εἰ δέ
φησιν οὗτος, δειξάτω καὶ παρασχέσθω, κἀγὼ
καταβαίνω. ἀλλ' οὐκ ἔστιν. εἰ μὲν τοίνυν ταῦθ'
ἅπαντες ἐπρεσβεύομεν, δικαίως οὐδέν' ἐπῄνεσεν ἡ
βουλή· δεινὰ γὰρ ὡς ἀληθῶς τὰ πεπραγμένα πᾶσιν·
εἰ δ' οἱ μὲν τὰ δίκαι' ἔπραττον ἡμῶν, οἱ δὲ τἀναντία,
διὰ τοὺς πεπονηρευμένους, ὡς ἔοικε, τοῖς ἐπιεικέσι
συμβεβηκὸς ἂν εἴη ταύτης τῆς ἀτιμίας μετεσχη-
33 κέναι. πῶς οὖν ῥᾳδίως πάντες εἴσεσθε τίς ποτ'
ἔσθ' ὁ πονηρός; ἀναμνήσθητε παρ' ὑμῖν αὐτοῖς
τίς ἐσθ' ὁ κατηγορῶν τῶν πεπραγμένων ἐξ ἀρχῆς.
δῆλον γὰρ ὅτι τῷ μὲν ἠδικηκότι σιγᾶν ἐξήρκει καὶ
διακρουσαμένῳ τὸν παρόντα χρόνον μηκέτ' εἰς
λόγον περὶ τῶν πεπραγμένων ἑαυτὸν καθιστάναι,
τῷ δὲ μηδὲν ἑαυτῷ συνειδότι δεινὸν εἰσῄει, εἰ
δεινῶν καὶ πονηρῶν ἔργων δόξει κοινωνεῖν τῷ
σιωπῆσαι. εἰμὶ τοίνυν ὁ κατηγορῶν ἐξ ἀρχῆς
ἐγὼ τούτων, τούτων δ' οὐδεὶς ἐμοῦ.

34 Ἡ μὲν τοίνυν βουλὴ ταῦτα προὔβεβούλευκε, τῆς
δ' ἐκκλησίας γιγνομένης καὶ τοῦ Φιλίππου παρόντος
ἐν Πύλαις ἤδη—ἦν γὰρ τοῦτο πρῶτον ἁπάντων τῶν
ἀδικημάτων, τὸ τὸν Φίλιππον ἐπιστῆσαι τοῖς
πράγμασι τούτοις, καὶ δέον ὑμᾶς ἀκοῦσαι περὶ
τῶν πραγμάτων, εἶτα βουλεύσασθαι, μετὰ ταῦτα
δὲ πράττειν ὅ τι δόξαι, ἅμ' ἀκούειν κἀκεῖνον παρ-
εῖναι καὶ μηδ' ὅ τι χρὴ ποιεῖν ῥᾴδιον εἰπεῖν εἶναι—
35 πρὸς δὲ τούτοις τοῦτο μὲν οὐδεὶς ἀνέγνω τῷ δήμῳ
τὸ προβούλευμα, οὐδ' ἤκουσεν ὁ δῆμος, ἀναστὰς δ'

(The Deposition and the Resolution are read)

Here is no commendation, no invitation from the Council to the ambassadors to dine in the Town Hall. If Aeschines says that such a thing exists, let him produce and exhibit it, and I will sit down. But no ; there is none. Now, if all the envoys acted alike, the Council was right in thanking nobody,— for we had all in very truth behaved scandalously indeed. But if some acted rightly and others wrongly, the well-conducted, it would seem, must submit to a discourtesy provoked by those who had played the rogue. How then can you find an easy answer to the question, Who was the rogue ? Consult your own recollections, and mark who denounced the transactions at the outset. For it is clear that, if the evil-doer could hold his peace, escape immediate detection, and never afterwards allow himself to be called to account, that was good enough for him ; whereas the man with a good conscience bethought himself that it would be very hard if by keeping silence he should become a reputed accomplice in scandalous and wicked actions. Well then, it was I who denounced these men from the outset, and none of them denounced me.

Well, the Council adopted this resolution. When the Assembly met, Philip was already at Thermopylae. For that is the beginning of their misdeeds : they had surrendered control to Philip ; and then,— although the right course for you was, first to hear the facts, next to decide, and finally to carry out your decision,—you heard nothing until he was already on the spot, and it was no easy matter to advise you what to do. Further, no one read the resolution to the Assembly, and the people never heard it.

οὗτος ἐδημηγόρει ταῦθ᾽ ἃ διεξῆλθον ἄρτι πρὸς
ὑμᾶς ἐγώ, τὰ πολλὰ καὶ μεγάλ᾽ ἀγαθά, ἃ πεπεικὼς
ἔφη τὸν Φίλιππον ἥκειν καὶ διὰ τοῦτο χρήμαθ᾽
ἑαυτῷ τοὺς Θηβαίους ἐπικεκηρυχέναι. ὥσθ᾽ ὑμᾶς,
ἐκπεπληγμένους τῇ παρουσίᾳ τὸ πρῶτον τῇ τοῦ
Φιλίππου, καὶ τούτοις ὀργιζομένους ἐπὶ τῷ μὴ
προηγγελκέναι, πραοτέρους γενέσθαι τινός, πάνθ᾽
ὅσ᾽ ἐβούλεσθ᾽ ὑμῖν ἔσεσθαι προσδοκήσαντας, καὶ
μηδὲ φωνὴν ἐθέλειν ἀκούειν ἐμοῦ μηδ᾽ ἄλλου
36 μηδενός. καὶ μετὰ ταῦτ᾽ ἀνεγιγνώσκεθ᾽ ἡ ἐπιστολὴ
ἡ παρὰ τοῦ Φιλίππου, ἣν οὗτος ἔγραψεν ἀπολειφθεὶς
ἡμῶν, ἄντικρυς οὕτως καὶ διαρρήδην ἀπολογία
γεγραμμένη τῶν τούτοις ἡμαρτημένων. καὶ γὰρ
ὡς αὐτὸς κατεκώλυσεν αὐτοὺς βουλομένους ἐπὶ
τὰς πόλεις ἰέναι καὶ τοὺς ὅρκους ἀπολαμβάνειν,
ἔνεστι, καὶ ὡς ἵνα συνδιαλλάττωσιν αὐτῷ τοὺς
Ἁλέας πρὸς τοὺς Φαρσαλίους κατέσχεν αὐτούς·
καὶ πάντ᾽ ἀναδεχόμενος καὶ εἰς αὐτὸν ποιούμενος
37 τὰ τούτων ἁμαρτήματ᾽ ἐστίν. ὑπὲρ δὲ Φωκέων ἢ
Θεσπιῶν ἢ ὧν οὗτος ἀπήγγειλε πρὸς ὑμᾶς, ἀλλ᾽
οὐδὲ μικρόν. καὶ τοῦτ᾽ οὐκ ἀπὸ ταὐτομάτου
τοῦτον ἐπράχθη τὸν τρόπον, ἀλλ᾽ ὑπὲρ μὲν ὧν
παρὰ τούτων ὑμᾶς ἔδει δίκην λαμβάνειν οὐ πεποιηκότων οὐδὲ διῳκηκότων οὐδὲν ὧν ὑμεῖς προσετάξατ᾽
ἐν τῷ ψηφίσματι, ἐκεῖνος ἐκδέχεται τὴν αἰτίαν καί
φησιν αὐτὸς αἴτιος γεγενῆσθαι, ὃν οὐκ ἐμέλλεθ᾽
38 ὑμεῖς, οἶμαι, δυνήσεσθαι κολάσαι, ἃ δ᾽ ἐκεῖνος
ἐξαπατῆσαι καὶ προλαβεῖν τῆς πόλεως ἐβούλετο,
[353] οὗτος ἀπήγγειλεν, ἵνα μηδ᾽ ἐγκαλέσαι μηδὲ μέμ-
ψασθαι μηδὲν ὕστερον ὑμεῖς ἔχοιτε Φιλίππῳ, μήτ᾽
ἐν ἐπιστολῇ μήτ᾽ ἄλλοθι μηδαμοῦ τῶν παρ᾽ ἐκείνου
τούτων ἐνόντων. λέγε δ᾽ αὐτοῖς αὐτὴν τὴν ἐπι-

However, Aeschines rose and delivered that oration
which I have already described, about the wonderful
advantages he had induced Philip to grant to you,
and the price set on his head by the Thebans in consequence ; and so, although you were at first alarmed
at Philip's approach, and indignant that the ambassadors had given you no warning, you became as
mild as lambs, expecting to get all that you desired,
and refused to hear a word from me or anyone else.
Then the letter from Philip was read. It had been
composed by Aeschines without our knowledge, and
was in fact a downright, explicit written defence of
the errors these men had committed. For it alleges
that Philip stopped them when they wanted to visit
the towns and receive the oaths, and that he detained
them in order that they might help him to reconcile
the Halians with the Pharsalians ; Philip takes on
his own shoulders the burden of all their delinquencies : but of the Phocians and the Thespians,
and of all the promises reported to you by Aeschines,
—not a word ! The job was not managed in this
fashion by mere accident. For derelictions of duty,
for which they ought to have been brought to justice,
and for their failure to do their work according to
your instructions, Philip takes all the blame. He
tells you it was his fault,—and of course you were
never likely to have any opportunity of punishing
him ! On the other hand, all the matters in which
he was trying to cheat you and overreach you were
left for Aeschines to report by word of mouth, so that
you might never have it in your power to incriminate
Philip or throw any blame on him, as the assertions
were not to be found in the letter or in any other
direct communication of his. Read to the jury the

στολήν, ἣν ἔγραψε μὲν οὗτος, ἔπεμψε δ᾽ ἐκεῖνος·
καὶ σκοπεῖθ᾽ ὅτι τοῦτον ἔχει τὸν τρόπον, ὃν διεξ-
ελήλυθ᾽ ἐγώ. λέγε.

ΕΠΙΣΤΟΛΗ

39 Ἀκούετ᾽, ὦ ἄνδρες Ἀθηναῖοι, τῆς ἐπιστολῆς, ὡς
καλὴ καὶ φιλάνθρωπος. περὶ δὲ Φωκέων ἢ Θηβαίων
ἢ τῶν ἄλλων ὧν οὗτος ἀπήγγειλεν, οὐδὲ γρῦ.
ταύτης τοίνυν οὐδ᾽ ὁτιοῦν ἐσθ᾽ ὑγιές. καὶ τοῦτ᾽
αὐτίκα δὴ μάλ᾽ ὑμεῖς ὄψεσθε. οἱ μὲν γὰρ Ἁλεῖς,
οὓς ἵνα συνδιαλλάττωσι κατασχεῖν φησι τούτους,
τοιαύτης τετυχήκασι διαλλαγῆς ὥστ᾽ ἐξελήλανται
καὶ ἀνάστατος ἡ πόλις αὐτῶν γέγονεν· τοὺς δ᾽
αἰχμαλώτους ὁ σκοπῶν τί ἂν ποιῶν ὑμῖν χαρίσαιτο
40 οὐδ᾽ ἐνθυμηθῆναί φησι λύσασθαι. μεμαρτύρηται δὲ
δήπουθεν ὑμῖν ἐν τῷ δήμῳ πολλάκις ὡς ἐγὼ τά-
λαντον ἔχων ἐπ᾽ αὐτοὺς ᾠχόμην, καὶ νῦν μαρτυ-
ρηθήσεται· διὸ καὶ τὴν ἐμὴν φιλοτιμίαν οὗτος ἀφαι-
ρούμενος τοῦτ᾽ ἔπεισεν ἐκεῖνον ἐγγράψαι. ὃ τοίνυν
μέγιστον ἁπάντων· ὁ γὰρ εἰς τὴν προτέραν γράψας
ἐπιστολήν, ἣν ἠνέγκαμεν ἡμεῖς, ὅτι " ἔγραφον δ᾽
ἂν καὶ διαρρήδην ἡλίχ᾽ ὑμᾶς εὖ ποιήσω, εἰ εὖ
ᾔδειν καὶ τὴν συμμαχίαν μοι γενησομένην," γεγονυίας τῆς συμμαχίας οὔ φησιν εἰδέναι τί ἂν ποιῶν
χαρίσαιτο, οὐδ᾽ ὃ αὐτὸς ὑπέσχετο· τοῦτο γὰρ ᾔδει
δηλονότι, εἴπερ μὴ ἐφενάκιζεν. ἀλλὰ μὴν ὅτι
[354] ταῦθ᾽ οὕτω τότ᾽ ἔγραψε, λέγε μοι λαβὼν ἐκ τῆς προτέρας ἐπιστολῆς αὐτὸ τοῦτ᾽, ἐνθένδε. λέγε.

letter written by Aeschines and dispatched by Philip.
You will observe that it agrees exactly with my
description. Read.

(*The Letter is read*)

You hear the letter, men of Athens,—such a nice,
courteous letter! But about the Phocians, about the
Thebans, about everything that Aeschines reported
—not a scrape of the pen! There is nothing in it
that is honest, as you shall see at once. For he tells
you that he detained them that they might help him
to reconcile the Halians. Well, the reconciliation
of the Halians consisted in their being cast out of their
homes, and their country devastated. As for the
prisoners, this man, who wanted to know what he
could do to oblige you, declares that the idea of getting
them liberated never entered his head. You know
that evidence has already been given before the
Assembly,—and that evidence shall now be repeated,
—that I had started with a talent in my pocket for
their ransom ; and therefore, to rob me of a patriotic
act, Aeschines persuaded Philip to write these words.
Now for the most important point. The man who,
in the first letter, which we brought home, wrote
these words : " I would write more explicitly of the
benefits I intend to confer on you, if I were certain
that the alliance will be made,"—this man, now that
the alliance has been made, says that he does not
know how he can gratify you. Not know the very
thing he promised! Why, he must have known it,
unless he was hoodwinking us throughout. To
prove, however, that he did so write at that time,
please take and read the actual passage from the
first letter,—beginning here. Read.

ΕΞ ΕΠΙΣΤΟΛΗΣ

41 Οὐκοῦν πρὶν μὲν εἰρήνης τυχεῖν, εἰ καὶ συμμαχία
προσγένοιτ᾽ αὐτῷ, γράψειν ὡμολόγει ἡλίκα τὴν
πόλιν εὖ ποιήσει· ἐπειδὴ δ᾽ ἀμφότερ᾽ αὐτῷ γέγονεν,
οὐκ εἰδέναι φησὶ τί ἂν ποιῶν χαρίσαιτο, ἐὰν δ᾽
ὑμεῖς λέγητε, ποιήσειν ἃ μήτ᾽ αἰσχύνην μήτ᾽
ἀδοξίαν αὐτῷ φέρει, εἰς ταύτας τὰς προφάσεις
καταφεύγων, κἂν ἄρ᾽ εἴπητέ τι καὶ προαχθῇθ᾽
ὑμεῖς ἐπαγγείλασθαι, ἀναχώρησιν ἑαυτῷ κατα-
λείπων.

42 Ταῦτα τοίνυν καὶ πόλλ᾽ ἕτερ᾽ ἐνῆν παραχρῆμα
τότ᾽ εὐθὺς ἐξελέγχειν καὶ διδάσκειν ὑμᾶς καὶ μὴ
προέσθαι τὰ πράγματ᾽ ἐᾶν, εἰ μὴ Θεσπιαὶ καὶ
Πλαταιαὶ καὶ τὸ Θηβαίους αὐτίκα δὴ μάλα δώσειν
δίκην ἀφείλετο τὴν ἀλήθειαν. καίτοι ταῦτα, εἰ
μὲν ἀκοῦσαι μόνον ἔδει καὶ φενακισθῆναι τὴν
πόλιν, ὀρθῶς ἐλέγετο, εἰ δὲ πραχθῆναι τῷ ὄντι,
σιωπᾶσθαι συνέφερεν. εἰ μὲν γὰρ ἐνταῦθ᾽ ἦν ἤδη
τὰ πράγμαθ᾽ ὥστε μηδ᾽ αἰσθομένοις τοῖς Θηβαίοις
πλέον εἶναι μηδέν, τί οὐ γέγονεν; εἰ δὲ παρὰ τὸ
43 προαισθέσθαι κεκώλυται, τίς ὁ ἐκλαλήσας; οὐχ
οὗτος; ἀλλ᾽ οὔτ᾽ ἔμελλεν οὔτ᾽ ἐβουλήθη ταῦτ᾽
οὔτ᾽ ἤλπισεν οὗτος, ὥστε τοῦ γ᾽ ἐκλελαληκέναι
μηδ᾽ αἰτίαν ἐχέτω· ἀλλὰ φενακισθῆναι τοῖς λόγοις
τούτοις ὑμᾶς ἔδει, καὶ ἐμοῦ τἀληθῆ μὴ ἐθελῆσαι
ἀκοῦσαι, καὶ αὐτοὺς οἴκοι καταμεῖναι, καὶ ψήφισμα

(The Excerpt is read)

You see that, before he got his peace, he covenanted that, if you should make alliance with him as well, he would specify in writing the great benefits that he would confer on Athens. But now that both peace and alliance are concluded, he says that he does not know what he can do to oblige you, but that, if you will tell him, he will do anything "that is consistent with his own honour and reputation"—taking refuge in this saving clause, and leaving himself a loop-hole in case you make any proposal or are induced to ask any favour.

All this chicanery, and much besides, might have been instantly detected, and you might have been informed and spared the sacrifice of your interests, if you had not been cheated out of the truth by that story of Thespiae and Plataea and the imminent punishment of the Thebans. Yet if Philip's promises were merely for show, and if the city was to be deluded, it was right to mention them; if, on the other hand, they were really to be fulfilled, it was best to say nothing about them. For if the project was so far matured that the Thebans could gain nothing by hearing of it, why has it not been executed? But if it has been thwarted because they had news of it in time, who let the secret out? Aeschines? Oh no; it was never meant to come off, and he neither wanted it nor expected it; let him be quit of the imputation of blabbing! The truth is that his purpose required that you should be hoodwinked by that talk; that you should refuse to hear the truth from me and should stay at home; and that they should triumphantly carry a decree

273

νικῆσαι τοιοῦτο δι' οὗ Φωκεῖς ἀπολοῦνται. διὰ
[355] ταῦτ' ἐσπαθᾶτο ταῦτα καὶ διὰ ταῦτ' ἐδημηγορεῖτο.
44 Ἀκούων τοίνυν ἐγὼ τηλικαῦτα καὶ τοιαῦτ'
ἐπαγγελλομένου τούτου τότε, καὶ ἀκριβῶς εἰδὼς
ὅτι ψεύδεται,—καὶ ὅθεν, φράσω πρὸς ὑμᾶς· πρῶτον
μὲν ἐκ τοῦ, ὅτε τοὺς ὅρκους ἔμελλε Φίλιππος
ὀμνύναι τοὺς περὶ τῆς εἰρήνης, ἐκσπόνδους ἀπο-
φανθῆναι τοὺς Φωκέας ὑπὸ τούτων, ὃ σιωπᾶν καὶ
ἐᾶν εἰκὸς ἦν, εἴπερ ἔμελλον σῴζεσθαι· ἔπειτ' ἐκ
τοῦ μὴ τοὺς παρὰ τοῦ Φιλίππου πρέσβεις ταῦτα
λέγειν μηδὲ τὴν ἐπιστολὴν τὴν Φιλίππου, ἀλλὰ
45 τοῦτον—ἐκ τούτων οὖν τεκμαιρόμενος, ἀναστὰς
καὶ παρελθὼν ἐπειρώμην μὲν ἀντιλέγειν, ὡς δ'
ἀκούειν οὐκ ἐθέλετε, ἡσυχίαν ἔσχον, τοσοῦτο
μόνον διαμαρτυράμενος (καὶ πρὸς Διὸς καὶ θεῶν
ἀναμιμνήσκεσθε), ὅτι ταῦτ' οὔτ' οἶδ' οὔτε κοινωνῶ,
προσέθηκα δ' ὡς οὐδὲ προσδοκῶ. τραχέως δ'
ὑμῶν τῷ μηδὲ προσδοκᾶν σχόντων, "καὶ ὅπως
γ', ὦ ἄνδρες Ἀθηναῖοι," ἔφην, "ἄν τι τούτων
γίγνηται, τούτους ἐπαινέσεσθε καὶ τιμήσετε καὶ
στεφανώσετε, ἐμὲ δὲ μή· καὶ μέντοι κἄν τι τῶν
ἐναντίων, ὅπως τούτοις ὀργιεῖσθε· ἐγὼ δ' ἀφ-
46 ίσταμαι." "μὴ νῦν," ὑπολαβὼν ἔφη Αἰσχίνης
οὑτοσί, "μὴ νῦν ἀφίστασο, ἀλλ' ὅπως τότε μὴ
προσποιήσει." "νὴ Δί', ἢ ἀδικήσω γ'," ἔφην.
ἐπαναστὰς δ' ὁ Φιλοκράτης μάλ' ὑβριστικῶς
"οὐδέν," ἔφη, "θαυμαστόν, ὦ ἄνδρες Ἀθηναῖοι,

ᵃ The clause excluding the Phocians from the benefit of
the peace had been rescinded by the Assembly (see § 159).
Aeschines and his friends were therefore acting *ultra vires* in
restoring the clause, when they administered the oath. Had
they been really convinced that Philip intended to spare the
Phocians, they would have retained the more general phrase,

ensuring the destruction of the Phocians. That is why this tissue of lies was woven; that is why it was made the theme of a popular harangue.

Now when I heard him making all these fine promises, and knew to a certainty that he was lying,— but let me tell you why I knew. First, because, when Philip was on the point of swearing the oath of ratification, the Phocians were expressly excluded from the treaty by these men; and that exclusion should have been passed over in silence, if the Phocians were to be delivered [a]; and secondly because none of the ambassadors from Philip, nor Philip's own letter, but only Aeschines, mentioned the promises. So drawing my conclusions, I rose and presented myself, and made an attempt to reply. When you refused me a hearing, I held my peace, except that I protested—and I entreat that you will recall this—that I had no knowledge of the promises, nothing to do with them, and, I added, no faith in them. At the words " no faith in them," you became exasperated; and I proceeded : " If any of these promises come true, men of Athens, be sure you give thanks and honours and decorations to these gentlemen; but not to me. If, however, things turn out otherwise, see that it is on them that you vent your wrath. I stand aside." " Not now," said Aeschines, interrupting me, " do not stand aside now; only do not put in your claim then." " Agreed ; " said I, " if I do, I shall be in the wrong." Then Philocrates rose, and said, in a very supercilious manner : " No wonder Demosthenes and I disagree,

the Athenians and their allies." It is more probable that Philip himself insisted on excluding the Phocians, and the ambassadors were as powerless as the Roman senators before Alaric.

μὴ ταῦτ' ἐμοὶ καὶ Δημοσθένει δοκεῖν· οὗτος μὲν
γὰρ ὕδωρ, ἐγὼ δ' οἶνον πίνω.'' καὶ ὑμεῖς
ἐγελᾶτε.

47 Σκέψασθε δὴ τὸ ψήφισμα, ὃ δίδωσι γράψας μετὰ
ταῦθ' ὁ Φιλοκράτης. ἀκοῦσαι μὲν γὰρ οὑτωσὶ
παγκάλως ἔχει· ἐπειδὰν δὲ τοὺς καιροὺς συλ-
[356] λογίσηταί τις ἐφ' ὧν ἐγράφη, καὶ τὰς ὑποσχέσεις
ἃς οὗτος ὑπισχνεῖτο τότε, οὐδὲν ἄλλο φανήσονται
πλὴν παραδόντες Φιλίππῳ καὶ Θηβαίοις Φωκέας,
μόνον οὐκ ὀπίσω τὼ χεῖρε δήσαντες. λέγε τὸ
ψήφισμα.

ΨΗΦΙΣΜΑ

48 Ὁρᾶτ', ὦ ἄνδρες Ἀθηναῖοι, τὸ ψήφισμα, ὅσων
ἐπαίνων καὶ.ὅσης εὐφημίας μεστόν ἐστι, καὶ τὴν
εἰρήνην εἶναι τὴν αὐτὴν ἥνπερ Φιλίππῳ καὶ τοῖς
ἐγγόνοις, καὶ τὴν συμμαχίαν, καὶ ἐπαινέσαι δὲ
Φίλιππον, ὅτι ἐπαγγέλλεται τὰ δίκαια ποιήσειν.
ἀλλ' οὐδὲν ἐκεῖνός γ' ἐπηγγέλλετο, ἀλλὰ τοσούτου
ἔδει ἐπαγγέλλεσθαι ὥστ' οὐδ' εἰδέναι φησὶ τί ἂν
49 ποιῶν ὑμῖν χαρίσαιτο. ἀλλ' οὗτος ἦν ὁ λέγων
ὑπὲρ αὐτοῦ καὶ ὑπισχνούμενος. πρὸς δὲ τοὺς παρὰ
τούτου λόγους ὡρμηκότας λαβὼν ὑμᾶς ὁ Φιλοκράτης ἐγγράφει τοῦτ' εἰς τὸ ψήφισμα· ἐὰν δὲ μὴ
ποιῶσι Φωκεῖς ἃ δεῖ καὶ παραδιδῶσι τοῖς Ἀμφικτύοσι τὸ ἱερόν, ὅτι βοηθήσει ὁ δῆμος ὁ Ἀθηναίων
50 ἐπὶ τοὺς διακωλύοντας ταῦτα γίγνεσθαι. οὐκοῦν,
ἄνδρες Ἀθηναῖοι, μενόντων μὲν ὑμῶν οἴκοι καὶ οὐκ
ἐξεληλυθότων, ἀπεληλυθότων δὲ τῶν Λακεδαιμονίων καὶ προῃσθημένων τὴν ἀπάτην, οὐδενὸς δ'
ἄλλου παρόντος τῶν Ἀμφικτυόνων πλὴν Θετταλῶν
καὶ Θηβαίων, εὐφημότατ' ἀνθρώπων τούτοις παρα-

276

men of Athens. He drinks water; I drink wine."
And then you all laughed.

Now look at the decree, which Philocrates afterwards drafted and handed to the clerk. It sounds
well enough to the ear; but if you will take into
account the occasion on which it was proposed, and
the promises which Aeschines was making at the
time, it will be clear that they were simply handing
over the Phocians to Philip and the Thebans—I
might almost say, with shackles on their wrists.
Read the decree.

(*The Decree is read*)

You observe, men of Athens, how full the decree
is of compliments and fine phrases; that it provides
that the peace, and also the alliance, made with
Philip shall be extended to his posterity; and that
thanks are given to Philip for his promise of just
dealings. But it was not Philip who had made any
promises; so far from promising he says that he
does not know what to do to oblige you. It was
Aeschines who was Philip's spokesman and gave
undertakings. Then Philocrates, taking advantage
of your ready acceptance of Aeschines' words, inserts
in the decree a clause providing that, if the Phocians
should not do what was right and give up the temple
to the Amphictyonic Council, the Athenian people
should send a force to coerce the recalcitrants. And
so, men of Athens, as you stayed at home instead of
taking the field, as the Lacedaemonians had discerned Philip's treachery and withdrawn, and as no
members of the Council were on the spot except
the Thessalians and the Thebans, he really has proposed, with the utmost civility, to hand the temple

DEMOSTHENES

δοῦναι γέγραφε τὸ ἱερὸν γράψας τοῖς Ἀμφικτύοσι
παραδοῦναι (ποίοις; οὐ γὰρ ἦσαν αὐτόθι πλὴν
Θηβαῖοι καὶ Θετταλοί), ἀλλ' οὐ συγκαλέσαι δὲ
τοὺς Ἀμφικτύονας, οὐδ' ἐπισχεῖν ἕως ἂν συλ-
λεγῶσιν, οὐδὲ βοηθεῖν Πρόξενον εἰς Φωκέας, οὐδ'
51 ἐξιέναι Ἀθηναίους, οὐδὲ τοιοῦτ' οὐδέν. καίτοι
[357] καὶ ἐπιστολὰς ἔπεμψεν ὁ Φίλιππος δύο καλούσας
ὑμᾶς, οὐχ ἵν' ἐξέλθητε· πώμαλα· οὐ γὰρ ἄν ποτε
τοὺς χρόνους ἀνελών, ἐν οἷς ἐδυνήθητ' ἂν ἐξελθεῖν,
τηνικαῦτ' ἐκάλει· οὐδ' ἂν ἐμέ, ἡνίκα δεῦρ' ἀποπλεῖν ἐβουλόμην, κατεκώλυεν· οὐδὲ τοιαῦτα λέγειν
τούτῳ προσέταττεν, ἐξ ὧν ἥκισθ' ὑμεῖς ἐμέλλετ'
ἐξιέναι· ἀλλ' ἵνα, ἃ ἐβούλεσθ' οἰόμενοι πράξειν
αὐτόν, μηδὲν ἐναντίον ψηφίσησθ' αὐτῷ, μηδ'
ἀμύνοιντο μηδ' ἀντέχοιεν οἱ Φωκεῖς ἐπὶ ταῖς παρ'
ὑμῶν ἐπανέχοντες ἐλπίσιν, ἀλλ' ἀπογνόντες ἅπανθ'
ἑαυτοὺς ἐγχειρίσαιεν. λέγε δ' αὐτοῖς αὐτὰς τὰς
ἐπιστολὰς τὰς τοῦ Φιλίππου.

ΕΠΙΣΤΟΛΑΙ

52 Αἱ μὲν τοίνυν ἐπιστολαὶ καλοῦσιν αὗται, καὶ νὴ
Δί' ἤδη γε· τούτοις δ', εἴπερ ἦν ὑγιές τι τούτων,
τί ἄλλο προσῆκεν ἢ συνειπεῖν ὅπως ἐξέλθηθ'
ὑμεῖς, καὶ τὸν Πρόξενον, ὃν περὶ τοὺς τόπους
ᾔδεσαν ὄντα, γράφειν εὐθέως βοηθεῖν; πάντα
τοίνυν τἀναντία τούτων φαίνονται πεποιηκότες.
εἰκότως· οὐ γὰρ οἷς ἐπέστελλε προσεῖχον τὸν νοῦν,

<hr>

ᵃ The force of ἤδη γε is not clear. Kennedy translates it
"for the first time," presumably meaning the first time that
Athens had ever taken instructions from Macedonia. The
previous paragraph rather suggests that Dem. is insinuating
that Philip, whose aim was to keep the Athenians inactive,
278

over to them. The wording is, " to the Amphictyons ; " but what Amphictyons ? There were none
there except Thessalians and Thebans. He makes
no such proposal as that the Amphictyonic Council
should be convened, or that operations should be
suspended until it meets, or that Proxenus should
march against the Phocians, or that the Athenians
should take the field. Philip, however, did send you
two letters of summons. Yes, but not with the
intention that you should take the field. That is
certain ; otherwise he would not have destroyed
your opportunity of going out before he summoned
you, nor would he have detained me when I wanted
to sail home, nor ordered Aeschines to make statements calculated to deter you from going out. No,
his object was that you, in the belief that he would
do all that you wanted, should make no decree pre-
judicial to him, and the Phocians might not stand
their ground and hold out in reliance upon hopes
afforded by you, but might make unconditional
surrender to him in sheer desperation. Read
Philip's actual letters.

(The two Letters are read)

These letters, then, do summon you,—yes, indeed,
at last ![a] But if there had been any honesty in the
letters, it was clearly the duty of these men to exhort
you to take the field, and to propose that Proxenus,
whom they knew to be in those parts, should at once
march to the aid of Philip. Their actual policy was
very different. Naturally ; for they did not apply
their minds to the phrasing of the letter ; they were

deferred the invitation till it was too late for them to put a
force in the field, whether to support Philip or the Phocians.

ἀλλ' ἃ φρονῶν ταῦτ' ἔγραφε συνῄδεσαν· τούτοις
οὖν συνέπραττον καὶ τούτοις συνηγωνίζοντο.

53 Οἱ μὲν τοίνυν Φωκεῖς, ὡς τὰ παρ' ὑμῶν ἐπύθοντ'
ἐκ τῆς ἐκκλησίας καὶ τό τε ψήφισμα τοῦτ' ἔλαβον
τὸ τοῦ Φιλοκράτους καὶ τὴν ἀπαγγελίαν ἐπύθοντο
τὴν τούτου καὶ τὰς ὑποσχέσεις, κατὰ πάντας τοὺς
τρόπους ἀπώλοντο. σκοπεῖτε γάρ. ἦσαν ἀπιστοῦν-
τές τινες αὐτόθι τῷ Φιλίππῳ καὶ νοῦν ἔχοντες·
οὗτοι πιστεύειν ὑπήχθησαν. διὰ τί; ὅτι ἡγοῦντο,
[358] οὐδ' εἰ δεκάκις Φίλιππος αὐτοὺς ἐξηπάτα, οὐδέποτ'
ἂν τούς γ' Ἀθηναίων πρέσβεις Ἀθηναίους ἐξαπατᾶν τολμῆσαι, ἀλλ' εἶναι ταῦτ' ἀληθῆ ἃ οὗτος
ἀπήγγειλε πρὸς ὑμᾶς, καὶ τοῖς Θηβαίοις ἥκειν
54 οὐχ αὑτοῖς ὄλεθρον. ἦσαν ἄλλοι τινὲς οἳ πάσχειν
ὁτιοῦν καὶ ἀμύνεσθαι δεῖν ᾤοντο· ἀλλὰ καὶ τούτους μαλακοὺς ἐποίησε τὸ τὸν Φίλιππον ὑπάρχειν
αὐτοῖς πεισθῆναι, καὶ τὸ ταῦτ' εἰ μὴ ποιήσουσιν
ὑμᾶς ἐπ' αὐτοὺς ἥξειν, οὓς βοηθήσειν αὐτοῖς ἤλπιζον
ἐκεῖνοι. ἀλλὰ καὶ μεταμέλειν ὑμῖν ᾤοντό τινες πε-
ποιημένοις τὴν πρὸς Φίλιππον εἰρήνην· τούτοις ὅτι
καὶ τοῖς ἐγγόνοις τὴν αὐτὴν ἐψηφίσασθ' ἐπέδειξαν,
ὥστε πανταχῇ τὰ παρ' ὑμῶν ἀπογνωσθῆναι. διόπερ
55 ἅπαντα ταῦτ' εἰς ἓν ψήφισμα συνεσκεύασαν. ὃ καὶ
μέγιστον ἔμοιγε δοκοῦσιν ἁπάντων ὑμᾶς ἠδικη-
κέναι· τὸ γὰρ πρὸς ἄνδρα θνητὸν καὶ διὰ καιρούς
τινας ἰσχύοντα γράφοντας εἰρήνην ἀθάνατον συνθέσθαι τὴν κατὰ τῆς πόλεως αἰσχύνην, καὶ ἀποστερῆσαι μὴ μόνον τῶν ἄλλων ἀλλὰ καὶ τῶν παρὰ
τῆς τύχης εὐεργεσιῶν τὴν πόλιν, καὶ τοσαύτῃ
περιουσίᾳ χρήσασθαι πονηρίας ὥστε μὴ μόνον τοὺς

in the secret of the intention with which it was written, and with that intention they concurred and co-operated.

When therefore the Phocians learned your policy from the proceedings of the Assembly, received the decree of Philocrates, and were informed of the report and promises of Aeschines, their ruin was complete. Just consider. There were some men in Phocis, sensible men, who had no confidence in Philip. They were induced to trust him. Why? Because they conceived that, though Philip had deceived them ten times over, he would never have dared to deceive Athenians and envoys of the Athenian people, that the report of Aeschines was true, and that destruction had overtaken not themselves but the Thebans. There were others who were ready at all hazards to hold out to the end; but even they were mollified by the persuasion that Philip was their friend, and that, if they refused compliance, you, from whom they were expecting succour, would turn against them. A third party supposed that you regretted your treaty of peace with Philip; but they were now informed that you had actually decreed an extension of the treaty to Philip's descendants, and so they abandoned all hope of your assistance. And that is why these men packed all those provisions into one decree. In my judgement they could not have done you a more grievous injury. To turn their treaty of peace with a mortal man, a mere potentate of occasion, into a covenant of immortal ignominy for the commonwealth; to strip their city of all she had, even of the largess of her good fortune; in the veriest extravagance of malice to heap injuries not only on the

ὄντας ᾿Αθηναίους ἀλλὰ καὶ τοὺς ὕστερόν ποτε
μέλλοντας ἔσεσθαι πάντας ἠδικηκέναι, πῶς οὐχὶ
56 πάνδεινόν ἐστι; τοῦτο τοίνυν οὐδέποθ᾿ ὑμεῖς
ὑπεμείνατ᾿ ἂν ὕστερον προσγράψαι πρὸς τὴν
εἰρήνην, τὸ καὶ τοῖς ἐγγόνοις, εἰ μὴ ταῖς παρ᾿
Αἰσχίνου ῥηθείσαις ὑποσχέσεσι τότ᾿ ἐπιστεύσατε,
αἷσπερ οἱ Φωκεῖς πιστεύσαντες ἀπώλοντο. καὶ
γάρ τοι παραδόντες αὐτοὺς Φιλίππῳ καὶ ἑκόντες
[359] ἐγχειρίσαντες ἐκείνῳ τὰς πόλεις ἁπάντων τῶν
ἐναντίων, ὧν πρὸς ὑμᾶς οὗτος ἀπήγγειλεν, ἔτυχον.
57 ῞Ινα δ᾿ εἰδῆτε σαφῶς ὅτι ταῦθ᾿ οὕτω καὶ διὰ
τούτους ἀπόλωλε, τοὺς χρόνους ὑμῖν λογιοῦμαι
καθ᾿ οὓς ἐγίγνεθ᾿ ἕκαστα. περὶ ὧν δ᾿ ἄν τις
ἀντιλέγῃ τούτων, ἀναστὰς ἐν τῷ ἐμῷ ὕδατι εἰπάτω.
ἡ μὲν τοίνυν εἰρήνη ἐλαφηβολιῶνος ἐνάτῃ ἐπὶ δέκα
ἐγένετο, ἀπεδημήσαμεν δ᾿ ἡμεῖς ἐπὶ τοὺς ὅρκους
τρεῖς μῆνας ὅλους· καὶ τοῦτον ἅπαντα τὸν χρόνον
58 ἦσαν οἱ Φωκεῖς σῷοι. ἥκομεν δὲ δεῦρ᾿ ἀπὸ τῆς
πρεσβείας τῆς ἐπὶ τοὺς ὅρκους τρίτῃ ἐπὶ δέκα τοῦ
σκιροφοριῶνος μηνός, καὶ παρῆν ὁ Φίλιππος ἐν
Πύλαις ἤδη καὶ τοῖς Φωκεῦσιν ἐπηγγέλλετο ὧν
οὐδὲν ἐπίστευον ἐκεῖνοι. σημεῖον δέ· οὐ γὰρ ἂν
δεῦρ᾿ ἧκον ὡς ὑμᾶς. ἡ δ᾿ ἐκκλησία μετὰ ταῦτα, ἐν
ᾗ πάντα τὰ πράγματ᾿ ἀπώλεσαν οὗτοι ψευσάμενοι
καὶ φενακίσαντες ὑμᾶς, τῇ ἕκτῃ ἐπὶ δέκα ἐγίγνετο
59 τοῦ σκιροφοριῶνος. ἀπὸ τοίνυν ταύτης πεμπταῖα
λογίζομαι τὰ παρ᾿ ὑμῶν ἐν τοῖς Φωκεῦσι γενέσθαι·
παρῆσαν γὰρ οἱ τῶν Φωκέων πρέσβεις ἐνθάδε, καὶ
ἦν αὐτοῖς καὶ τί ἀπαγγελοῦσιν οὗτοι καὶ τί ψη-
φιεῖσθ᾿ ὑμεῖς ἐπιμελὲς εἰδέναι. οὐκοῦν εἰκάς, ᾗ

---

[a] *in the time*, etc.: see *De cor.* 139.

Athenians of to-day but upon all who shall hereafter be Athenians,—is not that an appalling iniquity ? Never would you have consented to add to the treaty by afterthought the words *and to his posterity*, but for your confidence in the promises alleged by Aeschines. In those promises the Phocians confided, —and perished ! They surrendered themselves to Philip ; of their own accord they put their cities at his mercy ; and their treatment has exactly contradicted all the assurances of Aeschines.

To give you the clearest proof that that destruction was effected in this way by the contrivance of these men, I will submit a reckoning of the dates of the several transactions. If any of the defendants challenges my calculation, let him stand up and speak in the time *a* allotted to me. Now the treaty was made on the nineteenth of Elaphebolion, and we were abroad receiving the oaths for three entire months. During the whole of that time the Phocians were safe. We returned from the oath-taking embassy on the thirteenth of Scirophorion, when Philip was already at Thermopylae and making promises to the Phocians which they were not disposed to believe. The proof of that is that otherwise they would not have resorted to you. Then the Assembly, at which these men brought the whole business to ruin with their lies and cajolery, was held on the sixteenth of Scirophorion. Now I calculate that the news from Athens reached the Phocians on the fourth day after that date, for there were Phocian envoys in the city, and they were interested in knowing what report these men would submit and what decree you would adopt. Therefore the twentieth was the day on which we reckon that the

τίθεμεν πυθέσθαι τοὺς Φωκέας τὰ παρ' ὑμῶν· ἀπὸ
γὰρ τῆς ἕκτης εἰς ταύτην πέμπτη γίγνεται. ὑστέρα
τοίνυν δεκάτη, ἐνάτη, ὀγδόη· ταύτῃ ἐγίγνονθ' αἱ
σπονδαί, καὶ πάντα τἀκεῖ πράγματ' ἀπωλώλει καὶ
60 τέλος εἶχεν. τῷ τοῦτο δῆλον; τῇ τετράδι φθίνοντος ἠκκλησιάζετε μὲν τόθ' ὑμεῖς ἐν Πειραιεῖ περὶ
[360] τῶν ἐν τοῖς νεωρίοις, ἧκε δὲ Δερκύλος ἐκ Χαλκίδος, καὶ ἀπήγγειλεν ὑμῖν ὅτι πάντα τὰ πράγματ'
ἐγκεχείρικε Θηβαίοις ὁ Φίλιππος, καὶ πέμπτην εἶναι
ταύτην ἡμέραν ἐλογίζετ' ἀφ' οὗ γεγόνασιν αἱ
σπονδαί. ὀγδόη τοίνυν, ἑβδόμη, ἕκτη, πέμπτη,
τετράς· αὐτὸ συμβαίνει εἰς ταύτην εἶναι πέμπτην.
οὐκοῦν τοῖς χρόνοις, οἷς ἀπήγγελλον, οἷς ἔγραφον,
πᾶσιν ἐξελέγχονται συνηγωνισμένοι Φιλίππῳ καὶ
συναίτιοι γεγονότες τοῦ τῶν Φωκέων ὀλέθρου.
61 ἔτι τοίνυν τὸ μηδεμίαν τῶν πόλεων τῶν ἐν Φωκεῦσιν
ἁλῶναι πολιορκίᾳ μηδ' ἐκ προσβολῆς κατὰ κράτος,
ἀλλ' ἐκ τοῦ σπείσασθαι πάντας ἄρδην ἀπολέσθαι,
μέγιστόν ἐστι σημεῖον τοῦ διὰ τούτους πεισθέντας
αὐτοὺς ὡς ὑπὸ τοῦ Φιλίππου σωθήσονται ταῦτα
παθεῖν· οὐ γὰρ ἐκεῖνόν γ' ἠγνόουν. φέρε δή μοι
καὶ τὴν συμμαχίαν τὴν τῶν Φωκέων καὶ τὰ δόγμαθ'
ὑφ' ὧν καθεῖλον αὐτῶν τὰ τείχη, ἵν' εἰδῆθ' οἵων
ὑπαρχόντων αὐτοῖς παρ' ὑμῶν οἵων ἔτυχον διὰ
τούτους τοὺς θεοῖς ἐχθρούς. λέγε.

ΣΥΜΜΑΧΙΑ ΦΩΚΕΩΝ ΚΑΙ ΑΘΗΝΑΙΩΝ

62 Ἃ μὲν τοίνυν ὑπῆρχε παρ' ὑμῶν αὐτοῖς, ταῦτ'

284

DE FALSA LEGATIONE, 59–62

Phocians received the news, that is, the fourth day
after the sixteenth. Then followed the twenty-first,
twenty-second, twenty-third ; and on the twenty-
third the convention was made, and the fortunes of
Phocis perished and came to an end. How, then, is
this date proved ? On the twenty-seventh, when
you were holding an assembly at Peiraeus to discuss
dockyard business, Dercylus arrived from Chalcis
with the intelligence that Philip had put the whole
affair into the hands of the Thebans, and he com-
puted that it was then the fourth day after the
convention. Twenty-three, twenty-four, twenty-five,
twenty-six, twenty-seven : that makes it the fourth
day. Therefore these dates, together with their
own reports and decrees, all convict these men of
having co-operated with Philip, and they share with
him the guilt of the destruction of the Phocians.
Again, the consideration that not a city of the
Phocians was taken forcibly, whether by blockade
or assault, and yet that they were all brought to
utter ruin under the convention, is a convincing
proof that they perished because they had been
persuaded through these men that Philip would
deliver them ; for about *his* character they had no
illusions. Now give me our treaty with the Phocians,
and the Amphictyonic decrees, under which they
dismantled their defences. These documents will
show you on what footing you stood with them, and
what treatment they have received by the fault of
these wicked men. Read.

(*The Treaty of Friendship between the Athenians and
the Phocians is read*)

These are the relations that subsisted between

ἐστί, φιλία, συμμαχία, βοήθεια· ὧν δ' ἔτυχον διὰ
τοῦτον τὸν βοηθῆσαι κωλύσαντα ὑμᾶς, ἀκούσατε.
λέγε.

ΟΜΟΛΟΓΙΑ ΦΙΛΙΠΠΟΥ ΚΑΙ ΦΩΚΕΩΝ

'Ακούετ', ὦ ἄνδρες 'Αθηναῖοι. ὁμολογία Φιλίππου καὶ Φωκέων, φησίν, οὐχὶ Θηβαίων καὶ Φωκέων,
οὐδὲ Θετταλῶν καὶ Φωκέων, οὐδὲ Λοκρῶν, οὐδ'
ἄλλου τῶν παρόντων οὐδενός· καὶ πάλιν παρα-
63 δοῦναι δὲ τὰς πόλεις Φωκέας φησὶ Φιλίππῳ, οὐχὶ
[361] Θηβαίοις οὐδὲ Θετταλοῖς οὐδ' ἄλλῳ οὐδενί. διὰ
τί; ὅτι Φίλιππος ἀπηγγέλλετο πρὸς ὑμᾶς ὑπὸ
τούτου ἐπὶ τῇ τῶν Φωκέων σωτηρίᾳ παρεληλυθέναι.
τούτῳ δὴ πάντ' ἐπίστευον, καὶ πρὸς τοῦτον πάντ'
ἐσκόπουν, πρὸς τοῦτον ἐποιοῦντο τὴν εἰρήνην.
λέγε δὴ τἀπίλοιπα. καὶ σκοπεῖτε τί πιστεύσαντες
τί ἔπασχον. ἆρά γ' ὅμοι' ἢ παραπλήσι' οἷς οὗτος
ἀπήγγειλε; λέγε.

ΔΟΓΜΑΤΑ ΑΜΦΙΚΤΥΟΝΩΝ

64 Τούτων, ὦ ἄνδρες 'Αθηναῖοι, δεινότερ' οὐ γέγονεν
οὐδὲ μείζω πράγματ' ἐφ' ἡμῶν ἐν τοῖς "Ελλησιν,
οἶμαι δ' οὐδ' ἐν τῷ πρόσθεν χρόνῳ. τηλικούτων
μέντοι καὶ τοιούτων πραγμάτων κύριος εἷς ἀνὴρ[1]
γέγονε διὰ τούτους, οὔσης τῆς 'Αθηναίων πόλεως,
ᾗ προεστάναι τῶν Ἑλλήνων πάτριον καὶ μηδὲν
τοιοῦτον περιορᾶν γιγνόμενον. ὃν μὲν τοίνυν τρόπον οἱ ταλαίπωροι Φωκεῖς ἀπολώλασιν, οὐ μόνον

---

[1] After εἷς ἀνὴρ mss. have Φίλιππος, struck out by Cobet.

you and them—friendship, alliance, succour. Now hear what they have suffered through the man who thwarted the succour you owed them. Read.

(*The Convention between Philip and the Phocians is read*)

You hear it, men of Athens. A convention between Philip and the Phocians, it says, not between the Thebans and the Phocians, or the Thessalians and the Phocians, or the Locrians, or any other of the nationalities then present. Again, it says that the Phocians are to surrender their cities to Philip, not to the Thebans, or the Thessalians, or any other people. Why? Because you had been assured by Aeschines that Philip had come to deliver the Phocians. In Aeschines they had confidence; to Aeschines they looked for aid; with Aeschines they were making their peace. Read the other documents. Now you shall see to what sufferings they were brought by that confidence. Does the story agree with, does it in any way resemble, those reports of Aeschines? Read.

(*The Decrees of the Amphictyonic Council are read*)

Men of Athens, nothing more awful or more momentous has befallen in Greece within living memory, nor, as I believe, in all the history of the past. Yet through the agency of these men all these great and terrible transactions have been dominated by a single individual, though the city of Athens is still in being, the city whose ancestral prerogative it was to stand forth as the champion of the Hellenic race, and declare that such things shall not be. In what fashion these unhappy Phocians have perished you may learn, not from the decrees

287

65 ἐκ τῶν δογμάτων τούτων ἔστιν ἰδεῖν, ἀλλὰ καὶ ἐκ
τῶν ἔργων ἃ πέπρακται, θέαμα δεινόν, ὦ ἄνδρες
Ἀθηναῖοι, καὶ ἐλεινόν· ὅτε γὰρ νῦν ἐπορευόμεθ' εἰς
Δελφούς, ἐξ ἀνάγκης ἦν ὁρᾶν ἡμῖν πάντα ταῦτα,
οἰκίας κατεσκαμμένας, τείχη περιῃρημένα, χώραν
ἔρημον τῶν ἐν ἡλικίᾳ, γύναια δὲ καὶ παιδάρι' ὀλίγα
καὶ πρεσβύτας ἀνθρώπους οἰκτρούς· οὐδ' ἂν εἷς
δύναιτ' ἀφικέσθαι τῷ λόγῳ τῶν ἐκεῖ κακῶν νῦν
ὄντων. ἀλλὰ μὴν ὅτι τὴν ἐναντίαν ποτὲ Θηβαίοις
ψῆφον ἔθενθ' οὗτοι περὶ ἡμῶν ὑπὲρ ἀνδραποδισμοῦ
66 προτεθεῖσαν, ὑμῶν ἔγωγ' ἀκούω πάντων. τίν' ἂν
[362] οὖν οἴεσθ', ὦ ἄνδρες Ἀθηναῖοι, τοὺς προγόνους
ὑμῶν, εἰ λάβοιεν αἴσθησιν, ψῆφον ἢ γνώμην θέσθαι
περὶ τῶν αἰτίων τοῦ τούτων¹ ὀλέθρου; ἐγὼ μὲν γὰρ
οἶμαι κἂν καταλεύσαντας αὐτοὺς ταῖς ἑαυτῶν
χερσὶ καθαροὺς ἔσεσθαι νομίζειν. πῶς γὰρ οὐκ αἰσχρόν, μᾶλλον δ' εἴ τις ἔστιν ὑπερβολὴ τούτου,
τοὺς σεσωκότας ἡμᾶς τότε καὶ τὴν σῴζουσαν περὶ
ἡμῶν ψῆφον θεμένους, τούτους τῶν ἐναντίων τετυ-
χηκέναι διὰ τούτους, καὶ περιῶφθαι τοιαῦτα πεπον-
θότας οἷ' οὐδένες ἄλλοι τῶν Ἑλλήνων; τίς οὖν ὁ
τούτων αἴτιος; τίς ὁ ταῦτα φενακίσας; οὐχ οὗτος;
67 Πολλὰ τοίνυν ἄν τις, ὦ ἄνδρες Ἀθηναῖοι, Φίλιππον εὐδαιμονίσας τῆς τύχης, εἰκότως τοῦτο μάλιστ'
ἂν εὐδαιμονίσειεν ἁπάντων, ὃ μὰ τοὺς θεοὺς καὶ
τὰς θεὰς οὐκ ἔχω λέγειν ἔγωγ' ἄλλον ὅστις εὐτύχηκεν

¹ τοῦ τούτων: S τούτου τῶν: Shill. with other mss. τοῦ τῶν
Φωκέων.

ᵃ in the day of our trial: 404 B.C. when, after the naval
defeat at Aegospotami, and the surrender of the city to
Lysander, Athens lay at the mercy of Thebes, Sparta,
and Corinth. Grote, ch. lxv.

alone, but from the deeds that have been wrought—
a spectacle, men of Athens, to move us to terror and
pity indeed ! Not long ago, when we were travelling
to Delphi, necessity compelled us to look upon that
scene—homesteads levelled with the ground, cities
stripped of their defensive walls, a countryside all
emptied of its young men ; only women, a few little
children, and old men stricken with misery. No
man could find words adequate to the woes that exist
in that country to-day. And yet these are the people
—you take the words out of my mouth—these are
the people who in the day of our trial[a] openly cast
their vote against the Thebans, when the question
was the enslavement of us all ! Then what vote,
what judgement, men of Athens, do you think that
our forefathers would give, if they could recover
consciousness, at the trial of the men who devised the
destruction of the Phocians ? I conceive that they
would account even those who should stone them to
death with their own hands to be free of all blood-
guiltiness. For is it not an ignominy—or use a
stronger word if such there be—that, by the fault of
these men, the people who saved us at that crisis, and
gave for us the verdict of deliverance, have received
evil in requital of good, and have been abandoned
to the endurance of afflictions such as no people of
the Greeks has ever known ? And who is the author
of those wrongs ? Who is the contriver of that
deception ? Who but Aeschines ?

Men of Athens, Philip has many claims to
congratulation on his good fortune, but beyond
them all he might well be especially con-
gratulated for one thing, in which I solemnly
declare that I can name no man of our time who

ἐφ' ἡμῶν. τὸ μὲν γὰρ πόλεις μεγάλας εἰληφέναι
καὶ χώραν πολλὴν ὑφ' ἑαυτῷ πεποιῆσθαι καὶ
πάντα τὰ τοιαῦτα ζηλωτὰ μέν ἐστιν, οἶμαι, καὶ
λαμπρά· πῶς γὰρ οὔ; ἔχοι δ' ἄν τις εἰπεῖν πε-
68 πραγμένα καὶ ἑτέροις πολλοῖς. ἀλλ' ἐκεῖν' ἴδιον καὶ
οὐδενὶ τῶν πάντων γεγονὸς εὐτύχημα. τὸ ποῖον;
τὸ ἐπειδὴ πονηρῶν ἀνθρώπων εἰς τὰ πράγματ'
αὐτῷ ἐδέησε, πονηροτέρους εὑρεῖν ἢ ἐβούλετο.
πῶς γὰρ οὐχ οὗτοι τοιοῦτοι δικαίως ὑποληφθεῖεν
ἄν, οἵ γε, ἃ ὑπὲρ αὐτοῦ Φίλιππος τηλικούτων ὄντων αὐτῷ τῶν διαφόρων οὐκ ἐτόλμα ψεύσασθαι,
οὐδ' ἔγραψεν οὔτ' εἰς ἐπιστολὴν οὐδεμίαν, οὔτε
πρεσβευτὴς οὐδεὶς εἶπε τῶν παρ' ἐκείνου, ἐπὶ
ταῦθ' οὗτοι μισθώσαντες ἑαυτοὺς ὑμᾶς ἐξηπάτων;
69 καὶ ὁ μὲν Ἀντίπατρος καὶ ὁ Παρμενίων, δεσπότῃ
[363] διακονοῦντες καὶ οὐ μέλλοντες ὑμῖν μετὰ ταῦτ'
ἐντεύξεσθαι, ὅμως τοῦθ' ηὕροντο, μὴ δι' αὐτῶν
ὑμᾶς ἐξαπατηθῆναι· οἱ δ' Ἀθηναῖοι τῆς ἐλευθερω-
τάτης πόλεως πρέσβεις ταχθέντες ὑμᾶς, οἷς ἀπαν-
τῶντας ἐμβλέπειν, οἷς συζῆν ἀνάγκη τὸν λοιπὸν
βίον καὶ ἐν οἷς εὐθύνας ἔμελλον δώσειν τῶν πεπραγμένων, τούτους ἐξαπατᾶν ὑπέστησαν. πῶς ἂν
ἄνθρωποι κακίους ἢ μᾶλλον ἀπονενοημένοι τούτων
γένοιντο;
70 Ἵνα τοίνυν εἰδῆθ' ὅτι καὶ κατάρατός ἐστιν ὑφ'
ὑμῶν, καὶ οὐδ' ὅσιον ὑμῖν οὐδ' εὐσεβές ἐστι τοιαῦτ'
ἐψευσμένον αὐτὸν ἀφεῖναι, λέγε τὴν ἀρὰν καὶ
ἀνάγνωθι λαβὼν τὴν ἐκ τοῦ νόμου ταυτηνί.

ΑΡΑ

---

[a] Every meeting of the Assembly and of the Council
opened with a form of prayer, which included a curse on
the enemies of the state and was recited by the " marshal "

has been equally fortunate. Such achievements as the capture of great cities and the subjugation of a vast territory are, I suppose, enviable, as they are undoubtedly imposing ; yet we could mention many other men who have done the like. But the stroke of good fortune I have in mind is peculiar to him and has befallen no other man. What is it ? It is that, when he needed scoundrels for his purposes, he found bigger scoundrels than he wanted. For surely that is a fair description of the men who deceived you, hiring themselves out for lies which Philip, in spite of the great interests at issue, did not dare to tell on his own account, which he never wrote in any letter or put into the mouth of ambassadors of his own. Antipater and Parmenio, though they were in the service of a hard taskmaster, and though they were not likely to fall in with you again, nevertheless claimed exemption from serving as the agents of your beguilement ; and yet citizens of Athens, the appointed envoys of the freest of all cities, men who must needs encounter you and look you in the face, who must live with you all the rest of their life, who would have to render you a strict account of their actions, accepted a commission to beguile you ! Could any men be more wicked or more lost to all sense of shame ?

To show you that this man is already accursed by you, and that religion and piety forbid you to acquit one who has been guilty of such falsehoods,—recite the curse.[a] Take and read it from the statute : here it is.

(The Statutory Commination is read)

($\kappa\hat{\eta}\rho\upsilon\xi$) at the dictation of an under-clerk. The curse has nowhere been preserved, but a parody will be found in Aristoph. *Thesm.* 331 sqq.

DEMOSTHENES

Ταῦθ' ὑπὲρ ὑμῶν, ὦ ἄνδρες Ἀθηναῖοι, καθ'
ἑκάστην τὴν ἐκκλησίαν ὁ κῆρυξ εὔχεται νόμῳ
προστεταγμένα, καὶ ὅταν ἡ βουλὴ καθῆται, παρ'
ἐκείνῃ πάλιν. καὶ ταῦτ' οὐκ ἔνεστιν εἰπεῖν τούτῳ
ὡς οὐκ εὖ ᾔδει· ὑπογραμματεύων γὰρ ὑμῖν καὶ
ὑπηρετῶν τῇ βουλῇ αὐτὸς ἐξηγεῖτο τὸν νόμον
71 τοῦτον τῷ κήρυκι. πῶς οὖν οὐκ ἄτοπον καὶ
ὑπερφυὲς ἂν πεποιηκότες ὑμεῖς εἴητε, εἰ ἄρ', ἃ
προστάττετε, μᾶλλον δ' ἀξιοῦτε ποιεῖν ὑπὲρ ὑμῶν
τοὺς θεούς, ταῦτ' αὐτοὶ κύριοι γεγενημένοι τήμερον
μὴ ποιήσαιτε, ἀλλ' ὃν ἐκείνοις εὔχεσθ' ἐξώλη
ποιεῖν αὐτὸν καὶ γένος καὶ οἰκίαν, τοῦτον ἀφείητ'
αὐτοί; μηδαμῶς· ὃς γὰρ ἂν ὑμᾶς λάθῃ, τοῦτον
ἀφίετε τοῖς θεοῖς κολάζειν· ὃν δ' ἂν αὐτοὶ λάβητε,
μηκέτ' ἐκείνοις περὶ τούτου προστάττετε.

72 Εἰς τοίνυν τοῦτ' ἀναιδείας καὶ τόλμης αὐτὸν
ἥξειν ἀκούω, ὥστε πάντων τῶν πεπραγμένων
ἐκστάντα, ὧν ἀπήγγειλεν, ὧν ὑπέσχετο, ὧν πεφε-
νάκικε τὴν πόλιν, ὥσπερ ἐν ἄλλοις τισὶ κρινόμενος
[364] καὶ οὐκ ἐν ὑμῖν τοῖς ἅπαντ' εἰδόσι, πρῶτον μὲν
Λακεδαιμονίων, εἶτα Φωκέων, εἶθ' Ἡγησίππου
κατηγορήσειν. ἔστι δὲ ταῦτα γέλως, μᾶλλον δ'
73 ἀναισχυντία δεινή. ὅσα γὰρ νῦν ἐρεῖ περὶ τῶν Φωκέων ἢ τῶν Λακεδαιμονίων ἢ τοῦ Ἡγησίππου, ὡς
Πρόξενον οὐχ ὑπεδέξαντο, ὡς ἀσεβεῖς εἰσιν, ὡς
—ὅ τι ἂν δήποτ' αὐτῶν κατηγορῇ, πάντα δήπου
ταῦτα πρὸ τοῦ τοὺς πρέσβεις τούτους δεῦρ' ἥκειν
ἐπέπρακτο, καὶ οὐκ ἦν ἐμποδὼν τῷ τοὺς Φωκέας
σώζεσθαι, ὡς τίς φησιν; Αἰσχίνης αὐτὸς οὑτοσί.

292

This imprecation, men of Athens, is pronounced, as the law directs, by the marshal on your behalf at every meeting of the Assembly, and again before the Council at all their sessions. The defendant cannot say that he is not familiar with it, for, when acting as clerk to the Assembly and as an officer of the Council, he used to dictate the statute to the marshal. Would you not have acted absurdly and preposterously if to-day, when the power is in your own hands, you should preclude yourselves from doing what you enjoin, or rather require, the gods to do on your behalf; if you should yourselves release a man whom you have implored them to extirpate along with his household and his kindred? Never! Leave the undetected sinner to the justice of the gods; but about the sinner whom you have caught yourselves, lay no further injunctions on *them*.

I am informed that he has become so proficient in effrontery and hardihood that he will disavow all his acts—his reports, his promises, his deceptions of the city—as though he were not on trial before a jury that knows the whole truth, and that he will denounce first the Lacedaemonians, then the Phocians, and then Hegesippus. That is buffoonery, nay, barefaced impudence. Whatever he may say just now about the Phocians or the Lacedaemonians or Hegesippus,—that they did not receive Proxenus, that they are irreligious, that they are—anything he can say to their disadvantage,—surely all that was finished and done with before the return of the envoys to Athens, and therefore could not have stood in the way of the deliverance of the Phocians. Who says so? Why, Aeschines here, the defendant

DEMOSTHENES

74 οὐ γὰρ ὡς εἰ μὴ διὰ Λακεδαιμονίους, οὐδ' ὡς εἰ μὴ
Πρόξενον οὐχ ὑπεδέξαντο, οὐδ' ὡς εἰ μὴ δι' Ἡγήσιππον, οὐδ' ὡς εἰ μὴ διὰ τὸ καὶ τὸ ἐσώθησαν ἂν
οἱ Φωκεῖς, οὐχ οὕτω τότ' ἀπήγγειλεν, ἀλλὰ
πάντα ταῦθ' ὑπερβὰς διαρρήδην ἥκειν πεπεικὼς
ἔφη Φίλιππον Φωκέας σῴζειν, τὴν Βοιωτίαν
οἰκίζειν, ὑμῖν τὰ πράγματ' οἰκεῖα ποιεῖν· ταῦτα
πεπράξεσθαι δυοῖν ἢ τριῶν ἡμερῶν· διὰ ταῦτα
χρήμαθ' ἑαυτῷ τοὺς Θηβαίους ἐπικεκηρυχέναι.

75 μὴ τοίνυν ἃ πρὸ τοῦ τοῦτον ἀπαγγεῖλαι ταῦτ'
ἐπέπρακτ' ἢ Λακεδαιμονίοις ἢ Φωκεῦσιν ἀκούετε
μηδ' ἀνέχεσθε, μηδὲ κατηγορεῖν ἐᾶτε Φωκέων ὡς
πονηροί. οὐδὲ γὰρ Λακεδαιμονίους διὰ τὴν ἀρετὴν
αὐτῶν ποτ' ἐσώσατε, οὐδὲ τοὺς καταράτους Εὐβοέας τουτουσί, οὐδ' ἄλλους πολλούς, ἀλλ' ὅτι
συμφέρον ἦν σῶς εἶναι τῇ πόλει, ὥσπερ Φωκέας
νυνί. καὶ τί τῶν Φωκέων ἢ τῶν Λακεδαιμονίων
ἢ ὑμῶν ἢ ἄλλου τινὸς ἀνθρώπων μετὰ τοὺς παρὰ
τούτου λόγους ἐξαμαρτόντος οὐκ ἀπέβη τὰ πρὸς
[365] ὑμᾶς ὑπὸ τούτου ῥηθέντα; τοῦτ' ἐρωτᾶτε· οὐ

76 γὰρ ἕξει δεῖξαι. πέντε γὰρ γεγόνασιν ἡμέραι
μόναι, ἐν αἷς οὗτος ἀπήγγειλε τὰ ψευδῆ, ὑμεῖς
ἐπιστεύσατε, οἱ Φωκεῖς ἐπύθοντο, ἐνέδωκαν ἑαυτούς, ἀπώλοντο. ὅθεν, οἶμαι, καὶ δῆλόν ἐστι σαφῶς
ὅτι πᾶσ' ἀπάτη καὶ τέχνη συνεσκευάσθη τοῦ περὶ
Φωκέας ὀλέθρου. ὃν μὲν γὰρ χρόνον οὐχ οἷός
τ' ἦν ἐλθεῖν ὁ Φίλιππος διὰ τὴν εἰρήνην, ἀλλ' ἦν
ἐν παρασκευῇ, τοὺς Λακεδαιμονίους μετεπέμπετο,
πάντα τὰ πράγμαθ' ὑποσχόμενος πράξειν ἐκείνοις,
ἵνα μὴ δι' ὑμῶν αὐτοὺς οἱ Φωκεῖς ὑποποιήσωνται.

77 ἐπειδὴ δ' ἧκεν εἰς Πύλας, οἱ Λακεδαιμόνιοι δ'

294

himself. For he did not allege in his report that, but for the Lacedaemonians, but for their refusal to receive Proxenus, but for Hegesippus, but for this or that, the Phocians would have been delivered. He passed over all that, and declared explicitly that before his return he had persuaded Philip to deliver the Phocians, to repopulate Boeotia, and to put the whole business into your hands ; that it would all be accomplished within two or three days, and that in revenge the Thebans had set a price upon his head. Do not, then, listen to anything that had been done by Lacedaemonians or Phocians before he made his report ; do not let him talk about it ; do not permit him to denounce the Phocians and call them rascals. You saved the Lacedaemonians in old time, and those accursed Euboeans lately, and many other peoples, not because they were virtuous, but because their safety profited Athens, as that of the Phocians would to-day. What transgression did the Phocians or the Lacedaemonians or you or anyone else commit after Aeschines' speech, that the promises made by him to you then should not be fulfilled ? Ask him that question. He can point to none. For he made his lying report, you believed it, the Phocians heard of it, surrendered, and perished, all within a period of five days only. Hence it is clearly evident that the ruin of the Phocians was nothing but a concoction of deceit and artifice. For during the time when Philip was unable to march by reason of the peace, but was already laying his plans, he sent for the Lacedaemonians, promising to do everything for them, so that the Phocians might not, through your agency, secure their help. But when he had reached Thermopylae, and

αἰσθόμενοι τὴν ἐνέδραν ὑπεχώρησαν, τοῦτον αὖ
προκαθῆκεν ἐξαπατᾶν ὑμᾶς, ἵνα μὴ πάλιν, ὑμῶν
αἰσθομένων ὅτι Θηβαίοις τὰ πράγματα πράττει,
εἰς χρόνους καὶ πόλεμον καὶ τριβὴν ἐμπέσῃ, τῶν
μὲν Φωκέων ἀμυνομένων ὑμῶν δὲ βοηθούντων,
ἀλλ' ἀκονιτεὶ πάνθ' ὑφ' ἑαυτῷ ποιήσηται· ὅπερ
καὶ γέγονεν. μὴ οὖν ὅτι καὶ Λακεδαιμονίους καὶ
Φωκέας ἐξηπάτησε Φίλιππος, διὰ ταῦθ' ὧν ὑμᾶς
οὗτος ἐξηπάτησε μὴ δότω δίκην· οὐ γὰρ δίκαιον.

78 Ἃν τοίνυν ἀντὶ Φωκέων καὶ Πυλῶν καὶ τῶν
ἄλλων τῶν ἀπολωλότων Χερρόνησος ὡς περίεστι
τῇ πόλει λέγῃ, πρὸς Διὸς καὶ θεῶν μὴ ἀποδέξησθ',
ὦ ἄνδρες δικασταί, μηδ' ὑπομείνητε, πρὸς οἷς ἐκ
τῆς πρεσβείας ἠδίκησθε, καὶ ἐκ τῆς ἀπολογίας
ὄνειδος προσκατασκευασθῆναι τῇ πόλει, ὡς ἄρ'
ὑμεῖς τῶν ἰδίων τι κτημάτων ὑπεξαιρούμενοι τὴν
τῶν συμμάχων σωτηρίαν προήκασθε. οὐ γὰρ
ἐποιήσατε τοῦτο, ἀλλ' ἤδη τῆς εἰρήνης γεγονυίας
[366] καὶ τῆς Χερρονήσου σῴας οὔσης τέτταρας μῆνας
ὅλους ἐσῴζονθ' οἱ Φωκεῖς τοὺς ὕστερον, ἡ δὲ
τούτου ψευδολογία μετὰ ταῦθ' ὕστερον αὐτοὺς ἀπ-
79 ώλεσεν, ἐξαπατήσασ' ὑμᾶς. εἶτα καὶ νῦν ἐν μείζονι
κινδύνῳ τὴν Χερρόνησον οὖσαν εὑρήσετ' ἢ τότε.
πότερον γὰρ εὐπορώτερον ἂν δίκην ἔδωκε Φίλιππος
ἐξαμαρτὼν εἰς αὐτὴν πρὶν τούτων τι τῆς πόλεως
προλαβεῖν, ἢ νυνί; ἐγὼ μὲν οἶμαι, τότε πολλῷ.
τίς οὖν ἡ ταύτης περιουσία, τῶν φόβων ἀφῃρημένων
καὶ τῶν κινδύνων τῶν τοῦ βουληθέντος ἂν αὐτὴν
ἀδικῆσαι;

296

when the Lacedaemonians, detecting the snare, had withdrawn, he sent Aeschines as his agent in advance for your deception, lest, when you discovered that he was acting in the interest of the Thebans, he should be involved once more in delays and fighting and waste of time with the Phocians resisting him, and you helping them. In this way he hoped to obtain complete mastery without a struggle. And so it fell out. Aeschines, then, must not escape punishment for deceiving you, merely because Philip deceived the Lacedaemonians and the Phocians. That would be unjust indeed.

If as an offset to the Phocians and Thermopylae and all our other losses he tells you that the city still retains the Chersonese, I adjure you not to accept that excuse. In addition to the wrongs he has done you by his embassy, you must not suffer him by his defence also to fasten upon the city the reproach that, while stealthily securing some of your own possessions, you made sacrifice of the safety of your allies. You did no such thing. Peace was concluded; the Chersonese was secure; and then for the four ensuing months the Phocians were not imperilled, until you were deceived, and the Phocians destroyed, by this man's mendacity. Moreover, you will find that the Chersonese is in greater danger now than then. When would it have been easier to punish Philip for wrongful aggression upon that country— before he forestalled us at Thermopylae, or to-day? Surely far easier then! What, then, does it profit us that we still retain the Chersonese, if the man, who would have invaded it if he could, is freed from the apprehensions and perils that deterred him?

80 Ἔτι τοίνυν τοιοῦτό τι μέλλειν αὐτὸν ἀκούω
λέγειν, ὅτι θαυμάζει τί δήποτε Δημοσθένης αὐτοῦ
κατηγορεῖ, Φωκέων δ' οὐδείς. ὡς δὴ τοῦτ' ἔχει,
βέλτιον προακοῦσαι παρ' ἐμοῦ. Φωκέων τῶν
ἐκπεπτωκότων οἱ μέν, οἶμαι, βέλτιστοι καὶ με-
τριώτατοι φυγάδες γεγενημένοι καὶ τοιαῦτα πεπονθότες ἡσυχίαν ἄγουσι, καὶ οὐδεὶς ἂν αὐτῶν ἐθελή-
σειεν ὑπὲρ τῶν κοινῶν συμφορῶν ἰδίαν ἔχθραν
ἀνελέσθαι· οἱ δ' ὁτιοῦν ἂν ἀργυρίου ποιήσαντες τὸν
81 δώσοντ' οὐκ ἔχουσιν αὐτοῖς. οὐ γὰρ ἔγωγ' ἂν
ἔδωκ' οὐδενὶ οὐδὲν ὥστε μοι παραστάντας ἐνταυθὶ
βοᾶν οἷα πεπόνθασιν· ἡ γὰρ ἀλήθεια καὶ τὰ πεπραγμέν' αὐτὰ βοᾷ. ἀλλὰ μὴν ὅ γε δῆμος ὁ τῶν
Φωκέων οὕτω κακῶς καὶ ἐλεινῶς διάκειται,
ὥστε μὴ περὶ τοῦ κατηγορεῖν ἑκάστῳ τὰς Ἀθήνησιν
εὐθύνας εἶναι τὸν λόγον, ἀλλὰ δουλεύειν καὶ τε-
θνάναι τῷ φόβῳ Θηβαίους καὶ τοὺς Φιλίππου
ξένους, οὓς ἀναγκάζονται τρέφειν διῳκισμένοι
82 κατὰ κώμας καὶ παρῃρημένοι τὰ ὅπλα. μὴ δὴ
ταῦτα λέγειν αὐτὸν ἐᾶτε, ἀλλ' ὡς οὐκ ἀπολώλασι
[367] Φωκεῖς δεικνύναι, ἢ ὡς οὐχ ὑπέσχετο σώσειν
αὐτοὺς Φίλιππον. τοῦτο γάρ εἰσι πρεσβείας εὔθυναι, τί πέπρακται; τί ἀπήγγειλας; εἰ μὲν
ἀληθῆ, σώζου· εἰ δὲ ψευδῆ, δίκην δός· εἰ δὲ μὴ
πάρεισι Φωκεῖς, τί τοῦτο; οὕτω γὰρ διέθηκας
αὐτούς, οἶμαι, τὸ μέρος σύ, ὥστε μήτε τοῖς φίλοις
βοηθεῖν μήτε τοὺς ἐχθροὺς ἀμύνεσθαι δύνασθαι.

83 Καὶ μὴν ὅτι χωρὶς τῆς ἄλλης αἰσχύνης καὶ ἀ-
δοξίας, ἣν τὰ πεπραγμέν' ἔχει, καὶ μεγάλοι κίνδυνοι
περιεστᾶσιν ἐκ τούτων τὴν πόλιν, ῥᾴδιον δεῖξαι.
τίς γὰρ οὐκ οἶδεν ὑμῶν ὅτι τῷ Φωκέων πολέμῳ

I hear of another argument he will use : he will wonder why his accuser is Demosthenes and not one of the Phocians. I had better explain at once how the matter stands. The best and most respectable of the expatriated Phocians, being exiled and in distress, are living peaceably, and none of them would be willing to incur private animosity on account of the misfortunes of the nation, while those who might have done anything for a fee find that there is no one to pay it them. For I would never pay a man a farthing to stand here by my side and make an outcry about his sufferings, since truth and fact cry out loudly enough. Nay more, the commonalty of the Phocians are in such an evil and pitiable plight that there is no question with them of prosecuting at an Athenian scrutiny— only of living like slaves in mortal terror of Thebans and of Philip's mercenaries, who are billeted on them after they have been disarmed and distributed among villages. Do not allow this plea. No, Aeschines must prove either that the Phocians are not ruined, or that he did not promise that Philip would protect them. These are the questions for a scrutiny of an embassy : What has been accomplished ? What did you report ? If the truth,— go in peace ; if falsehood,—take your punishment. What matter if the Phocians are not in court ? You have played your part in reducing them to such straits that they can neither help their friends nor repel their enemies.

Moreover, apart from the discredit and infamy attached to these transactions, it is easy to show that they have involved the commonwealth in very serious perils. You all know that the prowess of

καὶ τῷ κυρίους εἶναι Πυλῶν Φωκέας ἤ τ' ἀπὸ
Θηβαίων ᾄδει' ὑπῆρχεν ἡμῖν, καὶ τὸ μηδέποτ' ἂν
ἐλθεῖν εἰς Πελοπόννησον μηδ' εἰς Εὔβοιαν μηδ' εἰς
84 τὴν Ἀττικὴν Φίλιππον μηδὲ Θηβαίους; ταύτην
μέντοι τὴν ἀπὸ τοῦ τόπου καὶ τῶν πραγμάτων
ἀσφάλειαν ὑπάρχουσαν τῇ πόλει ταῖς τούτων ἀπά-
ταις καὶ ψευδολογίαις πεισθέντες προήκασθ' ὑμεῖς,
καὶ τετειχισμένην ὅπλοις καὶ πολέμῳ συνεχεῖ καὶ
πόλεσι μεγάλαις συμμάχων ἀνδρῶν καὶ χώρᾳ
πολλῇ περιείδετ' ἀνασταθεῖσαν. καὶ ματαία μὲν
ἡ πρότερον βοήθει' εἰς Πύλας ὑμῖν γέγονεν, ἣν
μετὰ πλειόνων ἢ διακοσίων ταλάντων ἐποιήσασθε,
ἐὰν λογίσησθε τὰς ἰδίας δαπάνας τὰς τῶν στρα-
τευσαμένων, μάταιαι δὲ καὶ αἱ κατὰ Θηβαίων
85 ἐλπίδες. ὃ δέ, πολλῶν ὄντων καὶ δεινῶν ὧν οὗτος
ὑπηρέτηκε Φιλίππῳ, πλείστην ὕβριν ὡς ἀληθῶς
ἔχει κατὰ τῆς πόλεως καὶ ἁπάντων ὑμῶν, τοῦτ'
ἀκούσατέ μου, ὅτι τοῖς Θηβαίοις ἐγνωκότος ἐξ
[368] ἀρχῆς τοῦ Φιλίππου πάνθ' ἃ πεποίηκε ποιεῖν,
οὗτος ἀπαγγείλας τἀναντία καὶ φανεροὺς ἐπι-
δείξας ὑμᾶς οὐχὶ βουλομένους ὑμῖν μὲν τὴν ἔχθραν
τὴν πρὸς Θηβαίους μείζω, Φιλίππῳ δὲ τὴν χάριν
πεποίηκεν. πῶς ἂν οὖν ὑβριστικώτερον ἄνθρωπος
ὑμῖν ἐχρήσατο.
86 Λέγε δὴ τὸ ψήφισμα λαβὼν τὸ τοῦ Διοφάντου
καὶ τὸ τοῦ Καλλισθένους, ἵν' εἰδῆθ' ὅτι, ὅτε μὲν τὰ
δέοντ' ἐποιεῖτε, θυσιῶν καὶ ἐπαίνων ἠξιοῦσθε παρ'
ὑμῖν αὐτοῖς καὶ παρὰ τοῖς ἄλλοις, ἐπειδὴ δ' ὑπὸ τούτων παρεκρούσθητε, παῖδας καὶ γυναῖκας ἐκ τῶν
ἀγρῶν κατεκομίζεσθε καὶ τὰ Ἡράκλει' ἐντὸς
τείχους θύειν ἐψηφίζεσθ' εἰρήνης οὔσης. ὃ καὶ
θαυμάζω, εἰ τὸν μηδὲ τοὺς θεούς, καθ' ὃ πάτριον
300

the Phocians, and their control of the pass of Thermopylae, gave us security against the Thebans,
and ensured that neither Philip nor the Thebans
would invade either the Peloponnesus, or Euboea,
or Attica. But, overborne by the impostures and
falsehoods of these men, you have flung away the
security of position and circumstances which the
city enjoyed. That security was fortified by arms
and an unbroken front, by strongholds of our allies
and a broad territory ; and you have acquiesced in
its devastation. Your former expedition to Thermopylae, made at a cost of more than two hundred
talents, if you include the private expenses of the
troops, has gone to waste ; and so have all your
hopes respecting the Thebans. But of all the many
shameful services rendered by Aeschines to Philip,
let me mention the one that really implied the most
insolent disdain of the city and of you all. Philip
was resolved from the first to do for the Thebans
all that he has done, but Aeschines by the perversions
of his report revealed your repugnance, and so
intensified both your hostility and Philip's friendliness towards the Thebans. How could the man have
treated you more arrogantly ?

Now take and read the decrees of Diophantus
and of Callisthenes. They will show you how, when
you did your duty, you made it an occasion of
services of praise and thanksgiving, both at Athens
and abroad ; but when you had been led astray by
these men, you brought your wives and children in
from the country, and ordered the festival of Heracles
to be held within the walls, in time of peace. It
makes me wonder whether you will release unpunished

ἦν, τιμᾶσθαι ποιήσαντα, τοῦτον ἀτιμώρητον ἀφήσετε. λέγε τὸ ψήφισμα.

ΨΗΦΙΣΜΑ

Ταῦτα μὲν τότ' ἄξι', ὦ ἄνδρες 'Αθηναῖοι, τῶν πεπραγμένων ἐψηφίσασθε. λέγε δὴ τὰ μετὰ ταῦτα.

ΨΗΦΙΣΜΑ

87 Ταῦτα τότ' ἐψηφίζεσθ' ὑμεῖς διὰ τούτους, οὐκ ἐπὶ ταύταις ταῖς ἐλπίσιν οὔτε κατ' ἀρχὰς ποιησάμενοι τὴν εἰρήνην καὶ τὴν συμμαχίαν, οὔθ' ὕστερον ἐγγράψαι πεισθέντες εἰς αὐτὴν καὶ τοῖς ἐγγόνοις, ἀλλ' ὡς θαυμάσι' ἡλίκα πεισόμενοι διὰ τούτους ἀγαθά. καὶ μὴν καὶ μετὰ ταῦθ' ὁσάκις πρὸς Πορθμῷ ἢ πρὸς Μεγάροις ἀκούοντες δύναμιν Φιλίππου καὶ ξένους ἐθορυβεῖσθε, πάντες ἐπίστασθε. οὐ τοίνυν εἰ μήπω τῆς 'Αττικῆς ἐπιβαίνει δεῖ σκοπεῖν οὐδὲ ῥᾳθυμεῖν, ἀλλ' εἰ διὰ τούτους ἐξουσία γέγονεν αὐτῷ τοῦθ' ὅταν βούληται ποιῆσαι, τοῦθ' ὁρᾶν, καὶ πρὸς ἐκεῖνο τὸ δεινὸν βλέπειν, καὶ
[369] τὸν αἴτιον καὶ παρασκευάσαντα τὴν ἐξουσίαν ταύτην ἐκείνῳ μισεῖν καὶ τιμωρεῖσθαι.

88 Οἶδα τοίνυν ὅτι τοὺς μὲν ὑπὲρ τῶν κατηγορημένων αὐτοῦ λόγους Αἰσχίνης φεύξεται, βουλόμενος δ' ὑμᾶς ὡς πορρωτάτω τῶν πεπραγμένων ἀπάγειν διέξεισιν ἡλίκα πᾶσιν ἀνθρώποις ἀγάθ' ἐκ τῆς εἰρήνης γίγνεται καὶ τοὐναντίον ἐκ τοῦ πολέμου κακά, καὶ ὅλως ἐγκώμι' εἰρήνης ἐρεῖ, καὶ τοιαῦτ' ἀπολογήσεται. ἔστι δὲ καὶ ταῦτα κατηγορήματα τούτου. εἰ γὰρ ἡ τοῖς ἄλλοις ἀγαθῶν αἰτία τοσούτων πραγμάτων καὶ ταραχῆς ἡμῖν αἰτία γέγονε,

302

a man who has deprived even the gods of immemorial observances. Read the decree.

(The Decree of Diophantus is read)

So you decreed at that time, men of Athens, agreeably to your achievements. Now read the next.

(The Decree of Callisthenes is read)

That is the decree you then made ; and you owe it to these men. It was not with such expectations that you either made the first draft of the peace and alliance, or subsequently consented to add the words, *and to his posterity*, but in the hope of marvellous benefits through their agency. Yes, and since then you all remember how many times you have been agitated by news of Philip's army and auxiliaries at Porthmus or at Megara. True, he has not yet set foot in Attica ; but you must **not** look only at that and abate your vigilance,—you must bear in mind that, thanks to these men, he has it in his power to do so whenever he chooses. You must keep that danger before your eyes, and abhor and punish the author and purveyor of that power.

No doubt Aeschines will eschew a direct reply to the charges alleged, and in his desire to lead you as far as possible away from the facts, he will dilate on the great blessings that peace brings to the world, and set against them the evils of war. He will eulogize peace in general terms, and that will be his defence. But all those considerations tell against him. For, if peace, which brings blessings to others, has brought so much vexation and bewilderment

303

τί τις εἶναι τοῦτο φῇ πλὴν ὅτι δῶρα λαβόντες οὗτοι
89 καλὸν πρᾶγμα φύσει κακῶς διέθηκαν; τί δ'; " οὐ
τριήρεις τριακόσιαι καὶ σκεύη ταύταις καὶ χρήμαθ'
ὑμῖν περίεστι καὶ περιέσται διὰ τὴν εἰρήνην;"
ἴσως ἂν εἴποι. πρὸς δὴ ταῦτ' ἐκεῖν' ὑμᾶς ὑπο-
λαμβάνειν δεῖ, ὅτι καὶ τὰ Φιλίππου πράγματ'
ἐκ τῆς εἰρήνης γέγονεν εὐπορώτερα πολλῷ, καὶ
κατασκευαῖς ὅπλων καὶ χώρας καὶ προσόδων, αἳ
90 γεγόνασιν ἐκείνῳ μεγάλαι. γεγόνασι δὲ καὶ ἡμῖν
τινές. ἡ δέ γε τῶν πραγμάτων κατασκευὴ καὶ τῶν
συμμάχων, δι' ἣν ἢ αὑτοῖς ἢ τοῖς κρείττοσι τἀγαθὰ
πάντες κέκτηνται, ἡ μὲν ἡμετέρα πραθεῖσ' ὑπὸ
τούτων ἀπόλωλε καὶ γέγονεν ἀσθενής, ἡ δ' ἐκείνου
91 φοβερὰ καὶ μείζων πολλῷ. οὐ δὴ δίκαιον ἐκείνῳ
μὲν ἀμφότερ' ηὐξῆσθαι διὰ τούτους, καὶ τὰ τῶν
συμμάχων καὶ τὰ τῶν προσόδων, ἡμῖν δ' ἃ καὶ
ὡς[1] ἂν ὑπῆρχεν ἐκ τῆς εἰρήνης, ταῦτ' ἀνθ' ὧν
[370] ἀπέδοντ' αὐτοὶ λογίζεσθαι. οὐ γὰρ ταῦτ' ἀντ'
ἐκείνων γέγονεν, οὐδὲ πολλοῦ δεῖ, ἀλλὰ ταῦτα μὲν
ἦν ἂν ὁμοίως ἡμῖν, ἐκεῖνα δὲ τούτοις ἂν προσῆν,
εἰ μὴ διὰ τούτους.
92 Ὅλως δ', ὦ ἄνδρες Ἀθηναῖοι, δίκαιον δήπου
φήσαιτ' ἂν εἶναι μήτ', εἰ πολλὰ καὶ δεινὰ τὰ
συμβεβηκότ' ἐστὶ τῇ πόλει, μηδενὸς δ' Αἰσχίνης
αἴτιος τούτων, εἰς τοῦτον ἐλθεῖν τὴν ὀργήν, μήτ'
εἴ τι τῶν δεόντων πέπρακται δι' ἄλλον τινά, τοῦτο
σῶσαι τουτονί· ἀλλ' ὅσων οὗτος αἴτιος σκεψάμενοι
καὶ χάριν, ἂν ταύτης ἄξιος ᾖ, καὶ τοὐναντίον
ὀργήν, ἂν τοιαῦτα φαίνηται πεποιηκώς, ποιεῖσθε.

---

[1] ἃ καὶ ὡς Weil: ἃ δικαίως Shill. with mss.

to you, what are we to say except that these men with their bribe-taking have perverted to evil a thing in itself excellent ? What next ? Perhaps he will ask : " Do you not retain, and shall you not retain through the peace, three hundred war-galleys with stores and money for them ? "

In reply to that, you have to reflect that Philip also has greatly strengthened his position owing to the peace, as regards his material resources in arms, in territory, in revenues, which last have increased largely. And so indeed have ours, to some extent. But as to those other resources, of policy and of alliance,—and it is by them that all nations hold advantages for themselves or for stronger states—in our case, bartered away by these men, they have perished, or at least deteriorated : his are now formidable and far greater. It is surely unfair that, while Philip, thanks to these men, enjoys extended alliances and increased revenues, the advantages that we should in any case have gained from the peace should be reckoned by them as a set-off against those that they have sold. For our gains are not a compensation for our losses ; far from it ! No ; what we now have would equally have been ours, and what we have not would have been added to us, but for these men.

Speaking generally, men of Athens, you will doubtless agree that, however many misfortunes have befallen the city, if Aeschines had no hand in them, they ought not to be visited upon him. On the other hand, if the right policy has been taken by others, it is not fair that their success should save him. Take into account everything to which he contributed ; requite him with gratitude, if he deserves it, with resentment, if his conduct provokes

305

93 πῶς οὖν εὑρήσετε ταῦτα δικαίως; ἐὰν μὴ πάνθ' ἅμ'
ἐᾶτε ταράττειν αὐτόν, τὰ τῶν στρατηγῶν ἀδικήματα, τὸν πόλεμον τὸν πρὸς Φίλιππον, τἀπὸ τῆς
εἰρήνης ἀγαθά, ἀλλ' ἕκαστον ἐφ' ἑαυτοῦ σκοπῆτε.
οἷον· ἦν ἡμῖν πόλεμος πρὸς Φίλιππον· ἦν. ἐνταῦθ'
ἐγκαλεῖ τις Αἰσχίνῃ; βούλεταί τις τούτου κατηγορεῖν περὶ τῶν ἐν τῷ πολέμῳ πραχθέντων; οὐδὲ
94 εἷς. οὐκοῦν περὶ τούτων γ' ἀφεῖται, καὶ οὐδὲν
αὐτὸν δεῖ λέγειν· περὶ γὰρ τῶν ἀμφισβητουμένων
καὶ τοὺς μάρτυρας παρέχεσθαι καὶ τὰ τεκμήρια δεῖ
λέγειν τὸν φεύγοντα, οὐ τὰ ὁμολογούμεν' ἀπολο-
γούμενον ἐξαπατᾶν. ὅπως τοίνυν περὶ τοῦ πολέμου
μηδὲν ἐρεῖς· οὐδεὶς γὰρ οὐδὲν αἰτιᾶται περὶ αὐτοῦ
95 σε. μετὰ ταῦτ' εἰρήνην τινὲς ἡμᾶς ἔπειθον ποιή-
σασθαι· ἐπείσθημεν· πρέσβεις ἐπέμψαμεν· ἤγαγον
οὗτοι δεῦρο τοὺς ποιησομένους τὴν εἰρήνην. πάλιν
ἐνταῦθα περὶ τούτου μέμφεταί τις Αἰσχίνην;
φησί τις εἰσηγήσασθαι τοῦτον εἰρήνην, ἢ ἀδικεῖν
ὅτι δεῦρ' ἤγαγε τοὺς ποιησομένους; οὐδὲ εἷς.
[371] οὔκουν οὐδ' ὑπὲρ αὐτοῦ τοῦ ποιήσασθαι τὴν πόλιν
εἰρήνην οὐδὲν αὐτῷ λεκτέον· οὐ γὰρ οὗτος αἴτιος.
96 τί οὖν, ἄνθρωπε, λέγεις, εἴ τις ἔροιτό με, καὶ πόθεν
ἄρχει κατηγορεῖν; ὅθεν, ὦ ἄνδρες Ἀθηναῖοι, βου-
λευομένων ὑμῶν, οὐ περὶ τοῦ εἰ ποιητέον εἰρήνην
ἢ μή (ἐδέδοκτο γὰρ ἤδη τοῦτό γε) ἀλλ' ὑπὲρ τοῦ
ποίαν τινά, τοῖς γὰρ τὰ δίκαια λέγουσιν ἀντειπὼν
τῷ μισθοῦ γράφοντι συνεῖπε δῶρα λαβών, καὶ
μετὰ ταῦτ' ἐπὶ τοὺς ὅρκους αἱρεθείς, ὧν μὲν ὑμεῖς
97 προσετάξατε, οὐδ' ὁτιοῦν ἐποίησε, τοὺς δ' ἐπὶ τοῦ

resentment. How then will you reach a right conclusion ? Do not allow him to make a hotch-potch of the faults of the generals, the war with Philip, the blessings of peace ; but consider one thing at a time. For example, we were at war with Philip. True. Does anyone blame Aeschines for that ? Does anyone wish to arraign him for the events of the war ? Not a single man. Then so far he is acquitted ; he need not say a word. A defendant should adduce witnesses and submit proofs on the issues in dispute, not mislead the jury by addressing his defence to points of agreement. You are not to say anything about the war, Aeschines. No one blames you for that. Afterwards certain persons advised us to make peace ; we took their advice ; we sent ambassadors ; and they brought back to Athens envoys authorized to conclude peace. Here again no one blames Aeschines. Does anyone allege that he broached the question of peace ? Or that he acted wrongly when he brought the delegates here ? Not a single man. Then about the mere fact that the city made peace he need not say a word ; for that he is not chargeable. Suppose I am asked : " What do you mean, sir ? At what point do you begin your accusations ? " I begin at this point, men of Athens—at the time when you were deliberating, not whether peace should or should not be made—that question was already decided—but what sort of peace. Then he contra-dicted men who spoke honestly, and he supported the mover of a venal resolution, being himself bribed. Afterwards, when appointed to receive the oaths of ratification, he disobeyed every one of your instruc-tions ; he brought to ruin allies of ours whose safety

πολέμου διασωθέντας ἀπώλεσε τῶν συμμάχων,
καὶ τηλικαῦτα καὶ τοιαῦτ' ἐψεύσαθ' ἡλίκ' οὐδεὶς
πώποτ' ἄλλος ἀνθρώπων οὔτε πρότερον οὔθ'
ὕστερον. τὸ μὲν γὰρ ἐξ ἀρχῆς ἄχρι τοῦ λόγου
τυχεῖν Φίλιππον ὑπὲρ τῆς εἰρήνης, Κτησιφῶν καὶ
Ἀριστόδημος τὴν ἀρχὴν τὴν πρώτην ἔφερον τοῦ
φενακισμοῦ, ἐπειδὴ δ' εἰς τὸ πράττειν ἤδη τὰ
πράγμαθ' ἧκε, Φιλοκράτει καὶ τούτῳ παρέδωκαν,
98 ἐκδεξάμενοι δ' οὗτοι πάντ' ἀπώλεσαν. εἶτ' ἐπειδὴ
δεῖ λόγον καὶ δίκην ὑπέχειν τῶν πεπραγμένων,
ὧν, οἶμαι, πανοῦργος οὗτος καὶ θεοῖς ἐχθρὸς καὶ
γραμματεύς, ὡς ὑπὲρ τῆς εἰρήνης κρινόμενος
ἀπολογήσεται, οὐχ ἵνα πλειόνων ἢ κατηγορεῖ τις
αὐτοῦ δῷ λόγον· μανία γὰρ τοῦτό γε· ἀλλ' ὁρᾷ
τοῦθ' ὅτι ἐν μὲν τοῖς ὑφ' αὑτοῦ πεπραγμένοις
ἀγαθὸν μὲν οὐδέν ἐστιν, ἅπαντα δὲ τἀδικήματα, ἡ
δ' ὑπὲρ τῆς εἰρήνης ἀπολογία, καὶ εἰ μηδὲν ἄλλο,
99 τοὔνομα γοῦν ἔχει φιλάνθρωπον.
[372]   Ἣν δέδοικα μέν, ὦ ἄνδρες Ἀθηναῖοι, δέδοικα μὴ
λελήθαμεν ὥσπερ οἱ δανειζόμενοι ἐπὶ πολλῷ ἄγον-
τες· τὸ γὰρ ἀσφαλὲς αὐτῆς καὶ τὸ βέβαιον οὗτοι
προΰδοσαν, Φωκέας καὶ Πύλας· οὐ μὴν διὰ τοῦτόν
γ' ἐξ ἀρχῆς ἐποιησάμεθα, ἀλλ' ἄτοπον μέν ἐστιν
ὃ μέλλω λέγειν, ἀληθὲς δὲ πάνυ· εἰ γάρ τις ὡς
ἀληθῶς χαίρει τῇ εἰρήνῃ, τοῖς στρατηγοῖς, ὧν
κατηγοροῦσιν ἅπαντες, χάριν αὐτῆς ἐχέτω· εἰ
γὰρ ἐκεῖνοι ὡς ὑμεῖς ἐβούλεσθ' ἐπολέμουν, οὐδ'
100 ὄνομ' εἰρήνης ἂν ἠνέσχεσθε. εἰρήνη μὲν οὖν δι'

---

a Demosthenes often alludes scornfully to Aeschines' profession of γραμματεύς. Aeschines seems first to have been
private secretary to the statesmen Aristophon and Eubulus.
After his career on the stage, he obtained an under-clerkship

had never been imperilled in time of war ; and he told lies which both in quantity and quality exceed all records of human mendacity before or since. At the outset, until Philip got a hearing on the question of peace, Ctesiphon and Aristodemus undertook the first initiation of the imposture, but, when the business was ripe for action, they passed it on to Philocrates and the defendant, who took it over, and completed the enterprise of destruction. And now that he is answerable for his misdeeds, and must stand his trial, being as he is a knave, a scoundrel, and—a government clerk,[a] he will conduct his defence as if he were on trial for the peace, not to make his justification broader than his indictment—that would be folly—but because he can see in his own acts nothing that is good, nothing that is not criminal, while a defence of the peace, if it has no other merit, will enable him to pose as a Friend of Humanity.

Speaking of the peace, I fear, men of Athens, I sadly fear that we are unconsciously enjoying it like men who borrow money at a high rate of interest. For these men have betrayed the security and guarantee of the peace — the Phocians and Thermopylae. Anyhow, we have not to thank the defendant for peace. What I am going to say is strange, but quite true. If any man is really pleased with the peace, let him be grateful to those generals whom everyone denounces. For, had they fought to your satisfaction, you would have scorned the very name of peace. Peace, then, we owe to the

in the Civil Service, and subsequently became Clerk of the Council and Assembly. This was an official of some dignity ; he was appointed by popular election and enjoyed the privilege of free maintenance in the Prytaneum or Town Hall.

ἐκείνους, ἐπικίνδυνος δὲ καὶ σφαλερὰ καὶ ἄπιστος
διὰ τούτους γέγονε δωροδοκήσαντας. εἶργετ᾽ οὖν,
εἶργετ᾽ αὐτὸν τῶν ὑπὲρ τῆς εἰρήνης λόγων, εἰς δὲ
τοὺς ὑπὲρ τῶν πεπραγμένων ἐμβιβάζετε. οὐ γὰρ
Αἰσχίνης διὰ τὴν εἰρήνην κρίνεται, οὔ, ἀλλ᾽ ἡ
101 εἰρήνη δι᾽ Αἰσχίνην διαβέβληται. σημεῖον δέ· εἰ
γὰρ ἡ μὲν εἰρήνη ἐγεγόνει, μηδὲν δ᾽ ὕστερον ἐξηπά-
τησθ᾽ ὑμεῖς μηδ᾽ ἀπωλώλει τῶν συμμάχων μηδείς,
τίν᾽ ἀνθρώπων ἐλύπησεν ἂν ἡ εἰρήνη, ἔξω τοῦ
ἄδοξος γεγενῆσθαι; καίτοι καὶ τούτου συναίτιος
οὗτος συνειπὼν Φιλοκράτει. ἀλλ᾽ ἀνήκεστόν γ᾽
οὐδὲν ἂν ἦν γεγονός. νῦν δ᾽, οἶμαι, πολλῶν αἴτιος
οὗτος.

102 Ὅτι μὲν τοίνυν αἰσχρῶς καὶ κακῶς πάντα ταῦθ᾽
ὑπὸ τούτων ἀπόλωλε καὶ διέφθαρται, οἶμαι πάντας
ὑμᾶς εἰδέναι. ἐγὼ δ᾽, ὦ ἄνδρες δικασταί, τοσοῦτ᾽
ἀπέχω τοῦ συκοφαντίαν τινὰ τοῖς πράγμασι τούτοις
προσάγειν ἢ ὑμᾶς ἀξιοῦν, ὥστ᾽ εἰ ταῦθ᾽ ὑπ᾽ ἀβελ-
τερίας ἢ δι᾽ εὐήθειαν ἢ δι᾽ ἄλλην ἄγνοιαν ἡντινοῦν
οὕτω πέπρακται, αὐτός τ᾽ ἀφίημ᾽ Αἰσχίνην καὶ
103 ὑμῖν συμβουλεύω. καίτοι τῶν σκήψεων τούτων
[373] οὐδεμί᾽ ἐστὶ πολιτικὴ οὐδὲ δικαία. οὐδένα γὰρ τὰ
κοινὰ πράττειν ὑμεῖς κελεύετε οὐδ᾽ ἀναγκάζετε·
ἀλλ᾽ ἐπειδάν τις ἑαυτὸν πείσας δύνασθαι προσέλθῃ,
πρᾶγμα ποιοῦντες ἀνθρώπων χρηστῶν καὶ φιλαν-
θρώπων εὐνοϊκῶς δέχεσθε καὶ οὐ φθονερῶς, ἀλλὰ
καὶ χειροτονεῖτε καὶ τὰ ὑμέτερ᾽ αὐτῶν ἐγχειρίζετε.
104 ἐὰν μὲν οὖν κατορθοῖ τις, τιμήσεται καὶ πλέον
ἕξει τῶν πολλῶν κατὰ τοῦτο· ἐὰν δ᾽ ἀποτυγχάνῃ,
σκήψεις καὶ προφάσεις ἐρεῖ; ἀλλ᾽ οὐ δίκαιον. οὐ
γὰρ ἂν ἐξαρκέσειε τοῖς ἀπολωλόσι συμμάχοις

generals ; a perilous, insecure, and precarious peace to these men and their venality. Put a stop, then, to his eloquence about the peace. Make him address himself to his own performances. Aeschines is not on trial for the peace ; the peace is discredited through Aeschines. That is easily proved. Suppose that the peace had been concluded, and that you had not thereafter been deluded, and none of your allies destroyed—what human being would the peace have aggrieved ? I mean, apart from the consideration that it was not a glorious peace. For that fault Aeschines is indeed partly to blame, as he supported Philocrates. However, in the case supposed, no incurable mischief would have been done. As the case stands, he is answerable for a great deal.

Well, I suppose that you are satisfied that all this ruin and mischief was shamefully and wickedly perpetrated by these men. For my part, gentlemen of the jury, I am so reluctant to play the informer in these matters, or to ask you to do so, that, if we are dealing with blunders due to stupidity or simplicity or any other sort of ignorance, I acquit Aeschines, and invite you to do the like. And yet ignorance is not a fair excuse in public life ; for no man is required or compelled by you to handle politics. When a man puts himself forward with a persuasion of his own ability, you receive his advances, as kindly and courteous people should, with goodwill and without jealousy ; you give him appointments and entrust him with public business. If he succeeds, he will be honoured, and so far will gain an advantage over ordinary people ; but if he fails, shall he put forward excuses and apologies ? That would be unfair. For it would be very poor consolation indeed

311

οὐδὲ τοῖς παισὶν αὐτῶν οὐδὲ ταῖς γυναιξὶν οὐδὲ
τοῖς ἄλλοις διὰ τὴν ἀβελτερίαν τὴν ἐμήν, ἵνα μὴ
τὴν τούτου λέγω, τοιαῦτα πεπονθέναι· πολλοῦ γε
105 καὶ δεῖ. ἀλλ' ὅμως ὑμεῖς ἄφετ' Αἰσχίνῃ τὰ δεινὰ
ταῦτα καὶ ὑπερβάλλοντα, ἂν δι' εὐήθειαν ἢ δι' ἄλλην
ἄγνοιαν λελυμασμένος φανῇ. ἂν μέντοι διὰ πονηρίαν ἀργύριον λαβὼν καὶ δῶρα, καὶ τοῦτ' ἐξελεγχθῇ
σαφῶς ὑπ' αὐτῶν τῶν πεπραγμένων, μάλιστα
μέν, εἰ οἷόν τ', ἀποκτείνατε, εἰ δὲ μή, ζῶντα τοῖς
λοιποῖς παράδειγμα ποιήσατε. σκοπεῖτε δὴ τὸν
ὑπὲρ τούτων ἔλεγχον, ὡς δίκαιος ἔσται, μεθ' ὑμῶν.
106 Ἀνάγκη δήπου τοὺς λόγους τούτους Αἰσχίνην
πρὸς ὑμᾶς εἰπεῖν τουτονί, τοὺς περὶ τῶν Φωκέων
καὶ τῶν Θεσπιῶν καὶ τῆς Εὐβοίας, εἴπερ μὴ
πεπρακὼς αὑτὸν ἑκὼν ἐξηπάτα, δυοῖν θάτερον,
ἢ διαρρήδην ἀκούσανθ' ὑποσχομένου Φιλίππου
ὅτι πράξει ταῦτα καὶ ποιήσει, ἢ εἰ μὴ τοῦτο,
[374] γοητευθέντα καὶ φενακισθέντα τῇ περὶ τἆλλα φιλ-
107 ανθρωπίᾳ καὶ ταῦτ' ἐλπίσαντα παρ' αὐτοῦ. οὐκ
ἔνεστι τούτων οὐδὲ ἓν χωρίς. ἐκ τοίνυν τούτων
ἀμφοτέρων μάλιστα πάντων ἀνθρώπων μισεῖν
αὐτῷ προσήκει Φίλιππον. διὰ τί; ὅτι τὸ μὲν
ἐκείνου μέρος πάντ' αὐτῷ γέγονε τὰ δεινότατα καὶ
τὰ αἴσχιστα. ὑμᾶς ἐξηπάτηκεν, ἀδοξεῖ,[1] κρίνεται.
καὶ εἴ γέ τι τῶν προσηκόντων ἐγίγνετο, ἐν εἰσ-
αγγελίᾳ πάλαι ἂν ἦν· νῦν δὲ διὰ τὴν ὑμετέραν εὐήθειαν καὶ πρᾳότητ' εὐθύνας δίδωσι, καὶ ταύτας
108 ὁπηνίκα βούλεται. ἔστιν οὖν ὅστις ὑμῶν φωνὴν
ἀκήκοεν Αἰσχίνου κατηγοροῦντος Φιλίππου; τί δ';

---

[1] S has δικαίως ἀπόλωλε after ἀδοξεῖ; but the consequent
anticlimax seems impossible. Omit with Weil. Most mss.
δικαίως ἀπολωλέναι, showing the source of interpolation, 110.

to our ruined allies, or to their wives and children and the rest, to be told that their sufferings were due to stupidity on my part, not to say on his. Nevertheless, I ask you to overlook even the scandalous and outrageous misconduct of Aeschines, if it is shown that he did all this mischief because he was simple-minded or otherwise ignorant. But if he maliciously accepted money and rewards, and if that is clearly proved from the facts of the case, put him to death if possible, or, failing that, make him a living example to other malefactors. Now consider the proof of these matters and its justice, among yourselves.

Assuming that, when Aeschines made those speeches about the Phocians and Thespiae and Euboea, he had not sold himself, and was not wilfully deceiving you, we are reduced to one of two suppositions. Either he had taken an explicit promise from Philip that he would do and perform certain acts, or else, being spellbound and deluded by Philip's habitual courtesy, he honestly expected him to do them. There is no third alternative. Now, on either of those suppositions, he ought, of all men in the world, to detest Philip. Why? Because, thanks to Philip, he has fallen into the utmost danger and ignominy. He has deceived you; his reputation is shattered; he is on his trial. If he had been treated as he deserves, he would have been impeached long ago; but, in fact, by your simplicity and placability, he is only submitting to the usual scrutiny, and has chosen his own time. Is there then any man in that box who has ever heard the voice of Aeschines denouncing Philip, or has known him to press home,

ἐξελέγχοντ' ἢ λέγοντά τι τούτων ἑόρακεν; οὐδὲ
εἷς· ἀλλὰ πάντες Ἀθηναῖοι πρότερον κατηγοροῦσι
Φιλίππου, καὶ ὁ τυχὼν ἀεί, ὧν οὐδὲν οὐδεὶς ἠδίκηται
109 ἰδίᾳ δήπου. ἐγὼ δ' ἐκείνους τοὺς λόγους ἐζήτουν
παρὰ τούτου, εἴπερ μὴ πεπρακὼς αὑτὸν ἦν,
'' ἄνδρες Ἀθηναῖοι, ἐμοὶ μὲν χρήσασθ' ὅ τι βού-
λεσθε· ἐπίστευσ', ἐξηπατήθην, ἥμαρτον, ὁμολογῶ.
τὸν δ' ἄνθρωπον, ὦ ἄνδρες Ἀθηναῖοι, φυλάττεσθε·
ἄπιστος, γόης, πονηρός. οὐχ ὁρᾶθ' οἷα πεποίηκεν
ἐμέ; οἳ' ἐξηπάτηκεν;'' τούτων οὐδέν' ἀκούω τῶν
110 λόγων, οὐδ' ὑμεῖς. διὰ τί; ὅτι οὐ παρακρουσθεὶς
οὐδ' ἐξαπατηθείς, ἀλλὰ μισθώσας αὑτὸν καὶ
λαβὼν ἀργύριον ταῦτ' εἶπε, καὶ προὔδωκεν ἐκείνῳ,
καὶ γέγονε καλὸς κἀγαθὸς καὶ δίκαιος μισθωτὸς
ἐκείνῳ, πρεσβευτὴς μέντοι καὶ πολίτης ὑμῖν προδότης καὶ τρὶς οὐχ ἅπαξ ἀπολωλέναι δίκαιος.

111   Οὐ τοίνυν ἐκ τούτων μόνον δῆλός ἐσθ' ὅτι χρημάτων ἅπαντ' εἶπεν ἐκεῖνα. ἀλλ' ἧκον ὡς ὑμᾶς
[375] ἔναγχος Θετταλοὶ καὶ Φιλίππου πρέσβεις μετ'
αὑτῶν, ἀξιοῦντες ὑμᾶς Φίλιππον Ἀμφικτύον'
εἶναι ψηφίσασθαι. τῷ προσῆκεν οὖν ἀντειπεῖν
τούτοις μάλιστα πάντων ἀνθρώπων; Αἰσχίνῃ
τούτῳ. διὰ τί; ὅτι οἷς οὗτος ἀπήγγειλε πρὸς
112 ὑμᾶς, τούτοις τἀναντί' ἐποίησεν ἐκεῖνος· οὗτος
μὲν γὰρ ἔφη Θεσπιὰς καὶ Πλαταιὰς αὐτὸν τει-
χιεῖν, καὶ τοὺς μὲν Φωκέας οὐκ ἀπολεῖν, τὴν δὲ
Θηβαίων ὕβριν καταλύσειν· ὁ δὲ τοὺς μὲν Θηβαίους
μείζους ἢ προσῆκε πεποίηκε, τοὺς δὲ Φωκέας
ἄρδην ἀπολώλεκε, καὶ τὰς μὲν Θεσπιὰς καὶ Πλαταιὰς οὐ τετείχικε, τὸν δ' Ὀρχομενὸν καὶ τὴν
Κορώνειαν προσεξηνδραπόδισται. πῶς ἂν ἐναντιώ-
τερα πράγμαθ' ἑαυτοῖς τούτων γένοιτο; οὐ τοίνυν

or even mention, his grievance against Philip? Not a man! Every man in Athens is more ready than he is to denounce Philip, even casual people, who have suffered no personal wrong. I was expecting him, if he had not sold himself, to make this speech: " Men of Athens, deal with me as you choose. I was credulous; I was deceived; I made a blunder; I admit it. Beware of that man, men of Athens; he is double-faced, a trickster, a scoundrel. See how he has behaved to me; see how he has made me his dupe." But no; I have never heard him talk like that, nor have you. Why? Because he was not cajoled and hoodwinked; he had sold himself, and pocketed the money, before he made his speech and betrayed us to Philip. To Philip he has been a trusty and well-beloved hireling; to you a treacherous ambassador and a treacherous citizen, worthy of threefold destruction.

That is not the only proof that he was paid for all that he said. The other day there came to you some Thessalians, and envoys of Philip with them, to ask you to vote for Philip's admission to the Amphictyonic Council. Who ought to have been the very first to oppose them? Aeschines. Why? Because Philip's acts had falsified his report. For he had told you that Philip would fortify Thespiae and Plataea, would not destroy the Phocians, and would put a stop to the aggressions of the Thebans; but Philip has made the Thebans dangerously strong, he has exterminated the Phocians, and, instead of fortifying Thespiae and Plataea, he has enslaved Orchomenus and Coronea as well. Could contradiction go further? Yet Aeschines offered no

DEMOSTHENES

ἀντεῖπεν, οὐδὲ διῆρε τὸ στόμα, οὐδ' ἐφθέγξατ'
ἐναντίον οὐδέν. καὶ οὐχὶ τοῦτό πω δεινόν, τηλικοῦ-
τον ὄν· ἀλλὰ καὶ συνεῖπε μόνος τῶν ἐν τῇ πόλει
πάντων ἀνθρώπων. καίτοι τοῦτό γ' οὐδὲ Φιλοκράτης ἐτόλμησε ποιῆσαι ὁ μιαρός, ἀλλ' Αἰσχίνης
οὑτοσί. καὶ θορυβούντων ὑμῶν καὶ οὐκ ἐθελόντων

113 ἀκούειν αὐτοῦ καταβαίνων ἀπὸ τοῦ βήματος,
ἐνδεικνύμενος τοῖς πρέσβεσι τοῖς παρὰ τοῦ Φιλίππου παροῦσι, πολλοὺς ἔφη τοὺς θορυβοῦντας εἶναι,
ὀλίγους δὲ τοὺς στρατευομένους ὅταν δέῃ, (μέμνησθε γὰρ δήπου,) αὐτὸς ὤν, οἶμαι, θαυμάσιος
στρατιώτης, ὦ Ζεῦ.

114 Ἔτι τοίνυν, εἰ μὲν μηδένα μηδὲν ἔχοντ' εἴχομεν
δεῖξαι τῶν πρέσβεων, μηδ' ἦν ὥστ' ἰδεῖν ἅπαντας,
βασάνους καὶ τὰ τοιαῦθ' ὑπόλοιπον ἂν ἦν σκοπεῖν.
εἰ δὲ Φιλοκράτης μὴ μόνον ὡμολόγει παρ' ὑμῖν

[376] ἐν τῷ δήμῳ πολλάκις, ἀλλὰ καὶ ἐδείκνυεν ὑμῖν,
πυροπωλῶν, οἰκοδομῶν, βαδιεῖσθαι φάσκων κἂν
μὴ χειροτονῆθ' ὑμεῖς, ξυληγῶν, τὸ χρυσίον κατ-
αλλαττόμενος φανερῶς ἐπὶ ταῖς τραπέζαις, οὐκ ἔνι
δήπου τοῦτον εἰπεῖν ὡς οὐκ εἴληφε, τὸν αὐτὸν

115 ὁμολογοῦντα καὶ δεικνύντα. ἔστιν οὖν οὕτω τις
ἀνθρώπων ἀνόητος ἢ κακοδαίμων, ὥσθ' ἵνα λαμ-
βάνῃ μὲν Φιλοκράτης, ἀδοξῇ δ' αὐτὸς καὶ κινδυνεύῃ,
ἐξὸν αὐτῷ μετὰ τῶν μηδὲν ἠδικηκότων ἐξετάζε-
σθαι, τούτοις μὲν πολεμεῖν, πρὸς δ' ἐκεῖνον ἐλθὼν
κρίνεσθαι βούλεται; ἐγὼ μὲν οὐδέν' οἶμαι. ἀλλὰ
πάντα ταῦτ', ἐὰν ὀρθῶς σκοπῆτε. εὑρήσετε μεγάλ',
ὦ ἄνδρες Ἀθηναῖοι, καὶ ἐναργῆ σημεῖα τοῦ χρήματα
τοῦτον ἔχειν.

ᵃ torture : to get evidence from slaves.

316

opposition : he never opened his lips or made a single objection. That was bad—but not bad enough for him. He did what no other man in all Athens did—he spoke in support of the envoys. Even that miscreant Philocrates durst not go so far as that—only this man Aeschines. When you raised a clamour, and refused to hear him, he came down from the tribune, exclaiming, in order to cut a figure before Philip's ambassadors—you cannot have forgotten it :—" Plenty of shouters, but very few fighters, when it comes to fighting ! "—being himself, I suppose, such a marvellous fighter. O heavens !

Here is another point : if we were unable to prove that any one man among the ambassadors received anything, or if that were not as clear as daylight, we might have had recourse to torture *a* or the like. But when Philocrates not only confessed his gains repeatedly in the Assembly, but paraded them before your eyes, dealing in wheat, building houses, boasting that he would go abroad even if you did not appoint him, importing timber, changing his gold openly at the bankers,—he assuredly cannot deny that he has taken money, after that admission and that display. Think then of a man, who had it in his power to be counted among the innocent, choosing to fall out with them and to be accused as an adherent of Philocrates, merely to let Philocrates make money, while he accepts only the discredit and the peril ! Could any human being be so sense-less, or so unlucky ? No, indeed. You will find here, men of Athens, if you will only look at it in the right way, a strong and sufficient proof that Aeschines did take bribes.

DEMOSTHENES

116 Ὁ τοίνυν ὕστατον μὲν γέγονεν, οὐδενὸς δ᾽ ἐστὶν ἔλαττον σημεῖον τοῦ πεπρακέναι τοῦτον ἑαυτὸν Φιλίππῳ, θεάσασθε. ἴστε δήπου πρώην, ὅτ᾽ εἰσήγγειλεν Ὑπερείδης Φιλοκράτην, ὅτι παρελθὼν ἐγὼ δυσχεραίνειν ἔφην ἔν τι τῆς εἰσαγγελίας, εἰ μόνος Φιλοκράτης τοσούτων καὶ τοιούτων ἀδικημάτων αἴτιος γέγονεν, οἱ δ᾽ ἐννέα τῶν πρέσβεων μηδενός. καὶ οὐκ ἔφην τοῦθ᾽ οὕτως ἔχειν· οὐδαμοῦ γὰρ ἂν φανῆναι καθ᾽ αὑτὸν ἐκεῖνον, εἰ μὴ τοὺς συναγωνιζομένους τούτων τινὰς εἶχεν.

117 ἵν᾽ οὖν μήτ᾽ ἀφῶ μήτ᾽ αἰτιάσωμαι μηδένα, ἔφην ἐγώ, ἀλλὰ τὸ πρᾶγμ᾽ αὐτὸ τοὺς μὲν αἰτίους εὕρῃ τοὺς δὲ μὴ μετεσχηκότας ἀφῇ, ἀναστὰς ὁ βουλόμενος καὶ παρελθὼν εἰς ὑμᾶς ἀποφηνάσθω μὴ μετέχειν μηδ᾽ ἀρέσκειν αὐτῷ τὰ ὑπὸ Φιλοκράτους πεπραγ-
[377] μένα. καὶ τὸν τοῦτο ποιήσαντ᾽ ἀφίημ᾽ ἔγωγ᾽, ἔφην. ταῦτα γὰρ μνημονεύεθ᾽, ὡς ἐγὼ οἶμαι. οὐ τοίνυν παρῆλθεν οὐδεὶς οὐδ᾽ ἔδειξεν ἑαυτόν. καὶ

118 τῶν μὲν ἄλλων ἔστιν ἑκάστῳ τις πρόφασις· ὁ μὲν οὐχ ὑπεύθυνος ἦν, ὁ δ᾽ οὐχὶ παρῆν ἴσως, τῷ δὲ κηδεστὴς ἦν ἐκεῖ· τούτῳ δ᾽ οὐδὲν τούτων. ἀλλ᾽ οὕτω καθάπαξ πέπρακεν ἑαυτὸν καὶ οὐκ ἐπὶ τοῖς παρεληλυθόσι μεμισθάρνηκε μόνον, ἀλλὰ καὶ μετὰ ταῦτα δῆλός ἐστιν, ἄν περ ἐκφύγῃ νῦν, καθ᾽ ὑμῶν ὑπάρξων ἐκείνῳ, ὥσθ᾽, ἵνα μηδὲν ἐναντίον μηδὲ ῥῆμα πρόηται Φιλίππῳ, οὐδ᾽ ἀφιέντων ἀφίεται, ἀλλ᾽ ἀδοξεῖν, κρίνεσθαι, πάσχειν ὁτιοῦν αἱρεῖται παρ᾽ ὑμῖν μᾶλλον ἢ Φιλίππῳ τι ποιῆσαι μὴ πρὸς

119 ἡδονήν. καίτοι τίς ἡ κοινωνία, τίς ἡ πολλὴ πρόνοι᾽ ὑπὲρ Φιλοκράτους αὕτη; ὃς εἰ τὰ κάλλιστα καὶ πάντα τὰ συμφέροντ᾽ ἐπεπρεσβεύκει, χρήματα δ᾽ ὡμολόγει λαβεῖν ἐκ τῆς πρεσβείας, ὥσπερ ὡμολόγει,

318

Now look at a recent, but most convincing, proof that he sold himself to Philip. You know, I am sure, that, not long ago, when Hypereides impeached Philocrates, I rose and said that I was dissatisfied with the impeachment in one respect : it implied that all these grave misdemeanours had been committed by Philocrates alone, and not by any of the other nine ambassadors. That, I remarked, was impossible ; for by himself Philocrates would have counted for nothing, if he had none of his colleagues to act with him. " I do not wish," I said, " either to acquit or to accuse any man ; I want the guilty to be detected and the innocent cleared by plain fact. Therefore let any man who chooses stand up and come forward, and declare that he had no part in Philocrates' doings, and does not approve them. Every man who does this," I added, " I acquit." No doubt you remember the incident. Well, no one came forward or presented himself. The rest had various excuses : one was not legally accountable; another was not present ; a third had a brother-in-law in Macedonia. Aeschines had no such excuse. The truth is, he has sold himself once for all. Not only has he taken hire for past actions, but it is evident that, if he escapes now, he will henceforward, as against you, be Philip's man ; and so, for fear of uttering a single word injurious to Philip, even when you acquit him he does not accept acquittal. He prefers disrepute, prosecution, any punishment this court may inflict rather than to do anything disagreeable to Philip. But why this fellow-feeling ? Why this concern for Philocrates ? Though all his acts on embassy had been consistent with honour and sound policy, if Philocrates admitted, as he did

τοῦτό γ' αὐτὸ φυγεῖν καὶ διευλαβηθῆναι τῷ προῖκα
πρεσβεύοντι προσῆκε, καὶ διαμαρτύρεσθαι τὸ καθ'
αὑτόν. οὐ τοίνυν πεποίηκε τοῦτ' Αἰσχίνης. ταῦτ'
οὐ φανέρ', ὦ ἄνδρες Ἀθηναῖοι; ταῦτ' οὐχὶ βοᾷ
καὶ λέγει ὅτι χρήματ' εἴληφεν Αἰσχίνης, καὶ πονηρός ἐστιν ἀργυρίου συνεχῶς, οὐ δι' ἀβελτερίαν
οὐδὲ δι' ἄγνοιαν, οὐδ' ἀποτυγχάνων;

120 Καὶ τίς μου καταμαρτυρεῖ, φήσει, δῶρα λαβεῖν;
τοῦτο γάρ ἐστι τὸ λαμπρόν. τὰ πράγματ', Αἰσχίνη,
ἅπερ πιστότατ' ἐστὶν ἁπάντων, καὶ οὐκ ἔνεστ'
εἰπεῖν οὐδ' αἰτιάσασθαι, ὡς ἢ πεπεισμέν' ἢ χαριζό-
μενά τῴ ἐστι τοιαῦτα, ἀλλ' οἱάπερ αὐτὰ προδοὺς
[378] καὶ διαφθείρας σὺ πεποίηκας, τοιαῦτ' ἐξεταζόμενα
φαίνεται. πρὸς δὲ τοῖς πράγμασιν αὐτὸς αὐτίκα
δὴ σὺ σαυτοῦ καταμαρτυρήσεις. ἀπόκριναι γὰρ
δεῦρ' ἀναστάς μοι. οὐ γὰρ δὴ δι' ἀπειρίαν γ' οὐ
φήσεις ἔχειν ὅ τι εἴπῃς· ὃς γὰρ ἀγῶνας καινοὺς
ὥσπερ δράματα, καὶ τούτους ἀμαρτύρους, πρὸς
διαμεμετρημένην τὴν ἡμέραν αἱρεῖς διώκων, δῆλον
ὅτι πάνδεινος εἶ τις.

121 Πολλῶν τοίνυν καὶ δεινῶν ὄντων τῶν πεπραγμένων Αἰσχίνη τούτῳ, καὶ πολλὴν κακίαν ἐχόντων, ὡς
καὶ ὑμῖν οἶομαι δοκεῖν, οὐδέν ἐστιν οὗ μέλλω λέγειν,
ὡς ἐγὼ κρίνω, δεινότερον, οὐδ' ὅ τι μᾶλλον ἐπ'
αὐτοφώρῳ δεδωροδοκηκότ' αὐτὸν καὶ πεπρακότα
πάντ' ἐξελέγξει. ἐπειδὴ γὰρ ἀπεστέλλετ' αὖθις
αὖ τὸ τρίτον τοὺς πρέσβεις ὡς τὸν Φίλιππον, ἐπὶ
ταῖς καλαῖς καὶ μεγάλαις ἐλπίσι ταύταις αἷς οὗτος

---

a Demosthenes alludes to Aeschines' former profession of
actor and also to some recent trial in which Aeschines had
been engaged (possibly the action against Timarchus : see
Introd. pp. 234-5), when, owing to congestion in the law

admit, that he had taken bribes, an incorruptible ambassador would have taken infinite pains to avoid and disavow all association with him. Aeschines has not done so. Is not that a plain argument, men of Athens? Does it not proclaim aloud that he has taken bribes, and that from first to last he went wrong for money's sake,—not through stupidity, or ignorance, or blundering?

"What witness," he will ask, "testifies that I have taken bribes?" A brilliant argument! Facts, Aeschines, the most credible of all witnesses. You cannot find fault with facts, and say that they are what they are in deference to somebody, or to oblige somebody. They are what your treachery and perversion have made them, and such they appear on examination. But I have another witness besides the facts. You shall this very moment give evidence against yourself. Come here: stand up and answer me!—Nothing to say? You cannot plead inexperience. You, who take up a new prosecution as easily as you study a new play, and convict your man without witnesses and under a time-limit,—you must be an uncommonly clever speaker! [a]

Among the many flagrant misdeeds committed by Aeschines, the singular baseness of which I think you all appreciate, there is none more flagrant, in my judgement, than the action I am about to relate, none that will more palpably prove him to have taken bribes and sold everything. When for the third time you sent your ambassadors to Philip, for the fulfilment of those magnificent expectations which

courts, the time allotted to each speaker was cut down to a minimum. But the matter is obscure.

ὑπέσχητο, ἐχειροτονήσατε καὶ τοῦτον κἀμὲ καὶ
122 τῶν ἄλλων τοὺς πλείστους τοὺς αὐτούς. ἐγὼ μὲν
δὴ παρελθὼν ἐξωμοσάμην εὐθέως, καὶ θορυβούντων
τινῶν καὶ κελευόντων βαδίζειν, οὐκ ἂν ἔφην
ἀπελθεῖν· οὗτος δ᾽ ἐκεχειροτόνητο. ἐπειδὴ δ᾽ ἀν-
έστη μετὰ ταῦθ᾽ ἡ ἐκκλησία, συνελθόντες ἐβου-
λεύονθ᾽ οὗτοι τίν᾽ αὐτοῦ καταλείψουσιν. ἔτι γὰρ
τῶν πραγμάτων ὄντων μετεώρων καὶ τοῦ μέλλοντος
ἀδήλου, σύλλογοι καὶ λόγοι παντοδαποὶ κατὰ τὴν
123 ἀγορὰν ἐγίγνοντο τότε· ἐφοβοῦντο δὴ μὴ σύγκλητος ἐκκλησία γένοιτ᾽ ἐξαίφνης, εἶτ᾽ ἀκούσαντες
ὑμεῖς ἐμοῦ τἀληθῆ ψηφίσαισθέ τι τῶν δεόντων
ὑπὲρ τῶν Φωκέων, καὶ τὰ πράγματ᾽ ἐκφύγοι τὸν
[379] Φίλιππον. εἰ γὰρ ἐψηφίσασθε μόνον καὶ μικρὰν
ὑπεφήνατ᾽ ἐλπίδ᾽ ἡντινοῦν αὐτοῖς, ἐσώθησαν ἄν.
οὐ γὰρ ἐνῆν, οὐκ ἐνῆν μὴ παρακρουσθέντων ὑμῶν
μεῖναι Φιλίππῳ. οὔτε γὰρ σῖτος ἦν ἐν τῇ χώρᾳ,
ἀσπόρῳ διὰ τὸν πόλεμον γεγονυίᾳ, οὔθ᾽ ἡ σιτο-
πομπία δυνατὴ τριήρων οὐσῶν ὑμετέρων ἐκεῖ καὶ
τῆς θαλάττης κρατουσῶν, αἵ τε πόλεις πολλαὶ καὶ
χαλεπαὶ λαβεῖν αἱ τῶν Φωκέων, μὴ οὐ χρόνῳ καὶ
πολιορκίᾳ· εἰ γὰρ ἐν ἡμέρᾳ πόλιν ᾕρει, δύο καὶ
124 εἴκοσίν εἰσ᾽ ἀριθμῷ. διὰ δὴ ταῦτα πάντα, ἵνα
μηδὲν μετάθησθ᾽ ὧν ἐξηπάτησθε, τοῦτον αὐτοῦ
κατέλιπον. ἐξομόσασθαι μὲν δὴ μὴ μετ᾽ αἰτίας
τινὸς δεινὸν ἦν καὶ ὑποψία μεγάλη. " τί λέγεις;
ἐπὶ τηλικαῦτα καὶ τοιαῦτ᾽ ἀγαθὰ οὐχὶ βαδίζεις

---

^a A citizen appointed to any office could decline it, if he
took an oath before the Assembly that for reasons of health,
etc., he was unable to serve.

^b To watch and counteract Demosthenes.

Aeschines had guaranteed, you reappointed most
of the former envoys, including Aeschines and me.
I immediately declined the appointment on affidavit,[a]
and when certain persons were clamorous and insisted
that I should go, I declared that I would not leave
Athens ; but the nomination of Aeschines was still
valid. After the dispersal of the Assembly, the
envoys met and discussed which of them should be
left behind,[b] for the whole business was still in the
clouds, and the future uncertain, and all sorts of
conferences and discussions were going on in the
market-place. They were afraid that an extraordinary meeting of the Assembly might suddenly
be convened, and that then, on hearing the truth
from me, you might adopt some acceptable resolution
in favour of the Phocians, and that so Philip might
lose control. One friendly resolution, one gleam of
hope, and the Phocians might have been saved.
If you had not fallen into the trap, it was impossible
—yes, impossible—for Philip to remain at Thermopylae. There was no corn in the country, as the
war had prevented sowing ; and the conveyance
of corn was impossible so long as your fleet was
there and commanded the sea. The Phocian cities
were numerous, and not easy of capture, unless by
protracted siege. Even if Philip had taken a city
a day, there were twenty-two of them. For all
these reasons they left Aeschines at home, fearing
that you might be undeceived and change your
policy. Now to decline an appointment on affidavit
with no reason alleged was a strange move and
very suspicious. " What do you mean ? Are you
declining the embassy ? Are you not going to
Macedonia to realize all those grand benefits which

ἀπαγγείλας οὐδὲ πρεσβεύεις;'' ἔδει δὲ μένειν.
πῶς οὖν; ἀρρωστεῖν προφασίζεται, καὶ λαβὼν
Ἐξήκεστον τὸν ἰατρὸν ἀδελφὸς αὐτοῦ καὶ προσελθὼν τῇ βουλῇ ἐξώμοσεν ἀρρωστεῖν τουτονὶ καὶ
125 αὐτὸς ἐχειροτονήθη. ἐπειδὴ δ' ἀπωλώλεσαν οἱ
Φωκεῖς ὕστερον ἡμέραις πέντ' ἢ ἕξ, καὶ τέλος
εἶχε τὸ μίσθωμ' ὥσπερ ἂν ἄλλο τι τούτῳ, καὶ ὁ
Δερκύλος ἐκ τῆς Χαλκίδος ἧκεν ἀναστρέψας καὶ
ἀπήγγειλεν ὑμῖν ἐκκλησιάζουσιν ἐν Πειραιεῖ ὅτι
Φωκεῖς ἀπολώλασι, καὶ ὑμεῖς, ὦ ἄνδρες Ἀθηναῖοι,
ταῦτ' ἀκούσαντες εἰκότως κἀκείνοις συνήχθεσθε
καὶ αὐτοὶ ἐξεπέπληχθε, καὶ παῖδας καὶ γυναῖκας
ἐκ τῶν ἀγρῶν κατακομίζειν ἐψηφίζεσθε καὶ τὰ
φρούρι' ἐπισκευάζειν καὶ τὸν Πειραιᾶ τειχίζειν
126 καὶ τὰ Ἡράκλει' ἐν ἄστει θύειν,—ἐπειδὴ ταῦτ'
ἦν καὶ τοιαύτη ταραχὴ καὶ τοιοῦτος θόρυβος
[380] περιειστήκει τὴν πόλιν, τηνικαῦθ' ὁ σοφὸς καὶ
δεινὸς οὗτος καὶ εὔφωνος, οὔτε βουλῆς οὔτε δήμου
χειροτονήσαντος αὐτόν, ᾤχετο πρεσβεύων ὡς τὸν
ταῦτα πεποιηκότα, οὔτε τὴν ἀρρωστίαν, ἐφ' ᾗ
τότ' ἐξωμόσαθ', ὑπολογισάμενος, οὔθ' ὅτι πρεσβευτὴς ἄλλος ᾕρητ' ἀνθ' αὑτοῦ, οὔθ' ὅτι τῶν
τοιούτων ὁ νόμος θάνατον τὴν ζημίαν εἶναι κελεύει,
127 οὔθ' ὅτι πάνδεινόν ἐστιν ἀπηγγελκόθ' ὡς ἐπικεκή-
ρυκται χρήμαθ' αὑτῷ ἐν Θήβαις, ἐπειδὴ Θηβαῖοι
πρὸς τῷ τὴν Βοιωτίαν ἅπασαν ἔχειν καὶ τῆς Φωκέων χώρας ἐγκρατεῖς γεγόνασι, τηνικαῦτ' εἰς
μέσας τὰς Θήβας καὶ τὸ τῶν Θηβαίων στρα-
τόπεδον βαδίζειν· ἀλλ' οὕτως ἔκφρων ἦν καὶ ὅλος
πρὸς τῷ λήμματι καὶ τῷ δωροδοκήματι, ὥστε
πάντα ταῦτ' ἀνελὼν καὶ παριδὼν ᾤχετο.

you announced yourself?" However, he had to remain. What was to be done? He pleaded ill-health; and his brother, taking Execestus the physician with him, repaired to the council-house, made affidavit of the illness, and received the appointment himself. But afterwards, when within five or six days the Phocians were destroyed, when Aeschines' wages stopped as such things do, when Dercylus had returned from Chalcis and had informed you, at the assembly held at Peiraeus, of the destruction of the Phocians, when that news filled you with indignation on their account and alarm on your own, when you were resolving to bring in your women and children from the country, to reinstate the frontier fortresses, to fortify the Peiraeus, and to hold the festival of Heracles within the walls,—then at last, at that crisis, when the city was encompassed with confusion and terror, off marched this wise, clever, smooth-tongued gentleman, without waiting for Council or Assembly to reappoint him, on his embassy to the court of the chief malefactor. He forgot that he had sworn that he was too ill to travel; forgot that another ambassador had been chosen in his stead, and that the law visits such conduct with death; forgot that, with the Thebans not only holding all Boeotia but in possession of the territory of Phocis, it was a very odd thing for a man, who had solemnly announced that the Thebans had set a price upon his head, to walk straight into the middle of Thebes and the Theban encampment. Nevertheless, he was so excited, his appetite for money-making and bribe-taking was so keen, that he put aside and ignored all these obstacles, and off he went.

128 Καὶ τοιούτου τοῦ πράγματος ὄντος, ἔτι πολλῷ
δεινότερ' ἐστὶν ἃ ἐκεῖσ' ἐλθὼν διεπράξατο. ἁπάντων γὰρ ὑμῶν τουτωνὶ καὶ τῶν ἄλλων Ἀθηναίων
οὕτω δεινὰ καὶ σχέτλι' ἡγουμένων τοὺς ταλαιπώρους πάσχειν Φωκέας, ὥστε μήτε τοὺς ἐκ τῆς
βουλῆς θεωροὺς μήτε τοὺς θεσμοθέτας εἰς τὰ
Πύθια πέμψαι, ἀλλ' ἀποστῆναι τῆς πατρίου θεωρίας,
οὗτος εἰς τἀπινίκια τῶν πραγμάτων καὶ τοῦ
πολέμου, ἃ Θηβαῖοι καὶ Φίλιππος ἔθυον, εἱστιᾶτ'
ἐλθὼν καὶ σπονδῶν μετεῖχε καὶ εὐχῶν, ἃς ἐπὶ
τοῖς τῶν συμμάχων τῶν ὑμετέρων τείχεσι καὶ
χώρᾳ καὶ ὅπλοις ἀπολωλόσιν ηὔχετ' ἐκεῖνος, καὶ
συνεστεφανοῦτο καὶ συνεπαιώνιζε Φιλίππῳ καὶ
φιλοτησίας προὔπινεν.

129 Καὶ ταῦτ' οὐκ ἔνεστιν ἐμοὶ μὲν οὕτω τούτῳ δ'
[381] ἄλλως πως εἰπεῖν· ἀλλ' ὑπὲρ μὲν τῆς ἐξωμοσίας
ἐν τοῖς κοινοῖς τοῖς ὑμετέροις γράμμασιν ἐν τῷ
Μητρῴῳ ταῦτ' ἐστίν, ἐφ' οἷς ὁ δημόσιος τέτακται
καὶ ψήφισμ' ἄντικρυς περὶ τούτου τοῦ ὀνόματος
γέγραπται· ὑπὲρ δ' ὧν ἐκεῖ διεπράξατο, οἱ συμ-
πρεσβεύοντες καὶ παρόντες καταμαρτυρήσουσιν, οἵπερ ἐμοὶ ταῦτα διηγοῦντο· οὐ γὰρ ἔγωγ' αὐτοῖς
130 συνεπρέσβευσα, ἀλλ' ἐξωμοσάμην. καί μοι λέγε
τὸ ψήφισμα καὶ τὰ γράμματα, καὶ τοὺς μάρτυρας
κάλει.

ΨΗΦΙΣΜΑ. ΓΡΑΜΜΑΤΑ. ΜΑΡΤΥΡΕΣ

Τίνας οὖν εὐχὰς ὑπολαμβάνετ' εὔχεσθαι τοῖς
θεοῖς τὸν Φίλιππον ὅτ' ἔσπενδεν, ἢ τοὺς Θηβαίους;
ἆρ' οὐ κράτος πολέμου καὶ νίκην αὐτοῖς καὶ τοῖς
συμμάχοις διδόναι, καὶ τἀναντία τοῖς τῶν Φωκέων;
326

That was a remarkable proceeding, but far stranger still was his behaviour after his arrival in Macedonia. While you who are here and all other Athenians regarded the treatment of the Phocians as scandalous and outrageous, insomuch that you would not send any member of council or any judge to represent you at the Pythian games, but relinquished that time-honoured delegation, Aeschines attended the service of thanksgiving which the Thebans and Philip held to celebrate their victory and their political success, was a guest at the banquet, and took part in the libations and doxologies with which Philip thanked Heaven for the destruction of the fortresses, the territory, and the armies of your allies. He even joined Philip in wearing garlands and singing the Hymn of Praise, and drank to his health in the loving-cup.

Of these proceedings it is not possible for the defendant to give an account differing from mine. As for the affidavit of refusal, there is an entry in the record-office at the Temple of Demeter, of which the public caretaker is in charge, and a decree in which he is mentioned by name. As for his conduct over yonder, his own colleagues who were present, and from whom I got my information, will give evidence against him. I was not one of his colleagues, as I had declined on oath. Read the decree and the records, and call the witnesses.

(The Decree, Records, and Depositions are read)

What do you imagine were the prayers offered by Philip when he made libation ? Or by the Thebans ? Surely they implored strength and victory for themselves and their allies, weakness and defeat for the

327

οὐκοῦν ταῦτα συνηύχεθ' οὗτος καὶ κατηρᾶτο τῇ
πατρίδι, ἃ νῦν εἰς κεφαλὴν ὑμᾶς αὐτῷ δεῖ τρέψαι.

131 Οὐκοῦν ᾤχετο μὲν παρὰ τὸν νόμον, ὃς θάνατον
κελεύει τούτων τὴν ζημίαν εἶναι· ἐλθὼν δ' ἐκεῖσ'
ἑτέρων θανάτων ἄξια ποιῶν πέφανται· τὰ δὲ
πρόσθεν πεπραγμένα καὶ πεπρεσβευμένα ὑπὲρ
τούτων ἀποκτείνειεν ἂν αὐτὸν δικαίως. σκοπεῖτε
τοίνυν τί ἔσται τίμημα, ὃ ταύτην ἕξει τὴν ἀξίαν
ὥστε τοσούτων ἀδικημάτων ἀξιόχρεων φαίνεσθαι.

132 πῶς γὰρ οὐκ αἰσχρόν, ὦ ἄνδρες Ἀθηναῖοι, δημοσίᾳ
μὲν ἅπαντας ὑμᾶς καὶ ὅλον τὸν δῆμον πᾶσι τοῖς
πεπραγμένοις ἐκ τῆς εἰρήνης ἐπιτιμᾶν, καὶ μήτε
τῶν ἐν Ἀμφικτύοσι κοινωνεῖν ἐθέλειν, δυσκόλως
τ' ἔχειν καὶ ὑπόπτως πρὸς τὸν Φίλιππον, ὡς
[382] ἀσεβῶν καὶ δεινῶν ὄντων τῶν πεπραγμένων
καὶ οὔτε δικαίων οὔθ' ὑμῖν συμφερόντων, εἰς δὲ
τὸ δικαστήριον εἰσελθόντας τὰς ὑπὲρ τούτων εὐθύνας
δικάσοντας, ὅρκον ὑπὲρ τῆς πόλεως ὀμωμοκότας,
τὸν ἁπάντων τῶν κακῶν αἴτιον, καὶ ὃν εἰλήφατ' ἐπ'
αὐτοφώρῳ τοιαῦτα πεποιηκότα, τοῦτον ἀφεῖναι;

133 καὶ τίς οὐ δικαίως ἂν ὑμῖν ἐγκαλέσειε[1] τῶν ἄλλων
πολιτῶν, μᾶλλον δ' ἁπάντων τῶν Ἑλλήνων, ὁρῶν
Φιλίππῳ μὲν ὑμᾶς ὀργιζομένους, ὃς ἐκ πολέμου
ποιούμενος εἰρήνην παρὰ τῶν πωλούντων τὰς
πράξεις ἐωνεῖτο, πρᾶγμα πολλὴν συγγνώμην ἔχον
διαπραττόμενος, τουτονὶ δ' ἀφιέντας, ὃς τὰ ὑμέτερ'
οὕτως αἰσχρῶς ἀπέδοτο, τῶν νόμων τὰ ἔσχατα
ταττόντων ἐπιτίμια, ἐάν τις ταῦτα ποιῇ;

---

[1] ἂν ὑμῖν ἐγκαλέσειε A: ὑμῖν ἐγκαλέσει Shill. with SL;
but he agrees that this future-form is unauthorized.

allies of the Phocians. In that prayer Aeschines joined. He invoked a curse on his own fatherland. It is for you to make that curse recoil upon his own head.

So, when he took his departure, he was breaking a law whose penalty is death ; after his arrival, he is again proved guilty of conduct that deserves death ; and his earlier misconduct of this business of the embassy had been bad enough to bring him to death. You have therefore to consider what punishment shall be rigorous enough to afford a retribution adequate to all these transgressions. For assuredly, men of Athens, when all of you and the whole nation passed censure upon all the results of the peace, when you refused participation in the doings of the Amphictyonic Council, when your attitude towards Philip is still one of anger and suspicion, marking the whole of his conduct as sacrilegious and shameful, as well as unjust and injurious to yourselves,—it would be discreditable that you, who have entered this court to adjudicate at the scrutiny of those trans-actions, and have taken the judicial oath on behalf of the commonwealth, that you, I say, when the author of these wrongs has been placed in your power, caught red-handed after perpetrating such crimes, should return a verdict of acquittal. Is there a man among your fellow-citizens, nay, in all Greece, who will not justly upbraid you if he sees you venting your wrath upon Philip, whose offence admits of much excuse—for he was making peace after war, and buying his ways and means from willing sellers —and acquitting this man, who made infamous traffic of your interests, in defiance of laws that visit such offences with the severest retribution ?

134 Τάχα τοίνυν ἴσως καὶ τοιοῦτος ἥξει τις λόγος
παρὰ τούτων, ὡς ἀρχὴ γενήσεται πρὸς Φίλιππον
ἔχθρας, εἰ τῶν πρεσβευσάντων τὴν εἰρήνην καταψηφιεῖσθε. ἐγὼ δ', εἰ τοῦτ' ἐστὶν ἀληθές, οὐκ
ἔχω σκοπούμενος εὑρεῖν ὅ τι μεῖζον τούτου κατ-
ηγορήσω. εἰ γὰρ ὁ τῆς εἰρήνης χρήματ' ἀναλώσας
ὥστε τυχεῖν οὗτος οὕτω γέγονε φοβερὸς καὶ μέγας
ὥστε τῶν ὅρκων καὶ τῶν δικαίων ἀμελήσαντας
ὑμᾶς ἤδη τί Φιλίππῳ χαριεῖσθε σκοπεῖν, τί παθόν-
τες ἂν οἱ τούτων αἴτιοι τὴν προσήκουσαν δίκην
135 δεδωκότες εἶεν; οὐ μὴν ἀλλ' ὅτι καὶ φιλίας ἀρχὴ
συμφερούσης ὑμῖν οὕτω μᾶλλον ἐκ τῶν εἰκότων
γενήσεται, καὶ τοῦτ' οἴομαι δείξειν. εὖ γὰρ εἰδέναι
χρὴ τοῦθ', ὅτι οὐ καταφρονεῖ Φίλιππος, ὦ ἄνδρες
Ἀθηναῖοι, τῆς πόλεως τῆς ὑμετέρας, οὐδ' ἀχρη-
[333] στοτέρους νομίσας ὑμᾶς Θηβαίων ἐκείνους εἵλετ'
ἀνθ' ὑμῶν. ἀλλ' ὑπὸ τούτων ἐδιδάχθη καὶ ταῦτ'
ἤκουσεν, ἃ καὶ πρότερόν ποτ' εἶπον ἐγὼ πρὸς
ὑμᾶς ἐν τῷ δήμῳ καὶ τούτων οὐδεὶς ἀντεῖπεν,
136 ὡς ὁ μὲν δῆμός ἐστιν ἀσταθμητότατον πρᾶγμα τῶν
πάντων καὶ ἀσυνθετώτατον, ὥσπερ ἐν θαλάττῃ
πνεύματι κῦμα ἀκατάστατον, ὡς ἂν τύχῃ, κινού-
μενον. ὁ μὲν ἦλθεν, ὁ δ' ἀπῆλθεν· μέλει δ' οὐδενὶ
τῶν κοινῶν, ἀλλ' οὐδὲ μέμνηται. δεῖ δέ τινας φίλους ὑπάρχειν τοὺς ἕκαστα πράξοντας ἐν ὑμῖν αὐτῷ
καὶ διοικήσοντας, οἷον αὐτὸς δή· κἄνπερ αὐτῷ
τοῦτο κατασκευασθῇ, πᾶν ὅ τι ἂν βούληται παρ'
137 ὑμῖν ῥᾳδίως διαπράξεται. εἰ μὲν οὖν ἤκουσεν,
οἶμαι, τοὺς τότε ταῦτα πρὸς αὐτὸν εἰπόντας
παραχρῆμα, ὡς δεῦρ' ἐπανῆλθον, ἀποτετυμπανι-
σμένους, ἐποίησεν ἂν ταὐτὸ τῷ βασιλεῖ. τί δ' ἦν
ὃ ἐκεῖνος ἐποίησεν; ἐξαπατηθεὶς ὑπὸ Τιμαγόρου

Perhaps some such argument as this will be addressed to you,—that, if you condemn the diplomatists who negotiated the peace, it will be the beginning of enmity with Philip. If that is true, I do not think I could bring any more damaging charge against the defendant. If the potentate who spent his money to get the peace has indeed become so powerful and formidable that you are to ignore justice and the oath you have sworn, and consider only how to oblige Philip, what penalty can be too severe for the authors of his aggrandizement? However, I think I can satisfy you that their punishment will more probably sow the seed of a profitable friendship. Let me tell you, men of Athens, that Philip does not undervalue your city; it was not because he thought you less serviceable that he preferred the Thebans to you. But he was schooled by these men and was informed by them—I once told you this in Assembly, and none of them contradicted me—that a democracy is the most unstable and capricious thing in the world, like a restless wave of the sea ruffled by the breeze as chance will have it. One man comes, another goes; no one attends to, or even remembers, the common weal. Philip, they said, ought to have friends at Athens, who would manage his business for him as it arose, and carry it through—the person speaking, for example; if that provision were made, he would easily accomplish here whatever he desired. Now if he had heard that the persons who talked like that to him had been cudgelled to death immediately after their return home, I fancy he would have done what the King of Persia did. You remember what that was: the King had been inveigled by Tim-

καὶ τετταράκοντα τάλαντα, ὡς λέγεται, δεδωκὼς
αὐτῷ, ἐπειδὴ παρ' ὑμῖν ἐπύθετ' αὐτὸν τεθνεῶτα καὶ
οὐδὲ τοῦ ζῆν ὄντα κύριον αὐτῷ βεβαιῶσαι, μή τί γ'
ἃ ἐκείνῳ τόθ' ὑπέσχετο πρᾶξαι, ἔγνω τὴν τιμὴν
οὐχὶ τῷ κυρίῳ τῶν πραγμάτων δεδωκώς. καὶ
γάρ τοι πρῶτον μὲν Ἀμφίπολιν πάλιν ὑμετέραν
δούλην κατέστησεν, ἣν τότε σύμμαχον αὐτοῦ καὶ
φίλην ἔγραψεν· εἶτ' οὐδενὶ πώποτ' ἔδωκε χρήματα
138 τοῦ λοιποῦ. ταὐτὸ τοίνυν τοῦτ' ἂν ἐποίησε Φίλιππος, εἴ τινα τούτων εἶδε δίκην δόντα, καὶ νῦν,
ἂν ἴδῃ, ποιήσει. ἐπειδὰν δ' ἀκούῃ λέγοντας,
εὐδοκιμοῦντας ἐν ὑμῖν, ἑτέρους κρίνοντας, τί καὶ
[384] ποιήσῃ; ζητῇ πόλλ' ἀναλίσκειν, ἐξὸν ἐλάττω, καὶ
πάντας θεραπεύειν βούληται, δύ' ἢ τρεῖς ἐξόν;
μαίνοιτο μέντἄν. οὐδὲ γὰρ τὴν τῶν Θηβαίων
πόλιν εἵλετο δημοσίᾳ ποιεῖν ὁ Φίλιππος εὖ, πολλοῦ
139 γε καὶ δεῖ, ἀλλ' ὑπὸ τῶν πρέσβεων ἐπείσθη. ὃν
δὲ τρόπον, φράσω πρὸς ὑμᾶς ἐγώ. ἦκον ὡς αὐτὸν
πρέσβεις ἐκ Θηβῶν, ὅτε περ καὶ παρ' ὑμῶν ἡμεῖς
ἦμεν ἐκεῖ. τούτοις χρήματ' ἐκεῖνος ἐβούλετο
δοῦναι, καὶ πάνυ γ', ὡς ἔφασαν, πολλά. οὐκ
ἐδέξαντ' οὐδ' ἔλαβον ταῦθ' οἱ τῶν Θηβαίων πρέσβεις. μετὰ ταῦτ' ἐν θυσίᾳ τινὶ καὶ δείπνῳ πίνων
καὶ φιλανθρωπευόμενος πρὸς αὐτοὺς ὁ Φίλιππος
ἄλλα τε δὴ πόλλ', οἷον αἰχμάλωτα καὶ τοιαῦτα,
καὶ τελευτῶν ἐκπώματ' ἀργυρᾶ καὶ χρυσᾶ προὔπινεν αὐτοῖς. πάντα ταῦτ' ἐκεῖνοι διεωθοῦντο καὶ
140 οὐδαμῇ προΐενθ' ἑαυτούς. τελευτῶν δὲ Φίλων,
εἷς τῶν πρέσβεων, εἶπεν, ὦ ἄνδρες Ἀθηναῖοι,

agoras, and had made him a present, as the story goes, of forty talents ; but when he heard that the man had been put to death at Athens, and had not been competent to warrant his own life, much less to fulfil his undertaking, he realized that he had not paid the price to the man who could deliver the goods. The first result was that he again placed in subjection to you the city of Amphipolis, which he had put on his own list of friends and allies ; and the second, that he nevermore gave money to anybody. Philip would have done the same if he had seen any of these men brought to justice ; and he will do the same, if he sees that sight now. But when he sees these men holding up their heads here, making speeches, bringing other people to trial— what is he to do ? Is he to make a point of spending a great deal of money, when a little will do ? Is he to try to humour all of us, instead of two or three ? No ; that would be folly. For even his policy of public benevolence to the Thebans was by no means of his own choosing ; he was persuaded by their ambassadors, and I will tell you how. Ambassadors came to him from Thebes at the same time that we were there from you. He offered them money— a very large sum, by their own account. The Theban ambassadors declined the overture, and would not take the bribe. Afterwards, at a sacrificial banquet, when Philip was drinking with them, and showing them much civility, he kept offering them presents, beginning with captives and the like, and ending with gold and silver goblets. All these gifts they rejected, and would on no account give themselves away. At last Philo, one of the ambassadors, made a speech that deserved to have been spoken

λόγον οὐχ ὑπὲρ Θηβαίων ἀλλ' ὑπὲρ ὑμῶν ἄξιον
εἰρῆσθαι. ἔφη γὰρ τὸν Φίλιππον ὁρῶν καὶ με-
γαλοψύχως καὶ φιλανθρώπως ἔχοντα πρὸς αὑτοὺς
ἥδεσθαι καὶ χαίρειν· αὐτοὶ μὲν οὖν ὑπάρχειν
αὐτῷ φίλοι καὶ ξένοι καὶ ἄνευ τῶν δώρων τούτων,
εἰς δὲ τὰ τῆς πόλεως πράγματ', ἐν οἷς ἦν τότε,
τὴν φιλανθρωπίαν αὐτὸν ἠξίουν ταύτην προσθέντ'
ἄξιόν τι καὶ αὑτοῦ καὶ τῶν Θηβαίων πρᾶξαι, καὶ
ὅλην τε τὴν πόλιν οὕτω καὶ σφεῖς ὡμολόγουν
141 ὑπάρξειν αὐτῷ. καὶ γάρ τοι σκέψασθε τί τοῖς
Θηβαίοις γέγονεν ἐκ τούτων καὶ τί συμβέβηκε,
καὶ θεάσασθ' ἐπ' αὐτῆς τῆς ἀληθείας ἡλίκον ἐστὶ
τὸ μὴ πωλεῖν τὰ τῆς πόλεως. πρῶτον μὲν τοίνυν
[385] εἰρήνη γέγονεν αὐτοῖς πονοῦσι καὶ ταλαιπωρου-
μένοις ἤδη τῷ πολέμῳ καὶ ἡττωμένοις, εἶτα τῶν
ἐχθρῶν Φωκέων ἄρδην ὄλεθρος καὶ ὅλων τῶν
τειχῶν καὶ τῶν πόλεων ἀναίρεσις. ἆρα καὶ μόνα
ταῦτα; οὐ μὰ Δί', ἀλλ' ἔτι πρὸς τούτοις 'Ορχομε-
νός, Κορώνεια, Κορσιά, τὸ Τιλφωσαῖον, τῆς τῶν
142 Φωκέων χώρας ὁπόσην βούλονται. τοῖς μὲν δὴ
Θηβαίοις ταῦτ' ἐκ τῆς εἰρήνης γέγονεν, ὧν οὐδ'
ἂν εὔξαιντο δήπου μείζονα· τοῖς δὲ πρέσβεσι
τοῖς τῶν Θηβαίων τί; οὐδὲν πλὴν τὸ τούτων αἰτίοις
γεγενῆσθαι τῇ πατρίδι· τοῦτο δὲ καλόν, ὦ ἄνδρες
'Αθηναῖοι, καὶ σεμνὸν εἰς ἀρετῆς λόγον καὶ δόξης,
ἣν οὗτοι χρημάτων ἀπέδοντο.

'Αντιθῶμεν δὴ τί τῇ τῶν 'Αθηναίων πόλει
γέγονεν ἐκ τῆς εἰρήνης, καὶ τί τοῖς πρέσβεσι τοῖς
τῶν 'Αθηναίων, καὶ θεωρεῖτ' εἰ παραπλήσια τῇ
143 πόλει καὶ τούτοις αὐτοῖς. τῇ πόλει μὲν τοίνυν
ἀφεστηκέναι μὲν ἁπάντων καὶ τῶν κτημάτων

by your representatives, men of Athens, instead of by the spokesman of Thebes. He said that he was delighted and gratified to find Philip so courteously and generously inclined towards them ; that they were already his friends and guests, without those gifts ; would he be good enough to direct his benevolence to the public business on which he was engaged, and do something creditable both to himself and to the Thebans ? If so, they could promise him the friendship of all Thebes as well as their own. Now consider what the Thebans have gained in the end by this policy, and, in the light of actual truth, see what a fine thing it is to refuse to sell your country ! The Thebans have gained, in the first place, peace, when they were in trouble, hard pressed by the war, and in danger of defeat ; and secondly, the complete overthrow of their enemies, the Phocians, and the utter destruction of their strongholds and cities. Is that all ? No, indeed ; they have also gained Orchomenus, Coronea, Corsia, Tilphosaeum, and as much of the Phocian territory as they want. Such is the outcome of the peace for the Theban people ; and more they could not desire. And what have the ambassadors gained ? Nothing at all—except the satisfaction of having achieved these results for their country. Ah, but that is worth having, men of Athens ; a glorious reward, if you set any store by that honour and good repute which Aeschines and his friends bartered for a bribe.

Let us now set side by side the results of the peace to the commonwealth of Athens and to the ambassadors of Athens respectively, and you shall see whether there is any equivalence. To the commonwealth the result has been the loss of all those

καὶ τῶν συμμάχων, ὀμωμοκέναι δὲ Φιλίππῳ, κἂν
ἄλλος τις ἴῃ ποτ' ἐπ' αὐτὰ βουλόμενος σῴζειν,
ὑμᾶς κωλύσειν, καὶ τὸν μὲν ὑμῖν βουλόμενον παραδοῦναι ἐχθρὸν ἡγήσεσθαι καὶ πολέμιον, τὸν δ'
144 ἀπεστερηκότα σύμμαχον καὶ φίλον. ταῦτα γάρ
ἐσθ' ἃ συνεῖπε μὲν Αἰσχίνης οὑτοσί, ἔγραψε δ'
ὁ τούτου συνεργὸς Φιλοκράτης· καὶ κρατοῦντος
ἐμοῦ τὴν προτέραν ἡμέραν, καὶ πεπεικότος ὑμᾶς
τὸ τῶν συμμάχων δόγμα κυρῶσαι καὶ καλέσαι
τοὺς πρέσβεις τοὺς τοῦ Φιλίππου, ἐκκρούσας
οὗτος εἰς τὴν ὑστεραίαν τὴν Φιλοκράτους γνώμην
ἔπεισεν ἑλέσθαι, ἐν ᾗ καὶ ταῦτα καὶ πόλλ' ἄλλ'
145 ἔτι τούτων δεινότερ' ἐστὶ γεγραμμένα. τῇ μὲν
[386] δὴ πόλει ταῦτ' ἐκ τῆς εἰρήνης γέγονεν, ὧν οὐδ'
εὑρεῖν αἰσχίω ῥάδιον· τοῖς δὲ πρέσβεσιν τί τοῖς
ταῦτα πράξασιν; τὰ μὲν ἄλλα σιωπῶ πάνθ',
ὅσ' ἑοράκαθ' ὑμεῖς, οἰκίας, ξύλα, πυρούς· ἀλλ' ἐν
τῇ τῶν ἀπολωλότων συμμάχων χώρᾳ κτήματα
καὶ γεωργίαι παμπληθεῖς, Φιλοκράτει μὲν τά-
λαντον ἔχουσαι πρόσοδον, τούτῳ δ' Αἰσχίνῃ
146 τριάκοντα μνᾶς. καίτοι πῶς οὐ δεινόν, ὦ ἄνδρες
Ἀθηναῖοι, καὶ σχέτλιον τὰς τῶν ὑμετέρων συμμάχων συμφορὰς προσόδους τοῖς πρέσβεσι τοῖς
ὑμετέροις γεγενῆσθαι, καὶ τὴν αὐτὴν εἰρήνην τῇ
μὲν ἐκπεμψάσῃ πόλει τῶν μὲν συμμάχων ὄλεθρον,
τῶν δὲ κτημάτων ἀπόστασιν, ἀντὶ δὲ δόξης αἰσχύνην γεγενῆσθαι, τῶν δὲ πρέσβεων τοῖς κατὰ
τῆς πόλεως ταῦτα πράξασι προσόδους, εὐπορίας,
κτήματα, πλοῦτον ἀντὶ τῶν ἐσχάτων ἀποριῶν εἰργάσθαι; ἀλλὰ μὴν ὅτι ταῦτ' ἀληθῆ λέγω, κάλει
μοι τοὺς Ὀλυνθίων μάρτυρας.

possessions and all those allies, and a sworn promise to Philip that if any man shall at any time attempt to recover them, you will thwart him, and treat the man who would restore to you your own as an enemy and an adversary, and the man who robbed you as an ally and a friend. Such are the terms that Aeschines supported and his accomplice Philocrates proposed. On the first day I had the upper hand and persuaded you to confirm the decision of your allies and to summon Philip's ambassadors, but Aeschines forced an adjournment to the following day, and then persuaded you to adopt Philocrates' resolution, which included all these proposals and others still more objectionable. That is what the peace has brought to the city: you could not easily invent anything more dishonourable. What has it brought to the ambassadors who contrived that dishonour? I say nothing of the wealth that lies before your eyes—houses, timber, grain; but in the country of our ruined allies there are estates and extensive farms bringing in a rental of a talent to Philocrates and half a talent to Aeschines. Surely, men of Athens, it is strange and intolerable that the disasters of your allies have become the emolument of your envoys, and that one and the same peace should have brought, to the city sending ambassadors, the destruction of allies, dispossession of property, ignominy in exchange for honour, and to the ambassadors themselves who intrigued against the city, revenues, property, estates, and opulence in exchange for penury. To prove the truth of my statement, call the witnesses from Olynthus.

ΜΑΡΤΥΡΕΣ

147 Οὐ τοίνυν θαυμάσαιμ' ἂν εἰ καὶ τοιοῦτό τι τολμήσει λέγειν, ὡς οὐκ ἦν καλὴν¹ οὐδ' οἵαν ἠξίουν ἐγὼ
τὴν εἰρήνην ποιήσασθαι, κακῶς τῷ πολέμῳ τῶν
στρατηγῶν κεχρημένων. ἂν δὴ ταῦτα λέγῃ, πρὸς
θεῶν ἐρωτήσατ' αὐτὸν μεμνημένοι, πότερον ἐξ
ἑτέρας ᾤχετο πρεσβεύων πόλεως, ἢ ταύτης αὐτῆς.
εἰ μὲν γὰρ ἐξ ἑτέρας, ἣν κεκρατηκέναι τε τῷ πολέμῳ
φήσει καὶ χρηστοὺς ἔχειν στρατηγούς, εἰκότως
χρήματ' εἴληφεν· εἰ δ' ἐκ ταύτης αὐτῆς, τίνος ἕνεκα,
ἐφ' οἷς ἡ πέμψασα πόλις τῶν ἑαυτῆς ἀπέστη, ἐπὶ
[337] τούτοις οὗτος δῶρα προσλαβὼν φαίνεται; τῶν
γὰρ αὐτῶν ἔδει τήν τε πέμψασαν πόλιν τυγχάνειν
καὶ τοὺς ἐκ ταύτης πρέσβεις, εἴπερ τι τῶν δικαίων
ἐγίγνετο.

148 Ἔτι τοίνυν κἀκεῖνο σκέψασθ', ὦ ἄνδρες δικασταί.
πότερ' οἴεσθε πλέον Φωκέας Θηβαίων ἢ Φίλιππον
ὑμῶν κρατεῖν τῷ πολέμῳ; ἐγὼ μὲν γὰρ εὖ οἶδ' ὅτι
Φωκεῖς Θηβαίων. εἶχον γ' Ὀρχομενὸν καὶ Κορώνειαν καὶ τὸ Τιλφωσαῖον, καὶ τοὺς ἐν Νέωσιν
ἀπειλήφεσαν αὐτῶν, καὶ ἑβδομήκοντα καὶ δια-
κοσίους ἀπεκτόνεσαν ἐπὶ τῷ Ἡδυλείῳ, καὶ τρόπαιον εἱστήκει, καὶ ἱπποκράτουν, καὶ κακῶν
149 Ἰλιὰς περιειστήκει Θηβαίους. ὑμῖν δὲ τοιοῦτο
μὲν οὐδὲν οὔτ' ἦν μήτε γένοιτο τοῦ λοιποῦ, τοῦτο
δ' ἦν τὸ δεινότατον τοῦ πρὸς Φίλιππον πολέμου·
οὐκ ἐδύνασθε κακῶς ἡλίκ' ἐβούλεσθε ποιεῖν ἐκεῖνον·
τοῦ δὲ μὴ πάσχειν αὐτοὶ πᾶσαν ἄδειαν ἤγετε.
τί ποτ' οὖν ἐκ τῆς αὐτῆς εἰρήνης τοῖς μὲν Θηβαίοις,

¹ καλὴν AL : καλὴ Shill. with S, etc.

a An ambassador on the winning side can only be bribed

(Evidence of the Olynthian witnesses)

I shall not be surprised if he finds courage to tell you that we could not make an honourable peace, such as I required, because the generals mismanaged the war. If so, I beg that you will not forget to ask him whether he represented Athens or some other city. If another city, of which he can say that it had competent generals and has won the war, he has received bribes with some reason; but if he represented this city, how comes it that by terms of treaty the city that sent him has lost property and he has increased his property by his rewards? [a] In common justice, the city and its representatives should have fared alike.

Here is another point for your consideration, gentlemen of the jury. Who gained the greater advantage in the operations, the Phocians over the Thebans, or Philip over you? I reply, the Phocians over the Thebans. They held Orchomenus, and Coronea, and Tilphosaeum; they had kept within the walls the Theban garrison at Neon; they had slain two hundred and seventy Thebans at Hedyleum, and a trophy had been set up; they were superior in cavalry, and so an Iliad of woes encompassed the Thebans. No such disaster ever befell, nor, I hope, ever will befall, you. The worst misfortune of your war with Philip was that you could not do him as much harm as you wished; against defeat you were absolutely secure. Then why did the same peace mean, for the Thebans, who were so badly worsted

to gain concessions for the losers—a natural and comparatively harmless proceeding: an ambassador on the losing side is bribed by the winners to make their gain, and his country's loss, more complete.

τοῖς τοσοῦτο κρατουμένοις τῷ πολέμῳ, καὶ τὰ
ἑαυτῶν κομίσασθαι καὶ τὰ τῶν ἐχθρῶν προσλαβεῖν
γέγονε, τοῖς δ' Ἀθηναίοις ὑμῖν, καὶ ἃ τῷ πολέμῳ
διεσῴζετο, ταῦτ' ἐπὶ τῆς εἰρήνης ἀπολωλεκέναι;
ὅτι τἀκείνων μὲν οὐκ ἀπέδονθ' οἱ πρέσβεις, τὰ δ'
ὑμέτερ' οὗτοι πεπράκασιν.[1] ὅτι γὰρ ταῦθ' οὕτω
πέπρακται, καὶ ἐκ τῶν ἐπιλοίπων ἔτι μᾶλλον
εἴσεσθε.

150 Ἐπειδὴ γὰρ ἡ μὲν εἰρήνη τέλος εἶχεν αὕτη ἡ
τοῦ Φιλοκράτους, ᾗ συνεῖπεν οὗτος, οἱ δὲ πρέσβεις
[388] ἀπῆρκεσαν οἱ τοῦ Φιλίππου λαβόντες τοὺς ὅρκους
(καὶ μέχρι τούτου γ' οὐδὲν ἀνήκεστον ἦν τῶν
πεπραγμένων, ἀλλ' αἰσχρὰ μὲν ἡ εἰρήνη καὶ
ἀναξία τῆς πόλεως, ἀντὶ δὲ τούτων δὴ τὰ θαυμάσι'
ἀγάθ' ἡμῖν ἔμελλεν ἔσεσθαι), ἠξίουν ὑμᾶς ἐγὼ καὶ
τούτοις ἔλεγον πλεῖν τὴν ταχίστην ἐφ' Ἑλλησπόντου, καὶ μὴ προέσθαι μηδ' ἐᾶσαι κατασχεῖν
Φίλιππον μηδὲν ἐν τῷ μεταξὺ χρόνῳ τῶν ἐκεῖ
151 χωρίων. ᾔδειν γὰρ ἀκριβῶς ὅτι πάνθ', ὅσ' ἂν
ἐκ πολέμου γιγνομένης εἰρήνης προεθῇ, ταῦτα τοῖς
ἀμελήσασιν ἀπόλλυται· οὐδεὶς γὰρ πώποθ' ὑπὲρ
τῶν ὅλων πεισθεὶς εἰρήνην ἄγειν ὑπὲρ τῶν ἐγκατα-
λειφθέντων ἐξ ἀρχῆς ἠθέλησε πολεμεῖν, ἀλλὰ ταῦθ'
οἱ προλαβόντες ἔχουσιν. χωρὶς δὲ τούτων δυοῖν
χρησίμοιν οὐ διαμαρτήσεσθαι τὴν πόλιν ἡγούμην
πλευσάντων ἡμῶν· ἢ γὰρ παρόντων καὶ κατὰ τὸ
ψήφισμ' αὐτὸν ἐξορκωσάντων, ἃ μὲν εἰλήφει τῆς
152 πόλεως ἀποδώσειν, τῶν δὲ λοιπῶν ἀφέξεσθαι, ἢ μὴ
ποιοῦντος ταῦτ' ἀπαγγελεῖν ἡμᾶς εὐθέως δεῦρο, ὥστ'

---

[1] After πεπράκασιν all mss. have the words ἀλλὰ νὴ Δία
τοὺς συμμάχους ἀπειρηκέναι φήσει (or φησὶ) τῷ πολέμῳ: omitted
by Markland, and many edd., bracketed by Shill.

in the war, the recovery of their own possessions and the acquisition of possessions of their adversaries, and, for the Athenians, the loss in time of peace of advantages which were maintained in the war ? The reason is that their ambassadors did not sell them, but these men have sold you. That my account is true, you will find further proof as we proceed.

When the peace of Philocrates, which Aeschines supported in a speech, had been concluded, Philip's ambassadors accepted the oaths, and departed. So far no fatal mischief had been done. The peace was, indeed, discreditable and unworthy of Athens— but then we were going to get those wonderful advantages in exchange. I at once called upon you, and told the envoys, to sail for the Hellespont as speedily as possible, and not to abandon, or allow Philip to seize and hold, any of the positions there in the meantime ; for well I knew that indolent people lose for ever anything that they let slip in the transition from war to peace. No one, who has been induced by general considerations to sheathe the sword, is ever inclined to begin war over again for the recovery of his losses ; and so the appropriator retains possession. Apart from these considerations, I conceived that, if we sailed at once, the city would gain one of two advantages. For when we were on the spot and had accepted his oath according to the decree, either he would restore the places he had taken from Athens and keep his hands off the rest, or, if he refused, we could promptly report his refusal. In that case you, observing his grasping

ἐν ἐκείνοις τοῖς πόρρω καὶ ἐλάττοσι τὴν πλεονεξίαν
καὶ τὴν ἀπιστίαν ἰδόντας ὑμᾶς περὶ τῶνδε τῶν
ἐγγὺς καὶ μειζόνων, λέγω δὲ Φωκέων καὶ Πυλῶν,
οὐ προήσεσθαι· μὴ προλαβόντος δ' ἐκείνου ταῦτα
μηδ' ὑμῶν ἐξαπατηθέντων ἅπαντ' ἐν ἀσφαλεῖ
τὰ πράγμαθ' ὑμῖν ἔσεσθαι, καὶ παρ' ἑκόντος
153 ὑπάρξειν αὐτοῦ τὰ δίκαια. καὶ ταῦτ' εἰκότως
οὕτως ὑπελάμβανον ἕξειν. εἰ γὰρ ἦσαν, ὡς ἦσαν
τότε, Φωκεῖς σῷοι καὶ Πύλας εἶχον, ἐκεῖνος μὲν
[389] οὐδὲν ἂν ὑμῖν εἶχεν ἀνατείνασθαι φοβερόν, δι' ὃ
τῶν δικαίων ἄν τι παρείδετε· οὔτε γὰρ κατὰ γῆν
παρελθὼν οὔτε ναυσὶ κρατήσας εἰς τὴν Ἀττικὴν
ἥξειν ἔμελλεν· ὑμεῖς δ' ἐκείνου παραχρῆμα, εἰ
μὴ τὰ δίκαια ποιοίη, κλείσειν τὰ ἐμπόρια, καὶ
χρημάτων τ' ἐν σπάνει καὶ τῶν ἄλλων ἐν πολιορκίᾳ
πάλιν αὐτὸν καταστήσειν, ὥστ' ἐκεῖνος ὁ δουλεύσων
ἔμελλεν ἔσεσθαι τοῖς ἀπὸ τῆς εἰρήνης λυσιτελοῦ-
154 σιν, οὐχ ὑμεῖς. καὶ ταῦθ' ὅτι οὐκ ἐπὶ τοῖς συμ-
βεβηκόσι νυνὶ πλάττομαι καὶ προσποιοῦμαι, ἀλλὰ
τότ' εὐθὺς ἐγνώκειν καὶ προεωρώμην ὑπὲρ ὑμῶν
καὶ τούτοις ἔλεγον, ἐκεῖθεν εἴσεσθε. ἐπειδὴ γὰρ
ἐκκλησία μὲν οὐκέτ' ἦν ὑπόλοιπος οὐδεμία διὰ
τὸ προκατακεχρῆσθαι, οὗτοι δ' οὐκ ἀπῆσαν ἀλλ'
αὐτοῦ διέτριβον, γράφω ψήφισμα βουλεύων, τὴν
βουλὴν ποιήσαντος τοῦ δήμου κυρίαν, ἀπιέναι
τοὺς πρέσβεις τὴν ταχίστην, τὸν δὲ στρατηγὸν
Πρόξενον κομίζειν αὐτοὺς ἐπὶ τοὺς τόπους ἐν
οἷς ἂν ὄντα Φίλιππον πυνθάνηται, γράψας ὥσπερ
νῦν λέγω τοῖς ῥήμασιν οὕτως ἄντικρυς. καί μοι
λέγε τοῦτο τὸ ψήφισμα λαβών.

spirit and perfidy in those distant and comparatively unimportant places, would no longer be negligent of the more important concerns that lay nearer home—I mean the Phocians and Thermopylae. If he had not seized the positions, and if there had been no deception of you, all your interests were safe enough, and you would get fair treatment from him without compulsion. This was a reasonable expectation; for so long as the Phocians were safe, as they were at the time, and in possession of Thermopylae, there was no menace which Philip could have brandished in your face to make you disregard any of your just claims. He could not reach Attica either by a march across country or by getting command of the seas. If he refused justice, you could forthwith close his ports, stop his supply of money, and otherwise reduce him to a state of blockade; and so he, and not you, would be wholly dependent on the contingent benefits of the peace. I will now prove to you that I am not making up a story or claiming merit after the event, but that I formed my judgement, kept my eye on your interests, and told the envoys, without any delay. Finding that you had got to the end of the regular Assemblies, and that there was no meeting left, and observing that the envoys were still wasting time at Athens instead of starting at once, I proposed a decree as a member of the Council, to which the Assembly had given authority, directing the envoys to sail immediately, and the general Proxenus to convey them to any place in which he should ascertain that Philip was to be found. I drafted it, as I now read it, in those express terms. Please take and read the decree.

DEMOSTHENES

ΨΗΦΙΣΜΑ

155 Ἐνθένδε μὲν τοίνυν αὐτοὺς ἐξήγαγον οὕτως
ἄκοντας, ὡς καθαρῶς οἷς μετὰ ταῦτ' ἐποίουν
εἴσεσθε. ἐπειδὴ δ' ἀφικόμεθ' εἰς Ὠρεὸν καὶ
συνεμείξαμεν τῷ Προξένῳ, ἀμελήσαντες οὗτοι
τοῦ πλεῖν καὶ τὰ προστεταγμένα πράττειν ἐπορεύοντο κύκλῳ, καὶ πρὶν εἰς Μακεδονίαν ἐλθεῖν,
τρεῖς καὶ εἴκοσιν ἡμέρας ἀνηλώσαμεν· τὰς δ'
[390] ἄλλας πάσας καθήμεθ' ἐν Πέλλῃ, πρὶν Φίλιππον ἐλθεῖν, σὺν αἷς ἐπορεύθημεν ὁμοῦ πεντήκονθ'
156 ὅλας. ἐν δὲ τούτῳ Δορίσκον, Θρᾴκην, τἀπὶ
Τειχῶν, Ἱερὸν ὄρος, πάντα τὰ πράγματα, ἐν
εἰρήνῃ καὶ σπονδαῖς ᾕρει καὶ διῳκεῖθ' ὁ Φίλιππος,
πολλὰ λέγοντος ἐμοῦ καὶ θρυλοῦντος ἀεί, τὸ μὲν
πρῶτον ὡς ἂν εἰς κοινὸν γνώμην ἀποφαινομένου,
μετὰ ταῦτα δ' ὡς ἀγνοοῦντας διδάσκοντος, τελευ-
τῶντος δ' ὡς ἂν πρὸς πεπρακότας αὐτοὺς καὶ
ἀνοσιωτάτους ἀνθρώπους οὐδὲν ὑποστελλομένου.
157 ὁ δὲ τούτοις ἀντιλέγων φανερῶς καὶ ἅπασιν
ἐναντιούμενος οἷς ἔλεγον μὲν ἐγὼ ἐψήφιστο δ' ὑφ'
ὑμῶν, οὗτος ἦν. εἰ δὲ καὶ πᾶσιν ἤρεσκε ταῦτα
τοῖς ἄλλοις πρέσβεσιν, αὐτίκ' εἴσεσθε. ἐγὼ μὲν
γὰρ οὐδέν πω λέγω περὶ οὐδενὸς οὐδ' αἰτιῶμαι,
οὐδ' ἀναγκασθέντ' αὐτῶν οὐδένα δεῖ δοκεῖν χρηστὸν
εἶναι τήμερον, ἀλλὰ δι' αὐτὸν καὶ τὸ μὴ κεκοινω-
νηκέναι τῶν ἀδικημάτων. ὅτι μὲν γὰρ αἰσχρὰ
καὶ δεινὰ καὶ οὐ προῖκα τὰ πεπραγμένα, πάντες
ὑμεῖς ἑοράκατε· οἵτινες δ' οἱ τούτων μετεσχηκότες,
αὐτὸ δηλώσει.

ᵃ See Introd. p. 240.
ᵇ Those members of the embassy who were innocent may
come forward voluntarily and disavow Aeschines. Demo-

(The Decree of Demosthenes is read)

So I got them away from Athens, but quite against their will, as you will easily learn from their subsequent behaviour. When we had arrived at Oreus and joined Proxenus, instead of obeying their instructions and proceeding by sea, they started on a roundabout tour. We had wasted three-and-twenty days before we reached Macedonia ; and all the rest of the time, making, with the time consumed by the journey, fifty days in all, until the arrival of Philip, we were dawdling at Pella. Throughout that period Philip was occupying and disposing of Doriscus, Thrace, the Thracian fortresses, the Sacred Mount, and so forth, in spite of the peace and armistice.[a] All this time I did not spare words ; I talked to them first as one communicating his opinion, then as instructing the ignorant, and finally in uncompromising language, as dealing with corrupt and profligate persons. The man who openly contradicted me, and set himself in opposition to my advice and your formal resolutions, was Aeschines. You will learn presently whether his conduct was agreeable to his colleagues. For the moment, I have nothing to say of them by way of fault-finding. They may all show themselves honest men to-day, not by compulsion but of their own free will, and as having no share in those iniquities.[b] That the deeds done were disgraceful, monstrous, and venal, you have already discovered ; let facts disclose who were the participators.

sthenes will not force them to clear themselves ; he accuses none but the chief culprit. The next sentence, however, hints that, if they do not disavow him, they may share his disgrace.

158 Ἀλλὰ νὴ Δί᾽ ἐν τούτῳ τῷ χρόνῳ τοὺς ὅρκους
ἔλαβον παρὰ τῶν συμμάχων, ἢ τἄλλ᾽ ἃ προσῆκεν
ἐποίησαν. πολλοῦ γε καὶ δεῖ, ἀλλὰ τρεῖς μῆνας
ὅλους ἀποδημήσαντες καὶ χιλίας λαβόντες δραχ-
μὰς ἐφόδιον παρ᾽ ὑμῶν, παρ᾽ οὐδεμιᾶς πόλεως,
οὔθ᾽ ὅτ᾽ ἐκεῖσ᾽ ἐπορεύοντο οὔθ᾽ ὅτ᾽ ἐκεῖθεν δεῦρο,
τοὺς ὅρκους ἔλαβον, ἀλλ᾽ ἐν τῷ πανδοκείῳ τῷ πρὸ
τοῦ Διοσκορείου (εἴ τις ὑμῶν εἰς Φερὰς ἀφῖκται,
οἶδεν ὃ λέγω), ἐνταῦθ᾽ ἐγίγνονθ᾽ οἱ ὅρκοι, ὅτε δεῦρ᾽
ἤδη τὸ στράτευμ᾽ ἄγων ἐβάδιζε Φίλιππος, αἰσχρῶς,
159
[391] ὦ ἄνδρες Ἀθηναῖοι, καὶ ἀναξίως ὑμῶν. καίτοι
τοῦτο Φίλιππος ἁπάντων ἂν ἐτιμήσατο πλείστου
τοῦτον τὸν τρόπον πραχθῆναι. τήν τε γὰρ εἰρήνην οὐχὶ δυνηθέντων ὡς ἐπεχείρησαν οὗτοι τὸ
πρῶτον " πλὴν Ἀλέων καὶ Φωκέων " γράψαι,
ἀλλ᾽ ἀναγκασθέντος ὑφ᾽ ὑμῶν τοῦ Φιλοκράτους
ταῦτα μὲν ἀπαλεῖψαι γράψαι δ᾽ ἄντικρυς, Ἀθηναίους
καὶ τοὺς Ἀθηναίων συμμάχους, οὐκ ἐβούλετο
τοῦτον ὀμωμοκέναι τὸν ὅρκον οὐδένα τῶν αὑτοῦ
συμμάχων (οὐ γὰρ αὐτῷ συστρατεύσειν ἐφ᾽ ἃ νῦν
ἔχει τῶν ὑμετέρων ἔμελλον, ἀλλ᾽ ἕξειν πρόφασιν
160 τοὺς ὅρκους), οὔτε μάρτυρας γενέσθαι τῶν ὑπο-
σχέσεων ἐφ᾽ αἷς ηὑρίσκετο τὴν εἰρήνην, οὐδὲ τοῦτο
δειχθῆναι πᾶσιν, ὅτι οὐκ ἄρ᾽ ἡ πόλις ἡ τῶν Ἀθηναίων ἥττητο τῷ πολέμῳ, ἀλλὰ Φίλιππός ἐστιν ὁ
τῆς εἰρήνης ἐπιθυμῶν καὶ ὁ πόλλ᾽ ὑπισχνούμενος
τοῖς Ἀθηναίοις ἂν τύχῃ τῆς εἰρήνης. ἵνα δὴ μὴ
γένοιτο ταῦθ᾽ ἃ λέγω φανερά, διὰ ταῦτ᾽ οὐδαμόσ᾽
ᾤετο δεῖν τούτους βαδίζειν. οὗτοι δ᾽ ἐχαρίζοντο
346

But it may be urged that they spent all this time swearing in the allies, or discharging some other part of their duty. Not at all; though they were on their travels for three whole months, and received from you a thousand drachmas for journey-money, they did not get the oaths from any single city either on their outward journey or on their way home. The oaths were administered at the hostelry in front of the Temple of the Twins,—any of you who have been to Pherae will know the place I mean,— at the time when Philip was already on his march towards Athens with his army, and in a manner, men of Athens, that was thoroughly discreditable to the city. Yet Philip would have paid any sum to have matters managed in this way. For when these men had failed to draw the treaty, as they first tried to do, with a clause excepting the Halians and the Phocians, and Philocrates had been compelled by you to erase those words and write expressly, "the Athenians and the Allies of the Athenians," to the treaty so drawn Philip did not wish any of his allies to have sworn; for then they would have refused to join in his forcible occupation of those possessions of yours which he now holds, and the oath would have been their excuse. Nor did he desire witnesses of the promises on the strength of which he was obtaining the peace, nor any public disclosure of the fact that after all Athens had not been beaten in the war, and that it was Philip who was really eager for the peace, and was ready to make large promises to the Athenians if he could get it. Therefore he disapproved of these men going anywhere, lest the facts that I am stating should become generally known; and they were ready to

DEMOSTHENES

πάντ' ἐνδεικνύμενοι καὶ ὑπερκολακεύοντες ἐκεῖνον.
161 καίτοι ταῦθ' ὅταν ἐξελέγχωνται πάντα, τοὺς
χρόνους ἀνηλωκότες, τὰν Θράκῃ προειμένοι, μηδὲν
ὧν ἐψηφίσασθε πεποιηκότες μηδ' ὧν συμφέρον
ἦν, τὰ ψευδῆ δεῦρ' ἀπηγγελκότες, πῶς ἔνεστι παρ'
εὖ φρονοῦσι δικασταῖς καὶ βουλομένοις εὐορκεῖν
τούτῳ σώζεσθαι; ἀλλὰ μὴν ὅτι ταῦτ' ἀληθῆ λέγω,
λέγε πρῶτον μὲν τὸ ψήφισμα, ὡς ὀρκοῦν προσῆκεν ἡμῖν, εἶτα τὴν ἐπιστολὴν τὴν τοῦ Φιλίππου,
εἶτα τὸ Φιλοκράτους ψήφισμα καὶ τὸ τοῦ δήμου.

[392] ΨΗΦΙΣΜΑ. ΕΠΙΣΤΟΛΗ. ΨΗΦΙΣΜΑΤΑ

162 Καὶ μὴν ὅτι τὸν Φίλιππον ἐν Ἑλλησπόντῳ κατ-
ελάβομεν ἄν, εἴ τις ἐπείθετό μοι καὶ τὰ προσ-
τεταγμέν' ὑφ' ὑμῶν ἐποίει· κατὰ τὰ ψηφίσματα,
κάλει τοὺς ἐκεῖ παρόντας μάρτυρας.

ΜΑΡΤΥΡΕΣ

Λέγε δὴ καὶ τὴν ἑτέραν μαρτυρίαν, ἃ πρὸς
Εὐκλείδην ὕστερον ἐλθόντα τουτονὶ ἀπεκρίνατο
Φίλιππος.

ΜΑΡΤΥΡΙΑ

163 Ὅτι τοίνυν οὐδ' ἄρνησίς ἐστιν αὐτοῖς τὸ μὴ
ταῦθ' ὑπὲρ Φιλίππου πράττειν, ἀκούσατέ μου. ὅτε
γὰρ τὴν προτέραν ἀπήρομεν πρεσβείαν τὴν περὶ
τῆς εἰρήνης, κήρυχ' ὑμεῖς προαπεστείλαθ' ὅστις
ἡμῖν σπείσεται. τότε μὲν τοίνυν, ὡς τάχιστ'
εἰς Ὠρεὸν ἦλθον, οὐκ ἀνέμειναν τὸν κήρυκα οὐδ'
ἐποίησαν χρόνον οὐδένα, Ἅλου δὲ πολιορκουμένου
διέπλευσαν εἰς τοῦτον, καὶ πάλιν ἐντεῦθεν πρὸς

---

a *Eucleides*: sent to protest against Philip's invasion of
the dominions of Cersobleptes.

348

gratify him with ostentatious deference and extravagant adulation. Yet, when they are convicted of all these delinquencies, of having squandered their time, thrown away the Thracian outposts, done nothing agreeable either to your instructions or to sound policy, and sent lying dispatches to Athens, how can this man possibly find a way of escape before an intelligent and conscientious jury ? However, to prove the truth of my statements, read first the decree giving directions for the administration of the oath, then Philip's letter, and then the decree of Philocrates, and the decree of the Assembly.

(The Letter and the several Decrees are read)

To prove, moreover, that we should have caught Philip at the Hellespont, if my advice had been taken and your directions obeyed in the terms of the decrees, call the witnesses who were there present.

(Evidence is given)

Now read the other deposition testifying to the answer made by Philip to Eucleides [a] here, who arrived later.

(The Deposition is read)

Let me show you that there is no way of denying that they were acting in the interest of Philip. When we were setting out on the former embassy for peace, you sent forward a herald to arrange our safe-conduct. On that occasion, as soon as they reached Oreus, they wasted no time there waiting for the herald. Although Halus was beleaguered, they crossed the sea thither ; then left the town

Παρμενίωνα τὸν πολιορκοῦντ᾽ ἐξελθόντες ἀπῆραν
διὰ τοῦ πολεμίου στρατεύματος εἰς Παγασάς, καὶ
προϊόντες ἀπήντων ἐν Λαρίσῃ τῷ κήρυκι· τοσαύτῃ
164 σπουδῇ καὶ προθυμίᾳ τότ᾽ ἐχώρουν. ἐπειδὴ δ᾽
εἰρήνη μὲν ἦν, ἅπασα δ᾽ ἀσφάλει᾽ ἰέναι καὶ πρόσ-
ταγμα παρ᾽ ὑμῶν σπεύδειν, τηνικαῦτ᾽ οὔτ᾽ ἐπ-
είγεσθαι βαδίζουσιν οὔτε πλεῖν αὐτοῖς ἐπῄει. τί
δήποτε; ὅτι τότε μὲν τὸ τὴν εἰρήνην ὡς τάχιστα
γενέσθαι, τοῦτ᾽ ἦν ὑπὲρ Φιλίππου, νῦν δὲ τὸ ὡς
[393] πλεῖστον τὸν μεταξὺ χρόνον διατριφθῆναι τοῦ τοὺς
165 ὅρκους ἀπολαβεῖν. ἀλλὰ μὴν ὅτι καὶ ταῦτ᾽ ἀληθῆ
λέγω, λαβέ μοι καὶ ταύτην τὴν μαρτυρίαν.

ΜΑΡΤΥΡΙΑ

Ἔστιν οὖν ὅπως ἂν μᾶλλον ἄνθρωποι πάνθ᾽
ὑπὲρ Φιλίππου πράττοντες ἐξελεγχθεῖεν, ἢ τὴν
αὐτὴν ὁδὸν ἡνίκα μὲν σπεύδειν ὑπὲρ ὑμῶν ἔδει
καθήμενοι, ὅτε δ᾽ οὐδὲ βαδίζειν προσῆκε πρὶν
ἐλθεῖν τὸν κήρυκ᾽ ἐπειγόμενοι;
166 Ὃν τοίνυν χρόνον ἦμεν ἐκεῖ καὶ καθήμεθ᾽ ἐν
Πέλλῃ, σκέψασθε τί πράττειν ἕκαστος ἡμῶν προείλετο. ἐγὼ μὲν τοίνυν τοὺς αἰχμαλώτους ἀνασῴ-
ζειν καὶ ζητεῖν, καὶ παρ᾽ ἐμαυτοῦ τε χρήματ᾽ ἀναλίσκειν καὶ Φίλιππον ἀξιοῦν, ὧν ἡμῖν ἐδίδου ξενίων,
τούτους λύσασθαι· οὗτος δὲ αὐτίκ᾽ ἀκούσεσθε τί
ποιῶν διετέλεσεν. τί οὖν ἦν τοῦτο; τὸ κοινῇ
167 χρήμαθ᾽ ἡμῖν τὸν Φίλιππον διδόναι. ἵνα μηδὲ
τοῦτ᾽ ἀγνοῆτε, ἐκεῖνος ἡμᾶς διεκωδώνιζεν ἅπαντας·
τίνα τρόπον; ἑκάστῳ προσπέμπων ἰδίᾳ, καὶ πολὺ
350

and went to Parmenio, who was conducting the siege ; set off through the enemies' positions for Pagasae, and continued their journey till they met the herald at Larissa. Such was the energy and goodwill with which they travelled then ; but now, in time of peace, with complete security for travelling, and with your injunctions of haste, it never occurred to them to hasten their journey by land or to travel by sea. Why so ? Because then it was to Philip's advantage that peace should be concluded with all speed, but now that as much time as possible should be wasted before the administration of the oaths. To prove that this statement also is true, take and read this deposition.

(The Deposition is read)

Now could men be more clearly convicted of acting throughout in the interest of Philip ? It was the same journey : they loitered when they should have bestirred themselves in your service ; they hurried when they ought not to have moved a step until the arrival of the herald.

Take next the period of our loitering at Pella, and compare the employments which we severally chose for ourselves. Mine was to seek out and rescue the captives, spending money of my own, and asking Philip to apply to their ransom the money he was spending on hospitable gifts for us. But what Aeschines constantly tried to effect, you shall hear in a moment. What then was it ? It was that Philip should give us a lump sum as a collective present. You must know that Philip was already sounding us all in this way : he sent private messages to each of us in turn, with the offer, men of Athens,

351

DEMOSTHENES

γ', ὦ ἄνδρες Ἀθηναῖοι, διδοὺς χρυσίον. ὡς δ'
ἀπετύγχανεν ὁτουδήποτε (οὐ γὰρ ἐμέ γ' εἰπεῖν
ἐμαυτὸν δεῖ, ἀλλὰ τὰ ἔργα καὶ τὰ πεπραγμέν' αὐτὰ
δηλώσει), τὰ κοινῇ δοθέντα πάντας ἡγεῖτ' εὐήθως
λήψεσθαι· ἀσφάλειαν οὖν ἔσεσθαι τοῖς ἰδίᾳ πεπρακόσιν αὑτούς, εἰ καὶ κατὰ μικρὸν τοῦ λαβεῖν
κοινῇ πάντες μετάσχοιμεν. διὰ ταῦτ' ἐδίδοτο,
168 ξένια δὴ πρόφασιν. ἐπειδὴ δ' ἐκώλυσ' ἐγώ,
πάλιν προσδιενείμαντο τοῦθ' οὗτοι. τῷ Φιλίππῳ
δ', ἐπειδὴ ταῦτ' εἰς τοὺς αἰχμαλώτους ἠξίουν αὐτὸν
ἀναλίσκειν ἐγώ, οὔτε κατειπεῖν τούτων εἶχε
[394] καλῶς οὐδ' εἰπεῖν ὅτι "ἀλλ' ἔχουσιν ὁ δεῖνα καὶ
ὁ δεῖνα," οὔτε φυγεῖν τἀνάλωμα· ὡμολόγησε
μὲν δή, διεκρούσατο δ' εἰς τὰ Παναθήναια φήσας
ἀποπέμψειν. λέγε τὴν μαρτυρίαν τὴν Ἀπολλο-
φάνους, εἶτα τὴν τῶν ἄλλων τῶν παρόντων.

MAPTYPIA

169   Φέρε δὴ καὶ ὅσους αὐτὸς ἐλυσάμην τῶν αἰχμαλώτων εἴπω πρὸς ὑμᾶς. ἐν ὅσῳ γὰρ οὐχὶ παρόντος
πω Φιλίππου διετρίβομεν ἐν Πέλλῃ, ἔνιοι τῶν
ἑαλωκότων, ὅσοιπερ ἦσαν ἐξηγγυημένοι, ἀπιστοῦν-
τες, ὡς ἐμοὶ δοκεῖ, μὴ δυνήσεσθαι μετὰ ταῦτα
πεῖσαι τὸν Φίλιππον, ἑαυτοὺς ἔφασαν βούλεσθαι
λύσασθαι καὶ μηδεμίαν τούτου χάριν ἔχειν τῷ
Φιλίππῳ, καὶ ἐδανείζοντο ὁ μὲν τρεῖς μνᾶς, ὁ δὲ
πέντε, ὁ δ' ὅπως συνέβαινεν ἑκάστῳ τὰ λύτρα.
170 ἐπειδὴ τοίνυν ὡμολόγησεν ὁ Φίλιππος τοὺς λοι-
ποὺς λύσεσθαι, συγκαλέσας ἐγὼ τούτους οἷς
αὐτὸς ἔχρησα τἀργύριον, καὶ τὰ πεπραγμέν'

352

of a really large sum in gold. Having failed in some case or other,—in what case let the result disclose; it is not for me to name myself,—he conceived that a collective present might be accepted by all of us without misgiving ; and that there would be security for those who had individually sold themselves, if we all shared even to a trifling extent in the general acceptance. Accordingly it was offered, —nominally, as a form of hospitality. I stopped that manœuvre ; and then these men divided that money also among themselves. When I asked Philip to spend it on the captives, he could not with decency either inform against them by replying, " It is in so-and-so's pockets," or escape the outlay ; so he made me the promise, but evaded performance by saying that he would send the men home in time for the Panathenaic Festival. Read the deposition of Apollophanes, and then those of the other persons who were there.

(The Deposition is read)

Let me now tell you how many of the captives I ransomed myself. For while we were staying at Pella, before Philip's arrival, some of the prisoners, —all in fact who were out on bail,—having, I suppose, no confidence that they would afterwards be able to induce Philip to move, told me that they were willing to provide for their own ransom without putting themselves under obligation to Philip, and offered to borrow their ransom-money, three minas, five minas, or as the case might be. So when Philip agreed to get the release of the rest, I called together these men, to whom I had lent the money as a friendly loan, reminded them of the transaction, and made

ὑπομνήσας, ἵνα μὴ δοκοῖεν ἔλαττον ἔχειν ἐπ-
ειχθέντες μηδ᾽ ἐκ τῶν ἰδίων λελυτρῶσθαι πένητες
ἄνθρωποι, τῶν ἄλλων ὑπὸ τοῦ Φιλίππου προσ-
δοκωμένων ἀφεθήσεσθαι, ἔδωκα δωρεὰν τὰ λύτρα.
καὶ ὅτι ταῦτ᾽ ἀληθῆ λέγω, λέγε καὶ ταύτας τὰς
μαρτυρίας.

ΜΑΡΤΥΡΙΑΙ

171 "Οσα μὲν τοίνυν ἀφῆκα χρήματα καὶ δωρεὰν
ἔδωκα τοῖς ἀτυχήσασι τῶν πολιτῶν, ταῦτ᾽ ἐστίν.
ὅταν δ᾽ οὗτος αὐτίκα δὴ λέγῃ πρὸς ὑμᾶς "τί
δήποθ᾽, ὡς φῄς, ὦ Δημόσθενες, ἀπὸ τοῦ συνειπεῖν
ἐμὲ Φιλοκράτει γνοὺς οὐδὲν ἡμᾶς ὑγιὲς πράττοντας,
τὴν μετὰ ταῦτα πρεσβείαν τὴν ἐπὶ τοὺς ὅρκους
[395] συνεπρέσβευσας πάλιν καὶ οὐκ ἐξωμόσω;" ταῦτα
μέμνησθε, ὅτι τούτοις ὡμολογήκειν οὓς ἐλυσάμην
172 καὶ κομιεῖν λύτρα καὶ σώσειν εἰς δύναμιν. δεινὸν
οὖν ἦν ψεύσασθαι καὶ προέσθαι δυστυχοῦντας ἀνθρώπους πολίτας· ἰδίᾳ δ᾽ ἐξομοσάμενον οὐ πάνυ
καλὸν οὐδ᾽ ἀσφαλὲς ἦν ἐκεῖσε πλανᾶσθαι· ἐπεὶ εἰ
μὴ διὰ τὸ τούτους βούλεσθαι σῶσαι, ἐξώλης ἀπο-
λοίμην καὶ προώλης, εἰ προσλαβών γ᾽ ἂν ἀργύριον
πάνυ πολὺ μετὰ τούτων ἐπρέσβευσα. σημεῖον δέ·
ἐπὶ γὰρ τὴν τρίτην πρεσβείαν δίς με χειροτονησάντων ὑμῶν δὶς ἐξωμοσάμην. καὶ παρὰ ταύτην
τὴν ἀποδημίαν πάντα τἀναντί᾽ ἔπραττον τούτοις.
173 Ὧν μὲν τοίνυν αὐτοκράτωρ ἦν ἐγὼ κατὰ τὴν
πρεσβείαν, τοῦτον ἔσχε τὸν τρόπον ὑμῖν· ἃ δ᾽ οὗτοι
πλείους ὄντες ἐνίκων, ἅπαντ᾽ ἀπόλωλεν. καίτοι

ᵃ The Greek phrase, which occurs also at the end of the
De corona, suggests by its jingle the formula of some
curse, but cannot well be reproduced in English.

them a free gift of their ransom-money, lest they should seem to have been put into a worse position by their impetuosity, or to have been ransomed, though poor men, at their own expense, while the rest were expecting deliverance from Philip. To prove the truth of my statement, read these depositions also.

(The Depositions are read)

Well, these sums of money I gave away as a free gift to my fellow-citizens in distress. If Aeschines in addressing you should say presently : " Demosthenes, if you really inferred from my speech in support of Philocrates that our conduct was thoroughly corrupt, why did you join us on the subsequent embassy to receive the oaths, instead of excusing yourself ? " you must remember that I had promised the prisoners whom I delivered that I would bring the ransom-money and do my utmost for their rescue. It would therefore have been too bad to break my word and abandon fellow-creatures and fellow-citizens in misfortune. Had I declined on oath, a private excursion to Macedonia would have been neither decent nor safe. Except for my strong desire to liberate those men, may I die miserably before my time *a* if any reward would have induced me to accept an embassy with these men as my colleagues. I proved that by twice excusing myself when you twice appointed me to the third embassy, and also by my constant opposition to them on this journey.

So the business which I controlled by myself on the embassy turned out in this fashion to your advantage, although, where the majority prevailed, everything went to ruin. Indeed, if my advice had

355

καὶ τἆλλ᾽ ἂν ἅπαντ᾽ ἀκολούθως τούτοις ἐπέπρακτο,
εἴ τις ἐπείθετό μοι. οὐ γὰρ ἔγωγ᾽ οὕτως ἦν
ἄθλιος οὐδ᾽ ἄφρων ὥστε χρήματα μὲν διδόναι,
λαμβάνοντας ὁρῶν ἑτέρους, ὑπὲρ τῆς πρὸς ὑμᾶς
φιλοτιμίας, ἃ δ᾽ ἄνευ μὲν δαπάνης οἷά τ᾽ ἦν πραχθῆναι, πολλῷ δὲ μείζονας εἶχεν ὠφελείας πάσῃ τῇ
πόλει, ταῦτ᾽ οὐκ ἐβουλόμην γίγνεσθαι. καὶ σφόδρα
γ᾽, ὦ ἄνδρες Ἀθηναῖοι· ἀλλ᾽, οἶμαι, περιῆσαν οὗτοί
μου.

174 Φέρε δή, τί τούτῳ πέπρακται παρὰ ταῦτα καὶ τί
τῷ Φιλοκράτει θεάσασθε· παρ᾽ ἄλληλα γὰρ ἔσται
φανερώτερα. πρῶτον μὲν τοίνυν Φωκέας ἐκσπόνδους καὶ Ἀλέας ἀπέφηναν καὶ Κερσοβλέπτην
παρὰ τὸ ψήφισμα καὶ τὰ πρὸς ὑμᾶς εἰρημένα·
εἶτα τὸ ψήφισμ᾽ ἐπεχείρησαν κινεῖν καὶ μεταίρειν,
ἐφ᾽ ᾧ πρεσβεύοντες ἥκομεν· εἶτα Καρδιανοὺς
[396] Φιλίππῳ συμμάχους ἐνέγραψαν καὶ τὴν μὲν γρα-
φεῖσαν ἐπιστολὴν ὑπ᾽ ἐμοῦ πρὸς ὑμᾶς ἀπεψηφί-
σαντο μὴ πέμπειν, αὐτοὶ δ᾽ οὐδ᾽ ὁτιοῦν ὑγιὲς γρά-
175 ψαντες ἔπεμψαν. εἶθ᾽ ὁ γενναῖος οὑτοσὶ ἐμὲ μὲν
τὸν δῆμον ἔφη τὸν ὑμέτερον καταλύσειν ἐπηγγέλθαι
Φιλίππῳ, ὅτι ταῦτ᾽ ἐπέπληττον οὐ μόνον αἰσχρὰ
νομίζων, ἀλλὰ καὶ δεδιὼς μὴ συμπαραπόλωμαι
διὰ τούτους, αὐτὸς δ᾽ ἰδίᾳ πάντα τὸν χρόνον ἐν-
τυγχάνων οὐδ᾽ ὁτιοῦν ἐπαύσατο Φιλίππῳ. καὶ τὰ
μὲν ἄλλα σιωπῶ, Δερκύλος δ᾽ αὐτὸν ἐν Φεραῖς
τὴν νύκτ᾽ ἐφύλαττεν, οὐκ ἐγώ, τὸν παῖδ᾽ ἔχων τὸν
ἐμὸν τουτονί, καὶ λαβὼν ἐξιόντ᾽ ἐκ τῆς Φιλίππου
σκηνῆς ἐμοὶ τὸν παῖδ᾽ ἐκέλευσεν ἀπαγγέλλειν καὶ
αὐτὸν μεμνῆσθαι, καὶ τὸ τελευταῖον ὁ βδελυρὸς
καὶ ἀναιδὴς οὑτοσὶ νύκτα καὶ ἡμέραν ἀπιόντων

been taken, all our transactions might have had an equally fortunate issue ; for I was not so foolish and stupid as to lose money, while others were making money, out of sheer public spirit, and then object to a course of action that would have cost no expense, and that offered far greater advantages to the whole commonwealth. Yes, men of Athens, the issue might have been fortunate indeed ; only these men had their way.

And now I ask you to look at the acts of Aeschines and those of Philocrates, in comparison with mine ; for the contrast will help to expose them. First, in violation both of the decree and of assurances given to you, they excluded the Halians, the Phocians, and Cersobleptes, from the benefits of the treaty. Then they attempted to tamper with and repeal the decree from which our own authority was derived. Next they entered the Cardians as allies of Philip, and refused by a definite vote to send a dispatch written by me, but themselves composed and sent one that did not contain an honest word. Then, because I objected to their acts, not only thinking them dishonourable but fearing that I might share the ruin they were bringing on themselves, our chivalrous friend accused me of promising to Philip that I would overthrow the Athenian democracy, while all the time he was himself constantly holding private communications with Philip. I need only mention that not I but Dercylus, with the help of this servant of mine, watched him by night at Pherae, caught him emerging from Philip's tent, and told the servant to let me know, and not to forget it himself ; and that in the end this impudent black-guard stayed with Philip for a day and a night on

176 ἡμῶν ἀπελείφθη παρὰ Φιλίππῳ. καὶ ταῦθ' ὅτι
ἀληθῆ λέγω, πρῶτον μὲν αὐτὸς ἐγὼ συγγραψά-
μενος καὶ καταστήσας ἐμαυτὸν ὑπεύθυνον μαρ-
τυρήσω, εἶτα τῶν ἄλλων πρέσβεων ἕκαστον καλῶ,
καὶ δυοῖν θάτερον, ἢ μαρτυρεῖν ἢ ἐξόμνυσθαι ἀναγκάσω. ἐὰν δ' ἐξομνύωσιν, ἐπιορκοῦντας ἐξελέγξω
παρ' ὑμῖν φανερῶς.

ΜΑΡΤΥΡΙΑ

177 Οἵοις μὲν τοίνυν κακοῖς καὶ πράγμασι τὴν ἀποδημίαν πᾶσαν συνειχόμην ἑοράκατε. τί γὰρ αὐτοὺς
οἴεσθ' ἐκεῖ ποιεῖν ἐγγὺς ὄντας τοῦ διδόντος, ὅθ'
ὑμῶν ὁρώντων, τῶν καὶ τιμῆσαι κυρίων ὄντων καὶ
τοὐναντίον κολάσαι, τοιαῦτα ποιοῦσιν;

Συλλογίσασθαι δὴ βούλομαι τὰ κατηγορημέν'
ἀπ' ἀρχῆς, ἵν' ὅσ' ὑμῖν ὑπεσχόμην ἀρχόμενος τοῦ
λόγου, δείξω πεποιηκώς. ἐπέδειξ' οὐδὲν ἀληθὲς
[397] ἀπηγγελκότα ἀλλὰ φενακίσανθ' ὑμᾶς, μάρτυσι τοῖς
178 γεγενημένοις αὐτοῖς, οὐ λόγοις χρώμενος. ἐπέδειξ'
αἴτιον γεγενημένον τοῦ μὴ 'θέλειν ὑμᾶς ἀκούειν
ἐμοῦ τἀληθῆ ταῖς ὑποσχέσεσι καὶ τοῖς ἐπαγγέλμασι
τοῖς τούτου καταληφθέντας τότε, πάντα τἀναντία
συμβουλεύσαντ' ἢ ἔδει, καὶ τῇ μὲν τῶν συμμάχων
ἀντειπόντ' εἰρήνῃ, τῇ δὲ Φιλοκράτους συνηγο-
ρήσαντα, τοὺς χρόνους κατατρίψαντα, ἵνα μηδ'
εἰ βούλοισθε δύναισθ' ἐξελθεῖν εἰς Φωκέας, καὶ
ἄλλ' ἐπὶ τῆς ἀποδημίας πολλὰ καὶ δείν' εἰρ-
γασμένον, προδεδωκότα πάντα, πεπρακότα, δῶρ'

---

a It should be remembered that all evidence in the
Athenian courts was deposited in writing before the trial.
There was no verbal evidence and no cross-examination.
By attesting under oath the truth of his deposition, the

our departure. To prove the truth of these statements, in the first place I will give evidence myself, having duly written down my deposition and incurred legal responsibility *a* ; and I will then call the other ambassadors in turn, and compel them either to testify, or to take oath that they are unable to testify. If they take the oath, I shall easily convict them of perjury.

(The Deposition of Demosthenes is read)

You have seen how I was harassed by troubles and annoyance throughout the expedition. You can imagine how they behaved there, with their paymaster next door, when their conduct here, under the eyes of the people, who hold the power to reward and to chastise, is what we know it to be.

Now I wish to recapitulate the charges I have brought home, and to show that I have fulfilled the undertaking I gave at the outset of my speech. I have proved, not by words but by the testimony of facts, that there was no word of truth in the report of Aeschines, but that he successfully deceived you. I have proved that he is to blame for your refusal to hear the truth from me, captivated as you then were by his promises and assurances ; that his counsels were exactly opposed to right policy ; that he spoke against the terms of peace proposed by our allies, and in favour of the proposals of Philocrates ; that he purposely wasted your time to debar you from going to the aid of the Phocians if you should so desire ; that throughout his journey abroad his sins were many and grievous ; that he has betrayed everything, sold everything, taken bribes, witness of course made himself answerable to a charge of perjury.

ἔχοντα, οὐδὲν ἐλλελοιπότα μοχθηρίας. οὐκοῦν ταῦθ'
179 ὑπεσχόμην ἐν ἀρχῇ, ταῦτ' ἐπέδειξα. ὁρᾶτε τοίνυν
τὰ μετὰ ταῦτα· ἁπλοῦς γάρ ἐσθ' ὁ μέλλων λόγος
οὑτοσὶ πρὸς ὑμᾶς ἤδη. ὀμωμόκατε ψηφιεῖσθαι
κατὰ τοὺς νόμους καὶ τὰ ψηφίσματα τὰ τοῦ
δήμου καὶ τῆς βουλῆς τῶν πεντακοσίων· φαίνεται
δ' οὗτος πάντα τἀναντία τοῖς νόμοις, τοῖς ψηφίσμασι, τοῖς δικαίοις πεπρεσβευκώς· οὐκοῦν ἑαλωκέναι προσήκει παρά γε νοῦν ἔχουσι δικασταῖς.
εἰ γὰρ ἄλλο μηδὲν ἠδίκει, δύο τῶν πεπραγμένων
ἔσθ' ἱκάν' αὐτὸν ἀποκτεῖναι· οὐ γὰρ μόνον Φωκέας,
180 ἀλλὰ καὶ Θρᾴκην προδέδωκε Φιλίππῳ. καίτοι
δύο χρησιμωτέρους τόπους τῆς οἰκουμένης οὐδ'
ἂν εἷς ἐπιδείξαι τῇ πόλει, κατὰ μὲν γῆν Πυλῶν,
ἐκ θαλάττης δὲ τοῦ Ἑλλησπόντου· ἃ συναμφότερ'
οὗτοι πεπράκασιν αἰσχρῶς καὶ καθ' ὑμῶν ἐγκε-
χειρίκασι Φιλίππῳ. τοῦτο τοίνυν αὐτὸ ἄνευ τῶν
ἄλλων ἡλίκον ἔστ' ἀδίκημα, τὸ Θρᾴκην καὶ τὰ
Τείχη προέσθαι, μυρί' ἂν εἴη λέγειν, καὶ ὅσοι διὰ
[398] ταῦτ' ἀπολώλασι παρ' ὑμῖν, οἱ δὲ χρήματα πάμ-
πολλ' ὠφλήκασιν, οὐ χαλεπὸν δεῖξαι, Ἐργόφιλος,
Κηφισόδοτος, Τιμόμαχος, τὸ παλαιόν ποτ' Ἐργο-
κλῆς, Διονύσιος, ἄλλοι, οὓς ὀλίγου δέω σύμπαντας
181 εἰπεῖν ἐλάττω τὴν πόλιν βεβλαφέναι τούτου. ἀλλ'
ἔτι γὰρ τότ', ὦ ἄνδρες Ἀθηναῖοι, ἐκ λογισμοῦ τὰ
δείν' ἐφυλάττεσθ' ὑμεῖς καὶ προεωρᾶσθε· νῦν δ' ὅ
τι ἂν μὴ καθ' ἡμέραν ὑμᾶς ἐνοχλῇ καὶ παρὸν
λυπῇ, παρορᾶτε, εἶτα τὴν ἄλλως ἐνταῦθα ψηφί-
360

and stopped short of no iniquity. That, then, is what I undertook to prove ; and that is what I have proved. Now mark what follows ; for the argument I now put before you is plain and straightforward. You have sworn to give a verdict according to the laws, and to the decrees of the people and of the Council of Five Hundred ; the conduct of the defendant when holding the office of ambassador has manifestly violated those laws, those decrees, and the principles of justice ; therefore he must be convicted by an intelligent jury. If he had committed no other crime, two only of his transgressions are sufficient to put him to death, for he has betrayed Thrace as well as the Phocians to Philip. Yet no man could point out two places in the whole world of more importance to the commonwealth than Thermopylae by land and the Hellespont by sea ; and both of them these men have infamously sold and delivered into the hands of Philip. What an enormous offence, apart from all the rest, is the surrender of Thrace and the Thracian outposts, I could show by a thousand reasons ; and it would be easy to point to many men who for such betrayals have been sentenced to death or mulcted in large sums of money in this court,—Ergophilus, Cephisodotus, Timomachus, and, in old times, Ergocles, Dionysius, and others, of whom I may say that all of them together had inflicted fewer injuries upon the commonwealth than the defendant. But in those days, men of Athens, you were still careful to be on your guard against perils, and not sparing of precaution ; now you overlook anything that at any given moment does not disturb you or cause immediate annoyance. And then you come here and

ζεσθε, ἀποδοῦναι δὲ καὶ Κερσοβλέπτῃ Φίλιππον
τοὺς ὅρκους, μὴ μετέχειν δὲ τῶν ἐν Ἀμφικτύοσιν,
ἐπανορθώσασθαι δὲ τὴν εἰρήνην. καίτοι τούτων
οὐδενὸς ἂν τῶν ψηφισμάτων ἔδει, εἰ πλεῖν οὗτος
ἤθελε καὶ τὰ προσήκοντα ποιεῖν· νῦν δ᾽ ἃ μὲν ἦν
πλεύσασι σῶσαι, βαδίζειν κελεύων ἀπολώλεκεν,
ἃ δ᾽ εἰποῦσι τἀληθῆ, ψευδόμενος.

182 Ἀγανακτήσει τοίνυν αὐτίκα δὴ μάλα, ὡς ἐγὼ
πυνθάνομαι, εἰ μόνος τῶν ἐν τῷ δήμῳ λεγόντων
λόγων εὐθύνας ὑφέξει. ἐγὼ δ᾽ ὅτι μὲν πάντες ἂν
εἰκότως ὧν λέγουσι δίκην ὑπέχοιεν, εἴπερ ἐπ᾽
ἀργυρίῳ τι λέγοιεν, παραλείψω, ἀλλ᾽ ἐκεῖνο λέγω·
εἰ μὲν Αἰσχίνης ἰδιώτης ὢν ἀπελήρησέ τι καὶ δι-
ήμαρτε, μὴ σφόδρ᾽ ἀκριβολογήσησθε, ἐάσατε, συγγνώμην ἔχετε· εἰ δὲ πρεσβευτὴς ὢν ἐπὶ χρήμασιν
ἐπίτηδες ἐξηπάτηκεν ὑμᾶς, μὴ ἀφῆτε, μηδ᾽ ἀνά-
183 σχησθ᾽ ὡς οὐ δεῖ δίκην ὧν εἶπεν ὑποσχεῖν. τίνος
γὰρ ἄλλου δεῖ δίκην παρὰ πρέσβεων ἢ λόγων
λαμβάνειν; εἰσὶ γὰρ οἱ πρέσβεις οὐ τριήρων οὐδὲ
τόπων οὐδ᾽ ὁπλιτῶν οὐδ᾽ ἀκροπόλεων κύριοι
(οὐδεὶς γὰρ πρέσβεσι ταῦτ᾽ ἐγχειρίζει), ἀλλὰ
λόγων καὶ χρόνων. τοὺς μὲν τοίνυν χρόνους εἰ
[399] μὲν μὴ προανεῖλε τῆς πόλεως, οὐκ ἀδικεῖ, εἰ δ᾽
ἀνεῖλεν, ἠδίκηκε· τοὺς δὲ λόγους εἰ μὲν ἀληθεῖς
ἀπήγγελκεν ἢ συμφέροντας, ἀποφευγέτω, εἰ δὲ
καὶ ψευδεῖς καὶ μισθοῦ καὶ ἀσυμφόρους, ἁλι-
184 σκέσθω. οὐδὲν γὰρ ἔσθ᾽ ὅ τι μεῖζον ἂν ὑμᾶς
ἀδικήσειέ τις, ἢ ψευδῆ λέγων. οἷς γὰρ ἔστ᾽ ἐν
λόγοις ἡ πολιτεία, πῶς, ἂν οὗτοι μὴ ἀληθεῖς ὦσιν,

362

pass random resolutions,—that Philip shall swear fidelity to Cersobleptes,—that he shall have no share in Amphictyonic business,—that he shall revise the terms of peace. Yet all your resolutions would have been unnecessary, if only the defendant had chosen to travel by sea and to do his duty. What might have been saved by sailing, he has lost by insisting on travel by land ; and what might have been saved by telling the truth, he has lost by telling lies.

He will presently, as I am informed, make it a grievance that he, and he alone of all our debaters, is to be called to account for his speeches. I will spare him the retort that any man who takes money for his speeches might reasonably be brought to justice ; but there is one point on which I do insist. If Aeschines talked like an idiot and made blunders as an unofficial person, do not be hypercritical, leave him alone, make allowances. But if he has purposely deceived you for money while holding office as ambassador, do not let him off, do not listen to the suggestion that he is not to be put on his trial for mere words. For what are we to bring any ambassador to justice, if not for his words ? Ambassadors have control, not over war-ships, and military positions, and troops, and citadels,—these are never entrusted to them,—but over words and opportunities. If an ambassador has not wasted the opportunities of the state, he is no wrongdoer ; if he has wasted them, he has done wrong. If the words of his reports are true and profitable words, let him be acquitted ; if they are false, venal, and noxious, let him be convicted. A man can do no greater wrong than by telling lies to a popular assembly ; for, where the political system is based upon speeches, how can it

ἀσφαλῶς ἔστι πολιτεύεσθαι; ἐὰν δὲ δὴ καὶ πρὸς
ἃ τοῖς ἐχθροῖς συμφέρει δῶρά τις λαμβάνων λέγῃ,
πῶς οὐχὶ καὶ κινδυνεύσετε; οὐδέ γε τοὺς χρόνους
ἴσον ἔστ᾽ ἀδίκημ᾽ ὀλιγαρχίας ἢ τυράννου παρελέ-
185 σθαι καὶ ὑμῶν· οὐδ᾽ ὀλίγου γε δεῖ. ἐν ἐκείναις μὲν
γάρ, οἶμαι, ταῖς πολιτείαις πάντ᾽ ἐξ ἐπιτάγματος
ὀξέως γίγνεται· ὑμῖν δὲ πρῶτον μὲν τὴν βουλὴν
ἀκοῦσαι περὶ πάντων καὶ προβουλεῦσαι δεῖ, καὶ
τοῦθ᾽ ὅταν ᾖ κήρυξι καὶ πρεσβείαις προγεγραμ-
μένον, οὐκ ἀεί, εἶτ᾽ ἐκκλησίαν ποιῆσαι, καὶ ταύτην
ὅταν ἐκ τῶν νόμων καθήκῃ. εἶτα κρατῆσαι καὶ
περιγενέσθαι δεῖ τοὺς τὰ βέλτιστα λέγοντας τῶν
186 ἢ δι᾽ ἄγνοιαν ἢ διὰ μοχθηρίαν ἀντιλεγόντων. ἐφ᾽
ἅπασι δὲ τούτοις, ἐπειδὰν καὶ δεδογμένον ᾖ καὶ
συμφέρον ἤδη φαίνηται, χρόνον δεῖ δοθῆναι τῇ
τῶν πολλῶν ἀδυναμίᾳ, ἐν ᾧ καὶ ποριοῦνται ταῦθ᾽
ὧν ἂν δέωνται, ὅπως τὰ δόξαντα καὶ δυνηθῶσι
ποιῆσαι. ὁ δὴ τοὺς χρόνους τούτους ἀναιρῶν τῆς
οἵα παρ᾽ ἡμῖν ἐστι πολιτείας οὐ χρόνους ἀνῄρηκεν
οὗτος, οὔ, ἀλλὰ τὰ πράγμαθ᾽ ἁπλῶς ἀφῄρηται.
187 Ἔστι τοίνυν τις πρόχειρος λόγος πᾶσι τοῖς
ἐξαπατᾶν ὑμᾶς βουλομένοις "οἱ ταράττοντες τὴν
πόλιν, οἱ διακωλύοντες Φίλιππον εὖ ποιῆσαι τὴν
πόλιν." πρὸς οὓς ἐγὼ λόγον μὲν οὐδέν᾽ ἐρῶ,
τὰς δ᾽ ἐπιστολὰς ὑμῖν ἀναγνώσομαι τὰς τοῦ
Φιλίππου, καὶ τοὺς καιροὺς ἐφ᾽ ὧν ἕκαστ᾽ ἐξ-
[400] ηπάτησθ᾽ ὑπομνήσω, ἵν᾽ εἰδῆθ᾽ ὅτι τὸ ψυχρὸν τοῦτ᾽
ὄνομα, τὸ ἄχρι κόρου, παρελήλυθ᾽ ἐκεῖνος φενα-
κίζων ὑμᾶς.

ΕΠΙΣΤΟΛΑΙ ΦΙΛΙΠΠΟΥ

be safely administered if the speeches are false?
If he actually takes bribes and speaks in the interest
of our enemies, will not you be imperilled? Again, to
filch your opportunities is not an offence equivalent to
filching those of an oligarchy or a monarchy, but
far greater. For in those polities, I take it, everything
is done promptly at the word of command; but
with you, first the Council must be informed, and must
adopt a provisional resolution,—and even that not
at any time, but only after written notice given to
marshals and embassies; then the Council must
convene an Assembly, but only on a statutory date.
Then the most honest debaters have to make good
their advantage and argue down an ignorant or
dishonest opposition; and even then, after all these
proceedings, when a decision has been formed, and
its propriety demonstrated, further time must be
granted to the poverty of the populace for the provision of whatever is needed, to enable them to
execute the decision. Surely the man who, under
a constitution like ours, destroys the opportunities
for this procedure, has not destroyed opportunities
merely; he has absolutely robbed us of our control
over affairs.

Now there is an easy phrase at the disposal of
every one who wishes to delude you: " The dis-
turbers of the commonwealth; the thwarters of
Philip's public benefactions." I will not say a word
in reply; I will only read to you Philip's letters,
and remind you of the several occasions of your
deception, to show how " the Benefactor " has for-
feited by his beguilements that frigid and nauseating
title.

(*The Letters of Philip are read*)

DEMOSTHENES

188 Οὕτω τοίνυν αἰσχρὰ καὶ πολλὰ καὶ πάντα καθ᾽
ὑμῶν πεπρεσβευκὼς περιὼν λέγει " τί δ᾽ ἂν
εἴποι τις περὶ Δημοσθένους, ὃς τῶν συμπρέσβεων
κατηγορεῖ;" νὴ Δί᾽, εἴτε βούλομαί γ᾽ εἴτε μή
παρ᾽ ὅλην μὲν τὴν ἀποδημίαν ὑπὸ σοῦ τοιαῦτ᾽
ἐπιβεβουλευμένος, δυοῖν δ᾽ αἱρέσεως οὔσης μοι
νυνί, ἢ τοιούτων ὄντων τῶν πεπραγμένων δοκεῖν
189 κοινωνεῖν ὑμῖν, ἢ κατηγορεῖν. ἐγὼ δ᾽ οὐδὲ συμ-
πεπρεσβευκέναι φημί σοι, πρεσβεύειν μέντοι σὲ
μὲν πολλὰ καὶ δεινά, ἐμαυτὸν δ᾽ ὑπὲρ τουτωνὶ τὰ
βέλτιστα. ἀλλὰ Φιλοκράτης σοι συμπεπρέσβευ-
κε, κἀκείνῳ σύ, καὶ Φρύνων· ὑμεῖς γὰρ ταῦτ᾽
ἐπράττετε, καὶ ταῦτα πᾶσιν ὑμῖν ἤρεσκεν. "ποῦ
δ᾽ ἅλες; ποῦ τράπεζα; ποῦ σπονδαί;" ταῦτα
γὰρ τραγῳδεῖ περιών, ὥσπερ οὐχὶ τοὺς ἀδικοῦντας
τούτων ὄντας προδότας, ἀλλὰ τοὺς τὰ δίκαια
190 ποιοῦντας. ἐγὼ δ᾽ οἶδ᾽ ὅτι πάντες οἱ πρυτάνεις
θύουσιν ἑκάστοτε κοινῇ, καὶ συνδειπνοῦσιν ἀλλήλοις καὶ συσπένδουσιν· καὶ οὐ διὰ ταῦθ᾽ οἱ χρηστοὶ
τοὺς πονηροὺς μιμοῦνται, ἀλλ᾽ ἐὰν ἀδικοῦντα
λάβωσί τιν᾽ αὐτῶν, τῇ βουλῇ καὶ τῷ δήμῳ δηλοῦσιν.
ἡ βουλὴ ταὐτὰ ταῦτα, εἰσιτήρι᾽ ἔθυσε, συν-
ειστιάθη· σπονδῶν, ἱερῶν ἐκοινώνησαν οἱ στρατη-
γοί, σχεδὸν ὡς εἰπεῖν αἱ ἀρχαὶ πᾶσαι. ἆρ᾽ οὖν
διὰ ταῦτα τοῖς ἀδικοῦσιν ἑαυτῶν ἔδωκαν ἄδειαν;
191 πολλοῦ γε καὶ δεῖ. Λέων Τιμαγόρου κατηγόρει
[401] συμπεπρεσβευκὼς τέτταρ᾽ ἔτη, Εὔβουλος Θάρρηκος
καὶ Σμικύθου συσσεσιτηκώς, Κόνων ὁ παλαιὸς
ἐκεῖνος Ἀδειμάντου συστρατηγήσας. πότεροι οὖν

---

a The fifty Prytanes, belonging to one tribe, and performing for one tenth of the year the functions of the Council of
Five Hundred.

DE FALSA LEGATIONE, 188–191

Although so many, indeed all, of his acts on embassy were so discreditable and unpatriotic, he goes about asking : " And what are we to say of Demosthenes, who denounces his own colleagues ?" Yes, indeed ; I do and must denounce them, willingly or unwillingly, having been the victim of your machinations throughout the expedition, and being now reduced to the alternative of appearing as either the accomplice or the accuser of your crimes. I declare I was no colleague of yours ; yours was an embassy of flagrant wrong, mine was an embassy of loyal service. Your colleague was Philocrates, and you and Phryno were his ; for it was you and your friends who did these things and who approved of them. Hark to his melodramatic whine : " Where is the salt of friendship ? where is the genial board ? where is the cup of communion ? " as if doers of justice, not doers of iniquity, were traitors to those symbols ! I know that the Presidents [a] unite in a sacrificial service, dine together, and make libation together ; but it does not follow that the honest men take their cue from the knaves ; as soon as they detect one of themselves in misconduct, they lay information before the Council and the Assembly. In just the same way the Council holds its service of inauguration and its social banquet ; the commanders unite in worship and libation ; and so of all, or nearly all, the public authorities. Do they give impunity to delinquent colleagues on account of these observances ? No, indeed ! Leon denounced Timagoras, his fellow-ambassador for four years ; Eubulus his messmates, Tharrex and Smicythus ; and long ago Conon denounced Adeimantus after serving with him as general. Who were untrue to

367

τοὺς ἅλας παρέβαινον καὶ τὰς σπονδάς, Αἰσχίνη;
οἱ προδιδόντες καὶ οἱ παραπρεσβεύοντες καὶ οἱ
δωροδοκοῦντες ἢ οἱ κατηγοροῦντες; οἱ ἀδικοῦντες
δηλονότι τὰς ὅλης γε τῆς πατρίδος σπονδάς,
ὥσπερ σύ, οὐ μόνον τὰς ἰδίας.

192 Ἵνα τοίνυν εἰδῆθ᾽ ὅτι οὐ μόνον τῶν δημοσίᾳ ποτ᾽
ἐληλυθότων ὡς Φίλιππον ἀνθρώπων ἀλλὰ καὶ
τῶν ἰδίᾳ καὶ πάντων οὗτοι φαυλότατοι καὶ πονηρό-
τατοι γεγόνασι, μικρὸν ἀκούσατέ μου ἔξω τι τῆς
πρεσβείας ταύτης. ἐπειδὴ γὰρ εἷλεν Ὄλυνθον
Φίλιππος, Ὀλύμπι᾽ ἐποίει, εἰς δὲ τὴν θυσίαν
ταύτην καὶ τὴν πανήγυριν πάντας τοὺς τεχνίτας
193 συνήγαγεν. ἑστιῶν δ᾽ αὐτοὺς καὶ στεφανῶν τοὺς
νενικηκότας ἤρετο Σάτυρον τουτονὶ τὸν κωμικὸν
ὑποκριτήν, τί δὴ μόνος οὐδὲν ἐπαγγέλλεται, ἢ τίν᾽
ἐν αὐτῷ μικροψυχίαν ἢ πρὸς αὐτὸν ἀηδίαν ἐν-
εορακώς; εἰπεῖν δή φασι τὸν Σάτυρον ὅτι, ὧν
μὲν οἱ ἄλλοι δέονται, οὐδενὸς ὢν ἐν χρείᾳ τυγχάνει,
ἃ δ᾽ ἂν αὐτὸς ἐπαγγείλαιθ᾽ ἡδέως, ῥᾷστα μὲν ἐστι
Φιλίππῳ δοῦναι καὶ χαρίσασθαι πάντων, δέδοικε δὲ
194 μὴ διαμάρτῃ. κελεύσαντος δ᾽ ἐκείνου λέγειν καὶ
τι καὶ νεανιευσαμένου τοιοῦτον, ὡς οὐδὲν ὅ τι οὐ
ποιήσει, εἰπεῖν φασιν αὐτὸν ὅτι ἦν αὐτῷ Ἀπολλοφάνης ὁ Πυδναῖος ξένος καὶ φίλος, ἐπειδὴ δὲ
δολοφονηθεὶς ἐτελεύτησεν ἐκεῖνος, φοβηθέντες οἱ
συγγενεῖς αὐτοῦ ὑπεξέθεντο τὰς θυγατέρας παιδί᾽
ὄντ᾽ εἰς Ὄλυνθον. "αὗται τοίνυν τῆς πόλεως
[402] ἁλούσης αἰχμάλωτοι γεγόνασι καὶ εἰσὶ παρὰ σοί,
195 ἡλικίαν ἔχουσαι γάμου. ταύτας, αἰτῶ σε καὶ
δέομαι, δός μοι. βούλομαι δέ σ᾽ ἀκοῦσαι καὶ

ᵃ Not the great Olympian Games of Elis, but a Mace-

their salt and to the cup of friendship, Aeschines ? The traitors, the false ambassadors, and the bribe-takers, or their accusers ? The evil-doers, like you, broke covenant not with their friends alone but with the whole nation.

To show you, then, that these men are the basest and most depraved of all Philip's visitors, private as well as official,—yes, of all of them,—let me tell you a trifling story that has nothing to do with the embassy. After Philip had taken Olynthus, he was holding Olympian games,ᵃ and had invited all sorts of artists to the religious celebration and the festival. At the entertainment at which he crowned the suc-cessful competitors, he asked Satyrus, the comedian of our city, why he was the only guest who had not asked any favour ; had he observed in him any illiberality or discourtesy towards himself ? Satyrus, as the story goes, replied that he did not want any such gift as the others were asking ; what he would like to ask was a favour which Philip could grant quite easily, and yet he feared that his request would be unsuccessful. Philip bade him speak out, declaring with the easy generosity of youth that there was nothing he would not do for him. There-upon Satyrus told him that Apollophanes of Pydna had been a friend of his, and that after his death by assassination his kinsmen in alarm had secretly removed his daughters, who were then children, to Olynthus. These girls had been made captive when the town was taken, and were now in Philip's hands, and of marriageable age. " I earnestly beg you," he went on, " to bestow them on me. At the same

donian festival held at Dium. The date is probably the spring of 347 B.C.

μαθεῖν οἵαν μοι δώσεις δωρεάν, ἐὰν ἄρα δῷς· ἀφ'
ἧς ἐγὼ κερδανῶ μὲν οὐδέν, ἐὰν λάβω, προῖκα δὲ
προσθεὶς ἐκδώσω, καὶ οὐ περιόψομαι παθούσας
οὐδὲν ἀνάξιον οὔθ' ἡμῶν οὔτε τοῦ πατρός." ὡς
δ' ἀκοῦσαι τοὺς παρόντας ἐν τῷ συμποσίῳ, τοσοῦτον κρότον καὶ θόρυβον καὶ ἔπαινον παρὰ πάντων
γενέσθαι, ὥστε τὸν Φίλιππον παθεῖν τι καὶ δοῦναι.
καίτοι τῶν ἀποκτεινάντων ἦν τὸν Ἀλέξανδρον τὸν
ἀδελφὸν τὸν Φιλίππου οὗτος ὁ Ἀπολλοφάνης.

196 Ἐξετάσωμεν δὴ πρὸς τὸ τοῦ Σατύρου τοῦτο
συμπόσιον τὸ τούτων ἐν Μακεδονίᾳ γενόμενον, καὶ
θεάσασθ' εἰ παραπλήσιον τούτῳ καὶ ὅμοιον. κλη-
θέντες γὰρ οὗτοι πρὸς Ξενόφρονα τὸν υἱὸν τὸν
Φαιδίμου τοῦ τῶν τριάκοντ' ᾤχοντο· ἐγὼ δ'
οὐκ ἐπορεύθην. ἐπειδὴ δ' ἧκον εἰς τὸ πίνειν,
εἰσάγει τιν' Ὀλυνθίαν γυναῖκα, εὐπρεπῆ μέν,
ἐλευθέραν δὲ καὶ σώφρονα, ὡς τὸ ἔργον ἐδήλωσεν.

197 ταύτην τὸ μὲν πρῶτον οὑτωσὶ πίνειν ἡσυχῇ καὶ
τρώγειν ἠνάγκαζον οὗτοί μοι δοκεῖν, ὡς διηγεῖτ'
Ἰατροκλῆς ἐμοὶ τῇ ὑστεραίᾳ· ὡς δὲ προῄει τὸ
πρᾶγμα καὶ διεθερμαίνοντο, κατακλίνεσθαι καί τι
καὶ ᾄδειν ἐκέλευον. ἀδημονούσης δὲ τῆς ἀνθρώπου
καὶ οὔτ' ἐθελούσης οὔτ' ἐπισταμένης, ὕβριν τὸ
πρᾶγμ' ἔφασαν οὑτοσὶ καὶ ὁ Φρύνων καὶ οὐκ
ἀνεκτὸν εἶναι, τῶν θεοῖς ἐχθρῶν, τῶν ἀλειτηρίων
Ὀλυνθίων αἰχμαλώτων οὖσαν τρυφᾶν· καὶ "κάλει
παῖδα," καὶ "ἱμάντά τις φερέτω." ἧκεν οἰκέτης
[403] ἔχων ῥυτῆρα, καὶ πεπωκότων, οἶμαι, καὶ μικρῶν
ὄντων τῶν παροξυνόντων, εἰπούσης τι καὶ δακρυ-

time I wish you to understand what sort of gift you will be giving me, if you do give it. It will bring me no gain, for I shall provide them with dowries and give them in marriage ; and I shall not permit them to suffer any treatment unworthy of myself or of their father." It is said that, when the other guests heard this speech, there was such an outburst of applause and approval that Philip was strongly moved, and granted the boon. And yet Apollophanes was one of the men who had slain Philip's own brother Alexander.

Now let us compare the banquet of Satyrus with another entertainment which these men attended in Macedonia ; and you shall see whether there is any sort of resemblance. These men had been invited to the house of Xenophron, a son of Phaedimus, who was one of the Thirty Tyrants, and off they went; but I declined to go. When the drinking began, Xenophron introduced an Olynthian woman,—a handsome, but a freeborn and, as the event proved, a modest girl. At first, I believe, they only tried to make her drink quietly and eat dessert ; so Iatrocles told me the following day. But as the carouse went on, and they became heated, they ordered her to sit down and give them a song. The poor girl was bewildered, for she did not wish, and she did not know how, to sing. Then Aeschines and Phryno declared that it was intolerable impertinence for a captive,—and one of those ungodly, pernicious Olynthians too,—to give herself such airs. " Call a servant," they cried ; " bring a whip, somebody." In came a flunkey with a horsewhip, and—I suppose they were tipsy, and it did not take much to irritate them,—when she said something and began to cry,

371

σάσης ἐκείνης, περιρρήξας τὸν χιτωνίσκον ὁ οἰκέ-
198 της ξαίνει κατὰ νώτου πολλάς. ἔξω δ' αὐτῆς οὐδ'
ὑπὸ τοῦ κακοῦ καὶ τοῦ πράγματος ἡ γυνὴ ἀνα-
πηδήσασα προσπίπτει πρὸς τὰ γόνατα τῷ Ἰατρο-
κλεῖ, καὶ τὴν τράπεζαν ἀνατρέπει. καὶ εἰ μὴ
ἐκεῖνος ἀφείλετο, ἀπώλετ' ἂν παροινουμένη· καὶ
γὰρ ἡ παροινία τοῦ καθάρματος τουτουὶ δεινή.
καὶ περὶ ταύτης τῆς ἀνθρώπου καὶ ἐν Ἀρκαδίᾳ
λόγος ἦν ἐν τοῖς μυρίοις, καὶ Διόφαντος ἐν ὑμῖν
ἀπήγγελλεν ἃ νῦν μαρτυρεῖν αὐτὸν ἀναγκάσω, καὶ
κατὰ Θετταλίαν πολὺς λόγος καὶ πανταχοῦ.

199 Καὶ τοιαῦτα συνειδὼς αὑτῷ πεπραγμένα ὁ ἀ-
κάθαρτος οὗτος τολμήσει βλέπειν εἰς ὑμᾶς, καὶ τὸν
βεβιωμένον αὑτῷ βίον αὐτίκα δὴ μάλ' ἐρεῖ λαμπρᾷ
τῇ φωνῇ· ἐφ' οἷς ἔγωγ' ἀποπνίγομαι. οὐκ ἴσασιν
οὗτοι τὸ μὲν ἐξ ἀρχῆς τὰς βίβλους ἀναγιγνώσκοντά
σε τῇ μητρὶ τελούσῃ, καὶ παῖδ' ὄντ' ἐν θιάσοις καὶ
200 μεθύουσιν ἀνθρώποις καλινδούμενον; μετὰ ταῦτα
δὲ ταῖς ἀρχαῖς ὑπογραμματεύοντα καὶ δυοῖν ἢ
τριῶν δραχμῶν πονηρὸν ὄντα; τὰ τελευταῖα δ'
ἔναγχος ἐν χορηγίοις ἀλλοτρίοις ἐπὶ τῷ τριταγωνιστεῖν ἀγαπητῶς παρατρεφόμενον; ποῖον οὖν
ἐρεῖς βίον ὃν ποῦ βεβίωκας; [1] ἐπεὶ ὅ γε βεβιω-
μένος σοι τοιοῦτος φαίνεται. ἀλλὰ δὴ τὰ τῆς ἐξ-
ουσίας· οὗτος ἄλλον ἔκρινε παρ' ὑμῖν ἐπὶ πορνείᾳ.
ἀλλὰ μήπω ταῦτα, ἀλλὰ τὰς μαρτυρίας μοι λέγε
πρῶτον ταυτασί.

[404]   ΜΑΡΤΥΡΙΑΙ

[1] ποῖον οὖν ἐρεῖς βίον ὃν οὐ βεβίωκας; Shill. with mss. : ποῦ
Blass, from a parallel passage, p. 793 (xxv. 77).

[a] The Assembly of the Arcadian Confederacy, meeting at
Megalopolis.

he tore off her dress and gave her a number of lashes on the back. Maddened by these indignities, she jumped to her feet, upset the table, and fell at the knees of Iatrocles. If he had not rescued her, she would have perished, the victim of a drunken orgy, for the drunkenness of this blackguard is something terrible. The story of this girl was told even in Arcadia, at a meeting of the Ten Thousand [a] ; it was related by Diophantus at Athens in a report which I will compel him to repeat in evidence ; and it was common talk in Thessaly and everywhere.

With all this on his conscience the unclean scoundrel will dare to look you in the face, and before long he will be declaiming in sonorous accents about his blameless life. It makes me choke with rage. As if the jury did not know all about you : first the acolyte,[b] reading the service-books while your mother performed her hocus-pocus, reeling and tumbling, child as you were, with bacchanals and tipsy worshippers ; then the junior clerk, doing the dirty work of public offices for a few shillings a month : and at last, not so long ago, the parasite of the green-rooms, eking out by sponging what you earned as a player of trumpery parts ! What is the life you will claim, and where have you lived it, when such is too clearly the sort of life you really have lived ? And then the assurance of the man ! Bringing another man [c] before this court on a charge of un-natural crime ! However, I will let that go for the present. First read these depositions.

(The Depositions are read)

---

[b] *the acolyte*, etc. : see *De cor.* 259 ff.
[c] Timarchus ; see Introd. p. 234.

201 Τοσούτων τοίνυν καὶ τοιούτων ὄντων, ὦ ἄνδρες
δικασταί, ὧν ἀδικῶν ὑμᾶς ἐξελήλεγκται, ἐν οἷς τί
κακὸν οὐκ ἔνι; δωροδόκος, κόλαξ, ταῖς ἀραῖς
ἔνοχος, ψεύστης, τῶν φίλων προδότης, πάντ' ἔνεστι
τὰ δεινότατα· πρὸς ἓν οὐδ' ὁτιοῦν τούτων ἀπολογήσεται, οὐδ' ἕξει δικαίαν οὐδ' ἁπλῆν εἰπεῖν ἀπολογίαν οὐδεμίαν. ἃ δ' ἐγὼ πέπυσμαι μέλλειν αὐτὸν
λέγειν, ἔστι μὲν ἐγγυτάτω μανίας, οὐ μὴν ἀλλ'
ἴσως τῷ μηδὲν ἔχοντι δίκαιον ἀλλ' εἰπεῖν ἀνάγκη
202 πάντα μηχανᾶσθαι. ἀκούω γὰρ αὐτὸν ἐρεῖν ὡς
ἄρ' ἐγὼ πάντων ὧν κατηγορῶ κοινωνὸς γέγονα,
καὶ συνήρεσκε ταῦτά μοι καὶ συνέπραττον αὐτῷ,
ἔπειτ' ἐξαίφνης μεταβέβλημαι καὶ κατηγορῶ.
ἔστι δ' ὑπὲρ μὲν τῶν πεπραγμένων οὔτε δικαία
οὔτε προσήκουσ' ἡ τοιαύτη ἀπολογία, ἐμοῦ μέντοι
τις κατηγορία· ἐγὼ μὲν γάρ, εἰ ταῦτα πεποίηκα,
φαῦλός εἰμ' ἄνθρωπος, τὰ δὲ πράγματ' οὐδὲν
203 βελτίω διὰ τοῦτο, οὐδὲ πολλοῦ δεῖ. οὐ μὴν ἀλλ'
ἔγωγ' οἶμαί μοι προσήκειν ἀμφότερ' ὑμῖν ἐπιδεῖξαι,
καὶ ὅτι ψεύσεται ταῦτ' ἐὰν λέγῃ, καὶ τὴν δικαίαν
ἥτις ἐστὶν ἀπολογία. ἡ μὲν τοίνυν δικαία καὶ
ἁπλῆ, ἢ ὡς οὐ πέπρακται τὰ κατηγορημένα δεῖξαι,
ἢ ὡς πεπραγμένα συμφέρει τῇ πόλει, τούτων δ'
204 οὐδέτερον δύναιτ' ἂν οὗτος ποιῆσαι. οὔτε γὰρ ὡς
συμφέρει δήπου Φωκέας ἀπολωλέναι καὶ Πύλας
Φίλιππον ἔχειν καὶ Θηβαίους ἰσχύειν καὶ ἐν
Εὐβοίᾳ στρατιώτας εἶναι καὶ Μεγάροις ἐπι-
βουλεύειν καὶ ἀνώμοτον εἶναι τὴν εἰρήνην, ἔνεστι
[405] λέγειν αὐτῷ, οἷς τότ' ἐναντί' ἀπήγγειλε πρὸς
374

Of all these heinous crimes against the commonwealth, gentlemen of the jury, he has been proved guilty. No element of baseness is lacking. Bribetaker, sycophant, guilty under the curse, a liar, a traitor to his friends,—here are flagrant charges indeed! Yet he will not defend himself against any one of them; he has no honest and straightforward defence to offer. As for the topics on which, as I am informed, he intends to dwell, they border on insanity,—though, perhaps, a man devoid of any honest plea cannot help resorting to all manner of shifts. For I hear that he will tell you that I participated in all the acts I am denouncing, that I approved of them, and co-operated with him, and now have suddenly changed my mind and become his accuser. That is no honest and decent defence against specific charges; it is, however, an accusation against me; for if I acted as he says, I am a worthless person; but that is far from making his actions a whit better. However, it is incumbent on me, I suppose, first, to satisfy you that the allegation, if he makes it, will be false, and secondly, to show you what is an honest defence. Now it is an honest and straightforward defence to prove either that the acts alleged were never committed, or that, if committed, they were for the advantage of the state. But he cannot make good either of these positions He cannot claim as advantages the destruction of the Phocians, or Philip's occupation of Thermopylae, or the aggrandizement of Thebes, or the invasion of Euboea, or the designs against Megara, or the unratified peace; for he reported himself that exactly the opposite was going to happen and would be to your advantage. Neither

ὑμᾶς ὡς συμφέροντα καὶ γενησόμενα· οὔθ' ὡς οὐ
πέπρακται ταῦτα, δυνήσεται πεῖσαι τοὺς αὐτοὺς
205 ἑορακότας ὑμᾶς καὶ εὖ εἰδότας. οὐκοῦν ὡς οὐ
κεκοινώνηκα τούτοις οὐδενός, λοιπόν μοι δεῖξαι.
βούλεσθ' οὖν ὑμῖν, πάντα τἆλλ' ἀφείς, ἃ παρ'
ὑμῖν ἀντεῖπον, ἃ ἐν τῇ ἀποδημίᾳ προσέκρουον, ὡς
ἅπαντα τὸν χρόνον ἠναντίωμαι, αὐτοὺς παράσχωμαι μάρτυρας τούτους ὅτι πάντα τἀναντί' ἐμοὶ
καὶ τούτοις πέπρακται, καὶ χρήμαθ' οὗτοι μὲν
ἔχουσιν ἐφ' ὑμῖν, ἐγὼ δ' οὐκ ἠθέλησα λαβεῖν;
θεάσασθε δή.

206 Τίνα τῶν ἐν τῇ πόλει φήσαιτ' ἂν βδελυρώτατον
εἶναι καὶ πλείστης ἀναιδείας καὶ ὀλιγωρίας μεστόν;
οὐδεὶς οὐδ' ἂν ἁμαρτὼν ὑμῶν ἄλλον εὖ οἶδ' ὅτι
φήσειεν ἢ Φιλοκράτην. τίνα δὲ φθέγγεσθαι μέγιστον ἁπάντων καὶ σαφέστατ' ἂν εἰπεῖν ὅ τι βούλοιτο
τῇ φωνῇ; Αἰσχίνην οἶδ' ὅτι τουτονί. τίνα δ'
οὗτοι μὲν ἄτολμον καὶ δειλὸν πρὸς τοὺς ὄχλους
φασὶν εἶναι, ἐγὼ δ' εὐλαβῆ; ἐμέ· οὐδὲν γὰρ
πώποτ' οὔτ' ἠνώχλησα οὔτε μὴ βουλομένους
207 ὑμᾶς βεβίασμαι. οὐκοῦν ἐν πάσαις ταῖς ἐκκλησίαις,
ὁσάκις λόγος γέγονε περὶ τούτων, καὶ κατηγοροῦντος ἀκούετέ μου καὶ ἐλέγχοντος ἀεὶ τούτους
καὶ λέγοντος ἄντικρυς ὅτι χρήματ' εἰλήφασι καὶ
πάντα πεπράκασι τὰ πράγματα τῆς πόλεως.
καὶ τούτων οὐδεὶς πώποτ' ἀκούων ταῦτ' ἀντεῖπεν
208 οὐδὲ διῆρε τὸ στόμα, οὐδ' ἔδειξεν ἑαυτόν. τί ποτ'
οὖν ἐστι τὸ αἴτιον ὅτι οἱ βδελυρώτατοι τῶν ἐν τῇ
[406] πόλει καὶ μέγιστον φθεγγόμενοι τοῦ καὶ ἀτολμο-
τάτου πάντων ἐμοῦ καὶ οὐδενὸς μεῖζον φθεγγο-
μένου τοσοῦτον ἡττῶνται; ὅτι τἀληθὲς ἰσχυρόν,
καὶ τοὐναντίον ἀσθενὲς τὸ συνειδέναι πεπρακόσιν

can he convince you, against the evidence of your own eyes and your own knowledge, that these disasters are fabulous. My remaining duty is to prove that I had no partnership with these men in any of their doings. Is it your wish that I should put aside the rest of the story,—how I spoke against them in Assembly, how I fell out with them on the journey, how from first to last I persistently opposed them,—and should produce these men themselves as my witnesses to testify that my conduct and theirs has been utterly at variance, that they accepted money to thwart you, and that I refused it ? Then observe.

Whom would you call the most detestable person in all Athens, and the most swollen with impudence and superciliousness ? No one, I am sure, would name, even by a slip of the tongue, anyone but Philocrates. Who is the most vehement speaker,— the man who can express himself most emphatically with the aid of his big voice ? Undoubtedly Aeschines. Whom do these men call timid and faint-hearted, or, as I should say, diffident, in addressing a crowd ? Me ; for I never worried you ; I have never tried to dragoon you against your inclinations. Well, at every Assembly, whenever there is any discussion of this business, you hear me denouncing and incriminating these men, and declaring roundly that they have taken bribes and made traffic of all the interests of the commonwealth ; and no one of them ever contradicts me, or opens his mouth, or lets himself be seen. How comes it then that the most impudent men in Athens, and the loudest speakers, are overborne by me, the nervous man, who can speak no louder than another ? Because truth is strong, and consciousness of corrup-

DEMOSTHENES

αὐτοῖς τὰ πράγματα. τοῦτο παραιρεῖται τὴν θρα-
σύτητα τὴν τούτων, τοῦτ᾽ ἀποστρέφει τὴν γλῶτταν,
209 ἐμφράττει τὸ στόμα, ἄγχει, σιωπᾶν ποιεῖ. τὸ
τοίνυν τελευταῖον ἴστε δήπου πρώην ἐν Πειραιεῖ,
ὅτ᾽ αὐτὸν οὐκ εἰᾶτε πρεσβεύειν, βοῶνθ᾽ ὡς εἰσ-
αγγελεῖ με καὶ γράψεται καὶ ἰοὺ ἰού. καίτοι ταῦτα
μέν ἐστι μακρῶν καὶ πολλῶν ἀγώνων καὶ λόγων
ἀρχή, ἐκεῖνα δ᾽ ἁπλᾶ καὶ δύ᾽ ἢ τρί᾽ ἴσως ῥήματα,
ἃ κἂν ἐχθὲς ἐωνημένος ἄνθρωπος εἰπεῖν ἐδυνήθη,
" ἄνδρες Ἀθηναῖοι, τουτὶ τὸ πρᾶγμα πάνδεινόν
ἐστιν· οὑτοσὶ κατηγορεῖ ταῦτ᾽ ἐμοῦ ὧν αὐτὸς κοινωνὸς γέγονε, καὶ χρήματ᾽ εἰληφέναι φησὶν ἐμὲ
210 αὐτὸς εἰληφὼς ἢ μετειληφώς." τούτων μὲν τοίνυν
οὐδὲν εἶπεν οὐδ᾽ ἐφθέγξατο, οὐδ᾽ ἤκουσεν ὑμῶν οὐδείς, ἄλλα δ᾽ ἠπείλει. διὰ τί; ὅτι ταῦτα μὲν αὐτῷ
συνῄδει πεπραγμένα, καὶ δοῦλος ἦν τῶν ῥημάτων
τούτων. οὔκουν προσῄει πρὸς ταῦθ᾽ ἡ διάνοια,
ἀλλ᾽ ἀνεδύετο· ἐπελαμβάνετο γὰρ αὐτῆς τὸ συνειδέναι. λοιδορεῖσθαι δ᾽ ἄλλ᾽ ἄττ᾽ οὐδεὶς ἐκώλυεν
αὐτὸν οὐδὲ βλασφημεῖν.

211 Ὁ τοίνυν μέγιστον ἁπάντων, καὶ οὐ λόγος ἀλλ᾽
ἔργον· βουλομένου γὰρ ἐμοῦ τὰ δίκαια, ὥσπερ
ἐπρέσβευσα δίς, οὕτω καὶ λόγον ὑμῖν δοῦναι δίς,
προσελθὼν Αἰσχίνης οὑτοσὶ τοῖς λογισταῖς ἔχων
μάρτυρας πολλοὺς ἀπηγόρευε μὴ καλεῖν ἔμ᾽ εἰς τὸ
δικαστήριον ὡς δεδωκότ᾽ εὐθύνας καὶ οὐκ ὄνθ᾽
ὑπεύθυνον· καὶ τὸ πρᾶγμ᾽ ἦν ὑπεργέλοιον. τί
[407] οὖν ἦν τοῦτο; τῆς προτέρας ἐκείνης πρεσβείας,
ἧς οὐδεὶς κατηγόρει, δοὺς λόγον οὐκέτ᾽ ἐβούλετ᾽

---

a In this exclamation Demosthenes perhaps imitates the
melodramatic style and intonation of his adversary.
Aeschines is like our stage villain, crying, "Aha! A time
will come."

378

tion weak. Conscience paralyses their audacity ; conscience cripples their tongues, closes their lips, stifles them, puts them to silence. You remember the most recent occasion, at Peiraeus only the other day, when you refused to appoint Aeschines to an embassy, how he bellowed at me : " I will impeach you,—I will indict you,—aha ! aha ! " [a] And yet a threat of impeachment involves endless speeches and litigation ; but here are just two or three simple words that a slave bought yesterday could deliver : " Men of Athens, here is a strange thing ! This man accuses me of offences in which he himself took part. He says that I have taken bribes, when he took them, or shared them, himself." He never spoke, he never uttered a word of that speech ; none of you heard it ; he only vented idle menaces. The reason is that he was conscious of guilt ; he cowered like a slave before those words ; his thoughts did not approach them but recoiled from them, arrested by his evil conscience. Mere vague invective and abuse there was no one to stop.

And now comes the strongest possible point—not a matter of assertion but of fact. I wished to do the honest thing, and to give an account of myself twice, because I had been appointed ambassador twice ; but Aeschines approached the Court of Scrutiny, taking with him a crowd of witnesses, and forbade them to summon me, on the ground that I had already submitted to scrutiny, and was no longer liable. What was the real meaning of this ludicrous proceeding ? Having himself rendered his account of the earlier embassy, with which nobody found fault, he did not wish to come into court in

αὖθις εἰσιέναι περὶ ταύτης ἧς νῦν εἰσέρχεται, ἐν
212 ᾗ πάντα τἀδικήματ' ἐνῆν· ἐκ δὲ τοῦ δὶς ἔμ' εἰσελθεῖν ἀνάγκη περιίστατο καὶ τούτῳ πάλιν εἰσιέναι·
διὰ ταῦτ' οὐκ εἴα καλεῖν. καίτοι τοῦτο τὸ ἔργον,
ὦ ἄνδρες Ἀθηναῖοι, ἀμφότερ' ὑμῖν ἐπιδείκνυσι
σαφῶς, καὶ κατεγνωκόθ' ἑαυτοῦ τοῦτον, ὥστε
μηδενὶ νῦν ὑμῶν εὐσεβῶς ἔχειν ἀποψηφίσασθαι
αὐτοῦ, καὶ μηδὲν ἀληθὲς ἐροῦντα περὶ ἐμοῦ· εἰ γὰρ
εἶχε, τότ' ἂν καὶ λέγων καὶ κατηγορῶν ἐξητάζετο,
οὐ μὰ Δί' οὐκ ἀπηγόρευε καλεῖν.
213 Ὡς τοίνυν ταῦτ' ἀληθῆ λέγω, κάλει μοι τούτων
τοὺς μάρτυρας.

Ἀλλὰ μὴν ἐάν γέ τι ἔξω τῆς πρεσβείας βλασφημῇ
περὶ ἐμοῦ, κατὰ πόλλ' οὐκ ἂν εἰκότως ἀκούοιτ'
αὐτοῦ. οὐ γὰρ ἐγὼ κρίνομαι τήμερον, οὐδ' ἐγχεῖ
μετὰ ταῦθ' ὕδωρ οὐδεὶς ἐμοί. τί οὖν ἐστι ταῦτα
πλὴν δικαίων λόγων ἀπορία; τίς γὰρ ἂν κατηγορεῖν ἕλοιτο κρινόμενος, ἔχων ὅ τι ἀπολογήσεται;
214 ἔτι τοίνυν κἀκεῖνο σκοπεῖτ', ὦ ἄνδρες δικασταί.
εἰ ἐκρινόμην μὲν ἐγώ, κατηγόρει δ' Αἰσχίνης
οὑτοσί, Φίλιππος δ' ἦν ὁ κρίνων, εἶτ' ἐγὼ μηδὲν
ἔχων εἰπεῖν ὡς οὐκ ἀδικῶ κακῶς ἔλεγον τουτονὶ
καὶ προπηλακίζειν ἐπεχείρουν, οὐκ ἂν οἴεσθε
καὶ κατ' αὐτὸ τοῦτ' ἀγανακτῆσαι τὸν Φίλιππον,
εἰ παρ' ἐκείνῳ τοὺς ἐκείνου τις εὐεργέτας κακῶς
λέγει; μὴ τοίνυν ὑμεῖς χείρους γένησθε Φιλίππου,
ἀλλ' ὑπὲρ ὧν ἀγωνίζεται, περὶ τούτων ἀναγκάζετ'
ἀπολογεῖσθαι. λέγε τὴν μαρτυρίαν.

ᵃ Here and elsewhere (*e.g.* § 233) Demosthenes has time
to insert a few remarks while the witnesses are being collected
and before their depositions are read.

respect of the embassy for which he is now under examination ; and that is the embassy that includes all his misdeeds. But, if I came into court twice, he could not avoid a second appearance, and therefore he would not let me be summoned. Yet that act, men of Athens, proves two propositions : first, that Aeschines has pronounced his own condemnation, and therefore you cannot conscientiously acquit him to-day ; and secondly, that he will not have a truthful word to say about me, otherwise he would have spoken out and denounced me then, instead of trying to block my summons.

To prove the truth of these statements, please call the witnesses.[a]

If, however, he says scurrilous things about me, not pertinent to the question of the embassy, there are many reasons why you should not listen. I am not on my trial to-day, and I shall have no second opportunity [b] of speaking. It will only mean that he is destitute of honest arguments. No culprit would deliberately choose to prefer accusations, if he had any defence to offer. Or again, look at it in this light, gentlemen of the jury. Suppose that I were on trial, with Aeschines for my accuser, and Philip for my judge, and suppose that, being unable to deny my guilt, I were to vilify Aeschines and throw mud at him ; do you not think that that is just what would move Philip's indignation,—his own benefactors calumniated before his own tribunal ? Do not be less rigorous than Philip, but compel him to address his defence to the real issues of this controversy. Now read the deposition.

[b] *no second opportunity* : lit. " no one will hereafter pour water for me," *i.e.* into the clepsydra [57].

DEMOSTHENES

ΜΑΡΤΥΡΙΑ

215 Οὐκοῦν ἐγὼ μὲν ἐκ τοῦ μηδὲν ἐμαυτῷ συνειδέναι
καὶ λόγον διδόναι καὶ πάντα τἀκ τῶν νόμων ὑπέχειν
ᾤμην δεῖν, οὗτος δὲ τἀναντία. πῶς οὖν ταῦτ᾽ ἐμοὶ
καὶ τούτῳ πέπρακται; ἢ πῶς ἔνεστι τούτῳ ταῦτα
πρὸς ὑμᾶς λέγειν, ἃ μηδ᾽ ᾐτίαται πρότερον πώποτε;
οὐδαμῶς δήπου. ἀλλ᾽ ὅμως ἐρεῖ, καὶ νὴ Δί᾽ εἰκότως γε. ἴστε γὰρ δήπου τοῦθ᾽, ὅτι ἀφ᾽ οὗ γεγόνασιν ἄνθρωποι καὶ κρίσεις γίγνονται, οὐδεὶς
πώποθ᾽ ὁμολογῶν ἀδικεῖν ἑάλω, ἀλλ᾽ ἀναισχυν-
τοῦσιν, ἀρνοῦνται, ψεύδονται, προφάσεις πλάττον-
ται, πάντα ποιοῦσιν ὑπὲρ τοῦ μὴ δοῦναι δίκην.
216 ὧν οὐδενὶ δεῖ παρακρουσθῆναι τήμερον ὑμᾶς, ἀλλ᾽
ἀφ᾽ ὧν ἴστ᾽ αὐτοὶ τὰ πράγματα κρῖναι, μὴ τοῖς
ἐμοῖς λόγοις μηδὲ τοῖς τούτου προσέχειν, μηδέ γε
τοῖς μάρτυσιν, οὓς οὗτος ἑτοίμους ἕξει μαρτυρεῖν
ὁτιοῦν, Φιλίππῳ χορηγῷ χρώμενος· ὄψεσθε δ᾽ ὡς
ἑτοίμως αὐτῷ μαρτυρήσουσιν· μηδέ γ᾽ εἰ καλὸν
καὶ μέγα οὗτος φθέγξεται, μηδ᾽ εἰ φαῦλον ἐγώ.
217 οὐδὲ γὰρ ῥητόρων οὐδὲ λόγων κρίσιν ὑμᾶς τήμερον,
εἴπερ εὖ φρονεῖτε, προσήκει ποιεῖν, ἀλλ᾽ ὑπὲρ
πραγμάτων αἰσχρῶς καὶ δεινῶς ἀπολωλότων τὴν
ὑπάρχουσαν αἰσχύνην εἰς τοὺς αἰτίους ἀπώσασθε,
τὰ πεπραγμένα, ἃ πάντες ἐπίστασθε, ἐξετάσαντες.
218 τί οὖν ἐστι ταῦθ᾽ ἃ ὑμεῖς ἴστε καὶ οὐ παρ᾽ ἡμῶν
ὑμᾶς ἀκοῦσαι δεῖ; εἰ μὲν ἅπανθ᾽ ὅσ᾽ ὑπέσχονθ᾽
ὑμῖν ἐκ τῆς εἰρήνης γέγονε, καὶ τοσαύτης ἀν-
ανδρίας καὶ κακίας ὑμεῖς ὁμολογεῖτ᾽ εἶναι μεστοί,
ὥστε μήτ᾽ ἐν τῇ χώρᾳ τῶν πολεμίων ὄντων μήτ᾽
ἐκ θαλάττης πολιορκούμενοι μήτ᾽ ἐν ἄλλῳ μηδενὶ
δεινῷ τῆς πόλεως οὔσης, ἀλλὰ καὶ σῖτον εὔωνον

(*The Deposition is read*)

Thus in my consciousness of innocence I thought it my duty to render my account and accept my full legal liability, while Aeschines did not. Is my conduct then the echo of his? Is it competent for him to lay before this court charges which he has never made before? Assuredly not; and yet he will lay them, for a very good reason. For you know that, ever since mankind and the criminal law first came into being, no culprit has ever been convicted while confessing his guilt. They vapour, they gainsay, they tell lies, they forge excuses,—anything to evade justice. Do not be duped to-day by any of these stale tricks. You must pass judgement on the facts, according to your knowledge; you must pay no heed either to my assertions or to his, nor even to the witnesses whom he will have in waiting, with Philip as his paymaster,—and you will see how glibly they will testify. You must not notice what a fine loud voice he has, and what a poor voice I have. If you are wise, you must not treat this trial as a competition of forensic eloquence; but in regard to a dishonourable and perilous catastrophe, cast back upon the guilty the dishonour that attaches to it, after reviewing transactions that lie within the knowledge of you all. What, then, are the facts that you know and I need not recount? If all the promised results of the peace have come true, if you confess yourselves so effeminate and so cowardly that, with no enemy within your borders, no blockade of your ports, no imperilment of your capital, with corn-prices low and every other condi-

DEMOSTHENES

ὠνούμενοι καὶ τἄλλ' οὐδὲν χεῖρον πράττοντες ἢ
219 νῦν, προειδότες καὶ προακηκοότες παρὰ τούτων
καὶ τοὺς συμμάχους ἀπολουμένους καὶ Θηβαίους
ἰσχυροὺς γενησομένους καὶ τἀπὶ Θρᾴκης Φίλιππον
ληψόμενον καὶ ἐν Εὐβοίᾳ κατασκευασθησόμεν'
ὁρμητήρι' ἐφ' ὑμᾶς καὶ πάνθ' ἃ πέπρακται γενη-
σόμενα, εἶτα τὴν εἰρήνην ἐποιήσασθ' ἀγαπητῶς,
ἀποψηφίσασθ' Αἰσχίνου, καὶ μὴ πρὸς τοσούτοις
αἰσχροῖς καὶ ἐπιορκίαν προσκτήσησθε· οὐδὲν γὰρ
ὑμᾶς ἀδικεῖ, ἀλλ' ἐγὼ μαίνομαι καὶ τετύφωμαι
220 νῦν κατηγορῶν αὐτοῦ. εἰ δὲ πάντα τἀναντία
τούτων καὶ πολλὰ καὶ φιλάνθρωπ' εἰπόντες Φίλιππον, φιλεῖν τὴν πόλιν, Φωκέας σώσειν, Θηβαίους
παύσειν τῆς ὕβρεως, ἔτι πρὸς τούτοις μεῖζον' ἢ
κατ' Ἀμφίπολιν εὖ ποιήσειν ὑμᾶς, ἂν τύχῃ τῆς
εἰρήνης, Εὔβοιαν, Ὠρωπὸν ἀποδώσειν· εἰ ταῦτ'
εἰπόντες καὶ ὑποσχόμενοι πάντ' ἐξηπατήκασι καὶ
πεφενακίκασι καὶ μόνον οὐ τὴν Ἀττικὴν ὑμῶν
περιῄρηνται, καταψηφίσασθε, καὶ μὴ πρὸς τοῖς
ἄλλοις οἷς ὕβρισθε (οὐ γὰρ ἔγωγ' οἶδ' ὅ τι χρὴ
λέγειν ἄλλο) καὶ ὑπὲρ ὧν οὗτοι δεδωροδοκήκασιν
ὑμεῖς τὴν ἀρὰν καὶ τὴν ἐπιορκίαν οἴκαδ' ἀπενέγ-
κησθε.
221   Ἔτι τοίνυν κἀκεῖνο σκοπεῖτ', ὦ ἄνδρες δικασταί,
τίνος ἕνεκ' ἐγὼ μηδὲν ἠδικηκότων τούτων κατηγορεῖν ἂν προειλόμην. οὐ γὰρ εὑρήσετε. ἡδὺ
πολλοὺς ἐχθροὺς ἔχειν; οὐδέ γ' ἀσφαλές. ἀλλ'
ὑπῆρχέ μοι πρὸς τοῦτον ἀπέχθειά τις; οὐδεμία.
τί οὖν; ἐφοβοῦ περὶ σαυτοῦ, καὶ διὰ δειλίαν ταύτην
ἡγήσω σωτηρίαν· καὶ γὰρ ταῦτ' ἀκήκο' αὐτὸν

384

tion as favourable as it is to-day, and with foreknowledge on the assurance of your ambassadors that your allies would be ruined, that the Thebans would gain strength, that Philip would occupy the northern positions, that a basis of attack would be established against you in Euboea, and that everything that has in fact resulted would befall you, you thereupon cheerfully made the peace, by all means acquit Aeschines, and do not crown your other dishonours with the sin of perjury. He has done you no wrong, and I am a madman and a fool to accuse him. But if the truth is otherwise, if they spoke handsomely of Philip and told you that he was the friend of Athens, that he would deliver the Phocians, that he would curb the arrogance of the Thebans, that he would bestow on you many boons of more value than Amphipolis, and would restore Euboea and Oropus, if only he got his peace,—if, I say, by such assertions and such promises they have deceived and deluded you, and wellnigh stripped you of all Attica, find him guilty, and do not reinforce the outrages,—for I can find no better word,—that you have endured, by returning to your homes laden with the curse and the guilt of perjury, for the sake of the bribes that they have pocketed.

You should further ask yourselves, gentlemen of the jury, why, if they were not guilty, I should have gone out of my way to accuse them. You will find no reason. Is it agreeable to have many enemies? It is hardly safe. Perhaps I had an old standing feud with Aeschines? That is not so. "Well, but you were frightened on your own account, and were coward enough to seek this as a way of escape;" for that, I hear, is one of his suggestions. But, by

DEMOSTHENES

λέγειν. καίτοι μηδενός γ' ὄντος, Αἰσχίνη, δεινοῦ
[410] μηδ' ἀδικήματος, ὡς σὺ φῄς. εἰ γὰρ αὖ ταῦτ'
ἐρεῖ, σκοπεῖτ', ὦ ἄνδρες δικασταί, εἰ ἐφ' οἷς ὁ μηδ'
ὁτιοῦν ἀδικῶν ἐφοβούμην ἐγὼ μὴ διὰ τούτους
ἀπόλωμαι, τί τούτους προσήκει παθεῖν τοὺς
222 αὐτοὺς ἠδικηκότας; ἀλλ' οὐ διὰ ταῦτα. ἀλλὰ διὰ
τί σου κατηγορῶ; συκοφαντῶ νὴ Δία, ἵν' ἀργύριον
λάβω παρὰ σοῦ. καὶ πότερον κρεῖττον ἦν μοι
παρὰ Φιλίππου λαβεῖν τοῦ διδόντος πολὺ καὶ
μηδενὸς τούτων ἔλαττον, καὶ φίλον κἀκεῖνον ἔχειν
καὶ τούτους (ἦσαν γὰρ ἄν, ἦσάν μοι φίλοι τῶν
αὐτῶν κεκοινωνηκότι· οὐδὲ γὰρ νῦν ἔχθραν πα-
τρικὴν ἔχουσι πρός με, ἀλλ' ὅτι τῶν πεπραγμένων
οὐ μετέσχηκα), ἢ παρὰ τούτων ἀφ' ὧν εἰλήφασι
μεταιτεῖν, κἀκείνῳ τ' ἐχθρὸν εἶναι καὶ τούτοις;
καὶ τοὺς μὲν αἰχμαλώτους ἐκ τῶν ἰδίων τοσούτων
χρημάτων λύεσθαι, μικρὰ δ' ἀξιοῦν παρὰ τούτων
223 αἰσχρῶς μετ' ἔχθρας λαμβάνειν; οὐκ ἔστι ταῦτα,
ἀλλ' ἀπήγγειλα μὲν τἀληθῆ καὶ ἀπεσχόμην τοῦ
λαβεῖν τοῦ δικαίου καὶ τῆς ἀληθείας ἕνεκα καὶ
τοῦ λοιποῦ βίου, νομίζων, ὥσπερ ἄλλοι τινές, παρ'
ὑμῖν καὶ αὐτὸς ὢν ἐπιεικὴς τιμηθήσεσθαι, καὶ οὐκ
ἀνταλλακτέον εἶναί μοι τὴν πρὸς ὑμᾶς φιλοτιμίαν
οὐδενὸς κέρδους· μισῶ δὲ τούτους, ὅτι μοχθηροὺς
καὶ θεοῖς ἐχθροὺς εἶδον ἐν τῇ πρεσβείᾳ, καὶ ἀπ-
εστέρημαι καὶ τῶν ἰδίων φιλοτιμιῶν διὰ τὴν τούτων
δωροδοκίαν πρὸς ὅλην δυσχερῶς ὑμῶν τὴν πρεσβείαν ἐσχηκότων· κατηγορῶ δὲ νυνὶ καὶ ἐπὶ τὰς
εὐθύνας ἥκω τὸ μέλλον προορώμενος, καὶ βουλόμενος ἀγῶνι καὶ δικαστηρίῳ μοι διωρίσθαι παρ'

your own account, Aeschines, there is no crime, and therefore no jeopardy. If he repeats the insinuation, do you, gentlemen, consider this : in a case where I, who did no wrong whatever, was yet afraid lest these men's conduct should ruin me, what punishment ought they to suffer who were themselves the guilty parties ? However, that was not my reason. Then why am I accusing you ? Perhaps as a common informer, to get money out of you ? Which course was more profitable for me, to take money from Philip, who offered me a great deal,—as much as he gave them,—and so to make friends both with him and with them,—for indeed I might have had their friendship if I had been their accomplice, and even now there is no vendetta between us, only that I had no part in their malpractices,—or to levy blackmail on their takings, and so incur Philip's enmity and theirs ; to spend all my money on the ransom of captives, and then expect to get a trifle back dishonourably and at the cost of their hostility ? The thing is impossible ! No ; I made honest reports ; I kept my hands clean of corruption for the sake of truth and justice and of my future career, believing, as others have believed, that my honesty would be rewarded by your favour, and that my public spirit must never be bartered away for any emolument. I abhor these men because throughout the embassy I found them vicious and ungodly, and because by their corruption I have been robbed of the due reward of my patriotism, through your natural dissatisfaction with the whole business. I now denounce them, and I have attended this scrutiny, because I have a care for the future, and desire a decision recorded in this case and by

ὑμῖν ὅτι τἀναντί' ἐμοὶ καὶ τούτοις πέπρακται.
224 καὶ δέδοικα, δέδοικα (εἰρήσεται γὰρ πάνθ' ἃ φρονῶ
[411] πρὸς ὑμᾶς) μὴ τότε μὲν συνεπισπάσησθ' ἐμὲ
τὸν μηδ' ὁτιοῦν ἀδικοῦντα, νῦν δ' ἀναπεπτωκότες
ἦτε. παντάπασι γάρ, ὦ ἄνδρες Ἀθηναῖοι, ἐκ-
λελύσθαι μοι δοκεῖτε καὶ παθεῖν ἀναμένειν τὰ δεινά,
ἑτέρους δὲ πάσχοντας ὁρῶντες οὐ φυλάττεσθαι,
οὐδὲ φροντίζειν τῆς πόλεως πάλαι κατὰ πολλοὺς
καὶ δεινοὺς τρόπους διαφθειρομένης.

225 Οὐκ οἴεσθε δεινὸν εἶναι καὶ ὑπερφυές; (καὶ γὰρ
εἴ τι σιωπᾶν ἐγνώκειν, λέγειν ἐξάγομαι.) ἴστε
δήπου Πυθοκλέα τουτονὶ τὸν Πυθοδώρου. τούτῳ
πάνυ φιλανθρώπως ἐκεχρήμην ἐγώ, καὶ ἀηδὲς
ἐμοὶ καὶ τούτῳ γέγονεν εἰς τὴν ἡμέραν ταύτην
οὐδέν. οὗτος ἐκτρέπεταί με νῦν ἀπαντῶν, ἀφ' οὗ
πρὸς Φίλιππον ἀφῖκται, κἂν ἀναγκασθῇ που συντυχεῖν, ἀπεπήδησεν εὐθέως, μή τις αὐτὸν ἴδῃ
λαλοῦντ' ἐμοί. μετὰ δ' Αἰσχίνου περιέρχεται
226 τὴν ἀγορὰν κύκλῳ καὶ βουλεύεται. οὐκοῦν δεινόν,
ὦ ἄνδρες Ἀθηναῖοι, καὶ σχέτλιον τοῖς μὲν τὰ
Φιλίππου πράγμαθ' ᾑρημένοις θεραπεύειν οὕτως
ἀκριβῆ τὴν παρ' ἐκείνου πρὸς ἑκάτερ' αἴσθησιν
ὑπάρχειν, ὥσθ' ἕκαστον, ὥσπερ ἂν παρεστηκότος
αὐτοῦ, μηδ' ὧν ἂν ἐνθαδὶ πράξῃ μηδὲν ἡγεῖσθαι
λήσειν, ἀλλὰ φίλους τε νομίζειν οὓς ἂν ἐκείνῳ δοκῇ
καὶ μὴ φίλους ὡσαύτως, τοῖς δὲ πρὸς ὑμᾶς ζῶσι
καὶ τῆς παρ' ὑμῶν τιμῆς γλιχομένοις καὶ μὴ
προδεδωκόσι ταύτην τοσαύτην κωφότητα καὶ
τοσοῦτο σκότος παρ' ὑμῶν ἀπαντᾶν, ὥστε τοῖς
388

this court that my conduct has been exactly opposed to theirs. And yet I am afraid,—for all my thoughts shall be laid open to you,—I am afraid that hereafter you may destroy me with them in despite of my innocence, while to-day you are supine. For indeed, men of Athens, you seem to me to have become altogether slack, idly waiting for the advent of disaster. You see the distresses of others, but take no precaution for yourselves ; you have no thought for the steady and alarming deterioration of your commonwealth.

Do you not think this an extremely dangerous symptom ? (For though I had decided to say nothing, I am tempted to speak out.) Of course you know Pythocles, son of Pythodorus. I was on the most civil terms with him, and there has been no unpleasantness between us to this day. But now, since his visit to Philip, he turns aside whenever he meets me, and if he cannot avoid an encounter, he rushes off as soon as he can for fear he should be seen talking to me, while he will perambulate the whole market-place discussing plans with Aeschines. It is shocking and scandalous, men of Athens, that Philip has such an acute perception of the fidelity or treachery of the men who have made subservience to him their policy, that they all expect that nothing they do even in Athens will escape the master's eye, as though he stood at their very elbow, and that they must needs choose their private friends and enemies in obedience to his wishes ; while those whose lives are devoted to your service, and who covet and have never betrayed the honour that you can bestow, encounter in you such dullness of hearing, such darkness of vision, that here am I to-day

ἀλειτηρίοις τούτοις ἐξ ἴσου νῦν ἔμ' ἀγωνίζεσθαι,
227 καὶ ταῦτα παρ' ὑμῖν τοῖς ἅπαντ' εἰδόσιν. βούλεσθ'
οὖν εἰδέναι καὶ ἀκοῦσαι τὸ τούτων αἴτιον; ἐγὼ δὴ
[412] φράσω, ἀξιῶ δὲ μηδὲν ἄχθεσθαί μοι λέγοντι
τἀληθῆ. ὅτι ἐκεῖνος μὲν ἕν, οἶμαι, σῶμ' ἔχων καὶ
ψυχὴν μίαν παντὶ θυμῷ καὶ φιλεῖ τοὺς ἑαυτὸν εὖ
ποιοῦντας καὶ μισεῖ τοὺς τἀναντία, ὑμῶν δ' ἕκαστος
πρῶτον μὲν οὔτε τὸν εὖ ποιοῦντα τὴν πόλιν αὐτὸν
228 εὖ ποιεῖν ἡγεῖται οὔτε τὸν κακῶς κακῶς, ἀλλ'
ἕτερ' ἐστὶν ἑκάστῳ προυργιαίτερα, ὑφ' ὧν παρ-
άγεσθε πολλάκις, ἔλεος, φθόνος, ὀργή, χαρίσασθαι
τῷ δεηθέντι, ἄλλα μυρία· ἂν γὰρ ἅπαντά τις
ἐκφύγῃ τἆλλα, τούς γ' οὐδένα βουλομένους εἶναι
τοιοῦτον οὐ διαφεύξεται. ἡ δ' ἐφ' ἑκάστου τούτων
ἁμαρτία κατὰ μικρὸν ὑπορρέουσα ἀθρόος τῇ πόλει
βλάβη γίγνεται.
229 Ὧν μηδέν, ὦ ἄνδρες Ἀθηναῖοι, πάθητε τήμερον,
μηδ' ἀφῆτε τοῦτον ὃς ὑμᾶς τηλικαῦτ' ἠδίκηκεν.
καὶ γὰρ ὡς ἀληθῶς τίς ἔσται λόγος περὶ ὑμῶν, εἰ
τοῦτον ἀφήσετε; Ἀθήνηθεν ἐπρέσβευσάν τινες
ὡς Φίλιππον τουτονί, Φιλοκράτης, Αἰσχίνης, Φρύνων, Δημοσθένης. τί οὖν; ὁ μὲν πρὸς τῷ μηδὲν
ἐκ τῆς πρεσβείας λαβεῖν τοὺς αἰχμαλώτους ἐκ
τῶν ἰδίων ἐλύσατο· ὁ δ' ὧν τὰ τῆς πόλεως πράγματα χρημάτων ἀπέδοτο, τούτων πόρνας ἠγόραζε
230 καὶ ἰχθῦς περιιών. καὶ ὁ μὲν τὸν υἱὸν ἔπεμψε
Φιλίππῳ, πρὶν εἰς ἄνδρας ἐγγράψαι, ὁ μιαρὸς
Φρύνων· ὁ δ' οὐδὲν ἀνάξιον οὔτε τῆς πόλεως οὔθ'
αὑτοῦ διεπράξατο. καὶ ὁ μὲν χορηγῶν καὶ τριη-

contending on equal terms with these pernicious persons, even in a court well acquainted with the whole history. Would you like to know the reason? I will tell you, and I trust that you will not take offence at my candour. Philip, I take it, having one body and one soul loves those who help him and hates those who harm him with his whole heart, whereas no one of you regards the benefactor of the commonwealth as his benefactor, or the enemy of the commonwealth as his enemy. Each man has other motives, of more importance to him, and thereby you are often led astray,—compassion, jealousy, resentment, good nature, and a thousand more. For even though a man escape every other danger, he can never wholly escape those who do not want such a person as he is to exist. But, little by little, by accumulation of these errors, the foundation is sapped, and the integrity of public life collapses.

Do not, men of Athens, give way to these motives to-day. Do not acquit the man who has done you such grievous wrong. Think of the story that will be told, if you do acquit him. Once upon a time certain ambassadors went from Athens to see Philip, and their names were Philocrates, Aeschines, Phryno, and Demosthenes. One of them not only made no gain from his mission, but delivered captives at his own expense; but another went about buying harlots and fish with the money for which he had sold his country. One of them, named Phryno, a bold, bad man, sent his son to Philip before he had put him on the list of citizens; but another did not do anything that was unworthy of his country or himself. Though he was still paying for a chorus

ραρχῶν ἔτι καὶ ταῦτ' ᾤετο δεῖν, ἐθελοντὴς ἀναλίσκειν, λύεσθαι, μηδέν' ἐν συμφορᾷ τῶν πολιτῶν
[413] δι' ἔνδειαν περιορᾶν· ὁ δὲ τοσούτου δεῖ τῶν ὑπαρχόντων τιν' αἰχμάλωτον σῶσαι, ὥσθ' ὅλον τόπον
καὶ πλεῖν ἢ μυρίους μὲν ὁπλίτας, ὁμοῦ δὲ χιλίους
ἱππέας τῶν ὑπαρχόντων συμμάχων, ὅπως αἰχμά-
231 λωτοι γένωνται Φιλίππῳ, συμπαρεσκεύασεν. τί
οὖν μετὰ ταῦτα; Ἀθηναῖοι λαβόντες· ᾔδεσαν
μὲν γὰρ πάλαι· τί δαί; τοὺς μὲν χρήματ' εἰληφότας καὶ δῶρα, καὶ καταισχύναντας ἑαυτούς,
τὴν πόλιν, τοὺς ἑαυτῶν παῖδας, ἀφεῖσαν καὶ νοῦν
ἔχειν ἡγοῦντο καὶ τὴν πόλιν εὐθενεῖσθαι. τὸν δὲ
κατηγοροῦντα τί; ἐμβεβροντῆσθαι, τὴν πόλιν
ἀγνοεῖν, οὐκ ἔχειν ὅποι τὰ ἑαυτοῦ ῥίπτῃ.

232   Καὶ τίς, ὦ ἄνδρες Ἀθηναῖοι, τοῦτ' ἰδὼν τὸ
παράδειγμα δίκαιον αὑτὸν παρασχεῖν ἐθελήσει;
τίς προῖκα πρεσβεύειν, εἰ μήτε λαβεῖν μήτε τῶν
εἰληφότων ἀξιοπιστότερον παρ' ὑμῖν εἶναι δοκεῖν
ὑπάρξει; οὐ μόνον κρίνετε τούτους τήμερον, οὔ,
ἀλλὰ καὶ νόμον τίθεσθ' εἰς ἅπαντα τὸν μετὰ ταῦτα
χρόνον, πότερον χρημάτων αἰσχρῶς ὑπὲρ τῶν
ἐχθρῶν πρεσβεύειν ἅπαντας προσήκει ἢ προῖχ'
233 ὑπὲρ ὑμῶν τὰ βέλτιστ' ἀδωροδοκήτως. ἀλλὰ μὴν
περὶ μὲν τῶν ἄλλων οὐδενὸς προσδεῖσθε μάρτυρος·
ὡς δὲ τὸν υἱὸν ἔπεμψεν ὁ Φρύνων, κάλει μοι
τούτων τοὺς μάρτυρας.

Τοῦτον μὲν τοίνυν οὐκ ἔκρινεν Αἰσχίνης, ὅτι τὸν
αὑτοῦ παῖδ' ἐπ' αἰσχύνῃ πρὸς Φίλιππον ἔπεμψεν.
εἰ δέ τις ὢν ἐφ' ἡλικίας ἑτέρου βελτίων τὴν ἰδέαν,

ᵃ *i.e.* performing the "public services" (λῃτουργίαι) of the
choragia and the trierarchia.

and a man-of-war,[a] he thought it only right to spend more money of his own free will, to ransom captives, and to allow none of his countrymen to suffer distress through poverty. But another, instead of delivering any of the Athenians who were already in captivity, helped to bring a whole district, and ten thousand of the infantry and about a thousand of the cavalry of the allies into captivity to Philip. The sequel was that the Athenians caught these bad men, for they knew all about it, and—what do you think ? They released the men who had taken bribes and had disgraced themselves, the city, and their own children, because they thought that they were very sensible men, and that the city was going on nicely ; but they thought that the man who accused them had gone out of his mind, and that he did not understand Athens, and that he did not know even how to fling his money away.

With this example before his eyes, who, men of Athens, will ever wish to prove himself an honest man, or to go on embassy for nothing, if he is neither to make money nor to be held more worthy of your confidence than those who have made money ? To-day you are not merely adjudging this case : you are legislating for all future time, whether every ambassador is basely to serve your enemies for hire, or without fee or bribe to give his best service to you. On these matters you need no further witness ; but to prove that Phryno did send his son to Philip, please call the witnesses.

Now Aeschines never prosecuted Phryno for sending his own son to Philip with a dishonourable intention. But if a man [b] in the bloom of his youth

[b] Timarchus.

DEMOSTHENES

μὴ προϊδόμενος τὴν ἐξ ἐκείνης τῆς ὄψεως ὑποψίαν, ἰταμώτερον τῷ μετὰ ταῦτ' ἐχρήσατο βίῳ, τοῦτον [414] ὡς πεπορνευμένον κέκρικεν.

234 Φέρε δὴ περὶ τῆς ἑστιάσεως καὶ τοῦ ψηφίσματος εἴπω· μικροῦ γ', ἃ μάλιστά μ' ἔδει πρὸς ὑμᾶς εἰπεῖν, παρῆλθεν.[1] τῆς πρώτης ἐκείνης πρεσβείας γράφων τὸ προβούλευμ' ἐγὼ καὶ πάλιν ἐν τῷ δήμῳ ταῖς ἐκκλησίαις, ἐν αἷς ἐμέλλετε βουλεύεσθαι περὶ τῆς εἰρήνης, οὐδενὸς οὔτε λόγου πω παρὰ τούτων οὔτ' ἀδικήματος ὄντος φανεροῦ, τὸ νόμιμον ἔθος ποιῶν, καὶ ἐπήνεσα τούτους καὶ εἰς πρυτανεῖον 235 ἐκάλεσα. καὶ νὴ Δί' ἔγωγε καὶ τοὺς παρὰ τοῦ Φιλίππου πρέσβεις ἐξένισα, καὶ πάνυ γ', ὦ ἄνδρες Ἀθηναῖοι, λαμπρῶς· ἐπειδὴ γὰρ ἑώρων αὐτοὺς καὶ ἐπὶ τοῖς τοιούτοις ἐκεῖ σεμνυνομένους ὡς εὐδαίμονας καὶ λαμπρούς, εὐθὺς ἡγούμην ἐν τούτοις πρῶτον αὐτὸς περιεῖναι δεῖν αὐτῶν καὶ μεγαλοψυχότερος φαίνεσθαι. ταῦτα δὴ παρέξεται νῦν οὗτος λέγων ὡς αὐτὸς ἐπήνεσεν ἡμᾶς, αὐτὸς εἱστία 236 τοὺς πρέσβεις, τὸ πότ' οὐ διορίζων. ἔστι δὲ ταῦτα πρὸ τοῦ τὴν πόλιν ἠδικῆσθαί τι καὶ φανεροὺς τούτους πεπρακότας αὐτοὺς γενέσθαι, ὅτ' ἄρτι μὲν ἧκον οἱ πρέσβεις τὸ πρῶτον, ἔδει δ' ἀκοῦσαι τὸν δῆμον τί λέγουσιν, οὐδέπω δ' οὔθ' οὗτος συνερῶν δῆλος ἦν τῷ Φιλοκράτει οὔτ' ἐκεῖνος τοιαῦτα γράψων. ἂν δὴ ταῦτα λέγῃ, μέμνησθε τοὺς χρόνους ὅτι τῶν ἀδικημάτων εἰσὶ πρότεροι. μετὰ ταῦτα δ' οὐδὲν ἐμοὶ πρὸς τούτους οἰκεῖον οὐδὲ κοινὸν γέγονεν. λέγε τὴν μαρτυρίαν.

ΜΑΡΤΥΡΙΑ

[1] παρῆλθεν Y : παρῆλθον Shill. with S and most mss.

was more comely than others, and if, disregarding the suspicion that his personal charm might provoke, he has lived rather recklessly in later years, Aeschines must needs proceed against that man for immorality.

Now let me say a word about my entertainment and my decree. I had nearly forgotten those all-important topics ! When I was drafting the provisional resolution of the Council respecting the earlier embassy, and again in addressing the people at the Assemblies that were held to discuss the terms of peace, I followed the usual custom, and included a vote of thanks and an invitation to the public mess-table ; for at that time no wrongful word or act of theirs had been disclosed. It is also true that I entertained Philip's ambassadors, and did the thing very handsomely ; for, having observed in their own country that they take pride in such hospitality as evidence of wealth and splendour, I thought it my duty to outdo them with a more striking display of munificence. On the strength of these incidents, Aeschines will tell you : " Demosthenes thanked us, and entertained the ambassadors himself "—without marking the distinction of time. All this took place before the country had suffered wrong, and before it was evident that the envoys had sold themselves, immediately after the first return of the envoys, when the people had still to hear their report, and when it was not yet known that Aeschines would support Philocrates, or that Philocrates would move such a resolution. If he mentions the incidents, bear in mind that the dates were earlier than their offences, and that I have never since had any intimacy or any association with them. Read the deposition.

(The Deposition is read)

237 "Ισως τοίνυν ἀδελφὸς αὐτῷ συνερεῖ Φιλοχάρης
καὶ Ἀφόβητος· πρὸς οὓς ἀμφοτέρους ὑμῖν πολλὰ
[415] καὶ δίκαι᾽ ἔστιν εἰπεῖν· ἀνάγκη δ᾽, ὦ ἄνδρες
Ἀθηναῖοι, μετὰ παρρησίας διαλεχθῆναι, μηδὲν
ὑποστελλόμενον. ἡμεῖς, Ἀφόβητε καὶ σὺ Φιλό-
χαρες, σὲ μὲν τὰς ἀλαβαστοθήκας γράφοντα καὶ τὰ
τύμπανα, τούτους δ᾽ ὑπογραμματέας καὶ τοὺς
τυχόντας ἀνθρώπους (καὶ οὐδεμιᾶς κακίας ταῦτα,
ἀλλ᾽ οὐ στρατηγίας γ᾽ ἄξια) πρεσβειῶν, στρατη-
238 γιῶν, τῶν μεγίστων τιμῶν ἠξιώσαμεν. εἰ τοίνυν
μηδὲν ὑμῶν ἠδίκει μηδείς, οὐχ ἡμεῖς χάριν ὑμῖν
οὐδενός, ἀλλ᾽ ὑμεῖς ἡμῖν δικαίως ἂν εἴχετε τούτων·
πολλοὺς γὰρ ὑμῶν μᾶλλον ἀξίους τιμᾶσθαι παρέντες
ἡμεῖς ὑμᾶς ἐσεμνύνομεν. εἰ δὲ δὴ καὶ ἐν αὐτοῖς
οἷς ἐτιμᾶσθ᾽ ἠδίκηκέ τις ὑμῶν, καὶ ταῦτα τοιαῦτα,
πόσῳ μᾶλλον ἂν μισοῖσθε δικαίως ἢ σῴζοισθε;
ἐγὼ μὲν οἶμαι πολλῷ. βιάσονται τοίνυν ἴσως,
μεγαλόφωνοι καὶ ἀναιδεῖς ὄντες, καὶ τὸ " συγ-
239 γνώμη ἀδελφῷ βοηθεῖν " προσειληφότες. ὑμεῖς
δὲ μὴ ἡττᾶσθε, ἐκεῖν᾽ ἐνθυμούμενοι ὅτι τούτοις
μὲν τούτου προσήκει φροντίζειν, ὑμῖν δὲ τῶν
νόμων καὶ ὅλης τῆς πόλεως καὶ παρὰ πάντα τῶν
ὅρκων, οὓς αὐτοὶ κάθησθ᾽ ὀμωμοκότες. καὶ γὰρ
εἰ τινῶν δεδέηνται τουτονὶ σῴζειν, πότερ᾽ ἂν
μηδὲν ἀδικῶν φαίνηται τὴν πόλιν ἢ κἂν ἀδικῶν,
σκοπεῖτε. εἰ μὲν γὰρ ἂν μή, κἀγώ φημι δεῖν, εἰ
δ᾽ ὅλως κἂν ὁτιοῦν, ἐπιορκεῖν δεδέηνται. οὐ γὰρ
εἰ κρύβδην ἐστὶν ἡ ψῆφος, λήσει τοὺς θεούς, ἀλλὰ
τοῦτο καὶ πάντων ἄρισθ᾽ ὁ τιθεὶς τὸν νόμον εἶδε
396

Perhaps he will find a brother to speak for him, Philochares or Aphobetus ; to both of whom there is much that you can say with justice. (One must converse quite frankly, without any reserve.) We, Aphobetus and Philochares, although you, Philochares, were a painter of alabaster boxes and tambourines, and your brothers ordinary people, junior clerks and the like,—respectable occupations, but hardly suitable for commanding officers,—we, I say, dignified you with embassies, commands as generals, and other high distinctions. Even if none of the family had committed any crime, you would have no claim on our gratitude, but we should have a large claim on yours ; for we passed over many much more worthy claimants, and glorified you. But if in the actual enjoyment of those dignities one of you has committed a crime, and such a crime as this, do you not all deserve abhorrence much more than deliverance ? That is my view. However, they will storm and bluster,—for they have very loud voices and very little modesty,—and will remind you that " it is no sin to help your kin." Do not give way to them. It is their business to think of Aeschines ; it is your business to think of the laws, of the whole commonwealth, and above all of the oath in virtue of which you sit in that box. If they have besought any of you to deliver him, ask yourselves whether they mean in case he is not, or in case he is, guilty of a crime against the common weal. If they mean in case he is not guilty, I admit the plea ; but if they mean, deliver him in any case, they have entreated you to perjure yourselves. For though the vote is secret, it will not escape the eye of Heaven. The legislator wisely discerned herein

τὸ κρύβδην ψηφίζεσθαι, ὅτι τούτων μὲν οὐδεὶς
εἴσεται τὸν ἑαυτῷ κεχαρισμένον ὑμῶν, οἱ θεοὶ δ᾽
[416] εἴσονται καὶ τὸ δαιμόνιον τὸν μὴ τὰ δίκαια ψηφι-
240 σάμενον. παρ᾽ ὧν κρεῖττόν ἐστιν ἑκάστῳ τὰς
ἀγαθὰς ἐλπίδας τοῖς παισὶ καὶ ἑαυτῷ, τὰ δίκαια
γνόντα καὶ τὰ προσήκοντα, περιποιήσασθαι, ἢ τὴν
ἀφανῆ καὶ ἄδηλον χάριν τούτοις καταθέσθαι, καὶ
ἀφεῖναι τοῦτον ὃς αὐτὸς ἑαυτοῦ καταμεμαρτύρηκεν.
τίνα γάρ, Αἰσχίνη, μάρτυρα μείζω παράσχωμαι
τοῦ πολλὰ καὶ δεινὰ πεπρεσβεῦσθαί σοι ἢ σὲ κατὰ
σαυτοῦ; ὃς γὰρ ᾠήθης χρῆναι τὸν φανερόν τι
ποιῆσαι βουληθέντα τῶν σοὶ πεπρεσβευμένων τη-
λικαύτῃ καὶ τοιαύτῃ συμφορᾷ περιβαλεῖν, δῆλον
ὅτι δεινὸν ἄν τι παθεῖν σαυτὸν ἤλπιζες, εἰ πύθοινθ᾽
οὗτοι τὰ πεπραγμένα σοι.

241 Τοῦτο τοίνυν, ἄνπερ ὑμεῖς εὖ φρονῆτε, καθ᾽
αὑτοῦ συμβήσεται τούτῳ πεπρᾶχθαι, οὐ μόνον
κατὰ τοῦθ᾽ ὅτι παμμέγεθες σημεῖόν ἐστι τῶν πεπρεσβευμένων, ἀλλ᾽ ὅτι καὶ κατηγορῶν ἐκείνους
τοὺς λόγους εἶπεν οἳ κατ᾽ αὐτοῦ νῦν ὑπάρχουσιν· ἃ
γὰρ ὡρίσω σὺ δίκαια, ὅτε Τίμαρχον ἔκρινες, ταὐτὰ
δήπου ταῦτα καὶ κατὰ σοῦ προσήκει τοῖς ἄλλοις
242 ἰσχύειν. ἔλεγε τοίνυν τότε πρὸς τοὺς δικαστὰς
ὅτι ἀπολογήσεται δὲ Δημοσθένης ὑπὲρ αὐτοῦ, καὶ
κατηγορήσει τῶν ἐμοὶ πεπρεσβευμένων· εἶτ᾽, ἂν
ὑμᾶς ἀπαγάγῃ τῷ λόγῳ, νεανιεύσεται καὶ περιιὼν ἐρεῖ· πῶς; τί; τοὺς δικαστὰς ἀπαγαγὼν
ἀπὸ τῆς ὑποθέσεως ᾠχόμην τὸ πρᾶγμ᾽ αὐτῶν
ὑφελόμενος. μὴ σύ γε, ἀλλ᾽ ὑπὲρ ὧν ἀγωνίζει,
περὶ τούτων ἀπολογοῦ· τότε δ᾽, ἡνίκ᾽ ἐκεῖνον

the essence of secret voting, that no suppliant shall know the name of the juror who has granted his prayer, but the gods and the divine spirit will know him who has cast an unrighteous vote. Far better for each of you to make good his hopes of the blessing of Heaven for himself and his children, by recording a righteous and a dutiful verdict, than to bestow on these men a secret and unacknowledged favour, and acquit a man convicted by his own testimony. For what more powerful evidence, Aeschines, can I adduce for the many crimes of your embassy than the evidence you have given against yourself? You, who thought it necessary to implicate in so grievous a calamity one who purposed to bring a part of your misconduct to light, must surely have expected a terrible retribution if the jury should learn the true history of your deeds.

If you are wise, that performance of his will now be turned to his disadvantage, not only because it was a powerful indication of his misconduct, but because he employed in his prosecution arguments that are now valid against himself. For surely the principles which you, Aeschines, laid down when you prosecuted Timarchus ought to have equal weight for others against you. Now on that occasion he observed to the jury : " Demosthenes will conduct this man's defence, and will denounce my conduct of the embassy ; and then, if he leads you astray by his speech, he will go about in his conceited way, and boast : ' How did I do it? What did I say? Why, I led the jury clean away from the question ; filched the whole case from them, and came off triumphant.' " Then do not follow my example : address your defence to the real issue. You had

ἔκρινες, ἐξῆν σοι κατηγορεῖν καὶ λέγειν ὅ τι
ἐβούλου.
243 Ἀλλὰ μὴν καὶ ἔπη[1] τοῖς δικασταῖς ἔλεγες, οὐδένα
[417] μάρτυρ᾽ ἔχων ἐφ᾽ οἷς ἔκρινες τὸν ἄνθρωπον παρα-
σχέσθαι·

φήμη δ᾽ οὔ τις πάμπαν ἀπόλλυται, ἥντινα λαοὶ
πολλοὶ φημίξωσι· θεός νύ τίς ἐστι καὶ αὐτή.

οὐκοῦν, Αἰσχίνη, καὶ σὲ πάντες οὗτοι χρήματ᾽ ἐκ
τῆς πρεσβείας φασὶν εἰληφέναι, ὥστε καὶ κατὰ σοῦ
δήπουθεν "φήμη δ᾽ οὔ τις πάμπαν ἀπόλλυται,
244 ἥντινα λαοὶ πολλοὶ φημίξωσιν." ὅσῳ γὰρ αὖ σὲ
πλείους ἢ ἐκεῖνον αἰτιῶνται, θεώρησον ὡς εἴσει.[2]
τὸν μὲν Τίμαρχον οὐδ᾽ οἱ πρόσχωροι πάντες ἐγίγ-
νωσκον, ὑμᾶς δὲ τοὺς πρέσβεις οὐδεὶς Ἑλλήνων
οὐδὲ βαρβάρων ἔσθ᾽ ὅστις οὔ φησι χρήματ᾽ ἐκ
τῆς πρεσβείας εἰληφέναι. ὥστ᾽, εἴπερ ἐστ᾽ ἀληθὴς
ἡ φήμη, καθ᾽ ὑμῶν ἐστιν ἡ παρὰ τῶν πολλῶν, ἣν
ὅτι πιστὴν εἶναι δεῖ καὶ "θεός νύ τίς ἐστι καὶ αὐτή,"
καὶ ὅτι σοφὸς ἦν ὁ ποιητὴς ὁ ταῦτα ποιήσας,
σὺ διώρισας αὐτός.
245 Ἔτι τοίνυν ἰαμβεῖα δήπου συλλέξας ἐπέραινεν,
οἷον

ὅστις δ᾽ ὁμιλῶν ἥδεται κακοῖς ἀνήρ,
οὐ πώποτ᾽ ἠρώτησα, γιγνώσκων ὅτι
τοιοῦτός ἐστιν οἷσπερ ἥδεται ξυνών.

εἶτα τὸν εἰς τοὺς ὄρνεις εἰσιόντα καὶ μετὰ Πιττα-
λάκου περιόντα, καὶ τοιαῦτ᾽ εἰπών, ἀγνοεῖτ᾽, ἔφη,
ποῖόν τιν᾽ ἡγεῖσθαι δεῖ; οὐκοῦν, Αἰσχίνη, καὶ κατὰ

1 ἔπη Weil: ἐπὶ Shill. with mss.
2 εἴσει Butcher: εἴσῃ S: ἔχει Shill. and edd., with corrector of S.
400

your opportunity of denouncing and saying what you chose when you were the prosecutor.

Moreover, having no witnesses to produce in support of your accusations, you quoted verses to the jury:

> Rumour, that many people spread abroad,
> Dieth not wholly: Rumour is a god.[a]

And now, Aeschines, everybody says that you made money out of your embassy; so, of course, as against you, the rumour that many people spread abroad does not wholly die. That you may understand how far more numerous are your accusers than those of Timarchus, observe this. He was not known even to all his neighbours; but there is not a man in Greece or in foreign parts who does not aver that you ambassadors made gain of your embassy. If rumour is true, the rumour of the multitude is against you; and for the veracity, and even the divinity, of rumour, and for the wisdom of the poet who composed these verses, we have your own assurance.

After these heroics he naturally proceeds to collect and declaim some iambic poetry, for instance:

> Whoso delights to walk with wicked men,
> Of him I ask not, for I know him such
> As are the men whose converse pleases him.

Then follows the passage about "the man who frequented cockpits, and consorted with Pittalacus," and so forth; "do you not know what his character is?" Well, Aeschines, your iambics shall now serve

[a] From Hesiod, *Works and Days*, 761.

σοῦ τὰ ἰαμβεῖα ταῦθ' ἁρμόσει νῦν ἐμοί, κἂν ἐγὼ
λέγω πρὸς τούτους, ὀρθῶς καὶ προσηκόντως ἐρῶ,
ὅστις δ' ὁμιλῶν ἥδεται, καὶ ταῦτα πρεσβεύων,
Φιλοκράτει, οὐ πώποτ' ἠρώτησα, γιγνώσκων ὅτι
ἀργύριον εἴληφ' οὗτος, ὥσπερ Φιλοκράτης ὁ ὁμολογῶν.

246   Λογογράφους τοίνυν καὶ σοφιστὰς ἀποκαλῶν
[418] τοὺς ἄλλους καὶ ὑβρίζειν πειρώμενος, αὐτὸς ἐξελεγ-
χθήσεται τούτοις ὢν ἔνοχος. ταῦτα μὲν γὰρ τὰ
ἰαμβεῖ' ἐκ Φοίνικός ἐστιν Εὐριπίδου· τοῦτο δὲ
τὸ δρᾶμ' οὐδεπώποτ' οὔτε Θεόδωρος οὔτ' Ἀριστόδημος ὑπεκρίναντο, οἷς οὗτος τὰ τρίτα λέγων
διετέλεσεν, ἀλλὰ Μόλων ἠγωνίζετο καὶ εἰ δή τις
ἄλλος τῶν παλαιῶν ὑποκριτῶν. Ἀντιγόνην δὲ
Σοφοκλέους πολλάκις μὲν Θεόδωρος, πολλάκις δ'
Ἀριστόδημος ὑποκέκριται, ἐν ᾗ πεποιημέν' ἰαμβεῖα καλῶς καὶ συμφερόντως ὑμῖν πολλάκις αὐτὸς
εἰρηκὼς καὶ ἀκριβῶς ἐξεπιστάμενος παρέλιπεν.
247 ἴστε γὰρ δήπου τοῦθ', ὅτι ἐν ἅπασι τοῖς δράμασι
τοῖς τραγικοῖς ἐξαίρετόν ἐστιν ὥσπερ γέρας τοῖς
τριταγωνισταῖς τὸ τοὺς τυράννους καὶ τοὺς τὰ
σκῆπτρ' ἔχοντας εἰσιέναι. ταῦτα τοίνυν ἐν τῷ
δράματι τούτῳ σκέψασθ' ὁ Κρέων Αἰσχίνης οἷα
λέγων πεποίηται τῷ ποιητῇ, ἃ οὔτε πρὸς αὑτὸν
οὗτος ὑπὲρ τῆς πρεσβείας διελέχθη οὔτε πρὸς τοὺς
δικαστὰς εἶπεν. λέγε.

ΙΑΜΒΕΙΑ ΣΟΦΟΚΛΕΟΥΣ ΕΞ ΑΝΤΙΓΟΝΗΣ

ἀμήχανον δὲ παντὸς ἀνδρὸς ἐκμαθεῖν
ψυχήν τε καὶ φρόνημα καὶ γνώμην, πρὶν ἂν
ἀρχαῖς τε καὶ νόμοισιν ἐντριβὴς φανῇ.

my turn for an observation about you. I shall be speaking with the propriety of the Tragic Muse, when I say to the jury : Whoso delights to walk (especially on an embassy) with Philocrates, of him I ask not, for I know him well—to have taken bribes, as Philocrates did, who made confession.

Well, when he tries to insult other people by calling them speech-makers and charlatans, he shall be shown to be open to the same reproach. For those iambics come from the *Phoenix* of Euripides. That play was never acted by Theodorus or Aristodemus, for whom Aeschines commonly took the inferior parts ; Molon however produced it, and perhaps some other players of the old school. But Sophocles' *Antigone* was frequently acted by Theodorus, and also by Aristodemus ; and in that play there are some iambic lines, admirably and most instructively composed. That passage Aeschines omitted to quote, though he has often spoken the lines, and knows them by heart ; for of course you are aware that, in all tragic dramas, it is the enviable privilege of third-rate actors to come on as tyrants, carrying their royal sceptres. Now you shall weigh the merits of the verses which were specially written by the poet for the character of Creon-Aeschines, though he forgot to repeat them to himself in connexion with his embassy, and did not quote them to the jury. Read.

Iambics from the Antigone of Sophocles [a]

Who shall appraise the spirit of a man,
His mind, his temper, till he hath been proved
In ministry of laws and government?

[a] ll. 175-190.

ἐμοὶ γὰρ ὅστις πᾶσαν εὐθύνων πόλιν
μὴ τῶν ἀρίστων ἅπτεται βουλευμάτων,   5
ἀλλ᾽ ἐκ φόβου τοῦ γλῶσσαν ἐγκλείσας ἔχει,
κάκιστος εἶναι νῦν τε καὶ πάλαι δοκεῖ·
καὶ μεῖζον᾽ ὅστις ἀντὶ τῆς αὑτοῦ πάτρας

[419] φίλον νομίζει, τοῦτον οὐδαμοῦ λέγω.
ἐγὼ γάρ, ἴστω Ζεὺς ὁ πάνθ᾽ ὁρῶν ἀεί,   10
οὔτ᾽ ἂν σιωπήσαιμι τὴν ἄτην ὁρῶν
στείχουσαν ἀστοῖς ἀντὶ τῆς σωτηρίας,
οὔτ᾽ ἂν φίλον ποτ᾽ ἄνδρα δυσμενῆ χθονὸς
θείμην ἐμαυτῷ, τοῦτο γιγνώσκων ὅτι
ἥδ᾽ ἐστὶν ἡ σῴζουσα, καὶ ταύτης ἔπι   15
πλέοντες ὀρθῆς τοὺς φίλους ποιούμεθα.

248 Τούτων οὐδὲν Αἰσχίνης εἶπε πρὸς αὐτὸν ἐν τῇ
πρεσβείᾳ, ἀλλ᾽ ἀντὶ μὲν τῆς πόλεως τὴν Φιλίππου
ξενίαν καὶ φιλίαν πολλῷ μεῖζον᾽ ἡγήσαθ᾽ αὑτῷ καὶ
λυσιτελεστέραν, ἐρρῶσθαι πολλὰ φράσας τῷ σοφῷ
Σοφοκλεῖ, τὴν δ᾽ ἄτην ὁρῶν στείχουσαν ὁμοῦ, τὴν
ἐπὶ Φωκέας στρατείαν, οὐ προεῖπεν οὐδὲ προ-
εξήγγειλεν, ἀλλὰ τοὐναντίον συνέκρυψε καὶ συν-
έπραξε καὶ τοὺς βουλομένους εἰπεῖν διεκώλυσεν,
249 οὐκ ἀναμνησθεὶς ὅτι ἥδ᾽ ἐστὶν ἡ σῴζουσα καὶ
ταύτης ἔπι τελοῦσα μὲν ἡ μήτηρ αὐτοῦ καὶ καθ-
αίρουσα καὶ καρπουμένη τὰς τῶν χρωμένων οὐσίας ἐξέθρεψε τοσούτους τουτουσί, διδάσκων δ᾽ ὁ
πατὴρ γράμματα, ὡς ἐγὼ τῶν πρεσβυτέρων ἀκούω,
πρὸς τῷ τοῦ Ἥρω τοῦ ἰατροῦ, ὅπως ἐδύνατο, ἀλλ᾽
οὖν ἐν ταύτῃ γ᾽ ἕξῃ, ὑπογραμματεύοντες δ᾽ αὐτοὶ
καὶ ὑπηρετοῦντες ἁπάσαις ταῖς ἀρχαῖς ἀργύριον
εἰλήφεσαν, καὶ τὸ τελευταῖον ὑφ᾽ ὑμῶν γραμματεῖς

ᵃ Heros the physician: or, the Hero Physician; see
De cor. 129, and note.

I hold, and long have held, that man a knave
Who, standing at the helm of state, deserts
The wisest counsel, or in craven fear
Of any, sets a curb upon his lips.
Who puts his friend above his fatherland
I scorn as nothing worth ; and for myself,
Witness all-seeing Heaven ! I will not hold
My peace when I descry the curse that comes
To sap my citizens' security ;
Nor will I count as kin my country's foes ;
For well I wot our country is the ship
That saves us all, sailing on even keel :
Embarked in her we fear no dearth of friends.

Aeschines did not quote any of these lines for his own instruction on his embassy. He put the hospitality and friendship of Philip far above his country, —and found it more profitable. He bade a long farewell to the sage Sophocles ; and when he saw the curse that came,—to wit, the army advancing upon the Phocians,—he sounded no warning, sent no timely report ; rather he helped both to conceal and to execute the design, and obstructed those who were ready to tell the truth. He forgot the ship that saves ; forgot that embarked in her his own mother, performing her rites, scouring her candidates, making her pittance from the substance of her employers, here reared her hopeful brood to greatness. Here, too, his father, who kept an infant-school, lived as best he could,—next door to Heros the physician,[a] as I am told by elderly informants,— anyhow, he lived in this city. The offspring of this pair earned a little money as junior clerks and messengers in the public offices, until, by your

χειροτονηθέντες δύ ἔτη διετράφησαν ἐν τῇ θόλῳ,
πρεσβεύων δ' ἀπέσταλτο νῦν οὗτος ἐκ ταύτης.
250 τούτων οὐδὲν ἐσκέψατο, οὐδ' ὅπως ὀρθὴ πλεύσεται
προείδετο, ἀλλ' ἀνέτρεψε καὶ κατέδυσε καὶ τὸ
[420] καθ' αὑτὸν ὅπως ἐπὶ τοῖς ἐχθροῖς ἔσται παρ-
εσκεύασεν. εἶτ' οὐ σὺ σοφιστής; καὶ πονηρός γε.
οὐ σὺ λογογράφος; καὶ θεοῖς ἐχθρός γε· ὃς ἃ μὲν
πολλάκις ἠγωνίσω καὶ ἀκριβῶς ἐξηπίστασο, ὑπερ-
έβης, ἃ δ' οὐδεπώποτ' ἐν τῷ βίῳ ὑπεκρίνω, ταῦτα
ζητήσας ἐπὶ τῷ τῶν πολιτῶν βλάψαι τιν' εἰς μέσον
ἤνεγκας.
251   Φέρε δὴ καὶ περὶ τοῦ Σόλωνος ὃν εἶπε λόγον σκέψασθε. ἔφη τὸν Σόλων' ἀνακεῖσθαι τῆς τῶν τότε
δημηγορούντων σωφροσύνης παράδειγμα, εἴσω τὴν
χεῖρ' ἔχοντ' ἀναβεβλημένον, ἐπιπλήττων τι καὶ
λοιδορούμενος τῇ τοῦ Τιμάρχου προπετείᾳ. καίτοι
τὸν μὲν ἀνδριάντα τοῦτον οὔπω πεντήκοντ' ἔτη
φασὶν ἀνακεῖσθαι Σαλαμίνιοι, ἀπὸ Σόλωνος δ'
ὁμοῦ διακόσι' ἐστὶν ἔτη καὶ τετταράκοντ' εἰς τὸν
νυνὶ παρόντα χρόνον, ὥσθ' ὁ δημιουργὸς ὁ τοῦτο
πλάσας τὸ σχῆμα οὐ μόνον οὐκ αὐτὸς ἦν κατ'
252 ἐκεῖνον, ἀλλ' οὐδ' ὁ πάππος αὐτοῦ. τοῦτο μὲν
τοίνυν εἶπε τοῖς δικασταῖς καὶ ἐμιμήσατο· ὃ δὲ
τοῦ σχήματος ἦν τούτου πολλῷ τῇ πόλει λυσιτε-
λέστερον, τὸ τὴν ψυχὴν τὴν Σόλωνος ἰδεῖν καὶ τὴν
διάνοιαν, ταύτην οὐκ ἐμιμήσατο, ἀλλὰ πᾶν τοὐναντίον. ἐκεῖνος μέν γ' ἀφεστηκυίας Σαλαμῖνος Ἀθηναίων καὶ θάνατον ζημίαν ψηφισαμένων, ἄν τις

ᵃ The Prytaneum or Town Hall.

favour, they became full-fledged clerks, with free
maintenance for two years in the Rotunda.[a] Finally,
from this same city Aeschines received his commission
as ambassador. He cared for none of these obligations ; he took no thought that the ship of state
should sail on even keel ; he scuttled her and sank
her, and so far as in him lay put her at the mercy
of her foes. Are not you then a charlatan ? Yes,
and a vile one too. Are not you a speech-writer ?
Yes, and an unprincipled one to boot. You passed
over the speech that you so often spoke on the
stage, and knew by heart ; you hunted up rant that
in all your career you had never declaimed in character, and revived it for the undoing of your own
fellow-citizen.

Let us now turn to his remarks about Solon. By
way of censure and reproach of the impetuous style
of Timarchus, he alleged that a statue of Solon,
with his robe drawn round him and his hand enfolded,
had been set up to exemplify the self-restraint of
the popular orators of that generation. People who
live at Salamis, however, inform us that this statue
was erected less than fifty years ago. Now from
the age of Solon to the present day about two
hundred and forty years have elapsed, so that the
sculptor who designed that disposition of drapery
had not lived in Solon's time,—nor even his grand-
father. He illustrated his remarks by representing
to the jury the attitude of the statue ; but his mimi-
cry did not include what, politically, would have
been much more profitable than an attitude,—a
view of Solon's spirit and purpose, so widely different
from his own. When Salamis had revolted, and the
Athenian people had forbidden under penalty of

DEMOSTHENES

εἴπῃ κομίζεσθαι, τὸν ἴδιον κίνδυνον ὑποθεὶς ἐλεγεῖα
ποιήσας ᾖδε, καὶ τὴν μὲν χώραν ἀνέσωσε¹ τῇ πόλει,
253 τὴν δ' ὑπάρχουσαν αἰσχύνην ἀπήλλαξεν· οὗτος δ',
ἣν βασιλεὺς καὶ πάντες οἱ Ἕλληνες ὑμετέραν
ἔγνωσαν, Ἀμφίπολιν, ταύτην ἐξέδωκε καὶ ἀπέδοτο
[421] καὶ τῷ ταῦτα γράφοντι συνεῖπε Φιλοκράτει. ἄξιόν
γ', οὐ γάρ; ἦν Σόλωνος αὐτῷ μεμνῆσθαι. καὶ
οὐ μόνον ἐνταῦθα ταῦτ' ἐποίησεν, ἀλλὰ κἀκεῖσ'
ἐλθὼν οὐδὲ τοὔνομ' ἐφθέγξατο τῆς χώρας ὑπὲρ
ἧς ἐπρέσβευεν. καὶ ταῦτ' αὐτὸς ἀπήγγειλε πρὸς
ὑμᾶς· μέμνησθε γὰρ δήπου λέγοντ' αὐτὸν ὅτι
"περὶ δ' Ἀμφιπόλεως εἶχον μὲν κἀγὼ λέγειν·
ἵνα δ' ἐγγένηται Δημοσθένει περὶ αὐτῆς εἰπεῖν, παρ-
254 έλιπον." ἐγὼ δὲ παρελθὼν οὐδὲν ἔφην τοῦτον² ὧν
ἐβούλετ' εἰπεῖν πρὸς Φίλιππον ἐμοὶ παραλιπεῖν·
θᾶττον γὰρ ἂν τοῦ αἵματος ἢ λόγου μεταδοῦναί
τινι. ἀλλ', οἶμαι, χρήματ' εἰληφότ' οὐκ ἦν ἀντιλέγειν πρὸς Φίλιππον τὸν ὑπὲρ τούτου δεδωκότα,
ὅπως ἐκείνην μὴ ἀποδῷ. λέγε δή μοι λαβὼν καὶ
τὰ τοῦ Σόλωνος ἐλεγεῖα ταυτί, ἵν' ἴδηθ' ὅτι καὶ
Σόλων ἐμίσει τοὺς οἷος οὗτος ἀνθρώπους.

255 Οὐ λέγειν εἴσω τὴν χεῖρ' ἔχοντ', Αἰσχίνη, δεῖ, οὔ,
ἀλλὰ πρεσβεύειν εἴσω τὴν χεῖρ' ἔχοντα. σὺ δ'
ἐκεῖ προτείνας καὶ ὑποσχὼν καὶ καταισχύνας
τούτους ἐνθάδε σεμνολογεῖ, καὶ λογάρια δύστηνα
μελετήσας καὶ φωνασκήσας οὐκ οἴει δίκην δώσειν
τηλικούτων καὶ τοσούτων ἀδικημάτων, ἂν πιλίδιον

¹ ἀνέσωσε Herwerden : ἔσωσε Shill. with mss.
² τοῦτον A : τούτων Shill. with rest of mss.

408

death any proposal for its recovery, Solon, accepting the risk of death, composed and recited an elegiac poem, and so retrieved that country for Athens and removed a standing dishonour. Aeschines, on the other hand, gave away and sold Amphipolis, a city which the King of Persia and all Greece recognized as yours, speaking in support of the resolution moved by Philocrates. It was highly becoming in him, was it not ? to remind us of Solon ! Not content with this performance at home, he went to Macedonia, and never mentioned the place with which his mission was concerned. So he stated in his own report, for no doubt you remember how he said : " I, too, had something to say about Amphipolis, but I left it out to give Demosthenes a chance of dealing with that subject." I rose and told you that he had never once left to me anything that he wanted to say to Philip : he would sooner give a man a share of his life-blood than a share of his speech. The truth is that, having accepted money, he could hardly confront Philip, who gave him the money on purpose that he might not restore Amphipolis. Now, please, take and read these elegiac verses of Solon, to show the jury how Solon detested people like the defendant.

What we require, Aeschines, is not oratory with enfolded hands, but diplomacy with enfolded hands. But in Macedonia you held out your hands, turned them palm upwards, and brought shame upon your countrymen, and then here at home you talk magniloquently ; you practise and declaim some miserable fustian, and think to escape the due penalty of your heinous crimes, if you only don your

λαβὼν ἐπὶ τὴν κεφαλὴν περινοστῇς καὶ ἐμοὶ
λοιδορῇ. λέγε σύ.

ΕΛΕΓΕΙΑ

Ἡμετέρα δὲ πόλις κατὰ μὲν Διὸς οὔποτ᾽ ὀλεῖται
αἶσαν καὶ μακάρων θεῶν φρένας ἀθανάτων·
τοίη γὰρ μεγάθυμος ἐπίσκοπος ὀβριμοπάτρη
Παλλὰς ᾿Αθηναίη χεῖρας ὕπερθεν ἔχει.
αὐτοὶ δὲ φθείρειν μεγάλην πόλιν ἀφραδίησιν   5
[422]   ἀστοὶ βούλονται, χρήμασι πειθόμενοι,
δήμου θ᾽ ἡγεμόνων ἄδικος νόος, οἷσιν ἑτοῖμον
ὕβριος ἐκ μεγάλης ἄλγεα πολλὰ παθεῖν.
οὐ γὰρ ἐπίστανται κατέχειν κόρον, οὐδὲ παρούσας
εὐφροσύνας κοσμεῖν δαιτὸς ἐν ἡσυχίῃ.   10

πλουτοῦσιν δ᾽ ἀδίκοις ἔργμασι πειθόμενοι
. . . .
οὔθ᾽ ἱερῶν κτεάνων οὔτε τι δημοσίων
φειδόμενοι κλέπτουσιν ἐφ᾽ ἁρπαγῇ ἄλλοθεν ἄλλος, 15
οὐδὲ φυλάσσονται σεμνὰ Δίκης θέμεθλα,
ἣ σιγῶσα σύνοιδε τὰ γιγνόμενα πρό τ᾽ ἐόντα,
τῷ δὲ χρόνῳ πάντως ἦλθ᾽ ἀποτεισαμένη.
τοῦτ᾽ ἤδη πάσῃ πόλει ἔρχεται ἕλκος ἄφυκτον,
εἰς δὲ κακὴν ταχέως ἤλυθε δουλοσύνην,   20
ἣ στάσιν ἔμφυλον πόλεμόν θ᾽ εὕδοντ᾽ ἐπέγειρει,
ὃς πολλῶν ἐρατὴν ὤλεσεν ἡλικίην.
ἐκ γὰρ δυσμενέων ταχέως πολυήρατον ἄστυ
τρύχεται ἐν συνόδοις τοῖς ἀδικοῦσι φίλους.
ταῦτα μὲν ἐν δήμῳ στρέφεται κακά· τῶν δὲ πενι-
χρῶν   25
ἱκνοῦνται πολλοὶ γαῖαν ἐς ἀλλοδαπήν,
πραθέντες δεσμοῖσί τ᾽ ἀεικελίοισι δεθέντες.

little skull-cap,[a] take your constitutional, and abuse me. Now read.

Solon's Elegiacs

Not by the doom of Zeus, who ruleth all,
Not by the curse of Heaven shall Athens fall.
Strong in her Sire, above the favoured land
Pallas Athene lifts her guardian hand.
No ; her own citizens with counsels vain
Shall work her ruin in their quest of gain ;
Dishonest demagogues her folk misguide,
Foredoomed to suffer for their guilty pride.
Their reckless greed, insatiate of delight,
Knows not to taste the frugal feast aright ;
Th' unbridled lust of gold, their only care,
Nor public wealth nor wealth divine will spare.
Now here, now there, they raven, rob and seize,
Heedless of Justice and her stern decrees,
Who silently the present and the past
Reviews, whose slow revenge o'ertakes at last.
On every home the swift contagion falls,
Till servitude a free-born race enthralls.
Now faction reigns ; now wakes the sword of strife,
And comely youth shall pay its toll of life ;
We waste our strength in conflict with our kin,
And soon our gates shall let the foeman in.
Such woes the factious nation shall endure ;
A fate more hard awaits the hapless poor ;
For them, enslaved, bound with insulting chains,
Captivity in alien lands remains.

---

[a] *skull-cap* : a soft cap commonly worn by invalids ; also, according to Plutarch, by Solon, when he recited his verses on Salamis. Demosthenes ironically pretends that the defendant is still suffering from his sham illness [124].

οὕτω δημόσιον κακὸν ἔρχεται οἴκαδ᾽ ἑκάστῳ,
αὔλειοι δ᾽ ἔτ᾽ ἔχειν οὐκ ἐθέλουσι θύραι,   30
ὑψηλὸν δ᾽ ὑπὲρ ἕρκος ὑπέρθορεν, εὗρε δὲ πάντως,
εἰ καί τις φεύγων ἐν μυχῷ ᾖ[1] θαλάμου.
ταῦτα διδάξαι θυμὸς Ἀθηναίους με κελεύει,
ὡς κακὰ πλεῖστα πόλει δυσνομία παρέχει,
εὐνομία δ᾽ εὔκοσμα καὶ ἄρτια πάντ᾽ ἀποφαίνει, 35
καὶ θαμὰ τοῖς ἀδίκοις ἀμφιτίθησι πέδας,
[423] τραχέα λειαίνει, παύει κόρον, ὕβριν ἀμαυροῖ,
αὐαίνει δ᾽ ἄτης ἄνθεα φυόμενα,
εὐθύνει δὲ δίκας σκολιάς, ὑπερήφανά τ᾽ ἔργα
πραΰνει, παύει δ᾽ ἔργα διχοστασίης,   40
παύει δ᾽ ἀργαλέης ἔριδος χόλον· ἔστι δ᾽ ὑπ᾽ αὐτῆς
πάντα κατ᾽ ἀνθρώπους ἄρτια καὶ πινυτά.

256 Ἀκούετ᾽, ὦ ἄνδρες Ἀθηναῖοι, περὶ τῶν τοιούτων
ἀνθρώπων οἷα Σόλων λέγει, καὶ περὶ τῶν θεῶν, οὕς
φησι τὴν πόλιν σῴζειν. ἐγὼ δ᾽ ἀεὶ μὲν ἀληθῆ τὸν
λόγον τοῦτον ἡγοῦμαι καὶ βούλομαι, ὡς ἄρ᾽ οἱ θεοὶ
σῴζουσιν ἡμῶν τὴν πόλιν· τρόπον δέ τιν᾽ ἡγοῦμαι
καὶ τὰ νῦν συμβεβηκότα πάντ᾽ ἐπὶ ταῖς εὐθύναις
ταυταισὶ δαιμονίας τινὸς εὐνοίας ἔνδειγμα τῇ πόλει
257 γεγενῆσθαι. σκοπεῖτε γάρ. ἄνθρωπος πολλὰ
καὶ δεινὰ πρεσβεύσας, καὶ χώρας ἐκδεδωκὼς ἐν
αἷς τοὺς θεοὺς ὑφ᾽ ὑμῶν καὶ τῶν συμμάχων
τιμᾶσθαι προσῆκεν, ἠτίμωσεν ὑπακούσαντά τιν᾽
αὑτοῦ κατήγορον. διὰ τί; ἵνα μήτ᾽ ἐλέου μήτε
συγγνώμης ἐφ᾽ οἷς αὐτὸς ἠδίκηκε τύχῃ. ἀλλὰ
καὶ κατηγορῶν ἐκείνου κακῶς λέγειν προείλετ᾽ ἐμέ,

---

[1] καὶ . . . ᾖ edd. (also Bergk): γε . . . ἢ Shill. with
mss., declining to mend the metre.

To every hearth the public curse extends ;
The courtyard gate no longer safety lends ;
Death leaps the wall, nor shall he shun the doom
Who flies for safety to his inmost room.
 Ye men of Athens, listen while I show
How many ills from lawless licence flow.
Respect for Law shall check your rising lust,
Humble the haughty, fetter the unjust,
Make the rough places plain, bid envy cease,
Wither infatuation's fell increase,
Make crooked judgement straight, the works prevent
Of insolence and sullen discontent,
And quench the fires of strife.   In Law we find
The wisdom and perfection of Mankind.

You have heard, men of Athens, what Solon says
of men of such character, and of the gods who
protect our city.   That saying about the protection
of our city by the gods is, as I hope and firmly
believe, eternally true ; and in a manner I think
that even the events of this scrutiny furnish the
commonwealth with a new example of the divine
favour.   For consider this : a man who had scandalously misconducted his embassy, and who had given
away whole provinces in which the gods should have
been worshipped by you and your allies, disfranchised
one who had prosecuted him at duty's call.[a]   And
all for what ?   That he himself may win neither
compassion nor indulgence for his own transgressions.
Moreover, in accusing him, he went out of his way

---

[a] Demosthenes asserts that Timarchus prosecuted Aeschines from purely patriotic motives.   The Greek, however,
admits of more than one interpretation.

DEMOSTHENES

καὶ πάλιν ἐν τῷ δήμῳ γραφὰς ἀποίσειν καὶ τοιαῦτ'
ἠπείλει. ἵνα τί; ἵν' ὡς μετὰ πλείστης συγγνώμης
παρ' ὑμῶν ὁ τὰ τούτου πονηρεύματ' ἀκριβέστατ'
εἰδὼς ἐγὼ καὶ παρηκολουθηκὼς ἅπασι κατηγορῶ.
258 ἀλλὰ καὶ διακρουόμενος πάντα τὸν ἔμπροσθεν
χρόνον εἰσελθεῖν εἰς τοιοῦτον ὑπῆκται καιρόν, ἐν
ᾧ τῶν ἐπιόντων ἕνεκα, εἰ μηδενὸς ἄλλου, οὐχ
οἷόν τ' οὐδ' ἀσφαλὲς ὑμῖν δεδωροδοκηκότα τοῦτον
ἀθῷον ἐᾶσαι· ἀεὶ μὲν γάρ, ὦ ἄνδρες Ἀθηναῖοι,
[424] προσήκει μισεῖν καὶ κολάζειν τοὺς προδότας καὶ
δωροδόκους, μάλιστα δὲ νῦν ἐπὶ καιροῦ τοῦτο
γένοιτ' ἂν καὶ πάντας ὠφελήσειεν ἀνθρώπους
259 κοινῇ. νόσημα γάρ, ὦ ἄνδρες Ἀθηναῖοι, δεινὸν
ἐμπέπτωκεν εἰς τὴν Ἑλλάδα, καὶ χαλεπὸν καὶ
πολλῆς τινος εὐτυχίας καὶ παρ' ὑμῶν ἐπιμελείας
δεόμενον. οἱ γὰρ ἐν ταῖς πόλεσι γνωριμώτατοι
καὶ προεστάναι τῶν κοινῶν ἀξιούμενοι, τὴν αὑτῶν
προδιδόντες ἐλευθερίαν οἱ δυστυχεῖς, αὐθαίρετον
αὑτοῖς ἐπάγονται δουλείαν, Φιλίππου ξενίαν καὶ
ἑταιρίαν καὶ φιλίαν καὶ τοιαῦθ' ὑποκοριζόμενοι·
οἱ δὲ λοιποὶ καὶ τὰ κύρι' ἄττα ποτ' ἔστ' ἐν ἑκάστῃ
τῶν πόλεων, οὓς ἔδει τούτους κολάζειν καὶ παρα-
χρῆμ' ἀποκτιννύναι, τοσοῦτ' ἀπέχουσι τοῦ τοιοῦτόν
τι ποιεῖν, ὥστε θαυμάζουσι καὶ ζηλοῦσι καὶ βού-
260 λοιντ' ἂν αὐτὸς ἕκαστος τοιοῦτος εἶναι. καίτοι
τοῦτο τὸ πρᾶγμα καὶ τὰ τοιαῦτα ζηλώματα
Θετταλῶν μέν, ὦ ἄνδρες Ἀθηναῖοι, μέχρι μὲν
ἐχθὲς καὶ πρώην τὴν ἡγεμονίαν καὶ τὸ κοινὸν
ἀξίωμ' ἀπωλωλέκει, νῦν δ' ἤδη καὶ τὴν ἐλευθερίαν

to speak evil of me, and again at the Assembly he declared he would lay an indictment, with other such threats. And why? In order that you may extend your best indulgence to me when I, who have the most accurate knowledge of his villainies, and have watched him closely throughout, appear as his prosecutor. Again, thanks to his continual evasions, he has at last been brought to trial at the very moment when, for the sake of the future if for no other reason, you cannot possibly, or consistently with your own security, allow a man so steeped in corruption to go scot-free; for, while it is always your duty, men of Athens, to abhor and to chastise traitors and bribe-mongers, a conviction at this crisis will be peculiarly seasonable and profitable to all mankind. A strange and distressing epidemic, men of Athens, has invaded all Greece, calling for extraordinary good fortune, and for the most anxious treatment on your part. The magnates of the several cities, who are entrusted with political authority, are betraying their own independence, unhappy men! They are imposing on themselves a servitude of their own choosing, disguising it by specious names, as the friendship of Philip, fraternity, good-fellowship, and such flummery. The rest of the people, and all the various authorities of the several states, instead of chastising these persons and putting them to death on the spot, as they ought, are filled with admiration and envy, and would all like to be Philip's friends too. Yet this infatuation, this hankering after Philip, men of Athens, until very recently had only destroyed the predominance of the Thessalians and their national prestige, but now it is already sapping their in-

παραιρεῖται· τὰς γὰρ ἀκροπόλεις αὐτῶν ἐνίων
Μακεδόνες φρουροῦσιν· εἰς Πελοπόννησον δ' εἰσελθὼν τὰς ἐν Ἤλιδι σφαγὰς πεποίηκε, καὶ τοσαύτης
παρανοίας καὶ μανίας ἐνέπλησε τοὺς ταλαιπώρους
ἐκείνους ὥσθ', ἵν' ἀλλήλων ἄρχωσι καὶ Φιλίππῳ
χαρίζωνται, συγγενεῖς αὐτῶν καὶ πολίτας μιαι-
261 φονεῖν. καὶ οὐδ' ἐνταῦθ' ἔστηκεν, ἀλλ' εἰς Ἀρκαδίαν εἰσελθὼν πάντ' ἄνω καὶ κάτω τἀκεῖ πεποίηκε,
καὶ νῦν Ἀρκάδων πολλοί, προσῆκον αὐτοῖς ἐπ'
ἐλευθερίᾳ μέγιστον φρονεῖν ὁμοίως ὑμῖν (μόνοι
γὰρ πάντων αὐτόχθονες ὑμεῖς ἐστὲ κἀκεῖνοι)
[425] Φίλιππον θαυμάζουσι καὶ χαλκοῦν ἱστᾶσι καὶ
στεφανοῦσι, καὶ τὸ τελευταῖον, ἂν εἰς Πελοπόννησον ἴῃ, δέχεσθαι ταῖς πόλεσίν εἰσιν ἐψηφισμένοι.
262 ταὐτὰ δὲ ταῦτ' Ἀργεῖοι. ταῦτα νὴ τὴν Δήμητρ',
εἰ δεῖ μὴ ληρεῖν, εὐλαβείας οὐ μικρᾶς δεῖται, ὡς
βαδίζον γε κύκλῳ καὶ δεῦρ' ἐλήλυθεν, ὦ ἄνδρες
Ἀθηναῖοι, τὸ νόσημα τοῦτο. ἕως οὖν ἔτ' ἐν
ἀσφαλεῖ, φυλάξασθε καὶ τοὺς πρώτους εἰσ-
αγαγόντας ἀτιμώσατε· εἰ δὲ μή, σκοπεῖθ' ὅπως
μὴ τηνικαῦτ' εὖ λέγεσθαι δόξει τὰ νῦν εἰρημένα,
ὅτ' οὐδ' ὅ τι χρὴ ποιεῖν ἕξετε.
263   Οὐχ ὁρᾶθ' ὡς ἐναργές, ὦ ἄνδρες Ἀθηναῖοι, καὶ
σαφὲς παράδειγμ' οἱ ταλαίπωροι γεγόνασιν Ὀλύν-
θιοι; οἳ παρ' οὐδὲν οὕτως ὡς τὸ τὰ τοιαῦτα
ποιεῖν ἀπολώλασιν, οἱ δείλαιοι. ἔχοιτε δ' ἂν
ἐξετάσαι καθαρῶς ἐκ τῶν συμβεβηκότων αὐτοῖς.
ἐκεῖνοι γάρ, ἡνίκα μὲν τετρακοσίους ἱππέας
ἐκέκτηντο μόνον καὶ σύμπαντες οὐδὲν ἦσαν πλείους
πεντακισχιλίων τὸν ἀριθμόν, οὔπω Χαλκιδέων

dependence, for some of their citadels are actually garrisoned by Macedonians. It has invaded Peloponnesus and caused the massacres at Elis. It infected those unhappy people with such delirious insanity that, to overmaster one another and to gratify Philip, they stained their hands with the blood of their own kindred and fellow-citizens. It has not stopped there. It has entered Arcadia, and turned Arcadian politics upside down; and now many of that nation, who ought to pride themselves as highly as you upon their independence— for you and they are the only indigenous peoples in Greece—admire Philip, set up his effigy in bronze, decorate it with garlands, and, to crown all, have enacted a decree that, if he ever visits Peloponnesus, he shall be made welcome within their walls. The Argives have followed their example. Holy Mother Earth! if I am to speak as a sane man, we stand in need of the utmost vigilance, when this infection, moving in its circuit, has invaded our own city. Therefore take your precautions now, while we are still secure. Let the men who have brought it here be punished with infamy. If not, beware lest you discern the wisdom of my words too late, when you have lost the power of doing what you ought.

Do you not see, men of Athens, what a conspicuous and striking example is offered by those miserable Olynthians, who owe their ruin, unhappy men, to nothing so much as to such conduct as I have described? You may easily discover the truth by a review of their experience. At the time when their cavalry was only four hundred strong, and their whole force numbered no more than five thousand, for there was then no coalition of all the Chalcidians,

DEMOSTHENES

264 πάντων εἰς ἓν συνῳκισμένων, Λακεδαιμονίων ἐπ᾽
αὐτοὺς ἐλθόντων πολλῇ καὶ πεζῇ καὶ ναυτικῇ
δυνάμει (ἴστε γὰρ δήπου τοῦθ᾽, ὅτι γῆς καὶ θαλάττης ἦρχον ὡς ἔπος εἰπεῖν Λακεδαιμόνιοι κατ᾽
ἐκείνους τοὺς χρόνους), ἀλλ᾽ ὅμως τηλικαύτης
ἐπ᾽ αὐτοὺς ἐλθούσης δυνάμεως οὔτε τὴν πόλιν
οὔτε φρούριον οὐδὲν ἀπώλεσαν, ἀλλὰ καὶ μάχας
πολλὰς ἐκράτησαν καὶ τρεῖς τῶν πολεμάρχων
ἀπέκτειναν καὶ τὸ τελευταῖον, ὅπως ἐβούλοντο,
265 οὕτω τὸν πόλεμον κατέθεντο. ἐπειδὴ δὲ δωροδοκεῖν ἤρξαντό τινες, καὶ δι᾽ ἀβελτερίαν οἱ πολλοί,
μᾶλλον δὲ διὰ δυστυχίαν, τούτους πιστοτέρους
ἡγήσαντο τῶν ὑπὲρ αὐτῶν λεγόντων, καὶ Λασθένης
[426] μὲν ἤρεψε τὴν οἰκίαν τοῖς ἐκ Μακεδονίας δοθεῖσι
ξύλοις, Εὐθυκράτης δὲ βοῦς ἔτρεφε πολλὰς τιμὴν
οὐδενὶ δούς, ἕτερος δέ τις ἧκεν ἔχων πρόβατα,
ἄλλος δέ τις ἵππους, οἱ δὲ πολλοὶ καὶ καθ᾽ ὧν
ταῦτ᾽ ἐγίγνετο οὐχ ὅπως ὠργίζοντο ἢ κολάζειν
ἠξίουν τοὺς ταῦτα ποιοῦντας, ἀλλ᾽ ἀπέβλεπον,
266 ἐζήλουν, ἐτίμων, ἄνδρας ἡγοῦντο· ἐπειδὴ δὲ ταῦθ᾽
οὕτω προήγετο καὶ τὸ δωροδοκεῖν ἐκράτησε,
χιλίους μὲν ἱππέας κεκτημένοι, πλείους δ᾽ ὄντες
ἢ μύριοι, πάντας δὲ τοὺς περιχώρους ἔχοντες
συμμάχους, μυρίοις δὲ ξένοις καὶ τριήρεσι πεντή-
κονθ᾽ ὑμῶν βοηθησάντων αὐτοῖς, καὶ ἔτι τῶν
πολιτῶν τετρακισχιλίοις, οὐδὲν αὐτοὺς τούτων
ἐδυνήθη σῶσαι, ἀλλὰ πρὶν μὲν ἐξελθεῖν ἐνιαυτὸν
τοῦ πολέμου τὰς πόλεις ἁπάσας ἀπωλωλέκεσαν
418

they were invaded by the Lacedaemonians with a large force, both naval and military ; and you will remember that in those days the Lacedaemonians may be said to have held command both of land and of sea. Yet in spite of the strength of the attacking force, they never lost a town or even an outpost, they won many engagements, they slew three of the enemy commanders, and finally brought the war to an end on their own terms.[a] But when some of them began to accept bribes, when the populace was so stupid, or, let us say, so unlucky, as to give more credence to those persons than to patriotic speakers, when Lasthenes had roofed his house with timber sent as a present from Macedonia, and Euthycrates was keeping a large herd of cattle for which he had paid nothing to anybody, when one man returned home with a flock of sheep and another with a stud of horses, when the masses, whose interests were endangered, instead of being angry and demanding the punishment of the traitors, stared at them, envied them, honoured them, and thought them fine fellows,—when, I say, the business had gone so far as that, and corruption had won the day, then, though they numbered more than ten thousand and had a thousand cavalry, though all their neighbours were in alliance with them, though you came to their aid with ten thousand mercenaries, fifty war-galleys, and four thousand of your citizen-force, nothing could save them. Before the war had lasted a year they had lost every town in Chalcidice through

[a] Some Chalcidian cities obtained Sparta's aid against the growing power of Olynthus, and the war lasted from 382 to 379, when the Olynthians sued for peace and became members of the Spartan Confederacy, not exactly " on their own terms."

τὰς ἐν τῇ Χαλκιδικῇ προδιδόντες,[1] καὶ Φίλιππος
οὐκέτ' εἶχεν ὑπακούειν τοῖς προδιδοῦσιν, οὐδ'
267 εἶχεν ὅ τι πρῶτον λάβῃ. πεντακοσίους δ' ἱππέας
προδοθέντας ὑπ' αὐτῶν τῶν ἡγουμένων ἔλαβεν
αὐτοῖς ὅπλοις ὁ Φίλιππος, ὅσους οὐδεὶς πώποτ'
ἄλλος ἀνθρώπων. καὶ οὔτε τὸν ἥλιον ᾐσχύνονθ'
οἱ ταῦτα ποιοῦντες οὔτε τὴν γῆν πατρίδ' οὖσαν,
ἐφ' ἧς ἔστασαν, οὔθ' ἱέρ' οὔτε τάφους οὔτε τὴν
μετὰ ταῦτα γενησομένην αἰσχύνην ἐπὶ τοιούτοις
ἔργοις· οὕτως ἔκφρονας, ὦ ἄνδρες Ἀθηναῖοι, καὶ
παραπλῆγας τὸ δωροδοκεῖν ποιεῖ. ὑμᾶς οὖν, ὑμᾶς
εὖ φρονεῖν δεῖ τοὺς πολλούς, καὶ μὴ ἐπιτρέπειν τὰ
τοιαῦτα, ἀλλὰ κολάζειν δημοσίᾳ. καὶ γὰρ ἂν
καὶ ὑπερφυὲς εἴη, εἰ κατὰ μὲν τῶν Ὀλυνθίους
προδόντων πολλὰ καὶ δείν' ἐψηφίσασθε, τοὺς δὲ
παρ' ὑμῖν αὐτοῖς ἀδικοῦντας μὴ κολάζοντες φαί-
νοισθε. λέγε τὸ ψήφισμα τὸ περὶ τῶν Ὀλυνθίων.

ΨΗΦΙΣΜΑ

268 Ταῦθ' ὑμεῖς, ὦ ἄνδρες δικασταί, ὀρθῶς καὶ
καλῶς πᾶσιν Ἕλλησι καὶ βαρβάροις δοκεῖτ'
ἐψηφίσθαι κατ' ἀνδρῶν προδοτῶν καὶ θεοῖς ἐχθρῶν.
ἐπειδὴ τοίνυν τὸ δωροδοκεῖν πρότερον τοῦ τὰ
τοιαῦτα ποιεῖν ἐστι καὶ δι' ἐκεῖνο καὶ τάδε πράτ-
τουσί τινες, ὃν ἄν, ὦ ἄνδρες Ἀθηναῖοι, δωροδοκοῦντ'
ἴδητε, τοῦτον καὶ προδότην εἶναι νομίζετε. εἰ δ'
ὁ μὲν καιροὺς ὁ δὲ πράγμαθ' ὁ δὲ στρατιώτας
προδίδωσιν, ὧν ἂν ἕκαστος, οἶμαι, κύριος γένηται,
ταῦτα διαφθείρει· μισεῖν δ' ὁμοίως τοὺς τοιούτους
269 πάντας προσήκει. ἔστι δ' ὑμῖν, ὦ ἄνδρες Ἀθη-

---

[1] οἱ προδιδόντες Shill.: οἱ om. SA. Markland and others
bracket προδιδόντες, which can well be spared.

treachery, and Philip could no longer pay any attention to the traitors, and hardly knew what to capture first. He took five hundred horsemen with all their equipment by the treason of their officers—a number beyond all precedent. The perpetrators of that infamy were not put to the blush by the sun that shone on their shame or by the soil of their native land on which they stood, by temples or by sepulchres, by the ignominy that waited on their deeds : such madness, men of Athens, such obliquity, does corruption engender ! Therefore it behoves you, you the commonalty of Athens, to keep your senses, to refuse toleration to such practices, and to visit them with public retribution. For indeed it would be monstrous if, after passing so stern a decree of censure upon the men who betrayed the Olynthians, you should have no chastisement for those who repeat their iniquity in your own midst. Read the decree concerning the Olynthians.

(The Decree is read)

Gentlemen of the jury, by the universal judgement of Greeks and barbarians alike, you acted well and righteously in passing this vote of censure upon traitors and reprobates. Therefore, inasmuch as bribe-taking is the forerunner of such treasons, and for the sake of bribes men commit them, whenever, men of Athens, you see any man taking bribes, you may be sure that he is also a traitor. If one man betrays opportunities, another negotiations, another soldiery, each one is making havoc of the business he controls, and all alike deserve your reprobation. In dealing with them you, men of

ναῖοι, περὶ τούτων μόνοις τῶν πάντων ἀνθρώπων
οἰκείοις χρῆσθαι παραδείγμασι, καὶ τοὺς προγόνους, οὓς ἐπαινεῖτε δικαίως, ἔργῳ μιμεῖσθαι.
καὶ γὰρ εἰ μὴ τὰς μάχας μηδὲ τὰς στρατείας μηδὲ
τοὺς κινδύνους, ἐν οἷς ἦσαν ἐκεῖνοι λαμπροί, συμβαίνει καιρός, ἀλλ’ ἄγεθ’ ἡσυχίαν ὑμεῖς ἐν τῷ παρόντι,
270 ἀλλὰ τό γ’ εὖ φρονεῖν αὐτῶν μιμεῖσθε. τούτου
γὰρ πανταχοῦ χρεία, καὶ οὐδέν ἐστι πραγματω-
δέστερον οὐδ’ ὀχληρότερον τὸ καλῶς φρονεῖν τοῦ
κακῶς, ἀλλ’ ἐν τῷ ἴσῳ χρόνῳ νυνὶ καθήμενος
ὑμῶν ἕκαστος, ἂν μὲν ἃ χρὴ γιγνώσκῃ περὶ τῶν
πραγμάτων καὶ ψηφίζηται, βελτίω τὰ κοινὰ
ποιήσει τῇ πόλει καὶ ἄξια τῶν προγόνων πράξει,
ἂν δ’ ἃ μὴ δεῖ, φαυλότερα καὶ ἀνάξια τῶν προγόνων
ποιήσει. τί οὖν ἐκεῖνοι περὶ τούτων ἐφρόνουν;
ταυτὶ λαβὼν ἀνάγνωθι, γραμματεῦ· δεῖ γὰρ ὑμᾶς
ἰδεῖν ὅτι ἐπὶ τοῖς τοιούτοις ἔργοις ῥαθυμεῖτε, ὧν
θάνατον κατεγνώκασιν οἱ πρόγονοι. λέγε.

[428]   ΣΤΗΛΗ

271   Ἀκούετ’, ὦ ἄνδρες Ἀθηναῖοι, τῶν γραμμάτων
λεγόντων Ἄρθμιον τὸν Πυθώνακτος τὸν Ζελείτην
ἐχθρὸν εἶναι καὶ πολέμιον τοῦ δήμου τοῦ Ἀθηναίων καὶ τῶν συμμάχων αὐτὸν καὶ γένος πᾶν.
διὰ τί; ὅτι τὸν χρυσὸν τὸν ἐκ τῶν βαρβάρων εἰς
τοὺς Ἕλληνας ἤγαγεν. οὐκοῦν ἔστιν, ὡς ἔοικεν,
ἐκ τούτων ἰδεῖν ὅτι οἱ πρόγονοι μὲν ὑμῶν, ὅπως
μηδ’ ἄλλος ἀνθρώπων μηδεὶς ἐπὶ χρήμασι μηδὲν
ἐργάσεται κακὸν τὴν Ἑλλάδα, ἐφρόντιζον, ὑμεῖς
δ’ οὐδὲ τὴν πόλιν αὐτὴν ὅπως μηδεὶς τῶν πολιτῶν
272 ἀδικήσει προορᾶσθε. νὴ Δί’, ἀλλ’ ὅπως ἔτυχε
ταῦτα τὰ γράμμαθ’ ἕστηκεν. ἀλλ’ ὅλης οὔσης
422

Athens, and you alone among the nations of the world, can find examples to imitate in your own history, and may emulate in act the forefathers whom you justly commend. For if at the present time you are at peace, and cannot emulate the battles, the campaigns, the hazards of war, in which they won renown, you may at least imitate their sound judgement. That is wanted in all circumstances; and an honest judgement costs you no more pains and vexation than a vicious judgement. Each of you will sit in this court for just as long a time, whether, by reaching a right decision and giving a right verdict upon this case, he amends the condition of the commonwealth and does credit to his ancestry, or, by a wrong decision, impairs that condition and dishonours that ancestry. What, then, was their judgement in such a case ?—Clerk, take this and read it.—For I would have you know that you are treating with indifference offences such as your forefathers once punished with death.

(A Public Inscription is read)

You hear, men of Athens, the record which declares Arthmius, son of Pythonax, of Zelea, to be enemy and foeman of the Athenian people and their allies, him and all his kindred. His offence was conveying gold from barbarians to Greeks. Hence, apparently, we may conclude that your ancestors were anxious to prevent any man, even an alien, taking rewards to do injury to Greece; but you take no thought to discountenance wrongs done by your own citizens to your own city. Does anyone say that this inscription has been set up just anywhere ? No;

ἱερᾶς τῆς ἀκροπόλεως ταυτησὶ καὶ πολλὴν εὐρυ-
χωρίαν ἐχούσης παρὰ τὴν χαλκῆν τὴν μεγάλην
Ἀθηνᾶν ἐκ δεξιᾶς ἔστηκεν, ἣν ἀριστεῖον ἡ πόλις
τοῦ πρὸς τοὺς βαρβάρους πολέμου, δόντων τῶν
Ἑλλήνων τὰ χρήματα ταῦτα, ἀνέθηκεν. τότε μὲν
τοίνυν οὕτω σεμνὸν ἦν τὸ δίκαιον καὶ τὸ κολάζειν
τοὺς τὰ τοιαῦτα ποιοῦντας ἔντιμον, ὥστε τῆς
αὐτῆς ἠξιοῦτο στάσεως τό τ᾽ ἀριστεῖον τῆς θεοῦ
καὶ αἱ κατὰ τῶν τὰ τοιαῦτ᾽ ἀδικούντων τιμωρίαι·
νῦν δὲ γέλως, ἄδεια, αἰσχύνη, εἰ μὴ τὴν ἄγαν
ταύτην ἐξουσίαν σχήσετε νῦν ὑμεῖς.

273   Νομίζω τοίνυν ὑμᾶς, ὦ ἄνδρες Ἀθηναῖοι, οὐ
καθ᾽ ἕν τι μόνον τοὺς προγόνους μιμουμένους
ὀρθῶς ἂν ποιεῖν, ἀλλὰ καὶ κατὰ πάνθ᾽ ὅσ᾽ ἔπραττον ἐφεξῆς. ἐκεῖνοι τοίνυν, ὡς ἅπαντες εὖ οἶδ᾽
ὅτι τὸν λόγον τοῦτον ἀκηκόατε, Καλλίαν τὸν
Ἱππονίκου ταύτην τὴν ὑπὸ πάντων θρυλουμένην
εἰρήνην πρεσβεύσαντα, ἵππου μὲν δρόμον ἡμέρας
[429] πεζῇ μὴ καταβαίνειν ἐπὶ τὴν θάλατταν βασιλέα,
ἐντὸς δὲ Χελιδονίων καὶ Κυανέων πλοίῳ μακρῷ
μὴ πλεῖν, ὅτι δῶρα λαβεῖν ἔδοξε πρεσβεύσας,
μικροῦ μὲν ἀπέκτειναν, ἐν δὲ ταῖς εὐθύναις πεντή-
274   κοντ᾽ ἐπράξαντο τάλαντα. καίτοι καλλίω ταύτης
εἰρήνην οὔτε πρότερον οὔθ᾽ ὕστερον οὐδεὶς ἂν
εἰπεῖν ἔχοι πεποιημένην τὴν πόλιν. ἀλλ᾽ οὐ τοῦτ᾽
ἐσκόπουν. τούτου μὲν γὰρ ἡγοῦντο τὴν αὐτῶν
ἀρετὴν καὶ τὴν τῆς πόλεως δόξαν αἰτίαν εἶναι,
τοῦ δὲ προῖκ᾽ ἢ μὴ τὸν τρόπον τοῦ πρεσβευτοῦ·
τοῦτον οὖν δίκαιον ἠξίουν παρέχεσθαι καὶ ἀδωρο-
275   δόκητον τὸν προσιόντα τοῖς κοινοῖς. ἐκεῖνοι μὲν
τοίνυν οὕτως ἐχθρὸν ἡγοῦντο τὸ δωροδοκεῖν καὶ

although the whole of our citadel is a holy place, and although its area is so large, the inscription stands at the right hand beside the great brazen Athene which was dedicated by the state as a memorial of victory in the Persian war, at the expense of the Greeks. In those days, therefore, justice was so venerable, and the punishment of these crimes so meritorious, that the retribution of such offenders was honoured with the same position as Pallas Athene's own prize of victory. To-day we have instead—mockery, impunity, dishonour, unless you restrain the licence of these men.

In my judgement, men of Athens, you will do well, not to emulate your forefathers in some one respect alone, but to follow their conduct step by step. I am sure you have all heard the story of their treatment of Callias, son of Hipponicus, who negotiated the celebrated peace[a] under which the King of Persia was not to approach within a day's ride of the coast, nor sail with a ship of war between the Chelidonian islands and the Blue Rocks. At the inquiry into his conduct they came near to putting him to death, and mulcted him in fifty talents, because he was said to have taken bribes on embassy. Yet no one can cite a more honourable peace made by the city before or since ; but that is not what they regarded. They attributed the honourable peace to their own valour and to the high repute of their city, the refusal or acceptance of money to the character of the ambassador ; and they expected an honest and incorruptible character in any man who entered the service of the state. They held the taking of bribes to be too inimical and unprofitable

[a] 470 B.C., after the battle of Eurymedon.

ἀλυσιτελὲς τῇ πόλει, ὥστε μήτ' ἐπὶ πράξεως
μηδεμιᾶς μήτ' ἐπ' ἀνδρὸς ἐᾶν γίγνεσθαι· ὑμεῖς
δ', ὦ ἄνδρες Ἀθηναῖοι, τὴν αὐτὴν εἰρήνην ἑορα-
κότες, τὰ μὲν τῶν συμμάχων τῶν ὑμετέρων τείχη
καθῃρηκυῖαν, τὰς δὲ τῶν πρέσβεων οἰκίας οἰκο-
δομοῦσαν, καὶ τὰ μὲν τῆς πόλεως κτήματ' ἀφῃρη-
μένην, τούτοις δ' ἃ μηδ' ὄναρ ἤλπισαν πώποτε
κτησαμένην, οὐκ αὐτοὶ τούτους ἀπεκτείνατε, ἀλλὰ
κατηγόρου προσδεῖσθε, καὶ λόγῳ κρίνεθ' ὧν ἔργῳ
τἀδικήματα πάντες ὁρῶσιν.

276 Οὐ τοίνυν τὰ πάλαι ἄν τις ἔχοι μόνον εἰπεῖν,
καὶ διὰ τούτων τῶν παραδειγμάτων ὑμᾶς ἐπὶ
τιμωρίαν παρακαλέσαι· ἀλλ' ἐφ' ὑμῶν τουτωνὶ
τῶν ἔτι ζώντων ἀνθρώπων πολλοὶ δίκην δεδώκασιν, ὧν ἐγὼ τοὺς μὲν ἄλλους παραλείψω, τῶν
δ' ἐκ πρεσβείας, ἣ πολὺ ταύτης ἐλάττω κακὰ
τὴν πόλιν εἴργασται, θανάτῳ ζημιωθέντων ἑνὸς
ἢ δυοῖν ἐπιμνησθήσομαι. καί μοι λέγε τουτὶ τὸ
ψήφισμα λαβών.

ΨΗΦΙΣΜΑ

277 Κατὰ τουτὶ τὸ ψήφισμ', ὦ ἄνδρες Ἀθηναῖοι,
τῶν πρέσβεων ἐκείνων ὑμεῖς θάνατον κατέγνωτε,
ὧν εἷς ἦν Ἐπικράτης, ἀνήρ, ὡς ἐγὼ τῶν πρεσβυτέρων ἀκούω, σπουδαῖος καὶ πολλὰ χρήσιμος τῇ
πόλει, καὶ τῶν ἐκ Πειραιῶς καταγαγόντων τὸν
δῆμον καὶ ἄλλως δημοτικός. ἀλλ' ὅμως οὐδὲν
αὐτὸν ὠφέλησε τούτων, δικαίως· οὐ γὰρ ἐφ' ἡμι-
σείᾳ χρηστὸν εἶναι δεῖ τὸν τὰ τηλικαῦτα δι-
οικεῖν ἀξιοῦντα, οὐδὲ τὸ πιστευθῆναι προλαβόντα
παρ' ὑμῶν εἰς τὸ μείζω δύνασθαι κακουρ-
γεῖν καταχρῆσθαι, ἀλλ' ἁπλῶς μηδὲν ὑμᾶς

to the state to be tolerated in any transaction or in any person ; but you, men of Athens, having before you a peace which at once has pulled down the walls of your allies and is building up the houses of your ambassadors, which robbed the city of her possessions and earned for them wealth beyond the dreams of avarice, instead of putting them to death of your own accord, wait for the appearance of a prosecutor. You are giving them a trial of words with their evil deeds before your eyes.

Yet we need not restrict ourselves to bygone history, or rely upon those ancient precedents in our appeal to retributive justice. Within your own lifetime, in the time of the generation now living, not a few men have been tried and condemned. Passing by other instances, let me recall to your memory one or two men who have been punished by death after an embassy far less mischievous to the city. Please take and read this decree.

(*The Decree is read*)

By the terms of this decree, men of Athens, you condemned to death the ambassadors named. One of them was Epicrates, who, as I am informed by persons older than myself, was an honest, useful, and popular politician, and one of the men who marched from Peiraeus and restored the democracy.[a] No such consideration availed him ; and that was right, for a man who accepts so important a mission is not to be virtuous by halves. He must not use the public confidence he has earned as an opportunity for knavery : his duty is simply to do you no wilful

---

[a] *restored the democracy* : under Thrasybulus [280], 403 B.C. (Grote, ch. lxv.).

278 ἀδικεῖν ἑκόντα. εἰ τοίνυν τι τούτοις ἄπρακτόν
ἐστι τούτων ἐφ' οἷς ἐκείνων θάνατος κατέγνωσται,
ἔμ' ἀποκτείνατ' ἤδη. σκοπεῖτε γάρ. "ἐπειδὴ
παρὰ τὰ γράμματα" φησίν " ἐπρέσβευσαν ἐκεῖνοι,"
καὶ τοῦτ' ἐστὶ τῶν ἐγκλημάτων πρῶτον. οὗτοι
δ' οὐ παρὰ τὰ γράμματα; οὐ τὸ μὲν ψήφισμ'
" Ἀθηναίοις καὶ τοῖς Ἀθηναίων συμμάχοις," οὗτοι
δὲ Φωκέας ἐκσπόνδους ἀπέφηναν; οὐ τὸ μὲν
ψήφισμα "τοὺς ἄρχοντας ὀρκοῦν τοὺς ἐν ταῖς
πόλεσιν," οὗτοι δ', οὓς Φίλιππος αὐτοῖς προσ-
έπεμψε, τούτους ὤρκισαν; οὐ τὸ μὲν ψήφισμ'
"οὐδαμοῦ μόνους ἐντυγχάνειν Φιλίππῳ," οὗτοι
279 δ' οὐδὲν ἐπαύσαντ' ἰδίᾳ χρηματίζοντες; " καὶ
ἠλέγχθησάν τινες αὐτῶν ἐν τῇ βουλῇ οὐ τἀληθῆ
ἀπαγγέλλοντες." οὗτοι δέ γε κἂν τῷ δήμῳ. καὶ
ὑπὸ τοῦ; τοῦτο γάρ ἐστι τὸ λαμπρόν. ὑπ' αὐτῶν
τῶν πραγμάτων· οἷς γὰρ ἀπήγγειλαν οὗτοι,
πάντα δήπου γέγονε τἀναντία. "οὐδ' ἐπι-
[431] στέλλοντες" φησὶ "τἀληθῆ." οὐκοῦν οὐδ' οὗτοι.
"καὶ καταψευδόμενοι τῶν συμμάχων καὶ δῶρα
λαμβάνοντες." ἀντὶ μὲν τοίνυν τοῦ "καταψευδόμενοι" παντελῶς ἀπολωλεκότες· πολλῷ δὲ
δήπου τοῦτο δεινότερον τοῦ καταψεύσασθαι. ἀλλὰ
μὴν ὑπέρ γε τοῦ δῶρ' εἰληφέναι, εἰ μὲν ἠρνοῦντο,
ἐξελέγχειν λοιπὸν ἂν ἦν, ἐπειδὴ δ' ὁμολογοῦσιν,
ἀπάγειν δήπου προσῆκεν.
280 Τί οὖν, ὦ ἄνδρες Ἀθηναῖοι; τούτων οὕτως
ἐχόντων ὑμεῖς ἐξ¹ ἐκείνων τῶν ἀνδρῶν ὄντες, οἱ
δὲ καί τινες αὐτῶν ἔτι ζῶντες, ὑπομενεῖτε τὸν
μὲν εὐεργέτην τοῦ δήμου καὶ τὸν ἐκ Πειραιῶς,

¹ ἐξ inserted by Dobree, cf. τοὺς ἐξ ἐκείνων 313: om. Shill., mss.

ª By the legal process known as ἀπαγωγή.

wrong at all. Well, if the present defendants have omitted any single one of the misdeeds for which those persons were sentenced to death, execute me on the spot. Look at the decree : " Whereas the said ambassadors have disobeyed their instructions." That is the first charge alleged. And did not these men disobey their instructions ? Did not the decree say, " for the Athenians and the Allies of the Athenians," and did not they declare the Phocians to be excluded ? Did it not instruct them to swear in the magistrates in the several cities, and did they not swear in only such persons as Philip sent to them ? Did not the decree say that they were not to meet Philip alone in any place whatsoever, and did they not continually have private dealings with Philip ? " Whereas," says the old decree, " certain of them are convicted of making untruthful reports to the Council." Why, these men are convicted of making untruthful reports even to the Assembly. On what evidence ?—you remember that brilliant quibble. On the evidence of facts : the report was exactly contradicted by the event. It goes on : " and of sending untruthful dispatches." So did they. " And of bearing false witness against allies, and of taking bribes." For " bearing false witness " read " utterly destroying "—a vastly greater injury. But as to their having taken bribes, we should still, if they denied it, have to make the charge good ; but since they admit it, surely there should have been a summary arrest and punishment.[a]

What follows, men of Athens ? Such being the facts, will you, the descendants of these men, some of whom are still living, be content that Epicrates, the champion of democracy, the hero of the march

Ἐπικράτην, ἐκπεσεῖν καὶ κολασθῆναι, καὶ πάλιν
πρώην Θρασύβουλον ἐκεῖνον τὸν Θρασυβούλου
τοῦ δημοτικοῦ καὶ τοῦ ἀπὸ Φυλῆς καταγαγόντος
τὸν δῆμον τάλαντα δέκ' ὠφληκέναι, καὶ τὸν ἀφ'
Ἁρμοδίου καὶ τῶν τὰ μέγιστ' ἀγάθ' ὑμᾶς εἰργασμένων, οὓς νόμῳ διὰ τὰς εὐεργεσίας, ἃς
ὑπῆρξαν εἰς ὑμᾶς, ἐν ἅπασι τοῖς ἱεροῖς ἐπὶ ταῖς
θυσίαις σπονδῶν καὶ κρατήρων κοινωνοὺς πεποίησθε, καὶ ᾄδετε καὶ τιμᾶτ' ἐξ ἴσου τοῖς ἥρωσιν
281 καὶ τοῖς θεοῖς, τούτους μὲν πάντας τὴν ἐκ τῶν
νόμων δίκην ὑπεσχηκέναι, καὶ μήτε συγγνώμην
μήτ' ἔλεον μήτε παιδία κλάονθ' ὁμώνυμα τῶν
εὐεργετῶν μήτ' ἄλλο μηδὲν αὐτοὺς ὠφεληκέναι,
τὸν δ' Ἀτρομήτου τοῦ γραμματιστοῦ καὶ Γλαυκοθέας τῆς τοὺς θιάσους συναγούσης, ἐφ' οἷς ἑτέρα
τέθνηκεν ἱέρεια, τοῦτον ὑμεῖς λαβόντες ἀφήσετε,
τὸν τῶν τοιούτων, τὸν οὐδὲ καθ' ἓν χρήσιμον τῇ
πόλει, οὐκ αὐτόν, οὐ πατέρα, οὐκ ἄλλον οὐδένα
282 τῶν τούτου; ποῖος γὰρ ἵππος, ποία τριήρης, ποία
[432] στρατεία, τίς χορός, τίς λῃτουργία, τίς εἰσφορά,
τίς εὔνοια, ποῖος κίνδυνος, τί τούτων ἐν παντὶ
τῷ χρόνῳ γέγονε παρὰ τούτων τῇ πόλει; καίτοι
κἂν εἰ ταῦτα πάνθ' ὑπῆρχεν, ἐκεῖνα δὲ μὴ προσῆν,
δικαίως καὶ προῖκα πεπρεσβευκέναι, ἀπολωλέναι
δήπου προσῆκεν αὐτῷ. εἰ δὲ μήτε ταῦτα μήτ'
283 ἐκεῖνα, οὐ τιμωρήσεσθε; οὐκ ἀναμνησθήσεσθ' ὧν
κατηγορῶν ἔλεγε Τιμάρχου, ὡς οὐδέν ἐστ' ὄφελος

---

[a] According to Ulpian her name was Nino and her crime
was mixing a love-potion.

from Peiraeus, should have been degraded and
punished ; that more recently Thrasybulus, a son
of Thrasybulus the great democrat, who restored
free government from Phyle, should have paid a
fine of ten talents ; that even a descendant of
Harmodius and of the greatest of all your benefactors, the men to whom, in requital of their glorious
deeds, you have allotted by statute a share of your
libations and drink-offerings in every temple and
at every public service, whom, in hymns and in
worship, you treat as the equals of gods and demi-
gods,—will you be content that all these men should
have been subjected to the inexorable penalty of
law ; that they should find no succour in mercy
or compassion, in weeping children bearing honoured
names, or in any other plea ?   And then, when you
have in your power a son of Atrometus the dominie,
and of Glaucothea, the fuglewoman of those bac-
chanalian routs for which another priestess [a] suffered
death, will you release the son of such parents, a
man who has never been of the slightest use to the
commonwealth, neither he, nor his father, nor any
member of his precious family ?   Has the state
ever had to thank any one of them in the whole
course of his life for so much as a horse, or a war-
galley, or a military expedition, or a chorus, or any
public service, assessed contribution, or free gift, or
for any deed of valour or any benefit whatsoever ?
Yet even if he could claim credit for all those services,
but could not add that he has been an honest and
disinterested ambassador, he ought assuredly to
suffer death. If he has neither the one claim nor
the other, will you not punish him ? Remember
what he told you himself when he prosecuted

πόλεως ἥτις μὴ νεῦρ᾽ ἐπὶ τοὺς ἀδικοῦντας ἔχει,
οὐδὲ πολιτείας ἐν ᾗ συγγνώμη καὶ παραγγελία
τῶν νόμων μεῖζον ἰσχύουσιν· οὐδ᾽ ἐλεεῖν ὑμᾶς
οὔτε τὴν μητέρα δεῖν τὴν Τιμάρχου, γραῦν γυναῖκα,
οὔτε τὰ παιδί᾽ οὔτ᾽ ἄλλον οὐδένα, ἀλλ᾽ ἐκεῖν᾽
ὁρᾶν, ὅτι εἰ προήσεσθε τὰ τῶν νόμων καὶ τῆς
πολιτείας, οὐχ εὑρήσετε τοὺς ὑμᾶς αὐτοὺς ἐλεή-
284 σοντας. ἀλλ᾽ ὁ μὲν ταλαίπωρος ἄνθρωπος ἠτίμω-
ται, ὅτι τοῦτον εἶδ᾽ ἀδικοῦντα, τούτῳ δ᾽ ἀθῴῳ
δώσετ᾽ εἶναι; διὰ τί; εἰ γὰρ παρὰ τῶν εἰς ἑαυτοὺς
ἐξαμαρτόντων τηλικαύτην ἠξίωσε δίκην Αἰσχίνης
λαβεῖν, παρὰ τῶν εἰς τὰ τῆς πόλεως τηλικαῦθ᾽
ἡμαρτηκότων, ὧν εἷς οὗτος ὢν ἐξελέγχεται,
πηλίκην ὑμᾶς προσήκει λαβεῖν τοὺς ὀμωμοκότας
285 καὶ δικάζοντας; νὴ Δί᾽, οἱ νέοι γὰρ ἡμῖν δι᾽
ἐκεῖνον ἔσονται τὸν ἀγῶνα βελτίους. οὐκοῦν καὶ
διὰ τόνδ᾽ οἱ πολιτευόμενοι, δι᾽ ὧν τὰ μέγιστα
κινδυνεύεται τῇ πόλει· προσήκει δὲ καὶ τούτων
φροντίζειν. ἵνα τοίνυν εἰδῆθ᾽ ὅτι καὶ τοῦτον
ἀπώλεσε, τὸν Τίμαρχον, οὐ μὰ Δί᾽ οὐχὶ τῶν
ὑμετέρων παίδων, ὅπως ἔσονται σώφρονες, προ-
[433] ορῶν (εἰσὶ γάρ, ὦ ἄνδρες Ἀθηναῖοι, καὶ νῦν
σώφρονες· μὴ γὰρ οὕτω γένοιτο κακῶς τῇ πόλει,
ὥστ᾽ Ἀφοβήτου καὶ Αἰσχίνου σωφρονιστῶν δεη-
286 θῆναι τοὺς νεωτέρους), ἀλλ᾽ ὅτι βουλεύων ἔγραψεν,
ἄν τις ὡς Φίλιππον ὅπλ᾽ ἄγων ἁλῷ ἢ σκεύη
τριηρικά, θάνατον εἶναι τὴν ζημίαν. σημεῖον δέ·
πόσον γὰρ ἐδημηγόρει χρόνον Τίμαρχος; πολύν·
οὐκοῦν τοῦτον ἦν Αἰσχίνης ἅπαντ᾽ ἐν τῇ πόλει,

Timarchus,—that there is no merit in a city that is nerveless in its dealings with malefactors, or in a polity where indulgence and importunity are stronger than the laws. You must not, he said, have any pity for Timarchus's mother, an aged woman, or his children, or anyone else : you must fix your mind on the thought that, if you desert the laws and the constitution, you will find no one to pity you. The unfortunate Timarchus is still disfranchised because he was a witness of Aeschines' misdeeds, and why should you allow Aeschines to go scot-free ? If he demanded such severity of retribution from men who had transgressed only against himself and his friends, what retribution are you, a legal jury bound by oath, to exact from men who have grievously transgressed against the commonwealth, and of whom he is proved to be one ? He will say that the trial of Timarchus will improve the morals of our young men. Then this trial will improve the integrity of our statesmen, on whom depend the gravest political hazards ; and they also have a claim on your consideration. But let me show you that he did not bring Timarchus to ruin because of his anxious care —Heaven help us !—for the modesty of your children. Your children, men of Athens, are already modest ; and God forbid that Athens should ever be in such evil case as to require an Aphobetus or an Aeschines to teach young people modesty ! He did it because Timarchus had moved in the Council a decree making the conveyance of arms or ships' tackle to Philip a capital offence. As evidence of that, let me ask how long Timarchus had been a public speaker ? A very long time ; and during all that time Aeschines was in Athens ; yet he

καὶ οὐδεπώποτ᾽ ἠγανάκτησεν οὐδὲ δεινὸν ἡγήσατ᾽
εἶναι τὸ πρᾶγμα, εἰ ὁ τοιοῦτος λέγει, ἕως εἰς
Μακεδονίαν ἐλθὼν ἑαυτὸν ἐμίσθωσεν. λέγε δή
μοι τὸ ψήφισμα λαβὼν αὐτὸ τὸ τοῦ Τιμάρχου.

ΨΗΦΙΣΜΑ

287 Ὁ μὲν τοίνυν ὑπὲρ ὑμῶν γράψας μὴ ἄγειν ἐν τῷ
πολέμῳ πρὸς Φίλιππον ὅπλα, εἰ δὲ μή, θανάτῳ
ζημιοῦσθαι, ἀπόλωλε καὶ ὕβρισται· ὁ δὲ καὶ τὰ
τῶν ὑμετέρων συμμάχων ὅπλ᾽ ἐκείνῳ παραδοὺς
οὑτοσὶ κατηγόρει, καὶ περὶ πορνείας ἔλεγεν, ὦ
γῆ καὶ θεοί, δυοῖν μὲν κηδεσταῖν παρεστηκότοιν,
οὓς ἰδόντες ἂν ὑμεῖς ἀνακράγοιτε, Νικίου τε τοῦ
βδελυροῦ, ὃς ἑαυτὸν ἐμίσθωσεν εἰς Αἴγυπτον
Χαβρίᾳ, καὶ τοῦ καταράτου Κυρηβίωνος, ὃς ἐν
ταῖς πομπαῖς ἄνευ τοῦ προσώπου κωμάζει. καὶ
τί ταῦτα; ἀλλὰ τὸν ἀδελφὸν ὁρῶν Ἀφόβητον.
ἀλλὰ δῆτ᾽ ἄνω ποταμῶν ἐκείνῃ τῇ ἡμέρᾳ πάντες
οἱ περὶ πορνείας ἐρρύησαν λόγοι.

288 Καὶ μὴν εἰς ὅσην ἀτιμίαν τὴν πόλιν ἡμῶν ἡ τούτου πονηρία καὶ ψευδολογία καταστήσασ᾽ ἔχει,
πάντα τἆλλ᾽ ἀφείς, ὃ πάντες ὑμεῖς ἴστε, ἐρῶ.
πρότερον μὲν γάρ, ὦ ἄνδρες Ἀθηναῖοι, τί παρ᾽
[434] ὑμῖν ἐψήφισται, τοῦτ᾽ ἐπετήρουν οἱ ἄλλοι πάντες
Ἕλληνες· νῦν δ᾽ ἤδη περιερχόμεθ᾽ ἡμεῖς τί δέδοκται
τοῖς ἄλλοις σκοποῦντες, καὶ ὠτακουστοῦντες τί
τὰ τῶν Ἀρκάδων, τί τὰ τῶν Ἀμφικτυόνων, ποῖ
289 πάρεισι Φίλιππος, ζῇ ἢ τέθνηκεν. οὐ τοιαῦτα

ᵃ *Cyrebio*, a nickname, " Offal " (κυρήβια = bran); the
man's real name was Epicrates.

never took offence, he never began to think it a shame that a man of such character should make speeches, until he had visited Macedonia and sold himself. Please take and read the actual decree of Timarchus.

(*The Decree is read*)

The man who for your sake proposed the prohibition, under penalty of death, of carrying arms to Philip is vilified and disgraced ; the man who surrendered to Philip the armaments of our allies is his accuser. Immorality—save the mark !—was the theme of his speech, while at his side stood his two brothers-in-law, the very sight of whom is enough to set you in an uproar,—the disgusting Nicias, who went to Egypt as the hireling of Chabrias, and the abominable Cyrebio,[a] the unmasked harlequin of the pageants. But that was nothing: under his eyes sat his brother Aphobetus. In truth, on that day all that declaiming against immorality was like water flowing upstream.[b]

And now, to illustrate the discredit into which our city has been dragged by this man's trickery and mendacity, omitting much that I might mention, I will point to a symptom that you have all observed. In former times, men of Athens, all Greece used to watch anxiously for your decisions. To-day we prowl the streets wondering what the other communities have resolved, all agog to hear what is the news from Arcadia, what is the news from the Amphictyons, what will be Philip's next movement, whether he is alive or dead. You know that such

[b] For this metaphor to express topsyturvydom *cf.* Eurip. *Med.* 410—

ἄνω ποταμῶν ἱερῶν χωροῦσι παγαί,
καὶ δίκα καὶ πάντα πάλιν στρέφεται.

ποιοῦμεν; ἐγὼ δ' οὐ δέδοικ' εἰ Φίλιππος ζῇ, ἀλλ'
εἰ τῆς πόλεως τέθνηκε τὸ τοὺς ἀδικοῦντας μισεῖν
καὶ τιμωρεῖσθαι. οὐδὲ φοβεῖ με Φίλιππος, ἂν τὰ
παρ' ὑμῖν ὑγιαίνῃ, ἀλλ' εἰ παρ' ὑμῖν ἄδεια γενήσεται τοῖς παρ' ἐκείνου μισθαρνεῖν βουλομένοις,
καὶ συνεροῦσί τινες τούτοις τῶν ὑφ' ὑμῶν πεπι-
στευμένων, καὶ πάντα τὸν ἔμπροσθεν χρόνον ἀρνού-
μενοι μὴ πράττειν ὑπὲρ Φιλίππου νῦν ἀναβήσονται,
290 ταῦτα φοβεῖ με. τί γὰρ δή ποτ', Εὔβουλε, Ἡγη-
σίλεῳ μὲν κρινομένῳ, ὃς ἀνεψιός ἐστί σοι, καὶ
Θρασυβούλῳ πρώην, τῷ Νικηράτου θείῳ, ἐπὶ μὲν
τῆς πρώτης ψήφου οὐδ' ὑπακοῦσαι καλούμενος
ἤθελες, εἰς δὲ τὸ τίμημ' ἀναβὰς ὑπὲρ μὲν ἐκείνων
οὐδ' ὁτιοῦν ἔλεγες, ἐδέου δὲ τῶν δικαστῶν συγγνώμην ἔχειν σοί; εἶθ' ὑπὲρ μὲν συγγενῶν καὶ ἀναγ-
καίων ἀνθρώπων οὐκ ἀναβαίνεις, ὑπὲρ Αἰσχίνου
291 δ' ἀναβήσει, ὅς, ἡνίκ' ἔκρινεν Ἀριστοφῶν Φιλό-
νικον καὶ δι' ἐκείνου τῶν σοὶ πεπραγμένων κατηγόρει, συγκατηγόρει μετ' ἐκείνου σοῦ καὶ τῶν
ἐχθρῶν τῶν σῶν εἷς ἐξητάζετο; ἐπειδὴ δὲ σὺ
μὲν τουτουσὶ δεδιξάμενος, καὶ φήσας καταβαίνειν
εἰς Πειραιᾶ δεῖν ἤδη καὶ χρήματ' εἰσφέρειν καὶ τὰ
θεωρικὰ στρατιωτικὰ ποιεῖν, ἢ χειροτονεῖν ἃ συνεῖπε μὲν οὗτος ἔγραψε δ' ὁ βδελυρὸς Φιλοκράτης,
ἐξ ὧν αἰσχρὰν ἀντ' ἴσης συνέβη γενέσθαι τὴν
292 εἰρήνην, οὗτοι δὲ τοῖς μετὰ ταῦτ' ἀδικήμασι πάντ'
[435] ἀπολωλέκασι, τηνικαῦτα διήλλαξαι; καὶ ἐν μὲν
τῷ δήμῳ κατηρῶ Φιλίππῳ, καὶ κατὰ τῶν παίδων
ὤμνυες, ἦ μὴν ἀπολωλέναι Φίλιππον ἂν βούλεσθαι·

---

[a] The verdict of " guilty " or " not guilty." A second vote
was in some cases (*e.g.* at the trial of Socrates) required to
decide the punishment.

is our behaviour. What alarms me is the thought, not that Philip is alive, but that in Athens the spirit that loathes and punishes evil-doers is dead. Philip does not terrify me, if only your condition is healthy ; but if there is to be impunity in this court for men who hunger after Philip's pay, and if men who have won your confidence, men who have hitherto scorned the imputation of intriguing for Philip, are to appear as their advocates, that does terrify me.—What does this mean, Eubulus ? At the trial of your cousin Hegesilaus, and recently at that of Thrasybulus, an uncle of Niceratus, before the first vote of the jury[a] you would not even answer when you were called ; on the question of damages you did get up to speak, but you had not a word to say in their favour, and merely asked the jury to excuse you. So you do not mount the tribune for your own kinsmen and for men who have a claim on your services, and will you mount it for Aeschines, who, when Aristophon prosecuted Philonicus, and in denouncing him denounced your own policy, joined in the attack upon you, and so ranged himself with your enemies ? After terrifying the people, and telling them that they must go down to Peiraeus at once, pay the war-tax and turn the theatric fund into a war-chest, or else vote for the resolution that was supported by Aeschines and moved by that abominable Philocrates, with the result that we got a discreditable instead of an equitable peace, and after all the ruin that has been wrought by their subsequent misdeeds, are you reconciled with them after that ? In the Assembly you solemnly cursed Philip ; you swore by the head of your children that you desired his utter destruction, and will you now be the defender

νῦν δὲ βοηθήσεις τούτῳ; πῶς οὖν ἀπολεῖται,
ὅταν τοὺς παρ' ἐκείνου δωροδοκοῦντας σὺ σῴζῃς;
293 τί γὰρ δήποτε Μοιροκλέα μὲν ἔκρινες, εἰ παρὰ
τῶν τὰ μέταλλ' ἐωνημένων εἴκοσιν ἐξέλεξε δραχ-
μὰς παρ' ἑκάστου, καὶ Κηφισοφῶντα γραφὴν
ἱερῶν χρημάτων ἐδίωκες, εἰ τρισὶν ὕστερον ἡμέραις
ἐπὶ τὴν τράπεζαν ἔθηκεν ἑπτὰ μνᾶς· τοὺς δ'
ἔχοντας, ὁμολογοῦντας, ἐξελεγχομένους ἐπ' αὐτοφώρῳ ἐπὶ τῷ τῶν συμμάχων ὀλέθρῳ ταῦτα
πεποιηκότας, τούτους οὐ κρίνεις, ἀλλὰ καὶ σῴζειν
294 κελεύεις; καὶ μὴν ὅτι ταῦτα μέν ἐστι φοβερὰ καὶ
προνοίας καὶ φυλακῆς πολλῆς δεόμενα, ἐφ' οἷς δ'
ἐκείνους σὺ ἔκρινες, γέλως, ἐκείνως ὄψεσθε. ἦσαν
ἐν Ἤλιδι κλέπτοντες τὰ κοινά τινες· καὶ μάλ'
εἰκός γε. ἔστιν οὖν ὅστις μετέσχεν αὐτόθι νῦν
τούτων τοῦ καταλῦσαι τὸν δῆμον; οὐδὲ εἷς. τί
δ'; ἦσαν, ὅτ' ἦν Ὄλυνθος, τοιοῦτοί τινες ἄλλοι;
ἐγὼ μὲν οἶμαι. ἆρ' οὖν διὰ τούτους ἀπώλετ'
Ὄλυνθος; οὔ. τί δ'; ἐν Μεγάροις οὐκ οἴεσθ'
εἶναί τινα κλέπτην καὶ παρεκλέγοντα τὰ κοινά;
ἀνάγκη. καὶ πέφηνέ τις αἴτιος αὐτόθι νῦν τούτων
295 τῶν συμβεβηκότων πραγμάτων; οὐδὲ εἷς. ἀλλὰ
ποῖοί τινες οἱ τὰ τηλικαῦτα καὶ τοιαῦτ' ἀδικοῦντες;
οἱ νομίζοντες αὑτοὺς ἀξιόχρεως εἶναι τοῦ Φιλίππου
ξένοι καὶ φίλοι προσαγορεύεσθαι, οἱ στρατηγιῶντες
καὶ προστασίας ἀξιούμενοι, οἱ μείζους τῶν πολλῶν
οἰόμενοι δεῖν εἶναι. οὐ Πέριλλος[1] ἐκρίνετ' ἔναγχος
[436] ἐν Μεγάροις ἐν τοῖς τριακοσίοις, ὅτι πρὸς Φίλιππον
ἀφίκετο, καὶ παρελθὼν Πτοιόδωρος αὐτὸν ἐξῃτή-

---

[1] Πέριλλος edd. : Shill. with mss. Πέριλαος. See *De cor.* 48.

of Aeschines ? How can Philip be utterly destroyed, if you rescue the men who take his bribes ? Why did you prosecute Moerocles, because he had extorted twenty drachmas apiece from the lessees of the silver-mines ; why did you indict Cephisophon for misappropriating sacred funds, because he was three days late in paying seven minas into the bank, if, instead of prosecuting, you now try to rescue men who have confessed, who have been caught in the act, who are convicted of taking bribes for the destruction of our allies ? Yes, these are formidable offences, calling for the utmost vigilance and precaution ; while the charges you brought against those two men were comparatively ludicrous, as these considerations will show. Were there any persons in Elis who embezzled public money ? In all probability, yes. Did any one of them take part in the recent overthrow of free government there ? Not one. When there was still such a city as Olynthus, were there any thieves there ? I take it there were. Did Olynthus perish through their sins ? No. Do you suppose there were no thieves and pilferers of public funds in Megara ? There must have been such. Has any one of them been shown to be responsible for the present political troubles there ? Not one. Then who are the people who commit these monstrous crimes ? Persons who fancy themselves important enough to be called friends of Philip, men itching for military commands and eager for political distinction, men who claim superiority over the common herd. At Megara the other day was not Perillus tried before the Three Hundred on a charge of visiting Philip ? And did not Ptoeodorus, the first man in all Megara for

σατο, καὶ πλούτῳ καὶ γένει καὶ δόξῃ πρῶτος
Μεγαρέων, καὶ πάλιν ὡς Φίλιππον ἐξέπεμψε,
καὶ μετὰ ταῦθ' ὁ μὲν ἧκεν ἄγων τοὺς ξένους, ὁ δ'
296 ἔνδον ἐτύρευε; τοιαῦτα. οὐ γὰρ ἔστιν, οὐκ ἔσθ'
ὅ τι τῶν πάντων μᾶλλον εὐλαβεῖσθαι δεῖ ἢ τὸ
μείζω τινὰ τῶν πολλῶν ἐᾶν γίγνεσθαι. μή μοι
σῳζέσθω μηδ' ἀπολλύσθω μηδείς, ἐὰν ὁ δεῖνα
ἢ ὁ δεῖνα βούληται, ἀλλ' ὃν ἂν τὰ πεπραγμένα
σῴζῃ καὶ τοὐναντίον, τούτῳ τῆς προσηκούσης
ψήφου παρ' ὑμῶν ὑπαρχέτω τυγχάνειν· τοῦτο
297 γάρ ἐστι δημοτικόν. ἔτι τοίνυν πολλοὶ παρ'
ὑμῖν ἐπὶ καιρῶν γεγόνασιν ἰσχυροί, Καλλίστρατος
ἐκεῖνος, αὖθις Ἀριστοφῶν, Διόφαντος, τούτων
ἕτεροι πρότερον. ἀλλὰ ποῦ τούτων ἕκαστος ἐπρώ-
τευεν; ἐν τῷ δήμῳ· ἐν δὲ τοῖς δικαστηρίοις οὐδείς
πω μέχρι τῆς τήμερον ἡμέρας ὑμῶν οὐδὲ τῶν
νόμων οὐδὲ τῶν ὅρκων κρείττων γέγονεν. μὴ
τοίνυν μηδὲ νῦν τοῦτον ἐάσητε. ὅτι γὰρ ταῦτα
φυλάττοισθ' ἂν εἰκότως μᾶλλον ἢ πιστεύοιτε,
τῶν θεῶν ὑμῖν μαντείαν ἀναγνώσομαι, οἵπερ ἀεὶ
σῴζουσι τὴν πόλιν πολλῷ τῶν προεστηκότων
μᾶλλον. λέγε τὰς μαντείας.

ΜΑΝΤΕΙΑΙ

298 Ἀκούετ', ὦ ἄνδρες Ἀθηναῖοι, τῶν θεῶν ἃ ὑμῖν
προλέγουσιν. εἰ μὲν τοίνυν πολεμούντων ὑμῶν
ταῦτ' ἀνῃρήκασι, τοὺς στρατηγοὺς λέγουσι φυλάτ-
τεσθαι· πολέμου γάρ εἰσιν ἡγεμόνες οἱ στρατηγοί·
εἰ δὲ πεποιημένων εἰρήνην, τοὺς ἐπὶ τῆς πολιτείας
ἐφεστηκότας· οὗτοι γὰρ ἡγοῦνται, τούτοις πεί-
[437] θεσθ' ὑμεῖς, ὑπὸ τούτων δέος ἐστὶ μὴ παρα-

wealth, birth, and reputation, come forward and beg him off, and then send him back to Philip ? The sequel was that one of the pair returned with an alien army at his back, while the other was hatching the plot at home. Take that as a specimen. Indeed, there is no danger, no danger whatsoever, that requires more anxious vigilance than allowing any man to become stronger than the people. Let no man be delivered, and let no man be destroyed, merely because this man or that so desires ; let him who is delivered or destroyed by the evidence of facts be entitled to receive from this court the verdict that is his due. That is the democratic principle. Furthermore, at Athens many men have upon occasion risen to power—the great Callistratus, for instance, Aristophon, Diophantus, and others of earlier date. But what was the field of their supremacy ? The popular assembly. In courts of justice no man to this day has ever been superior to the people, or to the laws, or to the judicial oath. Then permit no such superiority to Aeschines to-day. To enforce the warning that it is better to take those precautions than to be credulous, I will read to you an oracle of the gods,—to whom Athens owes her salvation far more than to her most prominent politicians. Read the oracles.

(*The Oracles are read*)

Men of Athens, you hear the admonitions of the gods. If they are addressed to you in time of war, they bid you beware of your commanders, for commanders are the leaders of warfare ; if after conclusion of peace, of your statesmen, for they are your leaders, they have your obedience, by them

κρουσθῆτε. καὶ τὴν πόλιν συνέχειν φησὶν ἡ μαντεία,
ὅπως ἂν μίαν γνώμην ἔχωσιν ἅπαντες καὶ μὴ
299 τοῖς ἐχθροῖς ἡδονὴν ποιῶσι. πότερον οὖν οἴεσθ᾽
ἄν, ὦ ἄνδρες Ἀθηναῖοι, τὸν τοσαῦτα κάκ᾽ εἰργα-
σμένον σωθέντ᾽ ἢ δίκην δόνθ᾽ ἡδονὴν Φιλίππῳ
ποιῆσαι; ἐγὼ μὲν οἶμαι σωθέντα. φησὶ δέ γ᾽ ἡ
μαντεία δεῖν ὅπως ἂν μὴ χαίρωσιν οἱ ἐχθροὶ ποιεῖν.
ἅπασι τοίνυν μιᾷ γνώμῃ παρακελεύεται κολάζειν
τοὺς ὑπηρετηκότας τι τοῖς ἐχθροῖς ὁ Ζεύς, ἡ
Διώνη, πάντες οἱ θεοί. ἔξωθεν οἱ ἐπιβουλεύοντες,
ἔνδοθεν οἱ συμπράττοντες. οὐκοῦν τῶν ἐπιβου-
λευόντων μὲν ἔργον διδόναι, τῶν συμπραττόντων
δὲ λαμβάνειν καὶ τοὺς εἰληφότας ἐκσῴζειν.

300 Ἔτι τοίνυν κἂν ἀπ᾽ ἀνθρωπίνου λογισμοῦ τοῦτ᾽
ἴδοι τις, ὅτι πάντων ἐχθρότατον καὶ φοβερώτατον
τὸ τὸν προεστηκότ᾽ ἐὰν οἰκεῖον γίγνεσθαι τοῖς μὴ
τῶν αὐτῶν ἐπιθυμοῦσι τῷ δήμῳ. τίσι γὰρ τῶν
πραγμάτων ἐγκρατὴς γέγονε Φίλιππος ἁπάντων,
καὶ τίσι τὰ μέγιστα κατείργασται τῶν πεπραγμένων, σκέψασθε. τῷ παρὰ τῶν πωλούντων τὰς
πράξεις ὠνεῖσθαι, τῷ τοὺς προεστηκότας ἐν ταῖς
301 πόλεσι διαφθείρειν καὶ ἐπαίρειν, τούτοις. ταῦτα
τοίνυν ἐφ᾽ ὑμῖν ἐστιν ἀμφότερα, ἐὰν βούλησθε,
ἀχρεῖα ποιῆσαι τήμερον, ἐὰν τῶν μὲν μὴ ᾽θέλητ᾽
ἀκούειν τῶν τοῖς τοιούτοις συνηγορούντων, ἀλλ᾽
ἐπιδείξητ᾽ ἀκύρους ὄντας ὑμῶν (νῦν γάρ φασιν
εἶναι κύριοι), τὸν δὲ πεπρακόθ᾽ ἑαυτὸν κολάσητε,
302 καὶ τοῦθ᾽ ἅπαντες ἴδωσιν. παντὶ μὲν γὰρ εἰκότως
[438] ἂν ὀργισθείητ᾽, ὦ ἄνδρες Ἀθηναῖοι, τοιαῦτα πε-
ποιηκότι καὶ προδεδωκότι συμμάχους καὶ φίλους
καὶ καιρούς, μεθ᾽ ὧν ἢ καλῶς ἢ κακῶς ἑκάστοις

you may haply be deceived. The oracle also bids you keep the commonwealth together, that all may be of one mind, and may not gratify the enemy. What do you think, men of Athens ? Will Philip be gratified by the deliverance or by the punishment of the man who has done all this mischief ? By his deliverance surely ; but the oracle bids you strive that the enemy shall not rejoice. Therefore, you are all exhorted by Zeus, by Dione, by all the gods, to punish with one mind those who have made themselves the servants of your enemies. There are foes without ; there are traitors within. It is the business of foes to give bribes, of traitors to take bribes, and to rescue those who have taken them.

Moreover, it can be shown by mere human reasoning that it is extremely injurious and dangerous to permit the intimacy of a prominent statesman with men whose purposes are at variance with those of the people. If you will consider by what means Philip acquired his political supremacy and performed his most signal achievements, you will find that it was by buying treachery from willing sellers, and by corrupting leading politicians and stimulating their ambition. Both these practices it is within your power, if you so choose, to frustrate to-day, if you will first refuse to listen to the defenders of treachery, and prove that they cannot exercise that authority over you of which they boast, and then punish before the eyes of the world the man who has traitorously sold himself. You have good reason, men of Athens, to be indignant with every man who by such conduct has thrown overboard your allies, your friends, and those opportunities on which, for any nation, success or failure depends, but with no

DEMOSTHENES

ἔχει τὰ πάντα, οὐ μὴν οὐδενὶ μᾶλλον οὐδὲ δικαιότερον ἢ τούτῳ. ὃς γὰρ ἑαυτὸν τάξας τῶν ἀ-
πιστούντων εἶναι Φιλίππῳ, καὶ μόνος καὶ πρῶτος
ἰδὼν ὅτι κοινὸς ἐχθρὸς ἐκεῖνός ἐστιν ἁπάντων τῶν
Ἑλλήνων, ηὐτομόλησε καὶ προὔδωκε καὶ γέγονεν
ἐξαίφνης ὑπὲρ Φιλίππου, πῶς οὐ πολλάκις οὗτος
303 ἄξιός ἐστ' ἀπολωλέναι; ἀλλὰ μὴν ὅτι ταῦθ' οὕτως
ἔχει, αὐτὸς οὐχ οἷός τ' ἀντειπεῖν ἔσται. τίς γάρ
ἐσθ' ὁ τὸν Ἴσχανδρον προσάγων ὑμῖν τὸ κατ'
ἀρχάς, ὃν παρὰ τῶν ἐν Ἀρκαδίᾳ φίλων τῇ πόλει
δεῦρ' ἥκειν ἔφη; τίς ὁ συσκευάζεσθαι τὴν Ἑλλάδα
καὶ Πελοπόννησον Φίλιππον βοῶν, ὑμᾶς δὲ καθ-
εύδειν; τίς ὁ τοὺς μακροὺς καὶ καλοὺς λόγους
ἐκείνους δημηγορῶν, καὶ τὸ Μιλτιάδου καὶ τὸ[1]
Θεμιστοκλέους ψήφισμ' ἀναγιγνώσκων καὶ τὸν ἐν
304 τῷ τῆς Ἀγλαύρου τῶν ἐφήβων ὅρκον; οὐχ οὗτος;
τίς ὁ πείσας ὑμᾶς μόνον οὐκ ἐπὶ τὴν ἐρυθρὰν
θάλατταν πρεσβείας πέμπειν, ὡς ἐπιβουλευο-
μένης μὲν ὑπὸ Φιλίππου τῆς Ἑλλάδος, ὑμῖν δὲ
προσῆκον προορᾶν ταῦτα καὶ μὴ προΐεσθαι τὰ
τῶν Ἑλλήνων; οὐχ ὁ μὲν γράφων τὸ ψήφισμ'
Εὔβουλος ἦν, ὁ δὲ πρεσβεύων εἰς Πελοπόννησον
Αἰσχίνης οὑτοσί; ἐλθὼν δ' ἐκεῖσε ἄττα μέν ποτε
διελέχθη καὶ ἐδημηγόρησεν, αὐτὸς ἂν εἰδείη, ἃ δ'
ἀπήγγειλε πρὸς ὑμᾶς, ὑμεῖς οἶδ' ὅτι μέμνησθε
305 πάντες. βάρβαρόν τε γὰρ πολλάκις καὶ ἀλάστορα
τὸν Φίλιππον ἀποκαλῶν ἐδημηγόρει, καὶ τοὺς
[439] Ἀρκάδας ὑμῖν ἀπήγγελλεν ὡς ἔχαιρον, εἰ προσέχει
τοῖς πράγμασιν ἤδη καὶ ἐγείρεται ἡ τῶν Ἀθηναίων

---

[1] τὸ before Θεμιστοκλέους added by Weil : Shilleto omits
with MSS.

man more fiercely or more righteously than with Aeschines. For a man who once ranged himself with those who distrusted Philip, and made unassisted the first discovery of Philip's hostility to all Greece, and then became a deserter and a traitor and suddenly appeared as Philip's champion—does he not deserve a hundred deaths ? Yet that such are the facts, he will not be able to deny. For who originally introduced Ischander to you, declaring him to have come as the representative of the Arcadian friends of Athens ? Who raised the cry that Philip was forming coalitions in Greece and Peloponnesus while you slept ? Who made those long and eloquent speeches, and read the decrees of Miltiades and Themistocles and the oath which our young men take in the temple of Aglaurus [a] ? Was it not Aeschines ? Who persuaded you to send embassies almost as far as the Red Sea, declaring that Greece was the object of Philip's designs, and that it was your duty to anticipate the danger and not be disloyal to the Hellenic cause ? Was it not Eubulus who proposed the decree, and the defendant Aeschines who went as ambassador to the Peloponnesus ? What he said there after his arrival, either in conversation or in public speeches, is best known to himself : what he reported on his return I am sure you have not forgotten. For he made a speech in which he repeatedly called Philip a barbarian and a man of blood. He told you that the Arcadians were delighted to hear that Athens was really waking

---

[a] *Aglaurus*: daughter of Cecrops, legendary king of Attica ; canonized for an act of patriotic self-devotion. In her chapel young Athenians, on admission to citizenship, received their arms, and took the oath of loyalty.

πόλις. ὃ δὲ πάντων μάλιστ' ἀγανακτῆσαι ἔφη·
συντυχεῖν γὰρ ἀπιὼν Ἀτρεστίδᾳ παρὰ Φιλίππου
πορευομένῳ, καὶ μετ' αὐτοῦ γύναια καὶ παιδάρι'
ὡς τριάκοντα βαδίζειν, αὐτὸς δὲ θαυμάσας ἐρέσθαι
τινὰ τῶν ὁδοιπόρων, τίς ἄνθρωπός ἐστι καὶ τίς
306 ὄχλος ὁ μετ' αὐτοῦ, ἐπειδὴ δ' ἀκοῦσαι ὅτι Ἀτρε-
στίδας παρὰ Φιλίππου τῶν Ὀλυνθίων αἰχμάλωτα
δωρεὰν ταῦτ' ἔχων ἀπέρχεται, δεινὸν αὐτῷ τι
δόξαι καὶ δακρῦσαι καὶ ὀδύρασθαι τὴν Ἑλλάδα,
ὡς κακῶς διάκειται, εἰ τοιαῦτα πάθη περιορᾷ
γιγνόμενα. καὶ συνεβούλευεν ὑμῖν πέμπειν τινὰς
εἰς Ἀρκαδίαν οἵτινες κατηγορήσουσι τῶν τὰ
Φιλίππου πραττόντων· ἀκούειν γὰρ ἔφη τῶν
φίλων, ὡς ἐὰν ἐπιστροφὴν ἡ πόλις ποιήσηται καὶ
307 πρέσβεις πέμψῃ, δίκην ἐκεῖνοι δώσουσιν. ταῦτα
μὲν τοίνυν τότε καὶ μάλ', ὦ ἄνδρες Ἀθηναῖοι,
καλὰ καὶ τῆς πόλεως ἄξι' ἐδημηγόρει. ἐπειδὴ
δ' ἀφίκετ' εἰς Μακεδονίαν καὶ τὸν ἐχθρὸν εἶδε
τὸν αὐτοῦ καὶ τῶν Ἑλλήνων,[1] ἆρά γ' ὅμοι' ἢ παραπλήσια τούτοις; πολλοῦ γε καὶ δεῖ, ἀλλὰ μήτε
τῶν προγόνων μεμνῆσθαι μήτε τρόπαια λέγειν
μήτε βοηθεῖν μηδενί, τῶν τε κελευόντων μετὰ
τῶν Ἑλλήνων περὶ τῆς πρὸς Φίλιππον εἰρήνης
βουλεύεσθαι θαυμάζειν, εἰ περὶ τῶν ὑμετέρων
308 ἰδίων ἄλλον τινὰ δεῖ πεισθῆναι· εἶναί τε τὸν
Φίλιππον αὐτόν, Ἡράκλεις, ἑλληνικώτατον ἀνθρώπων, δεινότατον λέγειν, φιλαθηναιότατον· οὕτω
δ' ἀτόπους τινὰς ἐν τῇ πόλει καὶ δυσχερεῖς ἀνθρώ-

---

[1] (After καὶ τῶν Ἑλλήνων) τὸν Φίλιππον Shilleto with
mss. : struck out by Cobet.

446

up and attending to business. He related an incident which, he said, had filled him with deep indignation. On his journey home he had met Atrestidas travelling from Philip's court with some thirty women and children in his train. He was astonished, and inquired of one of the travellers who the man and his throng of followers were ; and when he was told that they were Olynthian captives whom Atrestidas was bringing away with him as a present from Philip, he thought it a terrible business, and burst into tears. Greece, he sorrowfully reflected, is in evil plight indeed, if she permits such cruelties to pass unchecked. He counselled you to send envoys to Arcadia to denounce the persons who were intriguing for Philip ; for, he said, he had been informed that, if only Athens would give attention to the matter and send ambassadors, the intriguers would promptly be brought to justice. Such was his speech on that occasion ; a noble speech, worthy of our Athenian traditions. But after he had visited Macedonia, and beheld his own enemy and the enemy of all Greece, did his language bear the slightest resemblance to those utterances ? Not in the least : he bade you not to remember your forefathers, not to talk about trophies, not to carry succour to anybody. As for the people who recommended you to consult the Greeks on the terms of peace with Philip, he was amazed at the suggestion that it was necessary that any foreigner should be convinced when the questions were purely domestic. And as for Philip,—why, good Heavens, he was a Greek of the Greeks, the finest orator and the most thorough-going friend of Athens you could find in the whole world. And yet there were some queer,

DEMOSTHENES

πους εἶναι, ὥστ᾽ οὐκ αἰσχύνεσθαι λοιδορουμένους
[440] αὐτῷ καὶ βάρβαρον αὐτὸν ἀποκαλοῦντας.

309 Ἔστιν οὖν ὅπως ταῦτ᾽ ἄν, ἐκεῖνα προειρηκώς,
ὁ αὐτὸς ἀνὴρ μὴ διαφθαρεὶς ἐτόλμησεν εἰπεῖν; τί
δ᾽; ἔστιν ὅστις ἂν τὸν Ἀτρεστίδαν τότε μισήσας
διὰ τοὺς τῶν Ὀλυνθίων παῖδας καὶ γύναια ταὐτὰ
Φιλοκράτει νῦν πράττειν ὑπέμεινεν, ὃς γυναῖκας
ἐλευθέρας τῶν Ὀλυνθίων ἤγαγε δεῦρο ἐφ᾽ ὕβρει,
καὶ οὕτως ἐπὶ τῷ βδελυρῶς βεβιωκέναι γιγνώ-
σκεται, ὥστε μηδὲν ἔμ᾽ αἰσχρὸν εἰπεῖν νυνὶ περὶ
αὐτοῦ δεῖν μηδὲ δυσχερές, ἀλλὰ τοσοῦτον εἰπόντος
μόνον, ὅτι Φιλοκράτης γυναῖκας ἤγαγε, πάντας
ὑμᾶς εἰδέναι καὶ τοὺς περιεστηκότας τὰ μετὰ
ταῦτα, καὶ ἐλεεῖν εὖ οἶδ᾽ ὅτι τὰς ἀτυχεῖς καὶ ταλαιπώρους ἀνθρώπους, ἃς οὐκ ἠλέησεν Αἰσχίνης,
οὐδ᾽ ἐδάκρυσ᾽ ἐπὶ ταύταις τὴν Ἑλλάδα, εἰ παρὰ
τοῖς συμμάχοις ὑπὸ τῶν πρέσβεων ὑβρίζονται;

310 Ἀλλ᾽ ὑπὲρ αὑτοῦ κλαήσει τοῦ τὰ τοιαῦτα
πεπρεσβευκότος, καὶ τὰ παιδί᾽ ἴσως παράξει
κἀναβιβᾶται. ὑμεῖς δ᾽ ἐνθυμεῖσθ᾽, ὦ ἄνδρες δικασταί, πρὸς μὲν τὰ τούτου παιδία, ὅτι πολλῶν
συμμάχων ὑμετέρων καὶ φίλων παῖδες ἀλῶνται
καὶ πτωχοὶ περιέρχονται δεινὰ πεπονθότες διὰ
τοῦτον, οὓς ἐλεεῖν πολλῷ μᾶλλον ὑμῖν ἄξιον ἢ
τοὺς τοῦ ἠδικηκότος καὶ προδότου πατρός, καὶ
ὅτι τοὺς ὑμετέρους παῖδας οὗτοι, "καὶ τοῖς
ἐγγόνοις" προσγράψαντες εἰς τὴν εἰρήνην, καὶ
448

ill-conditioned fellows in Athens who did not blush to abuse him, and even to call him a barbarian !

Is it, then, conceivable that the man who made the earlier of those speeches should also have made the later unless he had been corrupted ? Is it possible that the same man who was then inflamed with abhorrence of Atrestidas on account of those Olynthian women and children, should now be content to co-operate with Philocrates, who brought free-born Olynthian ladies to this city for their dishonour ? Philocrates is now so notorious for the infamous life he has lived that I need not apply to him any degrading or offensive epithet. When I merely mention that he did bring the ladies, there is not a man in this court, whether on the jury or among the onlookers, who does not know the sequel, and who does not, I am sure, feel compassion for those miserable and unfortunate beings. Yet Aeschines had no compassion for them. He did not shed tears over Greece on their account, indignant that they should suffer outrage in an allied country at the hands of Athenian ambassadors.

No ; our discredited ambassador will keep all his tears for himself. Very likely he will bring his children into court and put them in a conspicuous position. But do you, gentlemen of the jury, as you look at those children of his, reflect how many children of your own friends and allies are wanderers, roaming the world in beggary, suffering hardships which they owe to this man ; and that they deserve your compassion infinitely more than the offspring of a malefactor and a traitor, while, by adding to the treaty of peace the words *and to their posterity*, he and his friends robbed your own children even

τῶν ἐλπίδων ἀπεστερήκασι, πρὸς δὲ τὰ αὐτοῦ
τούτου δάκρυα, ὅτι νῦν ἔχετ᾽ ἄνθρωπον, ὃς εἰς
Ἀρκαδίαν ἐκέλευεν ἐπὶ τοὺς ὑπὲρ Φιλίππου πράτ-
311 τοντας πέμπειν τοὺς κατηγορήσοντας. νῦν τοίνυν
[441] ὑμᾶς οὐκ εἰς Πελοπόννησον δεῖ πρεσβείαν πέμπειν,
οὐδ᾽ ὁδὸν μακρὰν βαδίσαι, οὐδ᾽ ἐφόδι᾽ ἀναλίσκειν,
ἀλλ᾽ ἄχρι τοῦ βήματος ἐνταυθὶ προσελθόνθ᾽ ἕκαστον ὑμῶν τὴν ὁσίαν καὶ τὴν δικαίαν ψῆφον ὑπὲρ
τῆς πατρίδος θέσθαι κατ᾽ ἀνδρός, ὅς, ὦ γῆ καὶ
θεοί, ἐκεῖν᾽ ἃ διεξῆλθον ἐν ἀρχῇ δεδημηγορηκώς,
τὸν Μαραθῶνα, τὴν Σαλαμῖνα, τὰς μάχας, τὰ
τρόπαια, ἐξαίφνης ὡς ἐπέβη Μακεδονίας, πάντα
τἀναντία τούτοις, μὴ προγόνων μεμνῆσθαι, μὴ
τρόπαια λέγειν, μὴ βοηθεῖν μηδενί, μὴ κοινῇ μετὰ
τῶν Ἑλλήνων βουλεύεσθαι, μόνον οὐ καθελεῖν
312 τὰ τείχη. καίτοι τούτων αἰσχίους λόγοι οὐδένες
πώποτ᾽ ἐν τῷ παντὶ χρόνῳ γεγόνασι παρ᾽ ὑμῖν.
τίς γάρ ἐστιν Ἑλλήνων ἢ βαρβάρων οὕτω σκαιὸς
ἢ ἀνήκοος ἢ σφόδρα μισῶν τὴν πόλιν τὴν ἡμετέραν,
ὅστις, εἴ τις ἔροιτ᾽, "εἰπέ μοι, τῆς νῦν οὔσης
Ἑλλάδος ταυτησὶ καὶ οἰκουμένης ἔσθ᾽ ὅ τι ταύτην
ἂν τὴν προσηγορίαν εἶχεν ἢ ᾠκεῖθ᾽ ὑπὸ τῶν νῦν
ἐχόντων Ἑλλήνων, εἰ μὴ τὰς ἀρετὰς ὑπὲρ αὐτῶν
ἐκείνας οἱ Μαραθῶνι καὶ Σαλαμῖνι παρέσχονθ᾽
οἱ ἡμέτεροι πρόγονοι;" οὐδ᾽ ἂν εἷς εὖ οἶδ᾽ ὅτι
φήσειεν, ἀλλὰ πάντα ταῦθ᾽ ὑπὸ τῶν βαρβάρων
313 ἂν ἑαλωκέναι. εἶθ᾽ οὓς μηδὲ τῶν ἐχθρῶν μηδεὶς
ἂν τούτων τῶν ἐγκωμίων καὶ τῶν ἐπαίνων ἀπο-
στερήσειε, τούτων Αἰσχίνης ὑμᾶς οὐκ ἐᾷ μεμνη-
450

of hope. When you witness his tears, remember that you hold in your power a man who bade you send accusers to Arcadia to testify against the agents of Philip. And so to-day you have no need to send a mission to Peloponnesus, to make a long journey, or to pay travelling expenses ; you have only to advance one by one to this platform, and there cast a just and a righteous vote for your country's sake against the man who, having at the outset, as I described to you, spoken so eloquently about Marathon and Salamis, about battles and victories, from the moment he set foot on Macedonian soil contradicted his own utterances, forbade you to remember the example of your forefathers, or recall old victories, or carry succour to your friends, or take common counsel with the Greeks, and well-nigh bade you to dismantle the defences of your city. No more disgraceful speeches have ever been made in your hearing during the whole course of your history. Lives there a man, Greek or barbarian, so boorish, so unversed in history, or so ill-disposed to our commonwealth that, if he were asked the question, " Tell me, in all the country that we call Greece and inhabit to-day, is there an acre that would still bear that name, or remain the home of the Greeks who now possess it, if the heroes of Marathon and Salamis, our forefathers, had not in their defence performed those glorious deeds of valour," is there one man who would not make reply : " No ; the whole country would have become the prey of the barbarian invaders " ? Even among your foes there is not a man who would despoil those heroes of their meed of praise and gratitude ; and does an Aeschines forbid you, their own descendants,

DEMOSTHENES

σθαι, τοὺς ἐξ ἐκείνων, ἵν' αὐτὸς ἀργύριον λάβῃ;
καὶ μὴν τῶν μὲν ἄλλων ἀγαθῶν οὐ μέτεστι τοῖς
τεθνεῶσιν, οἱ δ' ἐπὶ τοῖς καλῶς πραχθεῖσιν ἔπαινοι
τῶν οὕτω τετελευτηκότων ἴδιον κτῆμ' εἰσίν· οὐδὲ
[442] γὰρ ὁ φθόνος αὐτοῖς ἔτι τηνικαῦτ' ἐναντιοῦται.
ὧν ἀποστερῶν ἐκείνους οὗτος αὐτὸς ἂν τῆς ἐπι-
τιμίας δικαίως νῦν στερηθείη, καὶ ταύτην ὑπὲρ
τῶν προγόνων ὑμεῖς δίκην λάβοιτε παρ' αὐτοῦ.
τοιούτοις μέντοι λόγοις, ὦ κακὴ κεφαλή, σύ, τὰ
τῶν προγόνων ἔργα συλήσας καὶ διασύρας τῷ
314 λόγῳ, πάντα τὰ πράγματ' ἀπώλεσας. εἶτα γεωρ-
γεῖς ἐκ τούτων καὶ σεμνὸς γέγονας. καὶ γὰρ
αὖ τοῦτο· πρὸ μὲν τοῦ πάντα κάκ' εἰργάσθαι τὴν
πόλιν ὡμολόγει γεγραμματευκέναι καὶ χάριν ὑμῖν
ἔχειν τοῦ χειροτονηθῆναι, καὶ μέτριον παρεῖχεν
ἑαυτόν· ἐπειδὴ δὲ μυρί' εἴργασται κακά, τὰς
ὀφρῦς ἀνέσπακε, κἂν "ὁ γεγραμματευκὼς Αἰσχίνης" εἴπῃ τις, ἐχθρὸς εὐθέως, καὶ κακῶς φησιν
ἀκηκοέναι, καὶ διὰ τῆς ἀγορᾶς πορεύεται θοἰμά-
τιον καθεὶς ἄχρι τῶν σφυρῶν, ἴσα βαίνων Πυθοκλεῖ,
τὰς γνάθους φυσῶν, τῶν Φιλίππου ξένων καὶ
φίλων εἷς οὗτος ὑμῖν ἤδη, τῶν ἀπαλλαγῆναι τοῦ
δήμου βουλομένων καὶ κλύδωνα καὶ μανίαν τὰ
καθεστηκότα πράγμαθ' ἡγουμένων, ὁ τέως προσ-
κυνῶν τὴν θόλον.

315 Βούλομαι τοίνυν ὑμῖν ἐπανελθεῖν ἐπὶ κεφα-
λαίων, ὃν τρόπον ὑμᾶς κατεπολιτεύσατο Φίλιππος
προσλαβὼν τούτους τοὺς θεοῖς ἐχθρούς. πάνυ δ'

***

^a See § 249.

to commemorate their names—all for the sake of his miserable bribes? There are indeed rewards in which the dead have no part or lot; but the praise that waits on glorious achievements is the peculiar guerdon of those who have gloriously died —for then jealousy is no longer their adversary. Let the man who would rob the dead of their reward be stripped of his own honours: that retribution you will levy on him for your forefathers' sake. By those speeches of yours, you reprobate, you made havoc of our policy, traducing and disparaging with your tongue the achievements of our forefathers. And from these performances you emerge a land-owner, a person of high consideration! Take another point. Before he did all that mischief to the commonwealth, he used to admit that he had been a clerk; he was grateful to you for his appointments; his demeanour was quite modest. But since he has perpetrated wrongs without number, he has become mightily supercilious. If a man speaks of "Aeschines, the man who was once a clerk," he makes a private quarrel of it, and talks of defamation of character. Behold him pacing the market-place with the stately stride of Pythocles, his long robe reaching to his ankles, his cheeks puffed out, as who should say, "One of Philip's most intimate friends, at your service!" He has joined the clique that wants to get rid of democracy,—that regards the established political order as an inconstant wave, —mere midsummer madness. And once he made obeisance to the Rotunda![a]

Now I wish by a brief recapitulation to remind you of the manner in which Philip discomfited your policy with these scoundrels as his confederates.

DEMOSTHENES

ἄξιον ἐξετάσαι καὶ θεάσασθαι τὴν ἀπάτην ὅλην. τὸ μὲν γὰρ ἀπ' ἀρχῆς τῆς εἰρήνης ἐπιθυμῶν, διαφορουμένης αὐτοῦ τῆς χώρας ὑπὸ τῶν λῃστῶν καὶ κεκλειμένων τῶν ἐμπορίων, ὥστ' ἀνόνητον ἐκεῖνον ἁπάντων εἶναι τῶν ἀγαθῶν, τοὺς τὰ φιλάνθρωπα λέγοντας ἐκείνους ἀπέστειλεν ὑπὲρ αὐτοῦ, τὸν Νεοπτόλεμον, τὸν Ἀριστόδημον, τὸν 316 Κτησιφῶντα· ἐπειδὴ δ' ἤλθομεν ὡς αὐτὸν ἡμεῖς 443] οἱ πρέσβεις, ἐμισθώσατο μὲν τοῦτον εὐθέως, ὅπως συνερεῖ καὶ συναγωνιεῖται τῷ μιαρῷ Φιλο- κράτει καὶ τῶν τὰ δίκαια βουλομένων ἡμῶν πράττειν περιέσται, συνέγραψε δ' ἐπιστολὴν ὡς 317 ὑμᾶς, ᾗ μάλιστ' ἂν ᾤετο τῆς εἰρήνης τυχεῖν. ἦν δ' οὐδὲν μᾶλλον μέγ' αὐτῷ καθ' ὑμῶν οὐδ' οὕτω πρᾶξαι, εἰ μὴ Φωκέας ἀπολεῖ. τοῦτο δ' οὐκ ἦν εὔπορον· συνῆκτο γὰρ αὐτῷ τὰ πράγματα, ὥσπερ ἐκ τύχης, εἰς καιρὸν τοιοῦτον, ὥστ' ἢ μηδὲν ὧν ἐβούλετ' εἶναι διαπράξασθαι, ἢ ἀνάγκην εἶναι ψεύσασθαι κἀπιορκῆσαι καὶ μάρτυρας τῆς αὐτοῦ κακίας πάντας Ἕλληνας καὶ βαρβάρους ποιή- 318 σασθαι. εἰ μὲν γὰρ προσδέξαιτο Φωκέας συμ- μάχους καὶ μεθ' ὑμῶν τοὺς ὅρκους αὐτοῖς ἀποδοίη, τοὺς πρὸς Θετταλοὺς καὶ Θηβαίους ὅρκους παρα- βαίνειν εὐθὺς ἀναγκαῖον ἦν, ὧν τοῖς μὲν τὴν Βοιωτίαν συνεξαιρήσειν ὠμωμόκει, τοῖς δὲ τὴν Πυλαίαν συγκαταστήσειν· εἰ δὲ μὴ προσδέχοιτο, ὥσπερ οὐ προσίετο, οὐκ ἐάσειν ὑμᾶς παρελθεῖν αὐτὸν ἡγεῖτο, ἀλλὰ βοηθήσειν εἰς Πύλας, ὅπερ, εἰ μὴ παρεκρούσθητε, ἐποιήσατ' ἄν· εἰ δὲ τοῦτο

454

It is well worth while to examine and contemplate the whole imposition. At the outset he was really desirous of peace, for his whole country was overrun by banditti, and his ports were blockaded, so that he got no advantage from all his wealth. Accordingly he sent those envoys who addressed you in his name with so much courtesy—Neoptolemus, Aristodemus, and Ctesiphon. But as soon as he was visited by us ambassadors, he promptly took Aeschines into his pay, that he might support and co-operate with the infamous Philocrates, and overpower those of us whose intentions were honest. He then composed a letter to you, as the best means of obtaining the peace he desired. Even then it was still out of his power to achieve any important result to your disadvantage, unless he should destroy the Phocians. That was no easy task, for, as luck would have it, his affairs had reached a crisis of such a nature that either he could not realize any of his purposes, or else he was obliged to commit falsehood and perjury, with the whole world, both Greek and barbarian, to witness his wickedness. For if he should accept the Phocians as allies, and with your help take the oath of friendship to them, he must at once violate the oaths he had already sworn to the Thessalians and the Thebans, with the latter of whom he had covenanted to help them in the subjugation of Boeotia, and with the former to restore their rights at the Amphictyonic Council. If, on the other hand, he was loth to accept them—and in fact the prospect did not please him—he expected that you would send troops to Thermopylae to stop his passage, as indeed you would have done if you had not been outwitted. In that event, he calculated

455

319 γένοιτο, οὐκ ἐνεῖναι παρελθεῖν ἐλογίζετο. καὶ
τοῦτ' οὐ παρ' ἄλλων αὐτὸν ἔδει πυθέσθαι, ἀλλ'
αὐτὸς ὑπῆρχε μάρτυς ἑαυτῷ τοῦ πράγματος· ὅτε
γὰρ Φωκέας ἐκράτησε τὸ πρῶτον καὶ διέφθειρε
τοὺς ξένους αὐτῶν καὶ τὸν ἡγούμενον καὶ στρα-
τηγοῦντ' Ὀνόμαρχον, τότε τῶν ὄντων ἀνθρώπων
ἁπάντων οὐδενός, οὔθ' Ἕλληνος οὔτε βαρβάρου,
Φωκεῦσι βοηθήσαντος πλὴν ὑμῶν, οὐχ ὅπως
[444] παρῆλθεν ἢ διεπράξαθ' ὧν ἐβουλήθη τι παρελθών,
320 ἀλλ' οὐδὲ προσελθεῖν ἐγγὺς ἐδυνήθη. ᾔδει δὴ
σαφῶς, οἶμαι, τοῦθ' ὅτι νῦν, ἡνίκ' ἐστασίαζε μὲν
αὐτῷ τὰ Θετταλῶν, καὶ Φεραῖοι πρῶτον οὐ συν-
ηκολούθουν, ἐκρατοῦντο δὲ Θηβαῖοι καὶ μάχην
ἥττηντο καὶ τρόπαιον ἀπ' αὐτῶν εἱστήκει, οὐκ
ἔνεστι παρελθεῖν, εἰ βοηθήσεθ' ὑμεῖς, οὐδ', ἂν
ἐπιχειρῇ, χαιρήσειν, εἰ μή τις τέχνη προσγενή-
σεται. πῶς οὖν μήτε ψεύσομαι φανερῶς, μήτ'
ἐπιορκεῖν δόξας πάνθ' ἃ βούλομαι διαπράξομαι;
πῶς; οὕτως, ἂν Ἀθηναίων τινὰς εὕρω τοὺς Ἀθηναίους ἐξαπατήσοντας· ταύτης γὰρ οὐκέτ' ἐγὼ
321 τῆς αἰσχύνης κληρονομῶ. ἐντεῦθεν οἱ μὲν παρ'
ἐκείνου πρέσβεις προὔλεγον ὑμῖν ὅτι Φωκέας οὐ
προσδέχεται Φίλιππος συμμάχους, οὗτοι δ' ἐκ-
δεχόμενοι τοιαῦτ' ἐδημηγόρουν, ὡς φανερῶς μὲν
οὐχὶ καλῶς ἔχει τῷ Φιλίππῳ προσδέξασθαι τοὺς
Φωκέας συμμάχους διὰ τοὺς Θηβαίους καὶ τοὺς
Θετταλούς, ἐὰν δὲ γένηται τῶν πραγμάτων κύριος
καὶ τῆς εἰρήνης τύχῃ, ἅπερ ἂν συνθέσθαι νῦν
322 ἀξιώσαιμεν αὐτόν, ταῦτα ποιήσει τότε. τὴν μὲν
τοίνυν εἰρήνην ταύταις ταῖς ἐλπίσι καὶ ταῖς ἐπ-
αγωγαῖς εὕρετο παρ' ὑμῶν ἄνευ Φωκέων· τὴν δὲ

that he would be unable to get through. He did not need any information from others to reach that conclusion. He was himself a sufficient witness, for, after his first defeat of the Phocians and the overthrow of their leader and commander Onomarchus, although no one in the whole world, Greek or barbarian, sent aid to them save you alone, so far from getting through Thermopylae, or accomplishing any of the purposes of the passage, he had been unable even to approach the pass. I take it he was perfectly well aware that now, with Thessaly at variance with him—the Pheraeans, for example, refusing to join his following—with the Thebans getting the worst of the war, defeated in an engagement, and a trophy erected at their expense, he would be unable to force the passage if you sent troops to Thermopylae, and that he could not even make the attempt without serious loss unless he should also resort to some trickery. " How, then," he thought, " shall I escape open falsehood, and attain all my objects without incurring the charge of perjury ? Only if I can find Athenians to hoodwink the Athenian people, for then I shall have no share in the ensuing dishonour." Accordingly his own envoys warned you that he would not accept the Phocian alliance, but then Aeschines and his friends, taking up the tale, assured the people that, although for the sake of the Thebans and the Thessalians Philip could not with decency accept the alliance, yet if he should become master of the situation, and get his peace, he would thereafter do exactly what we should now ask him to agree to. So on the strength of these expectations and inducements he obtained his peace, with the Phocians

βοήθειαν ἔδει κωλῦσαι τὴν εἰς τὰς Πύλας, ἐφ᾿
ἣν αἱ πεντήκοντα τριήρεις ὅμως ἐφώρμουν, ἵν᾿,
323 εἰ πορεύοιτο Φίλιππος, κωλύοιθ᾿ ὑμεῖς. πῶς
οὖν; τίς τέχνη πάλιν αὖ γενήσεται περὶ ταύτης;
τοὺς χρόνους ὑμῶν ἀφελέσθαι καὶ ἐπιστῆσαι τὰ
[445] πράγματ᾿ ἀγαγόντας ἄφνω, ἵνα μηδ᾿ ἂν βούλησθε
δύνησθ᾿ ἐξελθεῖν. οὐκοῦν τοῦθ᾿ οὗτοι πράττοντες
φαίνονται, ἐγὼ δ᾿, ὥσπερ ἀκηκόατ᾿ ἤδη πολλάκις,
οὐχὶ δυνηθεὶς προαπελθεῖν, ἀλλὰ καὶ μισθωσάμε-
324 νος πλοῖον κατακωλυθεὶς ἐκπλεῦσαι. ἀλλὰ καὶ
πιστεῦσαι Φωκέας ἔδει Φιλίππῳ καὶ ἑκόντας
ἑαυτοὺς ἐνδοῦναι, ἵνα μηδεὶς χρόνος ἐγγένηται
τοῖς πράγμασι μηδ᾿ ἐναντίον ἔλθῃ ψήφισμα παρ᾿
ὑμῶν μηδέν. οὐκοῦν ὡς μὲν οἱ Φωκεῖς σωθήσονται, παρὰ τῶν Ἀθηναίων πρέσβεων ἀπαγγελθή-
σεται, ὥστε καὶ εἴ τις ἐμοὶ διαπιστεῖ, τούτοις
πιστεύσας αὐτὸν ἐγχειριεῖ· τοὺς δ᾿ Ἀθηναίους
αὐτοὺς μεταπεμψόμεθ᾿ ἡμεῖς, ἵνα πάνθ᾿, ὅσ᾿ ἂν
βούλωνται, νομίσαντες ὑπάρχειν σφίσι μηδὲν ἐναντίον ψηφίσωνται· οὗτοι δὲ τοιαῦτ᾿ ἀπαγγελοῦσι
παρ᾿ ἡμῶν καὶ ὑποσχήσονται, ἐξ ὧν μηδ᾿ ἂν
ὁτιοῦν ᾗ κινηθήσονται.

325 Τοῦτον τὸν τρόπον καὶ τοιαύταις τέχναις ὑπὸ
τῶν κάκιστ᾿ ἀπολουμένων ἀνθρώπων πάντα τὰ
πράγματ᾿ ἀπώλετο. καὶ γάρ τοι παραχρῆμα,
ἀντὶ μὲν τοῦ Θεσπιὰς καὶ Πλαταιὰς ἰδεῖν οἰκιζομένας, Ὀρχομενὸν καὶ Κορώνειαν ἠκούσατ᾿ ἠν-
δραποδισμένας, ἀντὶ δὲ τοῦ τὰς Θήβας ταπεινὰς
γενέσθαι καὶ περιαιρεθῆναι τὴν ὕβριν καὶ τὸ φρόνημ᾿
αὐτῶν, τὰ τῶν συμμάχων τῶν ὑμετέρων Φωκέων

excluded; but it was still necessary to stop the reinforcement of Thermopylae, for which fifty war-galleys were lying at anchor to enable you to check Philip's advance. How could it be done? What new artifice could he invent for that purpose? Some one must filch your opportunities of action, and surprise you with an unexpected crisis, so that you might lose the power, if not the will, of sending the expedition. That, then, was clearly what these men undertook. As you have often heard, I was unable to get away in time; I had chartered a ship, but was prevented from sailing. But it was further necessary that the Phocians should acquire confidence in Philip and make a voluntary surrender, so that no delay should intervene, and no unfriendly resolution come to hand from you. "Very well," thought Philip, "a report shall be made by the Athenian ambassadors that the Phocians are to be protected; and so, though they persist in mis-trusting me, they will deliver themselves into my hands through confidence in the Athenians. We will enlist the sympathy of the Athenian people in the hope that, supposing themselves to have got everything they want, they will pass no obstructive resolution. These men shall carry from us such flattering reports and assurances that, whatsoever may befall, they will make no movement."

In this manner and by the aid of this artifice our ruin was accomplished by men themselves doomed to perdition. For at once, instead of witnessing the restoration of Thespiae and Plataea, you heard of the enslavement of Orchomenus and Coronea. Instead of the humiliation of Thebes and the abase-ment of her pride and insolence, the walls of your

τείχη κατεσκάπτετο· Θηβαῖοι δ' ἦσαν οἱ κατα-
σκάπτοντες, οἱ διοικισθέντες ὑπ' Αἰσχίνου τῷ
326 λόγῳ. ἀντὶ δὲ τοῦ τὴν Εὔβοιαν ἀντ' Ἀμφιπόλεως
ὑμῖν παραδοθῆναι, ὁρμητήρι' ἐφ' ὑμᾶς ἐν Εὐβοίᾳ
Φίλιππος προσκατασκευάζεται καὶ Γεραιστῷ καὶ
[446] Μεγάροις ἐπιβουλεύων διατελεῖ. ἀντὶ δὲ τοῦ τὸν
Ὠρωπὸν ὑμῖν ἀποδοθῆναι, περὶ Δρυμοῦ καὶ τῆς
πρὸς Πανάκτῳ χώρας μεθ' ὅπλων ἐξερχόμεθα,
ἃ, τέως¹ ἦσαν Φωκεῖς σῷοι, οὐδὲ πώποτ' ἐποιή-
327 σαμεν. ἀντὶ δὲ τοῦ τὰ πάτρι' ἐν τῷ ἱερῷ κατα-
σταθῆναι καὶ τὰ χρήματ' εἰσπραχθῆναι τῷ θεῷ,
οἱ μὲν ὄντες Ἀμφικτύονες φεύγουσι καὶ ἐξελήλανται, καὶ ἀνάστατος αὐτῶν ἡ χώρα γέγονεν,
οἱ δ' οὐπώποτ' ἐν τῷ πρόσθεν χρόνῳ γενόμενοι,
Μακεδόνες καὶ βάρβαροι, νῦν Ἀμφικτύονες εἶναι
βιάζονται· ἐὰν δέ τις περὶ τῶν ἱερῶν χρημάτων
μνησθῇ, κατακρημνίζεται, ἡ πόλις δὲ τὴν προ-
328 μαντείαν ἀφῄρηται. καὶ γέγονε τὰ πράγματα
πάνθ' ὥσπερ αἴνιγμα τῇ πόλει. ὁ μὲν οὐδὲν ἔψευ-
σται καὶ πάνθ' ὅσ' ἐβουλήθη διαπέπρακται, ὑμεῖς
δ', ἅπερ εὔξαισθ' ἂν ἐλπίσαντες, τἀναντία τούτων
ἑοράκατε γιγνόμενα, καὶ δοκεῖτε μὲν εἰρήνην
ἄγειν, πεπόνθατε δὲ δεινότερ' ἢ πολεμοῦντες·
οὗτοι δὲ χρήματ' ἔχουσ' ἐπὶ τούτοις καὶ μέχρι τῆς
329 τήμερον ἡμέρας δίκην οὐ δεδώκασιν. ὅτι γὰρ
ταῦθ' ἁπλῶς δεδωροδόκηνται καὶ τιμὴν ἔχουσιν
ἁπάντων τούτων οὗτοι, πολλαχόθεν μὲν ἔγωγ'
οἶμαι δῆλον ὑμῖν εἶναι πάλαι, καὶ δέδοικα μὴ

¹ τέως so all mss.: ἕως Shilleto (after Dind.), but he suggests τέως, ἕως (see Buttmann, *Ind. Meid.*).
460

own allies the Phocians were demolished, and demolished by those very Thebans whom Aeschines in his speech had sent to live in scattered villages. Instead of the surrender to you of Euboea in exchange for Amphipolis, Philip is establishing positions in Euboea as a base of attack upon you, and is constantly plotting against Geraestus and Megara. Instead of recovering Oropus, we are making an armed expedition to secure Drymus *a* and the district of Panactus,*a* an operation in which we never engaged so long as the Phocians were safe. Instead of the re-establishment of ancient rites in the Temple of Apollo, and the restitution of treasure to the god, men who were once Amphictyons are fugitives and exiles, and men who never in all former time were members of it, Macedonians and barbarians, are now forcing their way into the Amphictyonic Council. If anyone says a word about the sacred treasure, he is thrown down the precipice; and Athens is robbed of her precedence in the consultation of the Oracle To Athens the whole business is an insoluble puzzle. Philip has escaped falsehood, and has accomplished all his purposes, while you, after expecting the complete fulfilment, have witnessed the entire disappointment, of your desires. You are nominally at peace ; yet peace has brought you greater calamities than war. Meantime these men have made money by your misfortunes, and until to-day have never been brought to justice. That they have done it all for bribes, and that they have the price of their perfidy in their pockets, has, I suppose, long ago been manifest to you for many reasons ; and I am afraid

---

a *Drymus, Panactus* : frontier-towns on the edge of Boeotia.

DEMOSTHENES

τοὐναντίον οὗ βούλομαι ποιῶ, σφόδρ' ἀκριβῶς
δεικνύναι πειρώμενος διοχλῶ πάλαι τοῦτ' αὐτοὺς
330 ὑμᾶς εἰδότας· ὅμως δ' ἔτι καὶ τόδ' ἀκούσατε. ἔστιν
ὄντιν' ὑμεῖς, ὦ ἄνδρες δικασταί, τῶν πρέσβεων
ὧν ἔπεμψε Φίλιππος χαλκοῦν στήσαιτ' ἂν ἐν
ἀγορᾷ; τί δέ; δοίητ' ἂν ἐν πρυτανείῳ σίτησιν
[447] ἢ ἄλλην τινὰ δωρεάν, αἷς τιμᾶτε τοὺς εὐεργέτας;
ἐγὼ μὲν οὐκ οἶμαι. διὰ τί; οὔτε γὰρ ὑμεῖς γ'
ἀχάριστοί ἐστ' οὔτ' ἄδικοι ἄνθρωποι οὔτε κακοί.
ὅτι πάνθ' ὑπὲρ Φιλίππου καὶ οὐδ' ὁτιοῦν ὑπὲρ
ἡμῶν ἔπραξαν, εἴποιτ' ἄν, καὶ ἀληθῆ καὶ δίκαια.
331 εἶτ' οἴεσθ' ὑμεῖς μὲν οὕτω γιγνώσκειν, τὸν δὲ
Φίλιππον οὐχ οὕτως, ἀλλὰ τούτοις διδόναι τηλι-
καύτας καὶ τοσαύτας δωρεάς, διότι ὑπὲρ ὑμῶν καλῶς καὶ δικαίως ἐπρέσβευσαν; οὐκ ἔστι ταῦτα.
τὸν γὰρ Ἡγήσιππον ὁρᾶτε καὶ τοὺς μετ' αὐτοῦ
πρέσβεις πῶς ἐδέξατο. τὰ μὲν ἄλλα σιωπῶ,
ἀλλὰ Ξενοκλείδην τουτονὶ τὸν ποιητὴν ἐξεκή-
ρυξεν, ὅτι αὐτοὺς ὑπεδέξατο πολίτας ὄντας. τοῖς
μὲν γὰρ ὑπὲρ ὑμῶν λέγουσι δικαίως ὅσ' ἂν φρονῶσι
τοῦτον τὸν τρόπον προσφέρεται, τοῖς δὲ πεπρακόσιν αὐτοὺς ὡς τούτοις. ταῦτ' οὖν μαρτύρων,
ταῦτ' ἐλέγχων τίνων ἔτι δεῖται μειζόνων; ταῦτ'
ἀφαιρήσεται τίς ὑμῶν;
332 Εἶπε τοίνυν μοί τις ἄρτι προσελθὼν πρὸ τοῦ
δικαστηρίου πρᾶγμα καινότατον πάντων, Χάρητος
κατηγορεῖν αὐτὸν παρεσκευάσθαι, καὶ διὰ τούτου
τοῦ τρόπου καὶ τούτων τῶν λόγων ἐξαπατήσειν

ᵃ *Hegesippus* [72]: recently sent to protest against
Philip's retention of Halonnesus; author of the speech
On Halonnesus attributed to Demosthenes.

ᵇ *Chares* : for thirty years an unlucky, or incompetent,
commander by land and sea; politically, a friend of

that, contrary to my desire, I may be wearying you by submitting detailed proofs of facts well known to you. However, I must ask you to listen to one more argument. Gentlemen of the jury, would you set up in the market-place a statue of any of the ambassadors whom Philip sent? Or would you give to them free maintenance in the Town Hall, or any of the other privileges with which you reward your benefactors? Surely not; but why not? For in *you* there is no lack of gratitude or justice or kindness. It is, you will say—and it is a fair and honest reply—because they did everything for Philip and nothing for us. Then do you suppose that Philip acts on an entirely different principle from yours, and gives all those handsome presents to Aeschines and his friends because they conducted their mission duly and honestly in your interest? That is not so. You have observed the reception he gave to the envoy Hegesippus[a] and his colleagues. Not to mention other details, he banished by proclamation the Athenian poet Xenocleides for offering them hospitality as fellow-citizens. Such is his behaviour towards your representatives when they honestly speak out what they think; those who have sold themselves he treats as he treated Aeschines and his friends. My argument requires no other witnesses and no stronger proofs; nor can anyone erase these proofs from your minds.

Some one came up to me just now in front of the court, and told me a very odd thing. Aeschines, he said, had prepared himself to denounce the general Chares,[b] hoping to cajole you by his eloquent treat-

Demosthenes; had commanded the unsuccessful expedition sent too late for the relief of Olynthus.

ὑμᾶς ἐλπίζειν. ἐγὼ δ᾽ ὅτι μὲν πάντα τρόπον
κρινόμενος Χάρης εὕρηται πιστῶς καὶ εὐνοϊκῶς,
ὅσον ἦν ἐπ᾽ ἐκείνῳ, πράττων ὑπὲρ ὑμῶν, διὰ δὲ
τοὺς ἐπὶ χρήμασι λυμαινομένους τοῖς πράγμασι
πολλῶν ὑστερῶν, οὐ σφόδρ᾽ ἰσχυρίζομαι, ἀλλ᾽
ὑπερβολὴν ποιήσομαι. ἔστω γὰρ πάντ᾽ ἀληθῆ
λέξειν περὶ αὐτοῦ τουτονί. καὶ οὕτω τοίνυν κομιδῇ
333 γέλως ἐστὶ κατηγορεῖν ἐκείνου τουτονί. ἐγὼ
γὰρ Αἰσχίνην οὐδενὸς αἰτιῶμαι τῶν ἐν τῷ πολέμῳ
[448] πραχθέντων (τούτων γάρ εἰσιν οἱ στρατηγοὶ ὑπ-
εύθυνοι), οὐδὲ τοῦ ποιήσασθαι τὴν πόλιν εἰρήνην,
ἀλλ᾽ ἄχρι τούτου πάντ᾽ ἀφίημι. τί οὖν λέγω καὶ
πόθεν ἄρχομαι κατηγορεῖν; τοῦ ποιουμένης τῆς
πόλεως εἰρήνην Φιλοκράτει συνειπεῖν, ἀλλὰ μὴ
τοῖς τὰ βέλτιστα γράφουσι, καὶ τοῦ δῶρ᾽ εἰληφέναι,
τοῦ μετὰ ταῦτ᾽ ἐπὶ τῆς ὑστέρας πρεσβείας τοὺς
χρόνους κατατρῖψαι καὶ μηδὲν ὧν προσετάξαθ᾽
ὑμεῖς ποιῆσαι, τοῦ φενακίσαι τὴν πόλιν, καὶ
παραστήσαντ᾽ ἐλπίδας, ὡς ὅσα βουλόμεθ᾽ ἡμεῖς
Φίλιππος πράξει, πάντ᾽ ἀπολωλεκέναι, τοῦ μετὰ
ταῦθ᾽, ἑτέρων προλεγόντων φυλάττεσθαι τὸν τοσ-
334 αῦτ᾽ ἠδικηκότα, τοῦτον ἐκείνῳ συνηγορεῖν. ταῦτα
κατηγορῶ, ταῦτα μέμνησθε, ἐπεὶ δικαίαν εἰρήνην
καὶ ἴσην καὶ μηδὲν πεπρακότας ἀνθρώπους μηδὲ
ψευσαμένους ὕστερον κἂν ἐπῄνουν καὶ στεφανοῦν
ἐκέλευον. στρατηγὸς δ᾽ εἴ τις ἠδίκηκεν ὑμᾶς,
οὐχὶ κοινωνεῖ ταῖς νῦν εὐθύναις. ποῖος γὰρ
στρατηγὸς Ἄλον, τίς δὲ Φωκέας ἀπολώλεκε;
464

ment of that topic. I will not lay too much stress on the observation that, whenever Chares has been brought to trial, he has been found to have acted faithfully and loyally, so far as in him lay, in your interests, though he has often failed of success by the fault of the people who do mischief for money. I will go so far as to grant for argument's sake that every word Aeschines will utter against him is true. But even on that assumption it is absolutely ridiculous that a man in Chares' position should be denounced by a man like Aeschines. Observe that I do not blame Aeschines for any of the misadventures of the war, for which the generals are duly called to account. Nor do I blame him because the city made the peace : so far I acquit him. What then is the basis of my speech and of my indictment ? That, when the city was making the peace, he supported Philocrates, and did not support speakers whose proposals were patriotic ; that he took bribes ; that thereafter, on the later embassy, he deliberately squandered his opportunities ; that he deceived the city, and confounded its policy, by suggesting the hope that Philip would satisfy all our desires ; and that subsequently, when others warned you to beware of the perpetrator of so many iniquities, he addressed you as his advocate. These are my accusations. Do not forget them. For a just and equitable peace I would be grateful ; I would have commended and advised you to decorate negotiators who had not first sold themselves and then deceived you with falsehoods. Granted that you were wronged by any commander,—he is not concerned in the present inquiry. Did any commander bring Halus to destruction ? or the Phocians ? or Doriscus ? or

DEMOSTHENES

τίς δὲ Δορίσκον; τίς δὲ Κερσοβλέπτην; τίς δ'
Ἱερὸν ὅρος; τίς δὲ Πύλας; τίς δὲ πεποίηκεν
ἄχρι τῆς Ἀττικῆς ὁδὸν διὰ συμμάχων καὶ φίλων
εἶναι Φιλίππῳ; τίς δὲ Κορώνειαν, τίς δ' Ὀρχο-
μενόν, τίς Εὔβοιαν ἀλλοτρίαν; τίς Μέγαρα πρώην
335 ὀλίγου; τίς Θηβαίους ἰσχυρούς; τούτων γὰρ
οὐδὲν τοσούτων καὶ τηλικούτων ὄντων διὰ τοὺς
στρατηγοὺς ἀπώλετο, οὐδ' ἐν τῇ εἰρήνῃ συγ-
χωρηθὲν πεισθέντων ὑμῶν ἔχει Φίλιππος, ἀλλὰ διὰ
τούτους ἀπόλωλε καὶ τὴν τούτων δωροδοκίαν. ἂν
τοίνυν ταῦτα μὲν φεύγῃ, πλανᾷ δὲ καὶ πάντα
[449] μᾶλλον λέγῃ, ἐκείνως αὐτὸν δέχεσθε. "οὐ στρα-
τηγῷ δικάζομεν, οὐ περὶ τούτων κρίνει. μὴ λέγ'
εἴ τις αἴτιός ἐστι καὶ ἄλλος τοῦ Φωκέων ὀλέθρου,
ἀλλ' ὡς οὐ σὺ αἴτιος δεῖξον. τί οὖν, εἴ τι Δημοσθένης ἠδίκει, νῦν λέγεις, ἀλλ' οὐχ ὅτε τὰς εὐθύνας
ἐδίδου κατηγόρεις; δι' αὐτὸ γὰρ εἶ τοῦτ' ἀπ-
336 ολωλέναι δίκαιος. μὴ λέγ' ὡς καλὸν εἰρήνη, μηδ'
ὡς συμφέρον· οὐδεὶς γὰρ αἰτιᾶταί σε τοῦ ποιήσασθαι τὴν πόλιν εἰρήνην· ἀλλ' ὡς οὐκ αἰσχρὰ
καὶ ἐπονείδιστος, καὶ πόλλ' ὕστερον ἐξηπατήμεθα,
καὶ πάντ' ἀπώλετο, ταῦτα λέγε. τούτων γὰρ
ἁπάντων ἡμῖν αἴτιος σὺ δέδειξαι. καὶ τί δὴ μέχρι
νυνὶ τὸν τὰ τοιαῦτα πεποιηκότ' ἐπαινεῖς;" ἂν
οὕτω φυλάττητ' αὐτόν, οὐχ ἕξει τί λέγῃ, ἀλλὰ

Cersobleptes ? or the Sacred Mount ? or Thermopylae ?
Was it a commander who gave Philip an open road
to Attica through the territory of friends and allies ?
Who has made Coronea and Orchomenus and Euboea
alien ground for us ? Who nearly did the same
with Megara only yesterday ? Who has made the
Thebans strong ? These are enormous losses, but
for none of them is any general to blame. Philip
does not hold any of these advantages as a concession
made with your consent in the terms of peace. We
owe them all to these men and to their venality.
If, then, Aeschines shirks the issue, if he tries to
lead you astray by talking of anything rather than
the charges I bring, I will tell you how to receive his
irrelevance. "We are not sitting in judgement on
any military commander. You are not being tried
on the charges you refute. Do not tell us that this
man or that man is to blame for the destruction of
the Phocians ; prove to us that you are not to
blame. If Demosthenes committed any crime, why
bring it up now ? Why did you not lay your complaint at the statutory investigation of his conduct ?
For that silence alone you deserve your doom. You
need not tell us that peace is a lovely and profitable
thing ; for nobody blames you because the city
concluded peace. Deny, if you can, that the peace
we have is a disgraceful and ignominious peace ;
deny that after its conclusion we were deceived,
and that by that deception all was lost. The
blame for all these calamities has been brought
home to you. Why do you still speak the praises
of the man who inflicted them ? " Keep guard
over his tricks in that fashion, and he will have
nothing to say He will only aggravate the

τὴν ἄλλως ἐνταῦθ᾽ ἐπαρεῖ τὴν φωνὴν καὶ πεφωνασκηκὼς ἔσται.

337 Καίτοι καὶ περὶ τῆς φωνῆς ἴσως εἰπεῖν ἀνάγκη·
πάνυ γὰρ μέγα καὶ ἐπὶ ταύτῃ φρονεῖν αὐτὸν ἀκούω,
ὡς καθυποκρινούμενον ὑμᾶς. ἐμοὶ δὲ δοκεῖτ᾽
ἀτοπώτατον ἁπάντων ἂν ποιῆσαι, εἰ ὅτε μὲν τὰ
Θυέστου καὶ τῶν ἐπὶ Τροίᾳ κάκ᾽ ἠγωνίζετο,
ἐξεβάλλετ᾽ αὐτὸν καὶ ἐξεσυρίττετ᾽ ἐκ τῶν θεάτρων
καὶ μόνον οὐ κατελεύεθ᾽ οὕτως ὥστε τελευτῶντα
τοῦ τριταγωνιστεῖν ἀποστῆναι, ἐπειδὴ δ᾽ οὐκ ἐπὶ
τῆς σκηνῆς ἀλλ᾽ ἐν τοῖς κοινοῖς καὶ μεγίστοις τῆς
πόλεως πράγμασι μυρί᾽ εἴργασται κακά, τηνικαῦθ᾽
338 ὡς καλὸν φθεγγομένῳ προσέχοιτε. μηδαμῶς· μηδὲν ὑμεῖς ἀβέλτερον πάθητε, ἀλλὰ λογίζεσθ᾽ ὅτι
δεῖ κήρυκα μὲν ἂν δοκιμάζητε, εὔφωνον σκοπεῖν,
πρεσβευτὴν δὲ καὶ τῶν κοινῶν ἀξιοῦντά τι πράττειν δίκαιον καὶ φρόνημ᾽ ἔχονθ᾽ ὑπὲρ μὲν ὑμῶν
μέγα, πρὸς δ᾽ ὑμᾶς ἴσον, ὥσπερ ἐγὼ Φίλιππον μὲν
[450] οὐκ ἐθαύμασα, τοὺς δ᾽ αἰχμαλώτους ἐθαύμασα,
ἔσωσα, οὐδὲν ὑπεστειλάμην. οὗτος δ᾽ ἐκείνου
μὲν προὐκυλινδεῖτο καὶ τοὺς παιᾶνας ᾖδεν, ὑμῶν
339 δ᾽ ὑπερορᾷ. ἔτι τοίνυν ὅταν μὲν ἴδητε δεινότητ᾽
ἢ εὐφωνίαν ἤ τι τῶν τοιούτων ἀγαθῶν ἐπὶ χρηστοῦ
καὶ φιλοτίμου γεγενημένον ἀνθρώπου, συγχαίρειν
καὶ συνασκεῖν πάντας δεῖ· κοινὸν γὰρ ὑμῖν πᾶσι
τοῖς ἄλλοις τοῦτ᾽ ἀγαθὸν γίγνεται· ὅταν δ᾽ ἐπὶ
δωροδόκου καὶ πονηροῦ καὶ παντὸς ἥττονος λήμ-
468

thunders of his voice, and exhaust himself with his own vociferation.

On that famous voice of his, however, I really must offer some observations. For I am informed that he sets great store thereby, and that he hopes to overawe you by an exhibition of histrionic talent. When he tried to represent the woes of the House of Thyestes, or of the men who fought at Troy, you drove him from the stage with hisses and cat-calls, and came near to pelting him with stones, insomuch that in the end he gave up his profession of actor of small parts ; and I think you would be behaving very strangely if now, when he has wrought immeasurable mischief, not on the stage, but in his dealings with the most momentous affairs of state, you should be favourably impressed by his beautiful voice. No, gentlemen ; you must not yield to unworthy emotion. If you are holding an ex-amination for the office of herald, you do well to look for a man with a fine loud voice ; but if you are choosing an ambassador or a candidate for public office, you seek an honest man, a man who exhibits a proud spirit as your representative, and a spirit of equality as your fellow-citizen. I, for example, showed no respect for Philip ; I kept my respect for the captives, I rescued them, I spared no effort. Aeschines, on the other hand, grovelled at Philip's feet, sang his Hymn of Victory, and disregards you altogether. Again, when you observe eloquence, or vocal power, or any such merit, in a right-minded and patriotic speaker, by all means congratulate him and help him to exercise his gift, for you all share in its advantages. But when you find such powers in the possession of a corrupt and

ματος, ἀποκλείειν καὶ πικρῶς καὶ ἐναντίως ἀκούειν,
ὡς πονηρία δυνάμεως δόξαν εὑρομένη παρ' ὑμῶν
340 ἐπὶ τὴν πόλιν ἐστίν. ὁρᾶτε δ', ἀφ' ὧν οὗτος
εὐδοκιμεῖ, ἡλίκα τῇ πόλει περιέστηκε πράγματα.
αἱ μὲν τοίνυν ἄλλαι δυνάμεις ἐπιεικῶς εἰσιν αὐτάρ-
κεις, ἡ δὲ τοῦ λέγειν, ἂν τὰ παρ' ὑμῶν τῶν ἀκουόντων ἀντιστῇ, διακόπτεται. οὕτως οὖν ἀκούετε
τούτου ὡς πονηροῦ καὶ δωροδόκου καὶ οὐδ' ὁτιοῦν
ἐροῦντος ἀληθές.

341 Ὅτι δ' οὐ μόνον κατὰ τἄλλα, ἀλλὰ καὶ τὰ πρὸς
αὐτὸν τὸν Φίλιππον πράγματα πανταχῶς συμφέρει
τοῦτον ἑαλωκέναι, θεάσασθε. εἴτε γὰρ ἥξει ποτ'
εἰς ἀνάγκην τῶν δικαίων τι ποιεῖν τῇ πόλει, τὸν
τρόπον μεταθήσεται· νῦν μὲν γὰρ ᾕρηται τοὺς
πολλοὺς ἐξαπατῶν ὀλίγους θεραπεύειν, ἂν δὲ
τούτους ἀπολωλότας πύθηται, ὑμῖν τοῖς πολλοῖς
καὶ πάντων κυρίοις τὰ λοιπὰ ποιεῖν βουλήσεται.
342 εἶτ' ἐπὶ τῆς αὐτῆς ᾗσπερ νῦν ἐξουσίας καὶ ἀ-
σελγείας μενεῖ, τοὺς ὁτιοῦν ἂν ἐκείνῳ ποιήσοντας[1]
ἀνῃρηκότες ἐκ τῆς πόλεως ἔσεσθε, ἂν τούτους
ἀνέλητε· οἳ γὰρ οἰόμενοι δίκην ὑφέξειν τοιαῦτ'
[451] ἔπραξαν, τούτους, ἐὰν τὰ παρ' ὑμῶν αὐτοῖς ἐφεθῇ,
τί οἴεσθε ποιήσειν; ποῖον Εὐθυκράτη, ποῖον
343 Λασθένη, τίν' οὐχ ὑπερβαλεῖσθαι προδότην; τίνα
δ' οὐ πάντων τῶν ἄλλων χείρω πολίτην ὑπάρξειν,
ὁρῶντα τοῖς μὲν ἅπαντα πεπρακόσι χρήματα,

---

[1] So Shilletto with S and vulg.: most edd. following A
read ποιήσαντας; cf. § 80.
470

evil-minded man, the slave of filthy lucre, discourage
him, and listen to him with aversion and animosity ;
for if knavery enjoys in your eyes the reputation of
ability, it becomes a peril to the commonwealth.
You have before your eyes the dangers with which
the city is encompassed as the result of the reputation
he has achieved. Now other forms of ability are
almost wholly independent of conditions ; but the
ability of the speaker is paralysed by the recalcitrance
of his audience. Listen to him, then, as to a knave
and a bribe-taker, who will have no truthful word to
utter.

Observe in conclusion that, apart from all other
reasons, the conviction of this man is eminently
desirable in view of your future relations with
Philip. For if Philip ever finds himself under the
necessity of treating Athens with common justice,
he will have to remodel his methods. At present
his chosen policy is to cheat the many and court
the few ; but, when he learns that his favourites
have been brought to ruin, he will wish for the future
to deal with the many, who are the real masters of
our state. Or if he persists in the lawlessness and
the insolence that he displays to-day, you, by
putting these men out of the way, will have
delivered Athens from men ready to go to all lengths
in his service. For if the fear that they would be
called to account did not deter them, what conduct
can you expect from them if you should give them a
licence to do what they please ? Will they not
outvie Euthycrates, Lasthenes, and all the traitors
of history ? Every other man will be a worse citizen,
when he sees that men who have made traffic of the
common interests emerge with wealth and reputation,

DEMOSTHENES

δόξαν, ἀφορμὴν τὴν Φιλίππου ξενίαν περιοῦσαν,
τοῖς δὲ δικαίους τε παρέχουσιν ἑαυτοὺς καὶ προσ-
ανηλωκόσι χρήματα πράγματα, ἀπεχθείας, φθόνον
περιόντα παρ' ἐνίων; μηδαμῶς· οὔτε γὰρ πρὸς
δόξαν οὔτε πρὸς εὐσέβειαν οὔτε πρὸς ἀσφάλειαν
οὔτε πρὸς ἄλλ' οὐδὲν ὑμῖν συμφέρει τοῦτον ἀφεῖναι,
ἀλλὰ τιμωρησαμένους παράδειγμα ποιῆσαι πᾶσι,
καὶ τοῖς πολίταις καὶ τοῖς ἄλλοις Ἕλλησιν.

and with all the advantages of Philip's friendship, while the lot of those who approved themselves honest men and spent their money in your service is vexation and ill-will, and the enmity of those whom I need not name. Let it not be so! For the sake of your honour, of your religion, of your security, of everything you value, you must not acquit this man. Visit him with exemplary punishment, and let his fate be a warning not to our own citizens alone but to every man who lives in the Hellenic world.

INDEX OF NAMES

[We have omitted from this list (a) all place-names, except where some information seemed desirable for the better understanding of the text; (b) names of well-known persons constantly recurring. The bare reference is given in cases where the necessary information is supplied by the context or by the occasional footnotes. The traitors of *Cor.* 295 we have allowed to remain in deserved obscurity. The numbers refer to the sections.]

ADEIMANTUS, Athenian general at end of Peloponnesian war, *F.L.* 191

Aeacus, judge of the underworld, *Cor.* 127

Aglauros, *F.L.* 303

Alexander, brother of Philip, *F.L.* 195

Alexander the Great, *Cor.* 51 f., 270, 296 f.

Amphipolis, Athenian dependency in Thrace, captured by Philip in 357 B.C., *Cor.* 69; *F.L.* 22, 137, 220, 253 f.; 326

Anaxinus of Oreus; came to Athens in B.C. 341 and was put to death with torture as a spy, *Cor.* 137

Antigone of Sophocles, *F.L.* 246 f.

Antipater, envoy of Philip and regent of Macedonia after Alexander's death, *F.L.* 69

Antiphon (not the orator), *Cor.* 132

Aphobetus, brother of Aeschines, *F.L.* 237, 285, 287

Apollophanes (1), *F.L.* 168

Apollophanes (2) of Pydna, *F.L.* 194 f.

Aristodemus, Athenian actor and member of Macedonian party; member of first embassy to Philip, *Cor.* 21; *F.L.* 12, 18, 97, 246, 315

Aristolaus, *Cor.* 197

Aristonicus, *Cor.* 83, 223, 312

Aristophon, Athenian statesman of first half of fourth century, often mentioned with praise by Demosthenes; there are perhaps two of this name, *Cor.* 70, 75, 162, 219; *F.L.* 291, 297

Aristratus (1), tyrant of Sicyon, *Cor.* 48

Aristratus (2) of Naxos, *Cor.* 197

Arthmius, *F.L.* 271

Athene, *F.L.* 272. The statue referred to is that commonly, but wrongly, known as the Athene Promachos

Atresidas of Mantinea, *F.L.* 305 ff.

Atrometus, father of Aeschines, *Cor.* 130; *F.L.* 281

BATTALUS, *Cor.* 180

Blue Rocks at N. entrance to Bosporus; the Symplegades of the Argonauts, *F.L.* 273

CALLIAS, Athenian ambassador to Persia, 470 B.C., *F.L.* 273

Callisthenes, *Cor.* 37; *F.L.* 86

Callistratus, Athenian statesman, tried and acquitted in 366 B.C. in connexion with loss of Oropus, *Cor.* 219; *F.L.* 297

Cardia, town in Thracian Chersonesus, *F.L.* 174

475

INDEX

Carystus, town in S. of Euboea, *Cor.* 319

Cephalus, Athenian statesman at time of expulsion of Thirty Tyrants, *Cor.* 219, 251

Cephisodotus, Athenian general tried and fined for neglect of duty about 359 B.C.; perhaps identical with orator praised by Demosthenes *c. Lept.* p. 501.

Cephisophon, *Cor.* 21, 75; *F.L.* 293

Cersobleptes, Thracian king subdued by Philip in 341 B.C., *F.L.* 174, 181, 334

Chabrias, one of the ablest Athenian generals of fourth century; won battle of Naxos in 376 B.C.; commanded Egyptian navy in revolt against Persia; killed at Chios in 357 B.C., *F.L.* 287

Chares, Athenian general, *F.L.* 332

Charidemus, native of Oreus and commander of mercenaries, first in service of Cersobleptes and then in that of Athens, *Cor.* 114

Chelidonian Islands, off coast of Lycia, *F.L.* 273

Chersonesus, the Thracian peninsula now known as Gallipoli, *Cor.* 79, 92 f., 139, 302; *F.L.* 78 f.

Cirrhaean Plain, between Delphi and Corinthian Gulf; consecrated to Apollo after first Sacred War about 590 B.C., *Cor.* 149, 152

Cleitarchus, tyrant of Eretria in Euboea, *Cor.* 71, 81 f.

Collytus, Attic deme within walls of Athens, N. of Acropolis; the Lesser Dionysia were held here, *Cor.* 180

Conon, Athenian general defeated at Aegospotami; won sea fight off Cnidus in 394 B.C. and restored Long Walls, *F.L.* 191

Coronea, town in W. of Boeotia, *F.L.* 112, 141, 148, 325, 334

Corsia or Corsiae, town in Boeotia, *F.L.* 141

Cottyphus, Thessalian, president of Amphictyonic Council, *Cor.* 151

Creon, in *Antigone* of Sophocles, *Cor.* 180; *F.L.* 247

Cresphontes, in tragedy of same name by Euripides, *Cor.* 180

Ctesiphon, member of first embassy to Philip; not the Ctesiphon of the *De Corona*, *F.L.* 12, 18, 97, 315

Cyrebion, *F.L.* 287

Cyrsilus, *Cor.* 204

Decelea, Attic deme 15 miles N. of Athens, *Cor.* 96

Demades, Athenian orator and member of Macedonian party; negotiated peace between Philip and Athens after Chaeronea, *Cor.* 285

Demomeles, *Cor.* 223

Dercylus, member of first embassy to Philip, *F.L.* 60, 125, 175

Dio, *Cor.* 129

Diondas, *Cor.* 222, 249

Dionysius, *F.L.* 180

Diopeithes, perhaps the Athenian general who was commanding in Thrace in 343 B.C., and whom Demosthenes defended in his speech on the Chersonesus, *Cor.* 70

Diophantus, *F.L.* 86, 198, 297. Probably two, or even three, different persons are meant

Diotimus, a wealthy Athenian and one of the generals whose surrender Alexander demanded after destruction of Thebes, *Cor.* 114

Doriscus, town in Thrace, *Cor.* 70; *F.L.* 256, 334

Elpias, *Cor.* 129

Empusa, a goblin who repeatedly changed her shape, *Cor.* 130

Epicrates, accused of corruption on an embassy to Artaxerxes and, according to Plutarch, acquitted; Demosthenes is therefore probably referring to another trial, *F.L.* 277, 280

Ergisce, unknown town in Thrace *Cor.* 27

Ergocles, Athenian general condemned for peculation; Lysias's speech against him is extant, *F.L.* 180

INDEX

Ergophilus, Athenian general condemned for treachery or incompetence on some unknown occasion, *F.L.* 180

Eubulus, Athenian statesman and leader of peace party, *Cor.* 21, 70, 75, 162; *F.L.* 191, 290, 304

Eucleides, Athenian envoy sent to remonstrate with Philip about his treatment of Cersobleptes, *F.L.* 162

Eudicus, *Cor.* 48

Euripides quoted, *F.L.* 246

Eurybatus, *Cor.* 24

Euthycrates, an Olynthian traitor, *F.L.* 265, 342

Execestus, *F.L.* 124

Geraestus, town and promontory in extreme S. of Euboea, *F.L.* 326

Glaucothea, mother of Aeschines, *Cor.* 130, 184; *F.L.* 281

Glaucus, of Carystus in Euboea, famous boxer in time of Persian wars, *Cor.* 319

Haliartus, town in Boeotia, *Cor.* 96

Halonnesus, small island in N. Aegean to which Athenians laid claim; captured by Philip and offered by him as a gift to Athens, *Cor.* 69

Halus, town in S. of Thessaly near coast, *F.L.* 36, 39, 159, 163, 174, 334

Harmodius, the tyrannicide, *F.L.* 280

Hedyleum, in Boeotia, *F.L.* 148

Hegemon, member of Macedonian party at Athens, *Cor.* 285

Hegesilaus (Hegesileos), Athenian general in Euboea, *F.L.* 290

Hegesippus, anti-Macedonian statesman; defended Timarchus, *F.L.* 72 ff., 331

Heros, the physician, *Cor.* 129; *F.L.* 249

Hieronymus, a philippizing Arcadian, *F.L.* 11

Hipponicus, *F.L.* 273

Hypereides, the famous Athenian orator, friend, and supporter of Demosthenes; impeached Philocrates, *Cor.* 134, 223; *F.L.* 116

Iatrocles, member of first embassy to Philip, *F.L.* 197 f.

Ischander, *F.L.* 10, 303

Larisa (or Larissa), town in centre of Thessaly, *F.L.* 163

Lasthenes, an Olynthian traitor, *Cor.* 48; *F.L.* 265, 342

Leon, Athenian ambassador at court of Persia, *F.L.* 191. See Introd. p. 242

Leuctra, in Boeotia, scene of victory of Thebans in 371 B.C., *Cor.* 18, 98

Megalopolis, capital of confederacy of Arcadia, *F.L.* 11

Melantus, *Cor.* 249

Miltiades, victor of Marathon, *F.L.* 303

Minos, judge of the underworld, *Cor.* 127

Moerocles, Athenian orator of anti-Macedonian party, *F.L.* 293

Molon, Athenian actor, *F.L.* 246

Myrtenum, Thracian town not named elsewhere, *Cor.* 27

Nausicles, general commanding Athenian force sent to Thermopylae in 352 B.C., *Cor.* 114

Neon or Neones, town in Phocis, *F.L.* 148

Neoptolemus (1), a philippizing Athenian, *Cor.* 114; *F.L.* 12, 315

Neoptolemus (2), *F.L.* 10

Niceratus, *F.L.* 290

Nicias, brother-in-law of Aeschines, *F.L.* 287

Oenomaus, in tragedy of same name by Sophocles, *Cor.* 180, 242

Onomarchus, Phocian general in Sacred War from 354 to 352 B.C., when he was defeated and slain by Philip in Thessaly, *F.L.* 319

Orchomenus, town in Boeotia, *F.L.* 112, 141, 148, 325, 334

Oreus, town in N. of Euboea, *Cor.* 71, 79, 81; *F.L.* 155, 163

Oropus, town in N. of Attica near Boeotian frontier, *Cor.* 99; *F.L.* 22, 220, 326

477

INDEX

PAGASAE, seaport in S. of Thessaly, *F.L.* 163

Parmenio, envoy of Philip and Alexander's chief general, *F.L.* 69, 163

Pella, capital of Macedonia, *Cor.* 68; *F.L.* 155, 166, 169

Peparethus, island off S.E. extremity of Thessaly, *Cor.* 70

Perillus (Perilaus), *Cor.* 48; *F.L.* 295

Perinthians, on N. shore of Propontis, *Cor.* 89

Phaedimus, one of the Thirty Tyrants: occurs as Phaedrias in Xenophon's list (*Hell.* iii. 3. 2), *F.L.* 196

Pherae, town in S.E. of Thessaly, *F.L.* 158, 175

Philammon, contemporary boxer and athlete, *Cor.* 319

Philistides, *Cor.* 71, 81 f.

Philo, Theban envoy, *F.L.* 140

Philochares, brother of Aeschines, *F.L.* 237

Philocrates of Eleusis (not author of peace of 346 B.C.), *Cor.* 249

Philonicus, *F.L.* 291

Phoenix, tragedy of Euripides, *F.L.* 246

Phormio, *Cor.* 129

Phryno, member of first embassy to Philip, *F.L.* 189, 197, 229 f., 233

Phyle, fortress on W. frontier of Attica, seized and held by Thrasybulus and exiled democrats, 404-3 B.C., *F.L.* 280

Pittalacus, public slave with whom Timarchus associated, *F.L.* 245

Plataea, town in S. of Boeotia near Attic frontier, *Cor.* 208; *F.L.* 21, 42, 112, 325

Porthmus, seaport in Euboea not far from Eretria, *Cor.* 71; *F.L.* 87

Potidaea, Corinthian colony in Chalcidian Chersonesus, subject to Athens; captured by Philip in 356 B.C. and handed over to Olynthus, *Cor.* 69

Proconnesus, island in Propontis, *Cor.* 302

Proxenus, Athenian general at Oreus, *F.L.* 50, 52, 73 f., 154 f.

Ptoeodorus, *F.L.* 295

Pydna, town in Pieria (S. Macedonia), subject to Athens; captured and retained by Philip in 356 B.C., *Cor.* 69; *F.L.* 194

Pytho, Byzantian rhetorician, pupil of Isocrates, *Cor.* 136

Pythocles, political opponent of Demosthenes, *Cor.* 285; *F.L.* 225, 314

Pythodorus, *F.L.* 225

Pythonax, *F.L.* 271

RHADAMANTHUS, judge of the underworld, *Cor.* 127

SACRED MOUNT, in Thrace, *F.L.* 156, 334

Satyrus, Athenian actor and friend of Demosthenes, who received from him hints in elocution, *F.L.* 193, 196

Serrium, promontory and fortress on coast of Thrace, *Cor.* 27, 70

Simus, one of the Aleuadae of Larissa, helped by Philip in their contest with Lycophron of Pherae, *Cor.* 48

Simylus (also spelt Simyccas or Simmycas), *Cor.* 262

Smicythus, *F.L.* 191

Socrates, actor, *Cor.* 262

Solon, Athenian lawgiver and poet, *Cor.* 6; *F.L.* 251 ff.

Sophocles quoted, *F.L.* 246, 248

Sosicles, *Cor.* 249

TANAGRA, town in Boeotia near Attic frontier, occupied by Spartans early in fourth century, *Cor.* 96

Tharrex, *F.L.* 191

Themiso, tyrant of Eretria; seized Attic frontier town of Oropus and handed it over to Thebes in 366 B.C., *Cor.* 99

Themistocles, victor of Salamis, *Cor.* 204; *F.L.* 303

Theocrines, *Cor.* 313

Theodorus (1), Euboean concerned in seizure of Oropus by Themiso, *Cor.* 99

Theodorus (2), actor, *F.L.* 246

Thespiae, town in Boeotia, *F.L.* 31, 42, 112, 325

INDEX

Thraso, *Cor.* 137

Thrasybulus (1), restorer of Athenian democracy, *Cor.* 219; *F.L.* 280

Thrasybulus (2), *F.L.* 290

Thyestes, in drama, *F.L.* 337

Tilphosaeum, hill and town in Boeotia near Lake Copais, *F.L.* 141, 148

Timagoras, Athenian ambassador at court of Persia, 367 B.C., *F.L.* 31, 137, 191. See Introd. p. 242

Timarchus, *F.L.* 241, 244, 251, 283, 285 f. See Introd. p. 234

Timolaus, Theban who betrayed his city to Philip, *Cor.* 48

Timomachus, Athenian general condemned on unknown charge, *F.L.* 180

Triballians, Thracian tribe between Danube and Haemus range, *Cor.* 44

Tromes = Atrometus, *Cor.* 129

Troy, in drama, *F.L.* 337

XENOCLEIDES, *F.L.* 331

Xenophron, *F.L.* 196

ZELEA town in Troad. *F.L.* 271

Printed in Great Britain by R. & R. CLARK, LIMITED, *Edinburgh*

INDEX

THE LOEB CLASSICAL LIBRARY

VOLUMES ALREADY PUBLISHED

LATIN AUTHORS

AMMIANUS MARCELLINUS. J. C. Rolfe. 3 Vols.

APULEIUS : THE GOLDEN ASS (METAMORPHOSES). W. Adlington (1566). Revised by S. Gaselee.

ST. AUGUSTINE : CITY OF GOD. 7 Vols. Vol. I. G. E. McCracken. Vol. VI. W. C. Greene.

ST. AUGUSTINE, CONFESSIONS OF. W. Watts (1631). 2 Vols.

ST. AUGUSTINE : SELECT LETTERS. J. H. Baxter.

AUSONIUS. H. G. Evelyn White. 2 Vols.

BEDE. J. E. King. 2 Vols.

BOETHIUS : TRACTS AND DE CONSOLATIONE PHILOSOPHIAE. Rev. H. F. Stewart and E. K. Rand.

CAESAR : ALEXANDRIAN, AFRICAN AND SPANISH WARS. A. G. Way.

CAESAR : CIVIL WARS. A. G. Peskett.

CAESAR : GALLIC WAR. H. J. Edwards.

CATO AND VARRO : DE RE RUSTICA. H. B. Ash and W. D. Hooper.

CATULLUS. F. W. Cornish ; TIBULLUS. J. B. Postgate ; and PERVIGILIUM VENERIS. J. W. Mackail.

CELSUS : DE MEDICINA. W. G. Spencer. 3 Vols.

CICERO : BRUTUS AND ORATOR. G. L. Hendrickson and H. M. Hubbell.

CICERO : DE FINIBUS. H. Rackham.

CICERO : DE INVENTIONE, etc. H. M. Hubbell.

CICERO : DE NATURA DEORUM AND ACADEMICA. H. Rackham.

THE LOEB CLASSICAL LIBRARY

CICERO: DE OFFICIIS. Walter Miller.

CICERO: DE ORATORE, etc. 2 Vols. Vol. I: DE ORATORE, Books I and II. E. W. Sutton and H. Rackham. Vol. II: DE ORATORE, Book III; DE FATO; PARADOXA STOICORUM; DE PARTITIONE ORATORIA. H. Rackham.

CICERO: DE REPUBLICA, DE LEGIBUS, SOMNIUM SCIPIONIS. Clinton W. Keyes.

CICERO: DE SENECTUTE, DE AMICITIA, DE DIVINATIONE. W. A. Falconer.

CICERO: IN CATILINAM, PRO MURENA, PRO SULLA, PRO FLACCO. Louis E. Lord.

CICERO: LETTERS TO ATTICUS. E. O. Winstedt. 3 Vols.

CICERO: LETTERS TO HIS FRIENDS. W. Glynn Williams. 3 Vols.

CICERO: PHILIPPICS. W. C. A. Ker.

CICERO: PRO ARCHIA, POST REDITUM, DE DOMO, DE HARUSPICUM RESPONSIS, PRO PLANCIO. N. H. Watts.

CICERO: PRO CAECINA, PRO LEGE MANILIA, PRO CLUENTIO, PRO RABIRIO. H. Grose Hodge.

CICERO: PRO CAELIO, DE PROVINCIIS CONSULARIBUS, PRO BALBO. R. Gardner.

CICERO: PRO MILONE, IN PISONEM, PRO SCAURO, PRO FONTEIO, PRO RABIRIO POSTUMO, PRO MARCELLO, PRO LIGARIO, PRO REGE DEIOTARO. N. H. Watts.

CICERO: PRO QUINCTIO, PRO ROSCIO AMERINO, PRO ROSCIO COMOEDO, CONTRA RULLUM. J. H. Freese.

CICERO: PRO SESTIO, IN VATINIUM. R. Gardner.

[CICERO]: RHETORICA AD HERENNIUM. H. Caplan.

CICERO: TUSCULAN DISPUTATIONS. J. E. King.

CICERO: VERRINE ORATIONS. L. H. G. Greenwood. 2 Vols.

CLAUDIAN. M. Platnauer. 2 Vols.

COLUMELLA: DE RE RUSTICA; DE ARBORIBUS. H. B. Ash, E. S. Forster, E. Heffner. 3 Vols.

CURTIUS, Q.: HISTORY OF ALEXANDER. J. C. Rolfe. 2 Vols.

FLORUS. E. S. Forster: and CORNELIUS NEPOS. J. C. Rolfe.

FRONTINUS: STRATAGEMS AND AQUEDUCTS. C. E. Bennett and M. B. McElwain.

FRONTO: CORRESPONDENCE. C. R. Haines. 2 Vols.

GELLIUS. J. C. Rolfe. 3 Vols.

HORACE: ODES AND EPODES. C. E. Bennett.

HORACE: SATIRES, EPISTLES, ARS POETICA. H. R. Fairclough.

JEROME: SELECT LETTERS. F. A. Wright.

JUVENAL AND PERSIUS. G. G. Ramsay.

2

THE LOEB CLASSICAL LIBRARY

LIVY. B. O. Foster, F. G. Moore, Evan T. Sage, A. C. Schlesinger and R. M. Geer (General Index). 14 Vols.

LUCAN. J. D. Duff.

LUCRETIUS. W. H. D. Rouse.

MARTIAL. W. C. A. Ker. 2 Vols.

MINOR LATIN POETS: from PUBLILIUS SYRUS to RUTILIUS NAMATIANUS, including GRATTIUS, CALPURNIUS SICULUS, NEMESIANUS, AVIANUS, with " Aetna," " Phoenix " and other poems. J. Wight Duff and Arnold M. Duff.

OVID: THE ART OF LOVE AND OTHER POEMS. J. H. Mozley.

OVID: FASTI. Sir James G. Frazer.

OVID: HEROIDES AND AMORES. Grant Showerman.

OVID: METAMORPHOSES. F. J. Miller. 2 Vols.

OVID: TRISTIA AND EX PONTO. A. L. Wheeler.

PETRONIUS. M. Heseltine: SENECA: APOCOLOCYNTOSIS. W. H. D. Rouse.

PLAUTUS. Paul Nixon. 5 Vols.

PLINY: LETTERS. Melmoth's translation revised by W. M. L. Hutchinson. 2 Vols.

PLINY: NATURAL HISTORY. 10 Vols. Vols. I-V and IX. H. Rackham. Vols. VI-VIII. W. H. S. Jones. Vol. X. D. E. Eichholz.

PROPERTIUS. H. E. Butler.

PRUDENTIUS. H. J. Thomson. 2 Vols.

QUINTILIAN. H. E. Butler. 4 Vols.

REMAINS OF OLD LATIN. E. H. Warmington. 4 Vols. Vol. I (Ennius and Caecilius). Vol. II (Livius, Naevius, Pacuvius, Accius). Vol. III (Lucilius, Laws of the XII Tables). Vol. IV (Archaic Inscriptions).

SALLUST. J. C. Rolfe.

SCRIPTORES HISTORIAE AUGUSTAE. D. Magie. 3 Vols.

SENECA: APOCOLOCYNTOSIS. Cf. PETRONIUS.

SENECA: EPISTULAE MORALES. R. M. Gummere. 3 Vols.

SENECA: MORAL ESSAYS. J. W. Basore. 3 Vols.

SENECA: TRAGEDIES. F. J. Miller. 2 Vols.

SIDONIUS: POEMS AND LETTERS. W. B. Anderson. 2 Vols.

SILIUS ITALICUS. J. D. Duff. 2 Vols.

STATIUS. J. H. Mozley. 2 Vols.

SUETONIUS. J. C. Rolfe. 2 Vols.

TACITUS: DIALOGUS. Sir Wm. Peterson: and AGRICOLA AND GERMANIA. Maurice Hutton.

TACITUS: HISTORIES AND ANNALS. C. H. Moore and J. Jackson. 4 Vols.

TERENCE. John Sargeaunt. 2 Vols.
TERTULLIAN: APOLOGIA AND DE SPECTACULIS. T. R. Glover;
  MINUCIUS FELIX. G. H. Rendall.
VALERIUS FLACCUS. J. H. Mozley.
VARRO: DE LINGUA LATINA. R. G. Kent. 2 Vols.
VELLEIUS PATERCULUS AND RES GESTAE DIVI AUGUSTI. F. W.
  Shipley.
VIRGIL. H. R. Fairclough. 2 Vols.
VITRUVIUS: DE ARCHITECTURA. F. Granger. 2 Vols.

GREEK AUTHORS

ACHILLES TATIUS. S. Gaselee.
AELIAN: ON THE NATURE OF ANIMALS. A. F. Scholfield.
  3 Vols.
AENEAS TACTICUS, ASCLEPIODOTUS AND ONASANDER. The
  Illinois Greek Club.
AESCHINES. C. D. Adams.
AESCHYLUS. H. Weir Smyth. 2 Vols.
ALCIPHRON, AELIAN AND PHILOSTRATUS: LETTERS. A. R.
  Benner and F. H. Fobes.
APOLLODORUS. Sir James G. Frazer. 2 Vols.
APOLLONIUS RHODIUS. R. C. Seaton.
THE APOSTOLIC FATHERS. Kirsopp Lake. 2 Vols.
APPIAN'S ROMAN HISTORY. Horace White. 4 Vols.
ARATUS. Cf. CALLIMACHUS.
ARISTOPHANES. Benjamin Bickley Rogers. 3 Vols. Verse
  trans.
ARISTOTLE: ART OF RHETORIC. J. H. Freese.
ARISTOTLE: ATHENIAN CONSTITUTION, EUDEMIAN ETHICS,
  VIRTUES AND VICES. H. Rackham.
ARISTOTLE: GENERATION OF ANIMALS. A. L. Peck.
ARISTOTLE: METAPHYSICS. H. Tredennick. 2 Vols.
ARISTOTLE: METEOROLOGICA. H. D. P. Lee.
ARISTOTLE: MINOR WORKS. W. S. Hett. " On Colours,"
  " On Things Heard," " Physiognomics," " On Plants,"
  " On Marvellous Things Heard," " Mechanical Problems,"
  " On Indivisible Lines," " Situations and Names of
  Winds," " On Melissus, Xenophanes, and Gorgias."
ARISTOTLE: NICOMACHEAN ETHICS. H. Rackham.

THE LOEB CLASSICAL LIBRARY

ARISTOTLE : OECONOMICA AND MAGNA MORALIA. G. C. Armstrong. (With Metaphysics, Vol. II.)

ARISTOTLE : ON THE HEAVENS. W. K. C. Guthrie.

ARISTOTLE : ON THE SOUL, PARVA NATURALIA, ON BREATH. W. S. Hett.

ARISTOTLE : THE CATEGORIES. ON INTERPRETATION. H. P. Cooke ; PRIOR ANALYTICS. H. Tredennick.

ARISTOTLE : POSTERIOR ANALYTICS. H. Tredennick ; TOPICS. E. S. Forster.

ARISTOTLE : SOPHISTICAL REFUTATIONS. COMING-TO-BE AND PASSING-AWAY. E. S. Forster. ON THE COSMOS. D. J. Furley.

ARISTOTLE : PARTS OF ANIMALS. A. L. Peck; MOTION AND PROGRESSION OF ANIMALS. E. S. Forster.

ARISTOTLE : PHYSICS. Rev. P. Wicksteed and F. M. Cornford. 2 Vols.

ARISTOTLE : POETICS ; LONGINUS ON THE SUBLIME. W. Hamilton Fyfe ; DEMETRIUS ON STYLE. W. Rhys Roberts.

ARISTOTLE : POLITICS. H. Rackham.

ARISTOTLE : PROBLEMS. W. S. Hett. 2 Vols.

ARISTOTLE : RHETORICA AD ALEXANDRUM. H. Rackham. (With Problems, Vol. II.)

ARRIAN : HISTORY OF ALEXANDER AND INDICA. Rev. E. Iliffe Robson. 2 Vols.

ATHENAEUS : DEIPNOSOPHISTAE. C. B. Gulick. 7 Vols.

ST. BASIL : LETTERS. R. J. Deferrari. 4 Vols.

CALLIMACHUS : FRAGMENTS. C. A. Trypanis.

CALLIMACHUS : HYMNS AND EPIGRAMS, AND LYCOPHRON. A. W. Mair ; ARATUS. G. R. Mair.

CLEMENT OF ALEXANDRIA. Rev. G. W. Butterworth.

COLLUTHUS. *Cf.* OPPIAN.

DAPHNIS AND CHLOE. *Cf.* LONGUS.

DEMOSTHENES I : OLYNTHIACS, PHILIPPICS AND MINOR ORATIONS : I-XVII AND XX. J. H. Vince.

DEMOSTHENES II : DE CORONA AND DE FALSA LEGATIONE. C. A. Vince and J. H. Vince.

DEMOSTHENES III : MEIDIAS, ANDROTION, ARISTOCRATES, TIMOCRATES, ARISTOGEITON. J. H. Vince.

DEMOSTHENES IV-VI : PRIVATE ORATIONS AND IN NEAERAM. A. T. Murray.

DEMOSTHENES VII : FUNERAL SPEECH, EROTIC ESSAY, EXORDIA AND LETTERS. N. W. and N. J. DeWitt.

DIO CASSIUS : ROMAN HISTORY. E. Cary. 9 Vols.

THE LOEB CLASSICAL LIBRARY

DIO CHRYSOSTOM. 5 Vols. Vols. I and II. J. W. Cohoon.
Vol III. J. W. Cohoon and H. Lamar Crosby. Vols. IV
and V. H. Lamar Crosby.

DIODORUS SICULUS. 12 Vols. Vols. I-VI. C. H. Oldfather.
Vol. VII. C. L. Sherman. Vol. VIII. C. B. Welles.
Vols. IX and X. Russel M. Geer. Vol. XI. F. R. Walton.

DIOGENES LAERTIUS. R. D. Hicks. 2 Vols.

DIONYSIUS OF HALICARNASSUS: ROMAN ANTIQUITIES. Spel-
man's translation revised by E. Cary. 7 Vols.

EPICTETUS. W. A. Oldfather. 2 Vols.

EURIPIDES. A. S. Way. 4 Vols. Verse trans.

EUSEBIUS: ECCLESIASTICAL HISTORY. Kirsopp Lake and
J. E. L. Oulton. 2 Vols.

GALEN: ON THE NATURAL FACULTIES. A. J. Brock.

THE GREEK ANTHOLOGY. W. R. Paton. 5 Vols.

THE GREEK BUCOLIC POETS (THEOCRITUS, BION, MOSCHUS).
J. M. Edmonds.

GREEK ELEGY AND IAMBUS WITH THE ANACREONTEA. J. M.
Edmonds. 2 Vols.

GREEK MATHEMATICAL WORKS. Ivor Thomas. 2 Vols.

HERODES. Cf. THEOPHRASTUS: CHARACTERS.

HERODOTUS. A. D. Godley. 4 Vols.

HESIOD AND THE HOMERIC HYMNS. H. G. Evelyn White.

HIPPOCRATES AND THE FRAGMENTS OF HERACLEITUS. W. H. S.
Jones and E. T. Withington. 4 Vols.

HOMER: ILIAD. A. T. Murray. 2 Vols.

HOMER: ODYSSEY. A. T. Murray. 2 Vols.

ISAEUS. E. S. Forster.

ISOCRATES. George Norlin and LaRue Van Hook. 3 Vols.

ST. JOHN DAMASCENE: BARLAAM AND IOASAPH. Rev. G. R.
Woodward and Harold Mattingly.

JOSEPHUS. 9 Vols. Vols. I-IV. H. St. J. Thackeray. Vol.
V. H. St. J. Thackeray and Ralph Marcus. Vols. VI
and VII. Ralph Marcus. Vol. VIII. Ralph Marcus and
Allen Wikgren.

JULIAN. Wilmer Cave Wright. 3 Vols.

LONGUS: DAPHNIS AND CHLOE. Thornley's translation revised by J. M. Edmonds; and PARTHENIUS. S. Gaselee.

LUCIAN. 8 Vols. Vols. I-V. A. M. Harmon; Vol. VI.
K. Kilburn; Vol. VII. M. D. Macleod.

LYCOPHRON. Cf. CALLIMACHUS.

LYRA GRAECA. J. M. Edmonds. 3 Vols.

LYSIAS. W. R. M. Lamb.

THE LOEB CLASSICAL LIBRARY

MANETHO. W. G. Waddell. PTOLEMY: TETRABIBLOS. F. E. Robbins.

MARCUS AURELIUS. C. R. Haines.

MENANDER. F. G. Allinson.

MINOR ATTIC ORATORS. 2 Vols. K. J. Maidment and J. O. Burtt.

NONNOS: DIONYSIACA. W. H. D. Rouse. 3 Vols.

OPPIAN, COLLUTHUS, TRYPHIODORUS. A. W. Mair.

PAPYRI. NON-LITERARY SELECTIONS. A. S. Hunt and C. C. Edgar. 2 Vols. LITERARY SELECTIONS (Poetry). D. L. Page.

PARTHENIUS. Cf. LONGUS.

PAUSANIAS: DESCRIPTION OF GREECE. W. H. S. Jones. 5 Vols. and Companion Vol. arranged by R. E. Wycherley.

PHILO. 10 Vols. Vols. I-V. F. H. Colson and Rev. G. H. Whitaker; Vols. VI-X. F. H. Colson; General Index. Rev. J. W. Earp.
Two Supplementary Vols. Translation only from an Armenian Text. Ralph Marcus.

PHILOSTRATUS: IMAGINES: CALLISTRATUS: DESCRIPTIONS. A. Fairbanks.

PHILOSTRATUS: THE LIFE OF APOLLONIUS OF TYANA. F. C. Conybeare. 2 Vols.

PHILOSTRATUS AND EUNAPIUS: LIVES OF THE SOPHISTS. Wilmer Cave Wright.

PINDAR. Sir J. E. Sandys.

PLATO: CHARMIDES, ALCIBIADES, HIPPARCHUS, THE LOVERS, THEAGES, MINOS AND EPINOMIS. W. R. M. Lamb.

PLATO: CRATYLUS, PARMENIDES, GREATER HIPPIAS, LESSER HIPPIAS. H. N. Fowler.

PLATO: EUTHYPHRO, APOLOGY, CRITO, PHAEDO, PHAEDRUS. H. N. Fowler.

PLATO: LACHES, PROTAGORAS, MENO, EUTHYDEMUS. W. R. M. Lamb.

PLATO: LAWS. Rev. R. G. Bury. 2 Vols.

PLATO: LYSIS, SYMPOSIUM, GORGIAS. W. R. M. Lamb.

PLATO: REPUBLIC. Paul Shorey. 2 Vols.

PLATO: STATESMAN. PHILEBUS. H. N. Fowler: ION. W. R. M. Lamb.

PLATO: THEAETETUS AND SOPHIST. H. N. Fowler.

PLATO: TIMAEUS, CRITIAS, CLITOPHO, MENEXENUS, EPISTULAE. Rev. R. G. Bury.

PLUTARCH: MORALIA. 15 Vols. Vols. I-V. F. C. Babbitt;

THE LOEB CLASSICAL LIBRARY

Vol. VI. W. C. Helmbold ; Vol. VII. P. H. De Lacy and
B. Einarson ; Vol. IX. E. L. Minar, Jr., F. H. Sandbach,
W. C. Helmbold ; Vol. X. H. N. Fowler ; Vol. XII. H.
Cherniss and W. C. Helmbold.

PLUTARCH : THE PARALLEL LIVES. B. Perrin. 11 Vols.
POLYBIUS. W. R. Paton. 6 Vols.
PROCOPIUS : HISTORY OF THE WARS. H. B. Dewing. 7 Vols.
PTOLEMY : TETRABIBLOS. *Cf.* MANETHO.
QUINTUS SMYRNAEUS. A. S. Way. Verse trans.
SEXTUS EMPIRICUS. Rev. R. G. Bury. 4 Vols.
SOPHOCLES. F. Storr. 2 Vols. Verse trans.
STRABO : GEOGRAPHY. Horace L. Jones. 8 Vols.
THEOPHRASTUS : CHARACTERS. J. M. Edmonds ; HERODES,
etc. A. D. Knox.
THEOPHRASTUS : ENQUIRY INTO PLANTS. Sir Arthur Hort.
2 Vols.
THUCYDIDES. C. F. Smith. 4 Vols.
TRYPHIODORUS. *Cf.* OPPIAN.
XENOPHON : CYROPAEDIA. Walter Miller. 2 Vols.
XENOPHON : HELLENICA, ANABASIS, APOLOGY, AND SYMPO-
SIUM. C. L. Brownson and O. J. Todd. 3 Vols.
XENOPHON : MEMORABILIA AND OECONOMICUS. E. C. Mar-
chant.
XENOPHON : SCRIPTA MINORA. E. C. Marchant.

VOLUMES IN PREPARATION

ARISTOTLE : HISTORIA ANIMALIUM (Greek). A. L. Peck.
BABRIUS (Greek) AND PHAEDRUS (Latin). B. E. Perry.
PLOTINUS (Greek). A. H. Armstrong.

DESCRIPTIVE PROSPECTUS ON APPLICATION

CAMBRIDGE, MASS.   LONDON
HARVARD UNIV. PRESS   WILLIAM HEINEMANN LTD